David J. Hand   Joost N. Kok
Michael R. Berthold (Eds.)

Advances in Intelligent Data Analysis

Third International Symposium, IDA-99
Amsterdam, The Netherlands, August 9-11, 1999
Proceedings

Springer

Series Editors

Gerhard Goos, Karlsruhe University, Germany
Juris Hartmanis, Cornell University, NY, USA
Jan van Leeuwen, Utrecht University, The Netherlands

Volume Editors

David J. Hand
Department of Mathematics, Imperial College, Huxley Building
180 Queen's Gate, London SW7 2BZ, UK
E-mail: d.j.hand@ic.ac.uk

Joost N. Kok
Leiden Institute for Advanced Computer Science, Leiden University
2300 RA Leiden, The Netherlands
E-mail: joost@wi.leidenuniv.nl

Michael R. Berthold
Berkeley Initiative in Soft Computing, University of California at Berkeley
329 Soda Hall, Berkeley, CA 94720, USA
E-mail: berthold@cs.berkeley.edu

Cataloging-in-Publication data applied for

Die Deutsche Bibliothek - CIP-Einheitsaufnahme

Advances in intelligent data analysis : third international
symposium ; proceedings / IDA-99, Amsterdam, The Netherlands,
August 9 - 11, 1999. David H. Hand ... (ed.). - Berlin ; Heidelberg ;
New York ; Barcelona ; Hong Kong ; London ; Milan ; Paris ;
Singapore ; Tokyo : Springer, 1999
     (Lecture notes in computer science ; Vol. 1642)
     ISBN 3-540-66332-0

CR Subject Classification (1998): H.3, I.2, G.3, I.5.1, I.4.5, J.2, J.1, J.3

ISSN 0302-9743
ISBN 3-540-66332-0 Springer-Verlag Berlin Heidelberg New York

© Springer-Verlag Berlin Heidelberg 1999
Printed in Germany

Typesetting: Camera-ready by author
SPIN: 10703511   06/3142 – 5 4 3 2 1 0   Printed on acid-free paper

Foreword

For many years the intersection of computing and data analysis contained menu-based statistics packages and not much else. Recently, statisticians have embraced computing, computer scientists have started using statistical theories and methods, and researchers in all corners have invented algorithms to find structure in vast online datasets. Data analysts now have access to tools for exploratory data analysis, decision tree induction, causal induction, function estimation, constructing customized reference distributions, and visualization, and there are intelligent assistants to advise on matters of design and analysis. There are tools for traditional, relatively small samples, and also for enormous datasets. In all, the scope for probing data in new and penetrating ways has never been so exciting.

The IDA-99 conference brings together a wide variety of researchers concerned with extracting knowledge from data, including people from statistics, machine learning, neural networks, computer science, pattern recognition, database management, and other areas. The strategies adopted by people from these areas are often different, and a synergy results if this is recognized. The IDA series of conferences is intended to stimulate interaction between these different areas, so that more powerful tools emerge for extracting knowledge from data and a better understanding is developed of the process of intelligent data analysis. The result is a conference that has a clear focus (one application area: intelligent data analysis) and a broad scope (many different methods and techniques).

IDA-99 took place in Amsterdam from 9–11 August 1999. The invited speakers were Jacqueline Meulman (Leiden University, The Netherlands), Zdzislaw Pawlak (Warsaw Institute of Technology, Poland), and Paul Cohen (University of Massachusetts, Amherst, United States). The conference received more than 100 submissions. During a meeting of the program committee organized by Xiaohui Liu at Birkbeck College in London, 21 papers were selected for oral presentation and 23 papers were selected for poster presentation.

We want to express our thanks to all the people involved in the organization of IDA-99: especially Paul Cohen for the initial discussions, Xiaohui Liu and Michael Berthold for all their work behind the scenes, once again Michael Berthold for the preparation of the proceedings, and Daniel Tauritz, Walter Kosters, Marloes Boon-van der Nat, Frans Snijders, Mieke Bruné, and Arno Siebes for the local organization.

May 1999   David J. Hand (General Chair)
                                            Joost N. Kok (Program Chair)

Organization

General Chair: David J. Hand
                          Department of Mathematics
                          Imperial College
                          Huxley Building
                          180 Queen's Gate
                          London, SW7 2BZ, UK
                          Email: d.j.hand@ic.ac.uk

Program Chair: Joost N. Kok
                          Leiden Institute of Advanced Computer Science
                          Leiden University
                          2300 RA Leiden, The Netherlands
                          Email: joost@wi.leidenuniv.nl

Program Co-Chairs: Michael R. Berthold
                          Berkeley Initiative in Soft Computing
                          University of California at Berkeley
                          329 Soda Hall, Berkeley, CA 94702, USA
                          Email: berthold@cs.berkeley.edu

                          Douglas H. Fisher
                          Department of Computer Science
                          Vanderbilt University
                          Nashville, TN 37235, USA
                          Email: dfisher@vuse.vanderbilt.edu

Local Chair: Walter A. Kosters
                          Leiden Institute of Advanced Computer Science
                          Leiden University
                          2300 RA Leiden, The Netherlands
                          Email: kosters@wi.leidenuniv.nl

Program Committee

Niall Adams	Open University, UK
Pieter Adriaans	Syllogic, The Netherlands
Russell Almond	Educational Testing Service, US
Thomas Bäck	Informatik Centrum Dortmund, Germany
Riccardo Bellazzi	University of Pavia, Italy
Paul Cohen	University of Massachusetts, US
Paul Darius	Leuven University, Belgium
Tom Dietterich	Oregon State University, US
Gerard van den Eijkel	Delft University of Technology, The Netherlands
Fazel Famili	National Research Council, Canada
Karl Froeschl	University of Vienna, Austria
Linda van der Gaag	Utrecht University, The Netherlands
Alex Gammerman	Royal Holloway London, UK
Jaap van den Herik	Universiteit Maastricht, The Netherlands
Rainer Holve	FORWISS Erlangen, Germany
Larry Hunter	National Library of Medicine, US
David Jensen	University of Massachusetts, US
Bert Kappen	Nijmegen University, The Netherlands
Hans Lenz	Free University of Berlin, Germany
Frank Klawonn	University of Applied Sciences Emden, Germany
Bing Liu	National University, Singapore
Xiaohui Liu	Birkbeck College, UK
David Madigan	University of Washington, US
Heikki Mannila	Helsinki University, Finland
Erkki Oja	Helsinki University of Technology, Finland
Wayne Oldford	Waterloo, Canada
Albert Prat	Technical University of Catalunya, Spain
Luc de Raedt	KU Leuven, Belgium
Rosanna Schiavo	University of Venice, Italy
Kaisa Sere	Abo Akademi University, Finland
Jude Shavlik	University of Wisconsin, US
Roberta Siciliano	University of Naples, Italy
Arno Siebes	Center for Mathematics and Computer Science, The Netherlands
Rosaria Silipo	International Computer Science Institute, US
Floor Verdenius	ATO-DLO, The Netherlands
Stefan Wrobel	University of Magdeburg, Germany
Jan Zytkow	University of North Carolina, Charlotte, US

Table of Contents

Section I: Learning

From Theoretical Learnability to Statistical Measures of the Learnable.......3
   M. Sebban and G. Richard

ALM: A Methodology for Designing Accurate Linguistic Models for
Intelligent Data Analysis 15
   O. Cordón and F. Herrera

A "Top-Down and Prune" Induction Scheme for Constrained Decision
Committees 27
   R. Nock and P. Jappy

Mining Clusters with Association Rules....................................39
   W.A. Kosters, E. Marchiori, and A.A.J. Oerlemans

Evolutionary Computation to Search for Strongly Correlated
Variables in High-Dimensional Time-Series 51
   S. Swift, A. Tucker, and X. Liu

The Biases of Decision Tree Pruning Strategies 63
   T. Elomaa

Feature Selection as Retrospective Pruning in Hierarchical Clustering.......75
   L. Talavera

Discriminative Power of Input Features in a Fuzzy Model...................87
   R. Silipo and M.R. Berthold

Learning Elements of Representations for Redescribing Robot
Experiences 99
   L. Firoiu and P. Cohen

"Seeing" Objects in Spatial Datasets 111
   X. Huang and F. Zhao

Intelligent Monitoring Method Using Time Varying Binomial
Distribution Models for Pseudo-Periodic Communication Traffic 123
   K. Matsumoto and K. Hashimoto

Section II: Visualization

Monitoring Human Information Processing via Intelligent Data Analysis
of EEG Recordings..137
   A. Flexer and H. Bauer

Knowledge-Based Visualization to Support Spatial Data Mining...........149
   G. Andrienko and N. Andrienko

Probabilistic Topic Maps: Navigating through Large Text Collections......161
   Th. Hofmann

3D Grand Tour for Multidimensional Data and Clusters...................173
   L. Yang

Section III: Classification and Clustering

A Decision Tree Algorithm for Ordinal Classification 187
   R. Potharst and J.C. Bioch

Discovering Dynamics Using Bayesian Clustering.........................199
   P. Sebastiani, M. Ramoni, P. Cohen, J. Warwick, and J. Davis

Integrating Declarative Knowledge in Hierarchical Clustering Tasks........211
   L. Talavera and J. Béjar

Nonparametric Linear Discriminant Analysis by Recursive
Optimization with Random Initialization 223
   M. Aladjem

Supervised Classification Problems: How to Be Both Judge and Jury 235
   M.G. Kelly, D.J. Hand, and N.M. Adams

Temporal Pattern Generation Using Hidden Markov Model
Based Unsupervised Classification 245
   C. Li and G. Biswas

Exploiting Similarity for Supporting Data Analysis and Problem Solving...257
   E. Hüllermeier

Multiple Prototype Model for Fuzzy Clustering...........................269
   S. Nascimento, B. Mirkin, and F. Moura-Pires

A Comparison of Genetic Programming Variants for Data Classification ...281
   J. Eggermont, A.E. Eiben, and J.I. van Hemert

Fuzzy Clustering Based on Modified Distance Measures....................291
   F. Klawonn and A. Keller

Building Classes in Object-Based Languages by Automatic Clustering 303
   P. Valtchev

Section IV: Integration

Adjusted Estimation for the Combination of Classifiers 317
    B.J.A. Mertens and D.J. Hand

Data-Driven Theory Refinement Using KBDistAl 331
    J. Yang, R. Parekh, V. Honavar, and D. Dobbs

Reasoning about Input-Output Modeling of Dynamical Systems 343
    M. Easley and E. Bradley

Undoing Statistical Advice 357
    R. Almond

A Method for Temporal Knowledge Conversion 369
    G. Guimarães and A. Ultsch

Section V: Applications

Intrusion Detection through Behavioral Data 383
    D. Gunetti and G. Ruffo

Bayesian Neural Network Learning for Prediction in the Australian
Dairy Industry 395
    P.E. Macrossan, H.A. Abbass, K. Mengersen, M. Towsey, and G. Finn

Exploiting Sample-Data Distributions to Reduce the Cost of
Nearest-Neighbor Searches with Kd-Trees 407
    D. Talbert and D. Fisher

Pump Failure Detection Using Support Vector Data Descriptions 415
    D.M.J. Tax, A. Ypma, and R.P.W. Duin

Data Mining for the Detection of Turning Points in Financial Time
Series 427
    T. Poddig and C. Huber

Computer-Assisted Classification of Legal Abstracts 437
    B. Yang-Stephens, M.C. Swope, J. Locke, and I. Moulinier

Sequential Control Logic Inferring Method from Observed Plant
I/O Data 449
    Y. Ikkai, K. Ikeda, N. Komoda, A. Yamane, and I. Tone

Evaluating an Eye Screening Test 461
    G. Cheng, K. Cho, X. Liu, G. Loizou, and J.X. Wu

Application of Rough Sets Algorithms to Prediction of Aircraft
Component Failure 473
    J.M. Peña, S. Létourneau, and F. Famili

Section VI: Media Mining

Exploiting Structural Information for Text Classification on the WWW 487
  J. Fürnkranz

Multi-agent Web Information Retrieval: Neural Network Based
Approach 499
  Y.S. Choi and S.I. Yoo

Adaptive Information Filtering Algorithms 513
  D.R. Tauritz and I.G. Sprinkhuizen-Kuyper

A Conceptual Graph Approach for Video Data Representation and
Retrieval 525
  N. Fatemi and P. Mulhem

Author Index 537

Section I:

Learning

From Theoretical Learnability to Statistical Measures of the Learnable.......3
   M. Sebban and G. Richard

ALM: A Methodology for Designing Accurate Linguistic Models for
Intelligent Data Analysis 15
   O. Cordón and F. Herrera

A "Top-Down and Prune" Induction Scheme for Constrained Decision
Committees 27
   R. Nock and P. Jappy

Mining Clusters with Association Rules.....................................39
   W.A. Kosters, E. Marchiori, and A.A.J. Oerlemans

Evolutionary Computation to Search for Strongly Correlated
Variables in High-Dimensional Time-Series 51
   S. Swift, A. Tucker, and X. Liu

The Biases of Decision Tree Pruning Strategies 63
   T. Elomaa

Feature Selection as Retrospective Pruning in Hierarchical Clustering.......75
   L. Talavera

Discriminative Power of Input Features in a Fuzzy Model...................87
   R. Silipo and M.R. Berthold

Learning Elements of Representations for Redescribing Robot
Experiences 99
   L. Firoiu and P. Cohen

"Seeing" Objects in Spatial Datasets 111
   X. Huang and F. Zhao

Intelligent Monitoring Method Using Time Varying Binomial
Distribution Models for Pseudo-Periodic Communication Traffic 123
   K. Matsumoto and K. Hashimoto

From Theoretical Learnability to Statistical Measures of the Learnable

Marc Sebban and Gilles Richard

TRIVIA Research Team
Université des Antilles et de la Guyane
Campus de Fouillole, 95159 - Pointe-à-Pitre (France)
{msebban,grichard}@univ-ag.fr

Abstract. The main focus of theoretical models for machine learning is to formally describe what is the meaning of learnable, what is a learning process, or what is the relationship between a learning agent and a teaching one. However, when we prove from a theoretical point of view that a concept is learnable, we have no *a priori* idea concerning the difficulty to learn the target concept. In this paper, after reminding some theoretical concepts and the main estimation methods, we provide a learning-system independent measure of the difficulty to learn a concept. It is based on geometrical and statistical concepts, and the implicit assumption that distinct classes occupy distinct regions in the feature space. In such a context, we assume the learnability to be identify by the separability level in the feature space. Our definition is constructive, based on a statistical test and has been implemented on problems of the UCI repository. The results are really convincing and fit well with theoretical results and intuition. Finally, in order to reduce the computational costs of our approach, we propose a new way to characterize the geometrical regions using a k-Nearest-Neighbors graph. We experimentally show that it allows to compute accuracy estimates near from those obtained by a leave-one-out-cross-validation and with smaller standard deviation.

1 Introduction

As in a lot of fields of computer science, we can distinguish two trends in the machine learning community: the *theoretical* one and the *practical* one. In the first one, people are interested in developing formal models describing as close as possible what is a learning process. [5] developed an exact learning model, restricted to recursive primitive functions and without any time or complexity requirements. It was a kind of idealized model (learning in the limit) capturing only a small part of human learning and really too far from practical requirements. The paper of Valiant [18] was an attempt to relax such an idealized model and to define a theory of the learnable where some algorithmic and statistic constraints are introduced. Today, this theory based on the PAC learnability, is often the starting point of new theoretical research works.

D.J. Hand, J.N. Kok, M.R. Berthold (Eds.): IDA'99, LNCS 1642, pp. 3–14, 1999.

On the other hand, because of theoretical constraints, we find researchers who develop tools and algorithms applicable in practical situations. Their aim consists in developing efficient machines able to correctly learn concepts more or less complicated. The relevance of these machines is often numerically estimated taking into account both algorithmic and statistical constraints, as presented in the PAC model. Statistical criteria [11, 14, 16, 17, 20] or accuracy estimates [3, 10] are then often used to measure a certain degree of learnability.

According to the different approaches of these two trends, one may well wonder if a learnable concept from a practical standpoint is still learnable from a theoretical point of view, and *vice versa*. In this article, starting from theoretical considerations about learnability [18, 19], we progressively show how we derive to practical estimation methods used in machine learning. We propose then a first statistical approach to measure learnability regardless of learning methods. Actually, we think that the learnability degree of a given concept is an intrinsic property of its representation in the feature space. The idea to assess the relevance of the feature space independently of a learning method is not new. It is the original concept of the filter models in the feature selection field [9]. Our approach is based on the construction on the well-known Minimum Spanning Tree (*MST*) from which we characterize homogeneous subsets, deleting some particular edges. We build a statistical test on this number of deleted edges and use the critical threshold of the test to assess a learnability degree. In order to show the interest of our approach, we present some experimental results on benchmarks of the UCI repository, comparing our *a priori* decision rule with *a posteriori* accuracy estimates computed by three induction methods: *C4.5* [13], *ID3* [12] and the k-Nearest Neighbors (*k-NN*).

The main drawback of the MST is its computational cost. In order to deal with very big databases that we often find with new data-acquisition technologies (the World Wide Web for instance), we propose in the last section to replace the *MST* by the *k-NN* graph, which has a lower complexity. This new way to proceed modifies a little the property of learning-method independence, without challenging its principles. Actually, even if we use the *k*-NN to characterize the homogeneous subsets, we do not appeal to any induction rule for classifying a new instance. We experimentally show that our statistical variable built from this new graph not only gives a good accuracy estimate, but also provides a smaller standard deviation. Experimental results seem to confirm this property.

2   Theoretical Considerations

2.1   PAC Learnability

The task assigned to a learning machine is to approximate a target *concept f* and such a machine could be decomposed in two parts consisting in a *learning protocol* and a *deduction procedure* [18]. The *learning protocol* describes the way to represent information we dispose to learn f and the way we access to this information. The machine has to recognize whether f is true or not for a given data belonging to a set Ω. One of the natural procedures to access to information is called EXAMPLE and provides a finite set of examples $\Omega_a \subset \Omega$, *the training set*, positively or negatively exemplifying the target concept. Ω is supposed to be given with an unknown but fixed probability distribution P. The *deduction process* is in fact an algorithm A invoking the protocol and which has to produce an approximation h of the target concept f.

Definition 1. *The target concept f is considered as learnable if and only if it exists an algorithm A producing a concept h in a finite number of steps and satisfying the following property usually denoted PAC (as Probably Approximately Correct). For each $\epsilon, \delta \in [0,1]$, with probability at least $1 - \delta$, we must have*

$$\sum_{\{\omega \in \Omega | f(\omega) \neq h(\omega)\}} P(\omega) \leq \epsilon$$

So PAC-learnability is just stated in terms of existence of an algorithm satisfying PAC property. The PAC-property has been refined [1, 7], and some more sophisticated learning protocols have been studied [4, 6], but the basic intuition has not been really modified. We may point out some drawbacks of such models. Since the P distribution is unknown, there is no way to compute the theoretical risk of error (the left term of the inequality). Furthermore, PAC learnability does not provide training algorithms but rather gives formal criteria to determine whether a given algorithm runs in a satisfactory way : in case of positive result, some concepts are "easily" learnable since others give rise to a lot of difficulties. PAC learnability does not differentiate such situations. In some sense, the works of [19] allow to overcome some of the previous drawbacks by giving an upper bound for the error probability and providing a general scheme of training algorithms, namely the *Support Vector Machines*.

2.2   Support Vector Machines

Support Vector Machines (SVM) have been introduced by Vapnik [19] and are theoretically founded on the Vapnik and Chervonenkis dimension theory. Let us recall here what is the VC dimension. Given a set Ω, we consider a finite subset (i.e. a concept) A of Ω and a family $\mathcal{F}$ of subsets of Ω. We denote $A \cap \mathcal{F} = \{A \cap F \mid F \in \mathcal{F}\}$: this set is often called the track of $\mathcal{F}$ over A. Of course, $A \cap \mathcal{F} \subseteq 2^{|A|}$ where $2^{|A|}$ is the powerset of A. So A is shattered by $\mathcal{F}$ iff $A \cap \mathcal{F} = 2^{|A|}$. If A is shattered by $\mathcal{F}$, this means that each partition of A can be described by $\mathcal{F}$. The VC-dimension h of $\mathcal{F}$ is just the least upper bound of the set $\{|A| \mid A \text{ is shattered by } \mathcal{F}\}$. So the VC-dimension is an integer (sometimes infinite) which measures, in some sense, the complexity of the given model $\mathcal{F}$. If the elements F of $\mathcal{F}$ are described by functions, we see that the VC-dimension h is linked to a family of functions used to discriminate input data, so the output of the training algorithm is supposed to be one of these functions (linear function, polynomials, potential functions, etc.). One of the main advantages of this approach is the fact that the general risk is bounded by the empirical risk which is computable, added to an other quantity Q depending on h. In the previous notation of PAC, we have:

$$\sum_{\{\omega \in \Omega | f(\omega) \neq h(\omega)\}} P(\omega) \leq \sum_{\{\omega \in \Omega_a | f(\omega) \neq h(\omega)\}} P(\omega) + Q(\frac{m}{h})$$

where Q is a quantity linked to m, the cardinality of the training space, and to h, the VC dimension of the given model. Q is a decreasing function of $\frac{m}{h}$. So, if $\frac{m}{h}$ has a huge value, it is then sufficient to reduce the empirical risk to control the real risk. Ideally, the best situation is when m is very large, but generally this is not the case: so it is necessary to control the VC dimension h. Starting from such considerations, Vapnik provides a training scheme called Support Vector Machines. In the simple case of a two class problem, the main idea is to discriminate two point sets by building a separating hyper-plane. This plane is chosen in such a way to maximize its distance (called the margin) with the closest data. This way not only fits with theoretical results but also with the intuition: such an hyper-plane would be more robust since when adding a new point close to an element of a given class, this point will be far from the hyper-plane and so will be (with high probability) correctly classified. However, a main drawback is yet to be pointed out: an *a priori* model is fixed (*i.e.* a set of functions) to tackle a problem and we are not sure that a function of this model will be a good separator.

3   Practical Considerations

3.1   Notations

Let consider a set Ω of instances, each instance ω being characterized by the values of p features. We associate to ω a p-vector, $X(\omega) = (x_1(\omega), \ldots, x_p(\omega)) \in X = X_1 \times \ldots \times X_p$, each x_i belonging to a set X_i. X is the representation space or the feature set of Ω. Ω is supposed to be portioned into a finite number of classes $c_1, .., c_m$. For only a finite number n of elements ω in Ω we know the corresponding class $c(\omega)$: it constitutes a finite subset $\Omega_a \subset \Omega$ often called the training set $(n = |\Omega_a|)$. The aim of the learning algorithm is to generate a mechanism allowing to compute the class of a new element ω which does not belong to Ω_a. Of course, the underlying hypothesis is that $c(\omega)$ only depends on the vector $X(\omega)$.

3.2   Accuracy Estimates

Instead of proving that a given concept is learnable or not, it is possible to estimate a learnability degree of the target concept with regard to a given learning algorithm, computing an *a posteriori* accuracy. Different *a posteriori* methods are thus available: (i) the *holdout method* [10], (ii) the *k-cross-validation method* [10], (iii) *the bootstrap procedure* [3]. However, these *a posteriori* methods not only may require high computational costs, but also are dependent on the learning method to compute the learnability degree, that is not our first objective.

Moreover, recent works have proven that the accuracy is not always a suitable criterion. In [8], a formal proof is given that explains why Gini criterion and the entropy should be optimized instead of the accuracy when a top-down induction algorithm is used to grow a decision tree. Same kind of conclusions are presented with another statistical criterion in [15].

3.3 Statistical Criteria

Another way to measure the learnability consists then in using *a priori* statistical criteria, regardless of the learning algorithm. This way to proceed is based on the intuition that the difficulty to learn a concept directly depends on the feature space, and not on the learning method applied. Actually, the same concept may be more learnable in a feature space than in an other. Then, *measuring the learnability of a concept can amount to estimate the relevance of the feature space* (see [2] for a survey of relevance definitions). We recall here different criteria used to assess relevance.

- *Interclass distance*: the average distance between instances belonging to different classes is a good criterion to measure the relevance of a given feature space. However, the use of this criterion is restricted to problems without mutual class overlaps.
- *Class Projection*: this approach estimates the relevance of a given feature using conditional probabilities [17].
- *Entropy*: one can speak about feature relevance in terms of information theory. One can then use the Shannon's mutual information [20]; see also [11] where the cross-entropy measure is used, or [16] which uses a quadratic entropy computed from a neighborhood graph.
- *Probabilistic distance*: in order to correctly treat class overlaps, a better approach consists in measuring distances between probability density functions. It often leads to the construction of homogeneity tests [14].

The homogeneity tests are very interesting because they provide rigorous tools giving a good idea about the difficulty to learn a concept. Unfortunately, none of these tests currently proposed in literature, is both non parametric and applicable in X^p, with any type of attributes (*nominal, continuous, discrete*). We present in the next section a new statistical test overcoming these constraints.

4   The Test of Edges

4.1   Introduction

In the context of probabilistic distances, we can bring to the fore two types of extreme situations:

1. The most difficult situations are those where classes have the same probability distribution, *i.e.*:
   $f_1(x) = f_2(x) = ... = f_k(x)$ (called the null hypothesis in our test)

   where $f_i(x)$ is the probability for a given vector $x \in X$ to be in c_i.

During the learning phase, instances belonging to these classes will just be learned by heart (*overfitting situation*).

2. On the contrary, the most comfortable situations are those where classes have totally separated probability distributions.

The goal of our test is then to measure how far we are from the worst situation (*i.e.* where distributions are the same ones). The notion of distance is subjacent to our definition. Introduced in [16] in the pattern recognition field, the first version of the *test of edges* was limited to continuous attributes *i.e.* when $X = I\!R^p$. Recent works dealing with nominal attributes thanks to specific distance functions [21] allow to generalize here this test to mixed spaces. We detail in this section the useful aspects of the test of edges.

4.2   Formalism

The main idea is to decompose the space X into disjoint subsets, each of these subsets representing elements of the same class: so these subsets are considered as homogeneous. To do that, we use information contained in the *MST*.

Definition 2. *A tree is a connected graph without cycles. A subgraph that spans all vertices of a graph is called a spanning subgraph. A subgraph that is a tree and that spans all vertices of the original graph is called a spanning tree.*

Definition 3. *Among all the spanning trees of a weighted and connected graph, the one with the least total weight is called a Minimum Spanning Tree (MST).*

So, if we have a distance d over X, we can easily build a MST considering the weight of an edge as the distance between its extremities. Our approach is based on the search in the MST for *homogeneous subsets*.

Definition 4. *Given $G = (V, E)$, a graph composed by $v = | V |$ vertices and $e = | E |$ edges. Given G' a subgraph of $G, G' = (V', E')$. G' is an homogeneous subset if and only if:*

1. *All points of G' belong to the same class. In our case where $V \subset X$, this means : $\forall X(\omega_i), X(\omega_j) \in V'$, $c(\omega_i) = c(\omega_j)$.*
2. *G' is connected.*

Starting from the training set Ω_a and given a distance d over X, we get the *homogeneous subsets* with the following natural procedure:

- step 1: Construction of the *MST* over Ω_a which is composed of $n-1$ edges.
- step 2: Deletion of edges which connect 2 points belonging to different classes.

We may notice that each deletion in step 2 means that two elements, whose representations are very similar, belong in fact to distinct classes: so the number D of deleted edges is a main factor to estimate a learnability degree. In fact, D has to be estimated with regard to the initial number of edges $n - 1$: so our random variable is $\frac{D}{n-1}$ (the proportion of deleted edges to obtain homogeneous subsets). In the case where the distribution of classes are equal, we will have a great probability p to remove an edge. **So the degree of learnability may be estimated according to the comparison between p and $\frac{D}{n-1}$.**

4.3 The Law of $\frac{D}{n-1}$

With n instances we can build $\frac{n(n-1)}{2}$ edges. Among these edges, only $n-1$ will be really built with the MST. Considering as a success (with a p success probability) the deletion of an edge of the MST, D corresponds to the number of success. We can then deduce that the law of D is an hyper-geometric one. If the n size is high enough, the asymptotic normality of D is verified.

4.4 The Value of p

Recall that p is the probability under the null hypothesis to delete an edge. In this case, 2 conditions must be verified: (i) the 2 points (ω_i, ω_j) linked by this edge must be neighbors in the MST; (ii) they do not belong to the same class. The probability to delete an edge is: $p = P[(N_{ij} = true) \cap (c(\omega_i) \neq c(\omega_j))]$, where $(N_{ij} = true)$ means that ω_i is the neighbor of ω_j. Under the null hypothesis, the events "to be neighbor" and "to belong to the same class" are independent. We deduce that $p = P(N_{ij} = true) \times P(c(\omega_i) \neq c(\omega_j))$.

We can easily find that,

- $P(N_{ij} = true) = \frac{n-1}{\frac{n(n-1)}{2}}$

- $P(c(\omega_i) \neq c(\omega_j)) = \frac{\sum_{i=1}^{k-1} \sum_{j=i+1}^{k} n_i n_j}{\frac{n(n-1)}{2}}$ for $k \geq 2$

Thus, the probability p to delete an edge is:

$$p = \frac{n-1}{\frac{n(n-1)}{2}} \times \frac{\sum_{i=1}^{k-1} \sum_{j=i+1}^{k} n_i n_j}{\frac{n(n-1)}{2}}$$

where n_i is the number of instances of the class i. In conclusion,

$$D \equiv H\left(\frac{n(n-1)}{2}, n-1, \frac{n-1}{\frac{n(n-1)}{2}} \times \frac{\sum_{i=1}^{k-1} \sum_{j=i+1}^{k} n_i n_j}{\frac{n(n-1)}{2}}\right).$$

We can use the α_c critical threshold of this test to measure the degree of learnability between the 2 extreme situations: unlearnability ($\alpha_c = 1$, i.e. $f_1(x) = f_2(x)$) and strong learnability ($\alpha_c = 0$, i.e. $f_1 \cap f_2 = \emptyset$). Thus, we define the $(1 - \alpha_c)$-learnability as follows :

Definition 5. A concept is $(1 - \alpha_c)$-learnable iff the test of edges provides a α_c critical threshold, satisfying $P[f_1(x) = ... = f_k(x)] = \alpha_c$.

4.5 Distance Functions

The construction of the MST requires a distance over the feature set X. When features have real values, standard Euclidean metric is sufficient. A lot of recent works have been devoted to define adequate distances for spaces with mixed features. In [21], new heterogeneous distance functions are proposed, called the Heterogeneous Euclidean-Overlap Metric (*HEOM*), the Heterogeneous Value Difference Distance (*HVDM*), the Interpolated Value Difference Metric (*IVDM*), and the Windowed Value Difference Metric (*WVDM*). These distance functions properly handle nominal and continuous input attributes and allow the construction of a MST in mixed spaces. They are inspired by the Value Difference Metric [17]. It defines the distance between two values x and y of a nominal attribute a:

$$vdm_a(x,y) = \sum_{i=1}^{k} \left| \frac{N_{a,x,c_i}}{N_{a,x}} - \frac{N_{a,y,c_i}}{N_{a,y}} \right|^q = \sum_{i=1}^{k} |P_{a,x,c_i} - P_{a,y,c_i}|^q$$

where

- $N_{a,x}$ is the number of instances that have value x for attribute a,
- N_{a,x,c_i} is the number of instances in Ω_a that have value x for attribute a and output class c_i,
- P_{a,x,c_i} is the conditional probability that the output class is c_i given that attribute a has the value x, *i.e.*, $P(c_i/x_a = x)$,
- k is the number of output classes, and q is a constant.

For continuous attributes, HEOM, HVDM, IVDM and WVDM uses different strategies (normalization, discretization). We have integrated these new distance functions into our test in order to compare our approach on any problem with any learning methods.

5   Experimental Comparisons and Results on the MST

In order to bring to the fore the interest of our approach, we have to compare the learnability degree *a priori* determined by our test with the ability to learn the problem by a given learning algorithm (*i.e.* the *a posteriori* accuracy). We worked on 10 databases extracted from the UCI Repository[1]. Moreover, we have simulated an artificial problem (called *Artificial*) for which we know the overlapping degree and the α_c (near from 1). For each dataset, we have applied the following experimental set-up:

1. we used the C4.5 learning algorithm [13] to determine an accuracy estimate by cross-validation.
2. we applied also the ID3 algorithm [12] to determine a second accuracy rate.
3. a k-Nearest Neighbors classifier was run with $k = 10$.
4. finally, we computed the proportion $\frac{D}{n-1}$ of deleted edges from the MST, and the associated critical threshold α_c.

---

[1] http://www.ics.uci.edu/~mlearn/MLRepository.html

Table 1. Critical Threshold, $1 - \frac{D}{n-1}$, and Accuracy Rates with 3 learning algorithms

Database	# feat.	n	C4.5	ID3	k-NN	α_c	$1 - \frac{D}{n-1}$
Artificial	10	1000	51.0	50.7	50.1	1	50.1
Monks-2	6	432	65.0	69.7	62.0	0.95	63.5
Vehicle	18	846	69.9	71.8	69.5	10^{-3}	70.2
Pima	8	768	72.7	73.8	70.2	5.10^{-20}	71.0
Horse	22	368	84.8	75.3	71.1	10^{-11}	72.0
Monks-1	6	432	75.7	82.4	71.0	10^{-13}	72.3
Cleveland	7	297	72.3	72.4	75.0	9.10^{-20}	74.7
Australian	14	690	85.6	80.4	80.0	10^{-15}	80.2
Monks-3	6	432	97.1	90.3	90.0	10^{-68}	90.0
Vote	15	435	95.6	94.0	91	10^{-143}	91.2
Breast Cancer	10	699	95.7	94.6	96.3	10^{-170}	95.8

A first way to present the results would consist in sorting the α_c critical thresholds to have a classification according to the learnability degree of each problem, and compare this order with the accuracies computed by the 3 learning algorithms. However, contrary to the critical threshold, the accuracy estimates do not take into account the number of classes and the number of instances of each class. A 80% accuracy rate on 2 classes can not be compare with a 80% accuracy on 10 classes. So, we can not directly compare the accuracies with α_c. To avoid a normalization of the accuracies, a best comparison would consist in using directly the statistical variable $1 - \frac{D}{n-1}$ instead of α_c. Actually, this quantity intuitively measures in a way the guarantee for a new instance to be surrounded by examples of the same classes, *i.e.* to be correctly classified. Moreover, this strategy does not challenge the interest of α_c to determine the unlearnable problems. Sorting datasets according to the value of $1 - \frac{D}{n-1}$, we obtain the table 1.

We can note that:

1. With a classical $\alpha = 5\%$ risk, we can *a priori* conclude that *Artificial* and *Monks-2* problems are statistically unlearnable ($\alpha_c > \alpha$). So, our conclusion is that it seems to be useless to try to learn these 2 problems, with any learning algorithm. This conclusion is *a posteriori* confirmed by the accuracy estimates computed with the 3 learning methods. (Note that the number of instances is different for each class and that the random accuracy on Monks-2 is then about 55.9%)
2. The order is strictly kept by the accuracies computed with a k-NN classifier. This phenomenon is not surprising because the MST is a particular neighborhood graph, not very far from the 1NN topology.
3. That is more interesting is the order obtained with the two other classifiers. Excluding one database (*Monks1*), ID3 keeps the same order. For C4.5, three permutations are necessary to keep the same classification.

Table 2. Difference d for different sample sizes, and different values of μ_2

d	μ_2			
n	**3.0**	**2.0**	**1.5**	**1.2**
50	0.6	1.0	1.9	2.3
100	0.7	1.0	1.2	2.2
150	0.5	0.9	1.0	1.9
200	0.2	0.9	0.9	1.2
300	0	0.2	0.6	0.9
400	0.3	0.1	0.5	0.7
500	0.1	0.3	0.5	0.7

So, in the majority of cases, we can advance that our approach gives an exact idea of the learnability degree of each studied problem. Actually, the experimental results *a posteriori* confirm the decision of our statistical test.

6   The Test of Edges on a k-NN Graph

While our approach provides good results, it presents a shortcoming: its complexity. Actually, the construction of the MST requires $\mathcal{O}(n^2 \log n)$. A solution will consist in replacing the MST by another neighborhood graph with lower complexity, and that keeps the notion of homogeneous subset. The simplest is certainly the k-NN graph, which requires with the worst algorithm $\mathcal{O}(n^2)$. Even if we use the k-Nearest Neighbors to characterize the homogeneous subsets, we do not appeal to any induction rule for classifying a new instance. So, in such a context we do not challenge our first objective to have an independent measure, even if the random variable now turns towards an accuracy estimate. Actually, with $k = 1$, compute the quantity $1 - \frac{D}{|E|}$ (with $| E |= kn$) is strictly equivalent to compute an accuracy estimate using a Leave-One-Out Cross-Validation procedure (LOOCV) with a 1-NN classifier. On the other hand, it is not the case when $k > 1$. Particularly when k is even, in case of ties, a *tie breaking rule* chooses randomly a nearest-neighbor. This uncertainty does not exist with our strategy because the random variable is only built from the number of deleted edges, without any induction rule. According to this remark, we can expect not only to compute good accuracy estimates (very close to the LOOCV) but also to assure smaller standard deviation on small learning samples.

Before to get a theoretical proof of this property in future works, we show here some first experimental results. We have simulated samples of two classes according to a *a priori*-known distributions (for class 1, $\forall X_i$, $X_i \equiv N(\mu_1 = 1, \sigma)$; for class 2, $\forall X_i$, $X_i \equiv N(\mu_2, \sigma)$, $\mu_1 < \mu_2$). We varied the number of instances, and we also modified the distributions in order to increase the degree of overlapping ($\mu_2 \leftarrow \mu_2 - \varepsilon$). For different values of k we have computed the distributions of the $1 - \frac{D}{|E|}$ quantity and the Acc accuracy estimate by LOOCV using a k-NN classifier. While in the majority of cases, means of $1 - \frac{D}{|E|}$ and Acc are very close, the difference between standard deviations $d = \sigma_{Acc} - \sigma_{1 - \frac{D}{|E|}}$ seems to be significant. Results for $k = 2$ are presented in table 2. We can note that the standard deviation of $1 - \frac{D}{|E|}$ is always smaller than the one computed by LOOCV $(d > 0)$. For small sample sets with a high overlapping degree $(\mu_2 \approx \mu_1 \approx 1)$, the difference is very important because of the *tie breaking rule*. Progressively, with bigger learning sets, this difference tends to zero.

7 Conclusion

In this paper, we have developed a statistical test to *a priori* compute a measure of learnability for a given problem, represented in any feature space. This test is based over a Bayesian approach: the underlying hypothesis is that distribution of classes in the training set is a good mirror of the difficulty to build a learning machine. So, we compute a probability measuring, in some sense, the overlapping of the target classes. This probability is considered as a good measure of learnability for a given representation space of the problem. We implement this test and experiment it over 11 databases: practical results are in accordance with the expected ones. The high complexity of our algorithm turns our researches onto new geometrical graphs to characterize the homogeneous subsets. A preliminary experimental study shows interesting results with the k-NN graph, that would deserve new investigations in future works.

References

[1] J.L. Balcazar, J. Diaz, and J. Gabarro. Structural Complexity. *Springer Verlag*, 118(2), 1988.

[2] A.L. Blum and P. Langley. Selection of relevant features and examples in machine learning. *Issue of Artificial Intelligence*, pages 487–501, 1997.

[3] B. Efron and R. Tishirani. *An introduction to the bootstrap*. Chapman and Hall, 1993.

[4] M. Frazier, S. Goldman, N. Mishra, and L. Pitt. Learning from a consistently ignorant teacher. *Journal of Computer and System Sciences*, 52(3):471–492, June 1996.

[5] I. M. Gold. Language identification in the limit. *Information and Control*, 10:447–474, 1967.

[6] S. A. Goldman and H. D. Mathias. Teaching a smarter learner. *Journal of Computer and System Sciences*, 52(2):255–267, April 1996.

[7] K. Hoffgen and H. Simon. Lower bounds on learning decision lists and trees. In *Proceedings of the Fifth Workshop on COmputational Learning Theory, COLT'92*, pages 428–439, 1992.

[8] M.J. Kearns and Y. Mansour. On the boosting ability of top-down decision tree learning algorithms. *Proceedings of the Twenty-Eighth Annual ACM Symposium on the Theory of Computing*, pages 459–468, 1996.

[9] R. Kohavi. Feature subset selection as search with probabilistic estimates. *AAAI Fall Symposium on Relevance*, 1994.

[10] R. Kohavi. A study of Cross-Validation and Bootstrap for Accuracy Estimation and Model Selection. In *Proceedings of the 14th International Joint Conference on Artificial Intelligence*, pages 1137 – 1143, 1995.

[11] D. Koller and R.M. Sahami. Toward optimal feature selection. In *Thirteenth International Conference on Machine Learning (Bari-Italy)*, 1996.

[12] J.R. Quinlan. Induction of decision trees. *Machine Learning 1*, pages 81–106, 1986.

[13] J.R. Quinlan. *C4.5 : Programs for Machine Learning*. Morgan Kaufmann, 1993.

[14] C. Rao. *Linear statistical inference and its applications*. Wiley New York, 1965.

[15] R. E. Schapire and Y. Singer. Improved boosting algorithms using confidence-rated predictions. In *Proceedings of the Eleventh Annual ACM Conference on Computational Learning Theory*, pages 80–91, 1998.

[16] M. Sebban. *Modèles Théoriques en Reconnaissance de Formes et Architecture Hybride pour Machine Perceptive*. PhD thesis, Université Lyon 1, 1996.

[17] C. Stanfill and D. Waltz. Toward memory-based reasoning. In *Communications of the ACM*, pages 1213–1228, 1986.

[18] L. G. Valiant. A Theory of the Learnable. In *Communications of the ACM*, pages 1134 – 1142, 1984.

[19] V. Vapnik. *Support vector learning machines*. Tutorial at NIPS*97, Denver (CO), December 1997, 1997.

[20] D. Wettschereck and T.G. Dietterich. An experimental comparison of the nearest neighbor and nearest hyperrectangle algorithms. In *Machine Learning*, pages 5–28, 1995.

[21] D. R. Wilson and T. R. Martinez. Improved heterogeneous distance functions. *Journal of Artificial Intelligence Research*, 6:1–34, 1997.

ALM: A Methodology for Designing Accurate Linguistic Models for Intelligent Data Analysis[*]

Oscar Cordón and Francisco Herrera

Dept. of Computer Science and Artificial Intelligence, E.T.S. de Ingeniería
Informática, University of Granada, 18071 - Granada, Spain,
{ocordon,herrera}@decsai.ugr.es
http://decsai.ugr.es/{~ocordon,~herrera}

Abstract. In this paper we introduce *Accurate Linguistic Modelling*, an approach to design linguistic models from data, which are accurate to a high degree and may be suitably interpreted. Linguistic models constitute an Intelligent Data Analysis structure that has the advantage of providing a human-readable description of the system modelled in the form of linguistic rules. Unfortunately, their accuracy is sometimes not as high as desired, thus causing the designer to discard them and replace them by other kinds of more accurate but less interpretable models. ALM has the aim of solving this problem by improving the accuracy of linguistic models while maintaining their descriptive power, taking as a base some modifications on the interpolative reasoning developed by the Fuzzy Rule-Based System composing the model. In this contribution we shall introduce the main aspects of ALM, along with a specific design process based on it. The behaviour of this learning process in the solving of two different applications will be shown.

1 Introduction

Nowadays, one of the most important areas for the application of Fuzzy Set Theory as developed by Zadeh in 1965 [14] are Fuzzy Rule-Based Systems (FRBSs). These kinds of systems constitute an extension of classical Rule-Based Systems, because they deal with fuzzy rules instead of classical logic rules.

In this approach, fuzzy IF-THEN rules are formulated and a process of fuzzification, inference and defuzzification leads to the final decision of the system. Although sometimes the fuzzy rules can be directly derived from expert knowledge, different efforts have been made to obtain an improvement on system performance by incorporating learning mechanisms guided by numerical information to define the fuzzy rules and/or the membership functions associated to them. Hence, FRBSs are a suitable tool for Intelligent Data Analysis where the structure considered to represent the available data is a Fuzzy Rule Base.

From this point of view, the most important application of FRBSs is *system modelling* [10], which in this field may be considered as an approach used to

---

[*] This research has been supported by CICYT TIC96-0778

D.J. Hand, J.N. Kok, M.R. Berthold (Eds.): IDA'99, LNCS 1642, pp. 15–26, 1999.
© Springer-Verlag Berlin Heidelberg 1999

model a system making use of a descriptive language based on Fuzzy Logic with fuzzy predicates [11]. In this kind of modelling we may usually find two contradictory requirements, accuracy and interpretability.

When the main requirement is the accuracy, descriptive Mamdani-type FRBSs [7] are considered which use fuzzy rules composed of linguistic variables that take values in a term set with a real-world meaning. This area is called *Fuzzy Linguistic Modelling* due to the fact that the linguistic model consists of a set of linguistic descriptions regarding the behaviour of the system being modelled [11]. Nevertheless, the problem is that sometimes the accuracy of these kinds of models is not sufficient to solve the problem in a right way. In order to solve this problem, in this paper, we introduce *Accurate Linguistic Modelling* (ALM), a Linguistic Modelling approach which will allow us to improve the accuracy of linguistic models without losing its interpretability to a high degree.

To do so, this contribution is set up as follows. In Section 2, a brief introduction to FRBSs is presented with a strong focus on descriptive Mamdani-type ones. Section 3 is devoted to introduce the basis of ALM. In Section 4, a Linguistic Modelling process based on it is proposed. In Section 5, the behaviour of the linguistic models generated to solve two different applications is analysed. Finally, in Section 6, some concluding remarks will be pointed out.

2   Fuzzy Rule-Based Systems

An FRBS presents two main components: 1) the *Inference Engine*, which puts into effect the fuzzy inference process needed to obtain an output from the FRBS when an input is specified, and 2) the *Fuzzy Rule Base*, representing the known knowledge about the problem being solved in the form of fuzzy IF-THEN rules.

The structure of the fuzzy rules in the Fuzzy Rule Base determines the type of FRBS. Two main types of fuzzy rules are usually found in the literature:

1. *Descriptive Mamdani-type fuzzy rules* [7] —also called linguistic rules— which present the expression:

$$\text{IF } X_1 \text{ is } A_1 \text{ and ... and } X_n \text{ is } A_n \text{ THEN } Y \text{ is } B_i$$

   with $X_1, \ldots, X_n$ and Y being the input and output linguistic variables, respectively, and $A_1, \ldots, A_n$ and B being linguistic labels, each one of them having associated a fuzzy set defining its meaning.

2. *Takagi-Sugeno-Kang (TSK) fuzzy rules* [12], which are based on representing the consequent as a polynomial function of the inputs:

$$\text{IF } X_1 \text{ is } A_1 \text{ and ... and } X_n \text{ is } A_n \text{ THEN } Y = p_1 \cdot X_1 + \ldots + p_n \cdot X_n + p_0$$

   with $p_0, p_1, \ldots, p_n$ being real-valued weights.

The structure of a descriptive Mamdani-type FRBS is shown in Figure 1. As can be seen, and due to the use of linguistic variables, the Fuzzy Rule Base

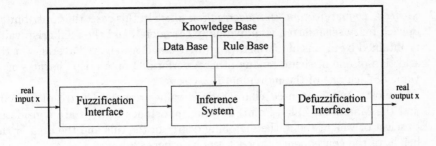

Fig. 1. Generic structure of a descriptive Mamdani-type Fuzzy Rule-Based System

becomes a Knowledge Base (KB) composed of the Rule Base (RB), constituted by the collection of linguistic rules joined by means of the connective *also*, and of the Data Base (DB), containing the term sets and the membership functions defining their semantics.

On the other hand, the Inference Engine is comprised by three components: a *Fuzzification Interface*, which has the effect of transforming crisp input data into fuzzy sets, an *Inference System*, that uses these together with the KB to perform the fuzzy inference process, and a *Defuzzification Interface*, that obtains the final crisp output from the individual fuzzy outputs inferred.

The *Inference System* is based on the application of the Generalized Modus Ponens, extension of the classical logic Modus Ponens. It is done by means of the Compositional Rule of Inference, which in its simplest form is reduced to [2]:

$$\mu_{B'}(y) = I(\mu_{A_i}(x_0), \mu_B(y))$$

with $x_0 = (x_1, \ldots, x_n)$ being the current system input, $\mu_{A_i}(x_0) = T(A_1(x_1), \ldots, A_n(x_n))$ being the matching degree between the rule antecedent and the input —T is a conjunctive operator (a t-norm)— and I being a fuzzy implication operator.

The Compositional Rule of Inference is applied to each individual rule, thus obtaining an output fuzzy set B_i' from each rule in the KB. The *Defuzzification Interface* aggregates the information provided by these fuzzy sets and transforms it into a single crisp value by working in one of the two following ways [2]:

1. *Mode A: Aggregation first, defuzzification after:* The individual fuzzy sets inferred are aggregated to obtain a final fuzzy set B' by means of a fuzzy aggregation operator G —which models the *also* operator that relates the rules in the base—. Then, a defuzzification method D is applied to transform the latter into a crisp value y_0 that will be given as system global output:

$$\mu_{B'}(y) = G\left\{\mu_{B_1'}(y), \mu_{B_2'}(y), \ldots, \mu_{B_n'}(y)\right\} \quad ; \quad y_0 = D(\mu_{B'}(y))$$

Usual choices for G and D are, respectively, the minimum and maximum operators and the Centre of Gravity and Mean of Maxima defuzzification methods.

2. *Mode B: Defuzzification first, aggregation after:* In this case, the contribution of each fuzzy set inferred is individually considered and the final crisp value is obtained by means of an operation (an average, a weighted average, or the selection of one of them, among others) performed on a crisp characteristic value of each one of the individual fuzzy sets.

   The most commonly used characteristic values are the Centre of Gravity and the Maximum Value Point. Several importance degrees are considered to select or weight them, the matching degree of the rule and the area or the height of the consequent fuzzy set among others [2].

3   ALM: An Approach for Generating Accurate Linguistic Models for Intelligent Data Analysis

One of the most interesting features of an FRBS is the interpolative reasoning it develops, which plays a key role in its high performance and is a consequence of the *cooperation among the fuzzy rules composing the KB*. As mentioned in the previous Section, the output obtained from an FRBS is not usually due to a single fuzzy rule but to the cooperative action of several fuzzy rules that have been fired, because they match the input to the system to some degree.

ALM will deal with the way in which the linguistic model make inference in order to improve its accuracy while not losing its description. Hence, it will be based on two main aspects that will be described in the two following subsections. The remaining one in this Section analyses some interesting remarks of the proposed approach.

3.1   A New Descriptive Knowledge Base Structure for Locally Improving the Model Accuracy

Some problems derived from the inflexibility of the concept of linguistic variable (see [1]) makes the usual linguistic model structure shown in the previous Section present low accuracy when working with very complex systems. Due to this reason, we consider obtaining a new more flexible KB structure that allows us to improve the accuracy of linguistic models without losing their interpretability.

In [9], an attempt was made to put this idea into effect first by designing a fuzzy model based on simplified TSK-type rules, i.e., rules with a single point in the consequent, and then transforming it into a linguistic model, which has to be as accurate as the former. To do so, they introduced a secondary KB, in addition to the usual KB, and proposed an Inference Engine capable of obtaining an output result from the combined action of both Fuzzy Rule Bases. Hence, what the system really does is to allow a specific combination of antecedents to have two different consequents associated, the first and second in importance, thus avoiding some of the said problems associated to the linguistic rule structure.

Taking this idea as a starting point, we allow a specific combination of antecedents to have two consequents associated, the first and second in importance in the fuzzy input subspace, but only in those cases in which it is really necessary to improve the model accuracy in this subspace, and not in all the possible ones as in [9]. Therefore, the existence of a primary and a secondary Fuzzy Rule Base is avoided, and the number of rules in the single KB is decreased, which makes easier to interpret the model.

These double-consequent rules will locally improve the interpolative reasoning performed by the model allowing a shift of the main labels making the final output of the rule lie in an intermediate zone between the two consequent fuzzy sets. They do not constitute an inconsistency from a Linguistic Modelling point of view due to the fact that they have the following interpretation:

IF x_1 is A_1 and ... and x_n is A_n THEN y is *between B_1 and B_2*

Other advantages of our approach are that we do not need the existence of a previous TSK fuzzy model and that we work with a classical fuzzy Inference Engine. In this contribution, we shall use the Minumum t-norm in the role of conjunctive and implication operator (although any other fuzzy operator may be considered for either of the two tasks). The only restriction is to use any defuzzification method working in mode B and considering the matching degree of the rules fired. We shall work with the *Centre of Gravity weighted by the matching degree* [2], whose expression is shown as follows:

$$y_0 = \frac{\sum_{i=1}^{T} h_i \cdot y_i}{\sum_{i=1}^{T} h_i}$$

with T being the number of rules in the KB, h_i being the matching degree between the ith rule and the current system input (see Section 2) and y_i being the centre of gravity of the fuzzy set inferred from that rule.

3.2 A New Way to Generate Fuzzy Rules for Globally Improving the Cooperation Between Them

The previous point deals with the local improvement of the fuzzy reasoning accuracy in a specific fuzzy input subspace. On the other hand, the second aspect deals with the cooperation between the rules in the KB, i.e., with the overlapped space zones that are covered by different linguistic rules. As is known, the generation of the best fuzzy rule in each input subspace does not ensure that the FRBS will perform well due to the fact that the rules composing the KB may not cooperate suitably. Many times, the accuracy of the FRBS may be improved if other rules different than the primary ones are generated in some subspaces because they cooperate in a better way with their neighbour rules.

Hence, we shall consider an operation mode based on generating a preliminary fuzzy rule set composed of a large number of rules, which will be single or double-consequent ones depending on the complexity of the specific fuzzy input subspace —no rules will be generated in the subspaces where the system is not defined—. Then, all these fuzzy rules will be treated as single-consequent ones (each double-consequent rule will be decomposed in two simple rules) and the subset of them with best cooperation level will be selected in order to compose the final KB.

3.3   Some Important Remarks about ALM

We may draw two very important conclusions from the assumptions made in the previous subsections. On the one hand, it is possible that, although the preliminary fuzzy rule set generated has some double-consequent rules, the final KB does not contain any rule of this kind after the selection process. In this case, the linguistic model obtained has taken advantage of the way in which the fuzzy rules has been generated because many rule subsets with different cooperation levels have been analysed. This is why it will present a KB composed of rules cooperating well, a fact that may not happen in other inductive design methods, such us Wang and Mendel's (WM-method) [13] and the Explorative Generation Method (EGM) [4] — an adaptation of Ishibuchi et al's fuzzy classification rule generation process [6] able to deal with rules with linguistic consequents— both of which are based on directly generating the best consequent for each fuzzy input subspace.

On the other hand, it is possible that the KB obtained presents less rules than KBs generated from other methods thanks to both aspects: the existence of two rules in the same input subspace and the generation of neighbour rules with better cooperation may mean that many of the rules in the KB are unnecessary to give the final system response. These assumptions will be corroborated in view of the experiments developed in Section 5.

4   A Linguistic Modelling Process Based on ALM

Following the assumptions presented in the previous Section, any design process based on ALM will present two stages: a preliminary *linguistic rule generation method* and a *rule selection method*. The composition of both stages in the learning process presented in this contribution, which takes as a base the WM-method, is shown in the next two subsections. Another ALM process based on the EGM is to be found in [4].

4.1   The Linguistic Rule Generation Method

Let E be an input-output data set representing the behaviour of the system being modelled. Then the RB is generated by means of the following steps:

1. *Consider a fuzzy partition of the input variable spaces*: It may be obtained from the expert information —if it is availaible— or by a normalization process. In this paper, we shall work with symmetrical fuzzy partitions of triangular membership functions (see Figure 2).
2. *Generate a preliminary linguistic rule set*: This set will be formed by the rule best covering each example —input-ouput data pair— contained in E. The structure of the rule $R_l = IF\ x_1\ is\ A_1^l\ and\ \ldots\ and\ x_n\ is\ A_n^l\ THEN\ y\ is\ B_l$ generated from the example $e_l = (x_1^l, \ldots, x_n^l, y^l)$ is obtained by setting each rule variable to the linguistic label associated to the fuzzy set best covering every example component.

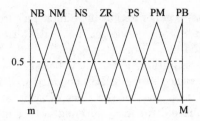

Fig. 2. Graphical representation of the type of fuzzy partition considered

3. *Give an importance degree to each rule*: The importance degree associated to R_l will be obtained as follows:

$$G(R_l) = \mu_{A_1^l}(x_1^l) \cdot \ldots \cdot \mu_{A_n^l}(x_n^l) \cdot \mu_{B_l}(y^l)$$

4. *Obtain a final RB from the preliminary linguistic rule set*: This step is the only one differing from the original WM-method. Whilst in that method the rule with the highest importance degree is the only one chosen for each combination of antecedents, in our case we allow the two most important rules in each input subspace —if they exist— to form part of the RB.
   Of course, a combination of antecedents may have no rules associated (if there are no examples in that input subspace) or only one rule (if all the examples in that subspace generated the same rule). Therefore, *the generation of double-consequent rules is only addressed when the problem complexity*, represented by the example set, *shows that it is necessary*.

4.2 The Rule Selection Genetic Process

In order to obtain a final KB composed of rules cooperating well and to achieve that more than a single rule is used only in those zones where it is really necessary, we shall use a rule selection process with the aim of selecting the best subset of rules from the initial linguistic rule set.

The selection of the subset of linguistic rules best cooperating is a combinatorial optimization problem [11]. Since the number of variables involved in it, i.e., the number of preliminary rules, may be very large, we consider an approximate algorithm to solve it, a Genetic Algorithm (GA) [5]. However, we should note that any other kind of technique can be considered without any change in ALM. Our rule selection genetic process [3] is based on a binary coded GA, in which the selection of the individuals is performed using the stochastic universal sampling procedure together with an elitist selection scheme, and the generation of the offspring population is put into effect by using the classical binary two-point crossover and uniform mutation operators.

The coding scheme generates fixed-length chromosomes. Considering the rules contained in the linguistic rule set derived from the previous step counted from 1 to T, a T-bit string $C = (c_1, ..., c_T)$ represents a subset of candidate rules to form the RB finally obtained as this stage output, B^s, such that,

$$\text{If } c_i = 1 \text{ then } R_i \in B^s \text{ else } R_i \notin B^s$$

The initial population is generated by introducing a chromosome representing the complete previously obtained rule set, i.e., with all $c_i = 1$. The remaining chromosomes are selected at random.

As regards the fitness funtion, $F(C_j)$, it is based on a global error measure that determines the accuracy of the FRBS encoded in the chromosome, which depends on the cooperation level of the rules existing in the KB. We usually work with the mean square error (SE), although other measures may be used. SE over the training data set, E, is represented by the following expression:

$$F(C_j) = \frac{1}{2|E|} \sum_{e_l \in E} (y^l - S(x^l))^2$$

where $S(x^l)$ is the output value obtained from the FRBS using the RB coded in C_j, when the input variable values are $x^l = (x_1^l, \ldots, x_n^l)$, and y^l is the known desired value.

5   Examples of Application

With the aim of analysing the behaviour of the proposed ALM process, we have chosen two different applications: the fuzzy modelling of a three-dimensional function [3] and the problem of rice taste evaluation [9]. In both cases, we shall compare the accuracy of the linguistic models generated from our process with the ones designed by means of other methods with different characteristics: two methods based on generating the RB rule by rule, i.e., without considering the cooperation among linguistic rules —the one proposed by Nozaki et al. (N-method) in [9], that has been mentioned in Section 3, and the simple WM-method— and another process based on working at the level of the whole KB —NEFPROX, the Neuro-Fuzzy approach proposed in [8].

5.1   Fuzzy Modelling of a Three-Dimensional Function

The expression of the selected function, the universes of discourse considered for the variables and its graphical representation are shown as follows. It is a simple unimodal function presenting two discontinuities at the points $(0,0)$ and $(1,1)$.

$$F(x_1, x_2) = 10 \cdot \frac{x_1 - x_1 x_2}{x_1 - 2x_1 x_2 + x_2},$$
$$x_1, x_2 \in [0,1], F(x_1, x_2) \in [0, 10]$$

In order to model this function, a training data set composed of 674 data uniformly distributed in the three-dimensional definition space has been obtained experimentally. On the other hand, another set composed of 67 data (a ten percent of the training set size) has been randomly generated for its use as a test set for evaluating the performance of the design methods. Of course, the latter set is only emploied to measure the generalization ability of the generated model, i.e., it is not considered in the learning stage. The DB used for all design

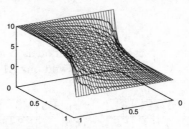

Fig. 3. Graphical representation of the function considered

methods is constituted by three normalised fuzzy partitions formed by *seven triangular-shaped fuzzy sets* (as shown in Fig. 2). The linguistic term set considered is $\{ES, VS, S, M, L, VL, EL\}$, standing E for Extremely, V for Very, and S, M, and L for Small, Medium and Large, respectively. Finally, the parameters considered for the rule selection genetic process are: Number of generations: 500, Population size: 61, Crossover probability: 0.6 and Mutation probability: 0.1 (per individual).

The results obtained in the experiments developed are collected in Table 1 where $\#R$ stands for the number of simple rules of the corresponding KB, and SE_{tra} and SE_{tst} for the values obtained in the SE measure computed over the training and test data sets, respectively. As may be observed, the results obtained by our process after each stage, generation and selection, are included.

Table 1. Results obtained in the fuzzy modelling of the selected function

Method	Generation			Selection		
	$\#R$	EC_{tra}	EC_{tst}	$\#R$	EC_{tra}	EC_{tst}
N-method	98	0.175382	0.061249	–	—	—
WM-method	49	0.194386	0.044466	–	—	—
NEFPROX	49	0.505725	0.272405	–	—	—
ALM	88	0.220062	0.146529	55	**0.019083**	**0.026261**

In view of these results, we should underline the good behaviour presented by our ALM process, that generates the most accurate model in the approximation of the training and test sets. As regards the number of rules in the KBs, we should note that our linguistic model only presents a few more rules than the ones generated from the WM-method and from NEFPROX. As shown in Table 2, by only adding eight new rules (and by removing two more) to the KB generated by means of the WM-method, a significantly more accurate model is obtained with a very small loss of interpretability (as mentioned, this KB only contains eight double-consequent rules). On the other hand, our model is more accurate to a high degree than the N-method one, presenting a very much simpler KB (55 rules against 98).

Table 2. Decision tables for the linguistic models obtained for the selected function by means of the WM-method (left) and our ALM process (right)

	x_2						
x_1	**ES**	**VS**	**S**	**M**	**L**	**VL**	**EL**
ES	*ES*	*ES*	*ES*	*ES*	*ES*	*ES*	*ES*
VS	*EL*	*M*	*S*	*VS*	*VS*	*ES*	*ES*
S	*EL*	*L*	*M*	*S*	*VS*	*VS*	*ES*
M	*EL*	*VL*	*L*	*M*	*S*	*VS*	*ES*
L	*EL*	*VL*	*VL*	*L*	*M*	*S*	*ES*
VL	*EL*	*EL*	*VL*	*VL*	*L*	*M*	*ES*
EL	*EL*	*EL*	*EL*	*EL*	*EL*	*EL*	*ES*

	x_2						
x_1	**ES**	**VS**	**S**	**M**	**L**	**VL**	**EL**
ES		*ES*	*ES*	*ES*	*ES*	*ES*	*ES*
VS	*EL*	*M*	*S*	*VS*	*S VS*	*ES*	*ES*
S	*EL*	*L*	*M*	*S*	*S VS*	*VS ES*	*ES*
M	*EL*	*VL*	*L*	*M*	*S*	*VS*	*ES*
L	*EL*	*VL EL*	*L VL*	*L*	*M*	*S VS*	*ES*
VL	*EL*	*EL*	*VL EL*	*VL VL*	*L VL*	*M*	*ES*
EL	*EL*	*EL*	*EL*	*EL*	*EL*	*EL*	

5.2   Rice Taste Evaluation

Subjective qualification of food taste is a very important but difficult problem. In the case of the rice taste qualification, it is usually put into effect by means of a subjective evaluation called the *sensory test*. In this test, a group of experts, usually composed of 24 persons, evaluate the rice according to a set of characteristics associated to it. These factors are: *flavor*, *appearance*, *taste*, *stickiness*, and *toughness* [9].

Because of the large quantity of relevant variables, the problem of rice taste analysis becomes very complex, thus leading to solve it by means of modelling techniques capable of obtaining a model representing the non-linear relationships existing in it. Moreover, the problem-solving goal is not only to obtain an accurate model, but to obtain a user-interpretable model as well, capable of putting some light on the reasoning process performed by the expert for evaluating a kind of rice in a specific way. Due to all these reasons, in this Section we deal with obtaining a linguistic model to solve the said problem.

In order to do so, we are going to use the data set presented in [9]. This set is composed of 105 data arrays collecting subjective evaluations of the six variables in question (the five mentioned and the overall evaluation of the kind of rice), made up by experts on this number of kinds of rice grown in Japan (for example, Sasanishiki, Akita-Komachi, etc.). The six variables are normalised, thus taking values in the real interval [0, 1].

With the aim of not biasing the learning, we have randomly obtained ten different partitions of the said set, composed by 75 pieces of data in the training set —to generate ten linguistic models in each experiment— and 30 in the test one —to evaluate the performance of the generated models—. To solve the problem, we use the same Linguistic Modelling processes considered in the previous Section. The values of the parameters of the rule selection genetic process are the same ones considered in that Section as well.

As was done in [9], we have worked with normalised fuzzy partitions (see Fig. 2) composed of a different number of linguistic labels for the six variables considered —two and three, to be precise—. The results obtained in the experiments developed are collected in Table 3. The values shown in columns SE_{tra} and SE_{tst} have been computed as an average of the SE values obtained on the training and test data sets, respectively, by the ten linguistic models generated in each case. The column $\#L$ stands for the number of labels considered in the fuzzy partitions in each experiment and $\#R$ stands for the average number of linguistic rules in the KBs of the models generated from each process.

Table 3. Results obtained in the rice taste evaluation

		Generation			Selection		
$\#L$	Method	$\#R$	EC_{tra}	EC_{tst}	$\#R$	EC_{tra}	EC_{tst}
	N-method	64	0.00862	0.00985	–	—	—
2	WM-method	15	0.01328	0.01311	–	—	—
	NefProx	15	0.00633	0.00568	–	—	—
	ALM	19.8	0.02192	0.02412	**5**	**0.00341**	**0.00398**
	N-method	364.8	0.00251	0.00322	–	—	—
3	WM-method	23	0.00333	0.00375	–	—	—
	NefProx	32.2	0.00338	0.00644	–	—	—
	ALM	25.7	0.00595	0.00736	**12.2**	**0.00185**	**0.00290**

From an analysis of these results, we may again note the good behaviour presented by the proposed ALM process. The linguistic models generated from it clearly outperform the ones designed by means of the other processes in the approximation of both data sets (training and test) in the two experiments developed (using 2 and 3 labels in the fuzzy partitions). On the other hand, even following the approach of double-consequent generation proposed in Section 3, our process generates the KBs with less rules, thus making the corresponding models simpler to be interpreted. In fact, none of the 20 KBs generated finally presents double-consequent rules due to the action of the selection process.

6   Concluding Remarks

In this paper, ALM has been proposed, that is a new approach to design linguistic models in the field of Intelligent Data Analysis, which are accurate to a high degree and suitably interpretable by human-beings. An ALM process has been introduced as well, and its behaviour has been compared to other Linguistic

Modelling techniques in solving two different problems. The proposed process has obtained very good results.

This leads us to conclude that, as mentioned in Section 3.3, our process has the capability of distinguishing the unnecesary rules and of generating KBs with good cooperation. The ALM operation mode based on: a) generating a preliminary fuzzy rule set with a large number of rules —considering double-consequent ones if it is necessary— and b) selecting the subset of them cooperating best allows us to obtain good results in the area of Linguistic Modelling.

References

1. Bastian, A.: How to handle the flexibility of linguistic variables with applications. International Journal of Uncertainty, Fuzziness and Knowledge-Based Systems **2:4** (1994) 463-484.
2. Cordón, O., Herrera, F., Peregrín, A.: Applicability of the fuzzy operators in the design of fuzzy logic controllers. Fuzzy Sets and Systems **86** (1997) 15-41.
3. Cordón, O., Herrera, F.: A three-stage evolutionary process for learning descriptive and approximative fuzzy logic controller knowledge bases from examples. International Journal of Approximate Reasoning **17:4** (1997) 369-407.
4. Cordón, O., Herrera, F.: A Proposal for Improving the Accuracy of Linguistic Modelling. Technical Report DECSAI-98113. Dept. of Computer Science and A.I. University of Granada. Spain (May, 1998).
5. Goldberg, D.E.: Genetic Algorithms in Search, Optimization, and Machine Learning. Addison-Wesley (1989).
6. Ishibuchi, H., Nozaki, K., Tanaka, H.: Distributed representation of fuzzy rules and its application to pattern classification. Fuzzy Sets and Systems **52** (1992) 21-32.
7. Mamdani, E.H., Applications of fuzzy algorithm for control a simple dynamic plant, Proceedings of the IEE, **121:12** (1974) 1585-1588.
8. Nauck, D., Klawonn, F., Kruse, R.: Fundations of Neuro-Fuzzy Systems. John Willey & Sons (1997).
9. Nozaki, K., Ishibuchi, H., Tanaka, H.: A simple but powerful heuristic method for generating fuzzy rules from numerical data. Fuzzy Sets and Systems **86** (1997) 251-270.
10. Pedrycz, W. (Ed.): Fuzzy Modelling: Paradigms and Practice. Kluwer Academic Press (1996).
11. Sugeno, M., Yasukawa, T.: A fuzzy-logic-based approach to qualitative modelling. IEEE Transactions on Fuzzy Systems **1:1** (1993) 7-31.
12. Takagi, T., Sugeno, M.: Fuzzy identification of systems and its application to modelling and control. IEEE Transactions on Systems, Man, and Cybernetics **15:1** (1985) 116-132.
13. Wang, L.X., Mendel, J.M.: Generating fuzzy rules by learning from examples. IEEE Transactions on Systems, Man, and Cybernetics **22** (1992) 1414-1427.
14. Zadeh, L.A.: Fuzzy sets. Information and Control **8** (1965) 338-353.

A "Top-Down and Prune" Induction Scheme for Constrained Decision Committees

Richard Nock[1] and Pascal Jappy[2]

[1] Univ. des Antilles-Guyane
Dept of Maths and CS, Campus de Fouillole,
97159 Pointe-à-Pitre, France
rnock@univ-ag.fr
[2] Léonard's Logic, 20 rue Thérèse,
75001 Paris, France
pjappy@leologic.com

Abstract. It was previously argued that Decision Tree learning algorithms such as CART or C4.5 can also be useful to build small and accurate Decision Lists. In that paper, we investigate the possibility of using a similar "top-down and prune" scheme to induce formulae from a much different class: Decision Committees. A decision committee contains rules, each of which being a couple (monomial, vector), where the vector's components are highly constrained with respect to classical polynomials. Each monomial is a condition that, when matched by an instance, returns its vector. When each monomial is tested, the sum of the returned vectors is used to take the decision. Decision Trees, Lists and Committees are complementary formalisms for the user: while trees are based on literal ordering, lists are based on monomial ordering, and committees remove any orderings over the tests. Our contribution is a new algorithm, WIDC, which learns using the same "top-down and prune" scheme, but building Decision Committees. Experimental results on twenty-two domains tend to show that WIDC is able to produce small, accurate, and interpretable decision committees.

1   Introduction

The ability to choose the output type (decision trees, lists, etc.) of an induction algorithm is crucial, at least for two reasons. First, the interpretation of the output depends on the user's natural preferences, and it may be easier using specific types of concept representations. Second, the problem adressed by the algorithm usually favors efficient encoding on some formalisms (*e.g.* linear separators) but not on others (*e.g.* ordinary decision trees). As an example [12] quote that

> "the clients [business users] found some interesting patterns in the decision trees, but they did not feel the structure was natural for them. They were looking for those two or three attributes and values (*e.g.* a combination of geographic and industries) where something "interesting" was happening. In addition, they felt it was too limiting that the nodes in a decision tree represent rules that all start with the same attributes."

D.J. Hand, J.N. Kok, M.R. Berthold (Eds.): IDA'99, LNCS 1642, pp. 27–38, 1999.
© Springer-Verlag Berlin Heidelberg 1999

Because classical induction algorithms provide only one, or very few choices of output types, the satisfaction of the user's preferences and/or the search for small (thus, interpretable) encodings are solved by browsing through the outputs of *various* algorithms. However, it is actually hard to compare such outputs for they can be built using different schemes, paradigms or principles. The usual error minimization principle is not always the only goal an induction algorithm has to realize, and various other parameters can be taken into account: time complexity, size restrictions over the output, vizualization requirements, by-classes errors, etc. As an example, consider CN2's decision list output [4], and the decision trees obtained from C4.5 [18]. It has been remarked that CN2's outputs are on average much bigger than the decision lists *equivalent* to C4.5's outputs [16]. This contradicts a *priori* observations on the expressive power of decision lists [20, 16]; in fact, the two algorithms are designed much differently from each other, and they optimize quite different criteria.

A previous study [16, 17] establishes that the particular induction scheme of C4.5 can be used to build decision lists, which in turn gives quite accurate comparisons with C4.5's decision trees, in the light of their theoretical relationships. In that paper, we propose to extend their general "top-down and prune" induction scheme to a much different class: decision committees (DC). DC is the Boolean multiclass extension of polynomial discriminant functions. A decision committee contains rules, each of these being a couple (monomial, vector). Each monomial is a condition that, when fired, returns its vector. After each monomial has been tested, the sum of the returned vectors is used to take the decision. This additive fashion for combining rules is absent from classical Boolean classifiers such as Decision Trees (DT) or Decision Lists (DL). Furthermore, unlike these two latter classes, the classifier contains absolutely no ordering, neither on variables (unlike DT), nor on monomials (unlike DL). When sufficiently small DCs are built and adequate restrictions are taken, a new dimension in interpreting the classifier is obtained, which does not exist for DT or DL. Namely, any example can satisfy many rules, and a DC can therefore be interpreted by means of various rule *subsets*. Decision committees share a common feature with decision tables [12]: they are all voting methods. However, decision tables classifiers are based on majority votings of the examples (and not of rules), over a restricted "window" of the description variables. They necessitate the storing of many examples, and the interpretations of the data can only be made through this window, according to this potentially large set of examples. Decision committees rather represent an efficient way to encode a large voting method into a small number of rules.

The algorithm we present is called WIDC, which stands for "Weak Induction of Decision Committees". It has the following key features. It uses recent results on partition boosting, ranking loss boosting [22] and some about pruning [10]. Second, it represents a weak learning algorithm as defined by [22], rather than a boosting algorithm as defined by [22]. In particular, no modification is made on the example's distribution, similarly to C4.5. Additionally, ADABOOST's procedure adapted to generate polynomials is not suited to calculate such constrained vectors as for DC. Finally, on multiclass problems, when it can be assumed that each example belongs to one class, WIDC proposes a polynomial solution for multiclass induction which is faster than that proposed by [22]. In addition, it avoids a NP-Hardness conjecture of [22].

This paper is organized as follows: in the following section, we present some definition about DC. We then proceed by a detailed exposition of each stage of the algorithm WIDC. In the last section, we present experiments that were carried out using WIDC, on twenty-two problems, most of which can be found on the UCI repository [2].

2 Definitions

Let c be the number of classes. An *example* is a couple (o, c_o) where o is an *observation* described over n variables, and c_o its corresponding *class* among $\{1, 2, ..., c\}$; to each example (o, c_o) is associated a weight $w((o, c_o))$, representing its appearance probability with respect to a learning sample LS which we dispose of. LS is itself a subset of a whole *domain* which we denote by $\mathcal{X}$. A decision committee contains two parts:

- A set of unordered couples (or rules) $\{(t_i, v_i)\}$ where each t_i is a monomial (a conjunction of literals) over $\{0, 1, *\}^n$ (n being the number of description variables), and each v_i is a vector in $\mathbb{R}^c$ (in the two-classes case, we add a single number rather than a 2-component vector).
- A Default Vector D in $[0, 1]^c$. Again, in the two-classes case, it is sufficient to replace D by a default class in $\{+, -\}$.

For any observation o and any monomial t_i, the proposition "o satisfies t_i" is denoted by $o \Rightarrow t_i$. The opposite proposition "o does not satisfy t_i" is denoted by "$o \not\Rightarrow t_i$. The classification of any observation o is made in the following way: define V_o as follows $V_o = \sum_{(t_i, v_i)|o \Rightarrow t_i} v_i$. The class assigned to o is then $\arg\max_{1 \leq j \leq c} V_o$ if $|\arg\max_{1 \leq j \leq c} V_o| = 1$, and $\arg\max_{j \in \arg\max_{1 \leq j \leq c} V_o} D$ otherwise. In other words, if the maximal component of V_o is unique, then the index gives the class assigned to o. Otherwise, we take the index of the maximal component of D corresponding to the maximal component of V_o.

Figure 1 presents the example of a simple decision committee having three rules, with $n = 4$. Let $x_1 x_2 x_3 x_4$ be some observation. Since it satisfies the first and the third monomial, its corresponding vector has respective components 2, -1 and 0. The greatest value is obtained for class c_1, which gives the class of the observation. Let $\bar{x}_1 \bar{x}_2 x_3 x_4$ be another observation. Its corresponding vector has respective components 0, -1, 0, which makes the default vector to assign a class. The largest value of the default vector among 0.2 and 0.5 is that of class c_3, which gives the class of the observation.

Let DC denote the whole class of decision committees. DC contains a subclass which is among the largest to be PAC-learnable [15], however this class is less

monomials	c_1	c_2	c_3
$x_1 \wedge x_2$	1	-1	1
$\overline{x}_1 \wedge x_3$	-1	-1	1
x_4	1	0	-1
default D	0.2	0.3	0.5

Fig. 1. A simple decision committee.

interesting from a practical viewpoint since rules can be numerous and hard to interpret. However, a subclass of decision committees [15] presents an interesting compromise between representational power and interpretability power. In this class, which is used by WIDC, each of the vector components are restricted to $\{-1, 0, 1\}$ and each monomial is present at most once. This subclass, to which we relate to as $DC_{\{-1,0,1\}}$, contains the example of figure 1; it suffers the same algorithmic drawbacks as decision trees [8] and decision lists [16]: the construction of small formulae with sufficiently high accuracy is hard[15]. In the case of $DC_{\{-1,0,1\}}$, this difficulty even comes from two sources: the size limitation, and the restriction over the vectors.

3   Overview of WIDC

[15] propose an algorithm, IDC, for building decision committees, which proceeds in two stages. The first stage builds a potentially large subset of different rules, each of which consists in a $DC_{\{-1,0,1\}}$ with only one rule. Then, in a second stage, it clusters gradually the decision committees, given that the union of two $DC_{\{-1,0,1\}}s$ with different rules is still a $DC_{\{-1,0,1\}}$. At the end of this procedure, the user obtains a population of DC, in which the most accurate one is chosen and returned. Results proved that IDC is efficient to build small DCs. In that paper, we provide an algorithm from learning decision committees which has a different structure since it builds only one DC ; it shares common features with algorithms such as C4.5 [18], CART [1], ICDL [16]. More precisely, WIDC is a three-stages algorithm. It first build a set of rules derived from the results of [22] on boosting decision trees. It then calculates the vectors using a scheme derived from Ranking loss boosting [22]. It then prunes the final $DC_{\{-1,0,1\}}$ using two possible schemes: pruning using the local convergence results and formulae of [10], to which we relate as "optimistic pruning", or a more conventional pruning to which we relate as "pessimistic pruning". The default vector is always chosen to be the observed distribution of ambiguously classified examples.

While it shares many common features with the "C4.5-family" of induction algorithms, WIDC is much different from the algorithms belonging to the so-called "AQ-family" [14, 13]. At least two fundamental parts of the induction are concerned. First, the goal itself is different. WIDC grows directly an overall concept for all classes instead of building a set of rules for each. Second, the main induction step, growing a single rule, is conducted from an empty, unconstrained rule, instead of being driven from a single observation.

3.1   Building a Large DC Using Partition Boosting

Suppose that the hypothesis (not necessarily a DC, it might be *e.g.* a decision tree) we build realizes a partition of the domain $\mathcal{X}$ into disjoint subsets $X_1, X_2, ..., X_N$. Fix as $[\![\pi]\!]$ the function returning the truth value of a predicate π. Define

$$W_+^{j,l} = \sum_{(o,c_o)\in LS} w((o,c_o))[\![(o,c_o) \in X_j \wedge c_o = l]\!]$$

$$W_-^{j,l} = \sum_{(o,c_o)\in LS} w((o,c_o))[\![(o,c_o) \in X_j \wedge c_o \neq l]\!]$$

In other words, $W_+^{j,l}$ represents the fraction of examples of class l present in subset X_j, and $W_-^{j,l}$ represents the fraction of examples of classes $\neq l$ present in subset X_j. According to [22], a weak learner should optimize the criterion:

$$Z = 2\sum_j \sum_l \sqrt{W_+^{j,l} W_-^{j,l}}$$

In the case of a decision tree, the partition is the one which is built at the leaves of the tree [18] ; in the case of a decision list, the partition is the one which is built at each rule, to which we add the subset associated to the default class [16]. Suppose that we encode the decision tree in the form of a subset of monomials, by taking for each leaf the logical-$\wedge$ of all attributes from the root to the leaf. All monomials are disjoint, and measuring Z over the tree's leaves is equivalent to measure Z over the partition realized by the set of monomials. However, due to the disjointness property, only t subsets can be realized with t monomials, or equivalently with a tree having t leaves.

Suppose that we generalize this observation by removing the disjointness condition over the monomials. Then a number of subsets of order $\mathcal{O}(2^t)$ can now be realized with only t monomials, and it appears that the number of realized partition can be exponentially larger using DC than DT. However, the expected running time is not bigger when using DC, since the number of partitions is in fact bounded by the number of examples $|LS|$, where $|.|$ denotes the cardinality. Thus, we may expect some gain in the size of the formula we build, which is of interest to interpret the classifier obtained.

Application of this principle in WIDC is straightforward: a large DC is built by growing repetively, in a top-down fashion, a current monomial. In this monomial, the literal added at the current step is the one which minimizes the current Z criterion, over all possible addition of literals, and given that the new monomial does not exist already in the current DC (in order to prevent multiple additions of a single monomial). When no further addition of a literal decreases the Z value, a new monomial is created and initialized at $\emptyset$, and then is grown using the same principle. When no further creation of a monomial decreases the Z, the algorithm stops and returns the current, large DC with still empty vectors. In the following step, WIDC calculates these vectors.

3.2   Calculation of the Rule Vectors Using Ranking Loss Boosting

[22] have investigated classification problems where the aim of the procedure is not to provide for some observation an accurate class. Rather, the algorithm outputs a set of values (one for each class) and we expect the class of the observation to receive the largest value of all, thus being ranked higher than all others. The *ranking loss* represents informally the number of times the hypothesis fails to rank higher the class of an observation, against a class to which it does not belong. Suppose that each example (o, c_o) is replaced by $c - 1$ new "examples" (o, y, c_o) where $y \neq c_o$, and renormalize the distribution of these new examples so that $\forall (o, c_o), \sum_{y \neq c_o} w((o, y, c_o)) = w((o, c_o))$. Thus, the weight of an arbitrary, newly defined example, $w((o, l_0, l_1))$, is 0 whenever $l_1 \neq c_o$ or $l_0 = l_1$, and equals otherwise $\frac{w((o, c_o))}{c-1}$. Take some monomial t_i obtained from the large DC, and all examples satisfying it. We now work with this restricted subset of examples, while calculating v_i. [22] propose a cost function which we should minimize in order to minimize the ranking loss. Adapted to our framework where the values of v_i are constrained to $\{-1, 0, 1\}$, we should find the vector v_i minimizing

$$Z = \sum_{o, l_0, l_1} w((o, l_0, l_1)) \times e^{-\frac{1}{2}(v_i[l_0-1]-v_i[l_1-1])}$$

(components of v_i are numbered from 0 to $c - 1$). [22] conjecture that finding the optimal vector (which is similar to an *oblivious* hypothesis according to their definitions) is NP-Hard when c is not fixed, when each example can be element of more than one class, and when new coefficients are predetermined to "adjust" the values of v_i. In our more restricted case however, the problem admits a solution which is polynomial-time with respect to $|LS|, n, c$. In the two following subsections, we present the algorithm for undetermined c, and then an exact and fast procedure for the two-classes case.

Polynomial Solution for Undetermined c   We calculate the vector v_i of some monomial t_i. We use the shorthands $W_0^+, W_1^+, ..., W_{c-1}^+$ to denote the sum of weights of the examples satisfying t_i and belonging respectively to classes $1, 2, ..., c$ (although not really relevant to the purpose of this paper, we could suppose that each example belongs to more than one class). We want to minimize Z as proposed above. Z can be rewritten as $Z = \sum_{l_0 \neq l_1} Z_{l_0, l_1}$, with

$$\forall l_0 \neq l_1, Z_{l_0, l_1} = \frac{W_{l_0}^+}{c-1} e^{-\frac{1}{2}\Delta_{l_0, l_1}} + \frac{W_{l_1}^+}{c-1} e^{\frac{1}{2}\Delta_{l_0, l_1}}$$

and
$$\Delta_{l_0, l_1} = v_i[l_0 - 1] - v_i[l_1 - 1]$$
Given only three possible values for each component of v, the testing of all 3^c possibilities is exponential and time-consuming. But we can propose a polynomial approach. Suppose without loss of generality that $W_0^+ \leq W_1^+ \leq \ldots \leq W_{c-1}^+$, otherwise, reorder the classes so that they verify this assertion. Then it comes $\forall 0 \leq l_0 < l_1 \leq c - 1, v_i[l_0 - 1] \leq v_i[l_1 - 1]$. Thus, the optimal v_i does not belong to a set of cardinality 3^c, but to a set of cardinality $\mathcal{O}(c^2)$ which is easy to explore in quadratic time. The solution when there are two classes is much more explicit, as we now show.

Explicit Solution in the Two-Classes Case For classical conventions, rename $W_0^+ = W^+$ and $W_1^+ = W^-$ representing the fraction of examples from the positive and negative class respectively, satisfying t_i. Due to the lack of space, we only present the algorithm. The proof is a straightforward minimization of Z in that particular case.

If $\frac{W_+}{W_-} < \frac{1}{e^{\frac{3}{2}}}$, then $v_i = (-1, +1)$;

If $\frac{1}{e^{\frac{3}{2}}} \leq \frac{W_+}{W_-} < \frac{1}{\sqrt{e}}$, then $v_i = (0, +1)$;

If $\frac{1}{\sqrt{e}} \leq \frac{W_+}{W_-} < \sqrt{e}$, then $v_i = (0, 0)$;

If $\sqrt{e} \leq \frac{W_+}{W_-} < e^{\frac{3}{2}}$, then $v_i = (+1, 0)$;

If $\frac{W_+}{W_-} \geq e^{\frac{3}{2}}$, then $v_i = (+1, -1)$.

3.3 Pruning a DC

The algorithm is a single-pass algoritm: each rule is tested only once, from the first rule to the last one. For each possible rule, a criterion Criterion(.) returns "TRUE" or "FALSE" depending on whether the rule should be removed or not. There are two versions of this criterion. The first one, to which we relate as "optimistic", is derived from the recent work of [10] on pruning decision-trees. The second one, more classic and "pessimistic", is strictly based on observed error minimization.

Optimistic Pruning [10] present a novel algorithm to prune decision trees, based on the a test over local observed errors. By using [10], lemma 1, we can obtain a similar test for DC, which seems however heuristic w.r.t. their general convergence results on DT. Its principle is the same : "can we compare, when testing some rule (t_i, v_i) and using the examples that satisfy the rule, the errors before and after removing the rule"? Name $\epsilon_{(t_i, v_i)}$ as the error before removing the rule, on the local sample $LS_{(t_i, v_i)}$ satisfying monomial t_i. Denote $\epsilon_\emptyset$ as the error before removing (t_i, v_i), still measured on the local sample $LS_{(t_i, v_i)}$. Then we define the "penalty"

$$\alpha'_{(t_i, v_i)} = \sqrt{\frac{(\text{Set}(v) + 2) \log(n) + 2 \log 1/\delta}{|LS_{(t_i, v_i)}|}}$$

Set(v) denotes the total number of literal of all other rules in the DC that an *arbitrary* example could satisfy. Remark that $\alpha'_{(t_i, v_i)}$ is fastly calculable, though it represents actually an combinatorial upperbound of the correct formula which would follow from [10], lemma 1. The value of Criterion((t_i, v_i)) is therefore "TRUE" iff $\epsilon_{(t_i, v_i)} + \alpha'_{(t_i, v_i)} \geq \epsilon_\emptyset$.

Pessimistic Pruning The test simply returns "TRUE" iff the error after pruning the tested rule is strictly lower than after. Otherwise, the rule is left.

4   Experimental Results

Experiments were carried out using both pruning stages for WIDC. We observed that the algorithm obtained poor results with the optimistc pruning, because the penalty factor was too large, particularly on small datasets. Remark that the penalty factor tends to zero as $|LS_{(t_i, v_i)}|$ tends to $+\infty$. We have chosen to uniformly resample LS into a much marger subset of 5000 examples, when the initial LS contained less than 5000 examples. By this, we uniformly resample each problem so that all mimic domains with identical sizes, with which reasonable comparions may be made on pruning.

Table 1 presents some results on datasets, which (except those marked by a "*") were taken from the UCI repository of machine learning database [2]. Experiments were carried out on each domain by averaging results over a ten-fold stratified cross validation procedure [19]. The results are presented for three types of execution of WIDC: with optimistic pruning (o), with pessimistic pruning (p), and without pruning ($\emptyset$). The terminology used for naming datasets is that of classical machine learning studies [6, 19]. The database LEDeven is exactly that of the LED recognition problem ([1], still with 10% noise over the attributes), except that the 10 classes over the digits are replaced by two (even/odd). Problem LEDeven+17 is LEDeven with 17 additional irrelevant attributes. Underlined numbers in error rates indicates better values. We did not underline better results in sizes, for they are systematically in favor of WIDC (o). Column "Others" points out previously cited results, relevant to our study.

Interpretation of table 1 by means of error comparisons gives a clear advantage for WIDC with pessimistic pruning. Results obtained also compare favourably to previously published results for induction algorithms, building decision trees, decision lists or decision committees. But they are all the more significant as we compare sizes obtained for the corresponding errors. For the "Echo" domain, WIDC with pessimistic pruning beats improved CN2 by two points, but the DC obtained contains roughly eight times less literals than CN2-POE's decision list. If we except "Vote0", on all other problems, we outperform CN2-POE on both accuracy and size. Finally, on "Vote0", note that WIDC with optimistic pruning is slightly outperformed by CN2-POE by 2.51%, but the DC obtained is *fifteen* times smaller than the decision list of CN2-POE. On many

Table 1. Experimental results using WIDC(least errors for WIDC are underlined for each problem).

Domain	WIDC (o)			WIDC (p)			WIDC ($\emptyset$)			Others
	err (%)	r_{DC}	l_{DC}	err (%)	r_{DC}	l_{DC}	err (%)	r_{DC}	l_{DC}	
Balance	22.38	4.1	10.5	13.33	16.4	39.9	14.29	18.7	44.9	32.1 (c)
Breast-W	7.46	1.1	4.5	4.08	5.4	22.8	6.90	7.7	29.3	4.0 (c)
Echo	32.14	1.8	3.9	30.71	1.9	4.3	31.42	24.6	38.8	$32.3_{35.4}$ (a)
Glass2	22.94	6.3	16.9	20.00	9.8	24.5	22.35	11.2	27.1	20.3 (c)
Heart-Statlog	24.07	3.1	8.9	19.26	9.1	32.7	21.85	12.5	40.8	21.5 (c)
Heart-C	22.90	2.9	9.1	21.93	8.4	30.1	25.48	13.3	46.2	$22.5_{52.0}$ (a)
Heart-H	22.67	3.9	10.9	20.33	9.2	28.2	20.00	14.3	43.5	$21.8_{60.3}$ (a)
Hepatitis	20.59	3.4	8.7	19.41	8.0	19.0	15.29	11.4	26.7	$19.2_{34.0}$ (a)
Iris	5.33	1.9	4.6	5.33	2.9	7.1	20.67	3.7	7.9	8.5 (c)
Labor	15.00	2.9	5.0	15.00	3.7	6.6	16.67	3.8	6.7	$16.31_{6.8}$ (d)
Lung	42.50	1.3	3.8	42.50	2.6	7.1	42.50	2.7	7.2	46.9 (e)
LED7	31.09	6.9	8.4	24.77	18.1	24.0	24.73	19.0	25.4	$25.73_{12.2}$ (d)
LEDeven *	23.48	5.4	9.6	16.88	6.1	10.8	34.43	12.1	18.4	
LEDeven+17 *	35.64	3.8	10.8	21.78	19.9	55.8	21.88	21.5	59.7	
Monk1	15.00	4.1	9.5	15.00	5.2	13.0	15.00	9.4	17.9	$16.66_{5.0}$ (d)
Monk2	24.43	9.0	38.4	21.64	18.6	66.5	31.80	24.8	82.1	$29.39_{18.0}$ (d)
Monk3	3.04	3.6	4.8	10.00	4.9	9.1	12.5	9.3	12.3	$2.67_{2.0}$ (d)
Pima	29.61	2.2	5.9	25.97	9.0	34.7	32.99	22.2	68.9	25.9 (c)
Vote0	6.81	1.9	3.0	8.86	6.6	13.5	10.00	9.5	18.9	$4.3_{49.6}$ (a)
Vote1	10.90	2.0	3.5	9.95	9.5	20.6	12.5	13.6	29.7	$10.89_{6.4}$ (d)
Waveform	30.49	4.8	8.2	23.33	7.8	19.0	20.24	40.1	65.0	$33.5_{21.8}$ (b)
XD6	22.29	5.4	13.0	18.80	10.3	27.0	35.7	37.1	67.1	$22.06_{14.8}$ (f)

- Conventions:

r_{DC} is the number of rules of the DC,

l_{DC} is the overall number of literals of the DC (if a literal is present k times, it is counted k times).

- References for "Others":

(a) [5], improved CN2 (CN2-POE) version, the small number indicates the size (number of literals) of the decision list, the large one indicates the error rate.

(b) [16], decision lists learning algorithm ICDL, notations follow (a).

(c) [6], C4.5's error.

(d) [15], DC learning algorithm IDC, notations follow (a).

(e) [2], nearest neighbors error.

(f) [3], best reported result on DT induction. The small number indicates the number of leaves (equiv. to a number of monomials).

problems, such a size reduction would be well worth the slight loss in accuracy, because we keep much informations on very small classifiers. This represents the main point of our experiments, and we go on further on explaining why it can be achieved by DC. Our main argument relies on the compromise between the formalism power [15] and the sizes of the experimental DC's we obtain. Consider the example of figure 2, obtained on the noisy problem LEDeven by WIDC with optimistic pruning. It is a very small DC achieving near-optimal prediction for the problem (13.04%). A LED is represented using seven binary descriptors. The fourth one is the one which is "off" on the "9" digit, and the fifth one is the lowest which is "on" on the "1" digit. Over the ten non-noisy digits, rule one is satisfied by all odd numbers, and by the "4" digit only (thus making an error). It is the rule having the highest correlation with the classes. Over the non-noisy digits, the second rule is only satisfied by the digit "2". Because the problem has 10% noise in the attributes, this rule has the particularity that any noisy odd digit that does not satisfy the first rule has a very *low* probability of satisfying this rule. In particular, it is much lower than the probability that a noisy even digit satisfy the second rule. Given the noise in the problem, this second rule somewhat "corrects" and adjusts the prediction of the first one. However, both rules can be interpreted independently. Though simple, this example shows how simple interpretations can be carried out using decision committees.

monomials	even	odd
$\overline{x}_4$	-1	1
$\overline{x}_5$	1	-1
default D	0.55	0.45

Fig. 2. An example of DC obtained on the problem LEDeven.

Consider now the problem XD6. In this problem, each example has 10 binary variables. The tenth is irrelevant in the strongest sense [9]. The target concept is a 3-DNF over the first nine variables: $(x_0 \wedge x_1 \wedge x_2) \vee (x_3 \wedge x_4 \wedge x_5) \vee (x_6 \wedge x_7 \wedge x_8)$. Such a formula is typically hard to encode using a decision tree. In our experiments with WIDC (o), we have remarked that the target formula itself is almost always an element of the classifier built, and the irrelevant attribute is always absent. On the "Vote0" and "Vote1" domains, which consist in predicting the classes democrat and republican from a set of poll questions, we also observed constant patterns in the DC built. In particular, problem "Vote1" was built from "Vote0" by removing the most informative literal, achieving itself ~ 5% errors. Even for "Vote1" where classical studies often report errors over 12%, and almost never around 10% [7], we observed on most of the runs a DC containing a rule wich could be translated as "If Not(adoption-of-the-budget-resolution) and el-salvador-aid, then republican". With such rules, the pessimistic pruning version of WIDC provided on average an error under 10%.

5   Conclusion

In this paper, we have presented a new algorithm for building voting procedures related to as Decision Committees. WIDC shares common features with the "C4.5-family" of induction algorithms, or more generally with the "Weak-induction" framework [21, 22], which previously proved useful in building Decision Trees or Decision Lists [18, 16, 17]. WIDC is a two-stages algorithm. A first stage uses recent results about Boosting to grow a large DC, which is pruned in a second stage to obtain a small formula. Experimental results tend to show that WIDC is able to build small and accurate formulae, whose interpretation is possible via single rules or directly via subsets of them.

References

[1]   L. Breiman, J. H. Freidman, R. A. Olshen, and C. J. Stone. *Classification and Regression Trees*. Wadsworth, 1984.

[2]   C. Blake, E. Keogh, and C.J. Merz. UCI repository of machine learning databases. 1998. http://www.ics.uci.edu/~mlearn/MLRepository.html.

[3]   W. Buntine and T. Niblett. A further comparison of splitting rules for Decision-Tree induction. *Machine Learning*, pages 75–85, 1992.

[4]   P. Clark and T. Niblett. The CN2 induction algorithm. *Machine Learning*, 3:261–283, 1989.

[5]   P. Domingos. A Process-oriented Heuristic for Model selection. In *Proc. of the 15 th ICML*, pages 127–135, 1998.

[6]   E. Franck and I. Witten. Using a Permutation Test for Attribute selection in Decision Trees. In *Proc. of the 15 th ICML*, pages 152–160, 1998.

[7]   R.C. Holte. Very simple classification rules perform well on most commonly used datasets. *Machine Learning*, pages 63–91, 1993.

[8]   L. Hyafil and R. Rivest. Constructing optimal decision trees is NP-complete. *Inform. Process. Letters*, pages 15–17, 1976.

[9]   George H. John, Ron Kohavi, and Karl Pfleger. Irrelevant features and the subset selection problem. In *Proc. of the 11 th ICML*, pages 121–129, 1994.

[10] M. J. Kearns and Y. Mansour. A Fast, Bottom-up Decision Tree Pruning algorithm with Near-Optimal generalization. In *Proc. of the 15 th ICML*, 1998.

[12] D. Kohavi and D. Sommerfield. Targetting Business users with Decision Table Classifiers. In *Proc. of the 4th Intl Conf. on KDD*, 1998.

[13] T. M. Mitchell. *Machine Learning*. McGraw-Hill, 1997.

[14] R. S. Michalski, I. Mozetic, J. Hong, and N. Lavrac. The AQ15 inductive learning system: An overview and experiments. In *Proc. of AAAI'86*, pages 1041–1045, 1986.

[15] R. Nock and O. Gascuel. On learning decision committees. In *Proc. of the 12 th ICML*, pages 413–420, 1995.

[16] R. Nock and P. Jappy. On the power of decision lists. In *Proc. of the 15 th ICML*, pages 413–420, 1998.

[17] R. Nock and P. Jappy. Decision Tree based induction of Decision Lists. *International Journal of Intelligent Data Analysis (accepted)*, 1999.
[18] J. R. Quinlan. *C4.5 : programs for machine learning*. Morgan Kaufmann, 1994.
[19] J. R. Quinlan. Bagging, Boosting and C4.5. In *Proc. of AAAI-96*, pages 725–730, 1996.
[20] R.L. Rivest. Learning decision lists. *Machine Learning*, pages 229–246, 1987.
[21] R. E. Schapire. The strength of weak learnability. *Machine Learning*, pages 197–227, 1990.
[22] R. E. Schapire and Y. Singer. Improved boosting algorithms using confidence-rated predictions. In *Proceedings of COLT'98*, pages 80–91, 1998.

Mining Clusters with Association Rules

Walter A. Kosters, Elena Marchiori, and Ard A.J. Oerlemans

Leiden Institute of Advanced Computer Science Universiteit Leiden
P.O. Box 9512, 2300 RA Leiden, The Netherlands
{kosters,elena,aoerlema}@cs.leidenuniv.nl

Abstract. In this paper we propose a method for extracting clusters in
a population of customers, where the only information available is the
list of products bought by the individual clients. We use association rules
having high confidence to construct a hierarchical sequence of clusters.
A specific metric is introduced for measuring the quality of the resulting
clusterings. Practical consequences are discussed in view of some experiments on real life datasets.

1 Introduction

The essence of clustering in databases is to identify homogeneous groups of
objects based on the values of their attributes. Various clustering techniques have
been proposed (e.g., [6,16]). In particular, in the database community several
systems have been introduced for clustering of data in large databases, see [8].
One can distinguish two main classes of clustering techniques: partitional and
hierarchical clustering. In partitional clustering ([11,13,17]) objects are grouped
into disjoint clusters such that objects in a cluster are more similar to each other
than to objects in other clusters. For instance, the well-known K-means and K-
medoid methods determine K cluster representatives and assign each object to
the cluster with its representative closest to the object in such a way that the
sum of the distances between the objects and their representatives is minimized.
Hierarchical clustering on the other hand is a nested sequence of partitions. In
the bottom-up method, larger and larger clusters are built by merging smaller
clusters, starting from atomic clustering where each object forms a cluster on its
own. In the top-down method however one starts with one cluster containing all
objects and constructs a subdivision of the cluster into smaller pieces, e.g., [10].
In this paper we introduce a top-down hierarchical clustering method for finding
clusters in a population of customers, where the only information available is the
list of products bought by the individual clients. The technique as well as the
metric we use are tailored for this specific class of data. However, the technique
gives satisfactory results also when applied to the more general problem of finding
clusters in a set of itemsets consisting of a sequence of binary attributes. In [11]
some theoretical questions for this setup are addressed, such as computational
complexity (NP-completeness) of possible embeddings in k-dimensional spaces,
and the associated clusterings.

D.J. Hand, J.N. Kok, M.R. Berthold (Eds.): IDA'99, LNCS 1642, pp. 39–50, 1999.

The idea is to use association rules for mining clusters. These rules relate groups of customers, and are of the form "80% of the customers that buy products A, B and C, buy product D too". Association rules (cf. [2]) are formalized by means of implication rules augmented with two parameters which describe their quality: the support which measures the frequencies of the products occurring in the rule, and the confidence which denotes the strength of the implication. A hierarchical clustering can be built using the following top-down method. First, association rules having support above a certain threshold are generated, using the efficient Apriori technique from [3]. Next, the "best" association rule is selected, where the selection criterion may depend on the number of products occurring on the left-hand side of the rules, as well as on the confidence and support of the rules. Finally, a cluster is constructed consisting of all the customers buying the products that occur in the left-hand side of the rule. The data set is then modified by removing the elements of that cluster. This procedure is iterated until a suitable stopping criterion is satisfied. Note that a small threshold for the support may bias the search towards clusters containing few, but strongly related clients, whereas a high support threshold allows one to construct larger clusters sharing less products.

In order to assess the effectiveness of this clustering method, we have conducted experiments on benchmark data sets from the literature, as well as on two real life datasets. The real life data sets contain different kinds of itemsets: in the first data set, items describe a small number of products, whereas in the second one items describe many products. The results of the experiments indicate that the success of this technique depends on the structure of the items in the data sets. If the set of possible products is large, whereas customers buy relatively few products, the association rules tend to be of lower confidence. The corresponding clustering may not be very informative in this case; however, the clusterings still make sense. On the other hand, if the customers buy (relatively) more products, for instance if the number of products is small, association rules tend to be more reliable—which holds for the implied clustering too. For measuring the quality of a cluster and comparing clusters, we introduce a metric for the space of customers which takes into account the specific structure of the itemsets.

The paper is organized as follows. In Section 2 we give some terminology on association rules and introduce an appropriate metric. Section 3 is devoted to a description of our method. In Section 4 we present some results from experiments. We conclude with a discussion.

2   Preliminaries

In this section we define the terminology and concepts that are used throughout the paper.

2.1   Discovering Association Rules

Suppose that we have n customers and a set S consisting of m products. Every customer i buys a subset $S_i \subseteq S$ of these products. The only information that is used for extracting regularities about the customers is the collection S_1, S_2, ..., S_n. An *association rule* is a rule of the form $R \Rightarrow T$ for disjoint subsets R and T of S, where $T \neq \emptyset$. Customer i is said to *satisfy* this rule if and only if $R \cup T \subseteq S_i$. The *support* of this rule is the number of customers that satisfy the rule, divided by the total number of customers. The *confidence* of a rule is the number of customers that satisfy it, divided by the number of clients i with $R \subseteq S_i$ (the confidence is set to zero if the denominator is zero). If $R \cup T$ has k elements, we say that the association rule has *order k*. In this paper we restrict ourselves to association rules whose right-hand side contains only one element. Association rules having both large support and confidence can be constructed using simple algorithms. However, if the database is very large, efficient methods are necessary (see [2,3,4,14]), like the well-known `Apriori` algorithm. This algorithm is based on the construction of subsets of S that are present in many customers, joining them to find ever larger subsets. These subsets are called large k-itemsets where k denotes their cardinality. Given minimum threshold $s\%$ for the support, the algorithm starts by constructing 1-itemsets having support greater than or equal to $s\%$. Then a large $(k+1)$-itemset is generated by merging two k-itemsets having exactly $(k-1)$ elements in common, and checking that its support is greater than or equal to $s\%$.

Once all large itemsets are generated, association rules can be easily derived as follows: suppose $\{A, B, C, D\}$ and consequently $\{A, B, C\}$ are large itemsets, then the rule $A, B, C \Rightarrow D$ (note that for simplicity we omit $\{$ and $\}$) can be derived. Clearly, any k-itemset gives rise to k association rules of order k.

2.2   A Metric for the Space of Customers

We turn the space of customers (i.e., subsets of S) into a metric space by means of the following distance measure. For subsets R and T of S we define

$$d(R, T) = \frac{|R \setminus T| + |T \setminus R|}{|R \cup T| + 1}$$

In this formula $\setminus$ denotes the set-theoretic difference ($X \setminus Y$ consists of those elements from X that are not in Y), and $|X|$ denotes the number of elements of X. So the numerator is the number of elements in the symmetric difference of R and T. This is the well-known Hamming distance when the list of products bought by a client is characterized by means of a string of bits whose length is equal to m, and where the i-th entry is 1 if the customer bought the i-th product, and 0 otherwise. The denominator in the definition of d is added in order to compensate for the size of the two sets. If for instance two customers differ in exactly one product, their distance is $2/(k+3)$, where k is the number of products bought in common. So their distance decreases as the number of common purchases increases. This allows for judging the distance between customers also in terms of the number of products they bought. The $+1$ in the denominator of the formula for the distance d is added to deal with the case $R = T = \emptyset$, but may also be omitted if one defines $d(\emptyset, \emptyset) = 0$. This approach leads to almost the same metric.

Note that $0 \leq d(\mathcal{R}, \mathcal{T}) \leq 1 - 1/(n+1) < 1$ for all subsets $\mathcal{R}$ and $\mathcal{T}$ of $\mathcal{S}$. (If necessary the measure can be renormalized by multiplying it by a suitable fixed factor.) Of course $d(\mathcal{R}, \mathcal{T}) = d(\mathcal{T}, \mathcal{R})$ for all subsets $\mathcal{R}$ and $\mathcal{T}$ of $\mathcal{S}$, and $d(\mathcal{R}, \mathcal{R}) = 0$. Finally the triangular inequality holds:

$$d(\mathcal{R}, \mathcal{T}) \leq d(\mathcal{R}, \mathcal{U}) + d(\mathcal{U}, \mathcal{T})$$

for all subsets $\mathcal{R}$, $\mathcal{U}$ and $\mathcal{T}$ of $\mathcal{S}$; this can be verified by some tedious calculations. Indeed, put $|\mathcal{R} \cap \mathcal{U} \cap \mathcal{T}| = a$, $|\mathcal{R} \cap \mathcal{U} \cap \overline{\mathcal{T}}| = b$, and so on; here $\overline{\mathcal{T}}$ denotes the complement of the subset $\mathcal{T}$ in $\mathcal{S}$. Now substitute these numbers in the inequality to be proved, remove the denominators and carefully check the remaining abundance of terms. We may conclude that d is a metric on the space of customers.

A cluster can be defined as a set of customers that are more near to each other than to clients in other clusters with respect to the distance d. Note that the construction of clusterings is biased towards customers buying many products. Therefore, when we encode the information of a customer as a string of bits, strings containing many ones are more liable to form a cluster. Also notice that the measure can be used for classification tasks, where the class of an item is defined to be the nearest cluster.

3   Association Rules Infer Clusters

Suppose that we have association rules of order 1, 2, 3 and so on. Now fix a minimum support threshold of say $s\%$. We consider the association rules having highest possible order, since they represent dependency among a larger set of products. These rules can be obtained by considering only the largest k-itemsets generated by the Apriori algorithm. The minimum support s has to be rather small for ensuring the existence of these rules. However, s should not be too small in order to avoid the generation of many rules which are satisfied by few customers. In the experiments we have conducted, the values of s have been chosen after tuning the algorithm on each specific dataset.

Once the association rules of highest order have been generated, we select the one with the highest confidence; if there exist more rules attaining this maximum, we choose one of them in a random way. We refer to the selected rule as $rule_1 = (\mathcal{R}_1 \Rightarrow \mathcal{T}_1)$. Now all customers that bought products in $\mathcal{R}_1$ constitute $cluster_1$. This means to include into the cluster not only the customers that satisfy the rule, but also those customers that bought all products from $\mathcal{R}_1$ but not those from $\mathcal{T}_1$. Because we consider rules having high confidence, it is expected that these extra customers are similar to those satisfying the rule. Next, we remove the customers occurring in $cluster_1$ from the original dataset. The process is iterated a suitable number of times, leading to a hierarchical clustering $cluster_1$, $cluster_2$, $cluster_3$, ... The termination condition we have used in the experiments consists of stopping when either a maximum number of clusters is generated (this maximum is given as an input parameter) or when the generated association rules do not reach the minimum support threshold.

The algorithm is illustrated below:

```
1    s := minimum support; i := 1;
2    Data := { all objects in the dataset }; Clust := ∅ ;
3    while (not termination-condition) do
4        H := { association rules over Data
                 having maximum order and support ≥ s };
5        best := rule from H with highest confidence;
6        cluster_i := { objects containing products in LHS(best) };
7        Data := Data \ cluster_i ; Clust := Clust ∪ {cluster_i};
8        i := i + 1;
9    od
```

Here LHS(*best*) denotes the set of elements on the left-hand side of the association rule *best*. The core of the algorithm consists of the statements in lines 4 and 5. In line 4 the association rules of maximum order are generated, by considering the objects in the dataset *Data*. Note that *Data* is initially equal to the original dataset, but it becomes smaller and smaller at each iteration (line 7). The generated cluster is inserted into the actual clustering *Clust* (assuming that this is an ordered set with respect to insertion) and the process is repeated on the smaller dataset *Data* obtained by removing the objects within the cluster.

In this way we obtain a partitioning of the set of customers into clusters. As the results of the experiments will show, the sequence of clusters has the property that the first clusters that are built are of good quality, while clusters that are generated later on may become less informative. The quality of the cluster is here only determined by considering the average distance of its elements and the confidence of the corresponding association rule. In this study we do not take into account other measures like the cluster diameter, i.e., the maximum distance between any two points of the cluster.

4   Experiments

For the experiments we used the so-called "Zoo Database", the artificial "LED Database" (both available from the Internet, see [15]), and two real life datasets generated from actual shop sales. The first two data sets are used for illustrating the effectiveness of our simple method in the case of classification problems. The other two datasets are used for illustrating the usefulness of the method for finding regularities in larger real life datasets—our original goal.

4.1   The Zoo Database

The zoo database contains 15 boolean attributes for $n = 101$ animals. In addition, there is one six-valued numeric attribute: the number of legs. For our algorithm to work it was necessary to turn this attribute into a boolean one, either by stating that "legs > 2 is equivalent to True" (or to False) or by introducing a boolean attribute for every possible numeric value. Here we choose the second option, the first one leading to almost identical results. So we have $m = 21$ "products": the terminology customer-product has to be interpreted as animal-attribute in this section. The original dataset also contains a classification of the animals into seven classes, referred to as A (41 mammals), B (20 birds), C (5 reptiles), D (13 fishes), E (4 amphibians), F (8 insects) and G (10 molluscs). The mean distance within the entire dataset is 0.577, which indicates that the attributes have several dependencies. In our experiments we discard information about the class to which an animal belongs.

support	cluster	number of animals	mean distance	mean Hamming distance	class contents	confidence
4%	1	12	0.030	0.333	$A(12)$	100%
	2	5	0.040	0.400	$A(5)$	100%
	3	6	0.000	0.000	$A(6)$	100%
	4	5	0.095	1.000	$B(5)$	100%
	5	9	0.074	0.778	$D(9)$	100%
	6	5	0.290	3.600	$A(5)$	100%
	7	11	0.123	1.200	$B(11)$	100%
	8	5	0.167	1.600	$A(5)$	100%
	9	5	0.149	1.400	$A(5)$	100%
	10	6	0.250	3.000	$A(2), D(4)$	100%
10%	1	12	0.030	0.333	$A(12)$	100%
	2	15	0.120	1.200	$A(15)$	100%
	3	16	0.158	1.608	$B(16)$	100%
	4	13	0.121	1.231	$D(13)$	100%
	5	11	0.345	4.036	$A(11)$	100%
	6	13	0.416	4.692	$A(1), B(4),$ $C(4), E(4)$	100%
	7	21	0.614	5.895	$A(2), C(1),$ $F(8), G(10)$	80%
40%	1	41	0.253	2.971	$A(41)$	100%
	2	42	0.451	5.573	$B(20), C(5),$ $D(13), E(4)$	97%

Fig. 1. Experimental results for the zoo database.

Figure 1 shows the results of some experiments. We considered three runs with different minimum threshold for the support: 4%, 10% and 40%. The maximum number of clusters to search for was set to 10. In the column "class contents" we mention the classes of the animals in the clusters (between brackets the number of animals of each class within the cluster). We also included the mean Hamming distance, since it might be a better measure for this database—the number of ones being relatively high.

The first and second run show that the classes are well separated; if the mean distance within the clusters gets higher, more classes may occur in the same cluster. The hierarchical nature of the clustering is also apparent. Note that when the support threshold is high, not all items are clustered in the end: not even rules of type "⇒ attribute" obtain this threshold anymore, just because the number of remaining animals is too small. The animals not clustered are exactly those from classes F and G. It would of course be possible to lower the threshold during the run, thus giving smaller clusters the opportunity to be discovered.

The rules found were of high order and confidence; for cluster 1 in the first and second run (it happens to be the same rule) the rule has order 9, for cluster 2 it has order 8 and 7, respectively. For the third run the first rule has order 3: "milk, breathes ⇒ backbone"; the second rule is: "backbone ⇒ eggs", so the animals not having a backbone remain unclustered. The mammal in cluster 6 of the second run is a platypus, the two mammals in cluster 7 are a dolphin and a porpoise; both classifications make some sense, at least for a non-biologist. The mean distances within the clusters are very small, see for instance cluster 3 in the first run. This also reveals some of the nature of the database.

4.2 The LED Database

The LED database is an artificial database, where each item corresponds with the "seven bit LED encoding" of one of the ten numbers $0, 1, 2, \ldots, 9$. Noise

support	cluster	number of strings	mean distance	class contents	confidence
7%	1	101	0.630	8(101)	100%
	2	120	0.654	9(120)	100%
	3	99	0.643	0(99)	100%
	4	117	0.656	6(117)	100%
	5	79	0.689	5(79)	100%
	6	92	0.693	2(92)	100%
	7	93	0.690	3(93)	100%
	8	95	0.716	4(95)	100%
	9	96	0.750	7(96)	100%
	10	108	0.800	1(108)	100%
7%	1	79	0.641	8(58), *(21)	91%
	2	83	0.669	6(78), *(5)	93%
	3	88	0.660	9(67), *(21)	88%
	4	90	0.703	2(70), *(20)	95%
	5	91	0.679	0(67), *(24)	94%
	6	90	0.716	5(58), *(32),	96%
	7	81	0.721	4(72), *(9)	90%
	8	81	0.712	3(58), *(23),	81%
	9	127	0.774	7(79), *(48)	84%
	10	122	0.814	1(93), *(29)	90%

Fig. 2. Experimental results for the LED database.

is introduced by appending at the end of the original string (with seven bits) a sequence of fixed length consisting of randomly chosen bits, as well as by corrupting some of the bits in the original string. The LED encoding shows which LED's out of seven are on in each case, for instance the topmost horizontal LED is activated for the numbers 0,2,3,5,7,8 and 9. This database is particularly interesting, since the noise may be added in such a way that there are lots of zeroes—a property also present in the real life data sets we use in the sequel.

As a typical example (see Figure 2) we added 93 random bits, giving a total of $m = 100$ bits; these extra bits had a 90% probability of being zero. We generated $n = 1000$ strings. The first experiment shows a situation where the original seven bits are not corrupted, whereas in the second run these bits had a 7% chance of being toggled (so on average 50% of the encoded strings contains a flaw). In the column "class contents" the classes of the strings, i.e., their numbers, in the clusters are given (between brackets the number of strings of each class within the cluster); a * denotes elements different from the majority within the class. Observe that some encodings are quite similar (for instance those of 0 and 8), giving understandable faults in case of noise.

The mean distance within the entire dataset is 0.764 and 0.778, respectively. The mean distance within the clusters is easily understood for the first experiment: the clustered strings may only differ in the 93 last bits, 9.3 of which are 1 on average. The association rules found are of high order, due to the exact nature of the database. The ordering of the clusters is as expected: note that the fact that our algorithm is biased towards ones implies that encodings with many zeroes (e.g., that for the number 1) are only detected in the end. We may conclude that the algorithm is capable of discovering clusters that respect the original classification, as it did for the zoo database.

4.3   Two Real Life Databases

In contrast with the previously discussed databases, the real life datasets considered here contain more customers, who may choose from many products. They are expected to show a less regular behaviour. Also, the division into classes is not known in advance. In all cases two or three of the biggest selling products were removed, since they do not contribute to the generation of interesting association rules. For example, in one of the datasets about 50% of the customers bought one particular product; this product is very likely to occur in a good association rule, but probably has not much discriminating ability.

The first database has $m = 7,500$ products, whereas the number of customers is of moderate size; we experimented with a subset consisting of $n = 800$ customers, buying 50 to 95 products each (sample **D1**), and a subset consisting of $n = 1,400$ customers, buying 8 to 10 products each (sample **D2**). For **D1** the mean number of products bought was 57.05, and the mean distance was 0.975, which is very high. For **D2** these numbers were 8.36 and 0.939, respectively.

The second database has $m = 100$ products, and we considered $n = 10,000$ customers (sample **D3**). It also contained purer data, i.e., there were less flaws present, probably because the products involved were more expensive. The mean number of products per customer was 2.11, with mean distance 0.720. Sample **D4** consisted of $n = 10,000$ other customers from the same database; here the mean number of products per customer was 2.35, with mean distance 0.733.

In all cases the support threshold was taken to be 2%, and the number of clusters to find was bounded by 10. Only for **D2** the support threshold was 0.5; larger values did not provide any significant clustering in that case. The results of the experiments are reported in Figure 3 and Figure 4. Except for the computation of the mean distance the runs took only a few minutes on a Pentium-based PC. The products that occur in the rules are arbitrarily named $s_1, s_2, \ldots, s_{19}$ and $t_1, t_2, \ldots, t_{13}$ for the first database, and $p_1, p_2, \ldots, p_{13}$ for the second one.

Note that the products in the rule for *cluster*$_3$ (sample **D3**) form a subset of those from *cluster*$_1$. In fact, in this database the rule $p_2 \Leftrightarrow p_3$ holds with high reliability. Since the algorithm tries to find association rules of the highest possible order first, having fixed support threshold, this rule is superseded by the rule $p_1, p_2 \Rightarrow p_3$ that constitutes *cluster*$_1$. In this case two separate clusters are found. If the support threshold were such that it was not met by $p_1, p_2 \Rightarrow p_3$, only one cluster, based on $p_2 \Rightarrow p_3$, would have resulted. This shows that human interference plays a crucial role in the process: the choice of the support threshold influences the clustering. In contrast, the triples $\{p_1, p_2, p_3\}$ and $\{p_4, p_5, p_6\}$ show some differences; the rule $p_5 \Rightarrow p_6$ has low confidence, and the clustering concerning these three products is not as clear as the one for $\{p_1, p_2, p_3\}$.

sample	cluster	number of customers	mean distance	rule	confidence
D1	1	26	0.947	$s_1, s_2 \Rightarrow s_3$	69%
	2	23	0.952	$s_4, s_5 \Rightarrow s_3$	69%
	3	35	0.952	$s_6, s_7 \Rightarrow s_2$	51%
	4	41	0.955	$s_3, s_8 \Rightarrow s_9$	43%
	5	22	0.962	$s_{10} \Rightarrow s_{11}$	72%
	6	32	0.965	$s_{12} \Rightarrow s_{13}$	50%
	7	41	0.964	$s_{14} \Rightarrow s_9$	46%
	8	46	0.964	$s_{15} \Rightarrow s_3$	45%
	9	55	0.964	$s_{16} \Rightarrow s_{17}$	43%
	10	62	0.966	$s_{18} \Rightarrow s_{19}$	38%
D2	1	14	0.832	$t_1 \Rightarrow t_2$	85%
	2	11	0.841	$t_3 \Rightarrow t_2$	72%
	3	10	0.841	$t_4 \Rightarrow t_5$	70%
	4	24	0.823	$t_5 \Rightarrow t_2$	87%
	5	14	0.855	$t_2 \Rightarrow t_6$	50%
	6	25	0.865	$t_7 \Rightarrow t_8$	40%
	7	50	0.868	$t_9 \Rightarrow t_{10}$	34%
	8	32	0.872	$t_{11} \Rightarrow t_{12}$	28%
	9	1220	0.939	$\Rightarrow t_{13}$	5%

Fig. 3. Experimental results for the first real life database.

sample	cluster	number of customers	mean distance	rule	confidence
D3	1	253	0.484	$p_1, p_2 \Rightarrow p_3$	98%
	2	337	0.443	$p_4, p_5 \Rightarrow p_6$	89%
	3	431	0.411	$p_2 \Rightarrow p_3$	99%
	4	320	0.372	$p_7 \Rightarrow p_8$	91%
	5	370	0.473	$p_9 \Rightarrow p_{10}$	72%
	6	2102	0.388	$p_5 \Rightarrow p_6$	67%
	7	6187	0.679	$\Rightarrow p_{11}$	20%
D4	1	216	0.455	$p_4, p_5, p_{12} \Rightarrow p_6$	96%
	2	202	0.557	$p_2, p_{13} \Rightarrow p_3$	100%
	3	312	0.428	$p_1, p_2 \Rightarrow p_3$	98%
	4	485	0.424	$p_4, p_5 \Rightarrow p_6$	90%
	5	376	0.450	$p_7 \Rightarrow p_8$	93%
	6	392	0.426	$p_9 \Rightarrow p_{10}$	85%
	7	1253	0.446	$p_6 \Rightarrow p_5$	63%
	8	6764	0.676	$\Rightarrow p_{11}$	26%

Fig. 4. Experimental results for the second real life database.

The last clusters do not seem to be of any importance. This holds in particular for $cluster_7$, resp. $cluster_8$, which resulted from a rule with empty left-hand side and consequently very low confidence. Also note the relatively high mean distance. No association rules of order 2 were present anymore, and the algorithm clusters all the remaining customers (remember that all customers buying the left-hand side, which is empty here, are clustered). Domain experts were capable of interpreting the most significant clusters. The experiments with many customers show higher coherence within the clusters, reflected by lower mean distance and higher confidence. In all cases the rules found had low order, also due to the abundance of products to choose from. But even for the case with fewer customers and less products per customer the clusters found made sense.

5   Conclusions

In this paper we have proposed a simple method for mining clusters in large databases describing information about products purchased by customers. The method generates a sequence of clusters in an iterative hierarchical fashion, using association rules for biasing the search towards good clusters. We have tested this method on various datasets. The results of the experiments indicate that the technique allows one to find informative clusterings.

As already mentioned, due to the hierarchical strategy employed to generate the clustering, it may happen that the cluster generated in the last iteration contains objects sharing few regularities. In this case, one can discard the last cluster and consider its objects as not belonging to the clustering, because they do not present enough regularities. Alternatively, one can redistribute the elements of the last cluster among the other clusters. For instance, a possible redistribution criterion can be the distance of the objects from the clusters, where an object is inserted in the cluster having minimal distance. More sophisticated techniques for redistributing objects of the last cluster can also be applied (e.g., [7,9]).

Clustering techniques have been studied extensively in the database community, yielding various systems such as CLARANS ([13]) and BIRCH ([17]). These systems are rather general: they apply techniques imported from clustering algorithms used in statistics, like in CLARANS, or sophisticated incremental algorithms, like in BIRCH. It is not our intention to advocate the use of our clustering algorithm as an alternative for such systems. Nevertheless, our clustering algorithm provides a simple tool for mining clusters in large databases describing sales data.

Several techniques based on association rules have been proposed for mining various kinds of information. However, to the best of our knowledge, our method provides a novel use of association rules for clustering. Some related techniques based on association rules are the following. In [1] an algorithm for finding profile association rules is proposed, where a profile association rule describes associations between customer profile information and behaviour information. In [12] association rules containing quantitative attributes on the left-hand side and a single categorical attribute on the right-hand side are considered. A method for clustering these rules is introduced, where rules having adjacent ranges are merged into a single description. This kind of clustering provides a compact representation of the regularities present in the dataset. Finally, in [5] the use of association rules for partial classification is investigated, where rules describing characteristics of some of the data classes are constructed. The method generates rules which may not cover all classes or all examples in a class. Moreover, examples covered by different rules are not necessarily distinct.

In this paper, we restricted ourselves to a specific type of datasets where the objects are vectors of binary attributes. We intend to investigate the effectiveness of the clustering method when multivalued attributes as well as quantitative ones are used: this amounts to considering more expressive forms of rules, like for instance the so-called profile association rules (see [1]).

An interesting topic for future work is the analysis of the integration of our technique into more sophisticated clustering systems. For instance, we would like to analyze the benefits of our clustering algorithm when used for generating a "good" initial clustering of the data that could be subsequently refined, either by means of iterative methods in the style of those from [7], or by means of methods based on evolutionary computation like genetic algorithms.

References

1. C.C. Aggarwal, Z. Sun and P.S. Yu, Online Generation of Profile Association Rules, in: R. Agrawal, P.E. Stolorz and G. Piatetsky-Shapiro (editors), *Proceedings of the Fourth International Conference on Knowledge Discovery and Data Mining (KDD-98)*, pp. 129–133, AAAI Press, 1998.
2. R. Agrawal, T. Imielinski and A. Swami, Mining Association Rules between Sets of Items in Large Databases, in: P. Buneman and S. Jajodia (editors), *Proceedings*

of the *1993 ACM SIGMOD International Conference on Management of Data*, pp. 207–216, ACM Press, 1993.

3. R. Agrawal, H. Mannila, R. Srikant, H. Toivonen and A.I. Verkamo, Fast Discovery of Association Rules, in: U.M. Fayyad, G. Piatetsky-Shapiro, P. Smyth and R. Uthurusamy (editors), *Advances in Knowledge Discovery and Data Mining*, pp. 307–328, AAAI/MIT Press, 1996.

4. R. Agrawal and R. Srikant, Fast Algorithms for Mining Association Rules in Large Databases, in: J.B. Bocca, M. Jarke and C. Zaniolo (editors), *Proceedings of the 20th International Conference on Very Large Data Bases (VLDB'94)*, pp. 478–499, Morgan Kaufmann, 1994.

5. K. Ali, S. Manganaris and R. Srikant, Partial Classification Using Association Rules, in: D. Heckerman, H. Mannila, D. Pregibon and R. Uthurusamy (editors), *Proceedings of the Third International Conference on Knowledge Discovery in Databases and Data Mining (KDD-97)*, pp. 115–118, AAAI Press, 1997.

6. P. Arabie and L.J. Hubert, An Overview of Combinatorial Data Analysis, in: P. Arabie, L.J. Hubert and G.D. Soete (editors), *Clustering and Classification*, pp. 5–63, World Scientific Pub., New Jersey, 1996.

7. G. Biswas, J.B. Weinberg and D.H. Fisher, ITERATE: A Conceptual Clustering Algorithm for Data Mining, *IEEE Transactions on Systems, Man, and Cybernetics* 28C (1998), 219–230.

8. M.S. Chen, J. Han and P.S. Yu, Data Mining: An Overview from a Database Perspective, *IEEE Transactions on Knowledge and Data Engineering* 8 (1996), 866–883.

9. D. Fisher, Iterative Optimization and Simplification of Hierarchical Clusterings, *Journal of Artificial Intelligence Research* 4 (1996), 147–180.

10. A.K. Jain and R.C. Dubes, *Algorithms for Clustering Data*, Prentice Hall, 1988.

11. W.A. Kosters, J.A. La Poutré and M.C. van Wezel, Understanding Customer Choice Processes Using Neural Networks, in: H.F. Arner Jr. (editor), *Proceedings of the First International Conference on the Practical Application of Knowledge Discovery and Data Mining (PADD97)*, pp. 167–178, The Practical Application Company, London, 1997.

12. B. Lent, A.N. Swami and J. Widom, Clustering Association Rules, in: A. Gray and P.-Å. Larson (editors), *Proceedings of the Thirteenth International Conference on Data Engineering*, pp. 220–231, IEEE Computer Society Press, 1997.

13. R.T. Ng and J. Han, Efficient and Effective Clustering Methods for Spatial Datamining, in: J.B. Bocca, M. Jarke and C. Zaniolo (editors), *Proceedings of the 20th International Conference on Very Large Data Bases (VLDB'94)*, pp. 144–155, Morgan Kaufmann, 1994.

14. J.-S. Park, M.-S. Chen, P.S.Yu, An Effective Hash Based Algorithm for Mining Association Rules, in: M.J. Carey and D.A. Schneider (editors), *Proceedings of the 1995 ACM SIGMOD International Conference on Management of Data*, pp. 175–186, ACM Press, 1995.

15. The UCI Machine Learning Repository, electronically available at http://www.ics.uci.edu/~mlearn/MLSummary.html

16. M. Zaït and H. Messatfa, A Comparative Study of Clustering Methods, *Future Generation Computer Systems* 13 (1997), 149–159.

17. T. Zhang, R. Ramakrishnan and M. Livny, BIRCH: An Efficient Data Clustering Method for Very Large Databases, in: H.V. Jagadish and I.S. Mumick (editors), *Proceedings of the 1996 ACM SIGMOD International Conference on Management of Data*, pp. 103–114, ACM Press, 1996.

Evolutionary Computation to Search for Strongly Correlated Variables in High-Dimensional Time-Series

Stephen Swift, Allan Tucker, and Xiaohui Liu

Department of Computer Science,
Birkbeck College, University of London,
Malet Street, London WC1E 7HX, United Kingdom

Abstract. If knowledge can be gained at the pre-processing stage, concerning the approximate underlying structure of large databases, it can be used to assist in performing various operations such as variable subset selection and model selection. In this paper we examine three methods, including two evolutionary methods for finding this approximate structure as quickly as possible. We describe two applications where the fast identification of correlation structure is essential and apply these three methods to the associated datasets. This automatic approach to the searching of approximate structure is useful in applications where domain specific knowledge is not readily available.

1 Introduction

If knowledge can be gained at the pre-processing stage, concerning the approximate underlying structure of very large databases, it can be used to assist in performing various operations, e.g. reducing the dimensionality of the database through the selection of variables for further analysis or grouping the variables into closely related subsets. In some applications it would be useful to gain this knowledge as quickly as possible. For example, if the procedure is part of a real time application or where the dataset is so large that a full analysis could take months.

One way to find the structure in a dataset is correlation analysis. In this paper we experiment with three methods in finding the approximate correlation structure and compare these with an exhaustive search method for verification. In this section we describe two applications and corresponding datasets where the fast identification of correlation structure is essential. Section 2 describes two methods for calculating correlations, one being a linear method and the other being able to calculate non-linear correlations. Section 3 describes various methods for performing fast, approximate search including our version of an evolutionary programming algorithm. Section 4 presents our results on the two datasets using the different algorithms and correlation coefficients. Finally, section 5 discusses the results and future work.

D.J. Hand, J.N. Kok, M.R. Berthold (Eds.): IDA'99, LNCS 1642, pp. 51–62, 1999.
© Springer-Verlag Berlin Heidelberg 1999

1.1   Oil Refinery Process Data

Many complex chemical processes record multivariate time-series data every minute. This data will be characterised by a large number of interdependent variables (in the order of hundreds per process unit). There can be large time delays between causes and effects (over 120 minutes in some chemical processes) and some variables may have no substantial impact on any others. Correlations can change within the system depending on how the process is being controlled. If we want to perform diagnosis automatically (in as close to real time as possible) a method to learn the current control structure would be required, which is calculated from the most recent data. In these situations sampling would be unsuitable because of the changes in control structure. One dataset used in this paper is from a Fluid Catalytic Cracker (FCC) [11] and has a total of approximately 300 variables. A dataset of this size would prevent the exhaustive search from being used as a comparison for other methods. Consequently steps were taken to use a sufficiently small dataset: 31 variables have been selected from the data containing approximately 10,000 data points.

1.2   Visual Field Data

The second data set is a section of Normal Tension Glaucoma (NTG) Visual Field (VF) Data. Glaucoma [8] is the name given to a family of eye conditions. The common trait of these conditions is a functional abnormality in the optic nerve, leading to a loss of visual field. This vision loss usually occurs only in part of the visual field, however untreated glaucoma can lead to blindness. Once diagnosed, a patient undergoes frequent outpatient appointments where their visual field is tested. The forecasting of a patient's visual field is important in order to diagnose, monitor and control the progression of glaucoma. Correlation between points at different time lags can play a useful role in the monitoring of the disease progression; since many mathematical methods for time-series forecasting need the correlations between variables to complete the models. It would be useful to be able to do this during a patient's regular consultation so that any decisions could be made while they wait, hence in as short a time as possible. The visual field dataset consists of 82 patients' right eyes measured approximately every six months for between five (a time-series length of ten) and 22 years (a time-series length of 44). The particular test used for this dataset results in 76 points being measured, which correspond to a 76 variable time-series.

2   Background

We are interested in developing an algorithm that finds a "good-but-not-optimal" selection of "interesting" highly correlated variables in as short a time as possible. The term interesting will, of course, depend on the application in question. For example, only *cross-correlations* will be of interest in the FCC domain. The number of correlations to be located would depend on the context in which the method is being used (from now on we shall refer to this parameter as the *rank size*).

Correlation analysis is a way to measure how "coupled" two or more variables are. Although this is not a reliable method with which to infer causality amongst variables, it can be useful in determining the underlying structure of a database. The correlation coefficient falls between the values -1 and +1 where -1 shows a strong negative correlation and +1 shows a strong positive. There exist various methods for calculating how correlated two variables are, the most common being Pearson's Correlation Coefficient.

Pearson's Correlation Coefficient (PCC) [12] measures the linear relationship between two continuous variables x and y.

$$\rho_{xy} = \frac{Cov(x,y)}{\sigma_x \sigma_y} Where - 1 \leq \rho_{xy} \leq 1 \tag{1}$$

$$Cov(x,y) = \frac{\sum_{i=1}^{n}(x_i - \mu_x)(y_i - \mu_y)}{n-1} \tag{2}$$

Where ρ_{xy} is the value of PCC between x and y, n is the number of x, y pairs, σ_x and σ_y are the standard deviations for x and y respectively, x_i and y_i are the *ith* instances of the variables x and y, and μ_x and μ_y are the expectations of the variables x and y. The calculation is, therefore, linear in computation time.

Spearman's Rank Correlation (SRC) [12] measures non-linear relationships between two variables, either discrete or continuous, by assigning a rank to each observation. It then incorporates the sums of the squares of the differences in paired ranks $(d_i)^2$ according to the formula:

$$R_s = \frac{6\sum_{i=1}^{n}(d_i)^2}{n(n^2-1)} \tag{3}$$

Where R_s is the value of SRC between the two variables, n is the number of pairs and each d_i is calculated by taking the difference between the ranks of each variable pair x_i and y_i. This means the calculation is of the order $nlog(n)$, since sorting must be used on data that is not already ranked.

Time-Series. Time-series data is a collection of observations made sequentially in time [3]. If one item is recorded at each time point, then the time-series is referred to as univariate. If more than one observation is made at each time point, then the series is multivariate. The medical, financial and process sectors are full of examples of time-series data sets, both univariate and multivariate.

If the data to be analysed is a time-series then the Cross-Correlation Function (CCF) can be used to explore how correlated two series are over differing time *lags*, therefore indicating the direction of influence. The Auto-Correlation Function (ACF) measures how closely correlated a variable is with itself over varying time lags. Both CCF and ACF may use one of the two correlation coefficients described above. For time-series in which the lags are large, many different coefficients must be calculated. If V is the number of variables and lag is the time lag that is under consideration, then the number of possible correlations is $lag \times V^2$. There may be various real-world applications where the number of possible correlations may pose a problem, for example, where the structure of a dataset would be required in real time as the data is produced, or where a dataset is so huge that it would take an unreasonable amount of time to process. The two real datasets described in the previous section illustrate these scenarios. Therefore, for the analysis of time-series with high dimensionality or large time lag influences, there is a need for fast approximate searches over the number of possible correlations.

For the FCC data, if the goal is to find a subset of highly correlated variables then auto-correlations will be considered irrelevant. For this reason only cross-correlations are explored. An assumption is made that the maximum time lag from cause to effect will be 60 minutes. Within the VF dataset, for each patient's visual field data, correlations will be calculated using the 76 visual field points at a time lag of up to five (30 months). Since the length of each time-series that makes up the VF dataset is significantly shorter than that in the FCC dataset, all of the 82 available patients are used to make the problem comparable in complexity. The combined correlations for all of the patients were averaged to get a single value for two points at a given time lag so that the general dependencies over a representative population can be compared with the medical literature [4,9] for verification.

3   Methods

This section describes the methods employed to find subsets of highly correlated variables through time. All of these methods use the absolute value of the correlation coefficients, in order to rank a relationship between 0 and 1 inclusive (the objective was to locate dependencies but not their nature). Four methods were implemented: Random Bag (RB), Genetic Algorithm (GA) [10], Evolutionary Programming (EP) [1,5,6] and an Exhaustive Search. These are described in the remainder of this section and all make use of a triple, (x, y, lag), to represent the correlation between variables x and y with a time lag of lag. It has proved hard to find any existing methods that do not rely on the data being categorical, for example [13]. Note that the standard statistical solution would be to explore the whole search space, sample the time-series, or restrict the search space through the use of expert knowledge; all of which are inappropriate for the applications used in this paper.

The Exhaustive Search. This method was performed on both data sets using Pearson's and Spearman's rank coefficients. Although in practice datasets could be of sufficiently large dimensionality and time-series length to preclude such a search, steps were taken to use sufficiently small datasets, so that the results could be used as a benchmark for the other methods. The exhaustive search consisted of simply exploring all of the variables, at each time lag. At time lag zero, the correlations $(x, y, 0)$ and $(y, x, 0)$ are effectively the same so duplicates are removed. The correlations $(x, x, 0)$ are all one, and hence these are removed too. This would result in a total of 31,730 correlations for the VF data, or 2,601,860 if all 82 patients' data are used. With the FCC data all correlations of the form (x, x, y) are removed since these are auto-correlations and do not show relationships *between* different variables. This will mean a total number of 55,335 different cross-correlations. This strategy of correlation *removal* was also performed in the other three methods.

The Random Bag. This is a heuristic approach whereby a random selection of triples is placed in a "bag" containing *Rank Size* triples. With each iteration a new random triple is added to the bag. When the bag overflows, the worst correlation falls out. This is repeated for a predefined number of iterations. The algorithm is described below:

> Set i = 0, R = Rank Size, Q = Empty Queue
> While $i < MAX$ Do
> > t = new random triple: (x, y, lag)
> > i = i + 1
> > If t is valid and t is not a member of Q Then insert t into Q
> > Sort Q in descending order of correlation
> > If *size of Q* = R+1 Then remove a triple from the tail of Q
> End While

Note that a triple is valid if it does not warrant removal. MAX is the maximum number of allowed calls to the correlation function. The final contents of the *Bag* represent the solution, i.e. the required *Rank Size* correlations.

Genetic Algorithm. A Genetic Algorithm is a method for search based on the mechanics of natural selection and genetics. A population of chromosomes that represents possible solutions is used to explore the search space. This is achieved by updating the population with the creation of new chromosomes, formed through the recombination of two existing chromosomes (using the *Crossover* operator), a small perturbation analogous to mutation (by the *Mutation* Operator), and the destruction of less fit chromosomes (through the *Survival* operator) [10]:

> Generate Population chromosomes
> For i = 1 to Generations do
> > Apply Crossover operator to Population
> > Apply Mutate operator to Population
> > Apply Survival operator to Population
> End For

For the correlation problem, a *chromosome* is represented by a number of genes corresponding to the required correlation rank size. Each *gene* consists of a correlation triple *(x, y, lag)* and each triple has three *elements*. Therefore each chromosome has a string of integer numbers, $element_i$, the length being equal to $3 \times RankSize$. One point linear crossover is used; the crossover point is restricted to multiples of three, thereby making sure that no gene will be split.

Mutation is defined as follows:

$element_i = $ U(1,Max($element_i$)), if $element_i$ is to mutate

Where $element_i$ is the *ith element* ($1 \le i \le 3 \times n$) of the chromosome, $U(a, b)$ returns a uniformly distributed random positive integer number between a and b inclusive, and $Max(element_i)$ returns the maximum value that variable $element_i$ could take.

The parameters were selected through experimentation for optimal performance. These are listed in Table 1 where RW uses the *Roulette Wheel* technique and DS uses *deterministic selection* (this is where the individuals carried over to the next generation are the best, thus not allowing for duplicates as with RW).

Table 1. GA Parameters

Mutation%		Crossover%		Population		Generations		Rank Size		Survival	
VF	FCC	VF	FCC	VF	FCC	VF	FCC	VF	FCC	VF	FCC
0.1	0.4	100	100	10	10	2500	28	100	250	RW	DS

Evolutionary Programming. Evolutionary Programming is based on a similar paradigm to Genetic Algorithms. However, the emphasis is on mutation and the method does not use any recombination. The basic algorithm is outlined as follows ([2,5]):

```
Generate Population chromosomes
For i = 1 to Generations do
         Duplicate the Population to Children
         Apply Mutate operator to Children
         Add the Children back to the Population
         Apply Survival operator to Population
End For
```

Traditionally, EP algorithms use *Tournament Selection* [1] during the survival of the fittest stage and the best chromosome out of the final population will be the solution to the problem. However, it was decided that the entire population would be the solution for our EP method as in the RB method. That is, each individual chromosome would represent a single correlation (a triple) while the population would represent the set of correlations found (*Population Size = Rank Size*). This therefore required a check for any duplicates after mutation, and for any invalid chromosomes. Any children that fell into this category were repeatedly mutated until they became valid. Although the entire population would represent the solution, it must be noted that the fitness of each individual would still be independent of the rest of the population. Each individual would try to maximise the correlation coefficient that it represents. This in turn would maximise the population's fitness by improving the set of correlations represented by the population. The number of *generations* required for the two applications is in the range of 10 and 25.

As can be seen with the GA method, a gene is a correlation triple (x, y, lag). Within the EP, however, a gene is either x, y, or the lag. We have used the idea of **Self-Adapting Parameters** [2] in this context. Here each gene, $gene_i$, in each chromosome is given a parameter, σ_i. Mutation is defined as follows:

$$gene_i' = gene_i + N(0, \sigma_i) \tag{4}$$

$$\sigma_i' = \sigma_i \times exp(s + s_i) \tag{5}$$

$$s = N(0, \frac{1}{\sqrt{2n}}) \tag{6}$$

$$s_i = N(0, \frac{1}{\sqrt{2\sqrt{n}}}) \tag{7}$$

Note that s is constant for each gene in each chromosome but different between chromosomes, and s_i is different for all genes. Both parameters are generated each time mutation occurs. Initial examination of the performance of the RB method found that the performance was better than the GA (see section 4). Similarities were drawn between this basic method and the EP algorithm. The major difference was, rather than adding a new random chromosome to the population, an existing member of the population is copied and mutated in a controlled manner. Each chromosome consisted of three parameters and their corresponding σ values. The value of n is the size of each chromosome, i.e. three. Each gene within a chromosome is mutated according to the Normal distribution with mean 0 and standard deviation equal to the gene's corresponding σ value (equation 4). The σ values, themselves, are mutated according to equation 5.

4   Results

For each dataset the different methods were run until the number of calls to the correlation function is equivalent to that of the exhaustive search. With the GA and the EP methods, this meant setting an artificially high number of generations. In practice this would be pointless. Figures 1-4 show the results from these experiments. Within these figures the logarithm has been taken of the number of function calls (to the appropriate correlation function) so as to highlight the difference in performance of the different algorithms. Next, an analysis was made of each method after approximately five percent of the total number of correlations was called.

4.1   FCC Results

The FCC results took a significantly longer time to run than with the VF data, since the time-series for this dataset was considerably larger. A rank size of 250 was decided upon for this dataset. The maximum average correlation for the top 250 correlations is shown in Figures 1 and 2 ("Top 250"). It can be seen that the EP method converges nearer to this maximum during the first 3,000 function calls (~ 3.5 in Figures 1 and 2) before slowing. The RB method does the next best, converging at a slower rate than EP but faster than the GA which is by far the slowest. The result for the GA was the best produced from a number of experiments using differing parameter values.

It was found that a very small mutation rate and a very high crossover rate was optimal in that it minimised function calls. It must be noted that although the function calls were reduced, the algorithm was still slowed drastically by the crossover operator. All methods eventually 'meet' at about 30,000 function calls (~ 4.5 in Figures 1 and 2) just below the maximum. The results are almost identical for Pearson's and Spearman's correlation coefficient.

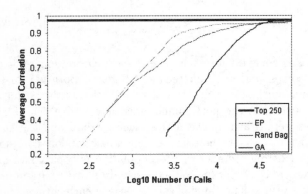

Fig. 1. Pearson's Correlation Coefficient for the FCC Data

Table 2 shows the analysis of the best correlations found. The exhaustive method shows the overall best, worst and average correlation in the entire possible 55,335. Top 250 shows these for only the top 250 correlations. The remaining three columns show the results after approximately five percent of the correlations were calculated ($\sim 3,000$ function calls) for the RB method, the EP method and the GA method. From the table, it can be observed that the EP method has the best average for both Pearson's and Spearman's correlation coefficient.

4.2   VF Results

A rank size of 100 was chosen as it is large enough to show if the relationships between the 76 points correspond to the same *nerve fibre bundles* [9]. The average

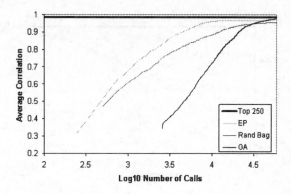

Fig. 2. Spearman's Correlation Coefficient for the FCC Data

Table 2. Five Percent Freeze for the FCC Data

	Exhaustive		Top250		RB		EP		GA	
	PCC	SRC	PCC	SRC	PCC	SRC	PCC	SRC	PCC	SRC
Num. of calls	55335	55335	55335	55335	3000	3001	3203	2821	3240	3283
% of calls	100	100	100	100	5.42	5.42	5.79	5.10	5.86	5.93
Best correlation	1	1	1	1	0.998	1	0.992	1	0.997	1
Ave. correlation	0.259	0.303	0.975	0.986	0.767	0.765	0.888	0.838	0.355	0.414
Worst correlation	0	0	0.961	0.958	0.624	0.639	0.775	0.709	0	0.015

correlation for the top 100 correlations is shown in Figures 3 and 4 ("Top 100").
It can be seen, as in the FCC dataset, that the EP method converges nearer to
this maximum during the first 130,000 function calls (~ 5.1 in Figures 3 and 4.)
before slowing. However, it can be seen, especially in the Pearson results, that the
EP method remains consistently higher than the other methods, more so than
in the FCC data. The RB method does the next best, converging at a slower
rate than EP. However the GA method catches up with the RB method, as the
number of calls increase. Again, the result for the GA was the best produced
from a number of experiments using differing parameter values. In the Spearman
experiments, the EP method is eventually outperformed by the GA and the RB
method. However, this is after approximately 50 percent of the number of calls
the exhaustive method made.

Table 3 shows the analysis of the best correlations found. The exhaustive
method shows the overall best, worst and average correlation in the entire possible 2,601,860. Top 100 shows these for only the top 100 correlations. The remaining three columns show the results after approximately five percent of the
correlations were calculated ($\sim 130,000$ function calls) for the RB method, the
EP method and the GA method. Once again the EP method has the best average
for both Pearson's and Spearman's correlation coefficient.

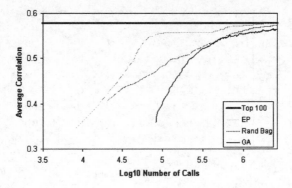

Fig. 3. Pearson's Correlation Coefficient for the VF Data

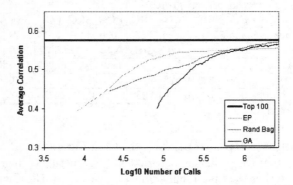

Fig. 4. Spearman's Correlation Coefficient for the VF Data

4.3   Discussion

To summarise the results, the EP method behaved better than the RB method and the GA in both datasets, using both correlation coefficients. It seemed that there was a larger difference in performance between EP and the others in the VF data. This is probably due to the fact that the numerical encoding of the variables map mathematically to spatial points upon the eye's retina. A mutation would result in a form of rotation or translation of co-ordinates. The self-adapting standard deviations would adjust to a level where certain transformations would result in many useful and high correlations, perhaps within the same nerve fibre bundle. In contrast, the variables in the FCC data are ordered in no meaningful way and so the self-adapting parameters can only adjust to the peaks within the cross correlation function. The GA performed the worst, particularly when the number of generations was set to a small number, because

Table 3. Five Percent Freeze for the VF Data

	Exhaustive		Top100		RB		EP		GA	
	PCC	SRC	PCC	SRC	PCC	SRC	PCC	SRC	PCC	SRC
N. calls	~2.6m	~2.6m	~2.6m	~2.6m	130052	130052	126362	130215	123082	120540
% calls	100	100	100	100	4.99	4.99	4.86	4.99	4.73	4.63
B. corr.	0.654	0.616	0.654	0.616	0.608	0.560	0.612	0.555	0.599	0.558
A. corr.	0.343	0.338	0.578	0.526	0.493	0.463	0.543	0.498	0.420	0.408
W. corr.	0.186	0.202	0.549	0.506	0.453	0.431	0.508	0.470	0.292	0.306

the crossover operator merely mixes correlation genes around. The crossover operator is additionally designed to carry forward good schema, which cannot exist within this context (i.e. all genes are independent and hence exhibit low epistasis). The GA could have been designed as in the EP method, with an individual representing a single correlation and the population representing the solution. However, unless a binary representation was used, the chromosome size would have been too small to fully exploit crossover. The binary representation would have been approximately 16 bits in the case of the FCC data. This is still very small, and some elementary experimentation has verified this.

5   Concluding Remarks

Within this paper we have explored several methods for quickly learning the correlation structure of a large dataset. We have applied these methods to two real world datasets that exhibit properties where this type of analysis is useful. That is, they are large multivariate time-series where the fast identification of the approximate correlation structure is needed. The results show that the EP method is by far the quickest to converge to a high average correlation. The self-adapting parameters appear ideally suited to finding meaningful clusters of correlations; however it still remains to be investigated where this method is appropriate, and where it falls down. We suggest that the EP method will perform no better than that of the RB method if there are no patterns within the underlying correlations of the dataset being explored. Here we are referring to the characteristics of the cross correlation function for the FCC data, and the spatial arrangement of the points within nerve fibre bundles in the VF data.

Extensive work has been carried out to investigate the usefulness of this data pre-processing method. For example we have found that the EP method is an efficient way of speeding up an algorithm to find a Dynamic Bayesian Network structure for the FCC data.

Acknowledgements

The authors wish to thank the project Sponsors: Moorfields Eye Hospital, UK; Honeywell Technology Centre, USA; Honeywell Hi-Spec Solutions, UK and the

Engineering and Physical Sciences Research Council, UK. We would also like to thank BP Oil, UK for supplying the FCC dataset. Finally we appreciate the helpful comments from the reviewers.

References

1. T. Baeck, G. Rudolph, H.-P. Schwefel, "Evolutionary Programming and Evolution Strategies: Similarities and Differences", D.B. Fogel and W. Atmar, editor: Proceedings of the Second Annual Conference on Evolutionary Programming, 11-22, 1993.
2. T. Baeck, "Evolutionary Algorithms: Theory and Practice", Oxford University Press, 1996.
3. C. Chatfield, "The Analysis of Time Series - An Introduction", Chapman and Hall, 4th edition, 1989.
4. D. Crabb, F. Fitzke, A. McNaught, R. Hitchings, "A Profile of the Spatial Dependence of Pointwise Sensitivity Across The Glaucomatous Visual Field", Perimetry Update, 1996/1997, pp. 301-310.
5. D.B. Fogel, "Evolutionary Computation - Toward a New Philosophy of Machine Intelligence", IEEE Press, 1995.
6. A. Ghozeil and D.B. Fogel, "Discovering Patterns in Spatial Data using Evolutionary Programming", Genetic Programming 1996: Proceedings of the First Annual Conference, J.R. Koza, D.E. Goldberg, D.B. Fogel, and R.L. Riolo (eds.), MIT Press, Cambridge, MA, pp. 521-527.
7. D. E. Goldberg, "Genetic Algorithms in Search, Optimisation, and Machine Learning", Addison Wesley, 1989
8. M. J. Haley, "The Field Analyzer Primer", Allergan Humphrey, 1987.
9. A. Heijl, A. Lindgren, G. Lindgren, "Inter-Point Correlations of Deviations of Threshold Values in Normal and Glaucomatous Visual Fields", Perimetry Update, 1988/89, pp. 177-183.
10. J.H. Holland, "Adaptation in Natural and Artificial Systems", University of Michigan Press, (1995).
11. R. Sadeghbeigi, "Fluid Catalytic Cracking Handbook", Gulf Publishing Company, 1995.
12. G. Snedecor and W. Cochran, "Statistical Methods", Iowa State University Press, 6th edition, 1967.
13. E.W. Steeg, D. Robinson and E. Willis, "Coincidence Detection: A Fast Method for Discovering Higher-Order Correlations in Multidimensional Data", Proceedings of the 4th International Conference on Knowledge Discovery and Data Mining, New York, 1998, pp. 112-120.

The Biases of Decision Tree Pruning Strategies

Tapio Elomaa

Department of Computer Science
P. O. Box 26 (Teollisuuskatu 23)
FIN-00014 University of Helsinki, Finland
elomaa@cs.helsinki.fi

Abstract. Post pruning of decision trees has been a successful approach in many real-world experiments, but over all possible concepts it does not bring any inherent improvement to an algorithm's performance. This work explores how a PAC-proven decision tree learning algorithm fares in comparison with two variants of the normal top-down induction of decision trees. The algorithm does not prune its hypothesis *per se*, but it can be understood to do pre-pruning of the evolving tree. We study a backtracking search algorithm, called *Rank*, for learning rank-minimal decision trees. Our experiments follow closely those performed by Schaffer [20]. They confirm the main findings of Schaffer: in learning concepts with simple description pruning works, for concepts with a complex description and when all concepts are equally likely pruning is injurious, rather than beneficial, to the average performance of the greedy top-down induction of decision trees. Pre-pruning, as a gentler technique, settles in the average performance in the middle ground between not pruning at all and post pruning.

1 Introduction

Pruning trades accuracy of the data model on the training data with syntactic simplicity in the hope that this will result in a better expected predictive accuracy on the unseen instances of the same domain. Pruning is just one *bias*—preference strategy—among a large body of possible ones, and it only works when it is appropriate from the outset. Schaffer [20] demonstrated that it is a misconception that pruning a decision tree, as compared to leaving it intact, would yield better expected generalization accuracy except for a limited set of target concepts. Suitably varying the setting of the learning situation gives rise to the better performance of the strategy which does not prune the tree at all. In particular, according to Schaffer's [20] experiments pruning a decision tree when classification noise prevails degrades the performance of decision tree learning.

We explore the practical value and generality of another kind of decision tree learning bias; one that is not geared towards avoiding overfitting nor minimizing the complexity of the resulting decision tree. In this approach one characteristic figure of the data model is, however, optimized. Inspired by the theoretical results of Ehrenfeucht and Haussler [6], we test how optimizing a secondary size and shape related parameter—the *rank* of a decision tree—affects the utility of the

D.J. Hand, J.N. Kok, M.R. Berthold (Eds.): IDA'99, LNCS 1642, pp. 63–74, 1999.
© Springer-Verlag Berlin Heidelberg 1999

resulting bias. By changing the values of the input parameters of the learning algorithm called *Rank* [7] we are tuning the fitting of the evolving decision tree to the training data. This is, in a sense, tempering with the level of pruning, but it happens in a controlled way: the fitting is taken into account already in growing the decision tree, when choosing the attributes and deciding the tree's shape. The combined data fit endorsement and model complexity penalization yields, in Domingos' [3,5] terms, *representations-oriented evaluation*.

The rank-optimizing algorithm works by backtracking, i.e., the algorithm may choose to revoke decisions it has made previously. The advantage of optimizing a size-related parameter is that the learning algorithm cannot suffer from pathology that affects decision tree learning algorithms using lookahead [12] nor is it as sensitive to the size of the training data as standard greedy top-down induction of decision trees [13]. Practical experience has shown the rank of a decision tree to be a very stable measure [7].

Elomaa and Kivinen [8] and Sakakibara [19] proved that rank-bounded decision trees can be learned—within the PAC framework of Valiant [1,22]—when classification noise prevails. The erroneous examples dictate that the fitting of the decision tree cannot be perfect. Relaxed fitting is obtained by pruning, not following full tree construction, but rather in *pre-pruning* fashion. Pre-pruning is a familiar technique from the early empirical decision tree learning algorithms like ID3 [14,15]. Recently it has, again, been advocated as an alternative to post pruning of decision trees [10,4]. Pre-pruning also implements early stopping of training [23], which aims to prevent overtraining and, through it, overfitting.

Our experiments confirm, in a slightly different setting, what was already reported by Shaffer [20]: over the space of equiprobable random Boolean concepts the *Naive* strategy to decision tree learning, which does not even attempt to prune the decision tree built, outperforms the *Sophisticated* one, which may choose to prune the tree, independent of the classification noise level affecting the domain. The latter strategy, though, has constantly obtained better results in empirical experiments. One opposite trend to those reported by Schaffer comes up in our experiments; viz. as the noise rate approaches maximal .5, the better performances start to even out between the learning strategies, rather than to steadily pile up in favor of the Naive strategy. This result is what one would intuitively expect.

The algorithm *Rank* has been previously observed to be competitive with other decision tree learning approaches on UCI data sets [7]. Our experiments here further confirm that in learning simple concepts without large amounts of noise prevailing, rank-minimization attains as good results as the straightforward top-down induction of decision trees. However, on concepts that are harder to express by decision trees, *Rank* cannot match the performance of the Naive strategy. As the noise rate increases, the rank-minimization algorithm catches up the advantage the Naive strategy possessed initially. In comparison with the Sophisticated strategy *Rank* steadily outperforms it.

In Section 2 we introduce briefly the learning of rank-bounded decision trees. In Section 3 a set of empirical experiments—inspired by those performed by

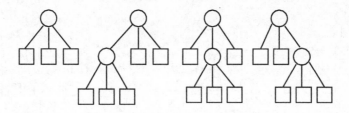

Fig. 1. Tree structures of rank 1 in $DT_3^1(2)$.

Schaffer [20]—is reported and discussed. Section 4 considers the outcome and implications of the experiments. Section 5 reviews further related research. Finally, Section 6 presents the conclusions of this study.

2 Learning Decision Trees of Minimum Rank

Ehrenfeucht and Haussler [6] showed that the function class represented by rank-bounded binary decision trees is learnable in the sense of the basic PAC model [22]. Its superclass—functions determined by arbitrary binary decision trees—is not learnable [9].

There is only one natural way to extend the original definition of the rank to general multivalued decision trees without losing the learnability property.

Definition 1. *The* rank *of a decision tree T, denoted by $r(T)$, is defined as:*

1. *If T consists of a single leaf, then $r(T) = 0$.*
2. *Else if T_{max} is a subtree of T with the maximum rank r_{max}, then*

$$r(T) = \begin{cases} r_{max} & \text{if } T_{max} \text{ is unique,} \\ r_{max} + 1 & \text{otherwise.} \end{cases}$$

This definition generalizes strictly that of Ehrenfeucht and Haussler [6]: The rank of a binary tree is the same as the rank of the subtree with a higher rank if the two subtrees have different ranks. Otherwise, the rank of the full tree is the rank of its both subtrees incremented by one.

Example 1. Let $DT_m^r(n)$ denote the set of all m-ary decision trees of rank at most r over n variables. We are concerned with *reduced* decision trees, where each variable appears at most once on any path from the root to a leaf. Observe that in a reduced tree n is the maximum rank of the tree.

Delimiting the rank of a decision tree (together with the value m) determines the tree structures in $DT_m^r(n)$. $DT_m^0(n)$ only contains the single-leaf tree structure, independent of the value of m. The number of possible labelings of that only leaf gives the number of functionally different equal-structured decision trees; $DT_m^0(n)$ always contains n separate one-leaf decision trees. For values $r > 0$ there exists more than just one possible tree structure (assuming $n > 1$).

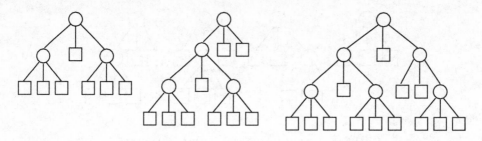

Fig. 2. Examples of tree structures in $DT_3^2(3)$.

For instance, Fig. 1 illustrates all (reduced) tree structures of rank 1 contained in $DT_3^1(2)$.

The decision trees are obtained from these structures by assigning each node with a label; the labeling must be legal, i.e., it has to keep the tree reduced. The function represented by a decision tree is not necessarily unique.

As the parameter values m, n, and r grow, the number of legal tree structures in $DT_m^r(n)$ and their possible labelings go up quickly. The tree structures in Fig. 2 are examples of those belonging to $DT_3^2(3)$.

In order to be able to construct decision trees of minimum rank in noisy domains one has to relax the fitting of examples by letting the decision tree give inconsistent decisions. Typically in top-down induction of decision trees as tightly fitted decision trees as possible are constructed and then, in the second phase, they are pruned back in order to avoid overfitting them to the false trends that happen to prevail in the training set [2,16]. Obviously, such pruning cannot be used in connection of rank-minimization.

In the algorithm *Rank* growing of a branch of the evolving tree is stopped when relaxed fitting is reached. Two *a priori* determined parameters control the degree of the required fitting. The relaxed fitting amounts to pre-pruning. The construction of a branch of the evolving decision tree is stopped when only a small portion of the examples under consideration deviates from the majority class or a minimal number of the examples belongs to a different class than the majority one [8,19]. The values for the input parameters determining the relative portion of consistent examples required (parameter γ) and the absolute number of errors allowed per class (parameter κ) before stopping the growing of a branch can be calculated exactly from the values of the standard PAC-parameters sample size, accuracy ε, confidence δ, and noise rate η [1,22]. The three latter parameters, of course, are unknown in practice.

We take γ and κ simply to be a real-valued and an integer-valued, respectively, input parameter for the learning algorithm. It is typical in inductive learning methods to expect the user to supply a value for a confidence level or a threshold parameter, which corresponds to γ parameter of *Rank*. For instance, C4.5 [16] is an example of such a program. Furthermore, in C4.5 the user is allowed to tune the value of a parameter (-m) that corresponds to κ.

Table 1. The programs implementing the relaxed rank-minimization. *Stopping-Condition* is the relaxed fitting rule that implements pre-pruning. *Find* is the subprogram that checks, by backtracking search, if a decision tree of the given rank exists. *Rank* is the main program controlling the value of the rank bound.

```
boolean StoppingCondition( Sample S, int κ, double γ )
{
    // Mᵢ is the number of instances of i in S. k is the majority class in S.
    if ( M_k ≥ γ|S| or M_j ≤ κ for all j ≠ k (and M_k > κ) ) return true;
    return false;
}
```

```
DecisionTree Find( Sample S, int r, Variables V, int κ, double γ )
{
    if ( StoppingCondition( S, κ, γ ) ) return T = k;   // k is the majority class in S.
    if ( r = 0 ) return none;
    for ( each informative variable v ∈ V ) {
        for ( each k ∈ [m] ) T_k^v ← Find(S_k^v, r − 1, V \ {v}, κ, γ);
        if ( ∀k ∈ [m] : T_k^v ≠ none )
            {T ← MakeTree(v, T_1^v, ..., T_m^v); return T;}
        if ( T_k^v = none for a single value k = ℓ ∈ [m] ) {
            T_ℓ^v ← Find(S_ℓ^v, r, V \ {v}, κ, γ);
            if ( T_ℓ^v ≠ none ) T ← MakeTree(v, T_1^v, ..., T_m^v);
            else T ← none;
            return T;
        }
    }
    return none;
}
```

```
DecisionTree Rank( Sample S, Variables V, int R, int κ, double γ )
{
    r ← R; T ← Find(S, R, V, κ, γ);
    if ( T = none ) {
        repeat { r ← r + 1; T ← Find(S, r, V, κ, γ); }
        until T ≠ none or r = |V|;
        if ( T = none ) T ← T = k;   // k is the majority class in S.
        return T;
    }
    r ← r(T);
    while ( r > 0 ) {
        Q ← Find(S, r − 1, V, κ, γ);
        if ( Q ≠ none ) { r ← r(Q); T ← Q; }
    }
    return T;
}
```

The programs implementing the learning algorithm *Rank* are described as code in Table 1. The main program *Rank* inputs five parameters: the training sample S, the variable set V, the initial rank candidate R, and the values for the parameters κ and γ. Depending on whether a decision tree is found by the subprogram *Find* using the initial rank candidate or not, a search proceeding to different directions for the true rank of the sample has to be performed. If, at the end, no decision tree is found—due to too tight fitting requirements—a single-leaf tree predicting the majority class of the sample is returned.

In the program *Find* it is assumed that all the variables in V are nominal and have the same arity; i.e., that their domain consists of the value set $[m] = \{1, \ldots, m\}$. This assumption is included here for the clarity of the code, it is not a restrictive assumption. *Find* carries out the backtracking search for a decision tree of at most the given rank bound. Observe that this search is not exhaustive—which would require exponential time—but avoids unnecessary recursion by carefully keeping track of the examined rank candidates. The asymptotic time requirement of this algorithm is linear in the size of the sample and exponential in the rank of the sample. However, the rank of the sample is constant, and usually very low in practice; hence, the algorithm is feasible. By S_k^v we denote the set of those examples in the sample S in which variable v has value k.

Finally, *StoppingCondition* checks whether the relaxed stopping condition holds in the sample under consideration. In other words, it returns value true if the conditions of pre-pruning are fulfilled and branch growing can be terminated.

3   Empirical Evaluation

We carry out a set of experiments inspired by those of Schaffer [20]. In them two strategies to decision tree learning implemented by the CART learning algorithm [2] were compared: Naive strategy chose the decision tree grown without a chance of ever pruning it and the Sophisticated strategy had the possibility of pruning the tree produced. The purpose of duplicating a part of these experiments is to assess the overall performance of the *Rank* algorithm and its pre-pruning strategy in contrast with two versions of the more familiar greedy top-down induction procedure.

3.1   Experiment Setting

Each experiment consists of 25 trials. We take all the trials into account, but pay special attention to the *discrepant trials*, those in which the the trees of the strategies differ in their accuracy. All experiments concern learning of Boolean functions on five attributes: named **a** through **e**. The number of training examples given to the learning algorithms is 50 randomly allotted instances. The prediction accuracy of a tree is analytically determined.

In testing the statistical significance of our findings we follow Schaffer [20] and use the non-parametric one-sided binomial sign test. Given n discrepant trials in an experiment, the test lets us reject the hypothesis that the strategies perform equally well with confidence $1 - \sum_{i=0}^{r} \left(\binom{n}{i}/2^n \right)$, where r, $0 \leq r \leq \lfloor n/2 \rfloor$, is the number of "wins" recorded by the strategy obtaining less wins. All trials, except when otherwise stated, have a .1 classification noise affecting them; i.e., each training example has a one tenth chance of having a corrupted (complemented) class value.

Instead of CART we use C4.5 (release 8) algorithm [16,17] to implement the basic learning strategies. As Schaffer [20] argues nothing should change through changing the top-down induction algorithm; the relative strengths and weaknesses of the strategies should stay constant. Sophisticated strategy is the default pruning of C4.5 and in the Naive strategy pruning has been turned off.

In C4.5, which uses global post pruning, the performance of the final decision tree is less sensitive to the values of the input parameters than that of *Rank*, built based on local pre-pruning. For *Rank* we adjust the values of its parameters κ and γ to suitable values empirically, but then keep the values constant throughout each experiment (25 trials). Only when large amounts of noise affect the learning situation will κ have a value different from 1. We do not leave the order of attribute inspection to be arbitrary as described in the code in Table 1. Instead, we use the evaluation function gini-index [2] to order the attributes. Nevertheless, the rank restriction ultimately decides whether an attribute is chosen to the tree or not.

3.2   Preliminary Experiments

Schaffer [20] started with two simple learning tasks, where the Sophisticated strategy emerged superior. In learning the first simple concept Class = a, there were 18 of 25 discrepant trials and in each of them the Sophisticated strategy was superior obtaining, indeed, the maximum achievable average accuracy of .9.

The learning algorithm *Rank* also attains the maximum achievable accuracy in each of the 25 trials using parameter value $\gamma = .75$. In this case the correct concept is a decision tree containing (at least) two leaves, which have to accommodate also all the corrupted examples. Therefore, relatively loose fitting is required for learning the correct concept.

In learning the second concept Class = a $\vee$ (b $\wedge$ c), there were 17 discrepant trials in Schaffer's experiment. The Sophisticated strategy chose a superior tree in 16 out of them, attaining the average accuracy of .854.

This time a correct decision tree contains at least four leaves. Thus, the fitting of the tree does not need to be as relaxed as in the previous experiment. Using parameter value $\gamma = .85$ *Rank* comes up with the correct concept in 18 of 25 trials attaining the average accuracy of .876.

In sum, these two simple concepts are at least as well learned by the backtracking rank-minimization as by growing a full decision tree and subsequently pruning it. This result supports our earlier finding—on the UCI data—that *Rank* performs comparably with C4.5 on the most commonly used machine learning test domains [7].

3.3   Parity and Random Functions

Parity function is true precisely when an odd number of the attributes take on the true value. It is hard to express by any representation using only single-attribute values. Parity serves to demonstrate the opposite case in Schaffer's [20] experiments: for it the fully-grown trees are more accurate than the pruned decision trees. Moreover, adding more noise to the training examples allows the Naive strategy to increase its lead over the Sophisticated strategy.

In the basic .1 classification noise case, when the C4.5 algorithm was used to implement the two strategies, the Naive strategy outperformed the Sophisticated one in each trial. The average accuracy of the Naive strategy over the 25 trials was .675 and that of the Sophisticated strategy was .542.

Parity is a worst-case function for rank-minimization since the correct decision tree for it has as high rank as possible. Therefore, any other matching concept of lower rank for the noisy training set is preferred over the true one. In light of this, one cannot expect *Rank* to attain the accuracy level of the Naive strategy. Using parameter value $\gamma = .9$ *Rank* obtained the average accuracy of .552. The number of discrepant cases with the Sophisticated strategy was 19 of 25, out of which in 12 trials *Rank* produced the superior decision tree. Naive strategy was superior to *Rank* in all trials.

A better understanding of the strategies' relative performance is obtained by repeating Schaffer's experiment of learning a random Boolean function on five attributes. In each trial we randomly fix a new target function. Parameter values for *Rank* need to be adjusted differently for each target function.

The number of discrepant trials between *Rank* and the Naive strategy is 23, out of which in 22 Naive produces the superior tree. *Rank* outperforms the Sophisticated strategy in 14 of 16 discrepant trials. The average accuracies over the 25 trials are .777 for the Naive strategy, .728 for the *Rank* algorithm, and .701 for the Sophisticated strategy.

These experiments go to show that when the correct decision tree has a syntactically complex tree description, close fitting of the tree to the training examples gives the best results. Learning random Boolean concepts demonstrates that the majority of concepts falls into this category.

3.4   The Effect of Classification Noise

The experiments reported by Schaffer [20] that bear most generality concern learning random Boolean functions. These experiments correspond to normal randomization analysis and give a measure of the average performance when all concepts are equally likely. However, as often pointed out [11,18,20], this does not necessary conform to real-world performance of the strategies.

Schaffer observed that as the classification noise rate of the training examples increases from .05 to .3, the number of discrepant trials steadily grows. The Sophisticated strategy is not able to conquer a larger proportion of those cases. Instead, the Naive strategy keeps advancing its superiority. This is a strong

Table 2. The effect of classification noise: random Boolean functions.

Error rate	Naive > Sophitic.		Naive > Rank		Rank > Sophistic.		Average accuracies		
							Naive	Rank	Sophistic.
.05	22 of 22	.99	19 of 20	.99	15 of 17	.99	.782	.738	.700
.1	23 of 23	.99	22 of 23	.99	14 of 16	.99	.777	.728	.701
.15	18 of 21	.99	15 of 20	.98	17 of 22	.99	.709	.691	.656
.2	21 of 22	.99	17 of 21	.99	18 of 21	.99	.695	.669	.622
.25	19 of 21	.99	12 of 19	.82	11 of 15	.94	.682	.663	.639
.3	15 of 21	.96	13 of 23	.66	12 of 19	.82	.625	.621	.584

demonstration of pruning lacking any inherent advantage in fighting against the effects of noise.

Table 2 lists the results of our experiment. The first column gives the noise rate. The next two record in how many out of the discrepant cases, the Naive strategy outperformed the Sophisticated one, and what is the confidence level by which we can trust the former to be superior in this experiment. Corresponding column pairs are given for the remaining two learning strategy pairs. The three last columns report the average accuracies of the algorithms over the 25 trials.

Our results are parallel to those reported by Schaffer; the Naive strategy is superior to the Sophisticated one independent of the error rate affecting the class attribute. However, there is also an opposite trend in here; when only a small error probability affects the learning situation the Naive strategy is with a very high confidence level significantly better than the Sophisticated strategy. As the error rate approaches .5, this confidence level starts to decline.

This effect is clearer in the comparison with the *Rank* algorithm. When .3 classification noise prevails, the confidence which we have for the Naive strategy's superiority is only .66 and the confidence for the superiority of *Rank* over the Sophisticated strategy has dropped down to .82. The decreasing confidences are due to the fact that the concept represented by the training examples approaches a random one. Thus, no data model can predict the class of an instance. The same can also be observed from the dropping average accuracies of all three strategies; they all gradually approach the random guess' accuracy .5.

In Schaffer's experiment the number of discrepant cases also increased along with the error rate. No such trend appears in the results of our experiment. In our experiment the noise rate as such has no bearing on the relative strengths of the learning strategies, none of them can be said to cope with classification noise better than the other strategies do.

3.5   Further Experiments

Schaffer [20] further explored the effects of, e.g., changing the representation of the concepts, adding different kinds of noise to the training examples, and on the number of instances belonging to different classes. We, however, leave performing similar tests as future work. It is evident that the representation changes would have similar effects on our test strategies as they had on those of Schaffer.

4   Discussion

The above experiments confirmed what Schaffer [20] already reported: In learning syntactically simple concepts, pruning leads to more accurate decision trees than leaving the tree be as it is after growing it. There are concepts that require a syntactically more complex description. In learning such concepts it is better to do as accurate fitting of the decision tree to the training examples as possible and not prune the tree. Most importantly, the concepts requiring a complex decision tree description are the ones that dominate the space of all possible concepts.

The last point is crucial for the practical applicability of decision trees. However, the empirical evidence overwhelmingly supports the hypothesis that most real-world learning domains have a syntactically simple decision tree representation [11,20]. There also exists some analysis to back up this claim [18].

An interesting difference in the results of the above comparison and those of Schaffer is that as the noise rate approaches the maximal .5 level, both the Naive strategy and the *Rank* algorithm start to lose the edge that they have over the Sophisticated strategy. This effect is intuitive; as the noise rate increases, the class associated with the instances tends towards a random assignment. Thus, it is impossible for any learning approach to predict the class of an instance. As Schaffer [20, pp. 163–165] analyses, exact fitting is the best prediction policy when all concepts are equiprobable. Therefore, the Naive strategy maintains some edge over the Sophisticated one even with as high error rate as .3.

Pre-pruning is not as aggressive as post pruning, which explains a substantial part of the differences observed in the performance of the *Rank* algorithm and the other two learning strategies. From these experiments it is hard to discern to what amount can we attribute these differences to the incomparable search procedures. However, in some trials the backtracking search clearly benefited and in others hampered the performance of decision tree learning.

5   Related Research

In a subsequent study Schaffer [21] generalized the main observations of the overfitting avoidance bias into the conservation law of generalization performance, which essentially observes that there cannot be a universally superior bias. More or less the same has been expressed in Wolpert's [24] "no free lunch" theorems. The relevance of these results for practical inductive learning can be questioned, since experience has shown that many of the learning domains encountered in practice have an extremely simple representation [11] and, hence, the bias of heavy pruning would suit practical learning tasks better than other biases.

Holder [10] has shown that the *intermediate decision trees*—subtrees pruned in a breadth-first order from the full trees grown by C4.5—perform better than the full and pruned trees in a large corpus of UCI data sets. Intermediate decision trees correspond to pre-prunings of the full tree. Holder's experiments also support our earlier observation: pre-pruning, if given a slight advantage by careful parameter adjusting, may be a competitive alternative to post pruning of decision trees on real-world domains.

Domingos [4] has considered the correctness of different interpretations of Occam's Razor. He compiles a substantial amount of analytical and empirical evidence against interpreting that the Law of Parsimony would somewhat qualify or justify pruning as an inherently beneficial technique in concept learning. No evidence supports assuming that lower syntactic complexity of a concept description would somehow transform into lower generalization error.

6 Conclusions

In this study we wanted to set into perspective of Schaffer's [20] results the bias induced by pre-pruning of decision trees and to compare the bias of the rank-minimization to that of the standard top-down induction of decision trees. The performance of pre-pruning on the scale of the complexity of concept representation settles down in between the Naive and the Sophisticated strategies. The bias resulting from rank-minimization was visible in some trials, but on the average level we cannot conclude much about it on the basis of these experiments.

The main findings of our experiments are similar to those that were reported by Schaffer [20]: Sophisticated strategy is the better choice in domains with a simple description, while the Naive one is the better choice otherwise. The differences that were observed in learning random Boolean concepts when classification noise prevails are interesting and worth attention.

In future work one could experiment with forcing a maximum rank bound for the decision trees—in the spirit of learning decision trees with stringent syntactic restrictions [11]—and observing such restriction's effects on the prediction accuracy of the resulting tree. Further experimentation with the effects of different noise generating schemes and other tests performed by Schaffer should be carried out in order to complete the study initiated in this paper.

References

1. Angluin, D., Laird, P.: Learning from noisy examples. Mach. Learn. **2** (1988) 343–370
2. Breiman, L., Friedman, J., Olshen, R., Stone, C.: Classification and Regression Trees. Wadsworth, Pacific Grove, CA (1984)
3. Domingos, P.: A process-oriented heuristic for model selection. In: Shavlik, J. (ed.): Machine Learning: Proceedings of the Fifteenth International Conference. Morgan Kaufmann, San Francisco, CA (1998) 127–135
4. Domingos, P.: Occam's two razors: the sharp and the blunt. In: Agrawal, R., Stolorz, P., Piatetsky-Shapiro, G. (eds.): Proceedings of the Fourth International Conference on Knowledge Discovery and Data Mining. AAAI Press, Menlo Park, CA (1998) 37–43
5. Domingos, P.: Process-oriented estimation of generalization error. In: Proceedings of the Sixteenth International Joint Conference on Artificial Intelligence. Morgan Kaufmann, San Francisco, CA (to appear)

6. Ehrenfeucht A., Haussler, D.: Learning decision trees from random examples. Inf. Comput. **82** (1989) 231–246

7. Elomaa, T.: Tools and techniques for decision tree learning. Report A-1996-2, Department of Computer Science, University of Helsinki (1996)

8. Elomaa, T., Kivinen, J.: Learning decision trees from noisy examples, Report A-1991-3, Department of Computer Science, University of Helsinki (1991)

9. Hancock, T., Jiang, T., Li, M., Tromp, J.: Lower bounds on learning decision lists and trees. Inf. Comput. **126** (1996) 114–122

10. Holder, L. B.: Intermediate decision trees. In: Proceedings of the Fourteenth International Joint Conference on Artificial Intelligence. Morgan Kaufmann, San Francisco, CA (1995) 1056–1061

11. Holte, R. C.: Very simple classification rules perform well on most commonly used data sets. Mach. Learn. **11** (1993) 63–90

12. Murthy S. K., Salzberg, S.: Lookahead and pathology in decision tree induction. In: Proceedings of the Fourteenth International Joint Conference on Artificial Intelligence. Morgan Kaufmann, San Francisco, CA (1995) 1025–1031

13. Oates, T., Jensen, D.: The effects of training set size on decision tree complexity. In: Fisher, D. H. (ed.): Machine Learning: Proceedings of the Fourteenth International Conference, Morgan Kaufmann, San Francisco, CA (1997) 254–261

14. Quinlan, J. R.: Learning efficient classification procedures and their application to chess end games. In: Michalski, R., Carbonell, J., Mitchell, T. (eds.): Machine Learning: An Artificial Intelligence Approach. Tioga, Palo Alto, CA (1983) 391–411

15. Quinlan, J. R.: Induction of decision trees. Mach. Learn. **1** (1986) 81–106

16. Quinlan, J. R.: C4.5: Programs for Machine Learning. Morgan Kaufmann, San Mateo, CA (1993)

17. Quinlan, J. R.: Improved use of continuous attributes in C4.5. J. Artif. Intell. Res. **4** (1996) 77–90

18. Rao, R. B., Gordon, D. F., Spears, W. M.: For every generalization action, is there really an equal and opposite reaction? Analysis of the conservation law for generalization performance. In: Prieditis, A., Russell, S. (eds.): Machine Learning: Proceedings of the Twelfth International Conference. Morgan Kaufmann, San Francisco, CA (1995) 471–479

19. Sakakibara, Y.: Noise-tolerant Occam algorithms and their applications to learning decision trees. Mach. Learn. **11** (1993) 37–62

20. Schaffer, C.: Overfitting avoidance as bias. Mach. Learn. **10** (1993) 153–178

21. Schaffer, C.: A conservation law for generalization performance. In: Cohen, W. W., Hirsh, H. (eds.): Machine Learning: Proceedings of the Eleventh International Conference. Morgan Kaufmann, San Francisco, CA (1994) 259–265

22. Valiant, L. G.: A theory of the learnable. Commun. ACM **27** (1984) 1134–1142

23. Wang, C., Venkatesh, S. S., Judd, J. S.: Optimal stopping and effective machine complexity in learning. In: Cowan, J. D., Tesauro, G., Alspector, J. (eds.): Advances in Neural Information Processing Systems, Vol. 6. Morgan Kaufmann, San Francisco, CA (1994) 303–310

24. Wolpert, D. H.: The lack of a priori distinctions between learning algorithms. Neural Comput. **8** (1996) 1341–1390

Feature Selection as Retrospective Pruning in Hierarchical Clustering

Luis Talavera

Departament de Llenguatges i Sistemes Informàtics
Universitat Politècnica de Catalunya
Campus Nord, Mòdul C6, Jordi Girona 1-3
08034 Barcelona, Spain
talavera@lsi.upc.es

Abstract. Although feature selection is a central problem in inductive learning as suggested by the growing amount of research in this area, most of the work has been carried out under the supervised learning paradigm, paying little attention to unsupervised learning tasks and, particularly, clustering tasks. In this paper, we analyze the particular benefits that feature selection may provide in hierarchical clustering. We propose a view of feature selection as a tree pruning process similar to those used in decision tree learning. Under this framework, we perform several experiments using different pruning strategies and considering a multiple prediction task. Results suggest that hierarchical clusterings can be greatly simplified without diminishing accuracy.

1   Introduction

The widespread use of information technologies produces an growing amount of data which is too huge to be analyzed by manual methods. There are large volumes of data containing both, many features and many examples. Inductive learning methods are a powerful method for automatically extracting useful information from this data or for assisting humans in this process. A problem related to this sort of data is the presence of a large number of features that might tend to decrease the effectiveness of learning algorithms, especially if most of these features appear to be irrelevant with regard to the learning task. In fact, feature selection is a central problem in inductive learning as suggested by the growing amount of research in this area [1, 9].

However, most of the work concerning feature selection has been carried out under the supervised learning paradigm, paying little attention to unsupervised learning tasks and, particularly, clustering tasks. Clustering is a form of unsupervised learning used to discover interesting patterns in data. Particularly, hierarchical clustering methods construct a tree-structured clustering where sibling clusters partition the observations covered by their parent. The particular knowledge organization and performance tasks of hierarchical clusterings suggest several dimensions to analyze the benefits of feature selection in hierarchical clustering tasks. In this paper, we propose a novel view of feature selection as

D.J. Hand, J.N. Kok, M.R. Berthold (Eds.): IDA'99, LNCS 1642, pp. 75–86, 1999.
© Springer-Verlag Berlin Heidelberg 1999

pruning in hierarchical clustering and propose some possible implementations. In addition, we perform an empirical comparison of these methods analyzing the results under the proposed dimensions.

2   Feature Selection in Hierarchical Clustering

Typically, the primary goal of feature selection is intended to make inductive learning algorithms more robust in the face of irrelevant features. Clearly, this may be a motivation for applying feature selection to hierarchical clustering tasks. However, it is important to highlight two specific factors that surround these tasks that may be relevant for feature selection. The first factor is the form of the *knowledge base*. Commonly, hierarchical clusterings are *polythetic* classifiers, that is, they divide objects based on their values along multiple features. Particularly, they tend to use the full set of features at each node to decide how to classify a new object. Note that, while in *monothetic* classifiers such as decision trees, a redundant feature adds one additional test when classifying a new observation, in polythetic classifiers it adds a test for each node in the classification path.

Secondly, we should take into account the *performance task* in which hierarchical clusterings should be useful. As in most inductive data analysis approaches, we can differentiate between *prediction* and *description* tasks [4]. As unsupervised approaches, hierarchical clustering systems are not restricted to predict a single class label. As remarked by several authors, unsupervised learning systems can support a *flexible prediction* task aimed to support prediction over all the features [5, 10]. Because of this multiple inference task, the presence of irrelevant features may be even more harmful in unsupervised systems. On the other hand, unsupervised learning may focus in *description* tasks, rather than in prediction. In such a case, we can view feature selection as a means of simplification of concept descriptions that may provide a more readable interpretation of the domain, without necessarily taking into account accuracy concerns.

In order to clarify further discussion, we now attempt to summarize four different dimensions to evaluate the particular benefits of feature selection in the hierarchical clustering task:

- *Irrelevant features.* The set of features used in an inductive learning task is a powerful representational bias that determines the performance a learning system. Irrelevant features may be particularly harmful in unsupervised systems since they try to form patterns around sets of correlated features without the guidance of external labeling.
- *Efficiency in the learning task.* As we have noted, hierarchical clusterings are polythetic classifiers. Since the decision of how to classify a new instance has to be made along several nodes in the tree, the number of features present in the data directly influences the complexity of the clustering process. If we apply feature selection to reduce this complexity, we should expect to obtain clusterings of similar or better quality that we would had obtained by using all the available features.

- *Efficiency in the performance task.* When using a hierarchical clustering to classify an unseen observation in order to infer unknown properties, the number of features still has a strong influence in the complexity of the process in the same manner we have described above. Again, selecting an appropriate subset of features may reduce this complexity. Since, in this case, the concern lies in exploiting feature selection to speed-up a prediction task, learning does not necessarily have to be affected by the feature selection process.
- *Comprehensibility of the results.* With the exception of logic-based approaches which select features by using the dropping conditions rule, clustering systems usually make use of all the available features at each node of the hierarchy. Reducing the number of features used in the clustering process allow to provide shorter cluster descriptions to the user. Short descriptions tend to be more readable and, hence more comprehensible. Comprehensibility has been recognized as a specially important concern in clustering [11].

3   Feature Selection as Pruning Concept Trees

Tree-based models are typical in inductive learning approaches. A powerful method for supervised classification tasks is the induction of decision trees [13]. In early approaches, the tree was expanded until all objects of a child were members of the same class. However, it has been found that this strategy may overfit the data by growing the tree more than is justified by the training set. To solve this problem, *pruning* strategies have been developed that either stop tree expansion during learning, or remove certain nodes in a post-processing step. Although the term of feature selection is usually used in supervised learning to denote a process external to the induction algorithm, pruning decision trees may be viewed as such a process, because we reduce the number of terms used in concept descriptions. In addition to avoid overfitting, pruning produces simpler trees and, thus, more comprehensible descriptions.

As remarked by Langley [10], pruning methods can be combined with any learning technique that deals with complex structures. Particularly, hierarchical clusterings may grow arbitrarily, producing lower levels that are not justified by the training data thus justifying the use of pruning methods. Because hierarchical clusterings can be used to predict many features, a pruning of the tree that is appropriate for one feature, may be innapropriate for other features. To cope with this problem, we can identify frontiers of clusters for prediction of each feature [6, 7]. With this strategy, in order to predict a feature value, classification has not necessarily to terminate at a leaf, but may stop in an intermediate node.

The mentioned approaches to pruning in both, decision trees and hierarchical clusterings, constraint the depth of the tree. Therefore, they may be viewed as *vertical* pruning strategies aimed to reduce the height of the resulting tree. In decision trees, this constrain results in a reduction of the number of terms used in the final descriptions, but as a polythetic classifier, removal of a node in a hierarchical clustering reduces the length of the classification path, but the full set of features is still used in concept descriptions. However, if we see a node

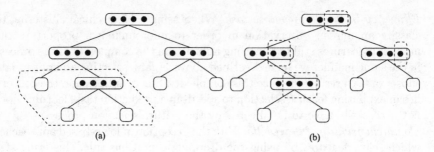

Fig. 1. Vertical (a) vs. horizontal (b) pruning. Dashed lines indicate pruned nodes or features.

in a hierarchical clustering as a set of tests to be made –one for each feature– to classify an instance through the children of this node, we can think about some sort of *horizontal* pruning strategy aimed to reduce the width of the levels of the tree by removing some features. Figure 1 graphically shows these ideas. Note that the complexity of classifying an object in a hierarchical clustering depends on both, the length of the path, and the number of features included in the computation of the metric used to decide the best host. Therefore, both horizontal and vertical pruning strategies, should improve the prediction task by reducing the path and the number of features used in computing the metric used for clustering, respectively. In addition, horizontal pruning can provide more readable concept descriptions, thus improving performance along two of the four evaluation dimensions presented in Section 2.

4   Horizontal Pruning Methods

Our proposal of viewing feature selection as pruning, constraints feature selection to be performed over an existing knowledge structure. This view contrasts with the traditional perspective of feature selection as a preprocessing step performed before learning occurs. There are two different points in the learning process in which this sort of feature selection can be performed, during learning and after learning. Note that this distinction is analogous to the traditional distinction into *prospective* (or prepruning) and *retrospective* (or postpruning) strategies.

Methods for deciding which features should be selected can be designed in a similar fashion to existing pruning methods for decision trees. Any pruning method must estimate the 'true' error rate of the pruned trees. For example, some pruning methods rely on some form of significance tests, such as χ^2, to determine whether the unpruned tree is significantly better that the pruned version. Other are based on resampling strategies such as holdout or cross-validation. These examples suggest a division of horizontal pruning strategies into *blind* and *feedback* methods. Blind methods consider features independently of the induction algorithm used, relying on some sort of estimation based on the data. Feedback methods use the results of the induction algorithm to obtain an estimate of performance. A similar distinction of feature selection methods is that into *filter* and *wrapper* methods.

Additionally, the pruning-based view suggest another interesting issue for feature selection. Existing methods of feature selection select a unique subset of features which is then used in the learning process. In our case, this means that all the nodes in all the levels are pruned in an homogeneous fashion. However, it appears reasonable to think about a more selective pruning strategy that considers different sets of features for each node. Different subsets of features may perform better at different local parts of the observation space than a single global set. Therefore, we can classify horizontal pruning strategies along a second dimension according to the scope of the pruning and distinguish into *local* and *global* methods. This view of feature relevance can be viewed as similar to the local weighting approaches used in lazy learning [15].

The presented dimensions may suggest a variety of strategies for horizontally pruning concept trees when combined with usual methods for organizing the search into the space of features. For example, we can start with the empty set of features and successively add features or we can start with all the features and successively remove them. These widely known strategies are called *forward selection (FS)* and *backward elimination (BE)* and may be used together with some error estimation method in order to find a suitable subset of features. Under our framework, we can choose between implementing blind or feedback based versions of the FS and BE strategies. Moreover, we can apply the procedures once for the whole hierarchical clustering, obtaining an homogeneous pruning or apply them locally to each node. Therefore, we can talk about local and global versions of FS and BE.

5   Experiments

In our experiments, we implemented several methods covering local, global, blind and feedback approaches. Particularly, we are interested in investigating the impact of horizontal pruning along two dimensions, namely, efficiency of the performance task and comprehensibility. The performance task considered is the flexible prediction task previously discussed, which is measured as the average accuracy over all of the features present in the data. This accuracy is computed for each instance by repeatedly masking out one feature and then using the cluster hierarchy to classify the instance and predict the masked value. Final accuracy is obtained by averaging the accuracy obtained for each individual feature. The predicted value always corresponds to the one found in the reached leaf.

We measured prediction efficiency empirically by recording the number of *feature tests* needed to classify an instance when making a prediction. For instance, if there are n features, for a given instance, the COBWEB algorithm first evaluates the utility of making an independent cluster and performs n tests to compute the category utility metric. Other operators such as evaluating the utility of incorporating the instance to an existing cluster among k different clusters, need $k \cdot n$ tests. The sum of all these tests averaged for all the predictions made, is used as an indicator of the complexity of making predictions. Finally, comprehensibility is evaluated simply by looking at the average number of features per node. We assume that shorter descriptions are more readable, and thus, more comprehensible.

The hierarchical clustering method used is the COBWEB system [5], since it is a well-known method and its basic strategy is the core of many unsupervised learning systems. Experiments were performed over three standard data sets from the UCI Repository: soybean small, soybean large and zoo database. The two first data sets are described by 35 features and the third by 16, thus they should give a good preliminary picture of the power of feature selection as horizontal pruning.

5.1 An Overview of COBWEB

COBWEB [5] is a hierarchical clustering system that constructs a tree from a sequence of observations. The system follows a strict *incremental* scheme, that is, it learns from each observation in the sequence without reprocessing previously encountered observations. An observation is assumed to be a vector of nominal values V_{ij} along different features A_i. COBWEB employs *probabilistic concept* descriptions to represent the learned knowledge. In this sort of representation, in a cluster C_k, each feature value has an associated conditional probability $P(A_i = V_{ij} \mid C_k)$ reflecting the proportion of observations in C_k with the value V_{ij} along the feature A_i.

The strategy followed by COBWEB is summarized in Table 1. Given an observation and a current hierarchical clustering, the system categorizes the observation by sorting it through the hierarchy from the root node down to the leaves. At each level, the learning algorithm evaluates the quality of the new clustering resulting from placing the observation in each of the existing clusters, and the quality resulting from creating a new cluster covering the new observation. In addition, the algorithm considers two more actions that can restructure the hierarchy in order to improve its quality. *Merging* attempts to combine the two sibling clusters which were identified as the two best hosts for the new observation; *splitting* can replace the best host and promote its children to the next higher level. The option that yields the high quality score is selected and the procedure is recursed, considering the best host as the root in the recursive call. The recursion ends when a leaf containing only the new observation is created.

In order to choose among the four available operators, COBWEB uses a cluster quality function called *category utility* defined for a partition $P = \{C_1, C_2, ..., C_n\}$ of n clusters as

$$\frac{\sum_k P(C_k) \sum_i \sum_j [P(A_i = V_{ij} \mid C_k)^2 - P(A_i = V_{ij})^2]}{n} \tag{1}$$

This function measures how much a partition P promotes inference and rewards clusters C_k that increase the predictability of feature values within C_k.

Function Cobweb(observation,root)
    1) Incorporate observation into the root cluster.
    2) **If** root is a leaf **then**
        return expanded leaf with the observation.
      else choose the best of the following operators:
        a) Incorporate the observation into the best host
        b) Create a new disjunct based on the observation
        c) Merge the two best hosts
        d) Split the best host
    3) If a), c) or d) recurse on the chosen host.

Table 1. The control strategy of COBWEB.

1. $F = \emptyset$
2. For each feature A_i not in F
    Estimate performance by classifying objects in the validation set starting from the root and using $F \cup \{A_i\}$ for the considered node.
3. Let be A_M the feature yielding the highest improvement.
4. If the performance of $F \cup \{A_M\}$ is higher than the performance of F, add A_M to F and goto 2.

Table 2. The FS algorithm for pruning features locally from a node.

Generally, the system is evaluated in terms of its predictive accuracy along all the features.

5.2 Experiment 1: Feedback Methods

Our first set of experiments is intended to explore the performance of feedback based methods. Our implementation uses a simple holdout strategy that divides the data set into three subsets: 40% for training, 40% for validation and 20% for test. A hierarchy is constructed using the training set and then, the validation set is used to estimate the performance of each of the different subsets of features considered. The final results shown correspond to the accuracy on the test set. We implemented four versions of this procedure by applying FS and BE strategies locally or globally. Table 2 shows the pseudo-code for the FS procedure applied locally to a node. Pruning starts by applying the procedure to the root node and it is recursively applied to the descendants until reaching a leaf node. The implementation of the BE strategy is analogous but starting with the full set of features and removing one feature at each step. The global strategies are implemented by estimating accuracy in step 2 using the selected subset of features in all the nodes, instead of only in a particular node. Recall

Table 3. Results for feedback-based methods: global and local FS and BE.

Dataset	Pruning	Accuracy	Tests	Features/Node
zoo	None	85.50 ± 2.72	162.76 ± 8.44	16.00 ± 0.00
	GFS	82.31 ± 4.55	75.76 ± 38.07	7.33 ± 3.78
	GBE	85.83 ± 2.53	117.13 ± 19.79	11.10 ± 1.76
	LFS	85.81 ± 2.68	25.52 ± 5.16	1.21 ± 0.12
	LBE	85.91 ± 3.14	42.51 ± 8.61	1.80 ± 0.18
soybean small	None	85.70 ± 2.35	277.48 ± 24.97	35.00 ± 0.00
	GFS	85.82 ± 2.35	55.68 ± 26.55	7.07 ± 3.12
	GBE	85.11 ± 3.00	134.25 ± 57.82	16.46 ± 6.52
	LFS	84.58 ± 2.78	18.37 ± 2.79	1.31 ± 0.23
	LBE	85.41 ± 2.21	40.12 ± 17.21	3.40 ± 1.17
soybean large	None	83.53 ± 1.46	466.33 ± 22.15	35.00 ± 0.00
	GFS	81.60 ± 3.48	240.87 ± 93.70	17.95 ± 6.75
	GBE	83.24 ± 1.27	385.01 ± 37.62	28.85 ± 2.12
	LFS	N/A		
	LBE	N/A		

that global methods select the same subset for all the nodes, so there is no need to recurse.

Table 3 shows the results from 30 trials with pruned clusterings generated with the four methods mentioned above from random instance orderings. For comparative purposes, we include the results obtained from unpruned trees constructed over the training set and tested on the test set, but without including the validation set. The lack of results of local pruning methods for the soybean large data set is due to the high processing time required. This highlights a first result: feedback-based local methods are likely to be impractical for data sets with high number of features. The reason is that we are trying to optimize a multiple prediction task, so that we need to run multiple tests when estimating performance instead of a single test of predicting a class label. For this extended task, the complexity of the implemented feedback methods for a data set with n features is $O(n^3)$, instead of the $O(n^2)$ required in supervised tasks.

Paradoxically, local methods appear to be the better performers, dramatically improving performance along both, prediction efficiency and comprehensibility dimensions. In the two first data sets, results suggest that the average number of tests required to classify an unseen object for prediction purposes may be improved in a range between 75-85% without diminishing accuracy. In addition, less than two features per node in the zoo data set and less than four in the small soybean appear to be enough for achieving accurate predictions, and presumably, for describing the resulting hierarchies in a more readable manner. On the other hand, FS methods are more likely to get stuck at local minima, thus producing lower accuracies. On the contrary, BE methods are more conservative but at the expense of obtaining larger feature subsets.

5.3 Experiment 2: Blind Methods

In our second set of experiments, we evaluate the performance of blind methods. Analogously to the first experiments, we can implement local and global versions of a blind method. However, since we have found evidence of the superiority of local over global strategies, we restrict our implementation of blind methods to the former.

We implemented a method that could be cast as a Critical Value Pruning (CVP) method [12]. This method is applied in decision tree induction by selecting a threshold or critical value for the attribute selection measure. A node is pruned if the value obtained by the measure does not exceed the critical value. In the case of horizontal pruning, we should use a measure estimating the predictive power of the features. A natural approach in COBWEB and related systems, is to use the evaluation metric used in the clustering process, since, it is supposed to promote partitions with high inference power. Therefore, for each feature, we can obtain a numerical estimate of performance by measuring the contribution of this feature to the category utility calculation and obtain what Gennari [8] terms the *salience* of a feature. The salience metric induces a partial order of relevance for the set of features that can be easily exploited to select a subset of features introducing a threshold. Specifically, for a given set of features $\{x_1, x_2, \ldots, x_n\}$ and a given τ value, we remove the features in the set

$$\{x \mid Salience(x) < \tau \cdot Max\{Salience(x_i) \mid i = 1, \ldots, n\}\}$$

The τ value is in the $[0,1]$ range, so that $\tau = 0$ means that no feature selection is performed because salience is always positive, while increasing τ values will select smaller subsets of features. The pruning procedure proceeds starting from the root node and recursively removing at each node the features scoring under the selected threshold. Note that, by considering individual nodes, we are considering different subsets of the object space and, therefore, different probability distributions for the features. Because of that, a different subset of features may be selected at each node as we expect from using local strategies.

Table 4 shows the results from 30 trials with pruned clusterings generated with different τ values from random instance orderings. We only used the training and test sets used in the first experiments, excluding the validation set in order to obtain comparable results. As expected, the degree of pruning increases for higher τ values. Again, we can observe that simpler clusterings perform as well as clusterings using the full feature set. The case of the large soybean data set is especially interesting, since we could not get a good picture of the performance that horizontal pruning can provide in our first experiment. Clearly, efficiency may be improved at least in a 50% and the set of defining features per node reduced around eight. From the results, it appears that blind methods select larger subsets of features that feedback methods in order to achieve comparable accuracies. This may be because feedback methods are less sensitive to feature dependences that can not be detected by the salience metric. This suggests that, although the results are very good, more drastic local pruning may be performed in the soybean large data set by selecting the correct set of features.

Table 4. Results for the blind method using different τ values.

Dataset	τ	Accuracy	Tests	Features/Node
	None	85.50 ± 2.72	162.76 ± 8.44	16.00 ± 0.00
	0.10	85.75 ± 2.91	79.89 ± 8.21	7.48 ± 1.17
	0.20	85.51 ± 3.54	69.09 ± 8.73	7.15 ± 1.23
	0.30	85.65 ± 3.66	60.45 ± 8.51	6.86 ± 1.23
	0.40	85.70 ± 3.85	54.85 ± 8.35	6.72 ± 1.23
zoo	0.50	85.14 ± 3.57	49.00 ± 7.94	6.52 ± 1.22
	0.60	84.50 ± 3.17	42.47 ± 7.43	6.32 ± 1.23
	0.70	83.91 ± 3.43	38.38 ± 8.51	6.13 ± 1.26
	0.80	82.61 ± 4.50	36.16 ± 7.76	5.97 ± 1.27
	0.90	81.07 ± 4.82	32.95 ± 8.57	5.86 ± 1.29
	None	85.70 ± 2.35	277.48 ± 24.97	35.00 ± 0.00
	0.10	85.70 ± 2.30	98.87 ± 15.27	7.55 ± 0.93
	0.20	85.50 ± 2.45	88.27 ± 15.60	7.00 ± 0.80
	0.30	85.46 ± 2.55	80.02 ± 15.62	6.54 ± 0.87
soybean	0.40	85.53 ± 2.69	69.24 ± 14.09	6.06 ± 0.91
small	0.50	85.53 ± 3.13	59.83 ± 10.79	5.55 ± 0.77
	0.60	85.16 ± 2.87	49.86 ± 10.81	4.93 ± 0.75
	0.70	85.16 ± 2.30	35.62 ± 7.82	3.73 ± 0.60
	0.80	84.56 ± 2.67	27.03 ± 5.54	3.12 ± 0.50
	0.90	83.99 ± 2.83	21.84 ± 4.76	2.71 ± 0.59
	None	83.53 ± 1.46	466.33 ± 22.15	35.00 ± 0.00
	0.10	83.65 ± 1.53	212.36 ± 17.58	8.30 ± 0.59
	0.20	83.17 ± 1.50	171.89 ± 18.25	7.58 ± 0.58
	0.30	82.25 ± 1.76	139.12 ± 17.42	6.89 ± 0.58
soybean	0.40	81.16 ± 1.86	111.89 ± 14.07	6.21 ± 0.53
large	0.50	79.65 ± 1.98	87.26 ± 11.71	5.50 ± 0.50
	0.60	78.47 ± 2.59	68.70 ± 10.43	4.84 ± 0.49
	0.70	77.87 ± 1.74	51.63 ± 7.41	3.88 ± 0.41
	0.80	75.90 ± 2.93	38.93 ± 5.98	3.29 ± 0.39
	0.90	74.85 ± 3.00	31.87 ± 3.88	2.90 ± 0.36

6   Related Work

As we have pointed out, there is a few body of work in feature selection for clustering tasks. Gennari [8] investigated a feature selection mechanism embedded in CLASSIT, a descendant of COBWEB, and made some preliminary experiments. However, his research differs from this work in that we focus in a complex flexible prediction task and not in predicting a single class label. Two works that apply feature selection as a preprocessing step are [2] and [3], but again, evaluation is performed over class labels (but see [14] for some results in a multiple prediction task using a preprocessing step).

In sum, our work is novel in two aspects. First, the retrospective pruning view makes feature selection a postprocessing step rather than a preprocessing one as is common in these tasks. Secondly, we focus in a multiple inference task that have been proposed for unsupervised learning systems instead of class label prediction. To our knowledge, no other works have approached the effect of feature selection in such a task.

7 Concluding Remarks

We have presented a view of feature selection as a retrospective tree pruning process similar to those used in decision tree learning. We think that this framework is a useful abstraction for the design and understanding of postprocessing approaches to feature selection in hierarchical clustering. This becomes especially important given the particular nature of the clustering task, that introduces additional factors of complexity with respect to supervised tasks. We have briefly outlined some of these factors such as the polythetic nature of hierarchical clusterings or the formulation of the performance task as a multiple inference task along all the features in the data. Additionally, the framework provides a single view of the complex problem of simplifying hierarchical clusterings, unifying feature selection and node removal procedures. This novel approach should lead to useful combinations of both approaches.

The empirical results show evidence on the power of feature selection in simplifying hierarchical clusterings. Particularly, local methods appear to dramatically reduce the number of features per node without diminishing accuracy. Our implementation of blind methods performed quite well, so suggesting that they are a promising alternative to more computationally expensive feedback methods.

Our work suggest that existing approaches to decision tree pruning may importantly inspire further research in novel methods for unsupervised feature selection. Future work should also evaluate the performance of integrated horizontal and vertical pruning methods for hierarchical clustering.

References

[1] A. L. Blum and P. Langley. Selection of relevant features and examples in machine learning. *Artificial Intelligence*, 97:245–271, 1997.

[2] M. Dash, H. Liu, and J. Yao. Dimensionality reduction for unsupervised data. In *Ninth IEEE International Conference on Tools with AI, ICTAI'97*, 1997.

[3] M. Devaney and A. Ram. Efficient feature selection in conceptual clustering. In *Machine Learning: Proceedings of the Fourteenth International Conference*, pages 92–97, Nashville, TN, 1997. Morgan Kaufmann.

[4] U. M. Fayyad, G. Piatetsky-Shapiro, and P. Smyth. From data mining to knowledge discovery: An overview. In U. M. Fayyad, G. Piatetsky-Shapiro, P. Smyth, and R. Uthurusamy, editors, *Advances in Knowledge Discovery and Data Mining*, pages 1–34. AAAI Press, Cambridge, MA, 1996.

[5] D. H. Fisher. Knowledge acquisition via incremental conceptual clustering. *Machine Learning*, 2:139–172, 1987.

[6] D. H. Fisher. Iterative optimization and simplification of hierarchical clusterings. *Journal of Artificial Intelligence Research*, (4):147–179, 1996.

[7] D. H. Fisher and J. C. Schlimmer. Concept simplification and prediction accuracy. In *Proceedings of the Fifth International Conference on Machine Learning*, pages 22–28, Ann Arbor, MI, 1988. Morgan Kaufmann.

[8] J. H. Gennari. Concept formation and attention. pages 724–728, 1991.

[9] G. H. John, R. Kohavi, and K. Pfleger. Irrelevant features and the subset selection problem. In *Proceedings of the Eleventh International Conference on Machine Learning*, pages 121–129. Morgan Kauffmann, San Mateo, CA, 1994.

[10] P. Langley. *Elements of machine learning*. Morgan Kaufmann, San Francisco, CA, 1995.

[11] R. S. Michalski and R. E. Stepp. Learning from observation: Conceptual clustering. In R. S. Michalski, J. G. Carbonell, and T. M. Mitchell, editors, *Machine Learning: An Artificial intelligence approach*, pages 331–363. Morgan Kauffmann, San Mateo, CA, 1983.

[12] J. Mingers. An empirical comparison of pruning methods for decision tree induction. *Machine Learning*, 4(2):227–243, 1989.

[13] J. R. Quinlan. *C4.5: Programs for Machine Learning*. Morgan Kaufmann, San Mateo, CA, 1993.

[14] L. Talavera. Feature selection as a preprocessing step for hierarchical clustering. In *Proceedings of the Sixteenth International Conference on Machine Learning*. Morgan Kaufmann, 1999. (To appear).

[15] D. Wettschereck and D. W. Aha. Weighting features. In *Proceedings of the First International Conference on Case-Based Reasoning*, Portugal, 1995. Lisbon.

Discriminative Power of Input Features in a Fuzzy Model

Rosaria Silipo[1] and Michael R. Berthold[2]

[1] International Computer Science Institute (ICSI)
1947 Center Street, Suite 600, Berkeley, CA 94704, USA
rosaria@icsi.berkeley.edu
[2] Berkeley Initiative in Soft Computing (BISC)
Dept. of EECS, CS Division, 329 Soda Hall
University of California, Berkeley, CA 94720, USA
berthold@cs.berkeley.edu

Abstract. In many modern data analysis scenarios the first and most urgent task consists of reducing the redundancy in high dimensional input spaces. A method is presented that quantifies the discriminative power of the input features in a fuzzy model. A possibilistic information measure of the model is defined on the basis of the available fuzzy rules and the resulting possibilistic information gain, associated with the use of a given input dimension, characterizes the input feature's discriminative power. Due to the low computational expenses derived from the use of a fuzzy model, the proposed possibilistic information gain generates a simple and efficient algorithm for the reduction of the input dimensionality, even for high dimensional cases. As real-world example, the most informative electrocardiographic measures are detected for an arrhythmia classification problem.

1   Introduction

In the last years it has become more and more common to collect and store large amounts of data from different sources [1]. However a massive recording of system's monitoring variables does not grant a better performance of further analysis procedures, if no new information is introduced in the input space. In addition the analysis procedure itself becomes more complicated for high dimensional input spaces and insights about the system's underlying structure more difficult to achieve.

An evaluation of the effectiveness of every input feature in describing the underlying system can supply new information and simplify further analysis. The detection of the most informative input features, that is the features characterizing at best the underlying system, reduces time and computational expenses of any further analysis and makes easier the detection of crucial parameters for data analysis and/or system modeling.

A quite common approach for the evaluation of the effectiveness of the input features defines some feature merit measures, on the basis of a statistical model

D.J. Hand, J.N. Kok, M.R. Berthold (Eds.): IDA'99, LNCS 1642, pp. 87–98, 1999.
© Springer-Verlag Berlin Heidelberg 1999

of the system [2, 1]. Assuming that a large database is available, the probability estimations, involved in the definition of the feature merit measures, are performed by means of the events frequencies, which require a precise definition of the input parameters and a clear identification of the output classes. In many real world applications, however, estimated frequencies are unavoidably altered by doubtful members of the output classes and by an inaccurate description of the input parameters. In addition the estimation of a probabilistic model is computationally expensive for high dimensional input spaces.

The concept of fuzzy sets was introduced in [3] with the purpose of a more efficient, though less detailed, description of real world events, allowing an appropriate amount of uncertainty. Fuzzy set theory yields also the advantage of a number of simple and computationally inexpensive methods to model a given training set. Based on the fuzzy set theory, some measures of fuzzy entropy have been established [4, 5] as measures of the degree of fuzziness of the model with respect to the training data. All the defined measures involve the data points into the fuzzy entropy calculation, in order to represent the uncertainty of the model in describing the training data.

In this paper an analysis "a posteriori" of fuzzy systems is proposed, to evaluate the discriminative power of the input features in characterizing the underlying system. A measure of possibilistic information is defined only on the basis of fuzzy rules. The separability of the different membership functions is measured on every input dimension and the input dimension with highest separability defines the most discriminative input feature, at least according to the analyzed fuzzy model. All that is based on the hypothesis that the fuzzy model describes with sufficient accuracy the data of the training set, that is that a sufficiently general training set has been used for the fuzzy rules inference. The main advantage of analyzing fuzzy rules, instead of fuzzy rules and training data as in [4, 5], consists of the highly reduced computational costs for the same amount of information, provided that the fuzzy model faithfully describes the underlying data structure.

The detection and ranking of the most effective input variables for a given task could represent one of the first steps in any data analysis process. The implementation of a fuzzy model requires generally a short amount of time even in case of very high dimensional input spaces and so does the corresponding evaluation of the discriminative power of the input features. Whenever a more accurate system's representation is wished, the analysis can continue with the application of more sophisticated and more computationally expensive analysis techniques on the most effective input features, pre-screened on the basis of the proposed possibilistic information.

2   Possibilistic Feature Merit Measures

2.1   A Possibility Measure

Given a number m of output classes C_i, $i = 1, \ldots, m$, and an n-dimensional input space, numerous algorithms exist, which derive a set of N_R fuzzy rules [3]

$\{R_k\}$, $k = 1, \ldots, N_R$, mapping the n-dimensional input into the m-dimensional output space. This set of rules models the relationships between the input data $x \in \mathcal{R}^n$ and the output classes C_i. Each input pattern $x = [x_1, \ldots, x_n]^T$ is associated to each output class C_i by means of a membership value $\mu_{C_i}(x)$. In figure 1.a an example is reported with a two-dimensional input space $\{x_1, x_2\}$, two output classes C_1 and C_2, and with trapezoids as membership functions $\mu_{C_1}(x)$ and $\mu_{C_2}(x)$ describing the relationships between the input data and the two output classes.

The membership function $\mu_{C_i}(x)$ quantifies the degree of membership of input pattern x to output class C_i. Its volume $V(C_i)$, as defined in eq. 1, therefore represents a measure of the possibility of output class C_i, on the basis of the given input space $D \subset \mathcal{R}^n$. Considering normalized membership functions $\mu_{C_i}(x)$, a larger volume $V(C_i)$ indicates a class of the output space with higher degree of possibility. An output class represented by a membership function, which takes value $+1$ everywhere on the input space, is always possible. A membership function with volume $V(C_i) = 0$ indicates an impossible class.

$$V(C_i) = \int_0^1 \int_{x \in D} \mu_{C_i}(x) \, dx \, d\mu \qquad (1)$$

The overall possibility of the whole output space $C = \{C_1, C_2, \ldots, C_m\}$ can be defined through the available fuzzy mapping system $\{R_k\} = \{R_1, R_2, \ldots, R_{N_R}\}$ as the sum of all the class possibilities $V(C_i)$, $i = 1, \ldots, m$. The relative contribution $v(C_i)$ of output class C_i to the whole output space's possibility is given in eq. 2.

$$v(C_i) = \frac{V(C_i)}{\sum_{j=1}^m V(C_j)} \qquad (2)$$

In case the output class C_i is described by $Q_i > 1$ fuzzy rules, the possibility of class C_i is given by the possibility of the union of these $q = 1, \ldots, Q_i$ fuzzy subsets of class C_i, each with membership functions $\mu_{C_i}^q(x)$. The possibility of the union of membership functions can be expressed as the sum of their possibilities, taking care of including the intersection possibility only once (eq. 3). If trapezoids are adopted as membership functions, the possibility of each fuzzy rule $V_q(C_i)$ becomes particularly simple to calculate [6].

$$V(C_i) = V\left(\cup_{q=1}^{Q_i} V_q(C_i)\right) = \int_0^1 \int_{x \in D} \cup_{q=1}^{Q_i} \mu_{C_i}^q(x) \, dx \, d\mu =$$

$$= \sum_{q=1}^{Q_i} \left[V_q(C_i) - \sum_{h=q+1}^{Q_i} V_q(C_i) \cap V_h(C_i) \right] \qquad (3)$$

2.2   A Possibilistic Information Measure

The variable $v(C_i)$ quantifies the possibility of class C_i relatively to the possibility of the whole output space and according to the fuzzy rules used to model the input-output relationships. $v(C_i)$, as defined in eq. 2, can then be adopted as the basic unit to measure the possibilistic information associated with class C_i. With respect to a probabilistic model, the employment of the relative possibility of class C_i, $v(C_i)$, takes into account the possible occurrence of multiple classes for any input pattern x and the calculation of the relative volume $v(C_i)$ is generally easier than the estimation of a probability function.

As in the traditional information theory, the goal is to produce a possibilistic information measure, that is [1]:

1. at its maximum if all the output classes are equally possible, i. e. $v(C_i) = \frac{1}{m}$ for $i = 1, \ldots, m$, m being the number of output classes;
2. at its minimum if only one output class C_i is possible, i. e. in case $v(C_j) = 0$ for $j \neq i$;
3. a symmetric function of its arguments, because the dominance of one class over the others must produce the same amount of possibilistic information, independently of which the favorite class is.

In order to produce a measure of the global possibilistic information $I(C)$ of the output space $C = \{C_1, \ldots, C_m\}$, the traditional functions employed in information theory – as the entropy function $I_H(C)$ (eq. 4) and the Gini function $I_G(C)$ (eq. 5) [1, 2] – can then be applied to the relative possibilities $v(C_i)$ of the output classes.

$$I_H(C) = -\sum_{i=1}^{m} v(C_i) \log_2 (v(C_i)) \tag{4}$$

$$I_G(C) = 1 - \sum_{i=1}^{m} (v(C_i))^2 \tag{5}$$

In both cases, entropy and Gini function, $I(C)$ represents the amount of possibilistic information intrinsically available in the fuzzy model. In particular not all the input features are effective the same way in extracting and representing the information available in the training set through the fuzzy model. The goal of this paper is to make explicit which dimension of the input space is the most effective in recovering the intrinsic possibilistic information $I(C)$ of the fuzzy model.

2.3   The Information Gain

Given a fuzzy description of the input space $\{R_k\}$ with intrinsic possibilistic information $I(C)$, a feature merit measure must describe the information gain derived by the employment of any input feature x_j in the model. Such information gain is expressed as the relative difference between the intrinsic information of the system before, $I(C)$, and after using that variable x_j for the analysis, $I(C|x_j)$, (eq. 6). The x_j input features producing the highest information gains are the most effective in the adopted model to describe the input space, and therefore the most informative for the proposed analysis.

$$g(C|x_j) = \frac{I(C) - I(C|x_j)}{I(C)} \tag{6}$$

Let us suppose that the input variable x_j is related to the output classes by means of a number N_R of membership functions $\mu_{C_i}^q(x_j)$, with $q = 1, \ldots, Q_i$ membership functions for every output class C_i, for $i = 1, \ldots, m$ output classes, and $N_R = \sum_{i=1}^m Q_i$. The use of input variable x_j for the final classification consists of the definition of an appropriate set of thresholds along input dimension j, that allow the best separation of the different output classes. A set of cuts is then created on the j-th input dimension, to separate the $F \leq N_R$ contiguous trapezoids related to different output classes.

If trapezoids are adopted as membership functions of the fuzzy model, the optimal cut between two contiguous trapezoids is located at the side intersection, if the trapezoids overlap on the sides; at the middle point of the overlapping flat regions, if the trapezoids overlap in their flat regions; at the middle point between the two trapezoids, if they do not overlap.

Between two consecutive cuts, a linguistic value L_k ($k = 1, \ldots, F$) can be defined for parameter x_j. Considering $x_j = L_k$ corresponds to isolating one stripe c_k on the input space. In stripe c_k new membership functions $\mu^q(C_i|x_j = L_k)$ to the output classes C_i are derived as the intersections of the original membership functions $\mu_{C_i}^q(x)$ with the segment $x_j = L_k$. Each stripe c_k is characterized by a local possibilistic information $I(c_k) = I(C|x_j = L_k)$ (eq. 4 or 5). The average possibilistic information $I(C|x_j)$, derived by the use of variable x_j in the fuzzy model, corresponds to the averaged sum of the local possibilistic information of stripes c_k (eq. 7).

$$I(C|x_j) = \frac{1}{F} \sum_{k=1}^F I(C|x_j = L_k) \tag{7}$$

The less effective the input feature x_j is in the original set of fuzzy rules, the closer the remaining $I(C|x_j)$ is to the original possibilistic information $I(C)$ of the model and the lower the corresponding information gain is, as described in eq. 6. Every parameter x_j produces an information gain $g(C|x_j)$ expressing its effectiveness in performing the required classification on the basis of the given fuzzy model. The proposed information gain can be adopted as a possibilistic feature merit measure.

2.4   An Example

In figure 1 an example is shown for a two-dimensional input space, two output classes, and with trapezoids as membership functions. The corresponding intrinsic possibilistic information of the original model $I(C)$ is reported in table 1. The average information of the system, $I(C|x_1)$ and $I(C|x_2)$, respectively after dimension x_1 and x_2 have been used for the classification, are reported in table 2 together with the corresponding information gains $g(C|x_1)$ and $g(C|x_2)$.

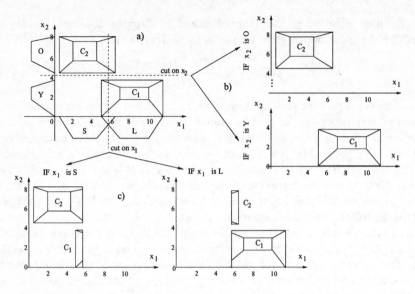

Fig. 1. New data spaces cutting on variable b) x_2 and c) x_1

A cut between the two membership functions on dimension x_2 (Fig. 1.b) produces a better separation than a cut on dimension x_1 (Fig. 1.c). That is the analysis on dimension x_2 offers a higher gain in information than the analysis on dimension x_1. This is indicated by $g(C|x_1) < g(C|x_2)$ either considering $I()$ as the entropy or the Gini function (Tab. 2). From the comparison of the information gains, $g(C|x_1)$ and $g(C|x_2)$, the analysis on variable x_2 supplies more of the information available in the fuzzy model than the analysis carried on variable x_1. The same conclusion could have been reached using $I(C|x_1) > I(C|x_2)$, but an information description through the gain function produces more clear results than using directly the possibilistic information parameter $I(C|x_j)$.

3   Real World Applications

The results in the previous section show the efficiency of the proposed possibilistic feature merit measures in detecting the input dimensions with maximum information content. In this section some experiments on real world databases are

Table 1. The fuzzy information measures for the two dimensional example

C_1	C_2	$I_H(C)$	$I_G(C)$
$V(C_1) = 13.0$	$V(C_2) = 12.6$	0.99	0.49
$v(C_1) = 0.51$	$v(C_2) = 0.49$		

Table 2. $I(C|x_j)$ and $g(C|x_j)$

$x_1 = S$	$x_1 = L$	$x_2 = Y$	$x_2 = O$
$V(C_1|x_1) = 0.53$	$V(C_1|x_1) = 13.0$	$V(C_1|x_2) = 13.0$	$V(C_1|x_2) = 0.00$
$V(C_2|x_1) = 12.6$	$V(C_2|x_1) = 0.53$	$V(C_2|x_2) = 0.00$	$V(C_2|x_2) = 12.6$
$v(C_1|x_1) = 0.04$	$v(C_1|x_1) = 0.96$	$v(C_1|x_2) = 1.0$	$v(C_1|x_2) = 0.00$
$v(C_2|x_1) = 0.96$	$v(C_2|x_1) = 0.04$	$v(C_2|x_2) = 0.00$	$v(C_2|x_2) = 1.0$
$I_H(C|x_1) = 0.24$		$I_H(C|x_2) = 0.00$	
$I_G(C|x_1) = 0.07$		$I_G(C|x_2) = 0.00$	
$g_H(C|x_1) = 0.76$		$g_H(C|x_2) = 1.0$	
$g_G(C|x_1) = 0.84$		$g_G(C|x_2) = 1.0$	

performed and the corresponding results reported, in order to observe whether these possibilistic feature merit measures are actually capable to detect the database features which controls the maximum information even on real-world data.

3.1 The IRIS Database

The first experiment is performed on the IRIS database. This is a relatively small database, containing data for three classes of iris plants. The first class is supposed to be linearly separable and the last two classes non linearly separable. The plants are characterized in terms of: 1) sepal length 2) sepal width 3) petal length and 4) petal width.

Both possibilistic information gains are very high for the third and the fourth input parameter, and almost zero for the first two input features (Tab. 3). In [8], where a detailed description of the parameters adopted in the IRIS database is produced, the sepal length and sepal width – parameter 1 and 2 – are reported to be more or less the same for all the three output classes, i. e. uninformative. Thus input parameter 1 and 2 should not contribute to the correct discrimination of the output classes. On the opposite, the petal features – parameters 3 and 4 – characterize very well the first class of iris (iris setosa) with respect to the other two.

In this case, the proposed possibilistic feature merit measures produce a very reliable description of the informative power of every input parameter. Hence parameters 1 and 2 could be removed and the analysis performed solely on the basis of parameters 3 and 4 without a relevant loss of information. The class correlation, reported in [9], is also very high for parameters 3 and 4 and much lower for the first two parameters. That confirms the results from the possibilistic feature merit measures.

3.2 Arrhythmia Classification

A very suitable area for fuzzy – or more generally imprecise – decision systems consists of medical applications. Medical reasoning is quite often a qualitative

Table 3. Information gain $g(C)$ of the iris features in the IRIS database

$I(C)$		x_1	x_2	x_3	x_4
$I_H(C) = 1.44$	$g_H(C)$	0.10	0.06	0.82	0.81
$I_G(C) = 0.61$	$g_G(C)$	0.10	0.06	0.84	0.79

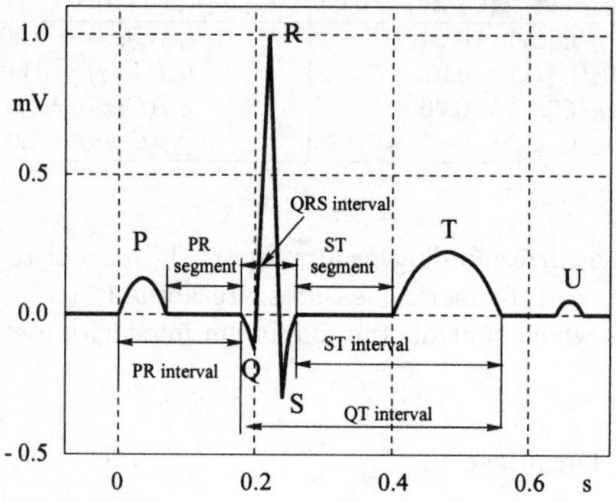

Fig. 2. The ECG waveshape.

and approximative process, so that the definition of precise diagnostic classes with crisp membership functions can sometimes lead to inappropriate conclusions. One of the most investigated fields in medical reasoning is the automatic analysis of the electrocardiogram (ECG), and inside that the detection of arrhythmic heart beats.

Some cells (the sino-atrial node) in the upper chambers (the atria) of the cardiac muscle (the myocardium) spontaneously and periodically change their electrical polarization, which progressively extends to the whole myocardium. This periodic and progressive electric depolarization of the myocardium is recorded as small potential differences between two different locations of the human body or with respect to a reference electrode. An almost periodic signal, the ECG, that describes the electrical activity of the myocardium in time, is the result. Each time period consists of a basic waveshape, whose waves are marked with the alphabet letters P, Q, R, S, T, and U (Fig. 2). The P wave describes the depolarization process of the two upper myocardium chambers, the atria; the QRS complex all together the depolarization of the two lower myocardium chambers, the ventricula; and the T wave the repolarization process at the end of each cycle. The U wave is often absent from the beat waveshape and, however, its origin is controversial. The heart contraction follows the myocardium depolarization phase. Anomalies in the PQRST waveshape are often connected to misconductions of the electrical impulse on the myocardium.

Table 4. Set of measures characterizing each beat waveshape.

RR	RR interval (ms)
RRa	average of the previous 10 RR intervals
QRSw	QRS width (ms)
VR	Iso-electric level (μV)
pA	Positive amplitude of the QRS (μV)
nA	Negative amplitude of the QRS (μV)
pQRS	Positive area of the QRS (μV * ms)
nQRS	Negative area of the QRS (μV * ms)
pT	positive area of the T wave (μV * ms)
nT	negative area of the T wave (μV * ms)
ST	ST segment level (μV)
STsl	slope of the ST segment (μV/ms)
P	P exist (yes 0.5, no -0.5)
PR	PR interval (ms)

A big family of cardiac electrical misfunctions consists of arrhythmic heart beats, deriving from an anomalous (ectopic) origin of the depolarization wavefront in the myocardium. If the depolarization does not originate in the sinoatrial node, a different path is followed by the depolarizing wavefront and therefore a different waveshape appears in the ECG signal. Arrhythmia are believed to occur randomly in time and the most common types have an anomalous origin in the atria (SupraVentricular Premature Beats, SVPB) or in the ventricula (Ventricular Premature Beats, VPB). With the development of automatic systems for the detection of QRS complexes and the extraction of quantitative measurements, large sets of data can be generated from hours of ECG signal. A larger number of measures though does not guarantee better performances of the upcoming classifier, if no significant new information is added. A pre-screening of the most significant measures for the analysis has the double advantage of lowering the input dimension and of improving the classifier's performance when poor quality measures are discarded.

The MIT-BIH database [10] represents a standard in the evaluation of methods for the automatic classification of the ECG signal, because of the wide set of examples of arrhythmic events provided. The MIT-BIH ECG records are two-channel, 30 minutes long and sampled at 360 samples/s. Two records (200 and 233) from the MIT-BIH database are analyzed in this study, because of their high number of arrhythmic beats. QRS complexes are detected and for each beat waveshape a set of 14 measures [11] is extracted by using the first of the two channels in the ECG record (Tab. 4). The first 2/3 of the beats of each record are used as training set and the last 1/3 as test set. A two-class, normal (N) vs. ventricular premature beats (VPB) is considered for record 200 and a three-class problem (N, VPB, and SVPB) for record 233, in order to quantify the discriminative power of the input features for both classification tasks.

Table 5. Information gain for different ECG beat measures (record 200). The amounts of correctly classified N and VPB and of uncertain beats are expressed in %.

	RR	RRa	QRSw	VR	pA	nA	pQRS	nQRS	pT	nT	ST	STsl	P	PR	N	VPB	unc.
g_H	.40	.00	**.78**	.09	.07	.00	.08	.04	.00	.61	.57	.01	.00	.00	99	97	1
g_G	.42	.01	**.80**	.11	.09	.01	.10	.05	.00	.63	.59	.02	.00	.00			
g_H	.47	-	.42	.14	.25	.25	.38	.21	-	.15	.36	.17	-	-	99	96	1
g_G	**.53**	-	.44	.18	.25	.27	.43	.26	-	.16	.38	.17	-	-			
g_H	**.74**	-	.08	-	.44	.42	.49	.28	-	-	.03	-	-	-	100	97	1
g_G	**.81**	-	.09	-	.48	.43	.55	.31	-	-	.04	-	-	-			
g_H	.52	-	-	-	.59	**.78**	.71	-	-	-	-	-	-	-	100	97	1
g_G	.56	-	-	-	.60	**.78**	.74	-	-	-	-	-	-	-			
g_H	-	-	-	-	.56	.38	**.59**	-	-	-	-	-	-	-	100	97	1
g_G	-	-	-	-	.57	.41	**.61**	-	-	-	-	-	-	-			
g_H	-	-	-	-	.41	-	**.72**	-	-	-	-	-	-	-	98	95	1
g_G	-	-	-	-	.45	-	**.76**	-	-	-	-	-	-	-			
g_H	-	-	-	-	.44	**.55**	-	-	-	-	-	-	-	-	100	97	1
g_G	-	-	-	-	.46	**.57**	-	-	-	-	-	-	-	-			
g_H	-	-	-	-	-	-	.29	-	-	-	-	-	-	-	74	50	0
g_G	-	-	-	-	-	-	.33	-	-	-	-	-	-	-			
g_H	-	-	.32	-	-	-	-	-	-	-	-	-	-	-	56	56	0
g_G	-	-	.38	-	-	-	-	-	-	-	-	-	-	-			
g_H	.48	-	-	-	-	-	-	-	-	-	-	-	-	-	89	31	0
g_G	.52	-	-	-	-	-	-	-	-	-	-	-	-	-			
g_H	-	-	-	-	.53	-	-	-	-	-	-	-	-	-	96	93	0
g_G	-	-	-	-	.57	-	-	-	-	-	-	-	-	-			
g_H	-	-	-	-	-	.60	-	-	-	-	-	-	-	-	95	95	0
g_G	-	-	-	-	-	.65	-	-	-	-	-	-	-	-			

At first all 14 measures are used for classification. The corresponding information gains $g_H(C)$ and $g_G(C)$ are listed in table 5, together with the percentages of correctly classified and uncertain beats on the test set, for record 200. Beats are labeled as uncertain if they are not covered by any rules of the fuzzy model. The percentage of uncertain beats (unc.) is defined with respect to the number of beats in the whole test set. The parameter with highest information gain is marked in bold. The ECG measures with smallest information gains are then progressively removed from the classification process. A similar table can be obtained for record 233.

Ventricular arrhythmia are mainly characterized by alterations in the QRS complex and T wave rather than in the PR segment. VPBs usually present a larger and higher QRS complex, and to a lower extent an altered ST segment. In table 5 some ECG measures produce from the very beginning no information gain, such as the presence of the P wave (P), the average RR interval of the previous 10 beats (RRa), and the PR interval (PR) as it was to be expected. Only 4-6 ECG features are characterized by a high information gain, that is are relevant for the classification process. An almost constantly used feature is the RR interval, that quantifies the prematurity of the beat and it is usually a sign for general arrhythmia. Also the QRS width, the positive and negative amplitude of the QRS complex and the corresponding areas, all parameters related to the QRS complex shape, play an important role, individually or together, in the classification procedure. If many input parameters are used, T wave features provide helpful information for classification, but they loose importance if no redundant input information is supplied. The low informative character of the past RR intervals, through the low information gain of the RRa parameter, confirms the unpredictability of VPBs. Individually, the positive and negative amplitude of the QRS complex present the highest information gain, confirmed by the highest performance on the test set, followed by the RR interval, the QRS width, and the QRS positive area.

All the estimated discriminative powers in table 5 find positive confirmation in clinical VPB diagnostics. The redundant or uninformative character of the input features with lowest information gain is proven by the fact that their removing does not affect the final performance on the test set, as long as at least two of the most significant ECG measures are kept. Indeed the same performance on the test set are observed both with the full input dimensionality and removing the least significant ECG measures.

Record 233 presents a new class of premature beats with supraventricular origin (SVPB) and a more homogeneous class of VPBs. Supraventricular arrhythmia can be differentiated from normal beats mainly by means of the RR interval and the PR segment, whenever the P wave can be reliably detected. Consequently the analysis of record 233, with respect to the analysis of record 200, shows a high information gain also for the PR measure, besides the negative amplitude and area of the QRS complex and the RR interval already used for VPB classification. However, if considered individually, none of the ECG measures produces a high information gain and good performance on the test set for all classes of beats. The PR interval shows to be useless if used alone for SVPB classification, but it gains a high discrimination power if any other significant ECG measure is added. The negative amplitude of the QRS complex and the RR interval alone show to be still highly discriminative for N/VPB classification, but helpless for SVPB recognition.

4 Conclusions

A methodology to estimate the discriminative power of input features based on an underlying fuzzy model is presented. Because of the approximative nature of fuzzy models, many algorithms exist to construct such models quickly from example data. Using properties of fuzzy logic, it is easy and computationally inexpensive to determine the possibilistic information gain associated with each input feature. The algorithm capability is illustrated by using an artificial example and the well-known IRIS data. The real-world feasibility was then demonstrated on a medical application.

The defined information gain provides a description of the class discriminability inside the adopted fuzzy model. This is related with classification performances, only if the fuzzy model was built on a sufficiently general set of training examples. The proposed algorithm represents a computationally inexpensive tool to reduce high-dimensional input spaces as well as to get insights about the system through the fuzzy model. For example, it can be used to determine which input features are exploited by fuzzy classifiers with better performance.

We believe that especially for large scale data sets in high dimensional feature spaces, such quick approaches to gain first insights into the nature of the data will become increasingly important to successfully find the underlying regularities.

5   Acknowledgments

The authors would like to thank Wei Zong, George. Moody, and prof. R.G. Mark from Harvard-MIT Division of Health Sciences and Technology M.I.T. (USA) for the ECG measures.

References

[1] V. Cherkassky and F. Mulier, "Learning from data", John Wiley and Sons Inc., 1998.

[2] C. Apte, S.J. Hong, J.R.M. Hosking, J. Lepre, E.P.D. Pednault, and B. K. Rosen, "Decomposition of heterogeneous classification problems", *Intelligent Data Analysis*, Vol. 2, n. 2, 1998.

[3] L.A. Zadeh, "A fuzzy-algorithmic approach to the definition of complex or imprecise concepts", *Int. J. Man-Machine Studies*, **8**: 249-291, 1976.

[4] A. De Luca, and S. Termini, "A definition of nonprobabilistic entropy in the setting of fuzzy sets theory",

[5] C.Z. Janikow, "Fuzzy Decision Trees: Issues and Methods", *IEEE Trans. Syst. Man and Cyb. PartB: Cybernetics*, **28**: 1-14, 1998.

[6] M. R. Berthold, K.P. Huber, "Comparing Fuzzy Graphs", Proc. of Fuzzy-Neuro Systems, pp. 234-240, 1998.

[7] M.R. Berthold, J. Diamond, "Constructive Training of Probabilistic Neural Networks", *Neurocomputing* 19: 167-183, 1998.

[8] R.A. Fisher, "The use of multiple measurements in taxonomic problems", *Annual Eugenics, II*, John Wiley, NY. **7**:179-188, 1950.

[9] C. Blake, E. Keogh, and C.J. Merz. UCI Repository of machine learning databases [http://www.ics.uci.edu/~mlearn/MLRepository.html]. Irvine, CA: University of California, Department of Information and Computer Science, 1998.

[10] MIT-BIH database distributor, Beth Israel Hospital, Biomedical Engineering, Division KB-26, 330 Brookline Avenue, Boston, MA 02215, USA.

[11] W. Zong, D. Jiang. "Automated ECG rhythm analysis using fuzzy reasoning", Proc. of Computers in Cardiology, pp. 69-72, 1998.

Learning Elements of Representations for Redescribing Robot Experiences

Laura Firoiu and Paul Cohen

Computer Science Department
University of Massachusetts at Amherst,
Amherst, MA 01003-4610
{lfiroiu, cohen}@cs.umass.edu

Abstract. This paper presents our first efforts toward learning simple logical representations from robot sensory data and thus toward a solution for the perceptual grounding problem [2]. The elements of representations learned by our method are states that correspond to stages during the robot's experiences, and atomic propositions that describe the states. The states are found by an incremental hidden Markov model induction algorithm; the atomic propositions are immediate generalizations of the probability distributions that characterize the states. The state induction algorithm is guided by the minimum description length criterion: the time series of the robot's sensor values for several experiences are redescribed in terms of states and atomic propositions and the model that yields the shortest description (of both model and time series) is selected.

1 Introduction

We are interested in learning without supervision elements of logical representations of episodes. The episodes in question are generated by robots interacting with their environments. Just as human infants bootstrap their sensorimotor experiences into a conceptual structure and language [4], so we want our robot to learn ontologies and language through interaction. Previous work has focused on learning *sensory prototypes*, which represent robot interactions in terms of how the interactions appear to the sensors [7]. For example, driving toward a wall and bumping into it is represented as a decreasing series of sonar values followed by the bump sensor going high. While sensory prototypes support some kinds of reasoning (e.g., predicting that the bump sensor will go high) they do not contain explicit elements that represent the robot, the wall, and the act of driving; and so do not support reasoning about the roles of entities in episodes [1]. This work takes the first step from sensory prototypes to logical representations. Logical representations have two advantages:

- Because they contain terms that denote the entities in a scene and the relationships between them, logical representations such as
  "push(robot, object)" are compact, and easily support planning and other

D.J. Hand, J.N. Kok, M.R. Berthold (Eds.): IDA'99, LNCS 1642, pp. 99–110, 1999.
© Springer-Verlag Berlin Heidelberg 1999

reasoning. The sensory prototype of pushing objects does not support these easily [8].

- Abstraction can be over predicates and properties of entities, rather than over patterns in sensory traces. For instance, the extensional category of pushable objects is the set of elements i such that the robot has experienced "push(robot, i)" in the past. Given the extensional category, one can imagine learning the intensional concept of pushable object, the properties that make objects pushable. Neither kind of categorization is feasible given only sensory prototypes.

If logical representations are so advantageous, why not build them into our robots, that is, make them part of the robots' innate endowment? The reason is that we want to explain how sensorimotor activity produces thought—classification, abstraction, planning, language—as it does in every human infant. So we start with sensors and actions, and in this paper we explain how elements of a logical representation might be learned from these sensorimotor beginnings.

The first step in the process of learning logical representations is to redescribe the episodes as state sequences. Our intuition is that experiences unfold through several relatively static stages. At least for simple robot activities, the robot's world tends to remain in the same state over some periods of time, so we expect the state sequences to be simple. For example, the experience of moving toward an object has some well defined stages: accelerating, approaching, being near the object. We want to identify the states that correspond to these stages and ground them in patterns of sensor values.

A technique that allows identification of states is that of hidden Markov model (HMM) induction. The assumption behind the HMM is that the data sequence is produced by a source that evolves in a state space and at each time step outputs a symbol according to the probability distribution of the current state. The states are thus characterized by stable probability distributions over the output alphabet. We identify the episode stages with the states of an HMM induced from all the data collected during a batch of episodes. Since they form a single vocabulary for all episodes, similar stages can be identified across experiences.

The second step in the process of learning logical representations is to find atomic propositions that denote facts in the current state. Since the states found by the HMM are characterized by probability distributions, the atomic propositions must be derived from them. We define the atomic propositions simply as disjunctions of the most likely sensor values according to these distributions. For example, the characterization of "accelerate" is given by some positive values of the acceleration sensor and by the velocity sensor varying within a range of values. A representation of an episode becomes a sequence of states described by these atomic propositions.

These representations are "passive" in the sense that, currently, they are not used by any problem solving system. These representations do not specify what to do in a certain situation or predict what will happen if an action is taken. In the absence of supervision and a problem solving task, we choose the principle of minimum description length to guide the learning process. This principle is implemented with the help of a cost function that measures both the size of the representations (atomic propositions, states, episodes as state sequences) and how well they describe the raw data. Our algorithm identifies the states and the atomic propositions that heuristically minimize the cost of these descriptions.

2 Identifying Experience Stages with Hidden Markov Models

2.1 Hidden Markov Models

A discrete hidden Markov model [6] is defined by a set of states and an alphabet of output symbols. Each state is characterized by two probability distributions: the transition distribution over states and the emission distribution over the output symbols. A random source described by such a model generates a sequence of output symbols as follows: at each time step the source is in one state; after emitting an output symbol according to the emission distribution of the current state, the source "jumps" to a next state according to the transition distribution of its current state. The activity of the source is observed indirectly, through the sequence of output symbols. A continuous HMM emits symbols from a continuous space, according to probability densities instead of probability distributions. For either discrete or continuous HMMs, efficient dynamic programming algorithms exist that:

- induce the HMM that maximizes (locally) the probability of emitting the given sequence (the Baum-Welch algorithm)
- find the state sequence that maximizes the probability of the given sequence, when the model is known (the Viterbi algorithm).

The HMM model definition can be readily extended to the multidimensional case, where a vector of symbols is emitted at each step, instead of a single symbol. The simplifying assumption that allows this immediate extension is conditional independence of variables given the state.

2.2 Input Preprocessing

We collected time series of sensor values from a Pioneer 1 robot. The robot has about forty sensors, and almost all of them return continuous values. While a continuous HMM appears more appropriate for this domain we chose discrete HMMs because our simple method of inducing atomic propositions works readily for probability distributions but not for probability densities. The sensor variables are discretized independently with unidimensional Kohonen maps [3]. Each continuous input value is mapped to one unit and the resulting symbols are the map units.

Not all of the robot's sensors are relevant to our experiments. Besides slowing down considerably the HMM induction algorithm, the irrelevant sensors introduce noise that leads the algorithm into creating meaningless states. We selected the sensors that we considered important and discarded the others from the sensor vector.

The sensor values are "jittery" and can bias the state induction algorithm toward frequent state changes. We correct this bias with one of our own: in a stable world, sensor values remain constant or change in a regular, not jittery, way. To introduce this bias, we create new variables by calculating the slopes (derivatives) of selected sensor variables and adding them to the sensor vector. The slopes are calculated by fitting lines piecewise to the time series. The algorithm has two steps:

1. Initialization: create a graph such that:
   - there is a node for each known point on the curve (time stamp);
   - there is one arc between any two distinct nodes; the arc points to the node with higher time stamp; the weight of the arc is the mean square error of the regression line fitted to the curve fragment defined by the two nodes (time stamps);
2. Find the shortest path in the above graph between the nodes corresponding to the first and last time step (Dijkstra's alg.).

The path calculated at step 2 defines a piecewise linear fit with the property that the sum over the individual fragments of the mean square error is minimized.

2.3   State Splitting Algorithm for HMM Induction

A limitation of HMM induction algorithms is that the number of states must be known in advance. Often, there are either too few states and the resulting propositions are too vague (for example a sensor can take any value) or there are too many states and propositions, such that the representation of experiences becomes long and not intelligible. Since we consider good representations to be "short" representations, our algorithm splits states as required to minimize the size of these representations, as measured[1] by a cost function. We designed the cost function according to the minimum message length (MML) principle [5], as a measure of the information needed to re-generate the original data (the time series of the experienced episodes). As in the MML paradigm, the robot must store two pieces of information. The first is its model, that is the collection of atomic propositions and states. The second is the encoding of each episode's time series by taking advantage of the model.

The cost function is a sum of two components: the model cost and the data cost. The cost of the model is a measure of the length of the model description. The data cost is a measure of the size of all the episode encodings. The two cost components are presented in section 2.5.

The state induction algorithm proceeds by recursively splitting states and re-training the resulting HMM until the cost cannot be improved:

---

[1]   The cost function is not the exact length of the encoded information, but a measure of it. For example we ignore string delimiters or the exact number of bits when defining the cost of encoding a number n as $log(n)$.

1. initialization: the HMM has only one state
2. iterate while cost is decreasing:
   - for each state, compute the cost resulting from splitting the state
   - select the state that yields the largest cost reduction and split it

State splitting stops because for the data cost to decrease, the model cost must increase , so the total cost cannot decrease indefinitely. By choosing to split the state that yields the largest cost reduction at the current iteration, the cost is minimized heuristically. We cannot attempt to minimize the cost globally, because an exhaustive search of all the splitting possibilities is exponential in the final number of states, and the HMM fitting algorithm is guaranteed to find only a local maximum, anyway.

2.4   State Characterization with Atomic Propositions

To characterize an HMM state by a set of logical propositions, we replace for each sensor the probability distributions over its values with logical descriptions of the distributions. These descriptions are disjunctions of the most likely sensor values, that is the values that have a probability higher than a certain threshold. An example of a proposition based on the distribution of the translational velocity (trans-vel) sensor is:

distribution:	0 0 0 0 0 0.14 0.33 0.54 0
atomic proposition:	$trans\_vel\_5\_6\_7$

In the example above, the proposition definition covers values 5 through 7. We consider that all the values in the proposition definition are equally likely to occur in a state in which the proposition holds. Thus, the proposition is defined as a generalization of the distribution from which it was derived to the uniform distribution over the covered values. This crude generalization reduces the proliferation of propositions and allows identification of common propositions across states.

Propositions are thus simple facts of the form "sensor S takes values x or y". Given a sensor model that describes the kind of information a sensor returns, we can transform these propositions into predicates. For example, if the sensor model specifies that the translational velocity sensor returns the translational velocity property of the constant $robot$, then the proposition $trans - vel\_5\_6\_7$ becomes the predicate $trans - vel\_5\_6\_7(robot)$. We can assume that for a simple experience, a sensor returns information about the same object throughout the experience. Transforming propositions into predicates and then composing them into more complex representation is the focus of our future work.

2.5   The Model and Data Encoding Costs

The model is a set of atomic propositions and states. We encode it by concatenating the descriptions of states and atomic propositions. An atomic proposition is described by enumerating the values it covers and its cost is:
$\# \ covered\_values \ * \ log(\# \ all\_sensor\_values)$.

The description of a state s_i has two parts. The first part specifies the codes for next states, according to its transition probability distribution. These codes are used in the encoding of time series [2] as follows: if the current state is s_i and the next state is s_j, then the optimal [3] code for s_j, given s_i, has $-log(prob(s_j|s_i))$ bits. The cost for all next state codes is $-\sum_{j=1}^{\#states} log(prob(s_j|s_i))$. If a transition probability $prob(s_k|s_i)$ is 0, then we replace the k-th term in the sum with $log(\#states)$.

The second part of a state encoding is its characterization with atomic propositions. This cost is defined as: $\#\,propositions\_in\_state * log(\#\,all\_propositions)$. The model cost is the sum of the costs of the descriptions of propositions and states.

The time series of experiences are encoded as the most likely state sequences in the induced HMM. A state specifies the set of atomic propositions that hold in the state and these propositions carry information about the sensor values. The propositions generalize over the distributions from which they were derived and lose information that was present in the distributions. Consequently, the propositions may be inaccurate, meaning they specify incorrect sensor values, or imprecise, meaning they specify a range of sensor values. For example, if a propositional characterization of an HMM state says "translational velocity is 2, 3, or 4." and the robot's translational velocity in the state is actually 5, then the proposition is inaccurate. If translational velocity is 3, then the proposition is imprecise.

To re-generate a time series of sensor values from logical state descriptions, one would have to store additional information, either for specifying one of the covered values when the proposition is not precise, or for correcting errors when the proposition does not hold at that time step. The cost of an individual experience is defined to include both the size of its encoding as a state sequence within the model and the additional information required for correcting the description, if necessary. Specifically, the cost is a sum over all time steps of:

1. the length of encoding with the optimal code the current state $s(t)$, given the previous state $s(t-1)$; as discussed above, this cost is either $-log(prob(s(t)|s(t-1)))$ or $log(\#\,states)$.
2. the length of encoding the sensor vector at the current time step, given the current state; for each sensor this component of the cost is either $log(\#\,covered\_values)$ if the proposition is imprecise, or $log(\#\,all\_sensor\_values)$ if the proposition is inaccurate

---

[2] Although these codes appear in the redescription of experiences, they must be specified in the model description because otherwise the encoded experiences cannot be decoded.

[3] We do not have to specify what this optimal code. For our cost function, we need to know only its length.

3   Experiment

3.1   Experiment Setting

Sensor value time series were collected from twelve simple experiences of the Pioneer 1 robot. The experiences fall into four categories: pass object on right, pass object on left, push object and approach object. There are three experiences of each kind. For all experiences, the object is perceived by the visual channel A, which was calibrated to detect blue objects. The perceived object will be referred from now on as "object A". The data were collected [4] in a less noisy environment, with the robot executing forward motions along an almost empty corridor. The noise reduction proved to be beneficial: no spurious objects – that usually mislead the state splitting algorithm – were detected in the visual field.

From the forty or so sensors of the Pioneer 1 robot, we selected six that we consider relevant for describing the twelve experiences in our experiment. These are:

- "trans-vel" is the robot's translational velocity
- "vis-A-area" is the area occupied by the object in the channel A visual field
- "vis-A-x" and "vis-A-y" are the coordinates in the visual field of object A
- "grip-front-beam" and "grip-rear-beam" return 1 when an object is between the two gripper arms and 0 otherwise

The slopes (derivatives) of the first four sensors were also added, yielding four more variables: "trans-acc" is the derivative of translational velocity and "diff-vis-A-xxx" are the derivatives of the visual sensors.

The sensor values were discretized with Kohonen maps, one unidimensional map for each sensor variable. Figure 1 shows the resulting discretization for the visual A area sensor. As it can be seen in this figure, the map is topologically ordered, that is $value(map\ unit\ 0) < value(map\ unit\ 1) < \ldots < value(map\ unit\ 8)$. Topological ordering is a property of unidimensional Kohonen maps, so the maps of all sensors are ordered. Due to this property, we can easily interpret the atomic propositions. For example, the atomic proposition "vis-A-area.0-1" tells us that a small object is seen in visual channel A, while "vis-A-area.7-8" signals the presence of a large object.

3.2   Results

The results of the state splitting algorithm for two of the twelve experiences, and the corresponding partitioning into stages are shown in fig. 2. For the states that occur during these two experiences, table 2 lists their probability distributions over sensor values and the induced atomic propositions. The most likely HMM state sequences for all experiences are shown in table 1.

---

[4] We thank Zack Rubinstein for providing the data and for collecting them in a less noisy environment.

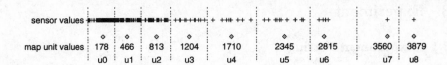

Fig. 1. Discretization of the "vis-A-area" sensor with a linear Kohonen map. The map has 9 units, u0 through u8, thus yielding 9 discrete symbols. The plot shows the values of the map units and the approximative intervals of sensor values allocated to each unit. It can be noticed that most of the sensor values are mapped to the first three units, while the last two units get only one value each.

Table 1. The middle column shows the most likely HMM state sequences for the twelve experiences and the right column shows their corresponding compressed stage sequences. In the compressed stage sequences, c_i stands for a composite stage and s_i stands for a simple stage.

experience	state sequence	compressed state sequence
pass-right-A	$s_1^+\ s_5^+\ s_4^+\ s_8^+\ s_0^+$	$c_{10}\ c_{13}$
pass-right-A	$s_1^+\ s_5^+\ s_4^+\ s_8^+\ s_0^+$	$c_{10}\ c_{13}$
pass-right-A	$s_2^+\ s_1^+\ s_5^+\ s_4^+\ s_8^+\ s_0^+$	$s_2\ c_{10}\ c_{13}$
pass-left-A	$s_2^+\ s_1^+\ s_5^+\ s_4^+\ s_8^+\ s_0^+$	$s_2\ c_{10}\ c_{13}$
pass-left-A	$s_2^+\ s_1^+\ s_5^+\ s_4^+\ s_8^+$	$s_2\ c_{10}\ s_8$
pass-left-A	$s_2^+\ s_1^+\ s_5^+\ s_8^+\ s_0^+$	$s_2\ c_9\ c_{13}$
push-A	$s_3^+\ s_1^+\ s_5^+\ s_4^+\ s_6^+\ s_7^+$	$c_{12}\ s_7$
push-A	$s_3^+\ s_1^+\ s_5^+\ s_4^+\ s_6^+\ s_7^+$	$c_{12}\ s_7$
push-A	$s_3^+\ s_1^+\ s_5^+\ s_4^+\ s_6^+\ s_7^+$	$c_{12}\ s_7$
approach-A	$s_3^+\ s_1^+\ s_5^+\ s_4^+\ s_6^+$	c_{12}
approach-A	$s_3^+\ s_1^+\ s_5^+\ s_4^+\ s_6^+$	c_{12}
approach-A	$s_3^+\ s_1^+\ s_5^+\ s_4^+\ s_6^+$	c_{12}

We can see from figure 2 and from table 1 that we can indeed identify a contiguous run of one HMM state, s_i^+, with an experience stage – call it s_i. Furthermore, some pairs of stages, for example $\langle s_1\ s_5 \rangle$ appear quite frequently. Such frequent pairs can be merged into composite stages. By replacing subsequences of simple stages with composite stages, even more simplified redescriptions of experiences are obtained. In order to explore this possibility, we implemented a simple compression algorithm that creates composite stages, guided again by the minimum description length principle. The description that must be minimized has two parts: the description of composite stages in terms of simple stages and the redescription of each individual experience with both composite and simple stages. The cost of each part is a measure of its description length. Creating a new composite stage has the effect that the cost of the first part increases, while that of the second part decreases. Therefore, the total cost, which is the sum of

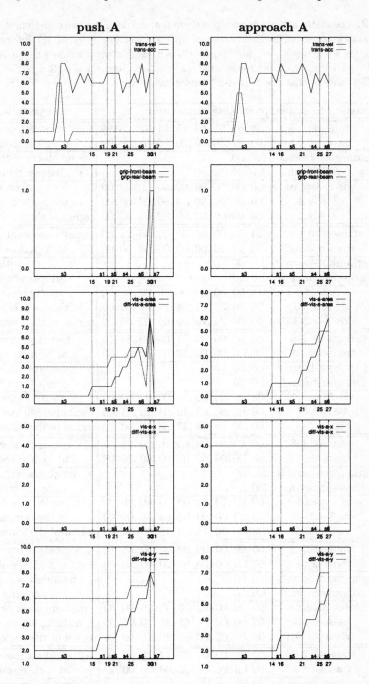

Fig. 2. HMM state fragmentation for two experiences: the left column contains the plots from a "push A" move and the right column from an "approach A" move. The units on the x-axis are time steps and the units on the y-axis are discretized sensor values.

Table 2. The states and atomic propositions that occur in the two experiences in figure 2. The states are listed in their order of appearance: $\langle s_3\ s_1\ s_5\ s_4\ s_6 \rangle$ for "approach A", and $\langle s_3\ s_1\ s_5\ s_4\ s_6\ s_7 \rangle$ for "push A". An atomic proposition like vis-A-x.3.5.6 means that the "vis-A-x" sensor mostly takes values from the set $\{3, 5, 6\}$, while "vis-A-area.5-8" means that the "vis-A-x" sensor takes values in the range $5 \ldots 8$.

state	atomic proposition	probability distribution	interpretation
s_3	trans-vel.0-8	.38 .01 .01 .03 .01 .01 .18 .28 .09	either accelerated or
	trans-acc.0.1.5.6	.06 .81 .00 .00 .06 .06 .00 .00	constant move
	grip-front-beam.0	1.0 .00	no object within
	grip-rear-beam.0	1.0 .00	gripper arms
	vis-A-area.0	1.0 .00 .00 .00 .00 .00 .00 .00	very small object
	vis-A-x.4	.00 .00 .00 .00 1.0 .00 .00 .00 .00	in the lower central
	vis-A-y.2	.00 .00 1.0 .00 .00 .00 .00 .00 .00	region of the visual field
s_1	trans-vel.0.1.6.7	.24 .05 .00 .00 .00 .00 .46 .24 .00	mostly constant move
	trans-acc.1-2	.00 .90 .10 .00 .00 .00 .00 .00 .00	at high speed
	grip-front-beam.0	1.0 .00	no object within
	grip-rear-beam.0	1.0 .00	gripper arms
	vis-A-area.0-1	.10 .90 .00 .00 .00 .00 .00 .00 .00	small object
	vis-A-x.2-6	.00 .00 .39 .02 .34 .17 .07 .00 .00	in the lower central
	vis-A-y.2-3	.00 .00 .24 .76 .00 .00 .00 .00 .00	region of the visual field
s_5	trans-vel.5-8	.00 .00 .00 .00 .00 .05 .50 .35 .10	constant move
	trans-acc.1.8	.00 1.0 .00 .00 .00 .00 .00 .00 .00	at high speed
	grip-front-beam.0	1.0 .00	no object within
	grip-rear-beam.0	1.0 .00	gripper arms
	vis-A-area.1	.00 1.0 .00 .00 .00 .00 .00 .00 .00	small object
	vis-A-x.1.2.4.5.6.7	.00 .02 .30 .00 .40 .04 .20 .04 .00	somewhere in the lower
	vis-A-y.3-4	.00 .00 .00 .78 .22 .00 .00 .00 .00	region of the visual field
s_4	trans-vel.5-8	.00 .00 .00 .00 .00 .16 .09 .63 .12	constant move
	trans-acc.1	.00 1.0 .00 .00 .00 .00 .00 .00 .00	at high speed
	grip-front-beam.0	1.0 .00	no object within
	grip-rear-beam.0	1.0 .00	gripper arms
	vis-A-area.2-3	.00 .00 .70 .30 .00 .00 .00 .00 .00	small object
	vis-A-x.1.4.6	.00 .23 .00 .00 .58 .00 .19 .00 .00	in the central
	vis-A-y.3-5	.00 .00 .00 .14 .70 .16 .00 .00 .00	region of the visual field
s_6	trans-vel.5-8	.00 .00 .00 .00 .00 .05 .50 .35 .10	constant move
	trans-acc.1	.00 1.0 .00 .00 .00 .00 .00 .00 .00	at high speed
	grip-front-beam.0	1.0 .00	no object within
	grip-rear-beam.0	1.0 .00	gripper arms
	vis-A-area.4-6	.00 .00 .00 .00 .45 .45 .10 .00 .00	medium sized object
	vis-A-x.4-5	.00 .00 .00 .00 .65 .35 .00 .00 .00	in the upper central
	vis-A-y.5-6	.00 .00 .00 .00 .00 .60 .40 .00 .00	region of the visual field
s_7	trans-vel.5-7	.00 .00 .00 .00 .00 .12 .25 .62 .00	constant move
	trans-acc.1	.00 1.0 .00 .00 .00 .00 .00 .00 .00	at high speed
	grip-front-beam.1	.00 1.0	object present within
	grip-rear-beam.0-1	.38 .62	gripper arms
	vis-A-area.5-8	.00 .00 .00 .00 .00 .38 .38 .12 .12	large object
	vis-A-x.3.5.6	.00 .00 .00 .25 .00 .13 .62 .00 .00	in the upper central
	vis-A-y.7-8	.00 .00 .00 .00 .00 .00 .00 .25 .75	region of the visual field

the costs of the two parts, may decrease as the result of creating a new composite stage. The algorithm continues to merge stages greedily, until the total cost stops decreasing. The results are shown in table 1 in the column "compressed stage sequence".

It can be noticed in table 1 that every "approach-A" experience is described by one composite stage, c_{12}, and every "push-A" experience is described by the same c_{12}, followed by the simple stage s_7. It can be seen in table 2 that state s_7, which defines stage s_7, is the only one to be characterized by the atomic propositions "grip-front-beam.1" and "grip-front-beam.0-1". These two propositions tell us that the robot is in "contact" with an object (the object is within the gripper arms). While it is obvious to us that "contact" is the difference between an "approach" and a "push", the algorithm does not get explicit information about the differences between experiences, and does not have the explicit goal of finding them. It is interesting then, that the minimum description length principle led to a re-representation of experiences that makes this distinction apparent.

It can be also noticed that the stage sequences allow a good clustering of experiences: the first two "pass-right-A" experiences share the same stage sequence and so do all the "push-A" and respectively, "approach-A", experiences.

While the above remarks are encouraging for the validity of our approach - applying the minimum description length criterion for inducing meaningful elements of representation - we can see in figure 2 that our algorithm fails to identify the acceleration stage for the two presented experiences. Although the first state in the sequence, s_3, is the only one that assigns nonzero probabilities to high acceleration values, the transition to the next state, s_1, is not triggered by the change in the acceleration regime, but by the change in the "vis-A-area" sensor from value 0 to 1. As a matter of fact, it can be noticed that for both experiences, there are other state changes triggered by this sensor as well: $s_5 \rightarrow s_4$ occurs when "vis-A-area" becomes 2 and $s_5 \rightarrow s_4$ when "vis-A-area" becomes 4. This indicates that the partitioning of these experiences into stages is mostly determined by the visual area of the object, and that the stages are identified with different degrees of closeness to the object. While this partitioning is not meaningless, it does not distinguish the important acceleration stage. The main reason is that the algorithm has no measure of the relative importance of the sensor variables, other than the reduction in description length obtained by distinguishing states based on their values. Another reason is that, as discussed in section 2.3, the cost of the description cannot be minimized globally.

4   Conclusions and Future Work

During the first year of an infant's life, she apparently develops increasingly rich and efficient representations of her environment (Mandler calls this process *re-description* [4]). We have shown how to re-describe multivariate time series of sensor values as rudimentary logical descriptions, by creating new objects that are associated with parts of the world at different abstraction levels. The objects at one level are grounded in, or mapped to, objects at the previous level. Because both memory and time are finite resources, the criterion of simple (short) descriptions must govern the process. In this work we tried to apply these ideas at the lowest levels of abstractions, by creating atomic propositions grounded in probability distributions over raw sensor values (physical level). The fragmentation of time series into states and their corresponding propositional characterizations often appear to agree with our interpretation of the evolution of experiences. But this fragmentation is not perfect: for example, as discussed in the previous section, there is no distinct "acceleration" stage, because the algorithm has no information that the acceleration sensor is more "important" than others. Meaningful representations must not be only simple, but also useful ([1]). We consider useful the elements of representations that predict the outcome of an experience, predict when a state change occurs, explain the differences between experiences or explain reward. Our next goal is to define the utility criterion for representation elements and redesign the learning algorithm to incorporate both the utility and the minimum description length criteria.

Acknowledgments

This research is supported by DARPA/AFOSRF and DARPA under contracts No. F49620-97-1-0485 and No. N66001-96-C-8504. The U.S. Government is authorized to reproduce and distribute reprints for governmental purposes notwithstanding any copyright notation hereon.The views and conclusions contained herein are those of the authors and should not be interpreted as necessarily representing the official policies or endorsements either expressed or implied, of the DARPA or the U.S. Government.

References

[1] Paul R. Cohen and Mary Litch. What are contentful mental states? Dretske's theory of mental content viewed in the light of robot learning and planning algorithms. To be presented at the *Sixteenth National Conference on Artificial Intelligence*, 1999.

[2] S. Harnad. The symbol grounding problem. *Physica D*, 42:335–346, 1990.

[3] Teuvo Kohonen. *Self-Organizing Maps*. Springer, 1995.

[4] Jean M. Mandler. How to build a baby: II. Conceptual primitives. *Psychological Review*, 99(4):587–604, 1992.

[5] J. J. Oliver and D. Hand. Introduction to minimum encoding inference. Technical Report 4-94, Statistics Dept., Open University, September 1994. TR 95/205 Computer Science, Monash University.

[6] Lawrence R. Rabiner. A tutorial on Hidden Markov Models and Selected Applications in Speech Recognition. *Proceedings of the IEEE*, 77(2):257–285, 1989.

[7] Michael Rosenstein and Paul R. Cohen. Concepts from time series. In *Proceedings of the Fifteenth National Conference on Artificial Intelligence*, pages 739–745. AAAI Press, 1998.

[8] Matthew D. Schmill, Tim Oates, and Paul R. Cohen. Learned models for continuous planning. In *Proceedings of Uncertainty 99: The Seventh International Workshop on Artificial Intelligence and Statistics*, pages 278–282, 1999.

"Seeing" Objects in Spatial Datasets

Xingang Huang[1] and Feng Zhao[2]

[1] Dept. of Computer and Information Science, The Ohio State University
2015 Neil Avenue, Columbus, Ohio 43210, U.S.A.,
huang@cis.ohio-state.edu
[2] Xerox Palo Alto Research Center
3333 Coyote Hill Road, Palo Alto, CA 94304, U.S.A.,
zhao@parc.xerox.com

Abstract. Regularities exist in datasets describing spatially distributed physical phenomena. Human experts often understand and verbalize the regularities as abstract spatial objects evolving coherently and interacting with each other in the domain space. We describe a novel computational approach for identifying and extracting these abstract spatial objects through the construction of a hierarchy of spatial relations. We demonstrate the approach with an application to finding troughs in weather data sets.

1 Introduction

In analyzing spatial datasets such as weather data or fluid motion, experts often perceive and reason about these physical fields in terms of abstract spatial objects (often described by the so-called features or patterns) that evolve and interact with each other. The benefits of doing this is at least twofold: (1) The fields are labeled by aggregate properties describing the macroscopic behaviors of the underlying phenomena so that the fields can be understood and manipulated on a scale more abstract than the point-wise description. (2) Just like the real-world phenomena they represent, the perceived objects are generally persistent both spatially and temporally and hence allow experts to understand them intuitively using common sense.

For example, when analyzing weather data, meterologists can perceive aggregate weather features such as high/low pressure centers, pressure troughs, thermal packings, fronts and jet streams and label them explicitly on the weather charts, as shown in Fig. 1. The experts then use weather rules to correlate these features and establish prediction patterns. Here is a sample of weather prediction rules [11]:

- "At 850mb, the polar front is located parallel to and on the warm side of the thermal packing."
- "Major and minor 500mb troughs are good indicators of existing or potential adverse weather."
- "Lows tend to stack toward colder air aloft while highs tend to stack toward warmer air aloft."

D.J. Hand, J.N. Kok, M.R. Berthold (Eds.): IDA'99, LNCS 1642, pp. 111–122, 1999.

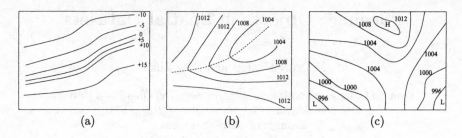

Fig. 1. Weather Features: (a) a thermal packing; (b) a pressure trough, where solid lines representing iso-bars and dashed line trough position; (c) highs "H" and lows "L" in a pressure map.

Modeling the abstraction and reasoning processes of scientists in these application domains is a goal of qualitative reasoning and common sense reasoning. The abstraction step extracts salient descriptions as spatial objects from raw spatial datasets. Without including this step, artificial systems that reason about physical systems will have to rely on domain experts to provide basic inputs. In the terminology of MD/PV in qualitative reasoning [3], this step corresponds to building place vocabulary (i.e., abstract spatial objects) from metric diagram (i.e., spatial datasets sampling the underlying physical fields).

The object-centered ontologies in qualitative reasoning assume the existence of base objects in the first place. Lundell's work deals with the physical fields, but the objects studied are only iso-clusters — sets of connected points with qualitatively equivalent parameter values [7]. Iso-clusters are easy to compute but inadequate for modeling more complex spatial objects, such as troughs and fronts in the weather analysis domain.

The spatial objects perceived by scientists have a common characteristics: they are all visually salient, at least to the trained eyes. On the other hand, these objects often do not admit a well-defined mathematical characterization with a small number of parameters. The identification and extraction of spatial objects share many similarities with the recognition and figure-ground separation problems in computer vision.

In this paper we develop a general approach to extracting abstract spatial objects from spatial datasets. It is built upon the framework of Spatial Aggregation (SA) that features a multi-layer representation and a set of generic operators to transform the representation [18]. This work extends the SA framework in three ways:

- It emphasizes the importance of internal structural information about spatial objects. A spatial object is not just a collection of constituent objects but with a rich internal structure that may influence the aggregate properties of the object including its identity.
- It classifies neighborhood relations into strong adjacencies and weak adjacencies. This classification explicates the connection between structural information and neighborhood relations and the connection between low-level

and high-level neighborhood relations, and enables high-level neighborhood relations to be built from primitive ones.
- It provides an algorithm for extracting structured spatial objects and extends the set of generic SA operators.

We have applied this approach to the trough extraction problem in weather analysis and obtained promising results.

The rest of the paper is organized as follows. Section 2 presents the proposed approach. Section 3 describes the trough application. The experimental results are shown in Section 4 and the related work is discussed in section 5.

2   Extracting Structured Spatial Objects

In this section, we first briefly review the Spatial Aggregation framework. We then introduce the notion of *strong adjacency* and *weak adjacency* as a refinement of neighborhood relations and discuss its use in aggregating objects and their neighborhood relations. Last we present a structure finding algorithm that incrementally extracts structured objects from spatial datasets.

2.1   Spatial Aggregation

Spatial Aggregation is a recently developed computational approach to hierarchical data analysis. It has been successfully applied to several difficult data analysis and control problems such as interpretation of numerical experiments [16,19], kinematics analysis of mechanisms [5], design of controllers [20] reasoning about fluid motion [17], and distributed control optimization [1].

SA features a multi-layer representation and a set of generic operators to transform spatial objects at a finer scale into ones at more abstract levels. The lowest level usually consists of the simplest, point-like spatial objects such as the image pixels in the raw data. From there on, domain knowledge is integrated into the generic operators to select salient objects, build appropriate neighborhood relations upon the objects, and aggregate them into more complex objects at the next higher level. After the aggregation, the newly formed higher level spatial objects generally contain richer domain-specific descriptions and aggregate spatial properties than their constituent spatial objects. These properties make the qualitative patterns more explicit and support the extraction of macroscopic behaviors. Details of the SA algorithm is described in the reference [18].

2.2   Strong Adjacencies and Weak Adjacencies

Neighborhood relation is essential in spatial object aggregation because, intuitively, a coherent spatial object has to be internally connected. We observe that neighborhood relations play two distinct roles in the aggregation process. Some bind a set of spatial objects into a single aggregate object and become "intra-relations" within the aggregate object after the aggregation. We call these neighborhood relations *strong adjacencies*. The others do not bind objects at the current level but stand out as "inter-relations" to reveal the spatial relations between the aggregate spatial objects after the aggregation. We call those *weak adjacencies*.

With the finer classification of neighborhood relations into strong and weak adjacencies, we then introduce a two-step classification for building increasingly more abstract objects: each connected component in the graph defined by the strong adjacencies is re-described into a higher level spatial object; the weak adjacencies are aggregated and summarized to build neighborhood relations among aggregate spatial objects. This classification is especially useful, compared to the original SA algorithm, when it is inappropriate to simplify and cluster aggregate spatial objects as points.

2.3   A Structure Finding Algorithm

Based on the adjacency classification, we present a structure finding algorithm for spatial objects, as illustrated in Fig. 2. At each level, the neighborhood relations are classified into strong adjacencies and weak adjacencies. Then the strong adjacencies and the spatial objects they bind together are re-described

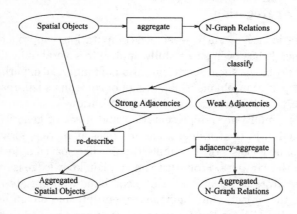

Fig. 2. The structure finding algorithm for one layer of aggregation. The output is fed into the next layer of aggregation that has the identical computational structure. Rectangles denote operators and ovals data.

into higher level spatial objects with the strong adjacencies serving as the internal structure. The weak adjacencies are then aggregated to build neighborhood relations between higher level spatial objects. Therefore, at the next level, with the internal structure of objects abstracted away and the relations among objects simplified by aggregation, the aggregate properties of the objects become more prominent. When object details are requested, the internal structure of the object is available at the lower level so that relevant information can be quickly located. In summary, the algorithm is capable of not only explicating structures from data, but also organizing information in a structured, hierarchical way.

A new SA operator, *adjacency-aggregate*, is introduced to support the aggregation of adjacencies with the following syntax:

– *adjacency-aggregate*: agg-objs * weak-adjacencies * constr-op → N-relations

It takes a collection of aggregate objects, the weak adjacencies among the constituents, and a constructor operator as inputs, and produces a set of neighborhood relations for the aggregate objects. The constructor operator *constr-op* constructs a neighborhood relation of two aggregate objects using all the pairwise weak adjacencies between their respective constituents. Different constructor operators may be employed according to the task requirements. The constructor operators currently supported by SAL are:

– *count*: return the number of weak adjacencies as the data value for the new N-relation.
– *minimal*: return the minimal weak adjacency as the data value for the new N-relation.
– *maximum*: return the maximum weak adjacency as the data value of the new N-relation.
– *pack*: return the set of weak adjacencies as the data value for the new N-relation.

Users can also supply other constructor operators. Fig. 3 demonstrates the *adjacency-aggregate* operation using the *count* constructor operator.

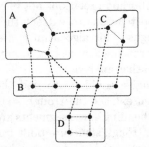   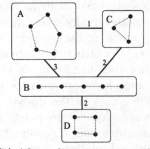

(a) Before adjacency-aggregation   (b) After adjacency-aggregation

Fig. 3. *Adjacency-aggregate* using the constructor *count*. A,B,C,D — aggregate objects; Dashed lines in (a) — weak adjacencies, Bold lines in (b) — computed N-relations.

We have introduced the concept of structured spatial objects, strong and weak adjacencies, and the structure finding algorithm. This approach supports the extraction of a hierarchy of structured spatial objects by iteratively aggregating the lowest level spatial objects and neighborhood relations. The original SAL library is extended to support the structure aggregation approach.

3   Application: Extracting Trough Structures from Weather Data

In this section, we use the weather application to demonstrate how the proposed approach can be used to extract abstract spatial objects from spatial datasets.

Troughs and ridges are important features in weather analysis. High-altitude troughs show the bending of the jet streams in the high-altitude air circulation and are important for extended weather forecast. Surface troughs are usually closely related to fronts and hence are useful for locating the fronts.

What are troughs and ridges? Visually, troughs and ridges are stacks of iso-bar segments bending consistently to one direction, with troughs corresponding to bendings pointing away from lower iso-bars and ridges away from higher iso-bars. Fig. 1 (b) shows a trough. Due to the Coriolis force, winds tend to follow iso-bars. So the bending of iso-bars is an indication of sharp direction change of wind, which usually brings more advection and causes more mixing of warm air with cold air, and therefore, the deteriorating weather.

Though the extraction of troughs seem effortless and immediate to human eyes, it is only qualitatively understood. Sometimes even experts may give different answers about the existence of a trough in a weather map because of their different "mind-judgment" criteria.

Intuitively, experts first observe the high bending segments of iso-curves in the chart and then extract the linear structures from these bending segments. Our trough finding algorithm emulates this process by first extracting the high bending segments of iso-bars, establishing neighborhood relations between these segments, and finally using these neighborhood relations to extract the linear structures among the segments to obtain troughs. This algorithm is a special instance of the earlier structure aggregation approach where aggregation parameters are chosen using domain knowledge in weather analysis.

An alternative approach to extracting troughs would be to find the high curvature points on the iso-bar curves and then extract the trough structures from these high curvature points. Since the high bending curve segments are more robust features than high curvature points, the trough structure built from the neighborhood relations of high bending curve segments is also more robust.

The complete algorithm has a pre-processing step, two levels of aggregation and a post-processing step:

- Pre-processing: Extract all the iso-points at the required contour levels.
- Level I aggregation:
  - *Aggregate*: Build neighborhood relations upon the iso-points using Delaunay triangulation.
  - *Classify*: Classify adjacency relations into strong adjacencies and weak adjacencies.

- *Re-describe*: Use strong adjacencies to aggregate iso-points into iso-curves.
- *Filter*: Extract salient objects, i.e., segment iso-curves and extract high bending curve segments.
  - Level II aggregation:
    - *Adjacency-aggregate*: Build neighborhood relations upon high bending curve segments by aggregating weak adjacencies.
    - *Classify*: Classify the neighborhood relations of curve segments into strong adjacencies and weak adjacencies.
    - *Re-describe*: Use strong adjacencies to aggregate curve segments into trough structures. Trim the trough structures into linear structures.
  - Post-processing: Locate and draw the trough line position as in the standard weather analysis chart.

The SA operators *aggregate*, *classify*, *re-describe*, *filter* and *adjacency-aggregate* are used in the above two-level aggregations. The filtering of curve segments at level I involves choosing an appropriate threshold for segmentation. We will discuss next the technical issues in computing a stable segmentation.

3.1 Curve Segmentation

We use curve fitting technique and *split and merge* algorithm [9,2,15] to segment curves. Because iso-bar curves are generally smooth, we use constant curvature curves (straight lines and circular arcs) to fit iso-bar curves, i.e., we first transform an iso-bar curve into $\psi - S$ space (ψ: the angle made between the tangent to the curve and a fixed line; S: the length of the curve from beginning), where constant curvature curves become line segments, and then use piecewise linear approximation to fit the transformed curve.

Split and merge algorithm requires an error threshold for segmentation if the desired number of segments of a curve is unknown. The algorithm generates a segmentation satisfying the error threshold constraint and seeking to minimize the number of segments, and minimize the approximation error if the number of segments can not be minimized any more. Because the shape of iso-bar curves varies in a large range, appropriate thresholds need to be selected according to the inherent properties of the underlying curves. We have developed the *iterative thresholding* technique to find appropriate thresholds for satisfactory segmentations of iso-bar curves. This technique generates a sequence of thresholds and use one of the two heuristics: *ATS* (Absolute Threshold Stability) or *RTS* (Relative Threshold Stability) to choose the most stable one from them. Because of the space limit, we are unable to go into the details of the iterative thresholding technique here. Interested readers are referred to our technical report [4]. Fig. 4 shows two sample outputs of our segmentation algorithm.

3.2 Extracting Bending Segments

After iso-bar curves are segmented, high-bending segments can be extracted by thresholding. One problem arises when the bending is sharp: the segmentation

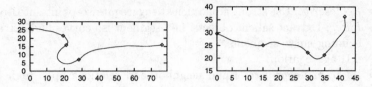

Fig. 4. Segmentation of two sample iso-bar curves.

algorithm extracts a short curve segment that has a large bending since the bending takes place in a very small interval; it is difficult for a short curve segment to establish spatial relations with other curve segments. However, the sharp bending is the main feature we want to detect. To facilitate the detection, we perform a *branch extension* operation on the extracted segments. The branch extension operation extends a short curve segment of large bending to its neighbors if its neighbor segments are flat. Fig. 5 gives an illustration of this operation.

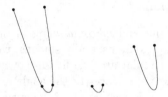

Fig. 5. The Branch Extension operation. Left: a curve and its segmentation; Center: segment extraction without branch extension; Right: segment extraction with branch extension.

4   Experimental Results

Fig. 6 shows a complete run of the trough extraction algorithm on a 500mb pressure data set. Each subgraph is labeled with the corresponding operation and the results obtained. Several things worth noting are:

1. (b) and (d) may look similar, but (d) does not have the short strong adjacency edges.
2. Because of the branch extension operation, the segments can overlap with each other. So in the (f), a square is used to denote the beginning of a segment and a circle the end of a segment.

Our algorithm detects one ridge (the longest one) and two troughs as expected.

Fig. 7 compares high altitude troughs detected by the algorithm and a trough drawn by meterologists from real datasets. Fig. 7 (b) is the national weather

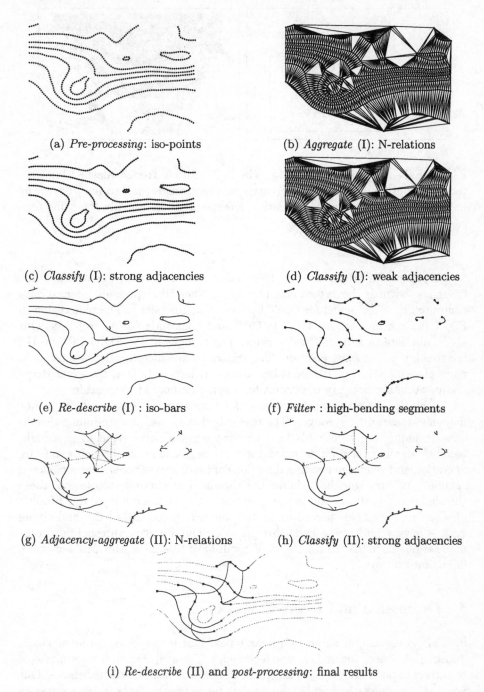

(a) *Pre-processing*: iso-points

(b) *Aggregate* (I): N-relations

(c) *Classify* (I): strong adjacencies

(d) *Classify* (I): weak adjacencies

(e) *Re-describe* (I) : iso-bars

(f) *Filter* : high-bending segments

(g) *Adjacency-aggregate* (II): N-relations

(h) *Classify* (II): strong adjacencies

(i) *Re-describe* (II) and *post-processing*: final results

Fig. 6. A complete run of the trough extraction algorithm

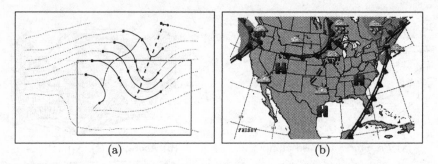

Fig. 7. Labeling weather chart: (a) The high-altitude trough (dashed line) detected by our algorithm. (b) The corresponding trough (dashed line) drawn by meterologists for the national weather forecast map for roughly the same area as the box in (a).

forecast map [1] for Friday, Jan. 15, 1999 (exact time unknown). The high altitude trough is shown as the dashed line. Our data is the 250mb pressure forecast data computed by ETA model for GMT 6am on Jan. 15, 1999 [2]. The plot region in Fig. 7 (a) is from Latitude 20°N to 59°N and Longitude 145°W to 65°W. Our algorithm detects a trough and a ridge. The troughs in the Fig. 7 (a) and (b) are roughly at the same position. The trough by the meterologists seems to be more pleasant visually because it is manually trimmed. In fact, the exact shape and position are not very important for a synoptic map at these scale.

Currently, the algorithm works well for high altitude pressure datasets but may miss some surface troughs. The reason is that we use predetermined thresholds, including the thresholds to determine when a curve segment is a high-bending segment, how far to extend a curve segment in the branch extension operation and when the bending directions of two curve segments are considered "similar" in our algorithm. Unlike the threshold in curve segmentation, these thresholds currently are not adaptively tuned by the underlying data. Finding appropriate thresholds according to the inherent properties of the underlying data is a very interesting and hard problem. Our iterative thresholding technique is an effort toward solving it. We will have to explore this problem more in our future work.

5   Discussion and Related Work

Spatial data mining is an active research field that leverages recent advances in information processing and storage technology. The goal of spatial data mining is to extract implicit knowledge, patterns, and relations from spatial databases. Our approach emulates the way human experts perceive structures in large datasets

---

[1] URL: http://www.weathersite.com/enlargetomorrow.html

[2] URL: ftp://nic.fb4.noaa.gov/pub/erl/eta.00z

in order for machines to "see" the same structures. It uses existing domain knowledge, expressed as parameters at various levels of aggregation, to aid the perception and understanding of spatial datasets. The two approaches are nonetheless complementary and can benefit from each other. Recent spatial data mining research also studies the aggregation techniques and spatial relations. For instance, Ng and Han [8] described a very efficient algorithm, CLARANS, to find spatial clusters of points in large databases. Knorr and Ng [6] presented the CRH algorithm for building proximity relations among aggregated spatial structures represented as point clusters and features represented as polygons.

This work is largely inspired by the pioneering work of Ken Yip in interpreting large fluid datasets [17]. It also shares a similar objective with the visualization work at Rutgers University[12,10]. The Rutgers group studies the *visiometrics* process that identifies, classifies, and tracks observable features (i.e., spatial objects in the terminology of this paper) in fluid datasets. The spatial objects studied by the Rutgers group are mostly iso-clusters, and classified by shape parameters such as area, curvature, torsion and moments. SA examines multiple levels of structural aggregation, whereas the *visiometrics* process corresponds to one layer of spatial aggregation. The Rutgers work introduces a rich vocabulary for spatial properties of fluid objects and a temporal object tracking mechanism that SA can build upon.

The importance of structural information in object recognition has long been recognized by computer vision researchers. In [13], Ullman described the well-known *scrambled face* example to show that individual features represent nothing meaningful unless they are properly arranged in space. Structural description [14] is one of the main approaches in object recognition in computer vision but is nonetheless under-researched because of the difficulties in computing structural information and representing the information suitably to facilitate robust and efficient matching. Our approach makes significant contribution to the computation of structural information by providing a systematic way of building neighborhood relations upon complex aggregated spatial objects.

6   Summary

We have presented a structure aggregation approach to extracting abstract spatial objects from spatial datasets. This work builds on SA to hierarchically derive neighborhood relations at different abstraction levels. Its application to trough extraction shows that it is capable of extracting visually salient and mathematically ill-defined spatial objects with relatively simple structures.

The work described here focuses on the extraction of spatial objects. Future work will study the identification of spatial objects that requires a suitable representation of structural information and an efficient and robust mechanism to match extracted structures against standard templates. We will continue to use the weather data analysis as the domain to explore these research issues.

Acknowledgment

The paper describes work conducted at Ohio State University, supported in part by NSF NYI grant CCR-9457802, ONR YI grant N00014-97-1-0599, and a Sloan Research Fellowship.

References

1. C. Bailey-Kellogg and F. Zhao. Influence-based model decomposition. In *Proceedings of AAAI*, to appear, 1999.
2. J.G Dunham. Optimum uniform piecewise linear approximation of planar curves. *IEEE Trans. Pattern Analysis Mach. Intell.*, **PAMI-8**:67–75, 1986.
3. K. Forbus, P. Nielsen, and B. Faltings. Qualitative kinematics: A framework. In *Proceedings of AAAI*, 1987.
4. X. Huang and F. Zhao. Segmentation of planar curves and the iterative thresholding technique. Technical Report OSU-CISRC-3/99-TR07, CIS, Ohio State Univ, 1999.
5. L. Joskowicz and E. Sacks. Computational kinematics. *Artificial Intelligence*, 51:381–416, 1991.
6. E.M. Knorr and R.T. Ng. Finding aggregate proximity relationships and commonalities in spatial data mining. *IEEE Trans. on Knowledge and Data Engineering*, 8:884–897, December 1996.
7. M. Lundell. A qualitative model of physical fields. In *Proceedings of AAAI*, 1996.
8. R.T. Ng and J. Han. Efficient and Effective Clustering Methods for Spatial Data Mining. In *Proceedings of the Twentieth International Conference on Very Large Databases*, pages 144–155, Santiago, Chile, 1994.
9. T. Pavlidis and S.L. Horowitz. Segmentation of plane curves. *IEEE Trans. Computer*, **C-22**:860–870, 1974.
10. R. Samtaney, D. Silver, N. Zabusky, and J. Cao. Visualizing features and tracking their evolution. *IEEE Computer Magazine*, July 1994.
11. Air Weather Service. Back to basics. In *AWS FOT Seminar STT-Q9-0004*, 1975.
12. D. Silver and N. Zabusky. Quantifying visualizations for reduced modeling in nonlinearscience: Extracting structures from data sets. *Journal of Visual Communication and Image*, 4:46–61, 1993.
13. S. Ullman. Visual routines. *Cognition*, 18, 1984.
14. S. Ullman. Chapter 2: Approaches to object recognition. In *High Level Vision*. MIT Press, 1996.
15. J.A. Ventura and J.M. Chen. Segmentation of two-dimensional curve contours. *Pattern Recognition*, 28:1129–1140, 1992.
16. K. M. Yip. *KAM: A system for intelligently guiding numerical experimentation by computer*. MIT Press, 1991.
17. K. M. Yip. Structural inferences from massive datasets. In *Proceedings of IJCAI*, 1997.
18. K. M. Yip and F. Zhao. Spatial aggregation: theory and applications. *J. Artificial Intelligence Research*, 5, 1996.
19. F. Zhao. Extracting and representing qualitative behaviors of complex systems in phase spaces. *Artificial Intelligence*, 69(1-2):51–92, 1994.
20. F. Zhao, Intelligent simulation in designing complex dynamical control systems. *Book chapter in Artificial Intelligence in Industrial Decision Making, Control, and Automation*, Tzafestas and Verbruggen (eds.), pp. 127-158, Kluwer, 1995.

Intelligent Monitoring Method Using Time Varying Binomial Distribution Models for Pseudo-Periodic Communication Traffic

Kazunori Matsumoto and Kazuo Hashimoto

KDD Laboratories Inc.
2-1-15 Ohara Kamifukuoka-Shi, Saitama 356-8502, Japan
{matsu, kh}@lab.kdd.co.jp

Abstract. In this paper, we deal with the degradation detection problem for telecommunication network gateways. The time series to be monitored is non-stationary but almost periodic (*pseudo-periodic*). The authors propose a technique called "optimization of partition model" which generates local stationary models for a *pseudo-periodic* time series. The optimization is based on the minimal AIC principle. The technique called SPRT is also applied to make efficient decisions. Experiments to evaluate methods for optimization, incremental model update, and the comparison with the conventional method are conducted with real data. The result shows the proposed method is effective and makes more precises decision than the conventional one.

1 Introduction

In a telecommunication network, multiple gateways work simultaneously to establish communication paths to a designated foreign network. As there exist many constraints in obtaining the detailed status of foreign networks, allocation of communication calls to gateways is decided by observing the *rate of established calls* on the gateways. When the *rate of established calls* significantly goes down on a certain gateway, the number of calls to be allocated to the gateway should be reduced. A major task of gateway monitoring is to find the degradation of the *rate of established calls* for each foreign network[1].

In modern networks, there are many kinds of communication traffic at one time, and the behavior of the traffic is not a simple stochastic process. Therefore many heuristic approaches are applied. Monitoring methods using expertise work well for some specific gateways. However, the rapid change of traffic behavior caused by new services spuars continual efforts to update heuristics in monitoring systems.

As a result there is a strong emphasis on intelligent data analysis techniques that can deal with real-time data streams from on-line monitor of gateways.

The method for dealing with this degradation detection problem requires the handling of real-time data streams, which are a non-stationary time series, and also the continuous updating of model parameters. The basic concept for solution of the above requirements is as follows:

D.J. Hand, J.N. Kok, M.R. Berthold (Eds.): IDA'99, LNCS 1642, pp. 123–134, 1999.

- Conventional methods deal with the *rate of established calls* directly. The definition of this rate is the ratio between the number of calls connected successfully and the number of attempted calls. We may regard these two values as the number of success occurrences and that of trials in *Bernoulli trials* respectively. The authors propose use of a *binomial distribution* model with these two values.
- The entire time series is non-stationary, but when we divide a time series into proper size segments, each segment can be regarded as stationary. Akaike's Information Criterion (AIC)[4] is useful for making partitions at proper positions in the time series. The authors propose to apply this technique to the degradation detection problem.
- In a short term range such as several weeks, the *rate of established calls* approximately depends on the day of the week, the rate is almost periodic and the interval of a cycle is a week long. The authors call this phenomenon *pseudo-periodic*, and call the interval of a cycle a *pseudo-period*. We can regard the time series of the segments, which belong to the same position in cycles within such a short range, as the same stochastic process. Authors propose to deal with such segments in the same model. By means of this approximation we can use more samples in each segment.
- The Sequential Probability Ratio Test (SPRT) developed by Wald[2] is suited for real-time decisions. It is popular in aerospace applications[3], but have not been used in this domain. The authors propose to apply this efficient stochastic test to our degradation detection problem.

2 Optimization of Partition Model for Pseudo-Periodic Time Series

2.1 Definition of Partition Model

Observations are repeated with an equal time interval. Let

$$S = (n_1, r_1), (n_2, r_2), \cdots, (n_{M+1}, r_{M+1}), (n_{M+2}, r_{M+2}), \cdots,$$
$$(n_{(m-1)M+1}, r_{(m-1)M+1}), (n_{(m-1)M+2}, r_{(m-1)M+2}), \cdots, (n_{mM}, r_{mM})$$

be a discrete time series, where (n_t, r_t) denotes the pair that consists of the number of trials and that of success occurrences at time t, M is the *pseudo period*, and m is the number of the pseudo-periodic cycles.

Let $\mathcal{P}^i = \{\pi_1^i, \pi_2^i, \cdots, \pi_{s(i)}^i\}$ be a set of partitions (called here *partition model*), where i is a unique identifier of the model and $s(i)$ is the number of partitions in $\mathcal{P}^i$.

Let $S_1^i, S_2^i, \cdots, S_{s(i)}^i$ be the set of observed data divided by $\mathcal{P}^i$ and F_j^i ($0 < F_j^i < M$) be the position of a partition π_j^i, where S_j^i is given as follows.

$$S_j^i = \{(n_{F_{j-1}^i}, r_{F_{j-1}^i}), \cdots, (n_{F_j^i-1}, r_{F_j^i-1}),$$
$$(n_{M+F_{j-1}^i}, r_{M+F_{j-1}^i}), \cdots, (n_{M+F_j^i-1}, r_{M+F_j^i-1}),$$

$$\cdots,$$

$$(n_{(m-1)M+F^i_{j-1}}, r_{(m-1)M+F^i_{j-1}}), \cdots, (n_{(m-1)M+F^i_j-1}, r_{(m-1)M+F^i_j-1})\}$$

S^i_j denotes the set of observed data which exists between π^i_{j-1} and π^i_j. Note that S is non-stationary but the distribution of S^i_j is binomial under our assumption.

2.2 Partition Model Selection Based on Minimal AIC Principle

Let $P(r|n, p)$ be the probability that r successes occurs in n trials, each of which has probability p of success.

Log-likelihood of S^i_j is

$$ll(S^i_j|p) = \sum_{(n,r)\in S^i_j} \log P(r|n, p)$$

$$= \sum_{(n,r)\in S^i_j} \log {}_nC_r \, p^r \, (1-p)^{n-r}$$

$$= \sum_{(n,r)\in S^i_j} \log {}_nC_r + R^i_j \log p + (N^i_j - R^i_j) \log(1-p),$$

$$\text{where} \quad R^i_j = \sum_{(n,r)\in S^i_j} r, \quad N^i_j = \sum_{(n,r)\in S^i_j} n.$$

When $\hat{p}^i_j$ is the maximum likelihood estimation of p for S^i_j, $\frac{\partial}{\partial p} ll(S^i_j|\hat{p}^i_j) = 0$. Thus, $\hat{p}^i_j = \frac{R^i_j}{N^i_j}$. The maximum log-likelihood of $\mathcal{P}^i$ is

$$MLL(\mathcal{P}^i) = \sum_{j=1}^{s(i)+1} ll(S^i_j|\hat{p}^i_j)$$

$$= \sum_{j=1}^{s(i)+1} \left\{ \sum_{(n,r)\in S^i_j} \log {}_nC_r + R^i_j \log \frac{R^i_j}{N^i_j} + (N^i_j - R^i_j) \log \frac{N^i_j - R^i_j}{N^i_j} \right\}$$

$$= \sum_{t=1}^{mM} \log {}_{n_t}C_{r_t} + \sum_{j=1}^{s(i)+1} \left\{ R^i_j \log \frac{R^i_j}{N^i_j} + (N^i_j - R^i_j) \log \frac{N^i_j - R^i_j}{N^i_j} \right\}.$$

Log-likelihood is inappropriate for comparing models when the number of parameters of each model is different. Akaike information Criterion (AIC) [4] in the next equation is known to be a correct measure for a general model comparison. Let $\theta, LL(\theta), |\theta|$ be the model to be compared, log-likelihood of the model θ, and the number of free parameters in the model.

$$AIC(\theta) = -2 \times LL(\theta) + 2 \times |\theta|$$

Based on the minimum AIC principle, the model θ which has the minimum $AIC(\theta)$ is the best model.

Note that $\sum_{t=1}^{mM} \log {}_{n_t}C_{r_t}$ in $MLL(\mathcal{P}^i)$ appears in all *partition models*, and we can ignore it. The most probable *partition model* $\mathcal{P}$ in $\{\mathcal{P}^1, \mathcal{P}^2, \cdots, \}$ is obtained by the following equations.

$$MLL'(\mathcal{P}^i) = \sum_{j=1}^{s(i)+1} \left\{ R_j^i \log \frac{R_j^i}{N_j^i} + (N_j^i - R_j^i) \log \frac{N_j^i - R_j^i}{N_j^i} \right\}$$

$$AIC'(\mathcal{P}^i) = -2 \times MLL'(\mathcal{P}^i) + 2 \times \{s(i) + 1\}$$

$$\mathcal{P} = \arg\min_i AIC'(\mathcal{P}^i)$$

3   Degradation Detection by SPRT

The conventional scheme of SPRT (Sequential Probability Ratio Test) is explained first and application of SPRT to our degradation detection problem is described.

3.1   Scheme of SPRT

SPRT is a well-known method for testing a hypothesis against an alternate one. Let $v_1, v_2, \ldots$ denotes the recent successive samples in a given time series vector. The basis for the SPRT is the recursive calculation of the logarithm of the likelihood ratio (LLR) function of the normal model and an alternate model with recent q samples

$$LLR(q) = \log \frac{p_q(v_1, v_2, \ldots, v_q | H_1)}{p_q(v_1, v_2, \ldots, v_q | H_0)},$$

where $p_q(v_1, \ldots, v_q | H_1)$ is the probability density function when the process is degraded (hypothesis H_1 is true), and $p_q(v_1, \ldots, v_q | H_0)$ is also the probability density function when the process is normal (H_0 is true). After assuming that v_i and v_j are independent, the above formula becomes additive and the LLR function is computed recursively

$$LLR(q) = LLR(q-1) + \log \frac{p(v_q | H_1)}{p(v_q | H_0)}$$

where $P(v_q | H_1)$ and $P(v_q | H_0)$ are probability density function yielding v_q when the process is degraded or normal, respectively. $LLR(q)$ is compared to two limits (degraded/normal), with a gray range between them. When it lies in the range, there is no decision. These two limits are derived from the *allowable false alarm rate* and the *allowable missed alarm rate* chosen by users.

3.2 SPRT for Degradation Detection in Binomial Models

SPRT requires two functions. One function evaluates the probability that the process is degraded and the other evaluates the probability that the process is normal. In the case of our degradation problem, LLR function is defined as below:

Let $\hat{p}$ be the maximum likelihood estimation of the segment in the most probable *partition model* to which the current observation belongs, let ϵ ($0 < \epsilon < 1$) be a weighting parameter which is introduced to control the sensitivity of degradation, and let $Prob(n, r|H_1)$ and $Prob(n, r|H_0)$ be the probability when the process is degraded and normal respectively.

$$
\begin{aligned}
LLR(n, r) &= \log \frac{Prob(n, r|H_1)}{Prob(n, r|H_0)} \\
&= \log \frac{P(r|n, p_w)}{P(r|n, p_g)} \\
&= \log \frac{{}_nC_r \, p_w^r \, (1 - p_w)^{n-r}}{{}_nC_r \, p_g^r \, (1 - p_g)^{n-r}} \\
&= r \log \frac{p_w}{p_g} + (n - r) \log \frac{1 - p_w}{1 - p_g} \, ,
\end{aligned}
$$

where p_w is an expected success probability under the degraded mode, and p_g is an expected success probability under the normal mode. p_w and p_g are defined as follows.

$$
p_w = \begin{cases} r/n & \text{if } \epsilon\hat{p} > r/n \\ \epsilon\hat{p} & \text{otherwise} \end{cases}
\tag{1}
$$

$$
p_g = \begin{cases} r/n & \text{if } \hat{p} < r/n \\ \hat{p} & \text{otherwise} \end{cases}
\tag{2}
$$

The rough meaning of $Prob(n, r|H_1)$ is the probability that the process is working under the condition that the success probability is lower than $\epsilon\hat{p}$. The smaller ϵ is, the smaller the number of detections becomes. Fig. 1 shows an example of $Prob(n, r|H_1)$ and $Prob(n, r|H_0)$.

By the above definitions, we can apply SPRT to our problem and make an efficient decision when new observed data is obtained.

4 Empirical Results with Real Traffic Data

In this section, experiments were conducted with the traffic data of international telephone and ISDN calls handled by KDD company. The data acquisition of real traffic was obtained by on-line monitors equipped with gateways, and carried out in two periods in 1994. The length of each period was 5 weeks long. The first period was from Jan. 23 to Feb. 26, and the second one was from Mar. 27 to Apr. 30. One national holiday is included in each period. In the experiments

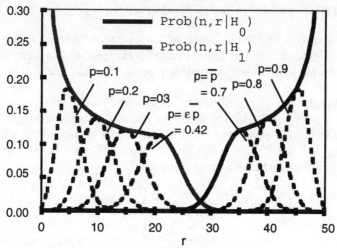

Fig. 1. The X-axis shows the number of success occurrences r, and the Y-axis shows the $Prob(n, r|H_1)$ and $Prob(n, r|H_0)$ when $n = 50, \hat{p} = 0.7, \epsilon = 0.6$. Probabilities for Bernoulli trials with a success probability $p = \hat{p}, \epsilon\hat{p}, 0.1, 0.2, \cdots$ are also indicated

in this paper, the first period is used for training data, and the second is used for test data. The time interval of data acquisition is 5 minutes. Thus the time series of each target foreign networks has 9,792 samples for the training and for the test, when the data of a national holiday is excluded. The number of target foreign networks was 1,516 in each periods.

Partition models may be generated by an exhaustive enumeration. But such a blind procedure often causes a computational explosion and makes infeasible *partition models*. Fig. 2 show the one of typical traffic behaviors in every day of the week. In this example, the behavior of the week-day is much different from that of week-end, and Monday is slightly different from other week-days. Domain experts knows such phenomena well, and prepared feasible *partition models*. Every segment in the prepared models starts at the beginning of a day and finishes at the end of a day. The number of prepared *partition models* (showed latter) becomes 11 when national holidays are not taken into account.

Execution of the optimization of *partition model*, incremental model update, and the degradation detection by SPRT is sufficiently fast in the following experiments, and the proposed method is able to satisfy real-time requirements.

4.1 Evaluation of Optimization of Partition Model

At first, all *partition models* for all target networks are generated from the training data. Then every model is applied to the test data, and log-likelihood of each model is measured for evaluating the fitness of the model. In this test, models are fixed and not updated.

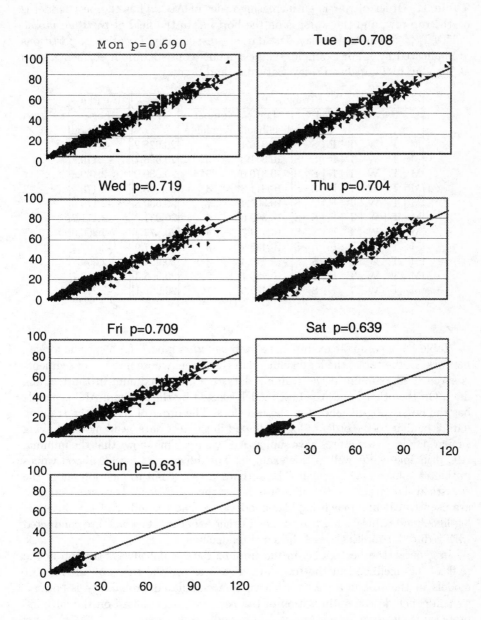

Fig. 2. These are the scatter graphs of observed time series in every day of the week. The X-axis shows the number of attempted calls, and Y-axis shows the number of calls connected sucessfully. Regression line and its gradient value are indicated.

Table 1. Order of row is an increasing order of AIC. Thus the best model is on the top row, and the worst is on the bottom. In the field of *partition model*, "M", "T", ⋯ denote Monday, Tuesday, ⋯ respectively. Location of partitions are indicated by |. For example, the best model consists of four segments, such as Monday to Thursday, Friday, Saturday, and Sunday

Training Phase								Log-likelihood	Number of segments	AIC	Test Phase Log-likelihood
M	T	W	T	F	S	S		-10,310.1	4	20,628.2	-2,169.7
M	T	W	T	F	S	S		-10,311.3	3	20,628.7	-2,170.8
M	T	W	T	F	S	S		-10,310.0	5	20,630.0	-2,169.8
M	T	W	T	F	S	S		-10,311.3	4	20,630.5	-2,170.9
M	T	W	T	F	S	S		-10,308.4	7	20,630.8	-2,170.6
M	T	W	T	F	S	S		-10,309.6	6	20,631.3	-2,171.7
M	T	W	T	F	S	S		-10,434.7	4	20,877.4	-2,206.8
M	T	W	T	F	S	S		-10,435.9	3	20,877.9	-2,207.9
M	T	W	T	F	S	S		-10,449.4	3	20,904.8	-2,209.7
M	T	W	T	F	S	S		-10,450.7	2	20,905.4	-2,210.7
M	T	W	T	F	S	S		-10,479.5	1	20,961.1	-2,217.9

Table 1 is a complete example of eleven *partition models* for a specific foreign network. In the table, the log-likelihood of the model whose number of segments is seven, is maximum in the training data, but not maximum in the training data. On the other hand, the best model selected by the minimal AIC principle has the largest log-likelihood in the test data. The order of AIC in the training data is similar to the order of log-likelihood in the test data. And models having similar partition structures have similar AIC values. This shows that the minimal AIC principle works well in this example. The diffrence of log-likelihood values in the test phase may be small. The authors are sorry not to mention about the statistical significance of the difference in the theory. But 9792 observed samples are used to calculate each log-likelihood value. The reliability of the obtained log-likelihood values is high. And more, other experiments which are conducted with reduced samples showed the same tendency.

In general, the best model in the training data is not always the top in the rank of log-likelihood in the test data. Fig. 3 shows the ranks of all the best models in the test data. As the curve of accumulated probability is convex, we can conclude the optimization of the *partition model* based on the authors' proposal is effective for a given pseudo-periodic time series.

4.2 Evaluation of Incremental Model Update

In this section, two methods are compared. The first method retains the same model selected in the training. The second one re-selects the best *partition model* and updates its parameters at the beginning of the day. Initial models generated from the training data are the same in both two methods.

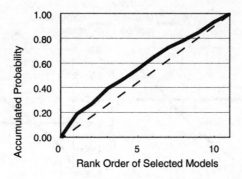

Fig. 3. X-axis shows the rank of selected models in the log-likelihood of the test data. Y-axis shows accumulation of probability

Table 2. Sum of log-likelihood for all foreign networks in the test data is described.

Type of method	Sum of log-likelihood
Fixed model	-7,857,152.0
Model updated incrementally	-7,852,232.9

Table 2 shows the result when two methods are applied to the test data. The log-likelihood of the incremental method is larger than that of the method using fixed models. As sufficient number of samples are used, the method proposed for the incremental model update is believed to be effective in practice.

4.3   Utility Comparison with a Conventional Method

In the conventional method used here, the *rate of established calls* is compared to the threshold at each observation. The threshold is basically decided by the distribution of the observed rate, which is assumed to be a Gaussian distribution, and fine tuning of the threshold is carried out by network operators continuously.

The comparison between the conventional method and the proposed one is made in the following two measures: One measure is the number of detections. It can be controlled by a sensitivity parameter ϵ in the proposed method, but fixed in the conventional one. The other measure is *Total Loss of Chance*. Let T be a set of time when degradation is detected, and $\bar{p}_t, n_t, r_t$ be an expected success probability at time t, and the number of trials and success occurrences respectively. *Total Loss of Chance* is defined as below.

$$\text{Total Loss of Chance} = \sum_{t \in T} \{n_t \bar{p}_t - r_t\}$$

Total Loss of Chance is also controllable by ϵ in the proposed method, but fixed in the conventional one.

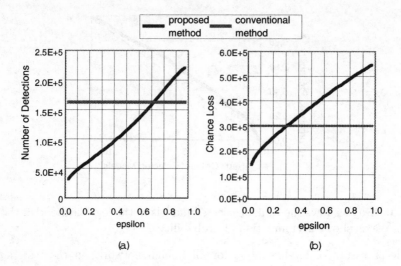

Fig. 4. (a) Relation between a sensitivity control parameter ϵ and the number of degradation detections, (b) Relation between a sensitivity control parameter ϵ and *Total Loss of Chance*

Fig. 4 shows the results of the two measures in the test data. In Fig. 4 (a), ϵ is 0.72 when the number of detections of each method is the same. In Fig. 4 (b), when ϵ is 0.72, *Total Loss of Chance* of the proposed method is about 4.6×10^5, which is 1.6×10^5 larger than that of the conventional one. These results show the proposed method can make more precise decision than the conventional method.

5   Related Works

Takanami and Kitagawa [6] shows an application which generates proper models called *locally stationary AR models* based on the minimal AIC principle from a non-stationary time series. The proposed method also uses the same principle, but is extended to a pseudo-periodic time-series. In our method, not only adjacent samples but also samples whose interval is *pseudo-periodic* are in the same stochastic model.

A long sequences of successive normal states are often observed in high quality networks. Such sequences are harmful for SPRT in the sense that the accumulation of LLR becomes too large. In order to solve this problem, Chien and Adams[5] propose that LLR be reset to zero when the accumulation reaches either of the limits. Uosaki[7] proposes another solution, a backward evaluation of LLR continuing backward until a decision is obtained. We adopted Chien's method because Uosaki's method requires much memory to keep the most recent log of LLR.

6   Conclusion

In this paper, the degradation detection problem for the rate of established calls on the gateway is dealt with. The time series to be monitored is non-stationary but almost periodic (*pseudo-periodic*). Methods for resolving this problem reqiure the continuous handling of pseudo-periodic time series and updating model parameters. To solve these requirements, the authors propose the following:

1. Binomial models using the number of sucessfully connected calls and attempted calls instead of the *rate of established calls.*
2. Applying the technique generating *local stationary* models to this problem. The technique generates candidates for division by time series, and selects the best division among candidates for division based on the minimal AIC principle.
3. Extending the above technique for a *pseudo-periodic* time series, in which non-adjacent *local stationary* segments, whose distance is a *pseudo-period*, are regarded as the same stochastic process.
4. Applying a technique called Sequential Probability Ratio Test (SPRT) to this problem in order to perform efficient degradation detection.

In section **2**, we showed the optimization of a *partition model* for this problem based on the above proposals 1,2,3. The optimization and updating of model parameters can be executed efficiently from the equations derived finally in the section.

In section **3**, we showed how to apply the technique called SPRT. This technique requires the two probabilities that the process is degraded or normal. Equations to calculate these probabilities are described.

Evaluation of the proposed method for real data is described in section **4**. A complete example of *partition models* is shown. In this example, the selected model based on the minimal AIC principle is also the best model in the test data. And the ranks of selected models in the test data are investigated. The result shows the proposed method for optimization is effective. The incremental model update is also tested. As the log-likelihood of incremental models is better than that of fixed models, the effectiveness is proven. Finally we compare the proposed method with a conventional method by two measures, the number of detections and *Total Loss of Chance*. The result shows the proposed method makes more precise decisions than the conventional one.

As the proposed method is proven to be more useful than the conventional one, the proposed method is scheduled to be used in systems at KDD this autumn, which monitor telephone and ISDN services.

References

1. ITU: Telephone Network and ISDN - Operation, Numbering, Routing and Mobile Service -. Rec. E.401-E.427, BLUE BOOK, Volume II, FascicleII.3, 1989.
2. Wald, A.: Sequential Analysis, Wiley, New York, 1947.

3. Gertler, J.: Survey of Model-Based Failure Detection and Isolation in Complex Plants. IEEE Control Systems Magazine, Dec. (1988) 3-11
4. Akaike, H.: A New Look at Statistical Model Identification. IEEE Transactions on Automatic Control, **19** (1974) 716-723
5. Chien, T. and M.B. Adams: A Sequential Failure Detection Technique and Its Application. IEEE Transactions on Automatic Control, Vol. **AC-21** (1976) 750-757
6. Takanami, T. and G. Kitagawa: A new efficient procedure for the estimation of onset times of seismic waves. Journal of Physics of the Earth, Vol.36, (1988) 267-290.
7. Uosaki, K.: Failure Detection Using Backward SPRT. Proceedings of IFAC Symposium on Identifications and System Parameter Estimation, York, UK, (1985) 1619-1624

Section II:

Visualization

Monitoring Human Information Processing via Intelligent Data Analysis
of EEG Recordings..137
    A. Flexer and H. Bauer

Knowledge-Based Visualization to Support Spatial Data Mining...........149
    G. Andrienko and N. Andrienko

Probabilistic Topic Maps: Navigating through Large Text Collections......161
    Th. Hofmann

3D Grand Tour for Multidimensional Data and Clusters....................173
    L. Yang

Monitoring Human Information Processing via Intelligent Data Analysis of EEG Recordings

Arthur Flexer[1] and Herbert Bauer[2]

[1] The Austrian Research Institute for Artificial Intelligence
Schottengasse 3, A-1010 Vienna, Austria
arthur@ai.univie.ac.at
[2] Department of Psychology, University of Vienna
Liebiggasse 5, A-1010 Vienna, Austria

Abstract. Human information processing can be monitored by analysing cognitive evoked potentials (EP) measurable in the electro encephalogram (EEG) during cognitive activities. In technical terms, both visualization of high dimensional sequential data and unsupervised discovery of patterns within this multivariate set of real valued time series is needed. Our approach towards visualization is to discretize the sequences via vector quantization and to perform a Sammon mapping of the codebook. Instead of having to conduct a time-consuming search for common subsequences in the set of multivariate sequential data, a multiple sequence alignment procedure can be applied to the set of one-dimensional discrete time series. The methods are described in detail and results obtained for spatial and verbal information processing are shown to be statistically valid, to yield an improvement in terms of noise attenuation and to be well in line with psychophysiological literature.

1 Introduction

Psychophysiological studies use the method of cognitive evoked potentials measurable in the encephalogram (EEG) during cognitive activities to monitor physiological correlates of human information processing. EEG is a non-invasive method to record electric brain potentials from the human scalp via a set of electrodes. We speak of cognitive evoked potentials (EPs) when the EEG is recorded from a test subject who is solving a cognitive task during recording. An EP is defined as the combination of the brain electric activity that occurs in association with the eliciting event and 'noise', which is brain activity not related to the event together with inference from non-neural sources. Since the noise contained in EPs is significantly stronger than the signal, the common approach is to compute an average across several EPs recorded under equal conditions to improve the signal-to-noise ratio. The average $\hat{s}(t)$ over the sample of N EPs is used to estimate the underlying signal $s(t)$:

$$\hat{s}(t) = \frac{1}{N} \sum_{i=1}^{N} x_i(t) = s(t) + \frac{1}{N} \sum_{i=1}^{N} n_i(t); \quad i = 1, 2, \ldots N; \quad 0 \le t < T \quad (1)$$

D.J. Hand, J.N. Kok, M.R. Berthold (Eds.): IDA'99, LNCS 1642, pp. 137–148, 1999.
© Springer-Verlag Berlin Heidelberg 1999

where $x_i(t)$ is the ith recorded EP, $s(t)$ the underlying signal, $n_i(t)$ the noise associated with the ith EP, and T the duration over which each EP is recorded. The crucial assumption behind averaging is that the evoked signal $s(t)$ is the same for each recorded EP $x_i(t)$. Whereas this is true for simpler sensoric or motoric events, cognitive activities do not elicit one specific EP waveform time locked to the onset of the recording. Only subsequences of the whole EPs that do not occur at fixed time after the onset of the recording can be expected to be due to the cognitive task.

Our approach towards the analysis of cognitive evoked potentials (EP) combines several intelligent data analysis methods (see Fig. 1) to tackle these problems. Since each EP is measured via a number of electrodes it is a multidimensional time series. After appropriate filtering, we visualize this high dimensional sequential set of data by replacing the sequence of the original vectors by a sequence of prototypical codebook vectors obtained from a clustering procedure. Additionally, a dimensionality reduction technique is applied to obtain an ordered one-dimensional representation of the high dimensional codebook vectors that allows for the depiction of the original sequence as a one-dimensional time series. Searching for common subsequences in the vast set of real valued multivariate sequential data is computationally prohibitive. Instead we can use the set of univariate discrete time series, the trajectories across codebook vectors, and apply a multiple sequence alignment procedure for comparison of sequences. Finally, we are able to compute an alternative selective average across the obtained subsequences.

Especially the analysis of the temporal structure of cognitive EPs is a largely unsolved problem in psychophysiology. Classical methods like [15,10,9] and [14] are designed for univariate time series of simpler motoric or sensoric EPs only. They usually assume that the recorded univariate signal is the same for all EPs during the whole duration of the recording but allow variable latencies of the common waveform. Therefore they cannot really cope with the harder problem of analysing cognitive EPs. Existing data mining approaches to processing of sequential patterns are not applicable to our problem for the following reasons: Template based approaches require a query pattern or frequent episode [8] to be defined before the search is started which is not possible for cognitive EPs since only very vague knowledge about the subsequences to be discovered exists. Template based approaches are also designed for univariate or symbolic sequences only. The same holds for specialized approaches given e.g. in [6] and [2] which have the additional problem of being hard to link to a model of cognitive EPs.

Our work is structured in the following way: First we describe the EP data sets and then all applied methods (clustering, visualization, sequence comparison) are presented in detail. Statistical significance is ensured via comparison with results obtained for artificial data sets, the gain in noise attenuation relative to common averaging is quantified and the results for spatial and verbal information processing are shown to be well in line with literature. All computer experiments have been done within a rigorous statistical framework using appropriate statistical tests.

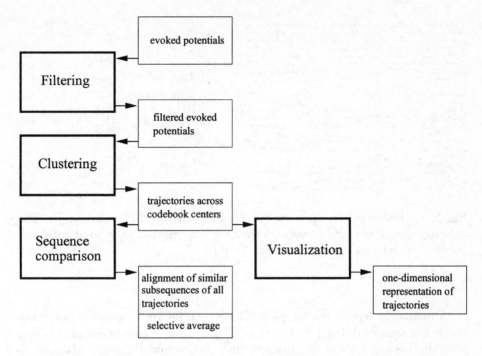

Fig. 1. Flow diagram of the spatio-temporal clustering approach.

2   The Data

The data stems from 10 good and 8 poor female spatializers who were subjected to both a spatial imagination and a verbal task. The complete data base of EP recordings is therefore divided into four groups: 319 EPs spatial/good, 167 EPs spatial/poor, 399 EPs verbal/good, 270 verbal/poor. After appropriate prepro-cessing (essentially limiting the signals to frequencies below $8Hz$ and eliminating the DC-like trend by subtracting a linear fit), each EP trial consists of 2125 sam-ples, each being a 22 dimensional real valued vector. One complete 22-channel EP trial (duration is 8.5 seconds) is depicted in Fig. 2(a). The discretization step described in Sec. 3 will make the analysis of this vast data set computationally tractable.

3   Clustering and Visualization

The EP time series are vector quantized together by using all the EP vectors at all the sample points as input vectors to a clustering algorithm disregarding their ordering in time. Then the sequence of the original vectors x is replaced by the sequence of the prototypical codebook vectors $\hat{x}$. There is a double benefit of this step: it is part of the visualization scheme and the sequences of $\hat{x}$ serve as input to the sequence comparison procedure.

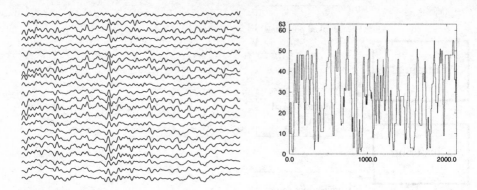

Fig. 2. (a) Example of a complete 8.5 second 22-channel EP recording. (b) The corresponding trajectory across codebook vectors depicted as ordered codebook numbers (y-axis) as a function of time (x-axis).

K-means clustering (see e.g. [3, p.201]) is used for vector quantization using the sum of squared differences $d(x, \hat{x}) = \sum_{i=0}^{k-1} \mid x_i - \hat{x}_i \mid^2$ as measure of distance, where both x and $\hat{x}$ are of dimension k. Since observation of the sum of distances $d(x, \hat{x})$ with growing size of codebooks did not indicate an optimal codebook size, we pragmatically decided to use 64 codebook vectors which is sufficient to preserve all important features in the sequence of codebook vectors. "Important" features are positive and negative topographical peaks and their development in time. The high number of different discrete symbols (64 codebook vectors) did not allow for a more principled information theoretic approach to obtain an optimal codebook size. Instead of a set of 22-dimensional time series, we now have sequences of discrete symbols, where each symbol is drawn from the alphabet of the 64 codebook vectors $\hat{x}$. For the 64 codebook vectors, we calculated a 64×64 distance matrix D_C.

The sequences of codebook vectors can be visualized in a graph where the x-axis stands for time and the y-axis for the number of the codebook vector. Since in the course of time, the trajectory moves only between codebook vectors that are close to each other in the 22 dimensional vector space, this neighbourhood should also be reflected by an appropriate ordering of the numbers of the codebook vectors. Such an ordered numbering results in smooth curves of the time vs. codebook number graphs and enables visual inspection of similarities between trajectories. We obtain such an ordered numbering by first performing a Sammon mapping [12] of the 22-dimensional codebook vectors to one output dimension and by then renumbering the codebook vectors according to a trivially achieved ordering of their one-dimensional representation. This combined technique of K-means clustering plus Sammon mapping of the codebook is described in [4] and an application to the analysis of EP data in [5]. An example for a trajectory across an ordered set of codebook vectors is given in Fig. 2(b).

Note that the ordering of the numbers of the codebook vectors is needed only for visualization and is not necessary for the subsequent sequence alignment.

4   Sequence Comparison

We chose a so-called *fixed length subsequence* approach for comparison of the sequences made of 64 discrete symbols (corresponding to 64 codebook vectors $\hat{x}$). Given two sequences E and F of length m, all possible overlapping subsequences having a particular window length W from E are compared to all subsequences from F. For each pair of elements the score taken from the distance matrix D_C is recorded and summed up for the comparison of subsequences. The distance between two subsequences of length W from two sequences E and F is therefore:

$$D_{align}(b_e, b_f, W) = \sum_{i=0}^{W-1} d(E_{b_e+i}, F_{b_f+i}) \tag{2}$$

The indices b_e and b_f are the beginning points of the subsequences in the sequences E and F and E_{b_e+i} and F_{b_f+i} are the corresponding codebook vectors. Successive application of this pairwise method allows for the alignment of more than two sequences. Such a *fixed subsequence* approach that is explicitly designed for *multiple sequence alignment* is given by [1]. It computes a multiple alignment by iteratively comparing sequences to the multiple alignment obtained so far, keeping always just the L best subsequences as an intermediate result.

This approach to multiple sequence alignment is called *progressive alignment*. It works by constructing a succession of pairwise alignments. Initially, two sequences are chosen at random and aligned via the *fixed length subsequence* approach described above. The L best pairwise alignments (i.e. pairs of subsequences) with minimum distances D_{align} are now fixed and stored in a heap. Then a third sequence is chosen at random and aligned to all the L pairwise alignments. The L best three-way alignments are now fixed and stored in the heap. This process is iterated until all sequences have been aligned.

When a subsequence is compared to an intermediate "more"-way (let us say p-way) subsequence, the resulting score is computed as the sum of the p pairwise comparisons of the subsequences in the intermediate solution with the new subsequence that is to be aligned. The number of all such crosswise comparisons within the final overall alignment is given by $P = \sum_{i=1}^{p-1} i$. The number of all element-wise comparisons within the final overall alignment is given by WP, and its average per element, the average element-wise within alignment distance, by:

$$\bar{D}_{align} = \frac{1}{WP} \sum_{i=1}^{p-1} \sum_{j=i+1}^{p-1} D_{align}(b_i, b_j, W) \tag{3}$$

Desired is a set of beginning points b_i^{min} for which $\bar{D}_{align}$ is minimal. The b_i^{min} are the same for all $d = 22$ channels of the corresponding ith EP. To diminish the variability of the results of this stochastic algorithm (random usage of sequences during iteration), we compute five such alignments and obtain an overall alignment and overall beginning points b_i^{min5} at the points in time where the sums of the five $\bar{D}_{align}$ are minimal. The number of single element-wise comparisons to obtain one alignment is $LW(m+1-W)P$. For a given L and m, this function is proportional to p^2, in contrast with m^p comparisons in "brute force" searching where not just the L best but all possible alignments are considered. As experiments with L equal 100, 1000 and 10000 showed, it is sufficient to keep 100 intermediate results to avoid the omission of good alignments that are weak in the first few sequences but strong in the later ones. Experiments varying the window length W from 31 to 62, 125 and 187 showed that $W = 125$ (corresponding to $500ms$ of EP) is short enough to yield alignments of satisfactory quality which are still long enough to be significant in terms of their psychophysiological interpretation. For more detail on tuning of the parameters L and W see [5].

For each channel of EP we can compute an alternative selective average $\hat{s}'(t)$ where the duration T is equal to the length of the subsequences, W, and the beginning points of the averaging are the parameters b_i^{min5}:

$$\hat{s}'(t) = \frac{1}{N} \sum_{i=1}^{N} x_i(b_i^{min5} + t); \quad 0 \le t < W \tag{4}$$

5 Results

In a related study [5] working on a subset of our EP data we have shown the statistical significance of our approach. We verified that our procedure yields better results for real human EPs than for unstructured random input in terms of average element-wise within alignment distance $\bar{D}_{align}$ (see Equ. 3). We compared results obtained from 21 EPs of one test subject with time-shuffled EPs and artificial EPs. The latter consisted of random Gaussian sequences whose power spectrum was changed appropriately to resemble the characteristics of real EPs. A one-way analysis of variance plus additional Duncan t-Tests allowed us to rank the result for real EP as being significantly better than the result for time-shuffled EP, which is again significantly better than the result for random Gaussian EP.

To compare the gain in noise attenuation of the common average and of our selective average, the respective estimated standard deviations of the background noise, $\hat{\sigma}(t)$ and $\hat{\sigma}'(t)$, are being compared.

$$\hat{\sigma}(t) = \left[\frac{\sum_{i=1}^{N} [x_i(t) - \hat{s}(t)]^2}{N-1} \right]^{\frac{1}{2}} \tag{5}$$

$$\hat{\sigma}'(t) = \left[\frac{\sum_{i=1}^{N} \left[x_i(b_i^{min5} + t) - \hat{s}'(t)\right]^2}{N-1} \right]^{\frac{1}{2}} \tag{6}$$

Since the $\hat{\sigma}(t)$ and $\hat{\sigma}'(t)$ are given for each of the $d = 22$ channels and for the duration of $t = m$ or $t = W$ respectively, the following average estimates of the standard deviations of the background noise are being computed:

$$\hat{S} = \frac{1}{dm} \sum_{j=1}^{d} \sum_{t=0}^{m-1} \hat{\sigma}_j(t) \qquad (7)$$

$$\hat{S}' = \frac{1}{dW} \sum_{j=1}^{d} \sum_{t=0}^{W-1} \hat{\sigma}'_j(t) \qquad (8)$$

$\hat{S}$ is the estimate for common averaging and $\hat{S}'$ for selective averaging. An $\hat{\sigma}_j(t)$ is the $\hat{\sigma}(t)$ for channel j given by Equ. 5. An $\hat{\sigma}'_j(t)$ is the $\hat{\sigma}'(t)$ for channel j given by Equ. 6. For all EPs of good and poor spatializers doing the spatial imagination task the common average $\hat{s}$ as well as five selective averages $\hat{s}'$ have been computed. Results for good spatializers were $\hat{S} = 7.68$ vs. mean $\hat{s}' = 4.35 \pm .068$ and for poor spatializers $\hat{S} = 7.84$ vs. mean $\hat{s}' = 4.37 \pm .048$. Computing Z-values shows the differences in noise attenuation to be significant:

$$Z_{good} = |(4.35 - 7.68)/(.068/\sqrt{5})| = |-109.5| > Z_{99} = 2.58;$$

$$Z_{poor} = |(4.37 - 7.84)/(.048/\sqrt{5})| = |-161.6| > Z_{99} = 2.58.$$

The estimated expected magnitude of the noise residual is now only ≈ 0.56 times that of the respective common averages. This is a gain in noise attenuation of more than 40%.

The results of computing selective averages via beginning points b_i^{min5} for both good and poor spatializers doing the spatial imagination task are given in Fig. 3 as sequences of topographical patterns. Each topography is a spherical spline interpolation of the 22 values at a single point in time of the selective averaging window. Given are topographies at $40, 80, \cdots, 440, 480 msec$ of the window for poor spatializers (top two rows) and good spatializers (lower two rows). We can see that for both groups there is one specific dominant topographical pattern visible, albeit at changing levels of amplitude. It is a pattern of more positive amplitudes at frontal to central regions relative to more negative amplitudes at occipital to parietal regions. This common topographical pattern is generally more negative for poor spatializers.

Our results obtained via the method of selective averaging have also been analysed by a series of analyses of variance (ANOVA). In accordance with the procedure of analysis of classical averages, selective averages of EPs are computed separately for each test subject and serve as inputs to the ANOVAs. A selective average $\hat{s}'(t)$ is computed separately for a test subject by averaging across all corresponding EPs, where the starting points of the averaging are the parameters b_i^{min5} and the duration is equal to the length of the subsequences, W.

Besides factors "Task" (spatial vs. verbal), "Performance" (good vs. poor) and "Location" (electrode position) we decided to include another factor "Time"

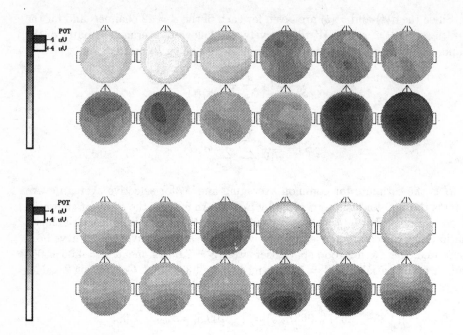

Fig. 3. Sequences of topographies for poor spatializers (top two rows) and good spatializers (lower two rows). Scale is from -4 to $+4mV$.

into our analyses. This factor is needed to describe the variation of the amplitude level of the selective averages within the course of time. Six evenly spaced points in time within the selective averaging window suffice to allow for a proper analysis of this temporal variation.

The first analysis of variance was computed to test for significance of the general differences between spatially and verbally evoked subsequences of topographies. The results of this Task (two repeated measures: spatial vs. verbal) × Time (6 repeated measures: amplitudes of the EPs at $0, 100, 200, 300, 400, 500ms$ in the selective averaging window) × Location (22 repeated measures: electrode positions) ANOVA are given in Tab. 5. The sample size is $N = 16$, since only 8 persons have been subjected to both the spatial and the verbal condition. On the chosen significance level of $\alpha = 5\%$ all three main effects as well as all two-way combined effects, except the Task × Location effect, and the three-way combined effect are highly significant. All corresponding values of the probability of the null hypothesis being true are very small, $P \leq 0.001$ most of the time, which is still true for the Greenhouse-Geisser (given in column ϵ_{GG}) adjusted probabilities $p_{adj.}$. The significant difference between spatial and verbal task in terms of their cortical activity distribution is of course well in line with psychophysiological literature. The more negative amplitudes at occipital to parietal regions

Table 1. ANOVA for spatial versus verbal task.

N=16 (8 spatial, 8 verbal)	Summary of all effects; Design: 1-TASK, 2-TIME, 3-LOCATION							
Effect	df Effect	df Error	ϵ_{GG}	$df_{adj.}$ Effect	$df_{adj.}$ Error	F	p-level	$p_{adj.}$
1	1	15	1.000	1.000	15.000	33.853	.000	.000
2	5	75	.497	2.485	37.280	6.425	.000	.002
3	21	315	.100	2.109	31.639	8.949	.000	.001
1 × 2	5	75	.539	2.695	40.432	7.360	.000	.001
1 × 3	21	315	.115	2.418	36.276	1.551	.060	.223
2 × 3	105	1575	.031	3.246	48.684	13.917	.000	.000
1 × 2 × 3	105	1575	.047	4.967	74.510	13.777	.000	.000

visible in Fig. 3 are as expected and we get the additional information that both kinds of information processing are accompanied by a series of activations and in-activations.

Table 2. ANOVA for spatial task, good versus poor performers.

N=18 (10 good, 8 poor)	Summary of all effects; Design: 1-PERFORMANCE, 2-TIME, 3-LOCATION							
Effect	df Effect	df Error	ϵ_{GG}	$df_{adj.}$ Effect	$df_{adj.}$ Error	F	p-level	$p_{adj.}$
1	1	16				7.999	.012	
2	5	80	.502	2.510	40.164	8.369	.000	.000
3	21	336	.131	2.758	44.122	7.187	.000	.001
1 × 2	5	80	.502	2.510	40.164	6.432	.000	.002
1 × 3	21	336	.131	2.758	44.122	3.962	.000	.017
2 × 3	105	1680	.076	8.015	128.238	10.002	.000	.000
1 × 2 × 3	105	1680	.076	8.015	128.238	18.537	.000	.000

Taking this difference into account, data of good vs. poor spatial performers were analysed separately within task "spatial" and task "verbal". The results of these Performance (good vs. poor) × Time (6 repeated measures: amplitudes of the EPs at $0, 100, 200, 300, 400, 500 ms$ in the selective averaging window) × Location (22 repeated measures: electrode positions) ANOVAs are given in Tab. 5 for spatial data and in Tab. 5 for verbal data. The sample size for the spatial data is $N = 18$, consisting of 10 good and 8 poor spatial performers. On the chosen significance level of $\alpha = 5\%$ all main and combined effects are significant, both before and after the Greenhouse-Geisser adjustment. For the verbal data, on the significance level of $\alpha = 5\%$ the main effect for the factor "Performance" is not significant, whereas most of the combined effects still are. Since the two performance levels "good" and "poor" represent extreme groups of spatial ability selected by psychological testing, they should be discriminable in their EP correlates during the spatial but not during the verbal task. This is exactly what we have found and others [13] have also reported and attributed to a higher investment of cortical effort visible as a more negative amplitude level of one similar pattern.

Table 3. ANOVA for verbal task, good versus poor performers.

N=16 (8 good, 8 poor)	Summary of all effects; Design: 1-PERFORMANCE, 2-TIME, 3-LOCATION							
Effect	df Effect	df Error	ϵ_{GG}	df_{adj} Effect	df_{adj} Error	F	p-level	p_{adj}
1	1	14				0.440	.518	
2	5	70	.469	2.345	32.832	19.873	.000	.001
3	21	294	.215	4.520	63.276	105.623	.000	.000
1 × 2	5	70	.469	2.345	32.832	2.916	.316	.318
1 × 3	21	294	.215	4.520	63.276	11.949	.000	.000
2 × 3	105	1470	.072	7.611	106.559	16.102	.000	.000
1 × 2 × 3	105	1470	.072	7.611	106.559	4.045	.000	.001

6   Discussion

The analysis of cognitive evoked potentials is a largely unsolved problem in psychophysiological research. Classical methods are designed for univariate time series of simpler motoric or sensoric EPs only and can therefore not really cope with the harder problem of analysing cognitive EPs. Nevertheless they are still state of the art.

We have developed a general approach to the visualization of high dimensional sequential data and the unsupervised discovery of patterns within multivariate sets of time series data by combining several intelligent data analysis techniques in a novel way. Our method allows the analysis of cognitive evoked potentials by finding common multivariate subsequences in a set of EPs which have fixed length but variable latencies and are sufficiently similar across all EP channels. With this new kind of selective averaging it is possible to better analyse the temporal structure of the cognitive processes under investigation.

We were able to validate our approach both on a statistical basis and in terms of the psychophysiological content of the obtained results: we demonstrated statistical significance by comparison with results obtained for artificial data and by quantifying the gain in noise attenuation; we showed the plausibility of our results by comparing them to what is already known about the psychophysiology of the human brain.

Our general approach to the visualization of high dimensional sequential data and the unsupervised discovery of patterns within multivariate sets of time series data is of course not restricted to the problem presented in this work. The methods described can either be applied to multivariate real valued data by using the full approach including the transformation to sequences of discrete symbols through vector quantization plus Sammon mapping or, if already symbolic sequences are available, the fixed segment algorithm alone can be applied. Our approach is also open to using more advanced techniques of sequence comparison, like e.g. Hidden Markov Models [11].

Acknowledgements: The EEG recordings have been made by R. Gstättner, Dept. of Psychology, University of Vienna. Parts of this work were done within the BIOMED-2 BMH4-CT97-2040 project SIESTA, funded by the EC DG XII. The Austrian Research Institute for Artificial Intelligence is supported by the Austrian Federal Ministry of Science and Transport. The author was supported by a doctoral grant of the Austrian Academy of Sciences.

References

1. Bacon D.J., Anderson W.F.: Multiple Sequence Alignment, Journal of Molecular Biology, 191, 153-161, 1986.
2. Boyd S.: Detecting and Describing Patterns in Time-Varying Data Using Wavelets, in [7].
3. Duda R.O., Hart P.E.: Pattern Classification and Scene Analysis, John Wiley & Sons, N.Y., 1973.
4. Flexer A.: Limitations of Self-Organizing Maps for Vector Quantization and Multidimensional Scaling, in Mozer M.C., et al.(eds.), Advances in Neural Information Processing Systems 9, MIT Press/Bradford Books, pp.445-451, 1997.
5. Flexer A., Bauer H.: Discovery of Common Subsequences in Cognitive Evoked Potentials, in Zytkow J.M. & Quafafou M.(eds.), Principles of Data Mining and Knowledge Discovery, Second European Symposium, PKDD '98, Proceedings, Lecture Notes in Artificial Intelligence 1510, p.309-317, Springer, 1998.
6. Howe A.E., Somlo G.: Modeling Discrete Event Sequences as State Transition Diagrams, in [7].
7. Liu X., Cohen P., Berthold M.(eds.): Advances in Intelligent Data Analysis, Second International Symposium, IDA-97, Lecture Notes in Computer Science, Springer Verlag, LNCS Vol. 1280, 1997.
8. Mannila H., Toivonen H., Verkamo A.I.: Discovery of Frequent Episodes in Event Sequences, Data Mining and Knowledge Discovery, Volume 1, Issue 3, 1997.
9. McGillem C.D., Aunon J.I.: Measurements of signal components in single visually evoked brain potentials, IEEE Transactions on Biomedical Engineering, 24, 232-241, 1977.
10. Pfurtscheller G., Cooper R.: Selective averaging of the intracerebral click evoked responses in man: an improved method of measuring latencies and amplitudes, Electroencephalography and Clinical Neurophysiology, 38: 187-190, 1975.

11. Rabiner L.R., Juang B.H.: An Introduction To Hidden Markov Models, IEEE ASSP Magazine, 3(1):4-16, 1986.
12. Sammon J.W.: A Nonlinear Mapping for Data Structure Analysis, IEEE Transactions on Comp., Vol. C-18, No. 5, p.401-409, 1969.
13. Vitouch O., Bauer H., Gittler G., Leodolter M., Leodolter U.: Cortical activity of good and poor spatial test performers during spatial and verbal processing studied with Slow Potential Topography, International Journal of Psychophysiology, Volume 27, Issue 3, p.183-199, 1997.
14. Weerd J.P.C.de, Kap J.I.: A Posteriori Time-Varying Filtering of Averaged Evoked Potentials, Biological Cybernetics, 41, 223-234, 1981.
15. Woody C.D.: Characterization of an adaptive filter for the analysis of variable latency neuroelectric signals, Medical and Biological Engineering, 5, 539-553, 1967.

Knowledge-Based Visualization to Support Spatial Data Mining

Gennady Andrienko and Natalia Andrienko

GMD - German National Research Center for Information Technology
Schloss Birlinghoven, Sankt-Augustin, D-53754 Germany
gennady.andrienko@gmd.de
http://allanon.gmd.de/and/

Abstract. Data mining methods are designed for revealing significant relationships and regularities in data collections. Regarding spatially referenced data, analysis by means of data mining can be aptly complemented by visual exploration of the data presented on maps as well as by cartographic visualization of results of data mining procedures. We propose an integrated environment for exploratory analysis of spatial data that equips an analyst with a variety of data mining tools and provides the service of automated mapping of source data and data mining results. The environment is built on the basis of two existing systems, Kepler for data mining and Descartes for automated knowledge-based visualization. It is important that the open architecture of Kepler allows to incorporate new data mining tools, and the knowledge-based architecture of Descartes allows to automatically select appropriate presentation methods according to characteristics of data mining results. The paper presents example scenarios of data analysis and describes the architecture of the integrated system.

1 Introduction

The notion of Knowledge Discovery in Databases (KDD) denotes the task of revealing significant relationships and regularities in data based on the use of algorithms collectively entitled "data mining". The KDD process is an iterative fulfillment of the following steps [6]:

1. Data selection and preprocessing, such as checking for errors, removing outliers, handling missing values, and transformation of formats.
2. Data transformations, for example, discretization of variables or production of derived variables.
3. Selection of a data mining method and adjustment of its parameters.
4. Data mining, i.e. application of the selected method.
5. Interpretation and evaluation of the results.

In this process the phase of data mining takes no more than 20 % of the total workload. However, this phase is much better supported methodologically

D.J. Hand, J.N. Kok, M.R. Berthold (Eds.): IDA'99, LNCS 1642, pp. 149–160, 1999.

and by software than all others [7]. This is not surprising because performing of these other steps is a matter of art rather than a routine allowing automation [8]. Lately some efforts in the KDD field have been directed towards intelligent support to the data mining process, in particular, assistance in the selection of an analysis method depending on data characteristics [2,4].

A particular case of KDD is knowledge extraction from spatially referenced data, i.e. data referring to geographic objects or locations or parts of a territory division. In analysis of such data it is very important to account for the spatial component (relative positions, adjacency, distances, directions etc.). However, information about spatial relationships is very difficult to represent in discrete, symbolic form required for the data mining methods. Known are works on spatial clustering [5] and use of spatial predicates [9], but a high complexity of data description and large computational expenses are characteristic for them.

2 Integrated Environment for Knowledge Discovery

For the case of analysis of spatially referenced data we propose to integrate traditional data mining instruments with automated cartographic visualization and tools for interactive manipulation of graphical displays. The essence of the idea is that an analyst can view both source data and results of data mining in the form of maps that convey spatial information to a human in a natural way. This offers at least a partial solution to the challenges caused by spatially referenced data: the analyst can easily see spatial relationships and patterns that are inaccessible for a computer, at least on the present stage of development. In addition, on the ground of such integration various KDD steps can be significantly supported.

The most evident use of cartographic visualization is in evaluation and interpretation of data mining results. However, maps can be helpful also in other activities. For example, visual analysis of spatial distributions of different data components can help in selection of representative variables for data mining and, possibly, suggest which derived variables would be useful to produce. On the stage of data preprocessing a map presentation can expose strange values that may be errors in the data or outliers. Discretization, i.e. transformation of a continuous numeric variable into one with a limited number of values by means of classification, can be aptly supported by a dynamic map display showing spatial distribution of the classes. With such a support the analyst can adjust the number of classes and class boundaries so that interpretable spatial patterns arise.

More specifically, we propose to build an integrated KDD environment on the basis of two existing systems, Kepler [11] for data mining and Descartes [1] for interactive visual analysis of spatially referenced data. Kepler includes a number of data mining methods and, what is very important, provides a universal plug-in interface for adding new methods. Besides, the system contains some tools for data and formats transformation, access to databases, querying, and is capable of graphical presentations of some kinds of data mining results (trees, rules, and groups).

Descartes [1] automates generation of maps presenting user-selected data and supports various interactive manipulations of map displays that can help to visually reveal important features of the spatial distribution of data. Descartes also supports some data transformations productive for visual analysis, and has a convenient graphical interface for outlier removal and an easy-to-use tool for generation of derived variables by means of logical queries and arithmetic operations over existing variables. It is essential that both systems are designed to serve the same goal: help to get knowledge about data. They propose different instruments that can complement each other and together produce a synergistic effect.

Currently, Kepler contains data mining methods for classification, clustering, association, rule induction, and subgroup discovery. Most of the methods require selection of a target variable and try to reveal relationships between this variable and other variables selected for the analysis. The target variable most often should be discrete. Descartes can be effectively used for finding "promising" discrete variables including, implicitly or explicitly, a spatial component. The following ways of doing this are available:

1. Classification by segmentation of a value range of a numeric variable into subintervals.
2. Cross-classification of a pair of numeric attributes. In both cases the process of classification is highly interactive and supported by a map presentation of the spatial distribution of the classes that reflects in real time all changes in the definition of classes.
3. Spatial aggregation of objects performed by the user through the map interface. Results of such an aggregation can be represented by a discrete variable. For example, the user can divide city districts into center and periphery or encircle several regions, and the system will generate a variable indicating to which aggregate each object belongs.

Results of most of the data mining methods are naturally presentable on maps. The most evident is the presentation of subgroups or clusters: painting or an icon can designate belonging of a geographical object to a subgroup or a cluster. The same technique can be applied for tree nodes and rules: visual features of an object indicate whether it is included in the class corresponding to a selected tree node, or whether a given rule applies to the object and, if so, whether it is correctly classified.

Since Kepler contains its own facilities for non-geographical presentation of data mining results, it would be productive to make a dynamic link between displays of Kepler and Descartes. This means that, when a cursor is positioned on an icon symbolizing a subgroup, a tree node, or a rule in Kepler, the corresponding objects are highlighted in a map in Descartes. And vice versa, selection of a geographical object in a map results in highlighting the subgroups or tree nodes including this object or marking rules applicable to it.

---

[1] See on-line demos in the Internet at the URL http://allanon.gmd.de/and/java/iris/

The above presented consideration can be summarized in the form of three kinds of links between data mining and cartographic visualization:

- From "geography" to "mathematics": using dynamic maps, the user arrives at some geographically interpretable results or hypotheses and then tries to find an explanation of the results or checks the hypotheses by means of data mining methods.
- From "mathematics" to "geography": data mining methods produce results that are then visually analyzed after being presented on maps.
- Linked displays: graphics representing results of data mining in the usual (non- cartographic) form are viewed in parallel with maps, and dynamic highlighting visually connects corresponding elements in both types of displays.

3   Scenarios of Integration

In this section we consider several examples of data exploration sessions where interactive cartographic visualization and different traditional methods of data mining were productively used together in data exploration.

3.1   Analysis with Classification Trees

In this session the user works with economic and demographic data about European countries [2]. He selects the attribute "National product per capita" and makes a classification of its values that produced interesting semantic and geographic clustering (Fig. 1). Then he asks the system to investigate how the classes are related to values of other attributes. The system starts the C4.5 algorithm and after about 15 seconds of computations produces the classification tree (Fig. 2).

It is important that displays of the map and the tree are linked:

- pointing to a class in the interactive classification window highlights the tree nodes relevant to this class (i.e. where this class dominates other classes);
- pointing to a geographical object on the map results in highlighting of the tree nodes representing groups including the object;
- pointing to a tree node highlights contours of objects on the map that form the group represented by this node (generally, in colors of classes)

3.2   Analysis with Classification Rules

In this session the user works with a database about countries of the world [3]. He selects the attribute "Trade balance" with an ordered set of values: Import much bigger than export, "import bigger than export", "import and export are

---

[2] The data have been taken from CIA World Book
[3] The data originate from ESRI world database

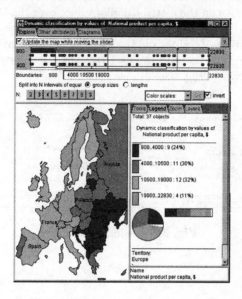

Fig. 1. Interactive classification of values of the target attribute

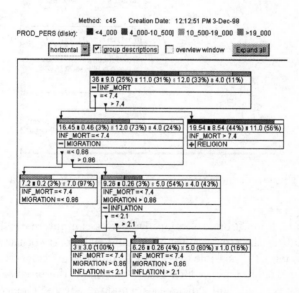

Fig. 2. The classification tree produced by the C4.5 algorithm

approximately equal", "export bigger than import", and "export much bigger than import". He looks on the distribution of values over the World and does not find any regularity. Therefore, he asks the system to produce classification rules explaining distribution of values on the basis of other attributes. After short computation by the C4.5 method the user receives a set of rules. Two examples of the rules are shown in Fig. 3.

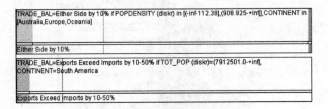

Fig. 3. Classification rules

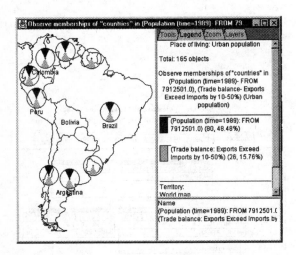

Fig. 4. Visualization of the rule for South America

For each rule, upon user's selection, Descartes can automatically produce a map that visualizes the truth values of left and right parts of the rule for each country. In this map it is possible to see which countries are correctly classified by the rule (both parts are true), which are misclassified (the premise is true while the consequence is false), and which cases remain uncovered (the consequence is true while the premise is false). Thus, in the example map in Fig. 4 (representing the second rule from Fig. 3) darker circle sectors indicate truth of the premise and lighter ones - truth of the concequence. One can see here seven cases of correct classification marked by signs with both sectors present and two cases of non-coverage where the signs have only the lighter sectors.

The user can continue his analysis with interactive manipulation facilities of maps to check the stability of relationships found. Thus, he can try to change boundaries of intervals found by the data mining procedure and see whether the correspondence between conditions in the left and the right parts of the rule will be preserved.

3.3   Selection of Interesting Subgroups

In this session the user wants to analyze the distribution of demographic attributes over continents. He selects a subset of these attributes and ran the SIDOS method to discover interesting subgroups (see some of the results in Fig. 5). For example, the group with "Death rate" less than 9.75 and "Life expectancy for female" greater than 68.64 includes 51 countries (31 % of the World countries), and 40 of them are African countries (78 % of African countries). To support the consideration of this group, Descartes builds a map (Fig. 6). The map shows all countries satisfying the description of the group. On the map the user can see specifically which countries form the group, which of them are in Africa and which are in other continents.

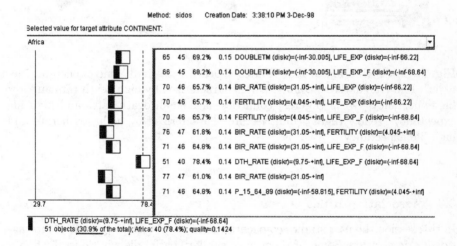

Fig. 5. Descriptions of interesting subgroups

It is necessary to stress once again that Descartes does the map design automatically on the basis of the knowledge base on thematic data mapping. The subgroups found give the user some hints for further analysis: which countries to select for closer look; collection of attributes that best characterizes the continents; groups of attributes with interesting spatial co-distribution. Thus, if the user selects the pair of attributes cited in the definition of the considered group

Fig. 6. Visualization of the subgroup

for further analysis, the system automatically creates a map for dynamic cross-classification on the basis of these attributes. The user may find other interesting threshold value(s) that leads to clear spatial patterns (Fig. 7).

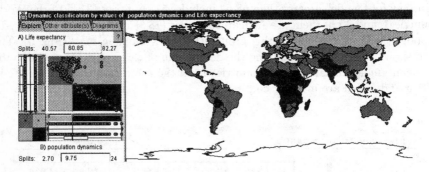

Fig. 7. Co-distribution of 2 attributes: "Death rate" and "Life expectancy, female". Red (the darkest) countries are characterized by high death rate and low life expectancy. Green (lighter) countries have small death rates and high life expectancy. Yellow (light) countries are characterized by high death rate and high life expectancy.

3.4   Association Rules

In this session the user studies co-occurrence of memberships in various international organization. Some of them have similar spatial distributions. To find a numeric estimation of the similarity the user selected "association rules" method. The method produced a set of rules concerning simultaneous membership in different organizations. Thus, it was found that 136 countries are members of UNESCO, and 128 of them (94 %) are also members of IBRD. This rule was supported by visualization of membership on automatically created maps. One of them demonstrates members of UNESCO not participating in IBRD (Fig. 8).

Generally, this method is applicable to binary (logical) variables. It is important that Descartes allows to produce various logical variables as results of data analysis. Thus, they can be produced by: marking table rows as satisfying

Fig. 8. Countries - members of UNESCO and non-members of IBRD

or contradicting some logical or territorial query, classifying numeric variables into two classes, etc. Association rules method is a convenient tool for analysis of such attributes.

3.5 Analysis of Sessions

It is clear that in all the sessions described above interactive visualization and data mining act as complementary instruments for data analysis. Their integration supported the iterative process of data analysis:

Interactive maps	Data mining	Interactive maps
1) Data preview, initial hypotheses; 2) Classification of values of attributes leading to interesting spatial patterns; 3) Definition of regions	1) Relationships among attributes; 2) Characterization of regions; 3) Attribute-based grouping of spatial objects	1) Relate general descriptions to individual instances 2) Instances that support or contradict discovered regularities 3) Spatial distribution of discovered groups

We should stress the importance of knowledge-based map design in all stages of the analysis. The ability of Descartes to automatically select presentation methods makes it possible for the user to concentrate on problem solving.

Generally, for the first prototype we selected only high-speed data mining methods to avoid long waiting time. However, currently there is a strategy in the development of data mining algorithms to create so called any time methods that can provide rough results after short computations and improve them with longer calculations. The open architecture of Kepler allows to add such methods later and to link them with map visualizations of Descartes.

One can note that we applied the system to already aggregated relatively small data sets. However, even with these data the integrated approach shows its advantages. Later we plan to extend the approach to large sets of raw data. The main problem is that maps are typically used for visualization of data aggregated over territories. A solution may be through automated or interactive aggregation of raw data and of results of data mining methods.

4   Software Implementation

The software implementation of the project is supported by the circumstance that both systems have client-server architecture and use socket connections and TCP/IP protocol for the client-server communication. The client components of both systems are realized in the Java language and provide the user interface. To couple the two systems, we implemented an additional link between the two servers. The Descartes server activates the Kepler server, establishes a socket connection, and commands Kepler to load the same application (workspace).

In the current implementation, the link between the two systems can be activated only in one direction: working with Descartes, the user can make Kepler apply some data mining method to selected data. A list of applicable methods is available to the user depending on the context (how many attributes are selected, what are their types, etc.). The selection of appropriate data analysis methods is done on the basis of an extension to the current visualization knowledge base existing in Descartes.

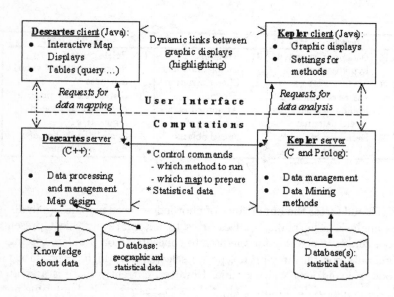

Fig. 9. The architecture of the integrated system

The link to data mining is available both from a table window and from some types of maps. Thus, classification methods (classification trees and rules) as well as subgroup discovery methods are available both from a table containing qualitative attribute(s) and from maps for interactive classification or cross-classification. The association rules method is available from a table with several logical attributes or from a map presenting such attributes.

When the user decides to apply a data mining method, the Descartes client allows him to specify the scope of interest (choose a target variable or value when necessary, select independent attributes, specify method-specific parameters, etc.) and then sends this information to the Descartes server. The server creates a temporary table with selected data and commands the Kepler server to import this table and to start the specified method. After finishing the computations, the Kepler server passes the results to the Kepler client, and this component visualizes the results. At this point a new socket connection between the Descartes client and the Kepler client is established for linking of graphics components. This link provides simultaneous highlighting of active objects on map displays in Descartes and graphic displays in Kepler.

Results of most data mining methods can be presented by maps created in Descartes. For this purpose the Kepler server sends commands to the Descartes server to activate map design, and the Descartes client displays the created maps on the screen.

5 Conclusions

To compare our work with others, we may note that exploratory data analysis has been traditionally supported by visualizations. Some work was done on linking of statistical graphics built in xGobi package with maps displayed in ArcView GIS [3] and on connecting clustering dendrograms with maps [10]. However, all previous works we are aware of utilize only a restricted set of predefined visualizations.

In our work we extend this approach by integrating data mining methods with knowledge-based map design. This allows us to create a general mapping interface for data mining algorithms. This feature together with the open architecture of Kepler gives an opportunity to add new data mining methods without system reengineering.

Acknowledgements

We are grateful to all members of GMD knowledge discovery group for numerous discussions about our work. Dr. H.Voss, D.Schmidt and C.Rinner made useful comments on the early version of the paper. We express our special thanks to Dr. D.Wettschereck (Dialogis GmbH) for the implementation of the link on Kepler's side.

References

1. Andrienko, G., and Andrienko, N.: Intelligent Visualization and Dynamic Manipulation: Two Complementary Instruments to Support Data Exploration with GIS. In: Proceedings of AVI'98: Advanced Visual Interfaces Int. Working Conference (L'Aquila Italy, May 24-27, 1998), ACM Press (1998) 66-75
2. Brodley, C.: Addressing the Selective Superiority Problem: Automatic Algorithm / Model Class Selection. In: Machine Learning: Proceedings of the 10th International Conference, University of Massachusetts, Amherst, June 27-29, 1993. San Mateo, Calif.: Morgan Kaufmann (1993) 17-24
3. Cook, D., Symanzik, J., Majure, J.J., and Cressie, N.: Dynamic Graphics in a GIS: More Examples Using Linked Software. Computers and Geosciences, **23** (1997) 371-385
4. Gama, J. and Brazdil, P.: Characterization of Classification Algorithms. In: Progress in Artificial Intelligence, Lecture Notes in Artificial Intelligence, Vol.990. Springer-Verlag: Berlin (1995) 189-200
5. Gebhardt, F.: Finding Spatial Clusters. In: Principles of Data Mining and Knowledge Discovery PKDD97, Lecture Notes in Computer Science, Vol.1263. Springer-Verlag: Berlin (1997) 277-287
6. Fayyad, U., Piatetsky-Shapiro, G., and Smyth, P.: The KDD Process for Extracting Useful Knowledge from Volumes of Data. Communications of the ACM, **39** (1996), 27-34
7. John, G.H.: Enhancements to the Data Mining Process. PhD dissertation, Stanford University. Available at the URL http://robotics.stanford.edu/~gjohn/ (1997)
8. Kodratoff, Y.: From the art of KDD to the science of KDD. Research report 1096, Universite de Paris-sud (1997)
9. Koperski, K., Han, J., and Stefanovic, N.: An Efficient Two-Step Method for Classification of Spatial Data. In: Proceedings SDH98, Vancouver, Canada: International Geographical Union (1998) 45-54
10. MacDougall, E.B.: Exploratory Analysis, Dynamic Statistical Visualization, and Geographic Information Systems. Cartography and Geographic Information Systems, **19** (1992) 237-246
11. Wrobel, S., Wettschereck, D., Sommer, E., and Emde, W.: Extensibility in Data Mining Systems. In Proceedings of KDD96 2nd International Conference on Knowledge Discovery and Data Mining. AAAI Press (1996) 214-219

Probabilistic Topic Maps: Navigating through Large Text Collections

Thomas Hofmann

Computer Science Division, UC Berkeley &
International CS Institute, Berkeley, CA
hofmann@cs.berkeley.edu

Abstract. The visualization of large text databases and document collections is an important step towards more flexible and interactive types of information retrieval. This paper presents a probabilistic approach which combines a statistical, model–based analysis with a topological visualization principle. Our method can be utilized to derive *topic maps* which represent topical information by characteristic keyword distributions arranged in a two–dimensional spatial layout. Combined with multi-resolution techniques this provides a three-dimensional space for interactive information navigation in large text collections.

1 Introduction

Despite of the great enthusiasm and excitement our time shows for all types of new media, it is indisputable that the most nuanced and sophisticated medium to express or communicate our thoughts is what Herder calls the 'vehiculum of our thoughts and the content of all wisdom and knowledge'[5] – our language. Consequently, prodigious benefits could result from the enhanced circulation and propagation of recorded language by todays digital networks, which make abundant repositories of text documents such as electronic libraries available to a large public. Yet, the availability of large databases does not automatically imply easy access to relevant information, since retrieving information from a glut of nuisance data can be tedious and extremely time consuming.

What is urgently needed are navigation aids, overlooks which offer uncomplicated and fast visual access to information, and maps that provide orientation, possibly on different level of resolution and abstraction. This paper deals with a statistical approach to provide such overlooks and maps for large collections of text documents. It aims at a concise visualization of conceptual and topical similarities between documents or aspects of documents in the form of *topic maps*. The proposed method has two building blocks:

i. A *latent semantic analysis* technique for text collections [3, 6] which models context–dependent word occurrences.
ii. A principle of *topology preserving* [11] which allows to visualize the extracted information, for example, in the form of a two–dimensional map.

D.J. Hand, J.N. Kok, M.R. Berthold (Eds.): IDA'99, LNCS 1642, pp. 161–172, 1999.
© Springer-Verlag Berlin Heidelberg 1999

Herein, data analysis and visualization are not treated as separate procedural stages; as we will discuss in more detail later on, it is a benefit of our procedure that it unites both problems. This is formally achieved by optimizing a single objective function which combines a statistical criterion with topological constraints to ensure visualization. This coupling makes sense, whenever the final end is not the analysis per se, but the presentation and visualization of regularities and patterns extracted from data to a user. As a general principle, the latter implies that the value of an analysis carried out by means of a machine learning algorithm depends on whether or not its results can be represented in a way which makes it amenable to human (visual) inspection and allow an effortless interpretation. Obviously it can be of great advantage, if this is taken into account as early as possible in the analysis and not in a post hoc manner.

Our approach is somewhat related in spirit to the WEBSOM learning architecture [10] which continues earlier work on semantic maps [15] and performs a topological clustering of words represented as context–vectors. However, the method presented here is based on a strictly probabilistic data model which is fitted by maximum likelihood estimation. The discrete nature of words is directly taken into account without deviation via a (randomized) vector space representation as in the WEBSOM. In addition, our model does not perform word *clustering*, but models topics via word *distributions*.

The rest of the paper is organized as follows: Section 2 briefly introduces a probabilistic method for latent semantic analysis [6], which is then extended to incorporate topological constraints in Section 3. Finally, Section 4 shows some exemplary results of multi-resolution maps extracted from document collections.

2   Probabilistic Latent Semantic Analysis

2.1   Data Representation

Probabilistic Latent Semantic Analysis (PLSA) [6, 7] is a general method for statistical factor analysis of two-mode and count data which we apply here to learning from document collections. Formally, text collections are represented as pairs over a set of documents $\mathcal{D} = \{d_1, \ldots, d_N\}$ and a set of words $\mathcal{W} = \{w_1, \ldots, w_M\}$, i.e, the elementary observations we consider are of the form (d, w), denoting the occurrence of a word w in a document d. Summarizing all observations by counts $n(d, w)$ of how often a word occurred in a document, one obtains a rectangular N by M matrix $\mathbf{N} = [n(d_i, w_j)]_{i,j}$ which is usually referred to as *term–document matrix*. The key assumption of this representation is the so-called 'bag-of-words' view which presupposes that conditioned on the identity of a particular document, word occurrences are statistically independent. This also the basis for the popular *vector-space model* of documents [16] and it is known that $\mathbf{N}$ will in many cases preserve most of the relevant information, e.g., for tasks like text retrieval based on keywords, which makes it a reasonable starting point for our purposes.

The term–document matrix immediately reveals the problem of *data sparseness*, which is one of the problems latent semantic analysis aims to address. A typical matrix derived from short texts like news stories, book summaries or paper abstracts may only have a tiny fraction of non-zero entries, because just a small part of the vocabulary is typically used in a single document. This has consequences, in particular for methods that are evaluating similarities between documents by comparing or counting common terms. The main goal of PLSA in this context is to map documents and words to a more suitable representation in a *probabilistic latent semantic space*. As the name suggests, the representation of documents and terms in this space is supposed to make semantic relations more explicit. PLSA is an attempt to achieve this goal in a purely data driven fashion without recourse to general linguistic knowledge, i.e, based exclusively on a document collection or corpus at hand. Given these expectations could be met, PLSA would offers great advantages in terms of flexibility as well as in terms of domain adaptivity.

2.2 Probabilistic Latent Semantic Analysis

PLSA is based on a latent class model which associates an unobserved class variable $z \in \mathcal{Z} = \{z_1, \ldots, z_K\}$ with each observation (d, w). As will be explained in more detail, the intention pursued by introducing latent variables is to model *text topics* such that each possible state $z \in \mathcal{Z}$ would ideally represent one particular topic or subject. Formally, let us define the following multinomial distributions: $P(d)$ is used to denote the probability that a word is observed in a particular document.[1] $P(w|z)$ denotes a word distributions conditioned on the latent class variable z, which represent different *topic factors*. Finally, $P(z|d)$ is used to denote document-specific distributions over the latent variable space $\mathcal{Z}$. We may now define the following probabilistic model over $\mathcal{D} \times \mathcal{W}$

$$P(d, w) = P(d)P(w|d), \quad \text{where} \quad P(w|d) = \sum_{z \in \mathcal{Z}} P(w|z)P(z|d) \ . \tag{1}$$

This model is based on a crucial conditional independence assumption, namely that d and w are independent conditioned on the state of the latent variable z associated with the observation (d, w). As a result, the conditional distributions $P(w|d)$ in (1) are represented as convex combinations of the K factors $P(w|z)$. Since in the typical case one has $K \ll N$, the latent variable z can be thought of as a bottleneck variable in predicting words conditioned on documents.

To demonstrate how this corresponds to a mixture decomposition of the term–document matrix, we switch to an alternative parameterization by applying Bayes' rule to $P(z|d)$ and arriving at

$$P(d, w) = \sum_{z \in \mathcal{Z}} P(z)P(d|z)P(w|z) \,, \tag{2}$$

which is perfectly symmetric in both entities documents and words. Based on (2) let us formulate the probability model (1) in matrix notation, by defining $\mathbf{U} = [P(d_i|z_k)]_{i,k}$, $\mathbf{V} = [P(w_j|z_k)]_{j,k}$, $\Sigma = \text{diag}[P(z_k)]_k$, so that $\mathbf{P} = [P(d_i, w_j)]_{i,j} =$

---

[1] This is intended to account for varying document lengths.

$\mathbf{U\Sigma V}^t$. The algebraic form of this decomposition corresponds exactly to the decomposition of $\mathbf{N}$ obtained by *Singular Value Decomposition* (SVD) in standard *Latent Semantic Analysis* (LSA) [3]. However, the statistical model fitting principle used in conjunction with PLSA is the likelihood principle, while LSA is based on the Frobenius or L_2–norm of matrices. The statistical approach offers important advantages since it explicitly aims at minimizing word perplexity[2]. The mixture approximation $\mathbf{P}$ of the co-occurrence table is a well-defined probability distribution and factors have a clear probabilistic meaning in terms of mixture component distributions. In contrast, LSA does not define a properly normalized probability distribution and the obtained approximation may even contain negative entries. In addition, the probabilistic approach can take advantage of the well-established statistical theory for model selection and complexity control, e.g, to determine the optimal number of latent space dimensions (cf. [6]). Last but not least, the statistical formulation can be systematically extended and generalized in various ways, an example being the model presented in Section 3 of this paper.

2.3   EM Algorithm for PLSA

In order fit the model in (1) we follow the statistical standard procedure and perform maximum likelihood estimation with the EM algorithm [4, 17]. One has to maximize

$$\mathcal{L} = \sum_{d \in \mathcal{D}} \sum_{w \in \mathcal{W}} n(d, w) \log P(d, w) \tag{3}$$

with respect to all multinomial distributions which define $P(d, w)$. EM is guaranteed to find a local maximum of $\mathcal{L}$ by alternating two steps: (i) an expectation (E) step where posterior probabilities for the latent variables are computed based on the current estimates of the parameters, (ii) a maximization (M) step, where parameters are updated based on the posterior probabilities computed in the E–step. For the E–step one simply applies Bayes' formula, e.g., in the parameterization of (1), to obtain

$$P(z|d, w) = \frac{P(z|d)P(w|z)}{\sum_{z' \in \mathcal{Z}} P(z'|d)P(w|z')} . \tag{4}$$

It is straightforward to derive the M–step equations [9]

$$P(w|z) \propto \sum_{d \in \mathcal{D}} n(d, w)P(z|d, w), \quad P(z|d) \propto \sum_{w \in \mathcal{W}} n(d, w)P(z|d, w) . \tag{5}$$

The estimation of $P(d) \propto \sum_w n(d, w)$ can be carried out independently. Alternating (4) and (5) initialized from randomized starting conditions results in a procedure which converges to a local maximum of the log–likelihood in (3).

"image processing"	"speech recognition"	"video coding"
image	speaker	video
segment	speech	sequence
textur	recognition	motion
color	signal	frame
tissue	train	scene
brain	hmm	segment
slice	source	shot
cluster	speaker	image
mri	segment	cluster
volume	sound	visual

Fig. 1. The 3 latent factors to most likely generate the word 'segment', derived from a $K = 128$ PLSA of the CLUSTER document collection. The displayed terms are the most probable in the class-conditional distribution $P(w|z)$.

2.4   Example: Analysis of Word Usage with PLSA

Let us briefly discuss an elucidating example application of PLSA at this point. We have run PLSA with 128 factors on two datasets: (i) CLUSTER: a collection of paper abstracts on clustering and (ii) the TDT1 collection (cf. Section 4 for details).

As a particularly interesting term in the CLUSTER domain we have chosen the word 'segment'. Figure 1 shows the most probable words of 3 out of the 128 factors which have the highest probability to generate the term 'segment'. This sketchy characterization reveals very meaningful sub-domains: The first factor deals with image processing, where "segment" refers to a region in an image. The second factor describes speech recognition where "segment" refers to a phonetic unit of an acoustic signal such as a phoneme. The third factor deals with video coding, where "segment" is used in the context of motion segmentation in image sequences. The factors thus seem to capture relevant topics in the domain under consideration.

Three factors from the decomposition of the TDT1 collections with a high probability for the term "UN" are displayed in Figure 2. The vocabulary clearly characterizes news stories related to certain incidents in the period of 1994/1995 covered by the TDT1 collection. The first factor deals with the war in Bosnia, the second with UN sanctions against Iraq, and the third with the Rwandan genocide. These example shows that the topic identified by PLSA might also correspond to something one might more appropriately refer to as *events*. De-

---

[2] Perplexity is a term from statistical language modeling which is utilized here to refer to the (log-averaged) inverse predictive probability $1/P(w|d)$.

"Bosnia"	"Iraq"	"Rwanda"
un	iraq	refugees
bosnian	iraqi	aid
serbs	sanctions	rwanda
bosnia	kuwait	relief
serb	un	people
sarajevo	council	camps
nato	gulf	zaire
peacekeepers	saddam	camp
nations	baghdad	food
peace	hussein	rwandan

Fig. 2. Three factors to most likely generate the word "UN" from a 128 factor decomposition of the TDT1 corpus.

pendent on the training collection and the specific domain the notion of topic has thus to be taken in a broader sense.

2.5   PLSA: What Is Missing?

From the example in Figure 1 one can see that the factors $P(w|z)$ extracted by PLSA provide a fairly concise description of *topics* or *events*, which can potentially be utilized for interactive retrieval and navigation. However, there is one major drawback: assuming that for large text collections one would like to perform PLSA with a latent space dimensionality of the order of several hundreds or even thousands, it seems inappropriate to expect the user to examine all factors in search for relevant documents and topics of interest. Of course, one may ask the user to provide additional keywords to narrow the search, but this is nothing more than an ad hoc remedy to the problem.

What is really missing in PLSA as presented so far, is a relationship between the different factors. Suppose for concreteness one had identified a relevant topic represented by some $P(w|z)$; the identity of z does not provide any information about whether or not another topic $P(w|z')$ could be relevant as well. The generalization we present in the following section, extends the PLSA model in a way that enables it to captures additional information about the relationships between topics. In the case of a two–dimensional map, this results in a spatial arrangement of topics on a two–dimensional grid, a format which may support different types of visualization and navigation. Other topologies can be obtained by exactly the same mechanism described in the sequel.

3   Topological PLSA

In order to extend the PLSA model in the described way, we make use of a principle that was originally proposed in the seminal work of Kohonen on Self–Organizing Maps (SOM) [11, 12]. While the formulation of the algorithm in [11] was heuristic and mainly motivated in a biological setting, several authors have subsequently proposed modifications which have stressed an information theoretic foundation of the SOM and pointed out the relations to vector quantization for noisy communication channels (cf. [14, 2, 8]). Moreover, it has been noticed [1] that the topology–preserving properties of the SOM are independent of the vectorial representation, most research on the SOM has been focusing on.

3.1   Topologies from Confusion Probabilities

The key step in the proposed generalization is to introduce an additional latent variable $v \in \mathcal{Z}$ of the same cardinality as z to define the probability model

$$P(d, w) = P(d)P(w|d), \quad P(w|d) = \sum_{z \in \mathcal{Z}} P(w|z) \sum_{v \in \mathcal{Z}} P(z|v)P(v|d). \quad (6)$$

It is straightforward to verify that from a purely statistical point of view this does not offers any additional modeling power. Whatever the choice for $P(z|v)$ and $P(v|d)$ might be, one can simply define $P(z|d) = \sum_v P(z|v)P(v|d)$ to obtain exactly the same distribution over $\mathcal{D} \times \mathcal{W}$ in the more parsimonious model of (1). Yet, we do *not* propose to fit all model parameters in (6) from training data, but to fix the *confusion probabilities*[3] $P(z|v)$ to prespecified values derived from a *neighborhood function* in the latent variable space $\mathcal{Z}$. We will focus on means to enforce a topological organization of the topic representations $P(w|z)$ on a two–dimensional grid with boundaries. Let us introduce the notation $z(x, y)$, $1 \leq x, y \leq L$, $x, y \in \mathbb{N}$ to identify latent states $z(x, y) \in \mathcal{Z}$ with points (x, y) on the grid. By the Euclidean metric, this embedding induces a distance function on $\mathcal{Z}$, namely

$$d(z(x, y), z(x', y')) = d((x, y), (x', y')) = \sqrt{(x - x')^2 + (y - y')^2}. \quad (7)$$

Now we propose to define $P(z|v)$ via a Gaussian with standard deviation σ

$$P(z|v) = \frac{\exp\left[-d(z, v)^2/(2\sigma^2)\right]}{\sum_{z'} \exp\left[-d(z', v)^2/(2\sigma^2)\right]}, \quad (8)$$

where σ is assumed to be fixed for now. To understand why this favors a topological organization of topics, consider a document d with its topic distribution $P(v|t)$. The confusion probabilities tilt this distribution to a distribution

---

[3] We use this terminology, because the relationship between z and v can be thought of in terms of a communication scenario: v represents the original message and z the message received after sending it via a noisy channel. $P(z|v)$ then correspond to the channel characteristic, i.e., how probable it is to receive z after sending v.

$P(z|d) = \sum_z P(z|v)P(v|d)$. For simplicity assume that $P(v|d) = 1$ for a particular $v \in \mathcal{Z}$, then the confusion probabilities will blend-in additional contributions mainly from neighboring states z of v on the two–dimensional grid. If these neighboring states represent very different topics, the resulting word distribution $P(w|d)$ in (6) will significantly deviate from the distribution one would get from (1), which – assuming that $P(v|d)$ was chosen optimal – will result in a poor estimate. If on the other hand the neighbors of v represent closely related topics, this deviation will in general be much less severe. A meaningful topological arrangement of topics will thus pay off in terms of word perplexity.

3.2   EM Algorithm for Topological PLSA

The next step consists in deriving the EM equations for topological PLSA. Standard calculations yield the M–step re-estimation formulae

$$P(w|z) \propto \sum_d n(d, w)P(z|d, w), \text{ and } P(v|d) \propto \sum_w n(d, w)P(v|d, w). \quad (9)$$

For the evaluation of (9) the marginal posterior probabilities are sufficient and it is not necessary to compute the joint posterior $P(v, z|d, w)$. The marginal posterior probabilities are given by

$$P(v|d, w) = \sum_z P(v, z|d, w) = \frac{P(v|d)P(w|v)}{\sum_{v'} P(v'|d)P(w|v')}, \quad \text{and} \quad (10)$$

$$P(z|d, w) = \sum_v P(v, z|d, w) = \frac{P(z|d)P(w|z)}{\sum_{z'} P(z'|d)P(w|z')}, \quad (11)$$

where $P(w|v) = \sum_z P(w|z)P(z|v)$ and $P(z|d) = \sum_v P(z|v)P(v|d)$. Notice also that the marginal posteriors are simply related by

$$P(v|d, w) = \sum_z P(v|z)P(z|d, w), \quad P(z|d, w) = \sum_v P(z|v)P(v|d, w). \quad (12)$$

In summary, one observes that the EM algorithm for topological PLSA requires the computation of marginal posteriors and document/word conditionals for both variables v and z. Moreover, these quantities are related by a simple matrix multiplication with the confusion matrix $[P(z_k|v_l)]_{k,l}$ or its counterpart $[P(v_k|z_l)]_{k,l}$.

3.3   Topologies and Hierarchies

There are two ways in which hierarchies are of interest in the context of topological PLSA: (i) To accelerate the PLSA by a multi-resolution optimization over a sequence of coarsened grids. (ii) To improve the visualization by offering multiple levels of abstraction or resolution on which the data can be visualized.

A significant computational improvement can be achieved by performing PLSA on a coarse grid, say starting on a 2×2 grid, and then recursively prolongating the found solution according to an quadtree–like scheme. This involves

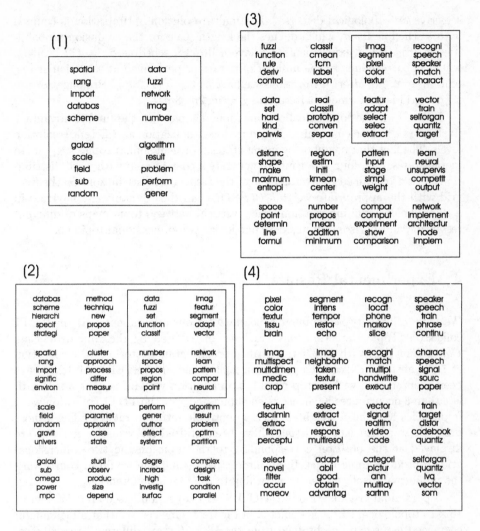

Fig. 3. Multi-resolution visualization of the CLUSTER collection with grid maps at 2 × 2 4×, 8 × 8 (upper left corner), and 16 (upper left corner). Subfigure (3) shows the 4 × 4 subgrid obtained by zooming the marked 2 × 2 window in subfigure (2). Similarly, subfigure (4) is a zoomed-in version of the marked window in subfigure (3).

copying the distributions $P(w|z)$ – with a small random disturbance – to the successors of z on the finer grid and distributing $P(v|d)$ from the coarse level among its four successor states on the finer grid. This procedure has the additional advantage that it often leads to better topological arrangements, since it is less sensitive to 'topological defects'.[4] The multi-resolution optimization is coupled with a schedule for σ, which defines the length-scale for the confusion probabilities in (8). In our experiments we have utilized a schedule $\sigma_n = (1/\sqrt[m]{2})^n \sigma_0$, where m corresponds to the number of iterations performed at a particular resolution level, i.e, after m iterations we have $\sigma_{n+m} = (1/2)\sigma_m$. Prolongations to a finer grid is performed at iterations $n = m, 2m, 3m, \ldots$.

Notice that the topological organization of topics has the further advantage to support a simple coarsening procedure for visualization at different resolution levels. The fact that neighboring latent states represent similar topics suggests to merge states, e.g., four at a time, to generate a coarser map with word distributions $P(w|z)$ obtained by averaging over the associated distributions on the finer grid with the appropriate weights $P(z)$. One can thus dynamically navigate in a three-dimensional information space: vertical between topic maps of different resolution and horizontally inside a particular two-dimensional topic map.

4   Experimental Results

We have utilized two document collections for our experiments: (i) the TDT1 collection (Topic Detection and Tracking, distributed by the *Linguistic Data Consortium* [13]) with 49,225 transcribed broadcast news stories, (ii) a collection of 1,568 abstract of research papers on 'clustering' (CLUSTER). All texts have been preprocessed with a stop word list, in addition very infrequent words with less than 3 occurrences have also been eliminated. For the TDT1 collection word frequencies have been weighted with an entropic term weight [16]. The 5 most probable words in factors $P(w|z)$ have been utilized for visualization and are displayed at the position corresponding to the topic on the two–dimensional grid to produce topic maps. In an interactive setting one would of course vary the number of displayed terms according to the user's preferences.

A pyramidal visualization of the CLUSTER collection based on a 256 factor, 16×16 topological PLSA is depicted in Figure 3. One can see that a meaningful coarsened maps can be obtained from the 16×16 map, different areas like astronomy, physics, databases, and pattern recognition can be easily identified. In particular on the finer levels, the topological organization is very helpful where the relation of different subtopics in signal processing, including image processing and speech recogniton, is well–preserved by the topic map. A similar map hierarchy for the TDT1 collection is depicted in Figure 4. Different topics and events can effortlessly be identified from the word distributions. Again, subtopics like the ones dealing with different events of international politics are mapped to neighboring positions on the lattice.

---

[4] There is a large body of literature dealing with the topology–preserving properties of SOMs. The reader is referred to [12] and the references therein.

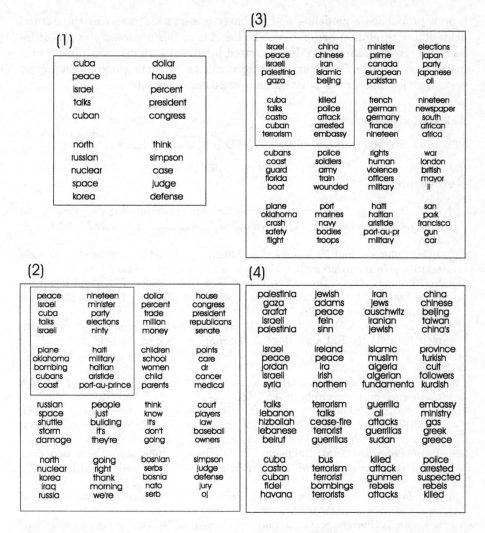

Fig. 4. Multi-resolution visualization of the TDT1 collection with grid maps at 2×2 $4 \times$, 8×8 (upper left corner), and 16 (upper left corner). Subfigure (3) shows the 4×4 subgrid obtained by zooming the marked 2×2 window in subfigure (2). Similarly, subfigure (4) is a zoomed-in version of the marked window in subfigure (3).

5   Conclusion

We have presented a novel probabilistic technique for visualizing text databases by *topic maps*. The main advantages are (i) a sound statistical foundation on a latent class model with EM as a fitting procedure, (ii) the principled combination of probabilistic modeling and topology-preservation, and (iii) the natural definition of resolution hierarchies. The benefits of this approach to support interactive retrieval have been demonstrated briefly with simple two–dimensional maps, however, since arbitrary topologies can be extracted, one might expect even more benefits in combination with more elaborate interfaces.

Acknowledgment

This work has been supported by a DAAD postdoctoral fellowship.

References

[1] J. M. Buhmann. Stochastic algorithms for data clustering and visualization. In M.I. Jordan, editor, *Learning in Graphical Models*. Kluwer Academic Publishers, 1998.

[2] J. M. Buhmann and H. Kühnel. Complexity optimized data clustering by competitive neural networks. *Neural Computation*, 5:75–88, 1993.

[3] S. Deerwester, G. W. Dumais, S. T. amd Furnas, Landauer. T. K., and R. Harshman. Indexing by latent semantic analysis. *Journal of the American Society for Information Science*, 1990.

[4] A.P. Dempster, N.M. Laird, and D.B. Rubin. Maximum likelihood from incomplete data via the EM algorithm. *J. Royal Statist. Soc. B*, 39:1–38, 1977.

[5] J. G. Herder. *Sprachphilosophische Schriften*. Felix Meiner Verlag, Hamburg, 1960.

[6] T. Hofmann. Probabilistic latent semantic analysis. In *Proceedings of the 15th Conference on Uncertainty in AI*, 1999.

[7] T. Hofmann. Probabilistic latent semantic indexing. In *Proceedings of the 22nd ACM-SIGIR International Conference on Research and Development in Information Retrieval, Berkeley, California*, 1999.

[8] T. Hofmann and J. M. Buhmann. Competitive learning algorithms for robust vector quantization. *IEEE Transaction on Signal Processing*, 46(6):1665–1675, 1998.

[9] T. Hofmann and J. Puzicha. Statistical models for co–occurrence data. Technical report, AI Memo 1625, M.I.T., 1998.

[10] S. Kaski, T. Honkela, K. Lagus, and T. Kohonen. WEBSOM–self-organizing maps of document collections. *Neurocomputing*, 21:101–117, 1998.

[11] T. Kohonen. *Self-organization and Associative Memory*. Springer, 1984.

[12] T. Kohonen. *Self-Organizing Maps*. Springer, 1995.

[13] Linguistic Data Consortium. TDT pilot study corpus. Catalog no. LDC98T25, 1998.

[14] S.P. Luttrell. Hierarchical vector quantization. *IEE Proceedings*, 136:405–413, 1989.

[15] H. Ritter and T. Kohonen. Self-organizing semantic maps. *Biological Cyberbetics*, 61:241–254, 1989.

[16] G. Salton and M. J. McGill. *Introduction to Modern Information Retrieval*. McGraw–Hill, 1983.

[17] L. Saul and F. Pereira. Aggregate and mixed–order Markov models for statistical language processing. In *Proceedings of the 2nd International Conference on Empirical Methods in Natural Language Processing*, 1997.

3D Grand Tour for Multidimensional Data and Clusters

Li Yang

Institute of High Performance Computing, National University of Singapore
89 Science Park Drive, #01-05/08 The Rutherford, Singapore 118261
yangli@ihpc.nus.edu.sg

Abstract. Grand tour is a method for viewing multidimensional data
via linear projections onto a sequence of two dimensional subspaces and
then moving continuously from one projection to the next. This paper
extends the method to 3D grand tour where projections are made onto
three dimensional subspaces. 3D cluster-guided tour is proposed where
sequences of projections are determined by cluster centroids. Cluster-
guided tour makes inter-cluster distance-preserving projections under
which clusters are displayed as separate as possible. Various add-on features, such as projecting variable vectors together with data points, interactive picking and drill down, and cluster similarity graphs, help further
the understanding of data. A CAVE virtual reality environment is at our
disposal for 3D immersive display. This approach of multidimensional
visualization provides a natural metaphor to visualize clustering results
and data at hand by mapping the data onto a time-indexed family of 3D
natural projections suitable for human eye's exploration.

1 Introduction

Visualization techniques have proven to be of high value in exploratory data
analysis and data mining. For data with a few dimensions, scatterplot is an
excellent means for visualization. Patterns could be efficiently unveiled by simply
drawing each data point as a geometric object in the space determined by one,
two or three numeric variables of the data, while its size, shape, color and texture
determined by other variables of the data. The ability to draw scatterplots is a
common feature of many visualization systems. Conventional scatterplots lose
their effectiveness, however, as dimensionality of data becomes large.

An idea comes out, then, to project higher dimensional data orthogonally
onto lower dimensional subspaces. It allows us to look at multidimensional data
in a geometry that is within the perceptibility of human eyes. Since there is
an infinite number of possibilities to project high dimensional data onto lower
dimensions, and information will eventually lose after the projection, the grand
tour[1,3] and other projection pursuit techniques[10,12] aim at automatically
finding the interesting projections or at least helping the users to find them.

Grand tour is an extension of data rotation for multidimensional data sets.
It is based on selecting a sequence of linear projections and moving continuously from one projection to the next. By displaying a number of intermediate

D.J. Hand, J.N. Kok, M.R. Berthold (Eds.): IDA'99, LNCS 1642, pp. 173–184, 1999.
© Springer-Verlag Berlin Heidelberg 1999

projections obtained by interpolation, the entire process creates an illusion of continuous, smooth motion through multidimensional displays. This helps to find interesting projections which is hard to find in the original data, owing to the curse of dimensionality. Furthermore, grand tour allows viewers to easily keep track of a specific group of data points throughout a tour. By examining where the data points go from one projection to the next, viewers have a much better understanding about data than using conventional visualization techniques such as bar charts or pie charts.

Now the question becomes how to choose "meaningful" projections and projection sequences to maximize the chance of finding interesting patterns. One simple way is choosing the span of any three arbitrary variables as a 3D subspace and then moving from this span to the next span of another three variables. This is what we call "simple projection". Each projection in the sequence is a 3D scatterplot of three variables. It is more than the 3D scatterplots, however, because more information could be unveiled by the animation moving from one projection to the next. Another straightforward way is random tour. By choosing randomly a 3D subspace and moving to the next randomly chosen 3D subspace, random tour creates a way for global dynamic browsing of multidimensional data. In the data preprocessing stage of a data mining project, simple projection and random tour are efficient ways to examine the distribution of values of each variable, the correlations among variables, and to decide which variables should be included in further analysis. Although real world databases have often many variables, these variables are often highly correlated, and databases are mercifully inherently low-dimensional. Simple projection and random tour are useful to identify the appropriate subspaces in which further mining is meaningful.

There are various ways of choosing interesting projections and projection sequences in a tour. For clustered data sets, one promising way is to use positions of data clusters to help choosing projections. Let us assume that a data set is available as data points in the p-dimensional Euclidean space and has been clustered into k clusters. Each cluster has a centroid which is simply an average of all the data points contained in the cluster. As we know, any four distinct and non-colinear points uniquely determine a 3D subspace. If we choose the centroids of any four clusters and project all data points onto a 3D subspace determined by these four cluster centroids, the Euclidean distance between any two of the four cluster centroids will be preserved and the four clusters will be displayed as separate as possible from each other. We call this a cluster-guided projection. Observe that there are $\binom{k}{4}$ possible cluster-guided projections. By using the grand tour to move from one cluster-guided projection to another, a viewer can have quickly a good sense of the positions of all data clusters.

There were both linear and nonlinear techniques[2] for dimension reduction of high dimensional data. Rather than nonlinear techniques such as Sammon's projection[15] which aims at preserving all inter-cluster distances by minimizing a cost function, we found linear projections more intuitive for the purpose of unveiling cluster structure and suitable for human eye's exploration. Linear projections and scatterplots could be found in many visualization systems (for example, the earlier Biplot[11]). The idea of using grand tour of lower dimensional projections to simulate higher dimensional displays was first proposed in [1]. Techniques were developed to design the path of a tour, for example, to principal component and canonical variate subspace[13], or to hill-climbing paths that follows gradients of projection pursuit indices[5,10]. An example visualization system which implements 2D projections and grand tour is XGobi[16]. For the visualization of data clusters, a 2D cluster-guided tour was proposed in [8].

To exploit human eyes' 3D nature of visual perception, we developed a visualization system for 3D projection and cluster-guided tour. A CAVE immersive virtual environment[6,7] is at our disposal for 3D immersive display. With the CAVE as a 3D "magic canvas", scatterplots can be drawn in mid-air in the 3D virtual space. This helps greatly data analysts visualize data and mining results. It helps to show 3D distributions of data points, locate similarity or dissimilarity between various clusters, and furthermore, determine which clusters to merge or to split further. Compared with other systems mentioned above, the grand tour in the CAVE virtual environment has characteristics such as: (1) 3D projection; (2) immersive virtual reality display; (3) cluster-guided projection determined by 4 data clusters; and (4) vary intuitive add-on tools for interaction and drilldown. It represents a novel tool to visualize multidimensional data and is now routinely employed for preprocessing data and analyzing mining results. It is also used to visually communicate mining results to clients.

The paper is organized as follows: Section 2 is to introduce grand tour . Section 3 discusses in detail the 3D cluster-guided projections and cluster-guided tour. Section 4 is for projection rendering inside the CAVE virtual environment. Section 5 presents add-on features such as projecting variable vectors together with data points, interactive picking and drill down, and cluster similarity graphs. Section 6 concludes the paper with future work and directions.

2   Grand Tour

For easy illustration, suppose we are to make a 2D tour in 3D Euclidean space (Fig. 1). A 2D oriented projection plan, or a 2-frame (a 2-frame is an orthonormal pair of vectors), can be identified by a unit index vector that is perpendicular to the plan. The most straight way to move from one 2D projection to the next is a sequence of interpolated projections to move the index vector to the next index vector on the unit sphere along a geodesic path.

For 3D grand tour of p-dimensional ($p > 3$) data sets, in the same way, it is necessary to have an explicitly computable sequence of interpolated 3-frames in p-dimensional Euclidean space. The p-dimensional data is then projected, in turn, onto the 3D subspace spanned by each 3-frame. For the shortest path to move from one 3D projection to another, the sequence of the interpolated 3-frames should be as straight as possible. Here "straight" means: If we think of the interpolated 3D subspaces as being evenly-spaced points on a curve in the space of 3D subspaces through the origin in Euclidean p-space (a so-called

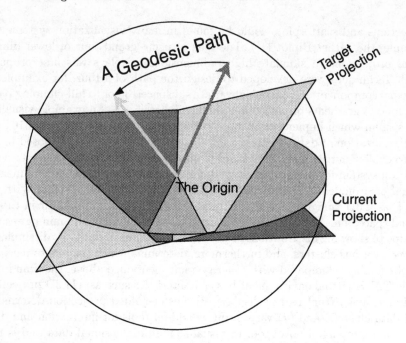

Fig. 1. Moving 2D projections along a geodesic path in 3D space.

"Grassmannian manifold")(Fig. 2), we should be able to choose that curve so that it is almost a geodesic.

Moving along a geodesic path creates a sequence of intermediate projections moving smoothly from the current to the target projection. This is a way of assuring that the sequence of projections is both comprehensible, and also that it moves rapidly to the target projection. For 3D projections, a geodesic path is simply a rotation in the (at most) 6-dimensional subspace containing both the current and the target 3D spaces. This implies that some pre-projection is necessary in implementation so that computing data projections is within the joint span of the current and the next 3D subspaces, the dimension of which can be substantially smaller than p. Various smoothness properties of such geodesic paths are explored in great detail in [3]. For a description of implementation details, see [13, Subsection 2.2.1].

3   3D Cluster-Guided Projection and Cluster-Guided Tour

Let $\{X_i\}_{i=1}^n$ denote a data set, that is, a set of n data points each taking values in the p-dimensional Euclidean space R^p, $p > 3$. Let $X \cdot Y$ denote the dot product of two points X and Y. Write the Euclidean norm of X as $\|X\| = \sqrt{X \cdot X}$, and the Euclidean distance between X and Y as $d(X, Y) = \|X - Y\|$. Let us suppose

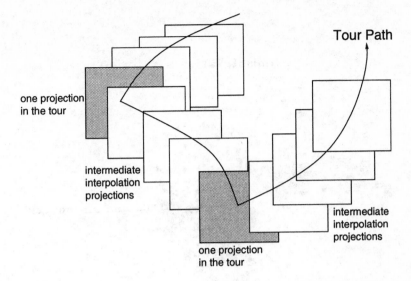

Fig. 2. A path of intermediate plans that interpolates a sequence of projection plans.

that we have partitioned the data set into k clusters, $k \geq 4$, and let $\{C_j\}_{j=1}^k$ denote the cluster centroids.

Any four distinct and non-colinear cluster centroids C_a, C_b, C_c and C_d in $\{C_j\}_{j=1}^k$ determine an unique 3D subspace in R^p. Let K_1, K_2 and K_3 constitute an orthonormal basis of the subspace (this could be obtained by orthonormalizing $C_b - C_a$, $C_c - C_a$, and $C_d - C_a$). We can then compute a 3D projection by projecting the data set $\{X_i\}_{i=1}^n$ onto the 3-frame (K_1, K_2, K_3). This projection preserves the inter-cluster distances, that is, the Euclidean distance between any two of the four cluster centroids $\{C_a, C_b, C_c, C_d\}$ is preserved after the projection. Specifically, let $X|p = (X \cdot K_1, X \cdot K_2, X \cdot K_3)$ denote the 3D projection of a p-dimensional point X, then $d(X|p, Y|p) = d(X, Y)$ for any $X, Y \in \{C_a, C_b, C_c, C_d\}$. This inter-cluster-distance-preserving projection is a right perspective of view that these four clusters are visualized as far as possible (Fig. 4).

There are various ways to choose the path (sequence of projections) of tour. One way is to simply choose a tripod from the variable unit vectors of p-dimension as the axes of one 3D projection and move from this projection to the next whose axes are another tripod. This is what we call "simple projection"(Fig. 3). It gives a way to continuously check a sequence of scatterplots of data against any three variables. Another straightforward way is random tour where each projection in the sequence is randomly generated. This gives a way for global dynamic browsing of multidimensional data.

Cluster-guided tour is a way to get cluster centroids involved in choosing projection sequences: Given k cluster centroids, there are at most $\binom{k}{4}$ combi-

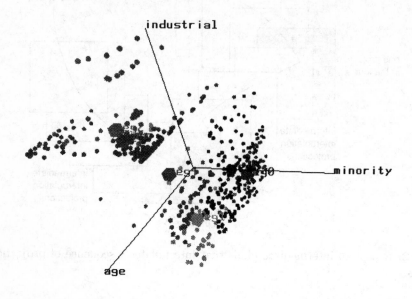

Fig. 3. Simple projection: a 3D scatterplot.

nations of unique 3D cluster projections. Each projection allows us to visualize the multidimensional data in relation to four cluster centroids. To visualize the multidimensional data in relation to all cluster centroids, we display a sequence of cluster-guided projections and use grand tour to move continuously from one projection in the sequence to the next.

The basic idea behind cluster-guided tour is simple: Choose a target projection from $\binom{k}{4}$ possible cluster-guided projections, move smoothly from the current projection to the target projection, and continue. We illustrate the 3D cluster-guided projection and guided-tour on the Boston housing data set from UCI ML Repository[4]. This data set has $n = 506$ data points and $p = 13$ real-valued attributes. The data set is typical (not in size, but in spirit) of the data sets routinely encountered in market segmentation. The 13 attributes measure various characteristics such as the crime rate, the proportion of old units, property tax rate, pupil-teacher ratio in schools, etc., that affect housing prices. We normalized all the 13 attributes to take values in the interval $[0, 1]$. To enable the cluster-guided tour, any clustering algorithm could be used to cluster the data set. Here we clustered the data set into 6 clusters by the Kohonen's Self-Organizing Map[14]. The six result clusters have 114, 46, 29, 107, 78, and 132 data points respectively. There are $\binom{6}{4} = 15$ possible 3D cluster-guided projections. We plot one of them in Fig. 4. To underscore the 3D cluster-guided

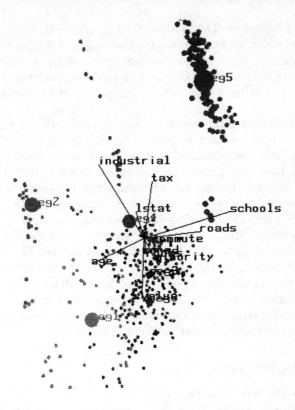

Fig. 4. A 3D cluster-guided projection determined by centroids (big balls with labels) of Clusters 1, 2, 4, 5. The four clusters are visualized as separate as possible. A *p*-pod of variable vectors is shown. Each ray of the *p*-pod represents the projection of a variable axis whose length represents the maximum value of the variable.

projections in locating interesting projections, compare Fig. 4 to Fig. 3 where we display a scatterplot of one of the attributes "industrial — proportions of non-retail business acres" against two of the other attributes "minority" and "ages of units." Unlike the scatterplot, the 3D cluster-guided projections reveal significant information about the positions of the clusters.

4   Rendering inside the CAVE Virtual Environment

CAVE is a projection-based virtual reality environment which uses 3D computer graphics and position tracking to immerse users inside a 3D space. The CAVE in IHPC has a 10 × 10 × 10 feet room-like physical space. Stereographic images are rear projected onto three side walls and front projected onto the floor. The four projected images are driven by 2 InfiniteReality graphics pipelines inside an SGI Onyx2 computer. The illusion of 3D is created through the use of LCD shutter glasses which are synchronized to the computer display through infrared emitters alternating the left and the right eye viewpoints. The CAVE allows multiple viewers to enter the CAVE and share the same virtual experience. But only one viewer can have the position/orientation of his/her head and hand captured.

With the CAVE as a 3D "magic canvas", 3D projection of high dimensional data is rendered as a galaxy in mid-air in the virtual space(Figure 5). The projection can be reshaped, moved back and forth, and rotated by using a wand (a 3D mouse). Each data point is painted as a sphere with its color representing the cluster it belongs. Spheres can be resized, and the speed of motion can be manually controlled anytime during a tour by adjusting an X-Y sensor attached on the wand. For easy identification, cluster centroids are painted as big cubs and labeled with cluster names. The variable vectors, which show the contribution to the projection of each variable, are visualized as lines in white color from the origin and marked by the names of variables at their far ends. There are two different ways of interactive picking: brushing with a resizable sphere brush; and cluster-picking by selecting a cluster's centroid. The CAVE has plenty of space for data rendering. At some future time, we may have multiple viewing projections synchronized and displayed simultaneously.

5   Add-On Features

5.1   Where We Are in a Tour?

A dizzy feeling besets many first-time viewers of high-dimensional data projections and they may ask "How do I know what I am looking at". In geometric terms, the task is to locate the position of a projection 3-frame in p-space. A visual way of conveying this information is to project the variable unit vectors in p-space like regular data, and render the result together with data points.

Examples of the application are shown through the Figures 3–5. A generalized tripod called "p-pod" is an enhanced rendition of the p variable unit vectors in p-space. Variable vectors in the p-pod can be treated as if they were real data, rendered as lines, and labeled by variable names in the far ends so that they are recognized as guide posts rather than data. In the figures, we choose the maximum value rather than the unit value of a variable as the length of its variable vector. The p-pod looks like a star with p unequal rays in 3D space, each indicating the contribution of a variable to the current projection.

5.2   Interactive Picking and Drill-Down

An advantage of grand tour is that an viewer can easily keep track of the movement of a certain group of data points during the whole journey of a tour. A cluster, or a set of data points, could be picked up by pointing to the cluster centroid or using a brushing tool. Data points picked up so far can be related back to the data, thus makes it possible for further analysis such as launching another mining process for drill down.

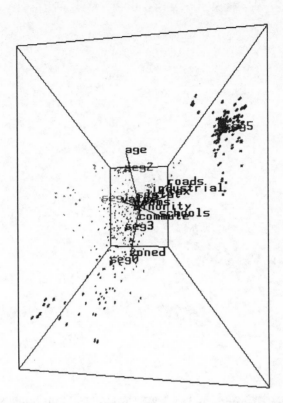

Fig. 5. This is a cluster-guided projection in the CAVE. The wireframe box indicates a 3D room where data points are plotted in mid-air. The cluster-guided projection is determined by centroids of Clusters 1, 2, 4, and 5.

5.3   Cluster Similarity Graphs

3D cluster-guided projection is continuous transformation of data. Two points which are close in R^p will remain close after projection. However, two points which are close in a 3D projection need not be close in R^p. There is a loss of information in projecting high-dimensional data to low-dimensions. To somewhat mitigate this information loss, we use cluster similarity graphs[9] as an enhancement to cluster-guided projection.

A cluster similarity graph can be defined as follows. Let vertices be a set of cluster centroids $\{C_j\}_{j=1}^k$, and add an edge between two vertices C_i and C_j if $d(C_i, C_j) \leq t$, where t is a user-controlled threshold. If t is very large, all cluster centroids will be connected. If t is very small, no cluster centroids will be connected. It is thus intuitively clear that changing the threshold value will reveal distances among cluster centroids. The cluster similarity graph can be overlaid onto the projections. For example, straight lines connecting the cluster centroids in the Fig. 6 represent a cluster similarity graph at a certain threshold. It can

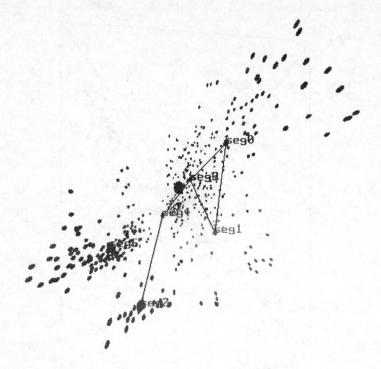

Fig. 6. An similarity graph adds yet another information dimension to cluster-guided projections.

be seen that the Clusters 0, 1, 3 are close to each other, among which Cluster 3 is close to Cluster 4 which is close to Cluster 2. Cluster 5 is a standalone cluster from all others. The cluster similarity graph adds yet another information dimension to cluster-guided projections, and hence, enhances the viewing experience.

6 Conclusion and Future Work

This paper discussed the use of 3D projections and grand tour to visualize higher dimensional data sets. This creates an illusion of smooth motion through a multidimensional space. The 3D cluster-guided tour is proposed to visualize data clusters. Cluster-guided tour preserves distances between cluster centroids. This allows us to fully capture the inter-cluster structure of complex multidimensional data. The use of the CAVE immersive virtual environment maximizes the chance of finding interesting patterns. Add-on features and interaction tools invite viewer's interaction with data.

The cluster-guided tour is a way to use data mining as a driver for visualization: Clustering identifies homogenous sub-populations of data, and the subpopulations are used to help design the path of tour. This method can also be applied to the results generated by other data mining techniques, for instance, to identify the significant rules produced by tree classification and rule induction. All these are possible ways to allow a user to better understand both results of mining and data at hand.

One important thing about an algorithm is its scalability. Grand tour scales well to large data sets. Its computational complexity is linear to the number of variables. The number of variables matters only in calculating projections, i.e. dot products, which has a linear complexity to the dimensionality of arguments. There are two major steps in grand tour, calculating a tour path and making projections. Calculating a tour path is nothing with the total number of data points. Making projections has a computational complexity linear to the number of data points. This is in the sense that all data points have to be projected one by one. For large data sets, this complexity can be greatly reduced by making density map instead of drawing points.

The following directions is being explored or will be explored in the future:

- *Working with categorical variables.* In relational databases it is quite common for many of the variables to be categorical rather than numerical. A categorical variable can be mapped onto a linear scatterplot axis in the same way as a numeric variable, provided that some order of distinct values of that variable is given along the categorical axis. Categorical values may be explicitly listed. The order of the values being listed will be the order these values be arranged on the axis. Categorical values could be grouped together, reflecting the natural taxonomy of values. Categorical values could also be sorted alphabetically, numerically by weight, or numerically by aggregate value of some other variable. We are working on having categorical variables involved in a tour, and some results may come up soon.
- *3D density projection and volume rendering.* Scatterplot loses its effectiveness as the number of points becomes very large. It has also a drawback that identical data records may coincide with each other. For a tradeoff between computational complexity, comprehensibility and accuracy, we plan to use dynamic projections of high dimensional density map as a model to visualize data sets which contain large number of data points. 3D density projection is important to study, especially when clusters are not balanced in size and when clusters overlap with each other. Research is now on finding solutions of problems such as: how to store the sparse, voxelized high dimensional data more efficiently; and how to fast render a volume of high dimensional voxels onto the projected 3-dimensional space.
- *Parallel implementation for better performance.* A parallel implementation is necessary for the rendering of very large data sets. Since data points are independently projected, it should be quite straightforward to parallelize the code, for instance, by using multithreads on a shared memory machine. Since our CAVE's backend computer, the SGI Onyx2, is quite busy with CAVE display, leaving few resources for projection calculation, a client-server implementation is also necessary. This will be done through a high speed

network connection to a more powerful SGI Origin2000. All projection data will be calculated on the server and sent in real time to the CAVE. One interesting issue here is how to transfer only the necessary projected data to the CAVE in order that the transferred data can be directly rendered.

References

1. D. Asimov. The grand tour: A tool for viewing multidimensional data. *SIAM Journal of Science and Statistical Computing*, 6(1):128–143, January 1985.
2. G. Biswas, A. K. Jain, and R.C. Dubes. An evaluation of projection algorithms. *IEEE Transactions on Pattern Analysis and Machine Intelligence*, PAMI-3:702–708, 1981.
3. A. Buja, D. Cook, D. Asimov, and C. Hurley. Theory and computational methods for dynamic projections in high-dimensional data visualization. Technical report, AT&T, 1996. http://www.research.att.com/~andreas/papers/dynamic-projections.ps.gz.
4. E. Keogh C. Blake and C.J. Merz. UCI repository of machine learning databases, 1998. http://www.ics.uci.edu/~mlearn/MLRepository.html.
5. D. R. Cook, A. Buja, J. Cabrera, and H. Hurley. Grand tour and projection pursuit. *Journal of Computational and Graphical Statistics*, 2(3):225–250, 1995.
6. C. Cruz-Neira. *Projection-based Virtual Reality: The CAVE and its Applications to Computational Science*. PhD thesis, University of Illinois at Chicago, 1995.
7. C. Cruz-Neira, D. J. Sandin, T. DeFanti, R. Kenyon, and Hart J, C. The cave audio visual experience automatic virtual environment. *Communications of the ACM*, 35(1):64–72, 1992.
8. I. S. Dhillon, D. S. Modha, and W. S. Spangler. Visualizing class structure of multidimensional data. In *Proceedings of the 30th Symposium on the Interface: Computing Science and Statistics*, Minneapolis, MN, May 1998.
9. R. O. Duda and P. E. Hart. *Pattern Classification and Scene Analysis*. Wiley, 1973.
10. J. Friedman and J. Tukey. A projection pursuit algorithm for exploratory data analysis. *IEEE Transactions on Computers*, 23:881–890, 1974.
11. K. R. Gabriel. Biplot display of multivariate matrices for inspection of data and diagnosis. In V. Barnett, editor, *Intrepreting multivariate data*, pages 147–173. John Wiley & Sons, New York, 1981.
12. P. J. Huber. Projection pursuit. *The Annals of Statistics*, 13(2):435–474, 1985.
13. C. Hurley and A. Buja. Analyzing high-dimensional data with motion graphics. *SIAM Journal on Scientific and Statistical Computing*, 11(6):1193–1211, 1990.
14. T. Kohonen. *Self-Organizing Maps*, volume 30 of *Springer Series in Information Sciences*. Springer, Berlin, Heidelberg, New York, second extended edition, 1997.
15. J. W. Sammon, Jr. A nonlinear mapping for data structure analysis. *IEEE Transactions on Computers*, C-18:401–409, 1969.
16. D. F. Swayne, D. Cook, and A. Buja. XGobi: Interactive dynamic data visualization in the X window system. *Journal of Computational and Graphical Statistics*, 7(1):113–130, 1998.

Section III:

Classification and Clustering

A Decision Tree Algorithm for Ordinal Classification 187
  R. Potharst and J.C. Bioch

Discovering Dynamics Using Bayesian Clustering 199
  P. Sebastiani, M. Ramoni, P. Cohen, J. Warwick, and J. Davis

Integrating Declarative Knowledge in Hierarchical Clustering Tasks 211
  L. Talavera and J. Béjar

Nonparametric Linear Discriminant Analysis by Recursive
Optimization with Random Initialization 223
  M. Aladjem

Supervised Classification Problems: How to Be Both Judge and Jury 235
  M.G. Kelly, D.J. Hand, and N.M. Adams

Temporal Pattern Generation Using Hidden Markov Model
Based Unsupervised Classification 245
  C. Li and G. Biswas

Exploiting Similarity for Supporting Data Analysis and Problem Solving ... 257
  E. Hüllermeier

Multiple Prototype Model for Fuzzy Clustering 269
  S. Nascimento, B. Mirkin, and F. Moura-Pires

A Comparison of Genetic Programming Variants for Data Classification ... 281
  J. Eggermont, A.E. Eiben, and J.I. van Hemert

Fuzzy Clustering Based on Modified Distance Measures 291
  F. Klawonn and A. Keller

Building Classes in Object-Based Languages by Automatic Clustering 303
  P. Valtchev

Section II

Classification and Clustering

A Decision Tree Algorithm for Ordinal Classification

Rob Potharst and Jan C. Bioch

Erasmus University Rotterdam
P.O. Box 1738, 3000 DR Rotterdam, The Netherlands

Abstract. In many classification problems the domains of the attributes and the classes are linearly ordered. For such problems the classification rule often needs to be order-preserving or monotone as we call it. Since the known decision tree methods generate non-monotone trees, these methods are not suitable for monotone classification problems. We provide an order-preserving tree-generation algorithm for multi-attribute classification problems with k linearly ordered classes, and an algorithm for repairing non-monotone decision trees. The performance of these algorithms is tested on random monotone datasets.

1   Introduction

Ordinal classification refers to an important category of real-world problems, in which the attributes of the objects to be classified and the classes are ordered. For this class of problems classification rules often need to be order-preserving. In that case we have a monotone classification problem. In this paper we study the problem of generating decision-tree-classifiers for monotone classification problems: the attributes and the set of classes are linearly ordered. Ordinal classification for multi-attribute decision making has been studied recently by Ben-David [1,2,3] for discrete domains, and by Makino et al. [5] for the two-class problem with continuous attributes. However, although the tree-generation method of Ben-David accounts for the ordering of the attributes and of the classes, order preserving is not guaranteed. Furthermore, the method of Makino et al. is restricted to the two-class problem. In this paper we propose a tree growing algorithm for the k-class problem that guarantees to induce monotone trees. In addition, we provide an algorithm that repairs non-monotone decision trees. These algorithms are also studied in our PhD-dissertation [8] and a technical report [6] in which we provide several algorithms for monotone classification problems with k classes and discrete or continuous domains. All proofs of the results of this paper will also be found in [6,8].

For motivation and examples of real world monotone classification problems we refer to [1,2,3]. Here we give a simple example of such a problem. Suppose a bank wants to base its loan policy on a number of features of its clients, for instance on income, education level and criminal record. If a client is granted a loan, it can be one in three classes: low, intermediate and high. So, together

D.J. Hand, J.N. Kok, M.R. Berthold (Eds.): IDA'99, LNCS 1642, pp. 187–198, 1999.
© Springer-Verlag Berlin Heidelberg 1999

Table 1. The bank loan dataset

client	income	education	crim.record	loan
cl1	low	low	fair	no
cl2	low	low	excellent	low
cl3	average	intermediate	excellent	intermediate
cl4	high	low	excellent	intermediate
cl5	high	intermediate	excellent	high

with the no loan option, we have four classes. Suppose further that the bank wants to base its loan policy on a number of credit worthiness decisions in the past. These past decisions are given in Table 1: A client with features at least as high as those of another client may expect to get at least as high a loan as the other client. So, finding a loan policy compatible with past decisions amounts to solving a monotone classification problem with the dataset of Table 1. In this paper we only discuss the main algorithm for discrete domains. In a companion paper [7] on quasi-monotone decision trees we also discuss continuous domains and the problem of dealing with noise.

2   Monotone Classification

In this paper we will assume that our *input space* $\mathcal{X}$ is a coordinate space. Elements of $\mathcal{X}$ will be vectors $(x_1, \ldots, x_n)$ with coordinates x_i which will take their values from a finite linearly ordered space $\mathcal{X}_i, i = 1, \ldots, n$. Without loss of generality we may assume that for $1 \leq i \leq n, \mathcal{X}_i = \{0, 1, \ldots, n_i\}$ for some integer n_i. Here the order relation $\leq$ on $\mathcal{X}$ is defined as $x \leq y$ iff $x_i \leq y_i$ for all $i = 1, \ldots, n$. This order relation is a partial ordering of the space $\mathcal{X}$. Of course, this includes the very common situation that our examples are measurements on n variables $X_1, \ldots, X_n$, where the individual measurement on variable X_i yields a value x_i from an ordered set $\mathcal{X}_i$. So each of the variables may take its values from a different set, as long as all these coordinate sets are linearly ordered.

Next, let $\mathcal{C}$ be a finite linearly ordered set of *classes*, with linear ordering $<$. A *classification rule* or *class labeling* is a function $\lambda : \mathcal{X} \to \mathcal{C}$ which assigns a class from $\mathcal{C}$ to every point in the input space $\mathcal{X}$. The minimal and maximal elements of $\mathcal{C}$ will be denoted by $c_{\min}$ and $c_{\max}$ respectively. A *classification problem* is the problem of finding a class labeling λ that satisfies certain constraints conditions, to be specified in the problem description. One possible constraint is that the labeling λ be monotone: a *monotone* classification rule is a function $\lambda : \mathcal{X} \to \mathcal{C}$ for which

$$x \leq y \Rightarrow \lambda(x) \leq \lambda(y) \tag{1}$$

for all points $x, y \in \mathcal{X}$.

A very common classification problem occurs, when there is a dataset or set of examples available. The usual constraint to be met in such a situation is that the classification rule one is looking for should correctly classify all examples in the dataset. With this situation we will deal in the sequel.

A dataset is a finite collection of examples from the input space, together with a class labeling of all these examples. Formally, we define a dataset as follows:

Definition 1 A *dataset* $\mathcal{D}$ is a pair (D, λ) where $D \subset \mathcal{X}$ is a finite subset of the input space $\mathcal{X}$ and $\lambda : D \to \mathcal{C}$ is a class labeling of the elements of D. The elements of D will be called the *examples* of the dataset.

Note first of all that the class labeling λ of a dataset $\mathcal{D} = (D, \lambda)$ is *not* a classification rule: it is only defined on D, a subset of $\mathcal{X}$, while a classification rule must be defined on all elements of the input space $\mathcal{X}$. Secondly, we do not allow an example to have two or more different classes: all elements of the dataset must be consistently labeled.

Given a dataset $\mathcal{D} = (D, \lambda)$ we can try to solve the corresponding *monotone classification problem* of finding a monotone classification rule $\hat{\lambda} : \mathcal{X} \to \mathcal{C}$ that extends the class labeling λ of the dataset $\mathcal{D}$ to the entire input space $\mathcal{X}$. Thus, $\hat{\lambda}(x) = \lambda(x)$ for all $x \in D$. Obviously, if one wants to find a solution for such a monotone classification problem, the dataset itself has to be monotone:

Definition 2 A dataset $\mathcal{D} = (D, \lambda)$ is called *monotone* if the implication (1) holds for all $x, y \in D$.

In order to save space we will often map the values of the attributes of a dataset to a set of numbers. For instance, Table 1 could be written as

X_1	X_2	X_3	$\mathcal{C}$
0	0	1	0
0	0	2	1
1	1	2	2
2	0	2	2
2	1	2	3

when we use the mapping low $\to 0$, average $\to 1$, high $\to 2$ for feature $X_1 =$ *income*, etc. We will even write concisely $\mathcal{D} = \{001{:}0,\ 002{:}1,\ 112{:}2,\ 202{:}2,\ 212{:}3\}$ for the above dataset.

As noted above the problem of finding a solution to a monotone classification problem amounts to finding a monotone extension $\hat{\lambda}$ of the class labeling λ of a dataset $\mathcal{D} = (D, \lambda)$. Formally, a function $\hat{\lambda} : \mathcal{X} \to \mathcal{C}$ is an *extension* of $\lambda : \mathcal{X} \to \mathcal{C}$, if the restriction of $\hat{\lambda}$ to D i.e. $\hat{\lambda}|D = \lambda$. Or, if $\hat{\lambda}(x) = \lambda(x)$ for all $x \in D$. If $\mathcal{D} = (D, \lambda)$ is monotone, we denote the collection of all monotone extensions of λ with $\Lambda(\mathcal{D})$. Note, that for classification rules $\lambda, \lambda' \in \Lambda(\mathcal{D})$ we mean by $\lambda \leq \lambda'$ that $\lambda(x) \leq \lambda'(x)$ for all $x \in \mathcal{X}$. $\Lambda(\mathcal{D})$ is partially ordered by this order relation $\leq$. We will now define two special elements of this collection $\Lambda(\mathcal{D})$.

Definition 3 If $\mathcal{D} = (D, \lambda)$ is a monotone dataset, we define $\lambda_{\min}^{\mathcal{D}} : \mathcal{X} \to \mathcal{C}$, and $\lambda_{\max}^{\mathcal{D}} : \mathcal{X} \to \mathcal{C}$, as follows: for all $x \in \mathcal{X}$

$$\lambda_{\min}^{\mathcal{D}}(x) = \begin{cases} \max\{\lambda(y) : y \in D, y \leq x\} & \text{if } x \geq y \text{ for some } y \in D \\ c_{\min} & \text{otherwise} \end{cases}$$

and

$$\lambda_{\max}^{\mathcal{D}}(x) = \begin{cases} \min\{\lambda(y) : y \in D, y \geq x\} & \text{if } x \leq y \text{ for some } y \in D \\ c_{\max} & \text{otherwise.} \end{cases}$$

The next lemma shows that the functions $\lambda_{\min}^{\mathcal{D}}$ and $\lambda_{\max}^{\mathcal{D}}$, as defined, are the minimal resp. maximal elements of $\Lambda(\mathcal{D})$.

Lemma *If $\mathcal{D} = (D, \lambda)$ is a monotone dataset, for the functions $\lambda_{\min}^{\mathcal{D}}$ and $\lambda_{\max}^{\mathcal{D}}$ the following statements hold:*

(i) $\lambda_{\min}^{\mathcal{D}}, \lambda_{\max}^{\mathcal{D}} \in \Lambda(\mathcal{D})$
(ii) $\Lambda(\mathcal{D}) = \{\hat{\lambda} : \lambda_{\min}^{\mathcal{D}} \leq \hat{\lambda} \leq \lambda_{\max}^{\mathcal{D}} \text{ and } \hat{\lambda} \text{ monotone}\}$.

Theoretically, we now have at least two solutions for a monotone classification problem with dataset $\mathcal{D} = (D, \lambda)$: the minimal and maximal extension of λ. These two classification rules we will call the *minimal rule* and the *maximal rule* respectively. In addition we have for every point x in the input space bounds that any rule $\hat{\lambda}$ must satisfy:

$$\lambda_{\min}^{\mathcal{D}}(x) \leq \hat{\lambda}(x) \leq \lambda_{\max}^{\mathcal{D}}(x).$$

Any monotone classification rule that satisfies these bounds will be another solution to our problem.

3   Induction of Monotone Decision Trees

From now on we will require the representation of our classification rule to have a specific form, viz. the form of a classification tree or decision tree. In this paper we will only consider *univariate binary* decision trees. However, we do consider non-binary trees in [6]. For univariate binary trees, at each node a split is made using a test of the form $X_i \leq c$ for some $c \in \mathcal{X}_i, 1 \leq i \leq n$. Thus, in each node the associated set $T \subset \mathcal{X}$ is split into the two subsets $T_L = \{x \in T : x_i \leq c\}$ and $T_R = \{x \in T : x_i > c\}$.

It is easily shown [6], that each subset T associated with a node or leaf can be written in the form $T = \{x \in \mathcal{X} : a \leq x \leq b\}$ for some $a, b \in \mathcal{X}$. We shall use the notation $T = [a, b]$ for a subset of this form.

We shall now show how we can generate from a data set $\mathcal{D}$ a binary decision tree $\mathcal{T}$. This process is also called *inducing* a binary decision tree $\mathcal{T}$ from a dataset $\mathcal{D}$. An algorithm for the induction of a decision tree $\mathcal{T}$ from a dataset $\mathcal{D}$ contains the following ingredients:

```
tree(𝒳, 𝒟₀):
    split(𝒳, 𝒟₀)

split(T, var 𝒟):
    𝒟 := update(𝒟, T);
    if ℋ(T, 𝒟) then
        assign class label ℒ(T, 𝒟) to leaf T
    else
        begin
            (T_L, T_R) := 𝒮(T, 𝒟);
            split (T_L, 𝒟);
            split (T_R, 𝒟)
        end
```

Fig. 1. Monotone Tree Induction Algorithm

- a *splitting rule* $\mathcal{S}$: defines the way to generate a split in each node,
- a *stopping rule* $\mathcal{H}$: determines when to stop splitting and form a leaf,
- a *labeling rule* $\mathcal{L}$: assigns a class label to a leaf when it is decided to create one.

If $\mathcal{S}, \mathcal{H}$ and $\mathcal{L}$ have been specified, then an *induction algorithm* according to these rules can be recursively described as in Figure 1.

In this algorithm outline there is one aspect that we have not mentioned yet: the *update rule*. In the algorithm we use, we shall allow the dataset to be updated at various moments during tree generation. During this process of updating we will incorporate in the dataset knowledge that is needed to guarantee the monotonicity of the resulting tree.

Note, that $\mathcal{D}$ must be passed to the split procedure as a *variable* parameter, since $\mathcal{D}$ is updated during execution of the procedure.

As noted in the beginning of this section, we only need to specify a splitting rule, a stopping rule, a labeling rule and an update rule. Together these are then plugged into the algorithm of Figure 2 to give a complete description of the algorithm under consideration. Note that each node T to be split or to be made into a leaf has the form $T = [a, b]$ for some $a, b \in \mathcal{X}$.

We start with describing the update rule. When this rule fires, the dataset $\mathcal{D} = (D, \lambda)$ will be updated. In our algorithm at most two elements will be added to the dataset, each time the update rule fires. Recall, that because T is of the form $T = [a, b]$, a is the minimal element of T and b is the maximal element of T. Now, either a or b, or both will be added to D, provided with a well-chosen labeling. If a and b both already belong to D, nothing changes. The complete update rule is displayed in Figure 2.

The splitting rule $\mathcal{S}(T, \mathcal{D})$ must be such that at each node the associated subset T is split into two nonempty subsets

$$\mathcal{S}(T, \mathcal{D}) = (T_L, T_R) \text{ with } T_L = \{x \in T : x_i \leq c\} \text{ and } T_R = \{x \in T : x_i > c\} \quad (2)$$

$$\text{update (var } \mathcal{D}, T):$$
$$\text{if } a \notin D \text{ then}$$
$$\text{begin}$$
$$D := D \cup \{a\};$$
$$\lambda(a) := \lambda_{\max}^{\mathcal{D}}(a)$$
$$\text{end;}$$
$$\text{if } b \notin D \text{ then}$$
$$\text{begin}$$
$$D := D \cup \{b\};$$
$$\lambda(b) := \lambda_{\min}^{\mathcal{D}}(b)$$
$$\text{end}$$

Fig. 2. The Update Rule of the Standard Algorithm

for some $i \in \{1, \ldots, n\}$, and some $c \in \mathcal{X}_i$. Note, that because of the assumption in section 2, T_R can also be written as $T_R = \{x \in T : x_i \geq c'\}$ for some $c' \in X_i$. Furthermore, the splitting rule must satisfy the following requirement: i and c must be chosen such that

$$\exists x, y \in D \cap T \text{ with } \lambda(x) \neq \lambda(y), x \in T_L \text{ and } y \in T_R. \tag{3}$$

Next, we consider the stopping rule $\mathcal{H}(T, \mathcal{D})$. As a result of the actions of the update rule, both the minimal element a and the maximal element b of T belong to D. Now, as a stopping rule we will use:

$$\mathcal{H}(T, \mathcal{D}) = \begin{cases} \textbf{true} & \text{if } \lambda(a) = \lambda(b), \\ \textbf{false} & \text{otherwise.} \end{cases} \tag{4}$$

Finally, the labeling rule $\mathcal{L}(T, \mathcal{D})$ will be simply:

$$\mathcal{L}(T, \mathcal{D}) = \lambda(a) = \lambda(b). \tag{5}$$

Now we can formulate the main theorem of this paper.

Theorem *If $\mathcal{D} = (D, \lambda)$ is a monotone dataset on input space $\mathcal{X}$ and if the functions $\mathcal{S}, \mathcal{H}, \mathcal{L}$ satisfy (2), (3), (4) and (5) , then the algorithm specified in Figure 1 and 2 will generate a monotone decision tree T with $\lambda_T \in \Lambda(\mathcal{D})$.*

Note, that this theorem actually proves a whole class of algorithms to be correct: the requirements set by the theorem to the splitting rule are quite general. Nothing is said in the requirements about how to select the attribute X_i and how to calculate the cut-off point c for a test of the form $t = \{X_i \leq c\}$. Obvious candidates for attribute-selection and cut-off point calculation are the well-known impurity measures like entropy, Gini or the twoing rule, see [4].

A useful variation of the above algorithm is the following. We change the update rule to

update (**var** $\mathcal{D}, T$):
    if T is homogeneous **then**
        begin
            body of update procedure of Figure 2
        end

Fig. 3. Update Rule of the Repairing Algorithm

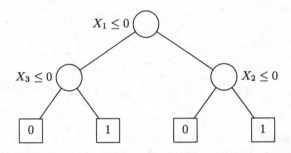

Fig. 4. Non-monotone Decision Tree

thus, only adding the corner-elements to the dataset if the node T is *homogeneous*, i.e. if $\forall x, y \in D \cap T : \lambda(x) = \lambda(y)$. If T is homogeneous, we will use the notation λ_T for the common value $\lambda(x)$ of all $x \in D \cap T$. The stopping rule becomes: $\mathcal{H}(T, \mathcal{D}) = $ **true**, if T is homogeneous and $\lambda(a) = \lambda(b)$, and **false** otherwise; and the labeling rule: $\mathcal{L}(T, \mathcal{D}) = \lambda(a) = \lambda(b) = \lambda_T$. With these changes the theorem remains true as can be easily seen. However, whereas with the standard algorithm from the beginning one works at 'monotonizing' the tree, this algorithm starts adding corner elements only when it has found a homogeneous node. For instance, if one uses maximal decrease of entropy as a measure of the performance of a test-split $t = \{X_i \leq c\}$, this new algorithm is equal to Quinlan's C4.5-algorithm, until one hits upon a homogeneous node; from then on our algorithm starts adding the corner elements a and b to the dataset, enlarging the tree somewhat, but making it monotone. We call this process *cornering*. Thus, this algorithm can be seen as a method that first builds a traditional (non-monotone) tree with a method such as C4.5 or CART, and next makes it monotone by adding corner elements to the dataset. This observation yields also the possible use of this variant: if one has an arbitrary (non-monotone) tree for a monotone classification problem, it can be 'repaired' i.e. made monotone by adding corner elements to the leaves and growing some more branches where necessary.

As an example of the use of this repairing algorithm, suppose we have the following monotone dataset $\mathcal{D} = \{000{:}0,\ 001{:}1,\ 100{:}0,\ 110{:}1\}$. Suppose further, that someone hands us the following decision tree for classifying the above dataset: This tree indeed classifies $\mathcal{D}$ correctly, but although $\mathcal{D}$ is monotone, the tree is not. In fact, it classifies data element 001 as belonging to class 1 and 101 as 0.

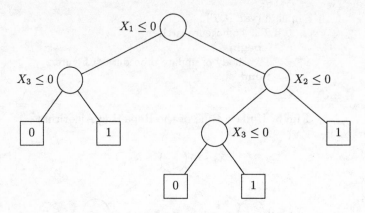

Fig. 5. The above tree, but repaired

Clearly, this conflicts with monotonicity rule (1). To correct the above tree, we apply the algorithm of Figure 3 to it. We add the maximal element of the third leaf 101 to the dataset with the value $\lambda_{\min}^{\mathcal{D}}(101) = 1$. The leaf is subsequently split and the resulting tree is easily found to be monotone, see Figure 5. Of course, if we would have grown a tree directly for the above dataset $\mathcal{D}$ with the Standard Algorithm we would have ended up with a very small tree with only three leaves.

4   Example

In this section we will use the presented Standard Algorithm to generate a monotone decision tree for the dataset of Table 1. As an impurity criterium we will use entropy, see [9]. Starting in the root, we have $T = \mathcal{X}$, so $a = 000$ and $b = 222$. Now, $\lambda_{\max}^{\mathcal{D}}(000) = 0$ and $\lambda_{\min}^{\mathcal{D}}(222) = 3$, so the elements 000:0 and 222:3 are added to the dataset, which then consists of 7 examples.

Next, six possible splits are considered: $X_1 \leq 0, X_1 \leq 1, X_2 \leq 0, X_2 \leq 1, X_3 \leq 0$ and $X_3 \leq 1$. For each of these possible splits we calculate the decrease in entropy as follows. For the test $X_1 \leq 0$, the space $\mathcal{X} = [000, 222]$ is split into the subset $T_L = [000, 022]$ and $T_R = [100, 222]$. Since T_L contains three data elements and T_R contains the remaining four, the average entropy of the split is $\frac{3}{7} \times 0.92 + \frac{4}{7} \times 1 = 0.97$. Thus, the decrease in entropy for this split is $1.92 - 0.97 = 0.95$. When calculated for all six splits, the split $X_1 \leq 0$ gives the largest decrease in entropy, so it is used as the first split in the tree.

Proceeding with the left node $T = [000, 022]$ we start by calculating $\lambda_{\min}^{\mathcal{D}}(022) = 1$ and adding the element 022:1 to the dataset $\mathcal{D}$, which will then have eight elements. We then consider the four possible splits $X_2 \leq 0, X_2 \leq 1, X_3 \leq 0$ and $X_3 \leq 1$, of which the last one gives the largest decrease in entropy, and leads to the nodes $T_L = [000, 021]$ and $T_R = [002, 022]$. Since $\lambda_{\min}^{\mathcal{D}}(021) = 0 = \lambda(000)$, T_L is made into a leaf with class 0.

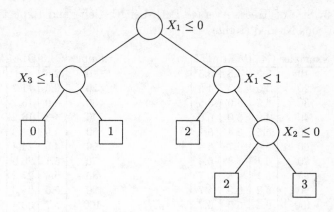

Fig. 6. Monotone Decision Tree for the Bank Loan Dataset

Proceeding in this manner we end up with the decision tree of Figure 6 which is easily checked to be monotone.

5   Experiments

We did some experiments to get an idea of the usefulness of our methods and to compare them with those of Ben-David[1,2,3] and Makino *et al.* [5]. First we did some experiments to investigate the size of the trees that our methods would generate, also in comparison with other methods. We generated random monotone datasets with 10, 20, 30, etc. examples and built trees with each of those datasets, using three different methods: C4.5 as a general method, which does not generate monotone trees, and two methods presented in this paper: MT1 is the repairing method of Figure 3, MT2 is the main method of Section 3 which we called the Standard Algorithm. As an aside, we use the abbreviation MT for Monotone Tree. In all experiments we used entropy as the impurity

Table 2. Size of trees: Number of Leaves

examples	C4.5	MT1	MT2
10	7.0	14.4	7.8
20	12.2	30.2	18.2
30	17.4	42.6	30.2
40	21.8	42.2	36.0
50	30.2	53.2	43.2
60	30.8	54.2	44.2
70	38.6	59.6	50.8
80	43.4	69.0	63.6
90	47.8	69.6	63.8
100	56.2	78.0	66.2
150	78.2	92.8	89.2

Table 3. Size of Trees: Average Path Length (left) and Expected Number of Comparisons Needed (right)

examples	C4.5	MT1	MT2
10	3.2	4.5	3.3
20	4.0	5.7	4.8
30	4.6	6.0	5.5
40	4.9	6.0	6.0
50	5.5	6.4	6.1
60	5.6	6.7	6.4
70	6.1	6.8	6.4
80	6.1	6.8	6.7
90	6.2	6.9	6.7
100	6.4	6.9	6.7
150	6.9	7.2	7.2

examples	C4.5	OLM	MT1	MT2
10	2.6	6.8	3.1	2.7
20	3.5	11.7	4.5	4.1
30	4.0	15.2	4.9	4.7
40	4.3	18.2	4.9	4.7
50	4.9	21.3	5.5	5.3
60	4.8	24.4	5.4	5.2
70	5.1	26.0	5.6	5.5
80	5.4	27.2	5.9	5.8
90	5.5	28.3	5.9	5.8
100	5.7	33.4	6.1	5.9
150	6.2	33.9	6.4	6.4

measure. For each number of examples we generated five different datasets, each from a universe with 5 attributes, each having 3 possible values, while all data elements where evenly divided over 4 classes. The results for the number of leaves of the generated trees are shown in Table 2. The figures shown are averages over the five datasets.

The size of a tree can also be measured by looking at the depth of a tree. One way to measure this depth is the average path length: the average length of a path from the root of the tree to a leaf. For instance, the average path length of the tree of Figure 6 is 2.4 since there are three paths of length 2 and two of length 3. Table 3(left) shows the results of our measurements, where the size of the generated trees is measured in average path length. Another measure of the depth of a tree is the expected number of comparisons needed to classify an arbitrary new example presented to the tree. If $T_1, \ldots, T_k$ are the leaves of a tree, this measure can be calculated as

$$\text{Expected Number of Comparisons Needed} = \sum_{i=1}^{k} \ell_i \frac{|T_i|}{|\mathcal{X}|}$$

where ℓ_i is the length of the path from the root to the leaf T_i. One advantage of this method of measuring the size of a tree is, that it can also be applied to a non-tree method such as OLM [1], where a new example also must be compared with a number of elements of the OLM-database. Thus, this last measure is also a measure of the efficiency of a classifier at classifying new examples. The results are shown in Table 3(right).

Thus, although both OLM and our decision tree methods MT1 and MT2 produce genuinely monotone classification rules, the decision tree methods appear to be much more efficient in classifying new examples. Of course, for OLM, the initial production of a classifier costs only a small fraction of the time it costs to build a new MT1 or MT2 tree, since OLM is only slightly more than a case-based system. However, when the classifiers are actually used, the situation is reversed, and our methods are superior. As a second experiment we did an

Table 4. Percentage Correctly Classified in 3-fold Cross Validation experiments

examples	C4.5	OLM	MT1	MT2
10	37.2	38.9	51.1	51.1
20	22.9	34.6	33.5	35.2
30	35.0	54.0	46.7	44.7
40	51.0	53.3	54.8	53.0
50	32.0	46.7	48.4	48.8
60	48.0	50.0	56.0	57.0
70	48.4	55.4	56.5	56.0
80	35.9	49.9	51.7	48.7
90	55.4	56.7	62.7	61.8
100	48.4	56.0	61.4	59.0
Average	41.5	49.6	52.3	51.5

Table 5. Comparison with Makino *et al.*

examples	# leaves			average depth			speed		
	Mak	MT1	MT2	Mak	MT1	MT2	Mak	MT1	MT2
10	5.8	12.2	8.0	3.0	4.1	3.2	0.4	1.0	0.6
20	7.0	14.6	10.6	3.2	4.4	4.0	0.8	1.2	0.8
30	13.0	19.2	15.2	4.2	5.1	4.5	1.8	1.2	1.8
40	15.6	21.0	18.8	4.8	5.4	5.1	2.4	2.0	2.4
50	13.6	18.8	17.6	4.3	4.9	4.8	2.4	1.6	2.4
60	19.4	23.0	20.8	5.1	5.4	5.0	3.6	2.0	3.2
70	22.4	26.0	22.2	5.3	5.6	5.2	4.6	2.4	4.8
80	25.6	31.6	30.8	5.6	6.0	5.6	5.6	3.4	6.8
90	26.8	32.4	30.2	5.7	5.7	5.6	5.8	3.6	6.8
100	31.8	32.8	31.6	5.9	5.8	5.7	7.6	4.4	8.0
150	44.8	46.2	44.2	6.3	6.2	6.1	13.8	6.4	17.6

attempt to investigate the generalizing power of the proposed methods. Again, we generated random monotone datasets of size 10, 20, etc. But now we used these datasets for 3-fold cross validation experiments. Each complete cross validation experiment was repeated four times with a different dataset. Thus, for each size and each method, we generated twelve different classifiers. The average percentage of correctly classified examples will be found in Table 4 for each of the five methods we tested. As a tentative result, it seems that our methods of Section 4 are slightly better in predicting a class for a new example than the other methods for these monotone problems. As a third and final experiment we wanted to compare our main methods with those of Makino *et al.* To do this we could only consider two class problems, since their method works only in that situation. Thus, we generated monotone datasets for two class problems with size 10, 20, etc., we generated trees with Makino and our methods MT1 and MT2, and we measured the size of the resulting trees, with the above three criteria. In addition, we measured the speed of the algorithm for generating the trees in seconds on our computer. The results are shown in Table 5. It appears that our algorithms MT1 and MT2 in the 2-class situation generate trees of comparable size, but our method MT1 seems to be faster than the method of Makino *et al.* and MT2.

6 Conclusion and Further Remarks

We have provided a tree generation algorithm for monotone classification problems with discrete domains and k classes. This improves and extends results of Ben-David [1] and Makino *et al.* [5]. This algorithm is to our knowledge the only method that guarantees to produce monotone decision trees for the k class problem. In addition, we show that our algorithm can be used to repair non-monotone decision trees that have been generated by other methods. We also discuss a number of experiments in order to test the performance of our algorithm for the k-class problem and to compare it with other methods. Our methods turn out to be much more efficient at classifying new examples than the only known existing method for monotone classification (OLM). The accuracy of our methods is at least of the same order. In the special case of the two-class problem it appears that the results of our algorithm (speed and tree size) are comparable with those of [5]. For real world monotone classification problems it would also be interesting to generate trees with different degrees of monotonicity not only in case the data set is not monotone due to noise, but also in case the data set is monotone. In our companion paper [7] on quasi-monotone decision trees we relax the requirement of full monotonicity, thereby giving an improvement of the results w.r.t. tree size, speed and generalisation. In that paper we also deal with the problem of noise.

References

1. Ben-David, A., Sterling, L., Pao, Y.H., (1989). Learning and classification of monotonic ordinal concepts. In: *Computational Intelligence*, vol. 5, pp. 45-49.
2. Ben-David, A., (1992). Automatic generation of symbolic multiattribute ordinal knowledge-based DSSs: methodology and applications. In: *Decision Sciences*, vol. 23, pp. 1357-1372.
3. Ben-David, A., (1995). Monotonicity maintenance in information-theoretic machine learning algorithms. In: *Machine Learning*, vol. 19, pp. 29-43.
4. Breiman, L., Friedman, J.H., Olshen, R.A., Stone, C.J., (1984). *Classification and regression trees.* Chapman and Hall, NewYork. Second Edition 1993.
5. Makino, K., Suda, T., Yano, K., Ibaraki, T., (1996). Data analysis by positive decision trees. In: *International symposium on cooperative database systems for advanced applications (CODAS)*, Kyoto, pp. 282-289.
6. Potharst, R., Bioch, J.C., Petter, T.C., (1997). Monotone decision trees. Technical Report EUR-FEW-CS-97-06, Erasmus University Rotterdam.
7. Potharst, R., Bioch, J.C., van Dordregt, R., (1998). Quasi-monotone decision trees for ordinal classification. Technical Report EUR-FEW-CS-98-01, Erasmus University Rotterdam.
8. Potharst, R., (1999). Classification using Decision Trees and Neural Nets. PhD-dissertation, Erasmus University Rotterdam, 1999.
9. J.R. Quinlan, (1993). *C4.5: Programs for Machine Learning*, Morgan Kaufmann, San Mateo, California.

Discovering Dynamics Using Bayesian Clustering

Paola Sebastiani[1], Marco Ramoni[2], Paul Cohen[3], John Warwick[3], and James Davis[3]

[1] Statistics Department, The Open University, Milton Keynes, United Kingdom
[2] Knowledge Media Institute, The Open University, Milton Keynes, United Kingdom
[3] Department of Computer Science, University of Massachusetts, Amherst, MA, USA

Abstract. This paper introduces a Bayesian method for clustering dynamic processes and applies it to the characterization of the dynamics of a military scenario. The method models dynamics as Markov chains and then applies an agglomerative clustering procedure to discover the most probable set of clusters capturing the different dynamics. To increase efficiency, the method uses an entropy-based heuristic search strategy.

1 Introduction

An open problem in exploratory data analysis is to automatically construct explanations of data [13]. This paper takes a step toward automatic explanations of time series data. In particular, we show how to reduce a large batch of time series to a small number of clusters, where each cluster contains time series that have similar dynamics, thus simplifying the task of explaining the data. The method we propose in this paper is a Bayesian algorithm for *clustering by dynamics*.

Suppose one has a set of univariate time series generated by one or more unknown processes, and the processes have characteristic dynamics. Clustering by dynamics is the problem of grouping time series into clusters so that the elements of each cluster have similar dynamics. For example, if a batch contains a time series of sistolic and diastolic phases, clustering by dynamics might find clusters corresponding to the pathologies of the heart. If the batch of time series represents sensory experiences of a mobile robot, clustering by dynamics might find clusters corresponding to abstractions of sensory inputs [10].

Our algorithm learns Markov chain (MC) representations of the dynamics in the time series and then clusters similar time series to learn prototype dynamics. A MC represents a dynamic process as a transition probability matrix. For each time series observed on a variable X, we construct one such matrix. Each row in the matrix represents a state of the variable X, and the columns represent the probabilities of transition from that state to each other state of the variable on the next time step. The result is a set of conditional probability distributions, one for each state of the variable X, that can be learned from a time series. A transition matrix is learned for each time series in a training batch of time series. Next, a Bayesian clustering algorithm groups time series that produce similar transition probability matrices.

D.J. Hand, J.N. Kok, M.R. Berthold (Eds.): IDA'99, LNCS 1642, pp. 199–209, 1999.

The main feature of our Bayesian clustering method is to regard the choice of clusters as a problem of Bayesian model selection and, by taking advantage of known results on Bayesian modeling of discrete variables [2], we provide closed form solutions for the evaluation of the likelihood of a given set of clusters and a heuristic entropy-based search. We note that recent work by [7, 11, 12] has investigated modeling approaches to clustering dynamic process.

While there are similarities between clustering by dynamics and learning Hidden Markov Models (HMMs), the former problem is different and somewhat simpler. An HMM has one probability distribution for the symbols emitted by each state, and also a matrix of probabilities of transitions between states [6, 4]. In our problem we fit a fully observable Markov model to each episode and then we search for the partition of these models into clusters that has maximum probability. In fact, in a related project, we developed an HMM approach to processing robot sensor data [3]. When trained on a batch of multivariate time series of sensor data, our HMM method learns a machine that generally has several paths from initial to ending states. Each training series is modeled as a sequence of state transitions along one of these paths, and so series that follow the same state transition paths might be viewed as members of a cluster. But the clustering is not based on overt similarity judgments, nor does the clustering satisfy any helpful properties, whereas clusters given by the technique in this paper constitute the maximum likelihood partition of sensor time series. In related work on clustering by dynamics, Oates has developed a method based on Dynamic Time Warping [5]. In this work, the "stretch" required to warp one multivariate time series into another is used as a similarity metric for agglomerative clustering. Because Dynamic Time Warping works on an entire time series, it is a good metric for comparing the *shape* of two series. The algorithm we discuss in this paper assumes the series are Markov chains, so clustering is based on the similarity of transition probability matrices, and some information about the shape of the series is lost. While there are undoubtedly applications where the shape of a time series is its most important feature, we find that Bayesian clustering of MCs produces meaningful groupings of time series, even in applications where the Markov assumption is not known to hold (see Section 4). Our algorithm is also very efficient and accurate, and it provides a way to include prior information about clusters and a heuristic search for the maximum likelihood clustering.

The reminder of this paper is organized as follows. We first describe the scenario on which we apply our clustering algorithm. The Bayesian clustering algorithm is described in Section 3. We apply the algorithm to a set of 81 time series generated in our application scenario and discuss the results in Section 4.

2   The Problem

The domain of our application is a simulated military scenario. For this work, we employ the *Abstract Force Simulator* (AFS) [1], which has been under development at the University of Massachusetts for several years. AFS uses a set of abstract agents called *blobs* which are described by a small set of physical features, including mass and velocity. A blob is an abstract unit; it could be an army, a soldier, a planet, or a political entity. Every blob has a small set of primitive actions that it can perform, primarily *move* and *apply-force*, to which more advanced actions, such as tactics in the military domain, can be added. AFS operates by iterating over all the units in a simulation at each clock tick and updates their properties and locations based on the forces acting on them. The physics of the world specifies probabilistically the outcomes of unit interactions. By changing the physics of the simulator, a military domain was created for this work.

Table 1. The tasks given to each blob in the scenario.

	Blob	Task
Primary Effort	Red 2	**retain** objective **Red Flag**
	Blue 2	**attack** objective **Red Flag**
Supporting Effort	Red 1	**attack** blob Blue 1
	Blue 1	**escort** blob Blue 1

The time series that we want to analyze come from a simple 2-on-2 *Capture the Flag* scenario. In this scenario, the blue team, *Blue 1* and *Blue 2*, attempt to capture the objective *Red Flag*. Defending the objective is the red team, *Red 1* and *Red 2*. The red team must defend the objective for 125 time steps. If the objective has not been captured by the 125th time step, the trial is ended and the red team is awarded a victory. The choice of goals and the number of blobs on each team provide a simple scenario. Each blob is given a task (or tactic) to follow and it will attempt to fulfill the task until it is destroyed or the simulation ends (Table 1).

In this domain, *retaining* requires the blob to maintain a position near the object of the retain — the Red Flag in this example — and protect it from the enemy team. When an enemy blob comes within a certain proximity of the object of the retain, the retaining blob will attack it. *Escorting* requires the blob to maintain a position close to the escorted blob and to attack any enemy blob that comes within a certain proximity of the escorted blob. *Attacking* requires the blob to engage the object of the attack without regard to its own state. These tactics remain constant over all trials, but vary in the way they are carried out based on environmental conditions such as mass, velocity and distance of friendly and enemy units. To add further variety to the trials, there are three initial mass values that a blob can be given. With four blobs, there are 81 combinations of

Table 2. Univariate representation of the scenario.

State #	State Description	Notes
0	(F1, FFR+, CFR+)	Strong Red
1	(F1, FFR+, CFR-)	
2	(F1, FFR-, CFR+)	
3	(F1, FFR-, CFR-)	
4	(F2, FFR+, CFR+)	Strong Red
5	(F2, FFR+, CFR-)	
6	(F2, FFR-, CFR+)	
7	(F2, FFR-, CFR-)	Strong Blue
8	(F3, FFR+, CFR+)	
9	(F3, FFR+, CFR-)	
10	(F3, FFR-, CFR+)	
11	(F3, FFR-, CFR-)	Strong Blue

these three mass values. At the end of each trial, one of three ending conditions is true:

A The trial ends in less than 125 time steps and the blue team captures the flag.

B The trials ends in less than 125 time steps and the blue team is destroyed.

C The trial is stopped at the 125th time step and the blue fails to complete its goal.

To capture the dynamics of the trials, we chose to define our state space in terms of the number of units engaged and force ratios. There are three possible engagement states at each time step. Red has more blobs "free" or unengaged (*F1*), both blue and red have an equal number of unengaged blobs (*F2*), or blue has more unengaged blobs (*F3*). In each of these states, either the red team or the blue team has more unengaged mass (*FFR+* or *FFR-* respectively). In each of the six possible combinations of the above states, either red or blue has more cumulative mass (*CFR+* or *CFR-* respectively). Altogether there are 12 possible world states, as shown in Table 2. The table shows states 0 and 4 to be especially advantageous for red and states 7 and 11 to be favorable to blue.

In the next section, we represent this set as the states of a univariate variable X, and show how to model the dynamics of each trial and then cluster trials having similar dynamics.

3   Clustering Markov Chains

We describe the algorithm in general terms. Suppose we have a batch of m time series, recording values of a variable X taking values $1, 2, ..., s$. We model the dynamics of each trial as a MC. For each time series, we estimate a transition matrix from data and then we cluster transition matrices with similar dynamics.

3.1   Learning Markov Chains

Suppose we observe a time series $x = (x_0, x_1, x_2, ..., x_{i-1}, x_i, ..)$. The process generating the sequence x is a MC if $p(X = x_t|(x_0, x_1, x_2, ..., x_{t-1})) = p(X = x_t|x_{t-1})$ for any x_t in x [8]. Let X_t be the variable representing the variable values at time t, then X_t is conditionally independent of $X_0, X_1, ..., X_{t-2}$ given X_{t-1}. This conditional independence assumption allows us to represent a MC as a vector of probabilities $p_0 = (p_{01}, p_{02}, ..., p_{0s})$, denoting the distribution of X_0 (the initial state of the chain) and a matrix of transition probabilities

$$P = (p_{ij}) = \begin{array}{c|cccc} & \multicolumn{4}{c}{X_t} \\ X_{t-1} & 1 & 2 & \cdots & s \\ \hline 1 & p_{11} & p_{12} & \cdots & p_{1s} \\ 2 & p_{21} & p_{22} & \cdots & p_{2s} \\ \vdots & & & \cdots & \\ s & p_{s1} & p_{s2} & \cdots & p_{ss} \end{array}$$

where $p_{ij} = p(X_t = j|X_{t-1} = i)$. Given a time series generated from a MC, we can estimate the probabilities p_{ij} from the data and store them in the matrix P. The assumption that the generating process is a MC implies that only pairs of transitions $X_{t-1} = i \rightarrow X_t = j$ are informative, where a transition $X_{t-1} = i \rightarrow X_t = j$ occurs when we observe the pair $X_{t-1} = i, X_t = j$ in the time series. Hence, the time series can be summarized into an $s \times s$ contingency table containing the frequencies of transitions $n_{ij} = n(i \rightarrow j)$ where, for simplicity, we denote the transition $X_{t-1} = i \rightarrow X_t = j$ by $i \rightarrow j$. The frequencies n_{ij} are used to estimate the transition probabilities p_{ij} characterizing the dynamics of the process that generated the data.

However, the observed transition frequencies n_{ij} may not be the only source of information about the process dynamics. We may also have some background knowledge that can be represented in terms of a hypothetical time series of length $\alpha + 1$ in which the α transitions are divided into α_{ij} transitions of type $i \rightarrow j$. This background knowledge gives rise to a $s \times s$ contingency table, homologous to the frequency table, containing these hypothetical transitions α_{ij} that we call *hyper-parameters*.

A Bayesian estimation of the probabilities p_{ij} takes into account this prior information by augmenting the observed frequencies n_{ij} by the hyper-parameters α_{ij} so that the *Bayesian estimate* of p_{ij} is

$$\hat{p}_{ij} = \frac{\alpha_{ij} + n_{ij}}{\alpha_i + n_i} \tag{1}$$

where $\alpha_i = \sum_j \alpha_{ij}$ and $n_i = \sum_j n_{ij}$. Thus, α_i and n_i are the numbers of times the variable X visits state i in a process consisting of α and n transitions, respectively. Formally, the derivation of Equation 1 is done by assuming Bayesian conjugate analysis with Dirichlet priors on the unknown probabilities p_{ij}. Further details are in [9]. By writing Equation 1 as

$$\hat{p}_{ij} = \frac{\alpha_{ij}}{\alpha_i} \frac{\alpha_i}{\alpha_i + n_i} + \frac{n_{ij}}{n_i} \frac{n_i}{\alpha_i + n_i} \tag{2}$$

we see that $\hat{p}_{ij}$ is an average of the classical estimate n_{ij}/n_i and of the quantity α_{ij}/α_i, with weights depending on α_i and n_i. Rewriting of Equation 1 as 2 shows that α_{ij}/α_i is the estimate of p_{ij} when the data set does not contain transitions from the state i — and hence $n_{ij} = 0$ for all j — and it is therefore called the *prior* estimate of p_{ij}, while $\hat{p}_{ij}$ is called the *posterior estimate*. The variance of the prior estimate α_{ij}/α_i is given by $(\alpha_{ij}/\alpha_i)(1 - \alpha_{ij}/\alpha_i)/(\alpha_i + 1)$ and, for fixed α_{ij}/α_i, the variance is a decreasing function of α_i. Since small variance implies a large precision about the estimate, α_i is called the *local precision* about the conditional distribution $X_t|X_{t-1} = i$ and it indicates the level of confidence about the prior specification. The quantity $\alpha = \sum_i \alpha_i$ is the *global* precision, as it accounts for the level of precision of all the s conditional distributions.

When n_i is large relative to α_i, so that the ratio $n_i/(\alpha_i + n_i)$ is approximately 1, the Bayesian estimate reduces to the classical estimate given by the ratio between the number n_{ij} of times the transition has been observed and the number n_i of times the variable has visited state i. In this way, the estimate of the transition probability p_{ij} is approximately 0 when $n_{ij} = 0$ and n_i is large. The variance of the posterior estimate p_{ij} is $\hat{p}_{ij}(1 - \hat{p}_{ij})/(\alpha_i + n_i + 1)$ and, for fixed $\hat{p}_{ij}$, it is a decreasing function of $\alpha_i + n_i$, the local precision augmented by the sample size n_i. Hence, the quantity $\alpha_i + n_i$ can be regarded as a measure of the *confidence* in the estimates: the larger the sample size, the stronger the confidence in the estimate.

3.2   Clustering

The second step of the learning process is an unsupervised agglomerative clustering of MCs on the basis of their dynamics. The available data is a set $S = \{S_i\}$ of m time series. The task of the clustering algorithm is two-fold: find the set of clusters that gives the best partition according to some measure, and assign each MC to one cluster. A partition is an assignment of MCs to clusters such that each time series belongs to one and only one cluster.

We regard the task of clustering MCs as a Bayesian model selection problem. In this framework, the model we are looking for is the most probable way of partitioning MCs according to their similarity, *given* the data. We use the probability of a partition given the data — i.e. the *posterior probability* of the partition — as scoring metric and we select the model with maximum posterior probability. Formally, this is done by regarding a partition as a hidden discrete variable C, where each state of C represents a cluster of MCs. The number c of states of C is unknown, but the number m of available MCs imposes an upper bound, as $c \leq m$. Each partition identifies a model M_c, and we denote by $p(M_c)$ its prior probability. By Bayes' Theorem, the posterior probability of M_c, given the sample S, is

$$p(M_c|S) = \frac{p(M_c)p(S|M_c)}{p(S)}.$$

The quantity $p(S)$ is the marginal probability of the data. Since we are comparing all the models over the same data, $p(S)$ is constant and, for the purpose of maximizing $p(M_c|S)$, it is sufficient to consider $p(M_c)p(S|M_c)$. Furthermore, if all models are *a priori* equally likely, the comparison can be based on the *marginal likelihood* $p(S|M_c)$, which is a measure of how likely the data are if the model M_c is true.

The quantity $p(S|M_c)$ can be computed from the marginal distribution (p_k) of C and the conditional distribution (p_{kij}) of $X_t|X_{t-1} = i, C_k$ — where C_k represents the cluster membership of the transition matrix of $X_t|X_{t-1}$ — using a well-known Bayesian method with conjugate Dirichlet priors [2, 9]. Let n_{kij} be the observed frequencies of transitions $i \to j$ in cluster C_k, and let $n_{ki} = \sum_j n_{kij}$ be the number of transitions observed from state i in cluster C_k. We define m_k to be the number of time series that are merged into cluster C_k. The observed frequencies (n_{kij}) and (m_k) are the data required to learn the probabilities (p_{kij}) and (p_k) respectively and, together with the prior hyper-parameters α_{kij}, they are all that is needed to compute the probability $p(S|M_c)$, which is the product of two components: $f(S, C)$ and $f(S, X_{t-1}, X_t, C)$. Intuitively, the first quantity is the likelihood of the data, if we assume that we can partition the m MCs into c clusters, and it is computed as

$$f(S, C) = \frac{\Gamma(\alpha)}{\Gamma(\alpha + m)} \prod_{k=1}^{c} \frac{\Gamma(\alpha_k + m_k)}{\Gamma(\alpha_k)}.$$

The second quantity measures the likelihood of the data when, conditional on having c clusters, we uniquely assign each time series to a particular cluster. This quantity is given by

$$f(S, X_{t-1}, X_t, C) = \prod_{k=1}^{c} \prod_{i=1}^{s} \frac{\Gamma(\alpha_{ki})}{\Gamma(\alpha_{ki} + n_{ki})} \prod_{j=1}^{s} \frac{\Gamma(\alpha_{kij} + n_{kij})}{\Gamma(\alpha_{kij})}$$

where $\Gamma(\cdot)$ denotes the Gamma function. Once created, the transition probability matrix of a cluster C_k — obtained by merging m_k time series — can be estimated as $\hat{p}_{kij} = (\alpha_{kij} + n_{kij})/(\alpha_{ki} + n_{ki})$.

In principle, we just need a search procedure over the set of possible partitions and the posterior probability of each partition as a scoring metric. However, the number of possible partitions grows exponentially with the number of MCs to be considered and, therefore, a heuristic method is required to make the search feasible. The solution we propose is to use a measure of similarity between estimated transition probability matrices to guide the search. Let P_1 and P_2 be transition probability matrices of two MCs. We adopt, as measure of similarity, the average Kulback-Liebler distance between the rows of the two matrices. Let p_{1ij} and p_{2ij} be the probabilities of the transition $i \to j$ in P_1 and P_2. The Kulback-Liebler distance of these two probability distributions is $D(p_{1i}, p_{2i}) = \sum_{j=1}^{s} p_{1ij} \log p_{1ij}/p_{2ij}$ and the average distance between P_1 and P_2 is then $D(P_1, P_2) = \sum_i D(p_{1i}, p_{2i})/s$.

Our algorithm performs a bottom-up search by recursively merging the closest MCs (representing either a cluster or a single trial) and evaluating whether the resulting model is more probable than the model where these MCs are separated. When this is the case, the procedure replaces the two MCs with the cluster resulting from their merging and tries to cluster the next nearest MCs. Otherwise, the algorithm tries to merge the second best, the third best, and so on, until the set of pairs is empty and, in this case, returns the most probable partition found so far. The rationale behind this ordering is that merging closer MCs first should result in better models and increase the posterior probability sooner. Note that the agglomerative nature of the clustering procedure spares us the further effort of assigning each single time series to a cluster, because this assignment comes as a side effect of clustering process.

We conclude this section by suggesting a choice of the hyper-parameters α_{kij}. We use uniform prior distributions for all the transition probability matrices considered at the beginning of the search process. The initial $m \times s \times s$ hyper-parameters α_{kij} are set equal to $\alpha/(ms^2)$ and, when two MCs are similar and the corresponding observed frequencies of transitions are merged, their hyper-parameters are summed up. Thus, the hyper-parameters of a cluster corresponding to the merging of m_k initial MCs will be $m_k\alpha/(ms^2)$. In this way, the specification of the prior hyper-parameters requires only the prior global precision α, which measures the confidence in the prior model. An analogous procedure can be applied to the hyper-parameters α_k associated with the prior estimates of p_k. We note that, since $\Gamma(x)$ is defined only for values greater than zero, the hyper-parameters α_{kij} must be non-negative.

4   Clusters of Dynamics

The 81 times series generated with AFS for the Capture the Flag scenario consist of 42 trials in which the blue team captures the red flag (end state A), 17 trials in which the blue forces are defeated (end state B) and 22 which were stopped after 125 time steps (end state C).

We used our clustering algorithm to partition the times series according to the dynamics they represent. A choice of a prior global precision $\alpha = 972$ — corresponding to the initial assignment $\alpha_{kij} = 1/12$ in the 81 transition probability matrices — yields 8 clusters. Table 3 gives the assignment of time series to each of the 8 clusters. By analyzing the dynamics represented by each cluster, it is possible to reconstruct the course of events for each trial. We did this "by hand" to understand and evaluate the clusters, to see whether the algorithm divides the trials in a significant way. We found that, indeed, the clusters correspond not only to end states, but different prototypical ways in which the end states were reached.

Clusters C_2, C_4 and C_5 consist entirely of trials in which blue captured the flag or time expired (end state A and C). While this may at first be seen as the algorithm's inability to distinguish between the two events, a large majority (though it is not possible to judge how many) of the "time-outs" were caused

Table 3. Summary of the clusters identified by the algorithm.

Cluster	A	B	C	Total
C_1	5	1	3	9
C_2	2	0	2	4
C_3	7	0	0	7
C_4	14	0	12	26
C_5	1	0	1	2
C_6	8	16	4	28
C_7	2	0	0	2
C_8	3	0	0	3
Total	42	17	22	81

by the blue team's inability to capitalize on a favorable circumstance. A good example is a situation in which the red team is eliminated, but the blue blobs overlap in their attempt to reach the flag. This causes them to slow to a speed at which they were unable to move to the flag before time expires. Only a handful of "time-outs" represent an encounter in which the red team held the blue team away from the flag. Clusters C_2, C_4 and C_5 demonstrate that the clustering algorithm can identify subtleties in the dynamics of trials, as no information about the end state is provided, implicitly or explicitly, by the world state.

Clusters C_1 and C_6 merge trials of all types. C_1 is an interesting cluster of drawn out encounters in which the advantage changes sides, and blobs engage and disengage much more than in the other clusters. For example, C_1 is the only cluster in which the MC visits all states of the variable and, in particular, is the only cluster in which state 8 is visited. By looking at the transition probabilities, we see that state 8 is more likely to be reached from state 6, and to be followed by state 0. Thus, from a condition of equal free units ($F2$) we move to a situation in which blue disengages a unit and has a free unit advantage ($F3$), which is immediately followed by a situation in which red has a free units advantage ($F1$). The "time-outs" (end state C) in this cluster represent the red team holding off the blue team until time runs out.

Cluster C_6, on the other hand, contains all but one of the trials in which the red team eliminated all of the blue units (end state B), as well as very similar trials where the red blobs appear dominant, but the blue team makes a quick move and grabs the flag. The cluster is characterized by having transitions among states 0, 4 and 10, with a large probability of staying in state 0 (in which the red forces are dominant) when reached. The large number of trials in which the blue team wins (especially large when we realize that C-endings are blue wins but for the fact that overlapping forces move very slowly) is a result of Blue 1 being tasked to escort Blue 2, a tactic which allows Blue 1 to adapt its actions to a changing environment more readily than other unit's tactics, and in many trials, gives blue a tactical advantage.

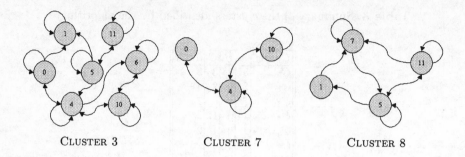

CLUSTER 3   CLUSTER 7   CLUSTER 8

Fig. 1. Markov Chains representing clusters C_3, C_7 and C_8.

Clusters C_3, C_7 and C_8 merge only times series of end state A, in which the blue team always captured the flag. Figure 1 displays the MC representing the three clusters (in which we have removed transitions with very low probability). Each cluster captures a different dynamics of how a blue victory was reached. For example, cluster C_8 is characterized by transitions among states 1, 5, 7 and 11 in which the blue team maintains dominance, and transitions to states 4 and 8 — in which the red forces are dominant — are given a very low probability. Indeed, the number of time steps of the trials assigned to cluster C_8 was always low, as the blue team maintained dominance throughout the trials and states 4 and 8 were never visited.

The trials in cluster C_7 visited states 0, 4, and 10 frequently and correspond to cases in which the blue team won despite a large mass deficit. In these cases, the objective was achieved by a break away of one of the blue blobs that outruns the red blobs to capture the flag. The trials assigned to cluster C_7 concluded with victory of the blue team despite a large mass deficit (the objective was achieved by a break away of one of the blue blobs that outruns the red blobs to capture the flag). Cluster C_3 displays transitions among states 0, 1, 4, 5, 6, 10 and 11 and represents longer, more balanced encounters in which the blue team was able to succeed.

5   Conclusions

Our overriding goal is to develop a program that automatically generates explanations of time series data, and this paper takes a step toward this goal by introducing a new method for clustering by dynamics. This method starts by modeling the dynamics as MCs and then applies a Bayesian clustering procedure to merge these MCs in a smaller set of prototypical dynamics. Explaining half a dozen clusters is much easier than explaining hundreds of time series. Although the explanations offered in this paper are still generated by human analysts — we have not yet achieved fully-automated explanation — the explanatory task is made much easier by our method.

Acknowledgments

This research is supported by DARPA/AFOSR under contract(s) No(s) F49620-97-1-0485. The U.S. Government is authorized to reproduce and distribute reprints for governmental purposes notwithstanding any copyright notation hereon. The views and conclusions contained herein are those of the authors and should not be interpreted as necessarily representing the official policies or endorsements either expressed or implied, of DARPA/AFOSR or the U.S. Government. This research was developed while Paola Sebastiani and Marco Ramoni were visiting fellows at the Department of Computer Science, University of Massachusetts, Amherst.

References

[1] M. Atkin, D. L. Westbrook, P. R. Cohen, and G D. Jorstad. AFS and HAC: The last agent development toolkit you'll ever need. In *Proceedings of the AAAI Workshop on Software Tools for Developing Agents*. American Association for Artificial Intelligence, 1998.

[2] G.F. Cooper and E. Herskovitz. A Bayesian method for the induction of probabilistic networks from data. *Machine Learning*, 9:309–347, 1992.

[3] L. Firoiu and P.R. Cohen. Experiments in abstracting from robot sensor data using hidden markov models. In *The Third Symposium on Intelligent Data Analysis*. Springer Verlag, Berlin, 1999.

[4] I.L. MacDonald and W. Zucchini. *Hidden Markov and other Models for discrete-values Time Series*. Chapman and Hall, London, 1997.

[5] T. Oates. Identifying distinctive subsequences in multivariate time series by clustering. In *Proceedings of the Sixteenth International Conference on Machine Learning*. Morgan Kaufmann Publishers, Inc., 1999. To appear.

[6] L. R. Rabiner. A tutorial on Hidden Markov Models and selected applications in speech recognition. In *Proceedings of the IEEE*, volume 77, pages 257–285, 1989.

[7] G. Ridgeway and S. Altschuler. Clustering finite discrete markov chains. In *Proceedings of the Joint Statistical Meetings, Section on Physical and Engineering Sciences*. ASA Press, 1998.

[8] S.M. Ross. *Stochastic Processes*. Wiley, New York, 1996.

[9] P. Sebastiani, M. Ramoni, and P.R. Cohen. Bayesian unsupervised classification of times series. Technical report, KMI, The Open University, 1999. Available at http://kmi.open.ac.uk/techreports/KMi-TR-76.

[10] P. Sebastiani, M. Ramoni, and P.R. Cohen. Unsupervised classification of sensory input in a mobile robot. In *Proceedings of the IJCAI Workshop on Neural, Symbolic and Reinforcement Methods for Sequence Learning*. 1999. To appear.

[11] P. Smyth. Clustering sequences with hidden Markov models. In M.C. Mozer, M.I.Jordan, and T.Petsche, editors, *Advances in Neural Information Precessing*, pages 72–93. MIT Press, Cambridge, MA, 1997.

[12] P. Smyth. Probabilistic model-based clustering of multivariate and sequential data. In *Proceedings of Artificial Intelligence and Statistics 1999*, pages 299–304. Morgan Kaufman, San Mateo CA, 1999.

[13] R. St. Amant and P. R. Cohen. Evaluation of a semi-autonomous assistant for exploratory data analysis. In *Proceedings of the First International Conference on Autonomous Agents*, pages 355–362, 1997.

Integrating Declarative Knowledge in Hierarchical Clustering Tasks

Luis Talavera and Javier Béjar

Departament de Llenguatges i Sistemes Informàtics
Universitat Politècnica de Catalunya
Campus Nord, Mòdul C6, Jordi Girona 1-3
08034 Barcelona, Spain
{talavera,bejar}@lsi.upc.es

Abstract. The capability of making use of existing prior knowledge is an important challenge for Knowledge Discovery tasks. As an unsupervised learning task, clustering appears to be one of the tasks that more benefits might obtain from prior knowledge. In this paper, we propose a method for providing declarative prior knowledge to a hierarchical clustering system stressing the interactive component. Preliminary results suggest that declarative knowledge is a powerful bias in order to improve the quality of clustering in domains were the internal biases of the system are inappropriate or there is not enough evidence in data and that it can lead the system to build more comprehensible clusterings.

1 Introduction

Clustering is a data mining task aiming to discover useful patterns in the data without any external advice. As opposed to classification tasks, where the goal is to build descriptions from labeled data, clustering systems must determine for themselves the way of dividing the objects. Several clustering methods have originated from statistics and pattern recognition, providing a wide range of choices. As pointed out by early machine learning work, a problem with most clustering methods is that they do not facilitate the interpretation task to users. A new proposal, referred to as *conceptual clustering* [3] was made in order to solve this problem. Importantly, the original formulation of conceptual clustering stated that learning should exploit any existing background knowledge. However, there is a lack of approaches concerned with this issue. From another point of view, Knowledge Discovery in Databases (KDD) has emerged as a new discipline combining methods from statistics, pattern recognition, machine learning and databases. The KDD process is described as an iterative task involving several steps with an important participation of users, especially providing background knowledge. However, clustering is often deemed as a knowledge-weak task and, in general, neither statistical nor machine learning methods make any assumption about the existence of prior knowledge.

Despite this lack of attention, clustering is a task that may obtain great benefits from using prior knowledge. The results of any inductive learning task

D.J. Hand, J.N. Kok, M.R. Berthold (Eds.): IDA'99, LNCS 1642, pp. 211–222, 1999.

are strongly dependent on the data. This is particularly true in the case of clustering, since there is no target variable to guide the process as in supervised tasks. Therefore, noise, incomplete or incorrect data may pose hard problems for building clusterings. For that reason, it appears desirable to build clustering systems with the capability of using external knowledge in the inductive process.

In this paper we present a method to incorporate prior knowledge into the process of constructing hierarchical clusterings. First we discuss the role of prior knowledge in unsupervised domains and point out some key issues. Next, we briefly review the ISAAC conceptual clustering system, which is the system employed in the experiments. Then, we propose a way of incorporating prior knowledge into the process and examine an example of using the method. An empirical study is performed using several data sets from the UCI Repository and some conclusions are presented.

2   Guiding Clustering with Prior Knowledge

We view the role of background knowledge in the clustering process under three different dimensions, namely, search, comprehensibility and validation. The influence of prior knowledge is easier to understand if we consider clustering as a search in a hypothesis space [4]. For any given data set, a potentially infinite number of hypotheses may be formulated and the problem of exploring all of them becomes intractable. To address this problem, clustering methods –and, in general, any inductive method– have to determine which hypotheses are better and discard the rest. The factors that influence the definition and selection of inductive hypotheses are called a *bias* [2]. It is easy to see that every inductive learning algorithm must include some form of bias, that is, it will always prefer some hypothesis over another. Since clustering is in nature a data-driven process, we can only expect to discover concepts that are clearly reflected in data. Of course, if the system uses the correct bias, it could discover any existing concept. However, in inductive systems, internal biases only take into account information provided by observed data, so they need some sort of external advice to change their behavior. In this sense, we can see the use of prior knowledge as an external bias that constraints the hypotheses generated and address the system towards the desired output. Therefore, prior knowledge overrides undesirable existing knowledge gathered from incomplete or incorrect data.

The second dimension related to using prior knowledge is *comprehensibility*. Comprehensibility have been typically addressed by incorporating a bias towards *simplicity*. Simplicity is often measured as the number of features used to describe the resulting concepts and hence, under two equally interesting hypotheses, systems would prefer the one which has the shorter description. However, this bias does not completely guarantee results to be comprehensible to users, rather it produces readable results. Readability is a desired property for results in order to be comprehensible, but it is not the only one. A system may present very readable results but ignore some important concept or relationship from the user point of view so that the results are not fully interpretable. In this sense,

Let $P = \{C_1, C_2, \ldots, C_K\}$ be the initial partition
Let NG be the level of generality desired

Function Isaac(P, NG)
   while Gen(P, NG) < 0 **do**
      Let C be the least general cluster in P
      Compute the similarity between C and the rest of clusters in P
      Merge C with the most similar concept in P
   endwhile

Table 1. The ISAAC algorithm.

comprehensibility may be viewed as strongly related with the user's goals and intuitions about the domain. Under this point of view, prior knowledge reflects specific user goals or reasoning paths about the concepts to be discovered and may contribute to obtain more interpretable results.

Finally, we can view prior knowledge as related to the *validation* of knowledge. The system can provide the user with the chance to alter its biases. With the selected bias, induction is performed and the results passed back to the user, who evaluates these results and decides whether they are satisfactory or not. In the later case, the user can choose a different bias. Prior knowledge acts just as another bias which can be provided by the user besides modifying the internal system biases. Validating the results of using some piece of knowledge implies to validate the correctness of this knowledge. Therefore, allowing users to express partial knowledge about the domain does not only serve as a guide for the clustering process, but also provides a mean of validating users theories.

In sum, we view the role of prior knowledge in clustering as highly related to user interaction. In unsupervised settings it is likely that it will be hard to obtain certain and complete knowledge from users. Providing clustering systems with the ability of using partial knowledge becomes an important concern and should help to confirm or reject this knowledge and obtaining additional one.

3   A Brief Introduction to ISAAC

In this section we give a brief explanation of the ISAAC system [7] which will be used to exemplify the use of prior knowledge in clustering. ISAAC is a conceptual clustering system that builds probabilistic concept hierarchies. A probabilistic description gives the feature-value distributions of the objects in a cluster. For each cluster C_k, the system stores the conditional probabilities $P(A_i = V_{ij} \mid C_k)$ for each feature A_i and each value V_{ij}. ISAAC works with nominal values estimating probabilities from the frequencies over the observed data.

ISAAC proceeds by using a typical agglomerative algorithm as shown in Table 1, in which clusters –or objects– are repeatedly merged. However, ISAAC differs from statistical agglomerative approaches in several ways. First, it is is intended to allow users to guide the construction of the cluster hierarchy which better suits their needs. The user can use the NG parameter, which is in the [0,1] range, to specify both the number of levels and their generality in the hierarchy. As the NG value increases, the system creates more general partitions with few concepts. Lower NG values instruct the system to build more specific partitions. The user can interact with the system experimenting with different sets of values for this parameter. Since the effect of modifying the NG values is semantically clear to the user, it is easier to deal with this parameter than, for instance, to specify distance thresholds to decide cut points in a tree. The algorithm shown in Table 1 presents only the procedure applied to one NG value, existing an outer loop that iterates over the different parameter values specified by the user. The initial partition P will be the set of singleton clusters for the first iteration, and for each subsequent iteration it will be the previously obtained set of clusters.

In addition, the system has not necessarily to construct binary trees as many hierarchical clustering algorithms do. Rather, it depends on the set of NG values provided by the user. This occurs because the system does not store all the intermediate mergings performed when computing a new level for the hierarchy. In order to decide when a level of generality given by the user have been reached, the system employs a probabilistic *generality* measure linked to the NG parameter. As shown in Table 1, the algorithm also takes advantage of the generality measure to choose the candidates to merge, trying to produce balanced levels formed by concepts of approximately the same level of abstraction. Although the system incorporates other capabilities such as a feature selection mechanism, they are not used in this work (see [7] for more details). Note that although incorporating some particular features, basically, the system is a hierarchical agglomerative clusterer and, therefore, the rest of the discussion and experiments might be generalized to similar algorithms as well.

4   Using Declarative Knowledge with ISAAC

Now we describe a method that enables ISAAC to exploit prior knowledge. Our focus is not only in finding a suitable bias to the system, but also in providing some feedback to the user about the relationship between their knowledge and that contained in the data. Users should experiment with different knowledge, in order to see the effect in the final results. This should provide users a mean to verify some uncertain hypotheses in the light of how they fit with the data.

We allow the user to define a set of classification rules expressed in a subset of first-order logic language (FOL). Rules always involve one universally quantified variable and an implication of the form

$$\forall x : P(x) \Rightarrow Q(x)$$

where $P(x)$ is a conjunction of predicates of the form $p(x, v)$ indicating that x takes the value v for the property p and $Q(x)$ is a predicate indicating that

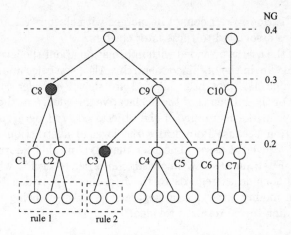

Fig. 1. Using declarative knowledge to constraint the clustering process

x belongs to class q (e.g. $\forall x : legs(x, 4) \wedge milk(x, yes) \Rightarrow mammal(x)$). In practice, we can omit the universal quantifier and express rules as a conjunctive combination of feature-value pairs:

$$(A_1 = V_{1j}) \wedge (A_2 = V_{2j}) \wedge ... \wedge (A_n = V_{nj}) \Rightarrow C_k$$

where A_i is one of the features present in the dataset and V_{ij} is one of the legal values for feature i. C_k is a dummy label for the set of objects that satisfy the rule and that may have some sense for the user (e.g. $legs = 4 \wedge milk = yes \Rightarrow mammal$). If the user defines several rules with the same label, they are considered as a disjunction and unified into a single rule. As presently defined, all the predicates must reference some feature present in the data set.

Under the ISAAC framework it is relatively easy to incorporate the bias provided by the set of rules to the clustering process. Specifically, we implemented a sort of meta-level that constraints the mergings that can be done during the agglomerative process. The goal is to obtain a cluster hierarchy consistent with the knowledge provided by the rules.

During the clustering process, there are clusters that partially represent some rule in the sense that by merging all these clusters together, we would have all the objects that the rule covers. The meta-level does not allow neither to merge any pair of clusters containing objects covered by different rules, nor merging a cluster with objects not covered by any rule with another with objects covered by some rule. For example, clusters $C1$ and $C2$ in Figure 1 cannot be merged with clusters $C3 - C7$, because this merging would prevent to finally form cluster $C8$ covering all the objects described by Rule 1. These constraints guarantee that, at certain level of generality, a cluster that completely satisfies each rule will be formed. Once a cluster includes all the instances covered by some rule, the meta-level removes all the constraints associated with this cluster. For example, cluster $C3$ covers all the objects of Rule 2 and, therefore, it can be merged with clusters $C4 - C7$. However, it cannot be merged with clusters $C1$ and $C2$ because of the constrains associated to these later clusters.

As a result, the user is provided with information about the level of generality in which the rule fits in the obtained hierarchy. Also, statistics about the number of mergings which have not been allowed are shown in order to give a rough approximation of the influence of the declarative knowledge in the process. The relative position in the hierarchy of the objects covered by a rule is a highly useful information because it indicates the level of abstraction of the rule in the context of a given dataset. The user may exploit this information in two different ways. First, he has new knowledge in order to decide which levels the hierarchy must include as regards to the hypotheses provided to the system. Second, he can modify the rules by generalizing or specializing the conditions included according to the results provided.

5   An Example of Interactive Clustering

In this section we present an example of application of the presented approach simulating interaction with a user. We used a subset of 1000 objects from the mushroom data set obtained from the UCI Repository, in which missing values have been substituted by the most frequent value. In these experiments the aim is to rediscover the original two-class division into edible and poisonous mushrooms. In a real world problem, a user would be present in order to provide background knowledge and evaluate the results. In this example, in the absence of a real user, we simulate the interaction using the number of correctly classified objects to evaluate the quality of the clusterings. Therefore, we assume that a user would prefer the more accurate cluster. Note that labels are used in the external evaluation and they are not used in any case during clustering.

Initially, assuming that no information is available, we constructed tentative clusterings by providing a set of NG values with an increment of 0.05 until obtaining two clusters at the top level. Recall that ISAAC is an agglomerative algorithm, so that it does not provide a single optimal partition, and that it needs a set of NG values in order to decide which are going to be the levels in the hierarchy. The best (i.e., the more accurate at the top level) of these clusterings was used in the rest of this experiments. Additionally, we ran the C4.5 supervised system [6] for inducing a decision tree over the same data. From the decision tree, we extracted some rules that were used to simulate the background knowledge provided by the user.

We observe that constructing a two-class top level partition provides a reasonably good description of the domain (89.50% of accuracy) but it is not completely satisfying. So we incorporate a rule that we think that classifies a class of mushrooms we will denote p:

    IF odor=f THEN p

The hierarchy reinforces this intuition since most objects covered by this rule have already been clustered together. Using this rule to bias clustering, we get a new partitioning at the top level that appears to be somewhat better

(92.90%). Additional knowledge suggest that another rule should hold for this data. Examining the hierarchy we note that an inner node contains a group that seems to correspond to our assumptions. However, the node is not clustered with our p class, as we would like. So we add the rule

```
IF odor=c THEN p
```

The resulting top level now appears to be a very good partition for this data set (95.60%). Note that, individually, these two rules do not provide completely new ways of grouping objects regarding the original decisions of the algorithm. However, considered together as describing a larger class (because they are both pointing to the same dummy label), they change the bias of the algorithm by forcing to group two subgroups that, originally, would have not been merged.

Despite these improvements, we still have an intuition about a type of p mushrooms defined by the rule:

```
IF odor=n AND spore-print-color=r THEN p
```

Again, we incorporate the rule to our process. Curiously, now we obtain a worst top level partition than before, even worst that the one obtained without using prior knowledge (70.20%). From the output of the system, we note that the last rule only covers 9 out of the 1000 objects, so we suspect that, perhaps, there is not enough evidence for supporting the addition of these few objects to our p class. A further exploration into the results reveals that the rule holds at the level obtained with $NG = 0.40$, a level partitioning the data into 7 clusters. By examining these clusters we observe that, effectively, a cluster representing the rule has been created, but the overall partition is not very good at this level either (83.70%). Is it the rule wrong? Not necessarily, since we have observed part of these objects grouped together before applying the rule. Figure 2 depicts the distribution of p and e mushrooms in part of the level formed with $NG = 0.40$. Figure 2 (a) represents the clusters formed by the original algorithm with no external guidance, while Figure 2 (b) shows the clusters obtained with the three rules. Note how the plain algorithm clusters 103 objects from the p class mixed with a number of objects of the e class. The improvement with the two first rules stems from forcing part of these objects to be clustered together with other objects from the p class forming a group of 296 objects. When adding the last rule, the group of objects induced increases only up to 305 objects. However, as shown in Figure 2 (b), forcing these few additional objects to be clustered together with our big p class, might be introducing a misleading bias. The problem is that the formed cluster is heterogeneous from the viewpoint of the data, because the last 9 objects were more similar to other objects in the e class than to these objects in the p class. By constraining a number of mergings suggested by the data, the algorithm comes up with an odd result. The lesson we learn from that is that, although we could be convinced that the 9 objects covered by the last rule effectively are part of the p class, the central tendency of the objects in the class is somewhat different, that is, these 9 objects are what could be deemed as an exception. In a probabilistic concept hierarchy, the way to represent this sort of exceptions is by allowing the special objects to be

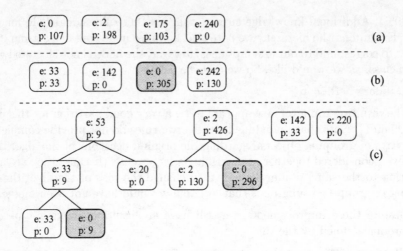

Fig. 2. Distributions of object labels in different mushroom hierarchies obtained with different levels of prior knowledge.

clustered with the wrong class at the top levels and creating internal disjuncts represented by inner nodes in the hierarchy.

We can obtain this behavior by using the same rule and changing the dummy label, so that the 9 objects are clustered together but they are not forced to be part of the big p class. The rule works as expected as shown in Figure 2 (c). Now we have the 9 objects clustered together in an inner level of the hierarchy as a child of the non-p class and the quality of the top level partition is maintained (95.60%). Finally, we think that mushrooms having odor=p should also be clustered in the p class. By examining the last hierarchy, we note that the system already has clustered together the objects satisfying this condition in an inner node in the fifth level. As in the previous case, it is unlikely that the system could cluster that small number of objects (32) correctly in the top level since they appear to be very similar to the non-p class mushrooms, being this internal disjunction the best solution.

6   Experiments

The following experiments compare the performance of the ISAAC clustering algorithm with and without using declarative knowledge. The evaluation is done on 3 data sets from the UCI Repository. Although agglomerative approaches are not as dependent on the ordering of presentation of instances as incremental systems, they depend on local merging decisions made during the clustering process. There might be several clusters in the initial stages of the process scoring the same similarities and the decision of which pair to merge first may result in

Table 2. Declarative knowledge used in the experiments

Data set	Rules	Objects

voting records	RULE 1:
	`IF physician-fee-freeze=n AND`
	`adoption-of-the-budget-resolution=y AND`
	`superfund-right-to-sue=y AND`
	`synfuels-corporation-cutback=y THEN democrat`
		37 (8.51%)

	RULE 2:
	`IF physician-fee-freeze=n AND`
	`adoption-of-the-budget-resolution=n THEN democrat`
		25 (5.75%)

	RULE 3: `IF physician-fee-freeze=n THEN democrat`	258 (59.31%)
mushroom	RULE 1: `IF odor=c THEN poisonous`	27 (2.70%)
	RULE 2: `IF odor=f THEN poisonous`	269 (26.90%)
promoters	RULE 1: `IF p-35=g AND p-12=t THEN -`	4 (3.77%)
	RULE 2: `IF p-35=t AND p-12=t AND p-10=t THEN +`	5 (4.71%)
	RULE 3: `IF p-35=t AND p-12=a THEN +`	19 (17.93%)

different final partitions. Therefore, all the results presented correspond to the average of 30 different runs of the system in order to account for this variability.

We used C4.5 to induce a decision tree for each data set. From this tree we extracted several classifying rules that were provided as background knowledge to ISAAC in additional runs. Table 2 shows the rules used for each data set and the number of total objects that each rule covers. Table 3 show the results obtained for different runs without background knowledge, with each rule and with combinations of some rules. As mentioned before, combinations of rules pointing to the same dummy label are treated as just one disjunctive rule, so that the total number of objects covered by the combined rule is the sum of the number of objects covered by its components. Results are the average percentage and standard deviations of correctly classified instances obtained by labeling each cluster with the label corresponding to the majority value of the class.

Results show that incorporating prior knowledge into the clustering process yields an important performance improvement. This improvement is especially interesting in the promoters data set, which combines a high dimensionality with a small number of objects that makes clustering very difficult and prone to high variability. It is worth to notice that it is not necessary to use very general rules in order to provide an appropriate bias to the system. In the three data sets, rules covering about a 15% of objects suffice to increase the performance of the clustering system. Of course, more general rules provide a stronger bias as shown by Rule 3 in the voting records data set. However, rules of intermediate generality appear to be powerful enough biases. The combination of rules 1 and 2 in the

Table 3. Results of using declarative knowledge on different data sets

Data set	Rule Base	Accuracy
	None	89.42 ± 2.03
voting	RULE 1	90.56 ± 0.96
records	RULE 2	92.36 ± 0.47
(435 objects, 16 feat.)	RULE 1+2	93.22 ± 0.48
	RULE 3	95.63 ± 0.00
	None	89.28 ± 0.25
mushroom	RULE 1	89.20 ± 0.25
(1000 objects, 22 feat.)	RULE 2	92.68 ± 0.25
	RULE 1+2	95.35 ± 0.25
	None	64.75 ± 11.00
	RULE 1	63.90 ± 8.75
promoters	RULE 2	57.89 ± 7.49
(106 objects, 57 feat.)	RULE 1+2	67.36 ± 9.22
	RULE 3	73.87 ± 6.96

mushroom data set and Rule 3 in the promoters data set, importantly boosts performance and covers about a 30% and 18% of objects, respectively. On the other hand, not every correct rule is a good bias for the system. For example, Rule 1 in the mushroom data set and Rules 1 and 2 applied alone in the promoters appear to decrease performance. This highlights an important issue of using prior knowledge in clustering: good rules are not only rules that correctly classify objects, but rules that appropriately modify the original biases of the system towards the desired results. Therefore, as a side result, experiments suggest the need for clustering systems of providing mechanisms of user interaction and comprehensible feedback in order to help users in validating his knowledge.

Besides modifying the bias of the system, we have pointed out that background knowledge should improve comprehensibility. In a hierarchical clustering, comprehensibility can be measured by counting the number of nodes that have to be considered in a classification path until achieving a classification. Note that testing nodes at the same level is roughly like testing disjunctions in a logical description, while descending into inner nodes is analogous to testing conjunctions. Ideally, one would like to make accurate predictions by descending only to a limited depth into the hierarchy and testing a limited number of nodes.

We run an additional experiment with the promoters data set by dividing the data into two disjoint subsets containing the 70% and 30% of objects, clustering the first subset, and using the second as a test set to predict the –unseen during learning– label. We made two sort of runs, one without background knowledge and another one using rule 3 from the previous experiments. For both, we recorded different accuracies by limiting the depth of the hierarchy at which predictions were made. These predictions are obtained from the majority value of the label in the reached node. Figure 3 shows the trade-off between accuracy and comprehensibility –measured as the number of tested nodes– obtained from 30 independent runs. Clearly, by using background knowledge, the system is able to make accurate predictions at the top levels of the hierarchy, so providing an

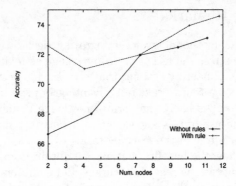

Fig. 3. Accuracy comprehensibility trade-off with and without background knowledge.

easy interpretation of the domain. By contrast, the original algorithm needs to test a higher number of nodes in order to achieve the same accuracy and, thus, suggests more complex explanations. Although the original algorithm attains a somewhat higher accuracy than using rules by descending deeper into the hierarchy, this improvement is achieved at the expense of a loss of comprehensibility. As a conclusion, results support our claims that using background knowledge improves the accuracy-comprehensibility trade-off in clustering tasks.

7 Related Work

The idea of combining declarative knowledge and inductive learning is not new. Explanation Based Learning (EBL) systems use the background knowledge contained in a domain theory to prove that an example is a member of a class and deduce a new rule which classifies more efficiently new similar examples. Most of the approaches integrating EBL and inductive learning stress the deductive component, so that they still rely strongly in a considerable amount of background knowledge [5]. Moreover, usually the inductive component is a supervised one, since EBL requires labeling of examples. On the contrary, we approach the integration of theory and data emphasizing the inductive component. Prior knowledge is viewed as a bias to help a data-driven process that, in turn, provides a confirmation on the validity of this knowledge.

Another paradigm that automatically integrates background knowledge into the learning process is Inductive Logic Programming (ILP),although there is a small body of research in clustering in this area. A recent exception is [1], although its evaluation is very limited with respect to the typical UCI data sets used for conceptual clustering. Moreover, agglomerative methods like ISAAC are common in hierarchical clustering. Since our method does not depend on any particular feature of the system, we think that it could be readily applied to any agglomerative approach, thus providing a way of integrating background knowledge without necessarily shifting to ILP tools.

8 Concluding Remarks

This work presents a methodology for integrating declarative knowledge into clustering tasks. We stress the use of prior knowledge as related to user interaction and advocate for clustering systems that can provide better interaction and feedback to the users in order to take full advantage of prior knowledge. Since in unsupervised settings it is likely that prior knowledge is uncertain and incomplete, we address the use of this knowledge as a bias to a data-driven process, which has the primary role in the learning task.

Results clearly show the benefits that we can obtain from using prior knowledge in the clustering task as regards accuracy and comprehensibility. We have also given a preliminary outline of the interactive use and validation of prior knowledge in clustering. Results highlight the important role of interaction and feedback in clustering in order to validate users theories. This becomes especially important because not every correct rule is a good bias for the clustering system, so that the user should be able of gain an appropriate insight into clustering results to decide which part of his knowledge is likely to be useful. With regard to this subject, we have outlined the benefits of a clustering system that allows the user to decide the degree of generality of the levels in a cluster hierarchy coupled with the use of prior knowledge. Other improvements such as providing feature relevances as a result of clustering may result in still better feedback.

Acknowledgments

We thank the anonymous referees for many valuable comments that greatly improved the quality of the paper. This work is partially supported by the Spanish Research Council (CICyT) project TIC96-0878.

References

[1] H. Blockeel, L. De Raedt, and J. Ramon. Top-down induction of clustering trees. In *Proceedings of the Fifteenth International Conference on Machine Learning*. Morgan Kaufmann, 1998.

[2] D. F. Gordon and M. Desjardins. Evaluation and selection of biases in machine learning. *Machine Learning*, 20(1-2):5–22, 1995.

[3] R. S. Michalski and R. E. Stepp. Learning from observation: Conceptual clustering. In R. S. Michalski, J. G. Carbonell, and T. M. Mitchell, editors, *Machine Learning: An Artificial intelligence approach*, pages 331–363. Morgan Kauffmann, 1983.

[4] T. M. Mitchell. Generalization as search. *Artificial Intelligence*, 18:203–226, 1982.

[5] D. Ourston and R. J. Mooney. Theory refinement combining analytical and empirical methods. *Artificial Intelligence*, (66):311–344, 1994.

[6] J. R. Quinlan. *C4.5: Programs for Machine Learning*. Morgan Kaufmann, San Mateo, CA, 1993.

[7] L. Talavera and J. Béjar. Efficient construction of comprehensible hierarchical clusterings. In *2nd. European Symposium on Principles of Data Mining and Knowledge Discovery*, volume 1510 of *Lecture Notes in Artificial Intelligence*, pages 93–101. Springer Verlag, 1998.

Nonparametric Linear Discriminant Analysis by Recursive Optimization with Random Initialization*

Mayer Aladjem

Department of Electrical and Computer Engineering,
Ben-Gurion University of the Negev, P.O.B. 653,
84105 Beer-Sheva, Israel
aladjem@ee.bgu.ac.il
http://www.ee.bgu.ac.il/faculty/m_a.html

Abstract. A method for the linear discrimination of two classes has been proposed by us in [3]. It searches for the discriminant direction which maximizes the distance between the projected class-conditional densities. It is a nonparametric method in the sense that the densities are estimated from the data. Since the distance between the projected densities is a highly nonlinear function with respect to the projected direction we maximize the objective function by an iterative optimization algorithm. The solution of this algorithm depends strongly on the starting point of the optimizer and the observed maximum can be merely a local maximum. In [3] we proposed a procedure for recursive optimization which searches for several local maxima of the objective function ensuring that a maximum already found will not be chosen again at a later stage. In this paper we refine this method. We propose a procedure which provides a batch mode optimization instead an interactive optimization employed in [3]. By means of a simulation we compare our procedure and the conventional optimization starting optimizers at random. The results obtained confirm the efficacy of our method.

1   Introduction

We discuss discriminant analysis which searches for a discriminant direction by maximizing the distance between the projected class-conditional densities. Unfortunately this distance is a highly nonlinear function with respect to the projected directions, and has more than one maximum. In most applications the optimal solution is searched for along the gradient of the objective function, hoping that with a good starting point the optimization procedure will converge to the global maximum or at least to a practical one. Some known techniques such as principal component analysis, Fisher discriminant analysis and their combination [1],[2] may be used for choosing a starting point for the optimization

---

* This work was supported in part by the Paul Ivanier Center for Robotics and Production Management, Ben-Gurion University of the Negev, Israel.

D.J. Hand, J.N. Kok, M.R. Berthold (Eds.): IDA'99, LNCS 1642, pp. 223–234, 1999.

procedure. Nevertheless, the observed maximum of the objective function can be merely a local maximum, which is far away from the global one in some data structures. In [3] we proposed a method for recursive optimization which searches for several large local maxima of the objective function. In this paper we refine this method. We propose a procedure for recursive optimization which ensures a batch mode optimization. Optimizing in this mode we replicate the recursive optimization using different starting points of the optimizer and then choose the best solutions from the trials done.

Section 2 describes our method for discriminant analysis [3], Section 3 presents our new proposal, and Sections 4 and 5 contain the results and analyses of the comparison based on the synthetic data sets.

2   Discriminant Analysis by Recursive Optimization

Suppose we are given training data $(\mathbf{z}_1, \mathbf{c}_1), (\mathbf{z}_2, \mathbf{c}_2), \ldots, (\mathbf{z}_{N_t}, \mathbf{c}_{N_t})$ comprising a set $Z_t = \{\mathbf{z}_1, \mathbf{z}_2, \ldots, \mathbf{z}_{N_t}\}$ of N_t training observations in n-dimensional sample space $(\mathbf{z}_j \in \mathbb{R}^n, n \geq 2)$ and their associated class-indicator vectors $\mathbf{c}_j$, $j = 1, 2, ..., N_t$. We discuss a two class problem and we require that $\mathbf{c}_j$ is a two-dimensional vector $\mathbf{c}_j = (c_{1j}, c_{2j})^T$ which shows that $\mathbf{z}_j$ belongs to one of the classes ω_1 or ω_2. The components c_{1j}, c_{2j} are defined to be one or zero according to the class-membership of $\mathbf{z}_j$, i.e. $c_{1j} = 1$, $c_{2j} = 0$ for $\mathbf{z}_j \in \omega_1$ and $c_{1j} = 0$, $c_{2j} = 1$ for $\mathbf{z}_j \in \omega_2$. The class-indicator vectors $\mathbf{c}_j$ imply decomposition of the set Z_t into two subsets corresponding to the unique classes. We denote by N_{t_i} the number of the training observations in class ω_i, for $i = 1, 2$.

Our method requires a normalization of the data, called sphering [6]. To achieve data sphering we perform an eigenvalue- eigenvector decomposition $\mathbf{S}_z = \mathbf{R}\mathbf{D}\mathbf{R}^T$ of the pooled sample covariance matrix $\mathbf{S}_z$ estimated over training set Z_t. Here $\mathbf{R}$ and $\mathbf{D}$ are $n \times n$ matrices; $\mathbf{R}$ is orthonormal and $\mathbf{D}$ diagonal. We then define the normalization matrix $\mathbf{A} = \mathbf{D}^{-1/2}\mathbf{R}^T$. The matrix $\mathbf{S}_z$ is assumed to be non-singular, otherwise only the eigenvectors corresponding to the non-zero eigenvalues must be used in the decomposition [6]. In the remainder of the paper, all operations are performed on the *sphered training data* $X_t = \{\mathbf{x}_j : \mathbf{x}_j = \mathbf{A}(\mathbf{z}_j - \mathbf{m}_z), \mathbf{z}_j \in Z_t, j = 1, 2, \ldots, N_t\}$ with $\mathbf{m}_z$ the sample mean vector estimated over $\mathbf{Z}_t$. For the sphered training data X_t the pooled sample covariance matrix becomes the identity matrix $\mathbf{A}\mathbf{S}_z\mathbf{A}^T = \mathbf{I}$.

We discuss discriminant analysis carried out by a linear mapping $y = \mathbf{w}^T\mathbf{x}$, $\mathbf{x} \in \mathbb{R}^n$, $y \in \mathbb{R}^1$, $n \geq 2$, with $\mathbf{x}$ an arbitrary n-dimensional observation, and $\mathbf{w}$ a direction vector. We require $\mathbf{w}$ to have unit length, and $y = \mathbf{w}^T\mathbf{x}$ can be interpreted geometrically as the projection of the observation $\mathbf{x}$ onto vector $\mathbf{w}$ in x-space (Fig.1).

We search for the discriminant vector $\mathbf{w}^*$

$$\mathbf{w}^* = \arg\max_{\mathbf{w}}\{PF(\mathbf{w})\}$$

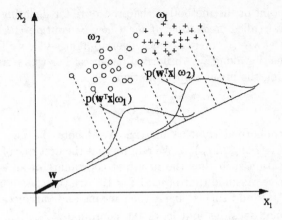

Fig. 1. Linear mapping $(y = \mathbf{w}^T\mathbf{x})$ in a two- dimensional $\mathbf{x}$-space. Class-conditional densities $p(\mathbf{w}^T\mathbf{x}|\omega_1)$ and $p(\mathbf{w}^T\mathbf{x}|\omega_2)$ along the vector $\mathbf{w}$.

which maximizes the *Patrick-Fisher (PF) distance* [5] between the class-conditional densities along it. $PF(\mathbf{w})$ denotes the PF distance along an arbitrary vector $\mathbf{w}$

$$PF(\mathbf{w}) = \left\{ \int_{\mathbb{R}^n} \left[\frac{N_{t1}}{N_t}\hat{p}(\mathbf{w}^T\mathbf{x}|\omega_1) - \frac{N_{t2}}{N_t}\hat{p}(\mathbf{w}^T\mathbf{x}|\omega_2) \right]^2 dx \right\}^{1/2} \qquad (1)$$

with

$$\hat{p}(\mathbf{w}^T\mathbf{x}|\omega_i) = \frac{1}{h\sqrt{2\pi}N_{ti}} \sum_{j=1}^{N_t} c_{ij} exp\left\{ \frac{-1}{2h^2} \left[\mathbf{w}^T(\mathbf{x} - \mathbf{x}_j) \right]^2 \right\} \ , i = 1, 2 \qquad (2)$$

the Parzen estimators with Gaussian kernels of the class-conditional densities of the projections $y = \mathbf{w}^T\mathbf{x}$. Here $\mathbf{x}$ is an arbitrary observation $(\mathbf{x} \in \mathbb{R}^n)$, c_{ij} is the class- indicator which constrains the summation in (2) on the ω_i- training observations ($\mathbf{x}_j$ corresponding to $c_{ij} = 1$), and h is a smoothing parameter.

$PF(\mathbf{w})$ is a nonlinear function with respect to $\mathbf{w}$. In order to search for several large local maxima of $PF(\mathbf{w})$ we have proposed a method for recursive maximization of $PF(\mathbf{w})$ [3]. We obtain a discriminant vector $\mathbf{w}^*$ related to a local maximum $PF(\mathbf{w}^*)$ and then we transform the data along $\mathbf{w}^*$ into data with greater overlap of the class-conditional densities (deflated maximum of $PF(\mathbf{w})$ at the solution $\mathbf{w}^*$), and iterate to obtain a new discriminant vector.

In our method we use the PF distance (1) because of the existence of an analytical expression of its gradient [5] used in the iterative optimization. Actually our method is not restricted to the PF distance only. It can be applied to any other discriminant criterion, which has several local maxima with respect to $\mathbf{w}$. In the case that an analytical expression of the gradient of the criterion can not be obtained we must estimate the gradient numerically.

The main point of the method is the procedure for deflating the local maximum of $PF(\mathbf{w})$ called *Reduction of the Class Separation* (RCS). In order to deflate $PF(\mathbf{w})$ at $\mathbf{w}^*$ (to increase class overlap along $\mathbf{w}^*$), we transform class-conditional densities along $\mathbf{w}^*$ to normal densities. For this purpose, we rotate the data applying the linear transformation

$$\mathbf{r} = \mathbf{U}\mathbf{x} \tag{3}$$

with $\mathbf{U}$ an orthonormal $(n \times n)$ matrix. We denote the new coordinates as $r_1, r_2, \ldots, r_n$ ($\mathbf{r} = (r_1, r_2, \ldots, r_n)^T$). We require that the first row of $\mathbf{U}$ is $\mathbf{w}^*$, which results in a rotation such that the new first coordinate of an observation $\mathbf{x}$ is $r_1 = y = (\mathbf{w}^*)^T \mathbf{x}$. Assume that $p(y|\omega_i), i = 1, 2$ are the class-conditional densities of $y = (\mathbf{w}^*)^T \mathbf{x}$ and $\mathbf{m}_{y|\omega_i}$, $\sigma^2_{y|\omega_i}$ their means and variances. We transform $p(y|\omega_i)$ to normal densities and leave the coordinates $r_2, r_3, \ldots, r_n$ unchanged. Let $\mathbf{q}$ be a vector function with components $q_1, q_2, \ldots, q_n$ that carries out this transformation: $r_1' = q_1(y)$ with r_1' having normal class-conditional distributions and $r_i' = q_i(r_i), i = 2, 3, \ldots, n$ each given by the identity transformations. The function q_1 is obtained by the percentile transformation method:

- for observations $\mathbf{x}$ from class ω_1:

$$q_1(y) = \left[\Phi^{-1}\left(F(y|\omega_1) \right) \right] (\sigma^2_{y|\omega_1} \pm \triangle\sigma^2)^{1/2} + (\mathbf{m}_{y|\omega_1} - \triangle\mathbf{m}_1); \tag{4}$$

- for observations $\mathbf{x}$ from class ω_2:

$$q_1(y) = \left[\Phi^{-1}\left(F(y|\omega_2) \right) \right] (\sigma^2_{y|\omega_2} \pm \triangle\sigma^2)^{1/2} + (\mathbf{m}_{y|\omega_2} - \triangle\mathbf{m}_2). \tag{5}$$

Here, $\triangle\sigma^2 (0 \leq \triangle\sigma^2 \leq 1)$, $\triangle\mathbf{m}_1$, $\triangle\mathbf{m}_2$ are user-supplied parameters, $F(y|\omega_i)$ is the class-conditional (cumulative) distribution function of $y = (\mathbf{w}^*)^T \mathbf{x}$ for $i = 1, 2$ and Φ^{-1} is the inverse of the standard normal distribution function Φ. Finally,

$$\mathbf{x}' = U^T \mathbf{q}(\mathbf{U}\mathbf{x}) \tag{6}$$

transforms the class-conditional densities along $\mathbf{w}^*$ to be normal densities

$$p(r_1'|\omega_i) = N(\mathbf{m}_{y|\omega_i} - \triangle\mathbf{m}_i, \sigma^2_{y|\omega_i} \pm \triangle\sigma^2) \tag{7}$$

leaving all directions orthogonal to $\mathbf{w}^*$ unchanged. If we set $\triangle\sigma^2 = 0$ and $\triangle\mathbf{m}_i = 0$, $i = 1, 2$ we make minimal changes of the data in the sense of the minimal relative entropy distance measure between the original and transformed class-conditional distributions [6, p.254] and [7, p.456]. If $\sigma^2_{y|\omega_i} \pm \triangle\sigma^2 = 1$ and $\mathbf{m}_{y|\omega_i} - \triangle\mathbf{m}_i = 0$, $i = 1, 2$ we transform the class-conditional densities along $\mathbf{w}^*$ to $N(0, 1)$ which results in full overlap of the classes along $\mathbf{w}^*$. This certainly eliminates the local maximum of the PF distance along $\mathbf{w}^*$, but it causes large changes of the distributions of the transformed data $\mathbf{x}'$ (6) in some applications. In order to direct the local optimizer to a new maximum of $PF(\mathbf{w})$, and to keep the class-conditional densities of $\mathbf{x}'$ (6) as close to the densities of the original data $\mathbf{x}$ as possible we search for the smallest values of the parameters $\triangle\sigma^2$,

$\triangle \mathbf{m}_1$, $\triangle \mathbf{m}_2$ that result in a deflated PF distance along $\mathbf{w}^*$. We start our search with $\triangle \sigma^2 = 0$ and $\triangle \mathbf{m}_i = 0, i = 1, 2$ (minimal changes of the data) and then we make trials increasing the values of $\triangle \sigma^2$ in the interval $(0 \leq \triangle \sigma^2 \leq 1)$. We choose the sign (+ or -) of the change ($\pm \triangle \sigma^2$) in order to approach $\sigma^2_{y|\omega_i} \pm \triangle \sigma^2$ to 1. We assign the latter value to 1 if it crosses 1. For each $\triangle \sigma^2$ we compute the values of $\triangle \mathbf{m}_1$ and $\triangle \mathbf{m}_2$ by an expression proposed by us in [3,p.294].

We presented the RCS in its abstract version based on probability distributions. The application to observed data is accomplished by substituting estimates of $F(y|\omega_i)$, $\mathbf{m}_{y|\omega_i}$ and $\sigma^2_{y|\omega_i}$ over the training set X_t.

3   Batch Mode Recursive Optimization Procedure

Here we refine our recursive optimization procedure developed in [3]. The idea is to ensure optimization in a batch mode instead of the optimization in an interactive mode proposed in [3]. For this purpose we propose a procedure which performs successive modification of the training data automatically (without man-machine interactions). In order to formalize this procedure we introduce the following nomenclature:

- X_t denotes the original (sphered) training data.
- $\mathbf{w}^*$ is the directional vector corresponding to the local maximum of the PF distance for the original data X_t.
- $\tilde{\mathbf{X}}_t$ denotes the training data used in the current iteration of the procedure.
- $\tilde{\mathbf{w}}$ is the directional vector corresponding to the local maximum of the PF distance for the current training data $\tilde{\mathbf{X}}_t$.
- $\tilde{\mathbf{X}}_t'$ denotes the modified training data which has a deflated PF distance along $\tilde{\mathbf{w}}$.
- $\tilde{\mathbf{w}}'$ is the directional vector corresponding to the local maximum of the PF distance for the modified training data $\tilde{\mathbf{X}}_t'$.

We propose the following computational procedure:

Step 1 *Starting from a directional vector we maximize the PF distance for the original training data* X_t. We save the optimal solution denoted by $\mathbf{w}^*$.

Step 2 *Initialization of the Reduction of the Class-Separation (RCS):* We initialize the current training data $\tilde{\mathbf{X}}_t$ with the original training data X_t ($\tilde{\mathbf{X}}_t = X_t$) and the current optimal solution $\tilde{\mathbf{w}}$ with the optimal solution $\mathbf{w}^*$ for X_t ($\tilde{\mathbf{w}} = \mathbf{w}^*$). We set $\triangle \sigma^2 = 0$ and $\triangle \mathbf{m}_i = 0$, for $i = 1, 2$. This setting implies minimal changes of the data during the RCS.

Step 3 *Running the RCS:* We estimate the class- conditional means, variances and (cumulative) distribution functions over the projections $y_j = (\tilde{\mathbf{w}})^T \tilde{\mathbf{x}}_i$ of the current training observations $\tilde{\mathbf{x}}_j \in \tilde{\mathbf{X}}_t$ onto the current optimal vector $\tilde{\mathbf{w}}$. We substitute these estimates into (4) and (5), transform $\tilde{\mathbf{x}}_j \in \tilde{\mathbf{X}}_t$ using (6), and obtain the modified training data $\tilde{\mathbf{X}}_t' = \{\mathbf{x}_j' : \mathbf{x}_j' = \mathbf{U}^T \mathbf{q}(\mathbf{U} \tilde{\mathbf{x}}_j) \ j = 1, 2 \ldots N_t\}$ which has a deflated PF distance along the optimal solution $\tilde{\mathbf{w}}$.

Step 4 *Starting from $\tilde{\mathbf{w}}$ we maximize the PF distance for the modified training data* $\tilde{\mathbf{X}}_t'$. We save the optimal solution denoted by $\tilde{\mathbf{w}}'$.

Step 5 *Starting from* $\tilde{\mathbf{w}}'$ *we maximize the PF distance for the original training data* X_t. We save the optimal solution $\mathbf{w}^*$.

Step 6 *Updating the control parameters* $\triangle\sigma^2$, $\triangle\mathbf{m}_1$, $\triangle\mathbf{m}_2$ *and the current training data* $\tilde{\mathbf{X}}_t$: We compare the last two solutions $\mathbf{w}^*$ saved in Step 5 and for the first trial in Step 1 and Step 5.

(a) If the last two solutions $\mathbf{w}^*$ are equal, we increase $\triangle\sigma^2$ (deflate more strongly the PF distance along $\tilde{\mathbf{w}}$) and update $\triangle\mathbf{m}_1$, $\triangle\mathbf{m}_2$ by an expression proposed by us in [3,p.294]. Our experience is that an increase of $\triangle\sigma^2$ with step-size 0.1 is suitable.

(b) If the last two solutions $\mathbf{w}^*$ are different (different local maxima of the PF distance have been identified) we update the current training data $\tilde{\mathbf{X}}_t$ with the modified training data $\tilde{\mathbf{X}}'_t$ ($\tilde{\mathbf{X}}_t = \tilde{\mathbf{X}}'_t$), update the current direction of the RCS $\tilde{\mathbf{w}}$ with the optimal solution $\tilde{\mathbf{w}}'$ for $\tilde{\mathbf{X}}'_t$ ($\tilde{\mathbf{w}} = \tilde{\mathbf{w}}'$) and restore the initial values of the control parameters $\triangle\sigma^2 = 0$, $\triangle\mathbf{m}_1 = 0$, $\triangle\mathbf{m}_2 = 0$.

Then we repeat Steps 3-6. We stop the iterations if several optimal solutions $\mathbf{w}^*$ corresponding to different values of the $PF(\mathbf{w}^*)$ (1) are obtained.

We replicate the proposed procedure (Steps 1-6) starting from different initial vectors in Step 1. We choose them by the preliminary principal component and Fisher discriminant analysis as we did in [3] and at random which is a usual initialization in the conventional optimization. Finally we choose from the vectors $\mathbf{w}^*$ saved in Step 5 those corresponding to large values of $PF(\mathbf{w}^*)$. We regard the selected $\mathbf{w}^*$, as "interesting" solutions.

4   An Interactive Run of the Recursive Optimization Procedure

Here we demonstrate the recursive optimization procedure in a run using two dimensional synthetic data. We used samples for two classes of the sample sizes $N_{t1} = N_{t2} = 50$, which were drawn from two-dimensional normal mixtures:

for class ω_1:

$$p(x_1, x_2|\omega_1) = \tfrac{1}{3}N([-1.5\ \ 0]^T, \varSigma) + \tfrac{1}{3}N([0.5\ \ -3]^T, \varSigma) + \tfrac{1}{3}N([-1\ \ -3]^T, \varSigma),$$

for class ω_2:

$$p(x_1, x_2|\omega_2) = \tfrac{1}{3}N([-0.5\ \ 3]^T, \varSigma) + \tfrac{1}{3}N([3\ \ 0]^T, \varSigma) + \tfrac{1}{3}N([0.5\ \ -3]^T, \varSigma).$$

Here, $N([\mu_1\ \mu_2]^T, \varSigma)$ denotes bivariate normal density with a mean vector $[\mu_1\ \mu_2]^T$ and a diagonal covariance matrix $\varSigma = diag(0.1, 0.2)$. Fig.2 presents the original (sphered) training data X_t.

For this data we computed the PF distances for 91 equally angled directions into the (x_1, x_2)-plane. The solid path "—" in Fig.3 presents $PF(\mathbf{w})$ (1) for the vectors $\mathbf{w}$ directed under different angles with respect to x_1-axis. We observe local maxima of $PF(\mathbf{w})$ at angles $19°$, $64°$, $105°$, $128°$ and $162°$. We ran our procedure described in Section 3. In Step 1 we chose $\mathbf{w}^*$ directed under $105°$

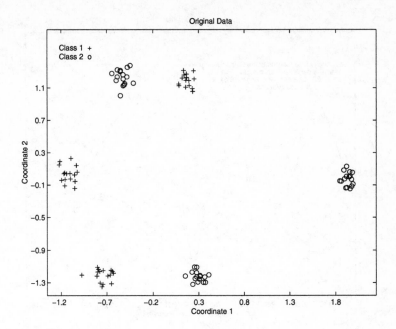

Fig. 2. Original data X_t.

with respect to x_1-axis and observed local maximum $PF(\mathbf{w}^*) = 0.52$ (see — in Fig.3). Then we ran Steps 3-6 three successive times keeping $\triangle\sigma^2 = 0$, $\triangle\mathbf{m}_1 = 0$, $\triangle\mathbf{m}_2 = 0$.

Here we analyze the result obtained in the first run of the Steps 3-6. In Fig. 4 we present the transformed data $\tilde{\mathbf{X}}_t'$ obtained in Step 3. Comparing $\tilde{\mathbf{X}}_t'$ (Fig.4) with the original data X_t (Fig.2), we observe that a significant class overlap was gained along the direction under 105° for the transformed data $\tilde{\mathbf{X}}_t'$. This is a desired result because our goal was to deflate the local maximum of the PF distance at 105° in order to direct the local optimizer to another solution. We calculated $PF(\mathbf{w})$ for $\tilde{\mathbf{X}}_t'$ using different directions of $\mathbf{w}$ and show the PF-path "..." in Fig.3. We observe that our procedure eliminated the maximum at 105° and smoothed the shape of the PF distance in the range 45° -180° causing some restructuring of its shape. It seems reasonable to search for other data transformations which cause less restructuring of the PF distance. In [4] we proposed a neural network implementation of the RCS which by performing highly nonlinear data transformation decreases the restructuring of the PF distance, but its complexity is higher than that of the procedure proposed in Section 3.

In the second and third iterations of Steps 3-6 we computed the PF distances for the successively transformed data $\tilde{\mathbf{X}}_t'$.The PF-paths are shown in Fig.3. The local maxima of these paths at 83°, 15° and 152° defined the starting points of the optimizer of PF distance for the original data X_t in Step 5. Using them our procedure converges to the solutions at 64°, 19° and 162° for the original data

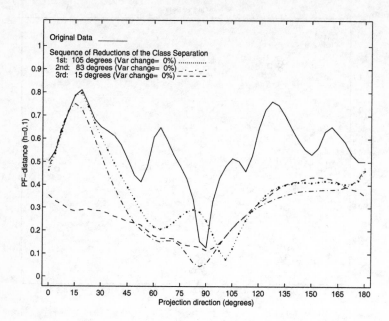

Fig. 3. PF distance for various directions into (x_1, x_2)-plane: original data —;
transformed data after successive RCS's at $105°$ ..., $83°$ -.-.- and $15°$ - - -.

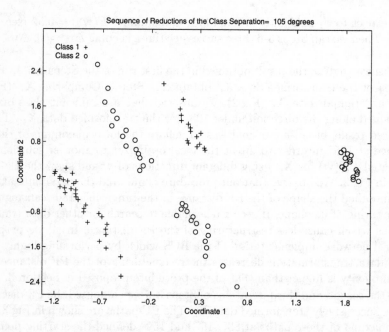

Fig. 4. Transformed data $X_t{'}$ after the RCS at $105°$.

"—" (see Fig.3). We found the two largest local maxima of the PF distance at $19°$ and $64°$, which are located far away from the starting initialization $105°$ used in Step 1. The latter can not be obtained by conventional optimization.

5   A Comparative Study

Here we compare the discrimination qualities of the discriminant vectors $\mathbf{w}^*$ obtained by our recursive procedure (Section 3) and those obtained by the conventional optimization with a random initialization of the starting directional vectors.

We ran experiments with observations drawn from six- dimensional distributions $p(\mathbf{x}|\omega_i) = p(x_1, x_2|\omega_i)p(x_3, x_4|\omega_i)p(x_5|\omega_i)p(x_6|\omega_i)$ for $i = 1, 2$. Here the densities were constructed with the following mixtures of the normal distributions:

for class ω_1:

$$p(x_1, x_2|\omega_1) = \tfrac{1}{3}N([0\ 1]^T, \mathbf{I}) + \tfrac{1}{3}N([5\ 3]^T, \mathbf{I}) + \tfrac{1}{3}N([0\ 6]^T, \mathbf{I})$$

$$p(x_3, x_4|\omega_1) = \tfrac{1}{3}N([-3\ 0]^T, 0.01\mathbf{I}) + \tfrac{1}{3}N([0.5\ 3]^T, 0.01\mathbf{I})$$

$$+ \tfrac{1}{3}N([-0.5\ -3]^T, 0.01\mathbf{I})$$

for class ω_2:

$$p(x_1, x_2|\omega_2) = \tfrac{1}{3}N([0\ 3]^T, \mathbf{I}) + \tfrac{1}{3}N([5\ 6]^T, \mathbf{I}) + \tfrac{1}{3}N([-5\ 6]^T, \mathbf{I})$$

$$p(x_3, x_4|\omega_2) = \tfrac{1}{3}N([-0.5\ 3]^T, 0.01\mathbf{I}) + \tfrac{1}{3}N([3\ 0]^T, 0.01\mathbf{I})$$

$$+ \tfrac{1}{3}N([0.5\ -3]^T, 0.01\mathbf{I})$$

and $p(x_5|\omega_i) = p(x_6|\omega_i) = N(0, 1)$. The classes were totally overlapped in the (x_5, x_6)-plane, partially overlapped in the (x_1, x_2)-plane and totally separated in the (x_3, x_4)-plane. We chose the data having several local maxima for $PF(\mathbf{w})$ (1). We observed two local maxima of $PF(\mathbf{w})$ into the (x_1, x_2)-plane and several local maxima into the (x_3, x_4)-plane including the global maximum of $PF(\mathbf{w})$. We set $N_{t1} = N_{t2} = 50$.

We carried out 150 runs of our procedure, starting from different initial directional vectors in Step 1. The components of the initial vectors were drawn at random from $N(0, 1)$.

We compared the discrimination quality of $\mathbf{w}^*$ in Step 1 and Step 5. In Step 1 we carried out the conventional optimization with random initialization of the starting directional vector while in Step 5 we employed our recursive optimization.

We evaluated the discrimination qualities of $\mathbf{w}^*$ by the resulting values of the $PF(\mathbf{w}^*)$ computed for the test (extra, validation) observations (500 per class).

In Steps 1, 4 and 5 we maximized $PF(\mathbf{w})$ (1) by a sequential quadratic programming method (routine E04UCF in the NAG Mathematical Library). We set the number of major iterations of the optimization routine E04UCF to 50. This setting was proved to be appropriate by a preliminary test.

We set $\mathbf{m}_{y|\omega_i} - \triangle \mathbf{m}_i = 0$ and $\sigma^2_{y|\omega_i} \pm \triangle \sigma^2 = 1$ for i=1,2 in (4) and (5) for all runs. This setting implies that the class- conditional densities of q_1 (4) and (5) are $N(0,1)$ which results in a modified training data $\tilde{\mathbf{X}}_t{}'$ (Step 3) with an approximately full overlap of the classes for the previously defined discriminant directions. This certainly eliminates the local maximum of $PF(\mathbf{w})$ at the previous solutions but it causes a large restructuring of $\tilde{\mathbf{X}}_t{}'$ which is highly unfavorable to our procedure.

We carried out three successive runs of Steps 3-6. In order not to favor our procedure by expanding the number of iterations in the optimization, we re-ran Step 1 with an extended number of the major iterations of the optimization routine E04UCF. We set it to $50 \times 2 \times N_{(steps3-6)}$, with $N_{(steps3-6)}$ the number of repetitions of Steps 3-6 (in our experiments $N_{(steps3-6)} = 3$). In the comparison we used the largest value of $PF(\mathbf{w}^*)$ obtained in Step 1.

We studied the situations (initial directional vectors) in which the conventional optimization failed with the value of $PF(\mathbf{w}^*)$ smaller then 0.35 (dashed path "- - -" in Fig.5). The solid path "—" in Fig.5 presents the results obtained by our procedure. The dots in the bottom of Fig.5 indicate the sequential number of the iteration which implies the largest value of $PF(\mathbf{w}^*)$ ($\cdot$ - first, $\cdot\cdot$ - second and $\cdot\cdot\cdot\cdot$ - third iteration). The dots which are missing indicate a case (random initializations 45, 55, 94) for which the conventional optimization was better then our procedure. Our recursive optimization (solid path) outperforms the conventional optimization in Step 1 (dashed path) for the most of the initializations.

We summarize the overall shape of the PF distance over the 100 replications by the boxplots shown in Fig.6. The boxplot in the left presents the values of $PF(\mathbf{w}^*)$ for the optimal solutions $\mathbf{w}^*$ obtained by the conventional optimization, the central boxplot illustrates the $PF(\mathbf{w}^*)$ for $\mathbf{w}^*$ obtained by our recursive optimization procedure, and the boxplot in the right presents the paired difference of the values of $PF(\mathbf{w}^*)$ (the difference of the solid and dashed paths of Fig.5). In Fig.6 the boxes show the values of the PF distances between quartiles; the lines represent the medians of the PF distances. Whiskers go out to the extremes of the PF distances. We observe that the values of $PF(\mathbf{w}^*)$ of our procedure tend to be larger than the values of $PF(\mathbf{w}^*)$ of the conventional optimization.

Finally we calculated the averaged difference of the values of $PF(\mathbf{w}^*)$ obtained by our recusive optimization and by the conventional optimization, which was 0.24. We evaluated the significance of this difference by the paired t-test and obtained the 99 percent confidence interval 0.24 ± 0.08 which confirms a significant increase of $PF(\mathbf{w}^*)$ for $\mathbf{w}^*$ obtained by our procedure.

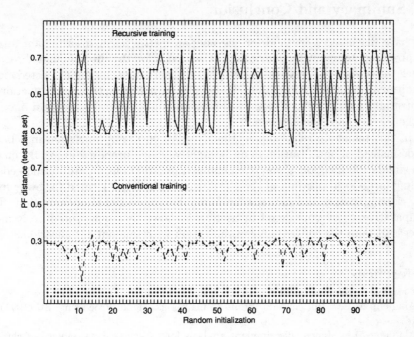

Fig. 5. Random initializations in which conventional optimization failed with the value of $PF(\mathbf{w}^*)$ smaller than 0.35.

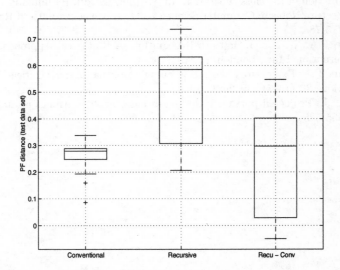

Fig. 6. Boxplots of the values of the $PF(\mathbf{w}^*)$ for $\mathbf{w}^*$ obtained by the conventional optimization and our recursive optimization.

6 Summary and Conclusion

We have discussed a method for the nonparametric linear discriminant analysis proposed by us in [3] previously. It searches for the discriminant direction which maximizes the Patrick-Fisher (PF) distance between the projected class-conditional densities. Since the PF distance is a highly nonlinear function, a sequential search for the directions corresponding to several large local maxima of the PF distance has been used.

In this paper we refine our method [3]. We ensure optimization in a batch mode instead of optimization in an interactive mode proposed in [3]. By means of a simulation (Section 4) we have demonstrated that our procedure succeeds in finding large local maxima of the PF distance which are located far away from the starting point, and can not be found by conventional optimization. The comparative study considered in Section 5 shows that our procedure is more successful than the conventional optimization with random initialization.

References

1. Aladjem, M.E.: Multiclass discriminant mappings. Signal Processing. **35** (1994) 1–18
2. Aladjem, M.E.: Linear discriminant analysis for two-classes via removal of classification structure. IEEE Trans. Pattern Anal. Mach. Intell. **19** (1997) 187–192
3. Aladjem, M.E.: Nonparametric discriminant analysis via recursive optimization of Patrick-Fisher distance. IEEE Trans. on Syst., Man, Cybern. **28B** (1998) 292–299
4. Aladjem, M.E.: Linear discriminant analysis for two classes via recursive neural network reduction of the class separation. In A.Amin, D.Dori, P.Pudil and H.Freeman (eds.), Lecture Notes in Computer Science **1451**: Advances in Pattern Recognition. (1998) 775-784
5. Devijver, P.A., Kittler, J.: Pattern Recognition: A Statistical Approach. Prentice-Hall International Inc., London. (1982)
6. Friedman, J.H.: Exploratory projection pursuit. Journal of the American Statistical Association. **82** (1987) 249–266
7. Huber, P.J.: Projected pursuit, including discussions. The Annals of Statistics. **13** (1985) 435-525

Supervised Classification Problems: How to Be Both Judge and Jury

Mark G. Kelly, David J. Hand, and Niall M. Adams

Department of Mathematics, Imperial College
The Huxley Building, 180 Queen's Gate, London, SW7 2BZ, UK
{m.g.kelly, d.j.hand, n.adams}@ic.ac.uk

Abstract. In many supervised classification problems there is ambiguity about the definitions of the classes. Sometimes many alternative but similar definitions could equally be adopted. We propose taking advantage of this by choosing that particular definition which optimises some additional criterion. In particular, one can choose that definition which leads to greatest predictive classification accuracy, so that any action taken on the basis of the predicted classes is most reliable.

1   Introduction

This paper is concerned with supervised classification problems, although the ideas described here may be applied more widely. In a supervised classification problem one has available a design set of data, containing values of variables describing the objects in a sample from the population of interest, as well as labels indicating to which of a set of classes each of the sampled objects belongs. The aim is to use this design set to construct a classification rule which will permit new objects to be assigned to classes purely on the basis of their vectors of measurements. For simplicity, in this paper we will restrict ourselves to the two class case.

Almost without exception, the formulations of such problems assume that the classes are well-defined. There has been some work on problems in which the class assignments in the design set may be made with error, but virtually none on problems in which there is ambiguity, uncertainty, or confusion about what, precisely, is meant by the different classes. This is the problem we consider in this paper.

Such problems are, in fact, surprisingly common. We conjecture that they may even be more prevalent than the 'standard' form of problem, where the classes are well-defined, but that researchers have tended to ignore the problems for practical operational reasons: one often needs a crisp classification into one of the possible classes so that some appropriate action can be taken (such as medical treatment or personnel authorisation, for example).

In this paper we focus mainly on the subclass of such problems in which the true classes are described by partitioning one or more underlying variables, and where the uncertainty and ambiguity arises because the positions of the partitioning thresholds are not definitively fixed. Here are some examples:

D.J. Hand, J.N. Kok, M.R. Berthold (Eds.): IDA'99, LNCS 1642, pp. 235–244, 1999.

- Student grades are often based on performance in examinations: a score of more than 70% may mean a student is assigned a grade A, a score between 60 and 70 may mean a grade B, and so on. Here the choices of 60 and 70 are not absolutes, but represent an arbitrary choice. It may be entirely reasonable to choose different values.
- When people apply for bank loans a predictive model is often built to decide whether or not they are likely to be good or bad risks. A 'bad risk' may be defined as one who is likely to become more than a certain number of months in arrears during the course of the loan. To produce well-defined classes (necessary so that an operational decision — accept or reject — can be made) a particular value has to be chosen for this 'certain number'. Thus an individual who is likely to fall more than *three* months in arrears might be regarded as bad. However, this choice — three — is somewhat arbitrary. One might, with almost equal justification, have chosen two or four. Indeed, as external circumstances change (the economic climate, the competitive banking environment, etc.) so one might prefer some different value to use in the definition of good and bad.
- More generally, still within the banking context, the good and bad classes may be defined in terms of several variables, for each of which a threshold must be chosen. Perhaps a bad bank account is one which is overdrawn by more than amount t_1, or by an amount t_2 in conjunction with a maximum balance during the past three months of less than t_3. Here all of the thresholds need to be chosen to define the classes, but there is nothing absolute about them.

From the perspective in which the class definitions are fixed and immutable, perhaps the most obvious strategy to tackle problems of the kind illustrated above is to develop models which are either invariant to a range of possible definitions of the classes or which can easily (even automatically) be adjusted to cope with different definitions. We have explored such models in Kelly and Hand([6]), Adams et al. ([1]), and Hand et al. ([4]). In particular, we looked at two classes of models. In one (Adams et al., [1], and Hand et al., [4]), we seek to predict the value that an individual is likely to have for the 'thresholding' variables (those variables on which thresholds are imposed to defined the classes), so that these predicted values can be compared with any chosen thresholds to produce a predicted classification. Note that the thresholds do not have to be specified at the time the model is built, but can be chosen immediately prior to the time at which the assignment to a class is desired. In the other class of models (Kelly and Hand, [6]), we model the probability that an individual is likely to have each value on the thresholding variable(s), so that we can estimate the probability that an individual will have a value greater than any chosen threshold. Again the threshold need not be specified in advance.

Such approaches are all very well, but the intrinsic arbitrariness (within limits, anyway) of the class definitions opens up a more radical possibility. If one is prepared to accept that alternative choices of the threshold may be equally legitimate, or at least that it is difficult to defend the position that one choice is superior to another (within limits, again), then perhaps advantage can be taken of this freedom of choice. In particular, perhaps one can choose the threshold(s), and hence the definitions of the classes, to optimise some criterion related to the performance of the classification rule. This idea is illustrated in Section 2. In Section 3 we point out that the situation is rather more subtle than might at first appear. Depending upon the measure used, one might expect performance to *appear* to improve, simply because of the changing threshold. This might mean that the apparent improvement is deceptive.

2   Taking Advantage of Uncertainty in the Class Definitions

In what follows, for convenience we shall call the variables used to define the classes the 'definition variables' and those used for the prediction the 'predictor variables'. Traditional supervised classification problems are asymmetric, in the sense that one is trying to predict the definition variable(s) from the predictor variables, and the issue is merely how to combine the values of the latter to yield a prediction. In our situation, however, the problem is more symmetric. Although one is still trying to predict the definition variable(s) from the predictor variables, one can now also choose how to combine the former so as to maximise the performance criterion of interest. This opens up a number of questions. For example, as we shall see below in Section 3, the choice of performance measure is critical, with different measures leading to qualitatively different kinds of results.

We shall suppose here that the classes are defined by imposing thresholds on several definition variables and combining the resulting intervals to yield classes — in the manner of the third example in the opening section. The example we will use commences with a baseline definition currently adopted by a bank (for commercial reasons the definition we are using is slightly different from that in everyday use). In this baseline definition, a bank account is 'bad' in a particular month if

(a) the excess amount overdrawn beyond the nominal limit is greater than £500;

OR

(b) this excess is greater than £100 AND the maximum balance over the course of the month is less than £0;

OR

(c) the total credit turnover in the month is less than 10% of the month's end balance.

A 'good' account is defined as the complement of this.

Now, discussions with the bank show that the choices of the threshold of £500 in (a), £100 and £0 in (b), and 10% in (c) are somewhat arbitrary. A value of £510 or £490 in the first would be equally legitimate in the definition. Of course, one may prefer £500 on aesthetic grounds, but that is hardly an appropriate argument in the competitive world of retail banking. Likewise, £500 is a convenient threshold for human comprehensibility but, since all of the numerical manipulations will be done by a computer, this seems hardly relevant. Of course, one can go to an extreme. It is entirely possible that £5000 would be an inappropriate threshold in (a). On this basis, one can define intervals of acceptable thresholds and, more generally, an *acceptable region* in the space of the definition variables which includes all sets of threshold values which would lead to acceptable definitions. (This may not be the simple product of the individual acceptable intervals since acceptable values of one variable may change according to the values of another variable.) Our aim is now to choose that point within this acceptable region which optimises the performance measure.

Performance measures are discussed in more detail in Section 3. Here we simply take the *Gini coefficient*, a commonly used measure in retail banking applications (Hand and Henley, [3]). This is a measure of the difference between two distributions, taking values between 0 and 1, larger values indicating better performance. It is defined as twice the area between the curve and the diagonal in a ROC curve. In our context these are the distributions of the estimated probabilities of belonging to the good class for the true good and bad classes respectively. Our aim, then, is to examine different definitions of these classes, calculate classification rules for them, and see how well these rules do in terms of Gini coefficient. We used logistic regression as the classification rule, and ten-fold cross-validation to evaluate the Gini coefficients.

Our data set consisted of 7956 bank accounts, and the acceptable region was defined by thresholds as follows (in fact, in this case, the acceptable region is the product of the acceptable intervals):

(a) $t_1 =$ (excess amount overdrawn beyond the nominal limit) $\in [200, 800]$
(b) $t_2 =$ (excess amount overdrawn beyond the nominal limit) $\in [50, 600]$;
$t_3 =$ (maximum balance over the course of the month) $\in [-150, 150]$
(c) $t_3 =$ (total credit turnover in the month $\div$ month's end balance) $\in [0.05, 0.50]$

One could simply apply a maximisation routine to find the definition within this region which optimises the Gini coefficient. However, so as to provide us with some insight into the behaviour of the model we evaluated the Gini at each point of a grid spanning the acceptable region (producing 5880 possible definitions of a bad account).

Table 1 shows four sample definitions and the resulting Gini coefficients. The first definition is that given at the start of the section — the slightly modified version of that currently used by the bank. It is clear from this table that Gini coefficients substantially greater than that currently obtained can be achieved — a difference of 0.05 is very important in the retail banking context, and can translate into millions of pounds.

Figure 1 shows a histogram of the Gini coefficients of the models for all 5880 definitions we tested. It is clear that many definitions permit models yielding

Table 1. Thresholds yielding four alternative definitions of 'bad account'.

Definition	t_1	t_2	t_3	t_4	Gini
1	500	100	0	0.10	0.41
2	400	150	-50	0.05	0.46
3	200	100	150	0.10	0.36
4	600	400	0	0.05	0.61

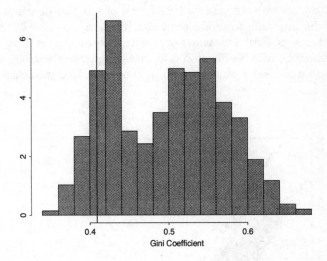

Fig. 1. Histogram of the Gini coefficients for the logistic regressions applied to the 5880 definitions.

Gini coefficients substantially greater than that achieved using the bank's current definition.

3   Is Improved Performance an Artefact?

Figure 1 is striking — but it is rather deceptive. Figure 2 shows a scatterplot of the proportions of the sample defined as bads by each definition against the Gini coefficient of the classifier built based on that definition. A negative correlation is clear: in general, a higher Gini coefficient is achieved by defining fewer accounts as bad. Of course, this is not a rigid relationship. For a given bad rate there are many different definitions, each associated with a different Gini coefficient; this is shown by the fact that a horizontal line at any given bad rate is associated with multiple classifiers and Gini coefficients. This means that there is still value in the notion of changing the definitions in the hope of improving class predictability. But it does mean that one has to be wary of the improvement arising simply as an artefact of such phenomena as changing priors. In this section we look at some aspects of such issues in more detail.

Many different measures of performance are used for assessing supervised classification rules (see Hand, [2], for a discussion). This is because different problems have different objectives. Some measures (the Gini coefficient is an example) focus on measuring the difference between the overall distributions of the estimated probabilities of belonging to class 0 for each of the two classes. Others reduce this to a comparison between summarising statistics of the two distributions (for example, the difference between their means, or this difference standardised by the average standard deviation of the two distributions). Yet others apply the threshold to produce the classification, and classify the objects into predicted classes, basing measures of performance on the resulting confusion matrix (for example, misclassification rate, cost-weighted misclassification rate, or the proportion of class 1 objects amongst those classified into class 0).

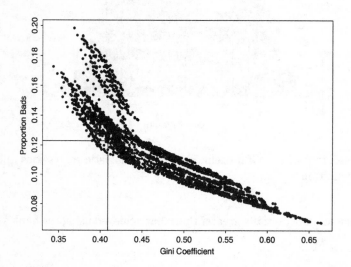

Fig. 2. Scatterplot of the bad rates for the 5880 definitions against the Gini coefficients of the logistic regressions.

Some measures — the Gini coefficient and the difference between the means, for example — are independent of the sizes of the classes. Others, however (for example, the misclassification rate, cost-weighted or not), are not. The standardised difference between the means will depend on the priors if the standard deviations of the two distributions are different, since then the larger class will dominate the estimate of the average standard deviation. If the distributions of the estimated probabilities are each normal for each class, and if they remain unchanged even though the priors alter, then the misclassification rate of the Bayes

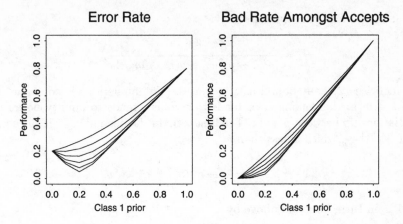

Fig. 3. Misclassification (error) rate and proportion classified into class 0 which are misclassified when, in both cases, 80% are classified as belonging to class 0.

classifier (that is, the minimum achievable misclassification rate) will decrease monotonically with the absolute difference between the priors (equal priors being associated with maximum error rate). On the other hand, (a) the misclassification rate obtained when fixed proportions are classified into each class, and (b) the proportion classified as class 0 when fixed proportions are classified into each class show the behaviour illustrated in Figure 3. This figure is based on univariate normal distributions for each class, both with unit standard deviation, the first with mean 0 and the second with mean $\mu = 0.5, 1.0, 1.5, ..., 3.0$ (with $\mu = 0.5$ being the top curve). In this example, 80% are classified as class 0 and the horizontal axis shows the prior for class 1. With this as the performance measure, we see that misclassification rate may not even be monotonic with increasing prior.

So much for behaviour as priors alone vary. Now what about behaviour as a threshold varies?

To get an analytical handle on things, suppose we have a bivariate normal population (x, y), with correlation ρ, and that we partition the y distribution at some threshold t, so that we are interested in a comparison between the distributions of x for objects whose y values are above and below this threshold. To measure performance, we use the ratio of the squared difference between the means to the weighted average variance within the two classes, where the weights are their relative sizes. Then (see Hand et al., [5]) the squared difference between the means is

$$\frac{1}{p^2(1-p)^2}\frac{\rho^2}{2\pi}e^{-t^2}$$

where p is the proportion of the population which has $y < t$, and the average variance is

$$1 - \rho^2 \frac{e^{-t^2}}{2\pi}\frac{1}{p(1-p)}$$

so that the performance measure is

$$T^2 = \frac{\rho^2/2\pi}{p^2(1-p)^2 e^{t^2} - p(1-p)\rho^2/2\pi}.$$

This increases without bound as t increases. (The numerator is constant. The second term in the denominator tends to zero as t tends to infinity because of the relationship between p and t. The first term in the denominator is the square of $p(1-p)e^{t^2/2}$, which is less than

$$(1-p)e^{t^2/2} = \frac{1}{\sqrt{2\pi}} e^{t^2/2} \int_t^\infty e^{-x^2/2}\, dx$$

which is, in turn, bounded above by

$$\frac{1}{\sqrt{2\pi}} e^{t^2/2} \int_t^\infty \frac{x}{t} e^{-x^2/2}\, dx = \frac{-1}{\sqrt{2\pi}} \frac{e^{t^2/2}}{t} \left[e^{-x^2/2}\right]_t^\infty = \frac{1}{t\sqrt{2\pi}}$$

which tends to zero as t tends to infinity.)

That is, as the definition threshold moves so that one of the classes becomes smaller and smaller, so this measure of performance improves. This may explain the pattern observed in Figure 2.

The above example assumed a bivariate normal distribution for the joint distribution of the estimated probability of belonging to class 0 (represented by x) and the distribution of the variable on which a threshold was imposed to define the classes. This meant that the conditional distribution of x had a mean which was a linear function of y. When this does not hold, the behaviour observed above may not arise.

To illustrate we take the difference between the means of the x distributions (the distribution of x for objects with y above the threshold, and the distribution for objects with y below the threshold) as the measure of performance. Different choices of the y threshold are likely to yield different values for the means of the x distributions. The values will depend on $f(y)$, the marginal distribution of y, and $M(x|y)$, the expected value of x given y. The difference between the means is

$$S = \frac{1}{p} \int_{-\infty}^t M(x|y) f(y)\, dy - \frac{1}{1-p} \int_t^\infty M(x|y) f(y)\, dy$$

where $p = \int_{-\infty}^t f(y)\, dy$. Since this relationship is not affected by arbitrary monotonic increasing transformations of y, we may take that transformation on which $f(y)$ is uniform. For example, if the distribution of y values is normal we may work with $u = \Phi(y)$, Φ being the cumulative normal distribution, yielding

$$S = \frac{1}{p} \int_0^{\Phi(t)} M(x|\Phi^{-1}(u))\, du - \frac{1}{1-p} \int_{\Phi(t)}^1 M(x|\Phi^{-1}(u))\, du$$

as the difference between the means. From this, it is obvious that the difference between the means depends on $M(x|\Phi^{-1}(u))$. Taking $M(x|\Phi^{-1}(u))$ to be a linear function of u results in a constant difference. On the other hand, taking $M(x|\Phi^{-1}(u)) = \Phi^{-1}(u)$ (which arises if we take the mean of the conditional distribution of x to be equal to y and take the distribution of y to be normal) then the difference between the means increases as t moves towards the extremes — as in the bivariate normal case above. Finally, suppose that $M(x|\Phi^{-1}(u))$ decreases linearly with u up to some point $u = T$ and is constant for u beyond that point. This corresponds to conditional distributions $f(x|y)$ which are the same for $y > \Phi^{-1}(T)$. Now, if we take the threshold t greater than $\Phi^{-1}(T)$ and increasing, the mean of the distribution for x values for objects with y greater than t remains constant, while the mean of the other approaches it as t increases — performance will decrease as t increases.

We see from these examples that performance can vary in different ways, depending on the underlying distributions and on the particular measure adopted. In particular, if the measure of performance is monotonically related to the position of a threshold, then the chosen definition of the classes will be at the edge of the region of acceptable definitions. This observation can simplify the process of optimising the performance measure.

4 Conclusion

We began with the premise that in many supervised classification problems there is intrinsic woolliness about the definition of the classes. In some cases this arises because the problem is dynamic, so that important factors can change over time, in others it arises because the classes are defined in terms of variables which are proxies for the real interests, and in yet others it arises because there is no real sense in which one definition is substantively better or more appropriate than another closely related definition. In such situations we suggest that advantage can be taken of the looseness of the definition of the classes by choosing that particular definition which optimises some additional criterion. If predictive classification accuracy is adopted as the criterion, such an approach means that one can have more confidence in the accuracy of one's predictions and conclusions.

Clearly such a strategy is not universally applicable. It is not appropriate if the classes are defined in a rigorous manner: for example, if a medical diagnosis is in terms of the definitive presence or absence of a tumour. It is only legitimate when there is some freedom to decide precisely what one means by the different classes.

Our practical example shows that significantly improved classification accuracy can be achieved by this method. In the banking situation, this means that the bank could base subsequent decisions and operations on the two classes, with greater confidence that the individual accounts really did lie in the predicted class. However, as we demonstrated in Section 3, the improvement in predictive classification performance may sometimes be a relatively simple consequence of the relationship between the definition variable, on which the threshold is imposed, and the distributions of estimated class membership probabilities. Sometimes this will mean that the optimum of the performance measure is located at the boundary of the region of acceptable definitions. This is, of course, precisely the place where the 'acceptability' is weakest.

The example in Section 2 used classification performance (in fact, Gini coefficient) as the criterion which was optimised by the choice of definition (as well as the predictive rule). However, other criteria could be used, and sometimes it is advantageous to use measures different from that which will be used to measure performance accuracy. Moreover, a radically different approach to defining the classes would be to formulate a linear combination (instead of a logical combination) of the definition variables, imposing a threshold on this to define the classes. This might be seen as a classical statistical approach. Putting these two suggestions together leads to the idea of measuring predictive power in terms of the multiple correlation coefficient between the predictor and definition variables. That is, we could use canonical correlations analysis to find that linear combination of the predictor variables, and that linear combination of the definition variables which are maximally correlated. This leads to a qualitatively different kind of definition for the classes from that used in Section 2, but one which may make perfectly sound sense, especially if the predictor variables are monotonically related to the perceived difference between the classes.

Acknowledgement

The work of MGK was supported by a CASE studentship from the UK's Engineering and Physical Sciences Research Council, with additional support from Abbey National Plc. We would like to express our appreciation to Sam Korman and Steve Bull for their interest in and encouragement of this work.

References

1. Adams, N.M., Hand, D.J., and Li, H.G.: A simulation study of indirect prognostic classification. In Proceedings in Computational Statistics, COMPSTAT-98, ed. R.Payne and P.Green, Heidelberg, Physica-Verlag, (1998) 149–154.
2. Hand, D.J.: Construction and Assessment of Classification Rules. Chichester: Wiley (1997).
3. Hand, D.J., Henley, W.E.: Statistical classification methods in consumer credit scoring: a review. Journal of the Royal Statistical Society, Series A, **160** (1997) 523–541.
4. Hand, D.J., Li, H.G., and Adams, N.M.: Supervised classification with structured class definitions. Technical Report (1998a).
5. Hand, D.J., Oliver, J.J. and Lunn, A.D.: Discriminant analysis when the classes arise from a continuum. Pattern Recognition, **31** (1998b), 641–650.
6. Kelly, M.G. and Hand, D.J.: Credit scoring with uncertain class definitions. Presented at Credit Scoring and Credit Control V, Edinburgh, September (1997).

Temporal Pattern Generation Using Hidden Markov Model Based Unsupervised Classification

Cen Li and Gautam Biswas

Department of Computer Science
Vanderbilt University, Nashville, TN 37235, USA
cen.li@vanderbilt.edu

Abstract. This paper describes a clustering methodology for temporal data using hidden Markov model(HMM) representation. The proposed method improves upon existing HMM based clustering methods in two ways: (i) it enables HMMs to dynamically change its model structure to obtain a better fit model for data during clustering process, and (ii) it provides objective criterion function to automatically select the clustering partition. The algorithm is presented in terms of four nested levels of searches: (i) the search for the number of clusters in a partition, (ii) the search for the structure for a fixed sized partition, (iii) the search for the HMM structure for each cluster, and (iv) the search for the parameter values for each HMM. Preliminary experiments with artificially generated data demonstrate the effectiveness of the proposed methodology.

1 Introduction

Unsupervised classification, or clustering, assumes data is not labeled with class information. The goal is to create structure for data by objectively partitioning data into homogeneous groups where the within group object similarity and the between group object dissimilarity are optimized. Data categorization is achieved by analyzing and interpreting feature descriptions associated with each group. The technique has been used extensively by researchers in discovering structures from databases where domain knowledge is not available or incomplete[21][17].

In the past, the focus of clustering analysis has been on data described with static features[21][17][6][16], i.e., values of the features do not change, or the changes are negligible, during observation period. In real world, most systems are dynamic and often are best described by temporal features whose values change significantly during observation period. Clustering data described with temporal features aimed at profiling behavior patterns for dynamic systems through data partitioning and cluster interpretation. Clustering temporal data is inherently more complex than clustering static data. First, the dimensionality of the data is significantly larger in temporal case. When data objects are characterized using static features, only one value is present for each feature. In temporal feature case, each feature is associated with a sequence of values. Also, the complexity of

D.J. Hand, J.N. Kok, M.R. Berthold (Eds.): IDA'99, LNCS 1642, pp. 245–256, 1999.
© Springer-Verlag Berlin Heidelberg 1999

cluster definition(modeling) and interpretation increases by orders of magnitude with dynamic data[27].

Time series may be considered similar if they share a similar global shape or some special local features, or have high correlation. We take a model based approach : time series are considered similar when the models characterizing individual series are similar. Models are similar when the probability of data generated by one model given the other model is high, and vise versa. We assume data has Markov property, and may be viewed as the result of a probabilistic walk along a fixed set of states. When states can be defined directly using feature values, a Markov chain model representation may be appropriate[29]. When the state definitions are not directly observable, or it is not feasible to define states by exhaustively enumerating feature values, they can be defined in terms of feature probability density functions. This corresponds to the hidden Markov model methodology. In this paper, we focus on temporal pattern generation using hidden Markov model representation.

A HMM is a non-deterministic stochastic Finite State Automata(FSA). The basic structure of a HMM consists of a connected set of states, $S = (S_1, S_2, ..., S_n)$. We use first order HMMs, where the state of a system at a particular time t is only dependent on the state of the system at the previous time point, i.e., $P(S_t|S_{t-1}, S_{t-2}, ..., S_1) = P(S_t|S_{t-1})$. A HMM of n states for data having m features can be characterized in terms of three sets of probabilities: (i) the initial state probabilities, π of size n, defines the probability any state being the initial state of a series, (ii) the transition probability matrix, A of size nxn, defines the probability of going from any one state to another state, and (iii) the emission probability matrix, B of size nxm, defines the probability of generating feature values at any given state[7]. We are interested in building HMMs for continuous temporal sequences. The emission probability density function(pdf) within each state is defined by a multivariate Gaussian distribution characterized by its mean vector, B_μ, and co-variance matrix, B_Σ. An example of a first order continuous density HMM with 3 states is shown in Figure 1. The π_is are the initial state probabilities for state i. The a_{ij}s are the transition probabilities from state i to state j and the (μ_i, Σ_i)s define the pdfs for emission probabilities for state i.

There are a number of advantages in the HMM representation for our temporal pattern generation problem:

- The hidden states of a HMM can be used to effectively model the set of potentially valid states of a dynamic process. While the set of states and the the exact sequence of states going through by a dynamic system may not be observed, it can be estimated based on observable behavior of the systems.
- HMMs represent a well-defined probabilistic model. The parameters of a HMM can be determined in a well-defined manner, using methods such as maximal likelihood estimates or maximal mutual information criterion.
- HMMs are graphical models of underlying dynamic processes that govern system behavior. Graphical models may aid the interpretation task.

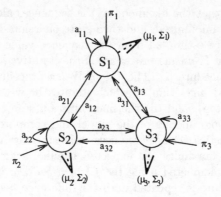

Fig. 1. An Example 3-State Continuous Density HMM

2   Proposed HMM Clustering Methodology

Clustering using HMMs was first studied by Rabiner *et al.* [8] for speech recognition problems. The idea has been further explored by other researchers including Lee [10], Dermatas and Kokkinakis [22], Lee [10], Kosaka *et al.* [20], and Smyth [26]. Two main problems that have been identified in these works are: (i) no objective criterion measure is used for determining the size of the clustering partition, and (ii) uniform, pre-specified HMM structure is assumed for different clusters of each partition. This paper describes a HMM clustering methodology that tries to remedy these two problems by developing an objective partition criterion measure based on model mutual information, and by developing an explicit HMM model refinement procedure that dynamically modify HMM structures during clustering process.

The proposed HMM clustering method can be summarized in terms of four levels of nested searches. From the outer most to the inner most level, the four searches are: the search for

1. the number of clusters in a partition,
2. the structure for a given partition size,
3. the HMM structure for each cluster, and
4. the parameters for each HMM structure.

Starting from the inner most level of search, each of these four search steps are described in more detail next.

2.1   Search Level 4: The HMM Parameters

This step tries to find the maximal likelihood parameters for the HMM of a fixed size. Segmental K-means procedure is employed[7] for this purpose. The model parameters are initialized using the Viterbi[2] heuristic procedure: given the current model parameters, the procedure first segments sequence values into different states such that the likelihood of the sequences along a single, unique path of the model is maximized, and then state emission definitions and transition probabilities are estimated from the sequence value segmentations. The core of the Segmental K-means procedure is the iterative Baum-Welch parameter reestimation procedure [1]. The *Baum-Welch* procedure is a variation of the more general EM algorithm[3], which iterates between two steps: (i) the expectation step(E-step), and (ii) the maximization step(M-step). The E-step assumes the current parameters of the model and computes the expected values of necessary statistics. The M-step uses these statistics to update the model parameters so as to maximize the expected likelihood of the parameters[24]. The procedure is implemented using the *forward-backward* computations. The Baum-Weltch procedure is repeated until the difference between the likelihood of the two consecutive model configurations is less than a certain threshold. In the following experiments, the model convergence criterion is set to $1.0 * 10^{-6}$. Like other maximum likelihood methods, this procedure may end up in local maximum values, especially when, in the case of a large HMM, there are a large number of parameters involved and the search space becomes very large and complex.

2.2   Search Level 3: The HMM Structure

This step attempts to replace an existing HMM for a group of objects by a more accurate and refined HMM model. Solcke and Omohundro [15] described a technique for inducing the structure of HMMs from data based on a general "model merging" strategy [13]. The procedure starts with a very large model which has one state defined for each value of each time series. Successfully, pairwise states are selectively merged until the posterior probability of the model stop to increase. The model that reaches the highest posterior probability is retained as the final model. Takami and Sagayama [14] proposed the Successive State Splitting(SSS) algorithm to model context-dependent phonetic variations. Ostendorf and Singer [25] further expanded the basic SSS algorithm by choosing the node and the candidate split at the same time based on likelihood gains. Casacuberta *et. al* [9] proposed to derive the structure of HMM through error correcting grammatical inference techniques.

Our HMM refinement procedure combines ideas from the past works. We start with an initial model configuration and incrementally grow or shrink the model through HMM state splitting and merging operations for choosing the right size model. The goal is to obtain a model that can better account for the data, i.e., having a higher model posterior probability. For both merge and split operations, we assume the Viterbi path does not change after each operation, that is for the split operation, the observations that were in state s will reside in either one of the two new states, q_0 or q_1. The same is true for the merge operation. This assumption can greatly simplify the parameter estimation process for the new states. The choice of state(s) to apply the split(merge) operation is dependent upon the state emission probabilities. For the split operation, the state that has the highest variances is split. For the merge operation, the two states that have the closest mean vectors are considered for merging. Next we describe the criterion measure used to perform heuristic model selection during HMM refinement procedure.

Marginal Likelihood Measure for HMM Model Selection Li and Biswas [28] proposed one possible HMM model selection criterion, the Posterior Probability of HMM(PPM), developed based on the computation for Bayesian model merging criterion in [15]. One problem with the PPM criterion is that it depends heavily on the base values for the exponential distributions used to compute prior probabilities of global model structures of HMMs.

Here, we present an alternative HMM model selection scheme. From Bayes theorem, given data, X, and a model, λ, trained from X, the posterior probability of the model, $P(\lambda|X)$, is given by:

$$P(\lambda|X) = \frac{P(\lambda)P(X|\lambda)}{P(X)},$$

where $P(X)$ and $P(\lambda)$ are prior probabilities of the data and the model respectively, and $P(X|\lambda)$ is the marginal likelihood of data. Since the prior probability of data remains unchanged for different models, for model comparison purpose, we have $P(\lambda|X) \propto P(\lambda)P(X|\lambda)$. By assuming uniform prior probability for different models, $P(\lambda|X) \propto P(X|\lambda)$. That is, the posterior probability of a model is directly proportional to the marginal likelihood. Therefore, the goal is to select the model that gives the highest marginal likelihood.

Computing marginal likelihood for complex models has been an active research area [19] [23] [12] [18]. Approaches include Monte-Carlo methods, i.e., Gibbs sampling methods [18] [11], and various approximation methods, i.e., the Laplace approximation [19] and approximation based on Bayesian information criterion [23]. It has been well documented that although the Monte-Carlo methods are very accurate, they are computationally inefficient especially for large databases. It is also shown that under certain regularity conditions, Laplace approximation can be quite accurate, but its computation can be expensive, especially for its component Hessian matrix computation. Next, we describe two efficient approximation methods developed for marginal likelihood computation: (i) the Bayesian Information Criterion(BIC), and (ii) the Cheeseman-Stutz(CS) approximation.

Bayesian Information Criterion In log form, BIC computes marginal likelihood of a model as:

$$\log P(\lambda|X) = \log P(X|\lambda, \hat{\theta}_\lambda) - \frac{d}{2} \log N,$$

where $\hat{\theta}_\lambda$ is Maximum Likelihood(ML) configuration of the model, d is the dimensionality of the model parameter space and N is the number of cases in data. The first term in BIC computation, $\log P(X|\lambda, \hat{\theta}_\lambda)$, is the likelihood term which tends to promote larger and more detailed models of data, whereas the second term, $-\frac{d}{2} \log N$, is the penalty term which favors smaller model having less parameters. BIC selects the best model for data by balancing these two terms.

Cheeseman-Stutz Approximation Cheeseman and Stutz first proposed the CS approximation method for their Bayesian clustering system, AUTOCLASS[21]:

$$P(X|\lambda) = P(X'|\lambda)\frac{P(X|\lambda)}{P(X'|\lambda)},$$

where X' represents complete data, i.e., data with known cluster labels. The first term is the complete data likelihood term. An exact computation of this term involves integration through all possible parameter configurations of the model:

$$P(X'|\lambda) = \int d\theta P(\theta|\lambda)P(X',\theta|\lambda),$$

where θ represents model parameter configuration. The integration can be approximated by a summation over a set of local maximum parameter configurations, θ_s, $\sum_{\theta \in \theta_s} P(\theta|\lambda)P(X',\theta|\lambda)$ [21][23]. To reduce computation, we have taken this approximation further by using a single maximum likelihood configuration, $\hat{\theta}_\lambda$, $\hat{\theta}_\lambda \in \theta_s$, to approximate the summation, i.e., $P(X'|\lambda) \approx P(\hat{\theta}_\lambda|\lambda)P(X',\hat{\theta}_\lambda|\lambda)$. The second term in CS approximation is a gross adjustment term. Both its nominator and denominator are expanded using BIC measure. Ignoring differences between the penalty terms in the nominator and the denominator, we obtain:

$$\log P(X|\lambda) \approx \log P(\hat{\theta}_\lambda|\lambda) + \log P(X|\hat{\theta}_\lambda, \lambda),$$

where X is the incomplete data and $P(\hat{\theta}|\lambda)$ is the prior probability of the model parameters. We assume that the transition probabilities out of individual states follow Dirichlet prior distribution, the feature mean values in each state are uniformly distributed, and the variances of each state follow Jeffery's prior distribution[21].

Apply Approximation Methods to HMM Structure Selection We experimentally illustrate how BIC and CS work for HMM structure selection. An artificial data set of 100 data objects is generated from a pre-defined five-state HMM. Each data object is described using two temporal features. The length of temporal sequences of each feature is 50. The same data set is modeled using HMMs of sizes ranging from 2 to 10. Results from BIC and CS are given in Figures 3. The dotted lines show the likelihoods of data modeled using HMMs of different sizes. The dashed lines show the penalty(Fig 2(a)) and the parameter prior probability (Fig2(b)) for each model. And the solid lines show BIC(Fig 2(a)) and CS(Fig 2(b)) as a combination of the above two terms. We observe, as the size of the model increases, the model likelihood also increases and the model penalty and parameter prior decreases monotonically. Both BIC and CS have their highest value corresponding to the correct model structure, the 5-state model.

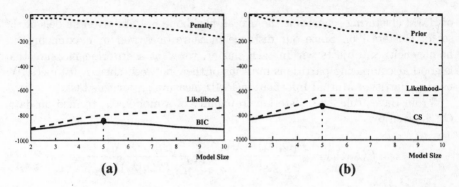

Fig. 2. HMM model selection using marginal likelihood approximation methods:
(a) BIC approximation (b) CS approximation

2.3 Search Level 2: The Partition Structure

The two most commonly used distance measures in the context of the HMM representation is the sequence-to-model likelihood measure [7] and the symmetrized distance measure between pairwise models [5]. We choose the sequence-to-model likelihood distance measure for our HMM clustering algorithm. Sequence-to-HMM likelihood, $P(O|\lambda)$, measures the probability that a sequence, O, is generated by a given model, λ. When the sequence-to-HMM likelihood distance measure is used for object-to-cluster assignments, it automatically enforces the maximizing within-group similarity criterion.

A K-means style clustering control structure and a depth-first binary divisive clustering control structure are proposed to generate partitions having different number of clusters. For each partition, the initial object-to-cluster memberships are determined by the sequence-to-HMM likelihood(See Section 2.2.1) distance measure. The objects are subsequently redistributed after HMM parameter reestimation and HMM model refinement have been applied in the intermediate clusters. For the K-means algorithm, the re-distribution is global for all clusters. For binary hierarchical clustering, the redistribution is carried out between the child clusters of the current cluster. Thus the algorithm is not guaranteed to produce the maximally probable partition of the data set. If the goal is to have a single partition of data, K-means style control structure may be used. If one wants to look at partitions at various levels of details, binary divisive clustering may be suitable. Partitions of different number of clusters are compared using the PMI criterion measure, described next. For K-means clustering, the search stops when PMI of the current partition is lower than that of the previous partition. For binary clustering, the search along a particular branch is terminated when dividing the current cluster decreases the overall PMI score.

2.4 Search Level 1: The Number of Clusters in a Partition

The quality of a clustering is measured in terms of its within cluster similarity and between cluster dissimilarity. A common criterion measure used by a number of HMM clustering schemes is the overall likelihood of data given models of the set of clusters [26]. Since our distance measure does well in maximizing the homogeneity of objects within each cluster, we want a criterion measure that is good at comparing partitions in terms of their between-cluster distances. We use the Partition Mutual Information(PMI) measure [4] for this task.

From Bayes rule, the posterior probability of a model, λ_i, trained on data, O_i, is given by:

$$P(\lambda_i|O_i) = \frac{P(O_i|\lambda_i)P(\lambda_i)}{P(O_i)} = \frac{P(O_i|\lambda_i)P(\lambda_i)}{\sum_{j=1}^{J} P(O_i|\lambda_j)P(\lambda_j)},$$

where $P(\lambda_i)$ is the prior probability of a data coming from cluster i before the feature values are inspected, and $P(O_i|\lambda_i)$ is the conditional probability of displaying the feature O_i given that it comes from cluster i. Let MI_i represent the average mutual information between the observation sequence O_i and the complete set of models $\lambda = (\lambda_1, ..., \lambda_J)$:

$MI_i = \log P(\lambda_i|O_i)$
$\quad = \log(P(O_i|\lambda_i)P(\lambda_i)) - \log \sum_{j=1}^{J} P(O_i|\lambda_j)P(\lambda_j).$

Maximizing this value is equivalent to separating the correct model λ_i from all other models on the training sequence O_i. Then, the overall information of the partition with J models is computed by summing over the mutual information of all training sequences: $PMI = \frac{\sum_{j=1}^{J} \sum_{i=1}^{n_j} MI_i}{J}$, where n_j is the number of objects in cluster j, and J is the total number of clusters in a partition. PMI is maximized when the J models are the most separated set of models, without fragmentation.

Next, we show how PMI measure is used to derive a good partition with the number of clusters and object-cluster membership. To better demonstrate the effects of PMI, we illustrate the process using the binary HMM clustering scheme, and we assume the correct model structure is known and fixed throughout the clustering process in this example. To generate data with K clusters, first we manually create K HMMs. From each of these K HMMs, we generate N_k objects, each described with M temporal sequences. The length of each temporal sequence is L. The total data points for such a data set is $K \cdot N_k \cdot M \cdot L$. In these experiments, we choose $K = 4$, $N_k = 30$, $M = 2$, and $L = 100$. The HMM for each cluster has 5 states.

First, the PMI criterion measure was not incorporated in the binary clustering tree building process. The branches of the tree is terminated either because there are too few objects in the node, or because the object redistribution process in a node ends with one cluster partition. The *full* binary clustering tree, as well as the PMI scores for intermediate and final partitions are computed and shown in Figure 3(a). The PMI scores to the right of the tree indicate the quality of the current partition, which includes all nodes at the frontier of the current tree. For example, the PMI score for the partition having clusters C_4 and C_{123} is 0.0, and PMI score for the partition having clusters C_4, $\frac{4}{30}C_2$, $\frac{26}{30}C_2$, and C_{13} is $-1.75 * 10^2$. The result of this clustering process is a 7-cluster partition, with six

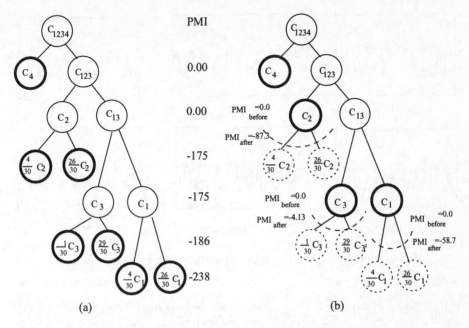

Fig. 3. The Binary HMM Clustering Tree

fragmented clusters, i.e., cluster C_2 is fragmented into $\frac{4}{30}C_2$ and $\frac{26}{30}C_2$, cluster C_3 is fragmented into $\frac{1}{30}C_3$, $\frac{29}{30}C_3$, and cluster C_1 is fragmented into $\frac{4}{30}C_1$ and $\frac{26}{30}C_1$. Figure 3(b) shows the binary HMM clustering tree where PMI criterion measure is used for determining branch terminations. The dotted lines cut off branches of the search tree where the split of the parent cluster results in a decrease in the PMI score. This clustering process re-discovers the correct 4-cluster partition.

3   Experiment

We generated an artificial data set from three random generative models, each of a different size. one with three states, one with four states, and one with five states. Based on each model, 50 data objects are created, each described by two temporal features. The length of values for each temporal feature is 50. Figure 4 shows six example data objects from this data set. The dotted lines and the solid lines represent values of the two temporal features for each object. It is observed that, from the feature values, it is quite difficult to differentiate which objects are generated from the same model. In fact, objects (a) and (f) are generated from the three-state HMM, objects (b) and (e) are generated from the four-state HMM, and objects (c) and (d) are generated from the five-state HMM. Due to space limitations, detailed parameters of these three models are omitted.

Given this data, our method successfully uncovers the correct clustering partition size, i.e., 3 clusters in the partition, and individual data object is assigned

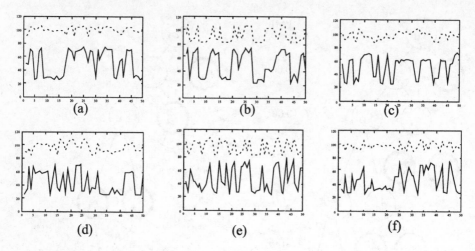

Fig. 4. Compare Data Objects Generated from Different Models

to the correct cluster, i.e., the cluster whose derived model corresponds to the object's generative model. Furthermore, for each cluster, our method accurately reconstructed the HMM with the correct model size and near perfect model parameter values.

4   Conclusion

We presented a temporal data clustering methodology based on HMM representation. HMMs have been used in speech recognition problems to model human pronunciations. Since the main objective in that study is recognition, it is not essential whether the true model structure is uncovered. A fixed size model structure can be used throughout data analyses, as long as the model structure is adequate in *differentiating* objects coming from different underlying models. On the other hand, in our case, HMMs are used to profile temporal behaviors of dynamic systems. Our ultimate objective is to characterize behavior patterns of dynamic systems by interpreting the HMMs induced from temporal data. Therefore, it is extremely important that the derived models are as close to the underlying models as possible. To facilitate this, we introduced a dynamic HMM refinement procedure to the clustering process and employed an objective measure, BIC, for model selection purposes. Furthermore, we have developed the PMI criterion measure for selecting the partition size. This allows an objective and automatic clustering process which can be very useful in many discovery tasks.

Our next step is to apply this method to real world problems. The application domain we are currently studying is about pediatric patients having Respiratory Distress Syndrome(RDS) and undergoing intensive hospital care. The goal of this application is to identify patient response patterns from temporal data recorded in the form of vital signs measured frequently throughout a patient's stay at the hospital.

References

1. Baum, L. E., Petrie, T., Soules, G., Weiss, N.: A maximization technique occurring in the statistical analysis of probabilistic functions of markov chains. The Annuals of Mathematical Statistics **4(1)** (1970) 164–171.
2. Forney, G.: The viterbi algorithm. Proceedings of the IEEE **61(3)** (1973) 268–277.
3. Dempster, A. P., Laird, N. M., Rubin, D. B.: Maximum likelihood from incomplete data via the em algorithm. Journal of Royal Statistical Society Series B(methodological) **39** (1977) 1–38.
4. Bahl, L. R., Brown, P. F., De Souza, P. V., Mercer, R. L.: Maximum mutual information estimation of hidden markov model parameters. Proceedings of the IEEE-IECEJ-AS International Conference on Acoustics, Speech, and Signal Processing **1** (1978) 49–52.
5. Juang, B. H., Rabiner, L. R.: A probabilistic distance measure for hidden markov models. AT&T Technical Journal **64(2)** (1985) 391–408.
6. Fisher, D.: Knowledge acquisition via incremental conceptual clustering. Machine Learning **2** (1987) 139–172.
7. Rabiner, L. R.: A tutorial on hidden markov models and selected applications in speech recognition. Proceedings of the IEEE **77(2)** (1989) 257–285.
8. Rabiner, L. R., Lee, C. H., Juang, B. H., Wilpon, J. G.: Hmm clustering for connected word recognition. Proceedings of the International Conference on Acoustics, Speech, and Signal Processing (1989).
9. Casacuberta, F., Vidal, E., and Mas B.: Learning the structure of hmm's through grammatical inference techniques. Proceedings of the International Conference on Acoustic, Speech, and Signal Processing (1990) 717–720.
10. Lee, K. F.: Context-dependent phonetic hidden markov models for speaker-independent continuous speech recognition. IEEE Transactions on Acoustics, Speech, and Signal Processing **38(4)** (1990) 599–609.
11. Casella G., George, E. I.: Explaining the gibbs sampler. The American Statistician **46(3)** (1992) 167–174.
12. Cooper, G. F., Herskovits, E.: A bayesian method for the induction of probabilistic network from data. Machine Learning **9** (1992) 309–347.
13. Omohundro, S. M.: Best-first model merging for dynamic learning and recognition. Advances in Neural Information Processing Systems **4** (1992) 958–965.
14. Takami, J., Sagayama, S.: A successive state splitting algorithm for efficient allophone modeling. Proceedings of the International Conference on Acoustics, Speech, and Signal Processing **1** (1992) 573–576.
15. Stolcke, A., Omohundro, S. M.: Best-first model merging for hidden markov model induction. Technical Report TR-94-003, International Computer Science Institute, 1994.
16. Wallace, C. S., Dowe, D. L.: Intrinsic classificatin by mml - the snob program. Proceedings of the Seventh Australian Joint Conference on Artificial Intelligence (1994) 37–44.
17. Biswas, G., Weinberg, J., Li, C.: Iterate: A conceptual clustering method for knowledge discovery in databases. Artificial Intelligence in Petroleum Industry: Symbolic and Computational Applications, Braunschweig, B. and Day, R. editors, Teditions Technip, 1995.

18. Chib, S.: Marginal likelihood from the gibbs sampling. Journal of the American Statistical Association (1995) 1313–1321.
19. Kass, R. E., Raftery, A. E.: Bayes factor. Journal of the American Statistical Association (1995) 773–795.
20. Kosaka, T., Masunaga, S., Kuraoka, M.: Speaker-independent phone modeling based on speaker-dependent hmm's composition and clustering. Proceedings of the ICASSP'95 (1995) 441–444.
21. Cheeseman, P., Stutz, J.: Bayesian classification(autoclass): Theory and results. Advances in Knowledge Discovery and Data Mining (1996) chapter 6 153–180, Fayyad, U. M., Piatetsky-Shapiro, G., Smyth, P., Uthurusamy, R. editors AAAI-MIT press.
22. Dermatas, E., Kokkinakis, G.: Algorithm for clustering continuous density hmm by recognition error. IEEE Transactions on Speech and Audio Processing 4(3) (1996) 231–234.
23. Chickering, D. M., Heckerman, D.: Efficient approximations for the marginal likelihood of bayesian networks with hidden variables. Machine Learning 29 (1997) 181–212.
24. Ghahramani, Z., Jordan, M. I.: Factorial hidden markov models. Machine Leaning 29 (1997) 245–273.
25. Ostendorf, M., Singer, H.: Hmm topology design using maximum likelihood successive state splitting. Computer Speech and Language 11 (1997) 17–41.
26. Smyth, P.: Clustering sequences with hidden markov models. Advances in Neural Information Processing (1997).
27. Li, C.: Unsupervised classification on temporal data. Technical Report VU-CS-TR-98-04, Vanderbilt University, April 1998.
28. Li, C., Biswas, G.: Clustering sequence data using hidden markov model representation. SPIE99 Conference on Data Mining and Knowledge Discovery: Theory, Tools, and Technology (1999) 14-21.
29. Sebastiani, P., Ramoni, M., Cohen, P., Warwick, J., Davis, J.: Discovering dynamics using bayesian clustering. Proceedings of the 3rd International Symposium on Intelligent Data Analysis (1999).

Exploiting Similarity for Supporting Data Analysis and Problem Solving

Eyke Hüllermeier[*]

IRIT - Institut de Recherche
en Informatique de Toulouse
Université Paul Sabatier
eyke@irit.fr

Abstract. Case-based reasoning relies on the hypothesis that "similar problems have similar solutions," which seems to apply, in a certain sense, to a large range of applications. In order to be generally applicable and useful for problem solving, however, this hypothesis and the corresponding process of case-based inference have to be formalized adequately. This paper provides a formalization which makes the "similarity structure" of a system accessible for reasoning and problem solving. A corresponding (constraint-based) approach to case-based inference exploits this structure in a way which allows for deriving a similarity-based prediction of the solution to a target problem in form of a set of possible candidates (supplemented with a level of confidence.)

1 Introduction

The problem solving method of case-based reasoning (CBR) relies on the assumption that "similar problems have similar solutions," subsequently referred to as the "CBR hypothesis." As an interesting aspect of this hypothesis we would like to emphasize that it implies certain *structural assumptions* of a system under consideration. These assumptions, however, are not related to the structure of the system directly. Rather, they concern the "similarity structure," which can be seen as a derived structure or a transformation of the system structure.

Consider, as an illustration, a simple data generating process P which transforms input values $x \in X$ into output values $y \in Y$. In order to explain a set $\{(x_1, y_1), \ldots, (x_n, y_n)\}$ of observed data, statistical methods or machine learning algorithms typically consider some *hypothesis space* $\mathcal{H}$. For $X = \mathbb{R}^n$ and $Y = \mathbb{R}$ this space might be given, for instance, as the class of linear functions $h(x) = \alpha_1 x_1 + \ldots + \alpha_n x_n$ $(\alpha_1, \ldots, \alpha_n \in \mathbb{R})$. Each of these functions corresponds to a certain hypothesis $h \in \mathcal{H}$. As in this example, the hypotheses are usually related to properties (attributes) of the *instances* $(x, y) \in X \times Y$, i.e., attributes of the output value are specified directly as a function $y = h(x)$ of the attributes of input values. As opposed to this, the CBR hypothesis postulates a certain

---

[*] This work has been supported by a TMR research grant funded by the European Commission.

D.J. Hand, J.N. Kok, M.R. Berthold (Eds.): IDA'99, LNCS 1642, pp. 257–268, 1999.
© Springer-Verlag Berlin Heidelberg 1999

relation between *similarity degrees* $\sigma(x, x')$ and $\sigma(y, y')$ associated with *pairs* of instances and, hence, makes structural assumptions about the process P not at the *system* or *instance level* but at the, say, *similarity level.*

Interpreted thus, the CBR hypothesis applies (at least to a certain extent) to many applicational domains. It seems, therefore, reasonable to exploit the information contained in the similarity structure of a system. Clearly, a necessary prerequisite for this is a suitable formalization of the CBR hypothesis and, hence, the process of case-based inference. So far, however, only few attempts have been made in this direction [3,6,15]. In this paper, we develop a formalization in which we proceed from a constraint-based interpretation of the CBR hypothesis, according to which the similarity of problems imposes a constraint on the similarity of associated solutions in form of a lower bound [3]. Based on this formalization, we propose an approach to case-based inference which seems to be particularly well-suited for supporting (well-structured) task types arising, e.g., data analysis and problem solving. The focus of the formal model we shall propose is on CBR as *case-based inference* (CBI), which essentially corresponds to the REUSE process within the (informal) R^4 model of the CBR cycle [1] and emphasizes the idea of case-based reasoning as a *prediction* method [3,7].

The remaining part of the paper is organized as follows: In Section 2, the basic framework of case-based inference is introduced, and a constraint-based realization of CBI is proposed. An application to data analysis and problem solving in knowledge-based configuration is outlined in Section 3. Section 4 concludes the paper with a summary.

2   The CBI Framework

In this section, we shall introduce the basic CBI framework we proceed from. Within this framework the primitive concept of a *case* is defined as a tuple consisting of a *situation* and a *result* or *outcome* associated with the situation. The meaning of a case might range from, e.g., example-category tuples in data analysis (classification) to problem-solution pairs in optimization. We do not make particular assumptions concerning the characterization of situations or results. Generally, an *attribute-value representation* will be utilized, i.e., situations as well as results will be marked as "feature" vectors of (not necessarily numeric) attribute values.

Definition 1 (CBI **set-up**). *A* CBI *set-up is defined as a 6-tuple*

$$\Sigma = \langle S, \mathcal{R}, \varphi, \sigma_S, \sigma_{\mathcal{R}}, \mathcal{M} \rangle,$$

where S is a countable set of situations, $\mathcal{R}$ is a set of results, and $\varphi : S \to \mathcal{R}$ assigns results to situations. The functions $\sigma_S : S \times S \to [0, 1]$ and $\sigma_{\mathcal{R}} : \mathcal{R} \times \mathcal{R} \to [0, 1]$ define similarity measures over the set of situations and the set of results, respectively. $\mathcal{M}$ is a finite memory $\mathcal{M} = \{\langle s_1, r_1 \rangle, \langle s_2, r_2 \rangle, \dots, \langle s_n, r_n \rangle\}$ of cases $c = \langle s, \varphi(s) \rangle \in S \times \mathcal{R}$. D_S resp. $D_{\mathcal{R}}$ denote the sets $\{\sigma_S(s, s') \mid s, s' \in S\}$ resp. $\{\sigma_{\mathcal{R}}(\varphi(s), \varphi(s')) \mid s, s' \in S\}$ of actually attained similarity degrees.

Clearly, the assumption that a situation $s \in S$ determines the associated outcome $r = \varphi(s) \in \mathcal{R}$ does not imply that the latter is *known* as soon as the situation is characterized. For example, let situations correspond to instances of a class of combinatorial optimization problems. Moreover, define the result associated with the situation as the (unique) optimal solution of the corresponding problem. Of course, deriving this solution from the description of the problem might involve a computationally complex process. In this connection, we refer to *case-based inference* as a method which supports the overall process of problem solving by predicting the result associated with a certain situation. To this end, CBI performs according to the CBR *principle*: it exploits experience in form of precedent cases, to which it "applies" background knowledge in form of the heuristic CBR hypothesis.

Definition 2 (CBI problem). *A CBI problem is a tuple $\langle \Sigma, s_0 \rangle$ consisting of a CBI set-up Σ and a new situation $s_0 \in S$. The task is to exploit the similarity structure[1] of Σ in conjunction with observed cases in order to predict resp. characterize the result $r_0 = \varphi(s_0)$ associated with s_0.*

It should be mentioned that the task of prediction is a very general one and contains several task types such as, e.g., *classification* or *diagnosis*, as special cases. The fact that a result is a function of a set of observable attributes (the situation) is the main characteristic of prediction.

2.1 CBI as Constraint-Based Inference

In this section, we will formalize the hypothesis of "similar situations having similar results." To this end, we adopt a constraint-based interpretation, according to which the similarity of situations constrains the similarity of the associated results (at a minimum level.)

Definition 3 (similarity profile). *For a CBI set-up Σ, the function $h_\Sigma : D_S \to [0, 1]$ defined by*

$$h_\Sigma(x) := \inf_{s,s' \in S, \sigma_S(s,s')=x} \sigma_\mathcal{R}(\varphi(s), \varphi(s'))$$

is called the similarity profile of the set-up Σ.

If we refer to the triple $(S, \mathcal{R}, \varphi)$ as the *system*, then φ can be seen as defining the *system structure* (or instance structure.) The similarity profile h_Σ is the "fingerprint" of this structure at the similarity level and (partly) defines the *similarity structure* of the set-up Σ. It can also be seen as a *condensed* representation of knowledge concerning the system structure φ. Indeed, the domain and the range of h_Σ are one-dimensional, whereas S and $\mathcal{R}$ will generally be of higher dimension.

---

[1] This term will be specified in Section 2.1.

Definition 4 (similarity hypothesis). *A similarity hypothesis is identified by a function* $h : [0,1] \to [0,1]$ *(and similarity measures* σ_S, σ_R.*) The intended meaning of the hypothesis* h *or, more precisely, the hypothesis* (h, σ_S, σ_R) *is that*

$$(\sigma_S(s,s') = x) \to (\sigma_R(\varphi(s), \varphi(s')) \geq h(x)) \tag{1}$$

holds true for all $s, s' \in S$. *A hypothesis* h *is called* stronger *than a hypothesis* h' *if* $h' \leq h$ *and* $h \nleq h'$. *We say that a* CBI *set-up* Σ *satisfies the hypothesis* h, *or that* h *is* admissible, *if* $h(x) \leq h_\Sigma(x)$ *for all* $x \in D_S$.

A similarity hypothesis h it thought of as an approximation of a similarity profile h_Σ. Thus, it defines a quantification of the CBR hypothesis for the set-up Σ. Since a similarity profile h_Σ is a condensed representation of the system structure φ, a similarity hypothesis h will generally be less constraining than a *system hypothesis* related to φ directly, i.e., an approximation $\widehat{\varphi} : S \to R$ of φ. On the other hand, a similarity profile has a relatively simple structure which facilitates the formulation, derivation, and adaptation of hypotheses.

Consider a CBI problem $\langle \Sigma, s_0 \rangle$ consisting of a set-up Σ and a new situation s_0. Moreover, suppose that Σ satisfies the hypothesis h. If the memory M contains the situation s_0, i.e., if M contains a case $\langle s, r \rangle$ such that $s = s_0$, then the outcome $r_0 = r$ can simply be retrieved from M. Otherwise, we can derive the following restriction:

$$r_0 \in C_{h,M}(s_0) := \bigcap_{\langle s,r \rangle \in M} \mathcal{N}_{h(\sigma_S(s_0,s))}(r), \tag{2}$$

where the α-*neighborhood* of a result $r \in R$ is defined as the set of all outcomes r' which are at least α-similar to r: $\mathcal{N}_\alpha(r) := \{r' \in R \,|\, \sigma_R(r,r') \geq \alpha\}$. Thus, in connection with the constraint-based view, the task of case-based inference can be seen as one of deriving and representing the set $C_{h,M}(s_0)$ in (2) or an approximation thereof. This may become difficult if, for instance, the definition of the similarity σ_R and, hence, the derivation of a neighborhood is complicated. The sets $\mathcal{N}_\alpha(r)$ in (2) may also become large, in which case they cannot be represented by simply enumerating their elements.

In the context of CBI it must generally be assumed that the similarity profile h_Σ of a CBI set-up Σ is unknown. Consequently, we cannot guarantee the admissibility of a certain hypothesis h. Nevertheless, suppose that h is indeed a good approximation of h_Σ. Then, it seems reasonable to utilize h for deriving a set $C_{h,M}(s_0)$ according to (2) as an approximation of $C_{h_\Sigma,M}(s_0)$ (while keeping the hypothetical character of h in mind.) This situation, which reflects the heuristic character of CBI as a problem solving method, is closely related to the aspect of *learning*. In [10], we have proposed an algorithm for learning similarity hypotheses from observed cases. It has been shown that corresponding hypotheses induce valid predictions, i.e., set-valued approximations (2) which cover r_0, with high probability. In fact, the probability of an invalid prediction can be made arbitrarily small by increasing the size of the memory.

The overall CBI process, as introduced in this section, is illustrated in Figure 1: (a) In a first step, the problem $\langle \Sigma, s_0 \rangle$ is characterized at the *similarity*

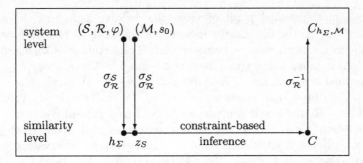

Fig. 1. Illustration of the case-based inference process.

level by means of its *similarity structure*, consisting of the similarity profile h_Σ resp. a corresponding hypothesis h and the similarity structure z_S of the (extended) memory $(\mathcal{M}, s_0)$. The latter can be thought of as the set of values $\{\sigma_S(s_0, s_k) \mid 1 \le k \le n\}$. In fact, h_Σ resp. z_S can be seen as the "image" of the system $(\mathcal{S}, \mathcal{R}, \varphi)$ resp. the (extended) memory $(\mathcal{M}, s_0)$ under the transformation defined by the similarity measures σ_S and $\sigma_\mathcal{R}$. (b) The main step of the CBI process is then to utilize the similarity structure of the problem for constraining the unknown outcome r_0 at the similarity level. The corresponding constraints C are *implicit* in the sense that they refer to the derived property of similarity but not to the result directly. (c) By applying the function $\sigma_\mathcal{R}^{-1} : \mathcal{R} \times [0, 1] \to 2^\mathcal{R}$, which is inversely related to $\sigma_\mathcal{R}$ via $\sigma_\mathcal{R}^{-1}(r, \alpha) = \mathcal{N}_\alpha(r)$, to the observed outcomes r_k ($1 \le k \le n$), the *similarity constraints* C are transformed into *constraints on outcomes*, which are combined via (2) to a constraint $C_{h_\Sigma, \mathcal{M}}$ resp. $C_{h, \mathcal{M}}$ at the system level.

Of course, the more "convenient" the similarity structure of a set-up Σ is, the more successful CBI will be. Within our framework, we have quantified this convenience, i.e., the degree to which the CBR hypothesis holds true for the set-up Σ, by means of the similarity profile h_Σ. This quantification, however, may appear rather restrictive. The existence of some "exceptional" pairs of cases, for instance, might call for small values $h_\Sigma(x)$ of the similarity profile h_Σ in order to guarantee the validity of (2). Then, the predictions (2) which reflect the success of the CBI process might become imprecise even though the similarity structure of Σ is otherwise strongly developed. In order to avoid this problem and to exploit the similarity structure of a system more efficiently we have developed a probabilistic generalization of the approach presented in this section. This approach extends the definition of a CBR set-up by endowing the set $\mathcal{S}$ with a probability measure modelling the occurence of situations. Then, the similarity of situations allows for deriving conclusions about the (conditional) probability distribution of the similarity of associated solutions, represented by a *probabilistic similarity profile*. A probabilistic formalization of the CBR hypothesis seems appropriate since it emphasizes the *heuristic* character of CBR and is particularly well-suited for modelling the "exception to the rule." Details concerning these extensions, which are not discussed in this paper, can be found in [11,12].

From a mathematical point of view, the decisive aspect of the inference scheme in Fig. 1 is the fact that it is based on the analysis of *transformed data* which depicts a certain *relation* between original observations. Considering these observations in pairs, the original data, represented by the memory $\mathcal{M} \subset \mathcal{S} \times \mathcal{R}$, is transformed into the set of data $\{(\sigma_{\mathcal{S}}(s, s'), \sigma_{\mathcal{R}}(r, r')) \mid \langle s, r \rangle, \langle s', r' \rangle \in \mathcal{M}\}$. As opposed to functional relations related to the instance level, which are of the form $\mathcal{S} \mapsto \mathcal{R}$, the result h of the analysis of this data provides information about the *relation* $\sigma_{\mathcal{R}}(\varphi(s), \varphi(s'))$ between outcomes $\varphi(s), \varphi(s')$, given the *relation* $\sigma_{\mathcal{S}}(s, s')$ between situations s and s'. Then, given an observation $\langle s, r \rangle$ and a new situation s_0 and, hence, the relation $\sigma_{\mathcal{S}}(s, s_0)$, h is used for specifying the relation $\sigma_{\mathcal{R}}(r, r_0)$ between r and $r_0 = \varphi(s_0)$. Finally, the inverse transformation $\sigma_{\mathcal{R}}^{-1}$ is used for translating the information about r and $\sigma_{\mathcal{R}}(r, r_0)$ into information about r_0 itself. Moreover, the *combination of evidence* concerning r_0 becomes necessary if this kind of information has been derived from different observations $\langle s_1, r_1 \rangle, \ldots, \langle s_n, r_n \rangle$.

In our case the relation between observations corresponds to their similarity, the function h defines an (estimated) upper bound in form of (an approximation of) the similarity profile, and the combination of evidence is realized as the intersection of individual predictions. This, however, does not seem compulsary. Indeed, we might think of basing inference procedures on alternative specifications such as, e.g., $\sigma_{\mathcal{S}}(s, s') = s - s'$ and $\sigma_{\mathcal{R}}(r, r') = r - r'$. Then, for instance, a least squares approximation h of the transformed data provides an estimation of the difference of two outcomes, given the difference of corresponding situations.

2.2   Case-Based Approximation

Given a hypothesis h and a memory $\mathcal{M}$, (2) can be extended to a set-valued function

$$C_{h,\mathcal{M}} : \mathcal{S} \to 2^{\mathcal{R}}, \, s \mapsto \bigcap_{\langle s', r' \rangle \in \mathcal{M}} N_{h(\sigma_{\mathcal{S}}(s, s'))}(r'), \qquad (3)$$

which is thought of as an (outer) approximation of φ (observe that $\varphi(s) \in C_{h,\mathcal{M}}(s)$ for all $s \in \mathcal{S}$ if h is admissible). Moreover, (3) is easily generalized such that only the k most similar cases, represented by a memory $\mathcal{M}_s \subset \mathcal{M}$, are used in order to derive a value $C_{h,\mathcal{M}}(s)$. Thus, (3) can be seen as an interesting *set-valued* version of the k-NEAREST NEIGHBOR (kNN) algorithm. As opposed to the latter, (3) also takes the quality of the similarity structure in connection with the prediction task into account. For instance, the function $C_{h,\mathcal{M}}$ will not be very constraining if this structure is poorly developed, which indicates that the application of the (original) kNN method does not seem advisable. Besides, the above-mentioned approach [10] to learning similarity hypotheses allows for quantifying the validity of predictions obtained from $C_{h,\mathcal{M}}$ by means of a probability bound α such that $\mathrm{P}(\varphi(y) \in C_{h,\mathcal{M}}(y)) \geq 1 - \alpha$. Thus, given a set $\mathcal{M}$ of observations and the induced hypothesis h, (3) does not only make a set-valued prediction of outcomes $\varphi(s)$ available, but also a corresponding level of confidence.

The comparison of the two algorithms makes also the difference between reasoning at the system level and reasoning at the similarity level obvious. Namely, the kNN algorithm applies the similarity measures directly to the instances in order to find the most similar ones and, hence, to derive a prediction. The similarity measures are used by more indirect means in our method, in the sense that they define the similarity structure h_Σ, which is then used (in connection with observed cases) for constraining outcomes.

It is interesting to study the approximation capability of (3). This, however, presupposes the system $(\mathcal{S}, \mathcal{R}, \varphi)$ to have a structure which allows us to quantify the quality of an approximation. To this end, let us endow $\mathcal{S}$ and $\mathcal{R}$ with a metric, i.e., let $(\mathcal{S}, d_\mathcal{S})$ and $(\mathcal{R}, d_\mathcal{R})$ be metric spaces. Clearly, a good approximation of φ can only be expected if the similarity measures $\sigma_\mathcal{S}$ and $\sigma_\mathcal{R}$ are somehow compatible with the distance measures $d_\mathcal{S}$ and $d_\mathcal{R}$. We can prove the following result.

Proposition 1. *Suppose that $\sigma_\mathcal{S} = f \circ d_\mathcal{S}$ and $\sigma_\mathcal{R} = g \circ d_\mathcal{R}$ with strictly decreasing functions f and g. For all $\varepsilon > 0$ suppose a finite set $\mathcal{S}' \subset \mathcal{S}$ to exist such that $\mathcal{S} = \bigcup_{s' \in \mathcal{S}'}\{s \in \mathcal{S} \mid d_\mathcal{S}(s, s') \leq \varepsilon\}$. Moreover, for some $L > 0$, assume the Lipschitz condition $d_\mathcal{R}(\varphi(s), \varphi(s')) \leq L d_\mathcal{S}(s, s')$ to hold on $\mathcal{S}$. Then, the function φ can be approximated by (3) to any degree of accuracy in the following sense: for all $\delta > 0$, a finite memory $\mathcal{M}$ exists such that $\|C_{h_\Sigma, \mathcal{M}}(s)\| := \max\{d_\mathcal{R}(r, r') \mid r, r' \in C_{h_\Sigma, \mathcal{M}}(s)\} \leq \delta$ for all $s \in \mathcal{S}$.*

PROOF: Let $\varepsilon > 0$ and $\mathcal{S}' \subset \mathcal{S}$ satisfy card$(\mathcal{S}') < \infty$ and $\mathcal{S} = \bigcup_{s' \in \mathcal{S}'}\{s \in \mathcal{S} \mid d_\mathcal{S}(s, s') \leq \varepsilon\}$. Moreover, define $\mathcal{M} := \bigcup_{s' \in \mathcal{S}'}\langle s', \varphi(s')\rangle$. For $s, s' \in \mathcal{S}$ such that $\sigma_\mathcal{S}(s, s') = x \in D_\mathcal{S}$ we have $d_\mathcal{S}(s, s') = f^{-1}(x)$. Thus, according to our assumptions, $\sigma_\mathcal{R}(\varphi(s), \varphi(s')) \geq g(Lf^{-1}(x))$, which means $h_\Sigma(x) \geq g(Lf^{-1}(x))$ for all $x \in D_\mathcal{S}$. Now, consider some $s \in \mathcal{S}$. From the property of $\mathcal{S}'$ follows that $\mathcal{M}$ contains a case $\langle s_0, r_0\rangle$ such that $d_\mathcal{S}(s, s_0) \leq \varepsilon$. Hence, $h_\Sigma(\sigma_\mathcal{S}(s, s_0)) \geq g(Lf^{-1}(\sigma_\mathcal{S}(s, s_0))) \geq g(L\varepsilon)$, which means $d_\mathcal{R}(r_0, r') \leq L\varepsilon$ for all $r' \in \mathcal{N}_{h_\Sigma(\sigma_\mathcal{S}(s, s_0))}(r_0)$. The result then follows from $d_\mathcal{R}(r, r') \leq d_\mathcal{R}(r, r_0) + d_\mathcal{R}(r_0, r')$ for all $r, r' \in \mathcal{N}_{h_\Sigma(\sigma_\mathcal{S}(s, s_0))}(r_0)$ and $C_{h_\Sigma, \mathcal{M}}(s) \subset \mathcal{N}_{h_\Sigma(\sigma_\mathcal{S}(s, s_0))}(r_0)$.   □

3   An Application to Combinatorial Optimization

3.1   Resource-Based Configuration

Resource-based configuration is a special approach to knowledge-based configuration. It is based on the idea that a technical system is composed of a set of primitive *components*, each of which is characterized by some set of *resources* or *functionalities* it provides and some other set of resources it demands. That is, the relation between components is modelled in an abstract way as the exchange of resources [13]. In its simplest form, a configuration problem is specified as a triple $\langle A, y, p\rangle$, where A is a set of components and y is an external demand of functionalities. Each component is characterized by some integer vector $a = (a_1, \ldots, a_m)$ with the intended meaning that it offers f_i, i.e., the i.th functionality, a_i times if $a_i > 0$ $(1 \leq i \leq m)$. Likewise, the component demands this functionality a_i times if $a_i < 0$. The set of components can be written compactly in form of an $m \times n$ integer matrix which we also refer to as A. The jth column a^j of A corresponds to the vector characterizing the jth component. The external demand is also specified as a vector $y \geq 0$, and the meaning of its entries y_i is the same as for the components except for the sign. The (integer) vector $p = (p_1, \ldots, p_n)$ defines the prices of the components, i.e., using the j.th component (once) within a configuration causes costs of $p_j > 0$. A configuration, i.e., the composition of a set of components, is written as a vector $x = (x_1, \ldots, x_n)$ with $x_j \geq 0$ the number of occurences of component a^j. A configuration x is *feasible* if the net result of the corresponding composition and the external demand y are "balanced," i.e., $A \times x = \sum_{j=1}^{n} x_j \, a^j \geq y$. If we speak of the *quality* of a configuration we always have its price in mind. Therefore, a feasible configuration (solution) x^* is called optimal if it causes minimal costs. In its basic form a resource-based configuration problem is obviously equivalent to an integer linear program.[2]

From an applicational point of view it seems reasonable to assume that configuration problems have to be solved repeatedly for varying demands y but a fixed set of components A and, hence, a fixed set of prices p. In this context, the tuple $\langle A, p \rangle$ is also referred to as the *knowledge base*, and a configuration problem is simply identified by the demand vector y. Obviously, this kind of *repetitive combinatorial optimization problem* is particularly interesting from a case-based reasoning perspective [14].

As two concrete examples let us consider the following knowledge bases $\langle A_1, p_1 \rangle$ and $\langle A_2, p_2 \rangle$:

$$
A_1 = \begin{pmatrix} 1 & 1 & 0 & 0 & 0 \\ 0 & 2 & -1 & 0 & 0 \\ 0 & 0 & 2 & 0 & 1 \\ 0 & 0 & 0 & 1 & -1 \\ 0 & 0 & 0 & 0 & 3 \end{pmatrix}, p_1 = \begin{pmatrix} 3 \\ 2 \\ 4 \\ 1 \\ 4 \end{pmatrix}, A_2 = \begin{pmatrix} 1 & 3 & 0 & -1 & 0 \\ 0 & 2 & -1 & 0 & 0 \\ 0 & -1 & 2 & 0 & 1 \\ 0 & 0 & 0 & 1 & -1 \\ 1 & 0 & 0 & 0 & 3 \end{pmatrix}, p_2 = \begin{pmatrix} 2 \\ 1 \\ 3 \\ 1 \\ 6 \end{pmatrix}
$$

In order to obtain CBI set-ups Σ_1 and Σ_2, which define corresponding *repetitive configuration problems*, we further formalize these examples within our framework as follows:

$$
S := \{y = (y_1, \ldots, y_5) \,|\, 0 \leq y_1, \ldots, y_5 \leq 6\}, \mathcal{R} := \mathbb{Z}_{\geq 0}
$$

$$
\sigma_S(y, y') := \exp\left(-0.1 \sum_{k=1}^{5} |y_k - y_k'|\right), \sigma_\mathcal{R}(r, r') := \exp\left(-0.1 \, |r - r'|\right)
$$

$$
\varphi(y) := \min\{x \times p \,|\, x \in \mathbb{Z}_{\geq 0}, A \times x \geq y\}
$$

That is, we consider demand vectors as situations, where the demand of a single functionality is at most six.[3] The result associated with a situation is the price of the corresponding optimal configuration.

---

[2] See [5] for extensions of the model under which this equivalence is lost.

[3] For the sake of simplicity we also allow for the "empty demand" $y = (0, 0, 0, 0, 0)$. Observe that these small examples already define problem classes of size 7^5.

3.2   Supporting Problem Solving

An obvious idea in connection with a repetitive configuration problem is to utilize the *experience* from previously solved problems in order to improve future problem solving. In this connection, a case-based approach seems particularly well-suited, since the problems under consideration are *similar* in the sense that they share the same knowledge-base.

Resource-based configuration problems can be approached efficiently by means of heuristic search methods [9]. Thus, one way of utilizing case-based experience is that of supporting the search process. Suppose, for instance, that we take the initial demand and the empty configuration as a point of departure and that a single search decision corresponds to adding a certain component a to the current (partial) configuration x. Such a decision, the cost of which is given by the cost of a, simply reduces the current problem y (associated with x) to the new configuration problem $y' = y - a$. Of course, the efficiency of the search procedure crucially depends on the quality of the heuristic rules which are used for guiding the search process, e.g., for deciding which components to add or when to break off a search path. The function $C_{h,\mathcal{M}}$ defined in (3) provides valuable information for supporting such decisions. Let us briefly comment on two possibilities of utilizing this function. A deeper discussion of corresponding approaches, however, is beyond the scope of this paper.

Since the depth of a search tree is generally not finite, an important problem consists of deciding when to break off a search path. The function $C_{h,\mathcal{M}}$ specifies bounds on the costs of the configuration problems (supplemented with levels of confidence,) which can be used in various ways for supporting this decision problem. The value $C_{h,\mathcal{M}}(y)$, for instance, defines a (heuristic) lower bound $l(y)$ and a corresponding upper bound $u(y)$ for the cost of the original configuration problem y (associated with the root of the search tree.) If the cost of the current frontier node exceeds $u(y)$, it seems likely that the corresponding path is not optimal. This argumentation also applies to all subtrees and, hence, can be used for guiding a generalized backtracking or an iterative deepening algorithm.

Another way of utilizing the cost bounds specified by $C_{h,\mathcal{M}}$ is to support the decision of which component to add next. If x and y denote the current configuration and the original demand, respectively, then $(x \times p + p_k + C_{h,\mathcal{M}}(y - A \times x - a^k))$ defines bounds on the optimal solution associated with the decision of adding the kth component to x, i.e., on the optimal solution located in the corresponding subtree. These bounds can be used for selecting the most promising component. More generally, $C_{h,\mathcal{M}}(y)$ can be combined with a heuristic estimation $\widehat{\varphi}(y)$ of a cost value $\varphi(y)$, where the function $\widehat{\varphi}$ is an approximation of the *cost function* $\varphi : \mathcal{S} \to \mathcal{R}$ (which maps demands to the cost of optimal solutions [8].) This approach to improving the accuracy of predictions is an interesting example for combining information provided by reasoning at the system level (respresented by φ) and reasoning at the similarity level. Let us elaborate on these ideas more closely.

3.3   Supporting Data Analysis

An obvious question in connection with the idea of basing search decisions on set-valued predictions of cost values concerns the quality of such predictions. We have quantified the latter for the first configuration problem by means of the expected width of an interval $C_{h_M,M}(y)$ and the probability of an invalid prediction $C_{h_M,M}(y) \not\supseteq \varphi(y)$, where M is chosen at random and h_M is derived from M according to the algorithm proposed in [10]. Figure 2 shows these values, which have been obtained by means of experimental studies, as a function of the size of the memory. (Please note the different scaling of the two x-axes.) As can be seen, the probability of an invalid prediction quickly converges toward 0. The non-monotonicity of the expected precision of predictions is caused by two opposite effects which occur in connection with the derivation of predictions from a memory M and the induced hypothesis h_M. Observe that $(h \leq h') \to (C_{h',M}(y) \subset C_{h,M}(y))$ and $(M' \subset M) \to (C_{h,M}(y) \subset C_{h,M'}(y))$ for all hypotheses h, h', memories M, M', and $y \in S$. The above-mentioned effect is then explained by the fact that $M' \subset M$ implies $h_M \leq h_{M'}$ according to the approch in [10].

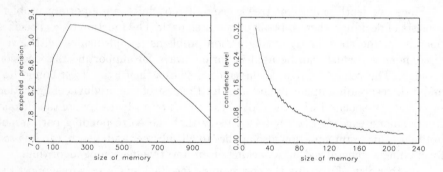

Fig. 2. Left: Expected width of a set-valued prediction $C_{h,M}(y)$ as a function of the size of the memory. Right: Expected probability of an invalid prediction.

Now, let us come back to the idea of combining a case-based approximation $C_{h,M}$ and an approximation $\widehat{\varphi}$ of a cost function. More specifically, suppose $\widehat{\varphi}$ to be defined as $\widehat{\varphi}(y) = [\alpha_1 y_1 + \ldots + \alpha_n y_m]$, where $[\cdot] : \mathbb{R} \to \mathbb{Z}$ maps real numbers to closest integer values. Given a set of observations in form of a memory M, the coefficients $\alpha_1, \ldots, \alpha_m$ can be determined by means of a least squares approximation. Moreover, an estimation $\widehat{\mu}_e$ of the distribution of the residuals $e = \varphi(y) - \widehat{\varphi}(y)$ for the complete problem class S can be derived from frequency information provided by the set $\{r - \widehat{\varphi}(s) \mid \langle s, r \rangle \in M\}$ of approximation errors.

Thus, $\widehat{\mu}_e(e)$ is an estimation of the probability that $\varphi(y) - \widehat{\varphi}(y) = e$ (if y is chosen from S at random.) Then, given a certain demand y, the value $\widehat{\mu}_y(p) = \widehat{\mu}_e(p - \widehat{\varphi}(y))$ can be considered as the probability that $\varphi(y) = p$.

Using the method proposed in [10], we can also derive a similarity hypothesis $h_{\mathcal{M}}$ and, hence, a case-based approximation $C_{h_{\mathcal{M}},\mathcal{M}}$ together with a confidence level α from the memory $\mathcal{M}$. The combination of predictions derived from $\widehat{\varphi}$ and $C_{h_{\mathcal{M}},\mathcal{M}}$ can be achieved, for instance, by applying Jeffrey's rule to $\widehat{\mu}_y$ and the (uncertain) event $C_{h_{\mathcal{M}},\mathcal{M}}(y)$.[4] This leads to the revised probability measure

$$\mu'_y = (1 - \alpha) \cdot \widehat{\mu}_y(\cdot \,|\, C_{h_{\mathcal{M}},\mathcal{M}}(y)) + \alpha \cdot \widehat{\mu}_y(\cdot \,|\, \mathcal{R} \setminus C_{h_{\mathcal{M}},\mathcal{M}}(y)), \qquad (4)$$

where $\widehat{\mu}_y(\cdot \,|\, A)$ denotes the measure $\widehat{\mu}_y$ conditioned on $A \subset \mathcal{R}$, $\widehat{\mu}_y(C_{h_{\mathcal{M}},\mathcal{M}}(y)) > 0$, and $\widehat{\mu}_y(\mathcal{R} \setminus C_{h_{\mathcal{M}},\mathcal{M}}(y)) > 0$. We might even think of replacing (4) by the simple conditional measure $\widehat{\mu}_y(\cdot \,|\, C_{h_{\mathcal{M}},\mathcal{M}}(y))$ if $\mathcal{M}$ is sufficiently large and, hence, α is close to 0. Experimental results[5] for the set-ups Σ_1 and Σ_2 clearly indicate that a combination of the two information sources via (4) improves the accuracy of predictions.

4   Summary

We have developed a formal approach to similarity-based reasoning which allows for deriving (set-valued) predictions of unknown outcomes (solutions). It has been argued that such predictions can be utilized for supporting, e.g., data analysis or optimization. The following points deserve mentioning:

• We have introduced a formal framework in which the task of *case-based inference* has been defined as one of predicting resp. characterizing the outcome associated with a new situation. The distinction between reasoning at the *system level* and reasoning at the *similarity level* has been emphasized.

• We have adopted a *constraint-based view* of CBI, according to which the CBR hypothesis imposes constraints on the relation between the similarity of situations and the similarity of corresponding outcomes.

• The concept of a *similarity profile* establishes a connection between the system level and the similarity level and (partly) represents the similarity structure of a CBI set-up. A *similarity hypothesis* defines an approximation of a similarity profile and can be seen as a quantification of the CBR hypothesis. This concept allows for realizing CBI in form of a constraint-based inference scheme.

---

[4] The uncertain information that $\varphi(y) \in C_{h_{\mathcal{M}},\mathcal{M}}(y)$ with a probability of (at least) $1 - \alpha$ (and $\varphi(y) \in \mathcal{R} \setminus C_{h_{\mathcal{M}},\mathcal{M}}(y)$ with a probability of (at most) α) is treated here as an *unreliable observation*, whereas, according to the usual interpretation of Jeffrey's rule, uncertain inputs are considered as constraints on the revised probability measure (which entails a certain dissymmetry between the role of the two information sources.) In fact, (4) should be seen as implementing the idea of *average focusing* [4], which coincides in our case with Jeffey's rule since $C_{h_{\mathcal{M}},\mathcal{M}}(y)$ and $\mathcal{R} \setminus C_{h,\mathcal{M}}(y)$ define a partition of $\mathcal{R}$.

[5] These results are omitted here due to reasons of space.

• The proposed prediction method takes also the quality of the similarity structure into account (as opposed to, e.g., the k-NEAREST NEIGHBOR algorithm.) Particularly, it is possible to provide a confidence level for the validity of predictions. The usefulness of this approach has been illustrated by means of an example from the field of knowledge-based configuration.

References

1. A. Aamodt and E. Plaza. Case-based reasoning: Foundational issues, methodological variations, and system approaches. *AI Communications*, 7(1):39–59, 1994.
2. D. Aha, D. Kibler, and M.K. Albert. Instance-based learning algorithms. *Machine Learning*, 6(1):37–66, 1991.
3. D. Dubois, F. Esteva, P. Garcia, L. Godo, R.L. de Mantaras, and H. Prade. Fuzzy set modelling in case-based reasoning. *Int. J. Intelligent Systems*, 13:345–373, 1998.
4. D. Dubois, S. Moral, and H. Prade. Belief change rules in ordinal and numerical uncertainty theories. In D.M. Gabbay and P. Smets, editors, *Handbook of Defeasible Reasoning and Uncertainty Management Systems, Vol. 3*, pages 311–392. Kluwer Academic Publishers, 1998.
5. I. Durdanovic, H. Kleine Büning, and M. Suermann. New aspects and applications in the field of resource-based configuration. Technical Report tr-rsfb-96-023, Department of Computer Science, University of Paderborn, 1996.
6. F. Esteva, P. Garcia, L. Godo, and R. Rodriguez. A modal account of similarity-based reasoning. *Int. J. Approximate Reasoning*, 16:235–260, 1997.
7. B. Faltings. Probabilistic indexing for case-based prediction. In *Proceedings ICCBR-97*, pages 611–622. Springer-Verlag, 1997.
8. E. Hüllermeier. Approximating cost functions in resource-based configuration. Technical Report tr-rsfb-98-060, Department of Computer Science, University of Paderborn, 1998.
9. E. Hüllermeier. A two-phase search method for solving configuration problems. Technical Report tr-rsfb-98-062, Department of Mathematics and Computer Science, University of Paderborn, October 1998.
10. E. Hüllermeier. Case-based inference as constraint-based reasoning: Learning similarity hypotheses. Submitted for publication, 1999.
11. E. Hüllermeier. A probabilistic approach to case-based inference. Technical Report 99-02 R, IRIT, Université Paul Sabatier, January 1999.
12. E. Hüllermeier. Toward a probabilistic formalization of case-based inference. In *Proceedings IJCAI-99*, 1999. To appear.
13. H. Kleine Büning, D. Curatolo, and B. Stein. Configuration based on simplified functional models. Technical Report tr-ri-94-155, Department of Computer Science, University of Paderborn, 1994.
14. D.R. Kraay and P.T. Harker. Case-based reasoning for repetitive combinatorial optimization problems, part I: Framework. *Journal of Heuristics*, 2:55–85, 1996.
15. E. Plaza, F. Esteva, P. Garcia, L. Godo, and R.L. de Mantaras. A logical approach to case-based reasoning using fuzzy similarity relations. *Journal of Information Sciences*, 106:105–122, 1998.

Multiple Prototype Model for Fuzzy Clustering

Susana Nascimento[1], Boris Mirkin[2], and Fernando Moura-Pires[1]

[1] Departamento de Informática
Faculdade Ciências e Tecnologia-Universidade Nova de Lisboa, Portugal
[2] DIMACS, Rutgers University
NJ, USA

Abstract. In partitional fuzzy clustering, each cluster is characterized
by two items: its centroid and its membership function, that are usually
interconnected through distances between centroids and entities (as in
fuzzy c-means).

We propose a different framework for partitional fuzzy clustering which
suggests a model of how the data are generated from a cluster structure
to be identified. In the model, we assume that the membership of each
entity to a cluster expresses a part of the cluster prototype reflected in
the entity. Due to many restrictions imposed, the model as is leads to
removing of unneeded cluster prototypes and, thus, can serve as an index
of the number of clusters present in data.

A comparative experimental study of the method fitting the model, its
relaxed version and the fuzzy c-means algorithm has been undertaken. In
general, the study suggests that our methods can be considered a model-
based parallel to the fuzzy c-means approach. Moreover, our generic version can be viewed as a device for revealing "the natural cluster structure" hidden in data.

1 Introduction

In hard partitional clustering [1,2], each entity belongs to only one cluster, and
thus, the membership functions are zero-one vectors. In fuzzy clustering, the
condition of exclusive belongingness for entities is relaxed, and the membership
becomes fuzzy expressing the degree of membership of an entity to a cluster.
Cluster prototypes are usually defined as weighted averages of the corresponding
entities. The most known example of this approach is the fuzzy c-means method
initially proposed by Dunn [3] and generalized by Bezdek [4,5,6].

Usually, membership functions are defined based on a distance function, such
that membership degrees express proximities of entities to cluster centers. Even
though the Euclidean distance is usually chosen, as in the original fuzzy c-means,
other distance functions like l_1 and l_∞ (belonging to the family of Minkowski
distances) and Mahalanobis distances, have been applied in partitional fuzzy
clustering (see [7,8]). These approaches, typically, fail to explicitly describe how
the fuzzy cluster structure relates to the data from which it is derived.

The present work proposes a framework for fuzzy clustering based on a model
of how the data is generated from a cluster structure to be identified. The underlying fuzzy c partition is supposed to be defined in such a way that the

D.J. Hand, J.N. Kok, M.R. Berthold (Eds.): IDA'99, LNCS 1642, pp. 269–279, 1999.

membership of an entity to a cluster expresses a part of the cluster's prototype reflected in the entity. This way, an entity may bear 60% of a prototype A
and 40% of prototype B, which simultaneously expresses the entity's membership to the respective clusters. The prototypes are considered as offered by the
knowledge domain. This idea can be implemented into a formal model differently, depending on the assumed relation between observed data and underlying
prototypes. A seemingly most natural assumption is that any observed entity
point is just a convex combination of the prototypes and the coefficients are the
entity membership values. This approach was developed by Mirkin and Satarov
as the so-called ideal type fuzzy clustering model [9] (see also [10]). It appears,
prototypes found with the ideal types model are extremes or even outsiders with
regard to the "cloud" of points constituting the data, which makes the ideal type
model very much different from the other fuzzy clustering techniques: the prototypes found with the other methods tend to be centroids rather than extremes,
in the corresponding clusters.

Thus, we consider here a different way for pertaining observed entities to
the prototypes: any entity may independently relate to any prototype, which
is similar to the assumption in fuzzy c-means criterion. This approach can be
considered as an intermediate between the fuzzy c-means clustering and ideal
type fuzzy clustering. It takes the adherence to the centroids from fuzzy c-means,
but it considers the membership as a multiplicative factor to the prototype in a
manner similar to that of the ideal type fuzzy clustering. The model is referred
to as the Fuzzy Clustering Multiple Prototype (FCMP) model.

The paper is organized as follows. Section 2 introduces fuzzy partitional
clustering with the fuzzy c-means algorithm. In section 3, the FCMP model for
fuzzy clustering is introduced as well as a clustering algorithm to fit the model.
Actually, two versions of the model are described: a generic one, FCMP-0, and
a relaxed version, FCMP-1. Section 4 discusses the results of a comparative
experimental study between FCMP models and the fuzzy c-means (FCM) using
simple data sets from the literature. To study the properties of the FCMP model
in a systematical way, a data generator has been designed. Section 5 discusses
the results of an experimental study using generated data. Conclusion on the
results and future work is in section 6.

2   Fuzzy c-Means Algorithm

The fuzzy c-means (FCM) algorithm [5] is one of the most widely used methods in
fuzzy clustering. It is based on the concept of fuzzy c-partition [11], summarized
as follows.

Let $\mathbf{X} = \{\mathbf{x}_1, \ldots, \mathbf{x}_n\}$ be a set of given data, where each data point $\mathbf{x}_k$
$(k = 1, \ldots, n)$ is a vector in $\Re^p$, U_{cn} be a set of real $c \times n$ matrices, and c be an
integer, $2 \leq c < n$. Then, the fuzzy c-partition space for X is the set

$$M_{fcn} = \{U \in U_{cn} : u_{ik} \in [0,1] \tag{1}$$
$$\sum_{i=1}^{c} u_{ik} = 1, \, 0 < \sum_{k=1}^{n} u_{ik} < n \},$$

where u_{ik} is the membership value of $\mathbf{x}_k$ in cluster i ($i = 1, \ldots, c$). The value of c is assumed to be known.

The aim of the FCM algorithm is to find an optimal fuzzy c-partition and corresponding prototypes minimizing the objective function

$$J_m(U, \mathbf{V}; X) = \sum_{k=1}^{m} \sum_{i=1}^{c} (u_{ik})^m \|\mathbf{x}_k - \mathbf{v}_i\|^2. \tag{2}$$

In (2), $V = (\mathbf{v}_1, \mathbf{v}_2, \ldots, \mathbf{v}_c)$ is a matrix of unknown cluster centers (prototypes) $\mathbf{v}_i \in \Re^p$, $\|\cdot\|$ is the Euclidean norm, and the weighting exponent m in $[1, \infty)$ is a constant that influences the membership values.

The FCM clustering criterion belongs to the class of least squares clustering criteria [2].

To minimize criterion J_m, under the fuzzy constraints defined in (1), the FCM algorithm is defined as an *alternating minimization* algorithm (cf.[5] for the derivations), as follows. Choose a value for c, m and ε, a small positive constant; then, generate randomly a fuzzy c-partition U^0 and set iteration number $t = 0$. A two-step iterative process works as follows. Given the membership values $u_{ik}^{(t)}$, the cluster centers $\mathbf{v}_i^{(t)}$ ($i = 1, \ldots, c$) are calculated by

$$\mathbf{v}_i^{(t)} = \frac{\sum_{k=1}^{n} \left(u_{ik}^{(t)}\right)^m \mathbf{x}_k}{\sum_{k=1}^{n} \left(u_{ik}^{(t)}\right)^m}. \tag{3}$$

Given the new cluster centers $\mathbf{v}_i^{(t)}$, update membership values $u_{ik}^{(t)}$:

$$u_{ik}^{(t+1)} = \left[\sum_{j=1}^{c} \left(\frac{\left\|\mathbf{x}_k - \mathbf{v}_i^{(t)}\right\|^2}{\left\|\mathbf{x}_k - \mathbf{v}_j^{(t)}\right\|^2} \right)^{\frac{2}{m-1}} \right]^{-1}. \tag{4}$$

The process stops when $\left|U^{(t+1)} - U^{(t)}\right| \leq \varepsilon$, or a predefined number of iterations is reached.

3 A Multiple Prototype Fuzzy Clustering Model

3.1 The Generic Model

Let the data matrix X be preprocessed into Y by shifting the origin to the data gravity center and scaling features by their ranges. Thus, $Y = [y_{kh}]$ is a $n \times p$ entity-to-feature data table where each entity, described by p features, is defined by the row-vector $\mathbf{y}_k = [y_{kh}] \in \Re^p$ ($k = 1 \cdots n$; $h = 1 \cdots p$). This data set can be structured according to a fuzzy c-partition which is a set of c clusters, any cluster i ($i = 1, \cdots, c$) being defined by: 1) its prototype, a row-vector $\mathbf{v}_i = [v_{ih}] \in \Re^p$, and 2) its membership values $\{u_{ik}\}$ ($k = 1 \cdots n$), so that the following constraints hold:

$$0 \leq u_{ik} \leq 1, \text{ for all } i = 1, \ldots, c, k = 1, \ldots, n; \tag{5}$$

$$\sum_{i=1}^{c} u_{ik} = 1, \text{ for all } k = 1, \ldots, n. \tag{6}$$

Notice that in this definition of fuzzy c-partition, the condition $0 < \sum_k u_{ik} < n$ in the original definition (1) is relaxed.

Let us assume that each entity $\mathbf{y}_k = [y_{kh}]$ of Y is related to each prototype $\mathbf{v}_i = [v_{ih}]$ ($i = 1, \cdots, c$) up to its membership degree u_{ik}; that is, u_{ik} expresses that part of $\mathbf{v}_i$ which is present in $\mathbf{y}_k$ in such a way that approximately $y_{kh} = u_{ik}v_{ih}$ for every feature h. More formally, we suppose that

$$y_{kh} = u_{ik}v_{ih} + \varepsilon_{ikh}, \tag{7}$$

where the residual values ε_{ikh} are as small as possible.

The ideal type fuzzy clustering model from [9] assumes that

$$y_{kh} = \sum_{i=1}^{c} u_{ik}v_{ih} + \varepsilon_{kh}, \tag{8}$$

which implies that all entity points $\mathbf{y}_k$ are convex combinations of the prototypes (up to the residuals). Thus, the prototypes according to this latter model must lie outside the area of entity points. This may be considered a formalization of the concept of ideal type in logics, which falls beyond the scope of current paper and will be omitted from consideration.

A clustering criterion according to (7) can be defined as fitting of each data point to each of the prototypes up to the degree of membership. This goal is achieved by minimizing all the residual values via the least-squares criterion

$$E_0(U, \mathbf{V}; Y) = \sum_{i=1}^{c} \sum_{k=1}^{n} \sum_{h=1}^{p} (y_{kh} - u_{ik}v_{ih})^2 \tag{9}$$

with regard to the constraints (5) and (6).

The equations in (7) along with the least-squares criterion (9) to be minimized by unknown parameters U and $V = (\mathbf{v}_1, \mathbf{v}_2, \ldots, \mathbf{v}_c) \in \Re^{cp}$ for Y given, will be referred to as the generic *fuzzy clustering multiple prototypes model*, FCMP-0, for short. In this model, the principle of the least-squares criterion in the fuzzy c-means is extended to a data-to-cluster model framework, which inevitably leads to a more complex form of the criterion.

3.2   Relaxing Restrictions of FCMP-0

In real domains of application (clinical findings for typical scenarios of diseases, personality traits in psychology, types of consumer in market research, and so on), the concept of prototype is meaningful in such a way that data entities can be described as sharing parts of prototypes. This is the idea underlying FCMP. However, the requirement of FCMP-0 that each entity be expressed as a part of each prototype is obviously too strong and unrealistic. The intuition leads us to consider that only meaningful sharings, those expressed by high membership values, should be taken into account in the equations (7).

There are two ways to implement this idea in the FCMP framework: in a hard manner and in a smooth one. A "hard" version should deal only with those equations in (7) that involve rather large values of u_{ik}. By specifying a threshold, β between 0 and 1, only those differences ε_{ikh} are left in the criterion (9) that satisfy the inequality, $u_{ik} \geq \beta$. In such a model, FCMP-β, entities may relate to as few prototypes as we wish. In particular, $\beta = 0.5$ leads to exclusive relationship of any entity to one prototype only. The idea of removing all small interactions between prototypes and entities from the criterion has been proposed in the context of fuzzy c-means clustering by Selim and Ismail [12] in several versions, one of which relates to directly thresholding the membership weights as suggested in this paragraph above. The authors of [12] referred to their approaches as to "soft clustering" as a kind of intermediate between crisp clustering and fuzzy clustering.

In this paper, we consider a different, smooth, manner of dealing with the unrealistic feature of FCMP-0. To smooth the members ε_{ikh} corresponding to small memberships, let us weight the squared residuals in (9) by corresponding u_{ik}:

$$E_1(U, V; Y) = \sum_{i=1}^{c} \sum_{k=1}^{n} \sum_{h=1}^{p} u_{ik}(y_{kh} - u_{ik}v_{ih})^2, \qquad (10)$$

subject to the fuzziness constraints (5) and (6).

The model with this criterion will be denoted as FCMP-1.

3.3 Minimizing FCMP Criteria

An alternating minimization algorithm FCM for fuzzy c-means clustering can be extended for minimization of both the FCMP-0 and FCMP-1 criteria subject to the fuzzy constraints (5) and (6).

Each iteration of the algorithm consists of two steps as follows. First, given membership matrix U, the optimal prototypes are determined according to the first-degree optimum conditions as

$$v_{ih}^{(t)} = \frac{\sum_{k=1}^{n} \left(u_{ik}^{(t)}\right)^a y_{kh}}{\sum k = 1^n \left(u_{ik}^{(t)}\right)^b} \ . \qquad (11)$$

The parameters a, b are $a = 1$ and $b = 2$ for FCMP-0 and $a = 2$ and $b = 3$, for FCMP-1.

Formula (11) is similar to expression (3) in FCM for the prototypes, which shows that the prototypes in FCMP are indeed centroids rather than extremes.

Second, given prototype matrix V, the optimal membership values are found by minimizing criterion (9) or (10), respectively. In contrast to FCM, minimization of the criteria subject to constraints (5) and (6) is not an obvious task; it requires an iterative solution on its own.

Upon preliminarily experimenting with several options, the gradient projection method [13,14] has been selected for finding optimal membership values (given the prototypes). It can be proven that the method converges fast for FCMP-0 with a constant (anti) gradient stepsize.

Let us denote the set of membership vectors satisfying conditions (5) and (6) by Q. The calculations of the membership vectors $\mathbf{u}_k^{(t)} = \left[u_{ik}^{(t)} \right]$ are based on vectors $\mathbf{d}_k^{(t)} = \left[d_{ik}^{(t)} \right]$:

$$d_{ik}^{(t)} = u_{ik}^{(t-1)} - \alpha(\langle v_i, v_i \rangle \, u_{ik}^{(t-1)} - \langle y_k, v_i \rangle), \tag{12}$$

where α is a stepsize parameter of the gradient method. Then, $\mathbf{u}_k^{(t)}$ is to be taken as the projection of $\mathbf{d}_k^{(t)}$ in Q, denoted by $P_Q(\mathbf{d}_k^{(t)})$[1]. The process stops when the condition $\left| U^{(t)} - U^{(t-1)} \right| \leq \varepsilon$ is fulfilled.

Finding membership vectors by minimizing FCMP-1 is performed similarly.

Thus, the algorithm consists of "major" iterations of updating matrices U and V and "minor" iterations of recalculation of membership values in the gradient projection method within each of the "major" iterations.

The algorithm starts with a set $V^{(0)}$ of c arbitrarily selected prototype points in $\Re^p$ and U^0; it stops when the difference between successive prototype matrices becomes small.

The algorithm converges only locally (for FCMP-1). Moreover, with a "wrong" number of clusters prespecified, FCMP-0 may not converge at all since FCMP-0 may shift some prototypes to infinity (see discussion in the next subsection). In our experiments, the number of major iterations in FCMP algorithms when they converge is small, which is exploited as a stopping condition: when the number of major iterations in an FCMP run goes over a large number (in our calculations, over 100), that means the process does not converge.

3.4   FCMP-0 as an Index of Data Structure

A feature of the FCMP-0 clustering criterion (9) is that it does not change if vectors $\mathbf{v}_i$ and $\mathbf{u}_i$ are changed for $\mathbf{v}_i\alpha$ and $\mathbf{u}_i/\alpha$ for some i, where α is an arbitary real. In particular, tending α to infinity, the prototype $\mathbf{v}_i$ tends to infinity, too, while its membership vector, $\mathbf{u}_i$, to zero, without any change in corresponding differences ε in criterion (9).

This way, some membership values needed to decrease some of the differences in (9) can be increased by simultaneously decreasing some other ones along with removing corresponding prototypes.

This is, in brief, an explanation of the empirically observed phenomenon of removing some initially set prototypes from the data set zone by the algorithm FCMP-0. In such a non-convergence case, the number of prototypes should

---

[1] The projection $P_Q(\mathbf{d}_k^{(t)})$ is based on an algorithm we developed for projecting a vector $\mathbf{d}_k^{(t)}$ over the simplex of membership vectors $\mathbf{u}_k^{(t)}$; its description is omitted here.

be decreased until FCMP-0 converges. The final number of prototypes can be considered a "natural" one relevant to the structure of the data set under consideration. Some results of experimentally testing of this feature of FCMP-0 are presented in two subsequent sections.

4 Experimental Study I

The main goal of all experiments is to compare FCMP-0, FCMP-1 and FCM (with its parameter $m = 2$). The emphasis will be done with regard to the clustering results rather than the performance of the algorithms. It is quite obvious that our criteria, (9) and, especially, (10), are more complex than that of FCM, (2), and thus require more calculations.

The results will be discussed in two sequential sections: (a) illustrative results with some simple data sets taken from the literature: butterfly [5], MS [9], wine and Iris [15] (this section); (b) general results found with a data generator designed for this study (next section).

In our experiments, each of the algorithms, FCM, FCMP-0, and FCMP-1, has been run on the same data set (with the same initial setting) for different values of c ($c = 2, 3, 4 \ldots$).

The clustering solutions found by FCMP-0 and FCMP-1, have been characterised by the following three features: 1) number of clusters found, c'; 2) separability; and 3) proximity to the FCM found prototypes. The separability index was also calculated for FCM solutions.

The separability index, $B_c = 1 - \frac{c}{c-1}\left(1 - \frac{1}{n}\sum_{k,i}\left(u_{ik}\right)^2\right)$, assesses the fuzziness of partition U; it takes values in the range $[0,1]$ such that $B_c = 1$ for hard partitions and $B_c = 0$ for the uniform memberships (cf. [5], pp. 157, for a detailed description).

The proximity between FCM and FCMP prototypes is defined as follows:

$$D_{FCM} = \frac{\sum_{i,h}(v'_{ih} - v_{ih})^2}{\sum_{i,h}(v_{ih})^2}.100, \tag{13}$$

where v_{ih}/v'_{ih} denote FCM/FCMP prototype feature values, respectively. Matching between FCMP prototypes and FCM prototypes is determined according to smallest distances. When the number of prototypes c' found by FCMP-0 is smaller than c, only c' prototypes participate in (13), in this case.

A summary of the results is presented in Table 1, where the number of (major) iterations, t_1, taken by each algorithm has also been registered. The boundary value $t_1 = 100$ corresponds to the non-convergence case.

These experiments show that FCMP-0 indeed converges sometimes to a smaller number of prototypes, c', by moving the other prototypes outside of the data set zone. For the butterfly, wine and MS's data sets the numbers of prototypes found by FCMP-0 correspond to those in the original data (2, 3, and 3, respectively). For the Iris data set, FCMP-0 converges only when $c' = 2$, even though the original data set contains three classes (i.e. c=3). This goes in line

Table 1. Results of running FCM, FCMP-0 and FCMP-1 algorithms for butterfly, wine, MS and Iris data sets.

			t_1		c'		B_c		$D_{FCM}(\%)$	
	c	FCM	MP-0	MP-1	MP-0	FCM	MP-0	MP-1	MP-0	MP-1
	2	22	12	9	2	0.47	0.9	0.83	4.1	7.4
Butt	3	27	100	17	2	0.44	0.87	0.69	33	42.4
(c=2)	4	72	100	32	2	0.49	0.84	0.6	15.7	26
	2	12	18	16	2	0.25	0.86	0.73	13.8	15.9
wine	3	21	20	13	3	0.26	0.79	0.87	7.1	6.6
(c=3)	4	66	100	19	3	0.17	0.7	0.89	18.4	36.4
MS	3	11	11	9	3	0.73	0.85	0.83	0.19	0.7
(c=3)	4	23	100	8	3	0.7	0.75	0.82	0.54	2.2
	2	10	7	10	2	0.67	0.94	0.8	0.36	1.1
Iris	3	15	100	16	2	0.56	0.9	0.77	8.71	10.4
(c=3)	4	28	100	18	2	0.48	0.78	0.76	6.2	13

with the claim made by some authors that, actually, the underlying structure in Iris data set consists of two clusters only [5].

The dissimilarity values, D_{FCM}, for FCMP-0 are small in the cases when the method converges and high in the other cases. This shows that in the case of convergence, FCMP-0 prototypes are very much similar to FCM ones.

The algorithm FCMP-1 always converges to a solution for the various values of c (i.e. $c' = c$). However, the pattern of D_{FCM} dissimilarity values for FCMP-1 closely follows that of FCMP-0.

Also, FCMP-0 and FCMP-1 partitions are more contrast than FCM ones, according to the separability coefficient, B_c. Finally, the numbers of major iterations for both FCMP-0 and FCMP-1 are always less than for FCM. Nevertheless, the former algorithms have their running times greater than FCM because of the time spent for "minor" iterations.

5   Experimental Study II

The main goal of this series of experiments is twofold. First, to perform a more extensive comparison of FCMP-0, FCMP-1 and FCM methods by using generated data sets. Second, to study the behavior of FCMP-0 as an index of the number of prototypes in data.

In order to study characteristics of the FCMP model in identifying a cluster structure, the model should be tested on data exhibiting its own cluster structure (a *cluster tendency* [2]). To accomplish this, a random data generator has been constructed as follows.

Data Generator

1. The dimension of the space (p), the number of clusters (c) and numbers $n_1, n_2, \ldots, n_c$ are randomly generated within prespecified intervals. The data set cardinality is defined as $n = \sum_{i=1}^{c} n_i$.
2. c cluster directions are defined as follows: vectors $\mathbf{o}_i \in \Re^p$ $(i = 1, \cdots, c)$ are randomly generated within a prespecified cube; then, their gravity center $\mathbf{o}$ is calculated.
3. For each i, define two p-dimensional sampling boxes, one within bounds $A_i = [.9\mathbf{o}_i, 1.1\mathbf{o}_i]$ and the other within $B_i = [\mathbf{o}, \mathbf{o}_i]$; then generate randomly $0.1 n_i$ points in A_i and $0.9 n_i$ points in B_i.
4. The data generated are normalized by centering to the origin and scaling by the range.

To visualize data, they are projected into a 2D/3D space of the best principal components as can be seen in Figure 1.

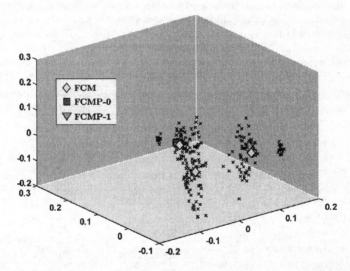

Fig. 1. A 3D plot of the best three principal components of generated data $(n = 225,\ p = 20,\ c = 3)$. The resulting prototypes for FCMP-0, FCMP-1 and FCM with $c' = 3$ are also projected in the same principal components.

Some 70 data sets have been generated with distinct numbers of prototypes (i.e. $c = 3, 4, 5, 6, \ldots$) and different space dimensions ($p = 20, 30, 50, \ldots 150$).

For each group of data sets of the same dimension (p) and generated prototypes (c), the three algorithms have been compared based on the same parameters used in experiment I: number of major iterations (t_1), number of prototypes found (c'), separability coefficient B_c and distances (D_{FCM}).

In general, the results follow those found for the illustrative data sets.

1. The dissimilarity values, D_{FCM}, for FCMP-0 prototypes are close to those of FCM when FCMP-0 converges. The distances are large when FCMP-0 does not converge. The pattern of similarities for FCMP-1 follows that for FCMP-0.
2. On average, the number of major iterations (t_1) in FCMP-1 is smaller than that in FCM, while in FCMP-0 this number does not differ significantly from that in FCM. However, the running time is greater for both of FCMP algorithms, because of the minor iterations with the gradient projection method.
3. The separability, B_c, of FCMP-0 and FCMP-1 solutions is always higher than that of FCM.
4. There is a percentage of cases when the number of clusters found by FCMP-0 is smaller than the number of generated prototypes. Also, it was found that FCM may also drastically reduce the number of prototypes (by making some of the prototypes equal to each other), especially when dimension of the space is high ($p \geq 100$). Moreover, in some cases, FCM leads to even smaller number of prototypes than FCMP-0.

These conclusions point to features of the models under investigation and should not be interpreted as advantages of one over others.

6   Conclusion

The fuzzy clustering approach proposed in this paper suggests a model of how the data is generated from a cluster structure to be identified. This implies direct interpretability of the fuzzy membership values, which alone should be considered a motivation for introducing the model-based methods.

Based on the experimental results obtained in this research, the FCMP-1 seems a model-based clustering approach that parallels FCM, and FCMP-0 can be viewed as a device for estimating the number of clusters in the underlying structure to be found.

This model-based clustering approach seems appealing in the sense that, on doing cluster analysis, the experts of a knowledge domain usually have a conceptual understanding of how the domain is organized in terms of prototypes. This knowledge, put into the format of tentative prototypes, may well serve as the initial setting for data based structurization of the domain. In such a case, the belongingness of data entities to clusters are based on how much they share the features of corresponding prototypes. This seems fair in such application areas as mental disorders in psychiatry or consumer behavior in marketing. However, the effective utility of the multiple prototypes model still remains to be demonstrated with real data.

Acknowledgments

This research has been carried out in the Department of Computer Science of FCT- Universidade Nova de Lisboa. Part of this research has been supported by DIMACS, a National Science Foundation Center for Discrete Mathematics and Theoretical Computer Science (a cooperative project of Rutgers University, Princeton University, AT&T Labs-Research, Bellcore and Bell Labs). One of the authors (S.N.) was also supported by a grant from PRAXIS XXI program, of the Portuguese Foundation for Science and Technology (FCT). The authors thank the anonymous reviewers for valuable comments.

References

1. Duda, R., Hart, P.: Pattern Classification and Scene Analysis. John Wiley & Sons, (1973)
2. Jain, A., Dubes, R.: Algorithms for Clustering Data. Prentice Hall, Englewood Cliffs, NJ, (1988)
3. Dunn, J.: A fuzzy relative of the isodata process and its use in detecting compact, well-separated clusters. Journal of Cybernetics, 3(3) (1973) 32–57
4. Bezdek, J.: Fuzzy Mathematics in Pattern Classification. PhD thesis, Applied Math. Center, Cornell University, Ithaca (1973)
5. Bezdek, J.: Pattern Recognition with Fuzzy Objective Function Algorithms. Plenum Press, New York (1981)
6. Bezdek, J., Hathaway, R.: Recent Convergence Results for the Fuzzy c-Means Clustering Algorithms. Journal of Classification, 5(2) (1988) 237–247
7. Bobrowski, L., Bezdek, J.: C-Means with l_1 and l_∞ norms. IEEE Transactions on Systems, Man and Cybernetics, 21(3) (1991) 545–554
8. Dave, R.: Fuzzy Shell-clustering and Applications to Circle Detection of Digital Images. International Journal of General Systems, 16(4) (1990) 343–355
9. Mirkin, B., Satarov, G.: Method of fuzzy additive types for analysis of multidimensional data: I, II. Automation and Remote Control, 51(5, 6) (1990) 683–688, 817–821
10. Mirkin, B.: Mathematical Classification and Clustering. Kluwer Academic Publishers (1996)
11. Ruspini, E.: A New Approach to Clustering. Information and Control, 15 (1969) 22–32
12. Selim, S. Z. and Ismail, M. A.: Soft Clustering of Multidimensional Data: A Semi-Fuzzy Approach. Pattern Recognition, 17(5) (1984) 559–568
13. Polyak, B.: Introduction to Optimization. Optimization Software, Inc., New York (1987)
14. Bertsekas, D.: Nonlinear Programming. Athena Scientific, Belmont, Massachusetts, USA (1995)
15. Blake, C., Keogh, E., Merz, C.: UCI Repository of machine learning databases. URL: http://www.ics.uci.edu/~mlearn/MLRepository.html. University of California, Irvine, Dept. of Information and Computer Sciences (1998)

A Comparison of Genetic Programming Variants for Data Classification

Jeroen Eggermont, Agoston E. Eiben, and Jano I. van Hemert

Leiden University
P.O. Box 9512
2300 CA Leiden
The Netherlands
{jeggermo,gusz,jvhemert}@cs.leidenuniv.nl

Abstract. In this paper we report the results of a comparative study on different variations of genetic programming applied on binary data classification problems. The first genetic programming variant is weighting data records for calculating the classification error and modifying the weights during the run. Hereby the algorithm is defining its own fitness function in an on-line fashion giving higher weights to 'hard' records. Another novel feature we study is the atomic representation, where 'Booleanization' of data is not performed at the root, but at the leafs of the trees and only Boolean functions are used in the trees' body. As a third aspect we look at generational and steady-state models in combination of both features.

1 Introduction

Binary data classification problems (with exactly two disjoint classes) form an important application area of machine learning techniques, in particular *genetic programming* (GP) [7, 1]. In this paper we compare a number of different variants for a GP applied to such problems. Rather than simply tuning on traditional GP parameters, we investigate the effect of two significant changes in a fixed GP setup (closely matching the setups in [7]) in combination with a generational, respectively steady-state model.

The first modification we consider amounts to using a fitness function based on weighting data records when calculating the total classification error and modifying the weights (thus the fitness function) on-line, during the run. This feature, called Stepwise Adaptation of Weights (SAW) has been first used in penalty functions for constraint satisfaction problems (see e.g. [3] and applied in one particular setup within a GP [2]. Here we conduct a systematic study of combinations of SAW-ing with a new representation in GP.

A specific representation forms the second line of investigation. In standard GP a function set of real valued operators is used and a special operator in the root of the tree 'Booleanizes' the outcome resulting in a (binary) classification of a given data record [7]. In our atomic representation 'Booleanization' of data is not performed at the root, but immediately at the leafs of a tree and only Boolean

D.J. Hand, J.N. Kok, M.R. Berthold (Eds.): IDA'99, LNCS 1642, pp. 281–290, 1999.
© Springer-Verlag Berlin Heidelberg 1999

functions are used in the tree's body. By such a relatively simple function set the flexibility to create different models, i.e. trees, is lower than in the standard representation, but the models become more transparent, i.e. better readable for humans. In practical applications this property is often more important than a lower classification error. The first experiments with this representation are reported in [6]

The third aspect we consider concerns steady-state and generational GP models. The standard GP approach is based on the generational population model and although some authors do use a steady-state model [2, 8], to our knowledge there is no experimental comparison available on the relative advantage of either model.

All the experiments were done using the *Library for Evolutionary Algorithm Programming* (LEAP)[1] system for the construction of the GPs, [6]. This library is currently under development using C++ and Design Patterns [5], and is aiming to be a framework that makes it easy to test out different methods within the field of evolutionary computation. Also it provides an easy way for users to incorporate their own techniques, representations and problems, thus assuring a fast and easy way of dealing with testing evolutionary algorithms in general.

2   Data Sets and Experiment Setup

For comparing different algorithm variants we use four different data sets from the Statlog collection[2]: the Australian Credit, the German Credit, the Heart Disease, and the Pima Indians Diabetes data set [9]. Each algorithm is evaluated using n-fold cross validation and the performance measure for different algorithms is the average classification error over the n-folds. Statlog uses a cost matrix for the reported results on the Heart Disease and German Credit data set. This influences the measured classification error as different penalties are given for each value of an attribute. For instance, misclassifying a patient with a heart disease receives a higher penalty than misclassifying a patient without a heart disease. We do not consider the Statlog cost matrix. In Table 1 we give the number of records for each data set and the number of folds done in the cross validation tests.

Besides the two tested features the other components and parameters of our GP are kept close to the experiments as described in [7], although we do use mutation in all cases (depending on the representation). The parameters that are common in each tested algorithm variants are summarized in Table 2.

3   SAW-ing

The rationale behind the Stepwise Adaptation of Weights (SAW) mechanism is to let the algorithm define the weights itself. The application domain of this

---

[1] Available on WWW at http://www.wi.leidenuniv.nl/~jvhemert/leap
[2] Available on WWW at http://www.ncc.up.pt/liacc/ML/statlog

Table 1. Test data sets

data set	number of records	cross validation
Australian Credit	690	10-fold
German Credit	1000	10-fold
Heart Disease	270	9-fold
Pima Indians Diabetes	768	12-fold

Table 2. Main GP parameters shared by all algorithm variants

Parameter	Value
Initial max. tree depth	5
Max. number of nodes	200
Initialization	ramped half-and-half
Population size	1000
Parent selection	linear ranking
Bias for linear ranked selection [10]	1.5
Replacement strategy	replace worst in population
Stop condition	perfect classification or 40000 evaluations
Mutation (atom/subtree) probability	0.1
Xover probability	0.9
Xover type	swap subtrees
Xover functions:atoms or functions:terminals ratio	4:1

mechanism is not restricted to GP and to data analysis, it can be used for any EA where the fitness function is composed in a manner represented by Equation 1. In fact, SAW-ing has been introduced and first applied in the context of constraint satisfaction [3, 4].

$$f(x) = \sum_{r \in D} w_r \cdot error(x, r) \tag{1}$$

where w_r is a weight assigned to the record r and $error(x, r)$ is a measure of misclassification. In the most simple case

$$error(x, r) = \begin{cases} 1 \text{ if } x \text{ classifies } r \text{ incorrectly} \\ 0 \text{ otherwise} \end{cases} \tag{2}$$

In a SAW-ing evolutionary algorithm the weights are initially all set at the same value and these weights are repeatedly increased with a certain step size Δw at predefined moments during the run. The general mechanism is presented in Figure 1.

Note that in a classification problem the overall quality of a candidate solution (the accuracy of a model on the whole data set) is determined by local scores on data records. In other words, the evaluation function (fitness function)

> *On-line weight update mechanism*
>   set initial weights (thus fitness function f)
>   **while not** EA is finished **do**
>   **for** the next T_p fitness evaluations **do**
>   let the EA run with this f
>   **end for**
>   redefine weights in f and recalculate fitness of individuals
>   **end while**

Fig. 1. Stepwise adaptation of weights (SAW)

measuring the total classification error is composed by the errors on particular data records. An evolutionary algorithm searching for a good model classifying the given records in a data set D could use the fitness function (to be minimized) defined as follows.

It is clear that a GP will primarily 'concentrate' on classifying those records correctly that carry the highest weights. Therefore, the weights need to be determined in accordance with the hardness of the records. Nevertheless, to determine how weights should be assigned to records appropriately, may require substantial insight into the problem, which may not be available, or only at substantial costs.

In the present SAW-ing GP implementation the weights are initially set as $w_r = 1$. Redefining the fitness function happens by adding Δw to the weights of those records that are misclassified by the best individual at the end of each period of T_p fitness evaluations. Obviously, the general rationale behind SAW-ing applies to our situation: records that are hard to classify correctly should have a higher weight, and by the on-line f adjust the weights according to its own experience.

The parameters of the SAW-ing mechanism as used through the present study are displayed in Table 3.

Table 3. SAW-ing parameters

Parameters	Value
Initial weights w_r	1
Δw	1
T_p steady-state	200 evaluations
T_p generational	1000 evaluations

As stated earlier, SAW-ing has been tested on various problems in the field of constraint satisfaction. The results obtained in these experiments are very promising. We therefore have extended the study of the SAW-ing mechanism to data classification using genetic programming. In Figure 2 we show typical runs of the SAW-ing mechanism on different binary CSPs [4]. Figures from other problems share a common feature; at first the fitness of the best individual is rising and then it suddenly drops to either a local optimum or eventually a global optimum. Also every fitness curve of a SAW-ing evolutionary algorithm shows a saw-shaped graph, due to redefinition of the weights every T_p fitness evaluations.

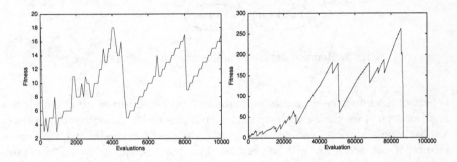

Fig. 2. Fitness curves for the SAW-ing EA on binary CSP. Figure on the left is a zoom in of the figure on the right for the first 10000 evaluations.

4   Atomic Representation

The motivation behind our so-called atomic representation comes from practical applications, where the selection of the best model to classify data is not only depending on classification accuracy. In practice, before adopting a certain model an intuitive verification by the users common sense takes place. To this end, it is crucial that models (trees in a GP based problem solver) are transparent, that is easy to read and understand for humans. Often, the size of the trees is limited to achieve a satisfactory level of transparency. Here we investigate another option. Rather than using a function set of numerical operators and a special operator in the root of the tree that 'Booleanizes' the outcome (resulting in a binary classification of a given data record), we process numerical information at the leafs of a tree, transform it into Boolean statements, and apply only Boolean functions in the body of the tree (see Figure 3).

Formally, an atom is syntactically a predicate of the form *operator*(*var*, *const*), built up from a variable indicating a field in the data set, a constant between 0 and 1, and a comparing operator, denoted by $A_<$ and $A_>$. In this representation the conditional part of a classification rule could look like:

$$(A_>(r_1, 0.3) \text{ nor } A_<(r_0, 0.6)) \text{ or } A_>(r_1, 0.2)$$

In this representation we use subatomic mutation. Every time an individual is selected for a mutation, we first choose a node in the tree to work on. If this node

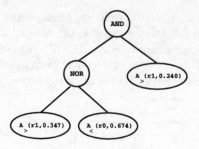

Fig. 3. Representation of a classification rule as a tree.

is part of the function set, a subtree mutation will be performed. If this node is a leaf (an atom), we choose with equal chance if this will be a subtree mutation or a subatomic mutation. A subatomic mutation works by first selecting, with equal chance, if the operation will be performed on the variable or on the constant. In case of a variable we randomly select a new variable. In case of the constant c a small number Δc $(-d < \Delta c < d)$ is generated which is then added to the constant as show in Equation 3. The values for all records are between 0 and 1 in the data sets we consider.

$$c' = \begin{cases} 0, & \text{if } c + \Delta c < 0, \\ 1, & \text{if } c + \Delta c > 1, \\ c + \Delta c, & \text{otherwise.} \end{cases} \tag{3}$$

With this representation we use the parameter setting displayed in Table 4 and with the standard GP representation we use the parameter setting displayed in Table 5.

Table 4. Parameters of the GP with an atomic representation.

Parameter	Value
Function set	$\{\text{and}, \text{or}, \text{nand}, \text{xnor}\}$
Atom set	attribute greater or less than a constant
Mutation type	1. subtree replacement
	2. subatomic mutation
Subatomic parameter d	0.1

5   Steady-State vs. Generational Model

Here we will look at steady-state and generational GP models. The standard GP approach is based on the generational population model [7] and although

Table 5. Parameters of the standard GP.

Parameter	Value
Function set	$\{+, -, \times, \%\}$
Terminal set	$\{x_1, \ldots, x_n\} \cup [0, 1]$
Mutation type	1. subtree replacement
	2. point mutation

some authors do use a steady-state model [2, 8], to our knowledge there is no experimental comparison available on the relative advantages of these models.

In the steady-state variant we update the population after creating two offspring, thus after one cycle of parent selection, crossover and mutation, and use $T_p = 200$ (recalculating the weights after 100 cycles). In the generational case, however, maintaining the same setup is not possible. Namely, for a generational GP the update interval T_p must be a multiple of the population size, otherwise a weight revision would be necessary in the middle of creating a new generation. This imposes a restriction on the combination of SAW-ing and the generational model, leaving less freedom for the user to determine an algorithm setup. In order to allow the maximal number of weight recalculations, while maintaining the population size 1000 we use $T_p = 1000$ in the experiments with the generational model. Notice that this implies a handicap for SAW-ing as the number of weight adjustments is reduced by a factor of five.

6   Results

We are presenting the results of the experiments arranged around the four data sets used in this study. For each algorithm variant we give the average classification error percentage as performance measure. The best result in each table is presented in italics.

Looking at the tables 6 through 9 we can make a number of observations. Under the steady-state model the SAW-ing variant has or shares the first place in five of the eight tests. Looking from a different perspective, the standard GP seems slightly better than the atomic representation. Having a better performance five times out of eight.

To give some insight of what influence the SAW-ing mechanism has on the behavior on the fitness function we give some figures of a typical run of the GP.

Table 6. Average classification error on the Australian Credit data set.

	steady state		generational	
algorithm	atom	standard	atom	standard
SAW	0.278	0.241	0.242	0.242
no-SAW	0.246	0.241	0.243	*0.232*

Table 7. Average classification error on the German Credit data set.

	steady state		generational	
algorithm	atom	standard	atom	standard
SAW	*0.281*	0.303	0.295	0.292
no-SAW	*0.281*	0.284	0.300	*0.281*

Table 8. Average classification error on the Heart Disease data set.

	steady state		generational	
algorithm	atom	standard	atom	standard
SAW	0.200	0.211	0.222	0.181
no-SAW	0.211	0.200	0.230	*0.170*

In Figure 4 we show plots of the steady-state GP, with and without the SAW-ing mechanism. The GP without SAW-ing shows the typical decrease of the fitness[3]. However, the plot of the GP with SAW-ing shows much fluctuation, in the range of 200. It is therefore crucial to stop the algorithm at the right time, i.e. when the fitness value is on its lowest point.

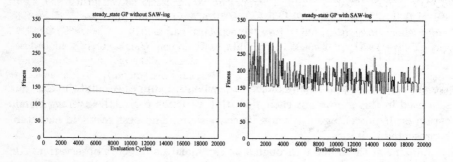

Fig. 4. Typical fitness curve for the steady-state GP without SAW-ing (left) and with SAW-ing (right) on the Australian Credit data set (first fold).

7   Comparison with Other Techniques

In order to compare our GP to other data mining techniques found in [9], we have chosen three algorithms outside the field of evolutionary computation. The algorithms we have chosen are LogDisc (a statistical method), C4.5 (a well-known decision trees algorithm) and Back-propagation (the standard algorithm

---

[3] Recall that we are trying to minimize the fitness function

Table 9. Average classification error on the Pima Indian Diabetes data set.

	steady state		generational	
algorithm	atom	standard	atom	standard
SAW-ing	0.263	0.257	0.267	0.257
no-SAW-ing	0.283	0.266	*0.250*	0.253

for training multi-layered feed-forward networks). Since the results reported in Statlog have used a cost matrix (Heart Disease and German Credit [9, 2]) which we have not, we only compare our results to the Australian Credit and Pima Indians Diabetes data sets. The results can be found in Table 10. As representative for GP we use the standard (generational) GP which has the best overall performance.

Table 10. Results on the Australian Credit and Pima Indians Diabetes Datasets.

data set	Australian Credit	Pima Indians Diabetes
BackProp	0.154	0.248
C4.5	0.155	0.270
standard GP	0.232	0.253
LogDisc	0.141	0.223

As we can clearly see in Table 10 the standard GP performs poorly on the Australian Credit data set when compared to the other 3 techniques. The performance of the standard GP on the Pima Indians data set not too bad. It is close to back-propagation and much better than C4.5.

8 Conclusions and Future Research

The comparison of the atomic and the standard representation indicates a hard trade-off situation. Giving up the flexibility of numerical operators for the sake of transparency achieved by using Boolean functions in the bodies of the trees comes at costs of performance. It seems that there is no generally advisable option, the choice between the two representations has to be made on a case-by-case basis, depending on the priorities in the given problem context.

Looking at the differences between the effects of the SAW-ing mechanism we should distinguish between the steady-state and the generational models. Using the steady-state model the SAW-ing variant helping the GP to a better performance three times out of eight, is not able to provide a constant improvement. This is in contrast to the results found in constraint satisfaction [3, 4] and it needs further investigation to pinpoint the exact reason of this observation. Although, one observation shows that the GP version with SAW-ing show much fluctuation in the fitness, causing a performance decrease when the algorithm is stopped at the wrong time, i.e. when the best solution in the population does not perform well.

These experiments are just the beginning of an extensive study of using genetic programming for data mining purposes. Research in the near future will focus on the comparison of techniques in this paper and the standard GP using commercial data as a benchmark.

References

[1] Wolfgang Banzhaf, Peter Nordin, Robert E. Keller, and Frank D. Francone. *Genetic Programming – An Introduction; On the Automatic Evolution of Computer Programs and its Applications*. Morgan Kaufmann, dpunkt.verlag, January 1998.

[2] J. Eggermont, A.E. Eiben, and J.I. van Hemert. Adapting the fitness function in GP for data mining. In P. Nordin and R. Poli, editors, *Proceedings of Second European Workshop on Genetic Programming*, LNCS. Springer, Berlin, 1999. in press.

[3] A.E. Eiben, J.K. van der Hauw, and J.I. van Hemert. Graph coloring with adaptive evolutionary algorithms. *Journal of Heuristics*, 4(1):25–46, 1998.

[4] A.E. Eiben, J.I. van Hemert, E. Marchiori, and A.G. Steenbeek. Solving binary constraint satisfaction problems using evolutionary algorithms with an adaptive fitness function. In A.E. Eiben, Th. Bäck, M. Schoenauer, and H.-P. Schwefel, editors, *Proceedings of the 5th Conference on Parallel Problem Solving from Nature*, number 1498 in LNCS, pages 196–205, Berlin, 1998. Springer.

[5] E. Gamma, R. Helm, R. Johnson, and J. Vlissides. *Design Patterns: elements of reusable object-oriented software*. Addison-Wesley, 1994.

[6] J.I. van Hemert. Applying adaptive evolutionary algorithms to hard problems. Master's thesis, Leiden University, 1998. Also available as http://www.wi.leidenuniv.nl/~jvhemert/publications/IR-98-19.ps.gz.

[7] J.R. Koza. *Genetic Programming*. MIT Press, 1992.

[8] W.B. Langdon. *Genetic Programming + Data Structures = Automatic Programming!* Kluwer, 1998.

[9] D. Michie, D.J. Spiegelhalter, and C.C. Taylor, editors. *Machine Learning, Neural and Statistical Classification*. Ellis Horwood, February 1994.

[10] D. Whitley. The GENITOR algorithm and selection pressure: Why rank-based allocation of reproductive trials is best. In J. David Schaffer, editor, *Proceedings of the Third International Conference on Genetic Algorithms (ICGA'89)*, pages 116–123, San Mateo, California, 1989. Morgan Kaufmann Publishers, Inc.

Fuzzy Clustering Based on Modified Distance Measures

Frank Klawonn[1] and Annette Keller[2]

[1] Department of Electrical Engineering and Computer Science
Ostfriesland University of Applied Sciences
Constantiaplatz 4
D-26723 Emden, Germany
[2] Institute for Flight Guidance
German Aerospace Center
Lilienthalplatz 7
D-38108 Braunschweig, Germany

Abstract. The well-known fuzzy c-means algorithm is an objective function based fuzzy clustering technique that extends the classical k-means method to fuzzy partitions. By replacing the Euclidean distance in the objective function other cluster shapes than the simple (hyper-)spheres of the fuzzy c-means algorithm can be detected, for instance ellipsoids, lines or shells of circles and ellipses. We propose a modified distance function that is based on the dot product and allows to detect a new kind of cluster shape and also lines and (hyper-)planes.

1 Introduction

Fuzzy clustering techniques aim at finding a suitable fuzzy partition for a given data set. For a fuzzy partition a datum is not necessarily assigned to a unique class or cluster, but has membership degrees between zero and one to each cluster. Fuzzy clustering algorithms are applied for various reasons:

- The membership degrees give information about the ambiguity of the classification.
- Fuzzy clustering can adapt to noisy data and classes that are not well separated.
- Since most fuzzy clustering approaches are based on optimizing an objective function, membership degrees represent continuous parameters so that a continuous optimization problem has to be solved.
- Fuzzy clustering can be applied to learning fuzzy rules from data.

In this paper we briefly review the principal objective function-based fuzzy clustering approach in section 2. Various modifications of the distance function in the objective function have been proposed in order to model different cluster forms. In section 3 we introduce a new angle-based distance measure that

---

[1] This work was supported by the European Union under grant EFRE 98.053

D.J. Hand, J.N. Kok, M.R. Berthold (Eds.): IDA'99, LNCS 1642, pp. 291–301, 1999.
© Springer-Verlag Berlin Heidelberg 1999

is suitable for data sets with a smaller number of extreme values and a large number of 'normal' values. Section 4 modifies this approach and we obtain a clustering algorithm to detect lines and (hyper-)planes that can be applied to line recognition as well as to constructing Takagi-Sugeno fuzzy rule systems (see for instance [13]) that describe a function in terms of local linear models.

2   Objective Function-Based Fuzzy Clustering

We cannot give a complete overview on fuzzy clustering here and mention only the basic ideas in order to provide the background for our new algorithms. For a thorough overview on fuzzy clustering we refer to [2,9]. Most fuzzy clustering algorithms aim at minimizing the objective function of weighted distances of the data to the clusters

$$J(X, U, v) = \sum_{i=1}^{c} \sum_{k=1}^{n} u_{ik}^{m} d^{2}(v_i, x_k) \qquad (1)$$

under the constraints

$$\sum_{k=1}^{n} u_{ik} > 0 \qquad \text{for all } i \in \{1, \ldots c\} \qquad (2)$$

and

$$\sum_{i=1}^{c} u_{ik} = 1 \qquad \text{for all } k \in \{1, \ldots n\}. \qquad (3)$$

$X = \{x_1, \ldots, x_n\} \subseteq \mathbb{R}^p$ is the data set, c is the number of fuzzy clusters, $u_{ik} \in [0, 1]$ is the membership degree of datum x_k to cluster i, v_i is the prototype or the vector of parameters for cluster i, and $d(v_i, x_k)$ is the distance between prototype v_i and datum x_k. The parameter $m > 1$ is called fuzziness index. For $m \to 1$ the clusters tend to be crisp, i.e. either $u_{ik} \to 1$ or $u_{ik} \to 0$ resulting in the hard c-means algorithm, for $m \to \infty$ we have $u_{ik} \to 1/c$. Usually $m = 2$ is chosen. (2) ensures that no cluster is empty, (3) enforces that for each datum its classification can be distributed over different clusters, but the sum of the membership degrees to all clusters has to be one for each datum. Therefore, for this approach the membership degrees can be interpreted as probabilities and the corresponding clustering approach is called probabilistic. The strict probabilistic constraint was relaxed by Davé who introduced the concept of noise clustering [6,7]. An additional noise cluster is added and all data have a (large) constant distant to this noise cluster. Therefore, noise data that are far away from all other clusters are assigned to the noise cluster with a high membership degree. Krishnapuram and Keller [12] developed possibilistic clustering by completely neglecting the probabilistic constraint (3) and adding a term to the objective function that avoids the trivial solution assigning no data to any cluster. We cannot discuss the details of these approaches here and restrict our considerations to the probabilistic fuzzy clustering approach. However, our algorithms can be applied in the context of noise and possibilistic clustering in a straight forward way.

We also do not consider the problem of determining the number of clusters in this paper and refer to the overview given in [9].

The basic fuzzy clustering algorithm is derived by differentiating the Lagrange function of (1) taking the constraint (3) into account. This leads to the necessary condition

$$u_{ik} = \frac{1}{\sum_{j=1}^{c} \left(\frac{d^2(v_i, x_k)}{d^2(v_j, x_k)} \right)^{\frac{1}{m-1}}} \tag{4}$$

for the membership degrees for a (local) minimum of the objective function, given the prototypes are fixed. In the same way, we can derive equations for the prototypes, fixing the membership degrees, when we have chosen the parameter form of the prototypes and a suitable distance function.

The corresponding clustering algorithm is usually based on the so-called alternating optimization scheme that starts with a random initialization and alternatingly applies the equations for the prototypes and the membership degrees until the changes become very small. Convergence to a local minimum or (in practical applications very seldom) a saddle point can be guaranteed [1,3].

The most simple fuzzy clustering algorithm is the fuzzy c-means (FCM) (see f.e. [2]) where the distance d is simply the Euclidean distance and the prototypes are vectors $v_i \in \mathbb{R}^p$. It searches for spherical clusters of approximately the same size and by differentiating (1) we obtain the necessary conditions

$$v_i = \frac{\sum_{k=1}^{n} u_{ik}^m x_k}{\sum_{k=1}^{n} u_{ik}^m} \tag{5}$$

for the prototypes that are used alternatingly with (4) in the iteration procedure.

Gustafson and Kessel [8] designed a fuzzy clustering method that can adapt to hyper-ellipsoidal forms. The prototypes consist of the cluster centres v_i as in FCM and (positive definite) covariance matrices C_i. The Gustafson and Kessel algorithm replaces the Euclidean distance by the transformed Euclidean distance

$$d^2(v_i, x_k) = (\det C_i)^{1/p} \cdot (x_k - v_i)^{\top} C^{-1} (x_k - v_i).$$

Besides spherical or ellipsoidal cluster shapes also other forms can be detected by choosing a suitable distance function. For instance, the prototypes of the fuzzy c-varieties algorithm (FCV) describe linear subspaces, i.e. lines, planes and hyperplanes [2,4]. The equations for the prototypes of this algorithm require the computation of eigenvalues and eigenvectors of (weighted) covariance matrices. FCV can be applied to image recognition (line detection) and to construct local linear (fuzzy) models. Shell clustering algorithms are another class of fuzzy clustering techniques that are mostly applied to image recognition and detect clusters in the form of boundaries of circles, ellipses, parabolas etc. (For an overview on shell clustering see [9,11].)

In principal any kind of prototype parameter set and distance function can be chosen in order to have flexible cluster shapes. However, the alternating optimization scheme, that can at least guarantee for some weak kind of convergence, can only be applied, when the corresponding distance function is differentiable. But even for differentiable distance functions we usually obtain equations for the prototypes that have no analytical solution (for instance [5]). This means that we have to cope with numerical problems and need in each iteration step a numerical solution of a coupled systems of non-linear equations. Other approaches try to optimize the objective function directly by evolutionary algorithms (for an overview see [10]). Nevertheless, fuzzy clustering approaches with distance functions that do not allow an analytical solution for the prototypes are usually very inefficient. In the following we introduce a new fuzzy clustering approach that admits also an analytical solution for the prototypes.

3   Clustering with Angle-Based Distances for Normalized Data

The idea of our approach is very similar to the original neural network competitive learning approach as it is for instance described in [14]. Instead of the Euclidean distance between a class representative and a given datum that Kohonen's self organizing feature maps use, the simple competitive learning approach computes the dot product of these vectors.

For normalized vectors the dot product is simply the cosine of the angle between the two vectors, i.e. the dot product is one if and only if the (normalized) vectors are identical, otherwise we obtain values between -1 and 1. Therefore, we define as the (modified) distance between a normalized prototype vector v and a normalized data vector x

$$d^2(v, x) \;=\; 1 - v^\top x. \tag{6}$$

Thus we have $0 \le d^2(v, x) \le 2$ and, in case of normalized vectors, $d^2(v, x) = 0 \Leftrightarrow x = v$.

Let us for the moment assume that the data vectors are already normalized. How we actually carry out the normalization will be discussed later on. With the distance function (6) the objective function (1) becomes

$$
J(X, U, v) = \sum_{i=1}^{c} \sum_{k=1}^{n} u_{ik}^m (1 - v_i^\top x_k)
$$
$$
= \sum_{i=1}^{c} \sum_{k=1}^{n} \left(u_{ik}^m - u_{ik}^m \sum_{\ell=1}^{p} v_{i\ell} x_{k\ell} \right)
$$

where $v_{i\ell}$ and $x_{k\ell}$ is the ℓth coordinate/component of vector v_i and x_k, respectively. By taking into account the constraint that the prototype vectors v_i have to be normalized, i.e.

$$
\| v_i \|^2 \;=\; \sum_{t=1}^{p} v_{it}^2 \;=\; 1 \tag{7}
$$

we obtain the Lagrange function

$$L = \sum_{i=1}^{c} \sum_{k=1}^{n} \left(u_{ik}^m - u_{ik}^m \sum_{\ell=1}^{p} v_{i\ell} x_{k\ell} \right) + \sum_{s=1}^{c} \lambda_s \left(\sum_{t=1}^{p} v_{st}^2 - 1 \right). \qquad (8)$$

The partial derivative of L w.r.t. $v_{i\ell}$ yields

$$\frac{\partial L}{\partial v_{il}} = -\sum_{k=1}^{n} u_{ik}^m x_{k\ell} + 2\lambda_i v_{i\ell}.$$

Since the first derivative has to be zero in a minimum, we obtain

$$v_{i\ell} = \frac{1}{2\lambda_i} \sum_{k=1}^{n} u_{ik}^m x_{k\ell}. \qquad (9)$$

Making use of the constraint (7), we have

$$1 = \frac{1}{4\lambda_i^2} \sum_{\ell=1}^{p} \left(\sum_{k=1}^{n} u_{ik}^m x_{k\ell} \right)^2,$$

which gives us

$$2\lambda_i = \sqrt{\sum_{\ell=1}^{p} \left(\sum_{k=1}^{n} u_{ik}^m x_{k\ell} \right)^2}$$

so that we finally obtain

$$v_{i\ell} = \frac{\sum_{k=1}^{n} u_{ik}^m x_{k\ell}}{\sqrt{\sum_{t=1}^{p} \left(\sum_{k=1}^{n} u_{ik}^m x_{kt} \right)^2}} \qquad (10)$$

as the updating rule for the prototypes.

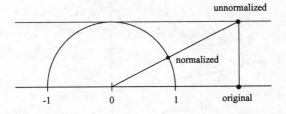

Fig. 1. Normalization of a datum

For this formula we have assumed that the data vectors are normalized. When we simply normalize the data vectors, we loose information, since collinear vectors are mapped to the same normalized vector. In order to avoid this effect

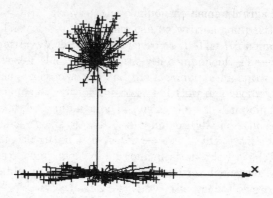

Fig. 2. Two clusters

we extend our data vectors by one component which we set one for all data vectors and normalize these $(p + 1)$-dimensional data vectors. In this way, the data vectors in $\mathbb{R}^p$ are mapped to the upper half of the unit sphere in $\mathbb{R}^{p+1}$. Figure 1 illustrates the normalization for one-dimensional data.

Figure 2 shows a clustering result for a two-dimensional data set (i.e. the clustering is actually carried out on the normalized three-dimensional data). The membership degrees are not illustrated in the figure. We have connected each datum with the cluster centre (that we obtain by reversing the normalization procedure) to which it has the highest membership degree.

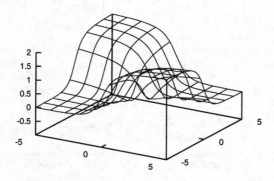

Fig. 3. The one-dimensional distance function

It can be seen in figure 2 that the prototype of the upper cluster is slightly lower than one might expect. The reason is that the distance function is not affine invariant. We can already see in figure 2 that vectors near zero keep almost their Euclidean distance when we normalize them, whereas very long vectors are all mapped to the very lower part of the semi-circle.

Figure 3 shows distance values of two one-dimensional vectors. (The distance is computed for the normalized two-dimensional vectors.) Of course, the distance is zero at the diagonal and increases when we go away from the diagonal. But the distance is increasing very quickly with the distance to the diagonal near zero, whereas it increases slowly, when we are far away from the diagonal.

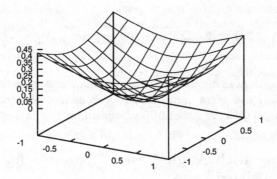

Fig. 4. Distance to the point $(0,0)$

Figures 4 and 5 also illustrate this effect. In Figure 4 the distance to the (non-normalized) two-dimensional vector (cluster centre) $(0,0)^\top$ is shown. It is a symmetrical distance function. However, when we replace the cluster centre $(0,0)^\top$ by the vector $(1,0)^\top$, we obtain the function in figure 5.

Here we can see that the distance is asymmetrical in the sense that it increases faster when we look in the direction of $(0,0)^\top$. This can be an undesired effect for certain data sets. But there are also data sets for which this effect has a positive influence on the clustering result. Consider for instance data vectors with the annual salary of a person as one component. When we simply normalize each component, the effect is that a few outliers (persons with a very high income) force that almost all data are normalized to values very near to zero. This means that the great majority simply collapses to one cluster (near zero) and few outliers build single clusters. Instead of a standard normalization, we can also choose a logarithmic scale in order to avoid this effect. But the above mentioned clustering approach offers an interesting alternative.

Figure 6 shows a clustering result of data of bank customers with the attributes age, income, amount in depot, credit, and guarantees for credits. The number of clusters was automatically determined by a validity criterion, resulting in three clusters. The axes shown in the figure are credit, income, and amount

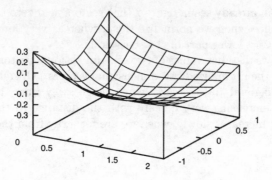

Fig. 5. Distance to the point $(1,0)$

in depot. It is worth noticing that there is a compact cluster in the centre, representing the majority of average customers, whereas there are two other clusters
covering custumers with high credit or a large amount of money, respectively.

4   Clustering with Angle-Based Distances for Non-normalized Data

In the previous section we have assumed that the data vectors are normalized
or that we normalize them for the clustering. In this section we discuss what
happens, when we refrain from normalizing the data vectors and the cluster
centres. In order to avoid negative distances, we have to modify the distance
function to

$$d^2(v, x) \;=\; (1 - v^\top x)^2. \tag{11}$$

The geometrical meaning of this distance function is the following. A datum
x has distance zero to the cluster v, if and only if $v^\top x = 1$ holds. This equation
describes a hyperplane, i.e. the hyperplane of all $x \in \mathbb{R}^p$ of the form

$$\frac{v}{\| v \|} + \sum_{s=1}^{p-1} \lambda_s w_s \tag{12}$$

where the vectors $w_1, \ldots, w_{p-1} \in \mathbb{R}^p$ span the hyperplane perpendicular to v
and $\lambda_1, \ldots, \lambda_{p-1} \in \mathbb{R}$.

This means that we can find clusters in the form of linear varieties like the
FCV algorithm. We will return to a comparison of FCV and this approach later
on. Figure 7 shows the distance to the prototype $v^\top = (0.5, 0)$. This prototype
describes the line

$$\begin{pmatrix} 2 \\ 0 \end{pmatrix} + \lambda \begin{pmatrix} 0 \\ 1 \end{pmatrix}.$$

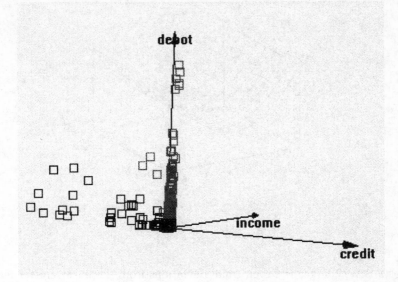

Fig. 6. Clustering result for bank customers

In order to derive equations for the prototypes we insert the distance function (11) into the objective function (1) and take the first derivative w.r.t. $v_{i\ell}$:

$$\frac{\partial J}{\partial v_{i\ell}} = -2 \sum_{k=1}^{n} u_{ik}^m (1 - v_i^\top x_k) x_{k\ell}$$

These derivatives have to be zero at a minimum and we obtain the system of linear equations

$$\sum_{k=1}^{n} u_{ik}^m (1 - v_i^\top x_k) x_k = 0.$$

Making use of the fact that $(v_i^\top x_k) x_k = (x_k x_k^\top) v_i$ holds, we obtain for the prototypes

$$v_i = \left(\sum_{k=1}^{n} u_{ik}^m x_k x_k^\top \right)^{-1} \sum_{k=1}^{n} u_{ik}^m x_k. \tag{13}$$

Note that the matrix $\sum_{k=1}^{n} u_{ik}^m x_k x_k^\top$ is the (weighted) covariance matrix (assuming mean value zero) and can therefore be inverted unless the data are degenerated.

An example of the detection of two linear clusters is shown in figure 8.

The difference of this approach to the FCV algorithm is in the computing scheme that requires inverting a matrix whereas for the FCV algorithm all eigenvalues and eigenvectors have to be computed. Another difference is caused by the non-Euclidean distance function that is again not affine invariant. Problems can arise when lines are near to $(0,0)^\top$, since then the corresponding prototype

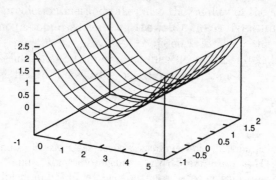

Fig. 7. Distance to $(0.5, 0)$

vector v is very large, and even small deviations from the linear cluster lead to large distances. These problems are well known for other fuzzy clustering algorithms with non-Euclidean distance functions [11] and have to be treated in a similar way.

5   Conclusions

We have introduced fuzzy clustering algorithms using dot product-based distance functions that lead to new cluster shapes in the normalized case and to linear clusters in the non-normalized case. They represent a further extension of the already known objective function-based fuzzy clustering approaches.

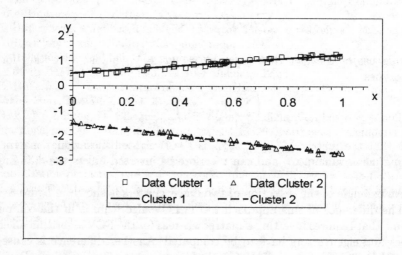

Fig. 8. Two linear clusters

References

1. Bezdek, J.C.: A Convergence Theorem for the Fuzzy ISODATA Clustering Algorithms. IEEE Trans. Pattern Analysis and Machine Intelligence **2** (1980) 1-8.
2. Bezdek, J.C.: Pattern Recognition with Fuzzy Objective Function Algorithms. Plenum Press, New York (1981).
3. Bezdek, J.C., Hathaway, R.H., Sabin, M.J., Tucker, W.T.: Convergence Theory for Fuzzy c-Means: Counterexamples and Repairs. IEEE Trans. Systems, Man, and Cybernetics **17** (1987) 873-877.
4. Bock, H.H.: Clusteranalyse mit unscharfen Partitionen. In: Bock, H.H. (ed.). Klassifikation und Erkenntnis: Vol. III: Numerische Klassifikation. INDEKS, Frankfurt (1979), 137-163.
5. Davé, R.N.: Fuzzy Shell Clustering and Application to Circle Detection in Digital Images. Intern. Journ. General Systems **16** (1990) 343-355.
6. Davé, R.N.: Characterization and Detection of Noise in Clustering. Pattern Recognition Letters **12** (1991) 657-664.
7. Davé, R.N.: On Generalizing Noise Clustering Algorithms. In: Proc. 7th Intern. Fuzzy Systems Association World Congress (IFSA'97) Vol. III, Academia, Prague (1997), 205-210.
8. Gustafson, D.E., Kessel, W.C.: Fuzzy Clustering with a Fuzzy Covariance Matrix. Proc. IEEE CDC, San Diego (1979), 761-766.
9. Höppner, F. Klawonn, F., Kruse, R., Runkler, T.: Fuzzy Cluster Analysis. Wiley, Chichester (1999).
10. Klawonn, F., Keller, A.: Fuzzy Clustering with Evolutionary Algorithms. Intern. Journ. of Intelligent Systems **13** (1998) 975-991.
11. Krishnapuram, R., Frigui, H., Nasraoui, O.: Fuzzy and Possibilistic Shell Clustering Algorithms and Their Application to Boundary Detection and Surface Approximation – Part 1 & 2. IEEE Trans. on Fuzzy Systems **3** (1995) 29-60.
12. Krishnapuram, R., Keller, J.: A Possibilistic Approach to Clustering. IEEE Trans. Fuzzy Systems **1** (1993) 98-110.
13. Kruse, R., Gebhardt, J., Klawonn, F.: Foundations of fuzzy systems. Wiley, Chichester (1994).
14. Nauck, D., Klawonn, F., Kruse, R.: Neuro-Fuzzy Systems. Wiley, Chichester (1997).

Building Classes in Object-Based Languages by Automatic Clustering

Petko Valtchev

INRIA Rhône-Alpes
655 av. de l'Europe, 38330 Montbonnot Saint-Martin, France

Abstract. The paper deals with clustering of objects described both by
properties and relations. Relational attributes may make object descriptions recursively depend on themselves so that attribute values cannot
be compared before objects themselves are. An approach to clustering is
presented whose core element is an object dissimilarity measure. All sorts
of object attributes are compared in a uniform manner with possible exploration of the existing taxonomic knowledge. Dissimilarity values for
mutually dependent object couples are computed as solutions of a system of linear equations. An example of building classes on objects with
self-references demonstrates the advantages of the suggested approach.

1 Introduction

Object-based systems provide a variety of tools for building software models of
real-world domains : classes and inheritance, object composition, abstract data
types, etc. As a result, the underlying data model admits highly structured descriptions of complex real-world entities. With the number of object applications
constantly growing the need of analysis tools for object datasets becomes critical
[7]. Although the importance of the topic has been recognized [4, 1], it has been
rarely addressed in the literature : a few studies concerning object knowledge
representation (KR) systems [3, 9, 1], or object-oriented (OO) databases [7] have
been reported in the past years.

Our own concern is the design of automatic class building tools for objects
with complex relational structure. A compact class can be built on-top of an
object cluster discovered by an automatic clustering procedure [5]. The main
difficulty that clustering application faces is the definition of a consistent comparison for all kinds of object attributes. Relations connect objects into larger
structures, object *networks*, and may lead to (indirect) self-references in object
descriptions. Self-references make it impossible to always compare object attributes before comparing objects. Consequently, most of the existing approaches
to clustering [6, 10] cannot apply on self-referencing descriptions.

We suggest an approach towards automatic class building whose core element
is an object dissimilarity measure. The measure evaluates object attributes in
a uniform way. Its values on mutually dependent object couples are computed

D.J. Hand, J.N. Kok, M.R. Berthold (Eds.): IDA'99, LNCS 1642, pp. 303–314, 1999.
© Springer-Verlag Berlin Heidelberg 1999

as solutions of a system of linear equations. Thus, even object sets with self-references may be processed by a clustering tool. The discovered clusters are turned to object classes and then provided with a intentional description.

The paper starts by a short presentation of an objects model together with a discussion of aspects which make objects similar (Section 2). A definition of a suitable dissimilarity measure is given in Section 3. The computation of the measure on mutually dependent object couples is presented. Section 4 shows an example of an application of the measure. Clustering and class characterization are discussed in Section 5.

2   Object Formalism

Object languages organize knowledge about a domain around two kinds of entities, classes and objects. Domain individuals are represented as objects, whereas groups of individuals, or categories, give rise to classes. Thus, each class is associated to a set of member objects, its *instances*. Both classes and objects are described in terms of attributes which capture particular aspects of the underlying individuals. A class description is a summary of instance descriptions.

In the following, only the descriptive aspects of object languages will be considered. The object model of TROPES, a system developed in our team [8] will be used to illustrate the object specific structure. However, the results presented later in the paper hold for a much larger set of object models.

2.1   Objects, Concepts, and Classes

A *structured object* in our model is a list of attribute values which are themselves objects or simple values. For instance, an object representing a flat within a real-estate knowledge base, may have fields for flat's rent, standing, owner, etc. Fig. 1 shows example of an object, `flat#5`, with three attributes, `rooms`, `owner` and `rent`.

Three kinds of attributes will be distinguished: *properties, components* and *links*. Properties model features of the individual being modeled, for example the rent of a flat, whereas components and links model relations to other individuals. Composition, or `part-of`, relation between individuals is expressed through component attributes. Such an attribute relates a composite object to one or a collection of component objects. Composition is distinguished due to its particular nature : it is a transitive and non-circular relation. On the above example, `owner` is a link and `rooms` is a component. Apart for nature, attributes have a `type` which delimits their possible values. Object-valued attributes are typed by object concepts whereas simple values are members of data types, further called *abstract data types* (ADT). Finally, attributes may have a single value or a collection of values in which case they are called *multi-valued* attributes. Collections are built on a basic type by means of a constructor, `list` or `set`. For instance, the values of `rooms` attribute in `flat#5` is a set of three instances of the `room` concept.

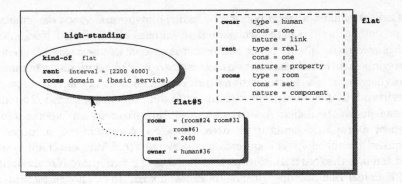

Fig. 1. Example of a concept, `flat`, a class, `high-standing` and an instance, `flat#5`. All three entities provide lists of attributes : concept attributes specify type, nature and constructor, which are necessary in interpreting values in instance attributes; class attributes provide value restrictions on instance attributes; instance attributes contain values.

Objects of a KB are divided into disjoint families, called *concepts*, e.g. `flat`, `human`, `room`. An object is thus an instance of a unique concept, for example, `flat#5` of the `flat` concept drawn as a rectangle. Concepts define the structure (set of object attributes with their types) and the identity of their instances. This may be seen on upper right part of Fig. 1 : `flat` defines the type, the nature and the constructor of the three attributes of the example. Concepts are comparable to big classes in a traditional OO application, or to tables in relational databases. A *class* defines a subset of concept instances called class *members*. Classes provide value restrictions on attribute values of member objects, that is sets of admissible values among all the values in the attribute basic type given by the concept. Restrictions on property attributes correspond to sub-types of the ADT, whereas restrictions on relations are classes of the underlying concept. For example, the class `high-standing` on Fig. 1 restricts the `rent` attribute to values in the interval [2200,4000] and the rooms attribute to sets composed of members of the classes `basic` and `service`. Classes of a concept are organized into a hierarchical structure called *taxonomy*.

An object KB is made up of a set concepts. For each concept, a set of instances are given which are organized into one or more class taxonomies. Objects and classes of different concepts are connected by means of relational attributes.

2.2 Summary on Objects as Data Model

An object is a member of the entire set of instances defined by its concept. A class defines a sub-set of instances. In quite the same way, simple values are members of the domain of their ADT whereas types define subsets of ADT values. Unlike objects, simple values have neither identity, nor attributes.

Objects can be seen as points in a multi-dimensional space determined by the object's concept where each dimension corresponds to an attribute. A class describes a region of that space and each member object lays exclusively within the region. Furthermore, dimensions corresponding to relational attributes are spaces themselves. Thus, a relation establishes a dependency between its source concept and its target concept : instances of the former are described by means of instances of the latter. An overview of all inter-concept dependencies is provided by a graphical structure, henceforth called *conceptual scheme* of the KB, composed by concepts as vertices and relational attributes as (labeled) edges. For example, the (partial) conceptual scheme of the real estate KB given on the left of Fig. 2 is made up of three concepts, human, flat and room, and three attributes: two links composing a circuit, owner and house, and a multi-valued component relation, rooms.

The scheme summarizes the relations that may exist between instances of different concepts in the KB. In fact, each object is embedded into a similar relational structure where each concept is replaced by one or a collection of its instances. The structure, which we call the *network* associated to an object *o*, includes all objects which are related to *o* by a chain of attributes. In a network, an edge corresponding to a multi-valued attribute may link a source object to a set of target objects. For example, on the left of Fig. 2, the network of the object flat#5 is drawn. Within the network, an edge rooms connects flat#5 to the three objects representing flat's rooms. Observe the similar topologies of both structures on Fig. 2. [1]

Finally, the network of *o* extended with classes of all its objects contains the entire amount of information about *o*. It is thus the maximal part of the KB to be explored for proximity computation.

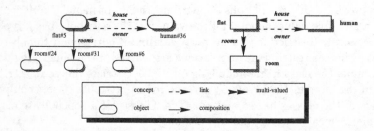

Fig. 2. Example of a KB conceptual scheme, on the right, and an object network that reflects the scheme structure, on the left. The network is obtained from the scheme by replacing a concept by an instance or a collection of instances.

---

[1] Actually, there is a label-preserving morphism from each instance network to the respective part of the conceptual scheme.

2.3   Analysis Issues

We are concerned with class design from a set of unclassified objects within an object KB. The problem to solve is an instance of the conceptual clustering problem [10] and therefore may be divided into two sub-tasks: constitution of member sets for each class and class characterization [6]. A conventional conceptual clustering algorithm would typically carry out both sub-tasks simultaneously using class descriptions to build member sets. With an object dataset where link attributes relate objects of the same concept this approach may fail. Let's consider the example of the spouse attribute which relates objects representing a married couple. Within a class of human, the spouse attribute refers to a possibly different class of the same concept. The attribute induces two-object circuits on instances of human and therefore may lead to circular references between two classes in the taxonomy. When classes are to be built in an automatic way, it is impossible to evaluate two classes, say c and c', referring to each other since the evaluation of each class would require, via the spouse attribute, the evaluation of the other one.

We suggest an approach to automatic class building which deals with both tasks separately. First, member sets are built by an automatic clustering procedure based on an object proximity measure. The measure implements principles suggested in [3] to compare object descriptions with self-references. Once all class member sets are available these are turned into undescribed classes. The characterization step is then straightforward since class attributes in particular those establishing circuits, may refer to any of the existing classes.

As our aim is to find compact classes, we require the discovered clusters to be homogeneous on all object attributes, inclusive relational ones. Thus, an object proximity measure is to be designed which combines in a consistent way the differences on both properties and relations. Keeping in mind the analogy between objects and simple values we can formulate the following general comparison principle. Given two points in a space, we shall measure their mutual difference with respect to the relative size of the smallest region that covers both of them. The smallest region is a type in case of primitive values and a class in case of objects. It is unique for an ADT, but it may be interpreted in two different ways for concepts. In a first interpretation, it corresponds to an existing class, the most specific common class of both objects. Thus, the corresponding region is not necessary the smallest possible one, but rather the smallest admissible by the taxonomy of the concept. The second interpretation is straightforward : the region is the effective smallest one, and is thus independent form the existing taxonomy.

In the next section we describe a dissimilarity function based on the above principle which deals successfully with circularity in object descriptions.

3   Dissimilarity of Objects

A proximity measure, here of *dissimilarity* kind [12], is usually defined over a set Ω of individuals ω described by n attributes $\{a_i\}_{i=1}^n$. Attribute-level functions

δ_i compute elementary differences on each attribute a_i, whereas global function $d = Aggr(\delta_i)$ combines those differences into a single value. In case of object KB, each concept C_l is assigned a separate object set Ω_l and hence a specific function $d_{C_l}^o$.

3.1 Object-Level Function

Let C be a concept, e.g. flat, with n attributes $\{a_1, .., a_n\}$ (we assume that each object has all attribute values). In our model, the *object dissimilarity function* $d_C^o : C^2 \rightarrow \mathbb{R}$ is a normalized linear combination of the attribute dissimilarities $\delta_i^f : type(a_i)^2 \rightarrow \mathbb{R}$. For a couple of objects o and o' in C, dissimilarity is computed as :

$$d_C^o(o, o') = \sum_{i=1}^n \lambda_i * \delta_i^f(o.a_i, o'.a_i) . \tag{1}$$

where λ_i is the weight of attribute a_i ($\sum_{i=1}^n \lambda_i = 1$). It is noteworthy that all real-valued functions are normalized.

With respect to what has been said in the previous section, the value of $d_C^o(o, o')$ may be interpreted in the following way. Suppose each δ_i^f evaluates the size of the smallest region that contains the values $o.a_i$ and $o'.a_i$ within the corresponding dimension. Then, $d_C^o(o, o')$ computes the weighted average of all such sizes. This is an estimation of the size of the smallest region covering o and o' within the space of C. The form of d^o has been chosen to enable the computation in case of circularity. In the following, possible definitions for δ_i^f are presented which are consistent with the general principle of the previous section.

3.2 Attribute-Level Functions

Following the attribute type, δ_i^f is substituted in Formula 1 either by a property dissimilarity, $\overline{\delta}_T^{pr}$ or by a relational dissimilarity $\overline{\delta}_{C'}^r$.

The dissimilarity of simple values depends on the ratio between the size of their most-specific common type and the size of the whole ADT value set. Formally, let T be an ADT of domain D. We shall denote by $range(t)$ the size of the sub-set of D described by the type t. This value may be a set cardinal, when T is a nominal or partially ordered type (structured as in [10]), or an interval length T is a totally ordered type. For a couple of values in D, v and v', let $v \vee v'$ denote their most specific common type within T. Then :

$$\overline{\delta}_T^{pr}(v, v') = \frac{range(v \vee v') - 0, 5 * (range(v) + range(v'))}{range(D)} . \tag{2}$$

The subtraction of the average of value ranges in the above formula allows $\overline{\delta}_T^{pr}$ to remain consistent with conventional functions on standard types. For example, with an integer type $T = [0 \ 10]$ the value of $\overline{\delta}_T^{pr}(2, 4) = 0, 2$.

In case of object-valued attribute, the relative size of the effective smallest region is estimated by applying a function of d^o kind. Doing that, the dissimilarity computation goes a step further in the object network structure, from objects to attribute values. In case of a strongly connected component[2] of the network the computation comes back to the initial couple of objects, o and o'. For example, comparing two flats requires the comparison of their owners which in turn requires the comparison of flats. In other words, the self-references in object structure lead to recursive dependence between dissimilarity values for object couples. Section 3.3 presents a possible way to deal with recursion.

The class dissimilarity δ^{cl} compares objects as members of a class and no more as attribute lists. More precisely, δ^{cl} estimates the relative size of the most specific common class of two objects. Of course, the function can only be used on an attribute a if a class taxonomy is available on $C' = type(a)$. Moreover, the computed values only make sense if the taxonomy structure reflects the similarities between instances of C'.

Formally, let C' be a concept, the type of an object-valued attribute a and let $root(C')$ be the root class of C'. Let also o'_1, o'_2 be a couple of instances of C' and let $c = o'_1 \vee o'_2$ be the most specific common class of o'_1, o'_2. Class dissimilarity is then the ratio of the number of objects in the class and the total number of concept instances. Thus, the more specific the class, the less dissimilar the objects.

$$\overline{\delta}^{cl}_{C'}(o'_1, o'_2) = \frac{\|(members(c))\| - 1}{\|members(root(C'))\|} . \tag{3}$$

where $members()$ returns the set of member objects of a class. Here one stands for the average of $members()$ on both objects.

The above function allows the existing taxonomic knowledge in the KB to be used for clustering, that is for building of new taxonomies.

In case of multi-valued attributes, both relational and of property nature, a specific comparison strategy must be applied since collections may have variable length. The resulting collection dissimilarity relies on a pair-wise matching of collection members prior to the computation. Space limitations do not allow the point to be extended here, but an interested reader will find a description of a multi-valued dissimilarity in [11]. All functions defined in that paper are consistent with the above dissimilarity model in that they are normalized and represent valid dissimilarity indices.

3.3 Dealing with Circularity

Circularity arises when strongly connected components occur in object networks. A simple example of such component is the two-way dependency between flat and human concepts established by the owner and house attributes. If the dissimilarity of a couple of humans who own their residences is to be computed, this depends, via the house attribute on the dissimilarity of the respective flats. The flat dissimilarity depends, in turn, on the dissimilarity of the initial objects via owner. Both values depend recursively on themselves. A possible way to deal with such a deadlock is to compute the values as solutions of a system of linear equations (see [2]).

---

[2] not to mix with component attributes

A single system is composed for each strongly connected component that occurs in *both* networks. In the system, the variables x_i correspond to pairs of objects which may be reached from the initial pair o, o' by the same sequences of relational links (no composition). For each couple, let's say there are m couples, an equation is obtained from Formula 1.

$$x_i = b_i + \sum_{i=j, i \neq j}^{m} c_{i,j} * x_j .$$ (4)

Here, b_i is the *local part* of the dissimilarity d_C^o, that is the sum of all dissimilarities on properties and components plus those links which does not appear in the strongly connected component (so there are no variables representing them in the system). The remaining dissimilarities are on link attributes which take part in the circular dependence.

The coefficients $c_{i,j}$ in each equation are computed as follows. If the objects of a couple corresponding to x_j are the respective values of an attribute a in the objects of the x_i couple, then $c_{i,j}$ is the weight of the attribute a. Otherwise, $c_{i,j}$ is 0.

The obtained system is quadratic (m variables and m equations).

$$\mathbf{C} * \mathbf{X} = \mathbf{B} .$$ (5)

The matrix C is *diagonal dominant* so the system has a unique solution. It can be computed in a direct way or by an iterative method.

The measures d_C^o, one per concept C, obtained by such a computation are valid dissimilarity indexes, since positive, symmetric and minimal. Moreover, it can be proved that if all δ_i^f functions are metrics, then d_C^o are metrics too.

4 An Example of Dissimilarity Computation

In the following, we shall exemplify the way d^o is computed and used to cluster objects. Due to space limitations, we only consider a sample dataset made exclusively of human instances with three attributes: age, salary and spouse (see Table 1). spouse attribute is of a link nature and its type is the human concept itself. It thus establishes tiny cycles of two instances of the human concept. The salary attribute indicates the month's income of a person in thousands of euros, it is of float type and ranges in [1.8, 3.3] whereas the age attribute is of integer type and ranges in [20, 35].

Let's now see how the value of d^o is computed for a couple of objects of the set, say o1 and o4. First, we fix the attribute weights at 0.4 for spouse, and 0.3 for both salary and age. According to Formula 1 the dissimilarity for o1 and o4 becomes:

$$d_{human}^o(o1,\ o4) = 0.3\ \overline{\delta}^f(26,\ 30) + 0.3\ \overline{\delta}^f(3,\ 2.7) + 0.4\ \overline{\delta}^f(o2,\ o3) .$$ (6)

Table 1. A sample dataset of human instances

attribute	o1 o2 o3 o4 o5 o6
age	26 23 27 30 32 35
salary	3 2.3 2.2 2.7 2.9 3.2
spouse	o2 o1 o4 o3 o6 o5

The first two differences are computed by a property function of $\overline{\delta}^f$ taking into account the respective domain ranges. The total of both computations amounts to $0,18$. As no taxonomy is provided, $\overline{\delta}^f$ on spouse is replaced by d^o_{human} :

$$d^o_{human}(o2,\ o3) = 0.3\ \overline{\delta}^f(23,\ 27) + 0.3\ \overline{\delta}^f(2.3,\ 2.2) + 0.4\ \overline{\delta}^f(o1,\ o4) \ . \tag{7}$$

Here we come to the mutual dependency of $d^o_{human}(o2,\ o3)$ and $d^o_{human}(o1,\ o4)$ due to the spouse circuit. Substituting a variable for each of them, lets say x_1 and x_2, the following linear equation system is obtained :

$$x_1 \ = \ 0.18 \ + \ 0.4 x_2 \tag{8}$$

$$x_2 \ = \ 0.14 \ + \ 0.4 x_1 \tag{9}$$

Table 2. Dissimilarity values for $\underline{d}^o_{human}$ and d^o_{human}

	o1	o2	o3	o4	o5	o6
o1	0	0.38	0.32	0.3	0.33	0.51
o2	0.38	0	0.23	0.48	0.65	0.9
o3	0.36	0.26	0	0.31	0.48	0.73
o4	0.28	0.43	0.31	0	0.17	0.42
o5	0.5	0.61	0.46	0.33	0	0.25
o6	0.56	0.74	0.57	0.44	0.25	0

The solutions for x_1 and x_2 are 0.28 and 0.26 respectively. The values of d^o_{human} for the whole dataset are given in Table 2. The table should be read as follows : whereas the entries below the main diagonal represent the results of the above d^o_{human} function, another function, lets call it $\underline{d}^o_{human}$, is given in the upper part of the matrix. $\underline{d}^o_{human}$ is computed only on age and salary attributes taken with equal weights. We put it here to exemplify the specific features of the relational measure in case of circularity.

A detailed examination of respective values for d^o_{human} and $\underline{d}^o_{human}$, leads to the following observation. Given a couple of objects o' and o'' which represent a couple of spouses, lets consider an arbitrary third object o and its dissimilarity with each of the initial objects. Suppose also $\underline{d}^o_{human}(o', o)$ is less than $\underline{d}^o_{human}(o'', o)$. Then, the following inequalities hold :

$$\underline{d}^o_{human}(o', o) \; < \; d^o_{human}(o', o) \; < \; \underline{d}^o_{human}(o'', o) . \qquad (10)$$

The same inequalities hold for $d^o_{human}(o'', o)$. Besides, the values of both measures for the initial couple remain the same:

$$d^o_{human}(o', o'') = \underline{d}^o_{human}(o', o'') . \qquad (11)$$

The underlying phenomenon is a kind of attraction between the objects of a couple, here o' and o''. Actually, the mutual influence of dissimilarity values for both objects to a third one tends to minimize their difference. This means that, within the space induced by the relational measure, both objects will lie somehow "nearer" than in the space induced by the simple measure, even if the absolute values of both functions remain equal.

Globally, the attraction results in a more compact dissimilarity matrices in the sense that the total variance of the values tends to decrease with respect to a non-relational measure with the same relative weights for property attributes. Of

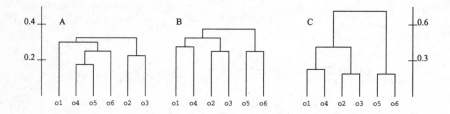

Fig. 3. Clustering results for the dataset: A. single linkage clustering with $\underline{d}^o_{human}$ as input; B. single-linkage clustering with d^o_{human} as input; C. complete-linkage clustering with d^o_{human} as input. The scale for first two dendrograms is given on the left and the scale of the last one on the right of the figure.

course, the above attraction phenomenon has been detected in a very particular situation where couples of objects of the same concept are strongly connected. However, a similar tendency can be observed in case of strongly connected components of greater size and of heterogeneous composition.

5   Clustering

The matrix obtained by the computation of d^o is used as an input for a hierarchical clustering algorithm which detects homogeneous object groups. An example of clustering results may be seen on Fig. 3 where input data has been taken from Table 2.

Thus, Fig. 3.A shows the result of a single linkage clustering on $\underline{d}^o_{human}$ values, whereas the dendrograms on Fig. 3.B and Fig. 3.C are obtained with d^o_{human} by a single-linkage and complete linkage algorithms respectively.

A first remark concerns the attraction between related objects which goes as far as to change the dissimilarity-induced order between object couples. This could be observed on the matrix, but the dendrogram shows it even better. In fact, whereas o4 forms a compact class with o5 in the first case, on the second dendrogram it is combined with o1. This shift is undoubtfully due to the influence of the o4's spouse, o3, which is nearer to the o1's spouse then to o5's. Both o1 and o4 are attracted to form a class with their spouses which may be seen on both dendrograms B and C.

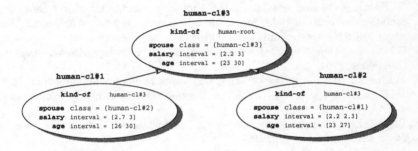

Fig. 4. Part of the class hierarchy obtained after characterization. of classes found by the hierarchical clustering.

As far as class inference is concerned, the clusterings with d^o_{human} suggest the existence of four classes below the root class. Before presenting them for user's validation, a characterization of each class in terms of attribute restrictions has to be provided. The description shows the limits of the region in the concept space represented by the class and thus helps in the interpretation. Fig. 4 shows the hierarchy made of three classes, corresponding to the object clusters {o1,o4}, {o2,o3} and {o1,o4,o2,o3}. Observe the cross-reference between classes human-cl#1 and human-cl#2 established via the spouse attribute.

6   Conclusion

An approach towards the automatic class design in object languages has been presented in the paper. Classes are built in two steps: first, member sets of classes are discovered by a proximity-based clustering procedure, then, each class is provided a characterization in terms of attributes.

The dissimilarity measure used for clustering compares objects with respect both to their properties and their relations. In case of self-references in object descriptions, the values of the measure are computed as solutions of a system of linear equations. In addition, the measure allows available taxonomic knowledge to be explored for object comparison, but does not require taxonomies to exist. In sum, the measure is complete with respect to object descriptions and therefore allows the detection of clusters which are homogeneous on all object attributes.

References

[1] H.W. Beck, T. Anwar, and S.B. Navathe. A conceptual clustering algorithm for database schema design. *IEEE Transactions on Knowledge and Data Engineering*, pages 396–411, 1994.

[2] G. Bisson. Conceptual clustering in a first order logic representation. In *Proceedings of the 10th European Conference on Artificial Intelligence, Vienna, Austria*, pages 458–462, 1992.

[3] G. Bisson. Why and how to define a similarity measure for object-based representation systems. In N.J.I. Mars, editor, *Towards Very Large Knowledge Bases*, pages 236–246, Amsterdam, 1995. IOS Press.

[4] G. Booch. *Object-oriented analysis and design with applications*. Benjamin-Cummings, 1994.

[5] J. Euzenat. Brief overview of t-tree: the tropes taxonomy building tool. In *Proceedings of the 4th ASIS SIG/CR classification research workshop, Columbus (OH US)*, pages 69–87, 1993.

[6] D.H. Fisher. Knowledge acquisition via incremental conceptual clustering. *Machine Learning*, 2:139–172, 1987.

[7] J. Han, S. Nishio, H. Kawano, and W. Wang. Generalization-based data mining in object-oriented databases using an object-cube model. *IEEE Transactions on Knowlwdge and Data Engineering*, 25(1):55–97, 1998.

[8] INRIA Rhône-Alpes, Grenoble (FR). *Tropes 1.0 reference manual*, 1995.

[9] J.-U. Kietz and K. Morik. A polynomial approach to the constructive induction of structural knowledge. *Machine Learning*, 14(2):193–217, 1994.

[10] R. Michalski and R. Stepp. *Machine learning: an Artificial Intelligence approach*, volume I, chapter Learning from observation: conceptual clustering, pages 331–363. Tioga publishing company, Palo Alto (CA US), 1983.

[11] P. Valtchev and J. Euzenat. Dissimilarity measure for collections of objects and values. In P. Coen X. Liu and M. Berthold, editors, *Proceedings of the 2nd Symposium on Intelligent Data Analysis.*, volume 1280 of *Lecture Notes in Computer Science*, pages 259–272, 1997.

[12] B. van Cutsem. *Classification and dissimilarity analysis*, volume 93 of *Lecture notes in statistics*. Springer Verlag, New York, 1994.

Section IV:

Integration

Adjusted Estimation for the Combination of Classifiers.....................317
   B.J.A. Mertens and D.J. Hand

Data-Driven Theory Refinement Using KBDistAl...........................331
   J. Yang, R. Parekh, V. Honavar, and D. Dobbs

Reasoning about Input-Output Modeling of Dynamical Systems...........343
   M. Easley and E. Bradley

Undoing Statistical Advice...357
   R. Almond

A Method for Temporal Knowledge Conversion...........................369
   G. Guimarães and A. Ultsch

Adjusted Estimation for the Combination of Classifiers

Bart J.A. Mertens[1] and David J. Hand[2]

[1] Trinity College Dublin, Dublin 2, Ireland.
bart.mertens@tcd.ie
[2] Imperial College, London SW7 2BZ, United Kingdom.
d.j.hand@ic.ac.uk

Abstract. An algorithm is proposed which adaptively and simultaneously estimates and combines classifiers originating from distinct classification frameworks for improved prediction. The methodology is developed and evaluated on simulations and real data. Analogies and similarities with generalised additive modeling, neural estimation and boosting are discussed. We contrast the approach with existing Bayesian model averaging methods. Areas for further research and development are indicated.

1 Introduction

There has been much recent interest in the combination of classifiers for improved classification. Much of this work applies to the combination of classifiers which are of a similar type or nature and is thus essentially concerned with estimation. An early example in the parametric context may be found in Friedman's regularized discriminant analysis [10]. Buntine [6], Hastie and Pregibon [13], Quinlan [18] and Oliver and Hand [17] generalize such approaches to the averaging of classification trees. From a conceptual point of view, these methods may be formulated either as direct applications or equivalent to Bayesian model averaging approaches within a fixed methodological framework. In some cases, such as parametric discrimination, we can postulate a 'global' probability model on the model probabilities within the framework. When such probability modeling is not straightforward, a careful consideration of the sources of variation in calibration may often suggest reasonable analogue implementations of model averaging to combine distinct within-framework model estimates [17][1,2].

While these developments to fully account for model uncertainty in a constrained and a priori methodological setting are encouraging, we could argue that the evaluation of model uncertainty in applied statistics and data analysis should be given a much broader interpretation. Above all, the assessment of model uncertainty should be concerned with the choice of the specific methodological framework itself within which any subsequent analysis is carried out. Classification studies provide an excellent example of this problem, as most studies are faced, at the first instance, with a choice between vastly different methodological approaches such as linear and quadratic (classical parametric) discrimination

D.J. Hand, J.N. Kok, M.R. Berthold (Eds.): IDA'99, LNCS 1642, pp. 317–330, 1999.
© Springer-Verlag Berlin Heidelberg 1999

versus machine learning approaches (such as CART), nearest neighbour methods or neural networks, among others. Furthermore, such issues of choice will often be much more subtle than those of estimation within any given framework and the effects of an unfortunate choice of classification method may be more serious, irrespective of the care and attention which could subsequently be applied in the calibration of a specific classifier. We could of course argue that model averaging methods could be generalised in practical applications to derive ad hoc combinations of predictions from a wider set of models. However, both theoretical argument [15] as well as empirical evidence would suggest that we may not be able to rely on such implementations to consistently provide good classification rules in all applications. As a consequence, and perhaps paradoxically, the Bayes paradigm would appear to break down precisely in those situations where model uncertainty is most acute.

This paper develops a methodology which can combine classifications from a class of conceptually distinct classification methods. We focus on the combination of linear discriminant rules with tree structured classifiers as an example. Our methodology derives from an interpretation of and an analogy with neural approaches to the combination of statistical models. We develop and illustrate the methodology through simulations and application on real data.

2   Adjusted Estimation

As a solution within the confines of classical Bayesian probability modeling does not readily suggest itself, we may explore related disciplines for inspiration to rejuvenate this area of research. A highly interesting class of models may be found in the artificial intelligence literature. Several interpretations of neural network modeling have already been put forward, among which those of generalised function estimation and prediction [19] and projection pursuit [20]. An alternative interpretation from a Bayes perspective would be to view neural estimation as averaging across the models in the interior layer of the network. However, notwithstanding the appeal of this analogy, a key difference between general model averaging-type methods and neural networks resides in the fact that the latter jointly calibrate the models in the hidden layer in some sense such that each model takes the best form in the context of the other data summaries which are present. In contrast, model averaging simply combines existing models. Restricting ourselves to the two-class problem, these considerations suggest that we may generalize model averaging to the between-model setting to allow calibrations of the type

$$f(1 \mid \mathbf{x}) = \alpha + \sum_{i \in I} g(\mathbf{x} \mid M_i),$$

where $\mathbf{x}$ is the measurement vector, each $g(\mathbf{x} \mid M_i)$ is a predictor within the model M_i, $\mathcal{M} = \{M_1, \ldots, M_I\}$ is the set of models and where the estimation of each predictor $g(\mathbf{x} \mid M_i)$ is adaptive or adjusted in the presence of the other models and their respective calibrations. Of course, for a completely general between-model set $\mathcal{M}$ the usual procedures for combined estimation and combination used in neural network estimation will break down. Specifically, for our model set of linear discrimination and CART, none of the traditional optimization methods seem to apply as there are no simple updating methods for the classification tree. Hence, we need to develop a general purpose algorithm which can adaptively combine and adjust, not just predicted class indicators or probabilities, but rather the optimization of the respective constituent models which we want to combine. We discuss the solution to this general problem by restricting to the case of the prediction of class indicators, and thus regression, first. The generalization to the prediction of class probabilities is discussed subsequently. We will restrict ourselves to two-class problems.

2.1   Predicting Class Indicators

The problem may be simplified by defining $f(1 \mid \mathbf{x}) \equiv \delta_{1j}$, with j the class indicator. This reduces the problem to the calibration of a regression equation for the prediction of class indicators. We can then propose an optimization criterion such as least squares and consider optimization of

$$\sum_{k=1}^{n} \{\delta_{1j_k} - \alpha - g(\mathbf{x}_k \mid \boldsymbol{\beta}, LR) - g(\mathbf{x}_k \mid \lambda, Tree)\}^2,$$

where δ_{1j_k}, $k = 1, \ldots, n$ are the class indicators for each of n observations, α is a constant and $g(\mathbf{x}_k \mid \boldsymbol{\beta}, LR)$ and $g(\mathbf{x}_k \mid \lambda, Tree)$ are predictions from a linear regression model and a regression tree and for each kth observation with feature vector $\mathbf{x}_k$. The parameters $\boldsymbol{\beta}$ and λ are the regression parameters of the linear model and a parameter which defines the size of the regression tree in some sense, respectively. Hence, we have for our choice of models that $g(\mathbf{x}_k \mid \boldsymbol{\beta}, LR) = \mathbf{x}_k^T \boldsymbol{\beta}$ and $g(\mathbf{x}_k \mid \lambda, Tree) = \sum_{l=1}^{m} a_l B_l(\mathbf{x}_k)$ is a regression tree, where the $B_l(\mathbf{x}_k) = I[\mathbf{x}_k \in R_l]$ are the basis functions defined on the hyper-rectangles R_l which are derived by the tree fitting algorithm [11].

The above simplification of the problem suggests optimization of the functions $g(\mathbf{x}_k \mid \boldsymbol{\beta}, LR)$ and $g(\mathbf{x}_k \mid \lambda, Tree)$ through an iterative scheme wherein we alternate between optimizations of LR and CART, each time keeping the predictions from the other constituent method fixed and then optimizing for the calibration of the residual which remains. The parameter α is kept fixed at the mean of the class indicator to reduce the redundancy of the specification. Thus, an alternating least squares scheme emerges which defines a backfitting procedure in a more statistical manner as compared to the more usual neural approach. It should be applicable to the combination of a wide class of models. Calibration of the classification tree at each iteration may require pruning or some other approach to reduce the variability of the predictor, which may be achieved through cross-validation or a set-aside test set. Table 1 shows the structure of the algorithm, which applies to general (univariate) regression problems.

Table 1. The alternating least squares combination algorithm.

(1.) *Initialize* Put iteration counter $i = 0$.

Put $y_k = \delta_{1j_k}$, $k = 1, \ldots, n$ and $\alpha_0 = \text{mean}(\mathbf{y})$, where $\mathbf{y} = (y_1, \ldots, y_n)^T$ and $g_0(\mathbf{x}_k \mid \boldsymbol{\beta}_0, LR) = g_0(\mathbf{x}_k \mid \lambda_0, Tree) = 0$, $k = 1, \ldots, n$. Mean-center both the matrix of predictors $\mathbf{X} = (x_1^T, \ldots, x_n^T)^T$ and predictant $\mathbf{y}$ and save the means.

(2.) *Update* Put iteration counter $i = i + 1$.

Fit the model $g_i(\mathbf{x}_k \mid \boldsymbol{\beta}_i, LR)$ to the residuals $y_k - g_{i-1}(\mathbf{x}_k \mid \lambda_{i-1}, Tree)$ and grow the tree $g_i(\mathbf{x}_k \mid Tree)$ to the residuals $y_k - g_i(\mathbf{x}_k \mid \boldsymbol{\beta}_i, LR)$. Derive the optimal constraining parameter λ_i for the unpruned tree $g_i(\mathbf{x}_k \mid Tree)$ (see later) and stabilize the tree size $\lambda_i \leftarrow f(\lambda_1, \ldots, \lambda_i)$. Apply to derive the pruned tree $g_i(\mathbf{x}_k \mid \lambda_i, Tree)$.

(3.) *Verify* Check convergence of the relative change of $L_i = \sum(y_k - g_i(\mathbf{x}_k \mid \boldsymbol{\beta}_i, LR) - g_i(\mathbf{x}_k \mid \lambda_i, Tree))^2$ and repeat step 2 if necessary.

Simulations We evaluate simulations as a first step in developing and validating the proposed methodology. Four simulated datasets were generated in two dimensions, each of which consists of 225 samples. For each of these simulations, 100 observations were generated from each of two bivariate normal distributions with means (0,1) and (0,-1) respectively and common covariance matrix diag(4, 0.25). We then simulated 25 observations from a contaminant spherical normal distribution with locations (4,2), (2,3), (0,-2) and (0,-1) for the first, second, third and fourth simulations respectively and a covariance matrix of diag(0.05,0.05). and all the data was rotated 45 degrees counter-clockwise. Figure 1 show pictures of each of the resulting simulations. Validated classifications were derived for each of the four simulation models which were considered. The validation samples were of the same size as those used for calibration. Although simulation could also have been used to prune the regression trees, we chose to use leave-one-out cross-validation to make the simulations more realistic.

Table 2 displays the validated classifications when shrinkage-based pruning [7][13] is used for constraining the fitting of each tree and based on cross-validated least squares lack-of-fit as a measure of the deviance of each tree. The shrinkage parameter was found to be highly variable during iterations and hence some constraint has to be placed on the choice of the pruning parameter λ. A criterion $f(\lambda_1, \ldots, \lambda_i)$ which depends on the pruning parameters calibrated in previous iterations and the newly proposed pruning parameter λ_i at the current iteration i and which becomes gradually increasingly resistant to changes in the pruning parameter seems appropriate. A simple rule based on a simple averaging of at most the past ten pruning parameters, possibly augmented by a form of robust averaging in later iterations was found to work well. Such a procedure is analogous to backstepping in more conventional Gauss-Newton approaches. The table shows the proportions of misclassified observations for the combination, ordinary linear discrimination and those from a regression tree fit to the class indicators. The parameters $\boldsymbol{\beta} = (\beta_1, \beta_2)$ of the final linear discriminant predictor $g(\mathbf{x}_k \mid \boldsymbol{\beta}, LR)$ within the optimized model combination are shown in the table together with their Euclidean norm and similarly, for the linear discriminant model only. An estimate of the size λ of the final regression tree $g(\mathbf{x}_k \mid \lambda, Tree)$ of the model combination is also given.

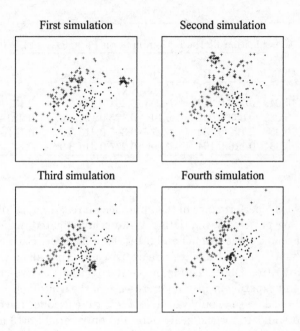

Fig. 1. Pictures of the simulated calibration data of two-class classification problems and for each of the first four simulations.

As may be seen from the table, the combination approach does extremely well for all simulations except for the second. The interpretation of these results is that the classification tree is able to remove the contaminating samples from the calibration of the linear discriminant model, as may be seen from the linear discriminant coefficients which are calibrated, particularly for the first simulation as one would expect. The second simulation is an exception, due to the failure of cross-validation-based shrinkage in the alternating least squares algorithm to sufficiently prune the tree. Recalibration of the model combination using newly simulated data from the appropriate model to select the pruning parameter gave similar results as for the other simulations. Generally and across all simulations, the tree sizes tend to be too large, which may again be explained by the use of cross-validatory estimation (see further in a discussion on convergence).

Data The above simulations have shown that the combination method can improve classifications across the constituents, but also, allows for a proper and correct identification of the relevant model constituents which are present. Hence,

Table 2. Validated classification results from the combination of models through alternating least squares as well as for linear discrimination and CART separately, using cross-validation based shrinkage for the calibration of the regression trees. * Failed to converge at iteration 100, relative change of the least squares criterion is 9.1e-4.

Simulation	Classification Method			Combination Parameters				LR Parameters		
	COMB	Tree	LR	β_1	β_2	$\|\beta\|$	λ	β_1	β_2	$\|\beta\|$
First	0.040	0.173	0.213	0.258	-0.262	0.368	2	0.131	-0.257	0.289
Second*	0.088	0.098	0.027	0.146	-0.125	0.192	6.6	0.220	-0.197	0.295
Third	0.058	0.129	0.138	0.277	-0.306	0.413	3.2	0.151	-0.172	0.229
Fourth	0.084	0.116	0.164	0.306	-0.277	0.413	3.9	0.247	-0.221	0.331

we investigated the performance of the approach on real data, all of which derive from the Statlog project. Seven data sets were investigated, for each of which both a calibration set was defined and a test set put aside. Each of these either represents (Pima Indians Diabetes, Heart Disease, Australian Credit) or was reduced (Handwritten Digits, Letter Image Recognition) to two-class problems. The analysis and experiment focused on the use of the continuous variables only. For the first three data sets, only variables 2 to 8 were used for the diabetes data, variables 1,4,5,8 and 10 for the heart data and only variables 13 and 14 for the Australian credit data. For the letter image data as well as the digits data, all sixteen attributes were used in the construction of the classification rules. Only discrimination between digits 1 and 7 was investigated for the digit data and similarly, the two-class classification problems for distinguishing between the letters o and q, i and j and b and e were investigated for the letter image data. All other classes were removed from the data in the investigation of each of these problems.

The results presented in table 3 (misclassified observations with misclassification proportions in brackets) are broadly favourable to the combination method, with the methodology either at least equivalent in terms of misclassification rate to the optimal single model or predictor (Heart, Credit, Letters (be)) or improving on the constituents (Diabetes, Letters (oq)). The Digit (17) data and the Letters (ij) are the exceptions. For the digits this appears due to insufficient shrinkage which eliminates the linear discriminant model from the combination, which seems to confirm previous results on potential cross-validation-based shrinkage problems from the simulation experiments. On the other hand the methodology appears capable of identifying a single optimal model if one exists (Heart data: $\lambda = 1$).

Convergence We have used and motivated alternating least squares as an ad hoc method for the combination of distinct models. Breiman and Friedman [3],

Table 3. Validated classification results on real data and for the comparison of the alternating least squares combination method, linear discrimination and CART separately. Both the number of misclassified observations and the misclassification rate are given.

	Classification Method			Model Parameters	
	Combination	Tree	LR	$\|\beta\|$	λ
Diabetes	39 (0.232)	43 (0.260)	44 (0.262)	0.118	1.4
Heart	32 (0.320)	40 (0.400)	32 (0.320)	0.147	1
Credit	92 (0.317)	91 (0.314)	118 (0.407)	0.048	3.6
Digits (17)	25 (0.014)	27 (0.015)	19 (0.011)	2.22e-3	5.9
Letters (oq)	9 (0.025)	19 (0.052)	18 (0.049)	0.213	17.3
Letters (ij)	28 (0.078)	23 (0.064)	33 (0.092)	0.132	9.4
Letters (be)	4 (0.010)	5 (0.012)	21 (0.052)	0.029	7.3

Buja, Hastie and Tibshirani [5], Buja [4] and Hastie and Tibshirani [14] investigate the existence of optima and convergence for alternating least squares and alternating conditional expectation algorithms and for the case of estimating optimal transformations. While our application is different, we have an additional problem in the use of cross-validation which is intrinsic in the fitting of the regression tree. This is analogous to difficulties in using alternating least squares with the supersmoother for estimating optimal transforms of data. As a consequence, the algorithm is no longer a strict alternation between pure least squares fits. The simulations confirm this problem (second simulation) and examples can be found where the sequence of models fails to settle, due to the inability of cross-validation to identify a realistic pruning parameter. In all cases we have seen however, convergence problems have been attributable to cross-validation and disappear when either a user-specified pruning parameter was supplied and kept fixed throughout alternations or by using set-aside test sets. A more subtle difficulty may reside in the use of a regression tree which may not have the required properties as a 'data smooth' [3]. As discussed above, we have not found evidence of this in practical applications, which mirrors experience by Breiman and Friedman.

Of potentially greater importance is the question whether and how the methodology can identify good and realistic model combinations in practice and from the point of view of classification. Figure 2 shows pictures of the first simulation with the separating surfaces from linear discrimination and the regression tree superimposed, as well as those from the same models within the alternating least squares model combination. It is not surprising that linear discrimination should have a problem with this simulation, as the estimation of the within-group covariance matrices for the model corresponding to the first 200 observations will be biased due to the presence of the contaminant model. As a consequence, the angle of the linear discriminant surface relative to the first axis is 27° (as opposed to 45°). All observations from the contaminant model are misclassified, in addition to misclassifications in the first 200 observations due to the inappropriate orientation of the separating surface relative to these data. Likewise, the regression tree can not well approximate the first diagonal due to the rectangular shape of the generated basis regions which is inherent in the specification of the method and this problem is exacerbated by the small sample sizes. More surprisingly however, it also fails to fully isolate the relatively compact cluster of contaminant data as well. As a consequence, neither model can cope with the data as given here. In contrast, the alternating least squares model combination separates the data by reducing the regression tree to a single split on the first axis only (coordinate value 3.2). This effectively removes the contaminant data from the calibration of the linear discriminant model and as a consequence, the angle of the calibrated linear discriminant surfaces returns to 45°. The model combination thus identifies what is effectively an optimally separating model. Similar conclusions and discussion apply for the other simulations.

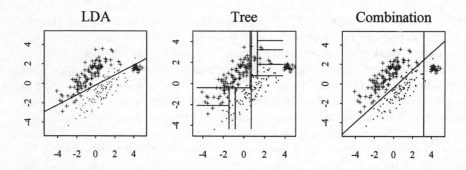

Fig. 2. Pictures of the simulated calibration data and discriminant models for the first simulation. The pictures on the left are for linear discrimination and the regression tree only. The right figure shows the separating surfaces from the same two models within the model combination derived by alternating least squares.

2.2 Predicting Probabilities

We may generalize the above approach to the prediction of the posterior probabilities of class membership by postulating the generalised dependent variable $f(1 \mid \mathbf{x}) \equiv \text{logit}(p(1 \mid \mathbf{x}))$. The alternating least squares method may then be applied to the linearisation of the corresponding prediction formula

$$\text{logit}(p(1 \mid \mathbf{x})) = \alpha + \sum_{i \in I} g(\mathbf{x} \mid M_i)$$

by deriving the adjusted dependent variable

$$z = \alpha + g(\mathbf{x} \mid \boldsymbol{\beta}, LR) + g(\mathbf{x} \mid \lambda, Tree) + \frac{y - p}{p * (1 - p)}$$

where $p = \rho(\alpha + g(\mathbf{x} \mid \boldsymbol{\beta}, LR) + g(\mathbf{x} \mid \lambda, Tree))$ with $\rho(x) = \exp(x)/(1 + \exp(x))$ (note p is short notation for $p(1 \mid \mathbf{x})$). We then fit the combination of classification models to the adjusted dependent variable through the above described weighted alternating least squares method, where the weights are given as $w = p * (1 - p)$. The fitted combined models define the update of the adjusted dependent variable and the weights for the next iteration and the procedure is repeated until convergence. This approach which is essentially an application of the local scoring algorithm thus embeds the previous iterative alternating least squares method for the calibration of class indicators in a second iterative layer and for the optimization of the log-likelihood

$$L = \sum y \ln(p) + (1 - y) \ln(1 - p).$$

The methodology proposed above was found to work on the strict condition that a backstepping procedure is enforced at each stage to ensure that the internal alternating least squares algorithm identifies model combinations which improve the log-likelihood. This may be done for the parameter α and the parameter vector $\boldsymbol{\beta}$ from the linear discriminant model by postulating mixing parameters $0 \leq \gamma_\alpha, \gamma_L \leq 1$ and then evaluate the log-likelihood for the backstep estimates $\alpha_i \leftarrow \gamma_\alpha * \alpha_{i-1} + (1 - \gamma_\alpha) * \alpha_i$ and $g_i(\mathbf{x}_k \mid \boldsymbol{\beta}_i, LR) \leftarrow \gamma_L * g_{i-1}(\mathbf{x}_k \mid \boldsymbol{\beta}_{i-1}, LR) + (1 - \gamma_L) * g_i(\mathbf{x}_k \mid \boldsymbol{\beta}_i, LR)$ where the subscripts i and $i - 1$ identify the estimates with respect to the corresponding models after and before the present iteration i, respectively. Devising a similar backstepping procedure for the regression tree is more complicated as both the redefinition of the spatial structure (basis functions) at each step as well as the use of pruning or shrinkage precludes a direct application of the above backstepping method. We may generalize the approach to trees in the following manner. Using similar notation as before, we will let $g_i(\mathbf{x}_k \mid Tree)$ and $g_{i-1}(\mathbf{x}_k \mid Tree)$ represent the *unpruned* trees from the present and previous iterations with proposed corresponding optimal pruning parameters λ_i and λ_{i-1}, as derived according to the algorithms described in the previous section. We may backstep with a two-stage approach by first backstepping the shrinkage parameter only $\lambda_i \leftarrow \gamma_T * \lambda_{i-1} + (1 - \gamma_T) * \lambda_i$ for some choice of $0 \leq \gamma_T \leq 1$ and then apply the backstep estimate λ_i to derive the backstep regression tree predictions $g_i(\mathbf{x}_k \mid \lambda_i, Tree) \leftarrow \gamma_T * g_{i-1}(\mathbf{x}_k \mid \lambda_i, Tree) + (1 - \gamma_T) * g_i(\mathbf{x}_k \mid \lambda_i, Tree)$ which may then be used to define the updated adjusted dependent variable z for the next iteration. The optimal combination of backstepping parameters $0 \leq \gamma_\alpha, \gamma_L, \gamma_T \leq 1$ may be identified by a three-dimensional grid search on the unit cube whereby the log-likelihood is evaluated for each choice and the minimum identified. The generalisation to the multiclass case is from the formulaic point of view identical to that of generalising logistic discrimination.

Table 4. Validated classification results from the combination of models through adjusted estimation as well as for linear discrimination and CART separately, using cross-validation based shrinkage for the calibration of the regression trees. Parameters are given for the combination.

	Classification Method			Model Parameters				
	Combination	Tree	LR	α	β_1	β_2	$\|\boldsymbol{\beta}\|$	λ
First simulation	8 (0.036)	32 (0.142)	48 (0.213)	-0.349	2.911	-3.030	4.202	2.2
Second simulation	7 (0.031)	21 (0.093)	6 (0.027)	-1.367	4.722	-3.839	6.086	7.4
Third simulation	17 (0.076)	30 (0.133)	31 (0.138)	-0.248	2.562	-2.845	3.828	4.2
Fourth simulation	19 (0.084)	27 (0.120)	37 (0.164)	-0.174	4.184	-4.122	5.873	2.8

Simulations Results from the application of this methodology to the simulations are shown in table 4. These are broadly in line with those from the prediction of class indicators (table 2) and with exception of the second simulation, where the adjusted estimation algorithm is clearly superior. This is due to the application of backstepping in the identification of the optimum, which does not feature in the basic alternating least squares algorithm. Problems with cross-validation and the choice of the optimum tree size apply to both algorithms and for this simulation specifically. Readers may note small differences between the results on CART as compared to those shown in table 2. This is because table 4 shows results from the fitting of a classification tree, which optimizes the log-likelihood and predicts probabilities, whereas previous results relate to those obtained from a regression tree which is fit to the class indicators using the sum of squares of deviations as a measure of homogeneity. The same problem does not apply to the linear model as the discriminant surface is identical in both cases. With respect to the first simulation, the fitted combined model is effectively the same (in terms of the separating surfaces) to that discussed in section 2.1.3 and with similar interpretation.

Data Table 5 shows results from the adjusted estimation algorithm for the same data as discussed before. Results are again comparable as before, with the exception of the digits (17) and the letters (ij) for which the adjusted algorithm clearly is superior. This again demonstrates the importance of the backstep. Most importantly, the combination either improves on the constituents or equals the best method, across all examples.

3   Interpretation and Discussion

We have developed and explored an ad hoc algorithm for the combination of predictors from models which originate from conceptually different classifica-

Table 5. Validated classification results on data and for the comparison of the adjusted estimation combination method, linear discrimination and CART separately. Both the number of misclassified observations and the misclassification rate are given.

	Classification Method			Model Parameters		
	Combination	Tree	LR	α	$\|\beta\|$	λ
Diabetes	39 (0.232)	43 (0.260)	44 (0.262)	-0.644	0.720	1.4
Heart	33 (0.330)	37 (0.370)	32 (0.320)	-0.335	0.870	1
Credit	97 (0.334)	94 (0.324)	118 (0.407)	-0.028	1.37e-3	3.3
Digits (17)	11 (0.006)	19 (0.011)	19 (011)	0.232	0.0783	4.9
Letters (oq)	11 (0.030)	23 (0.063)	18 (0.049)	0.247	4.970	16.9
Letters (ij)	26 (0.072)	27 (0.075)	33 (0.092)	0.082	2.276	17.1
Letters (be)	8 (0.020)	9 (0.023)	21 (0.052)	-0.053	2.839	8.2

tion frameworks. It is important to note that the methodology is of a crucially different nature from methods based on the combination of committees or ensembles of predictors, such as may be found in bagging [2] or stacking [1] approaches or more general model averaging and Bayesian procedures [16]. Model averaging effectively operates on models which have already been defined and combines them by removing variance through a smoothing of overcomplex models to avoid overfitting (e.g. regularized discrimination). In contrast to these methods, alternating least squares and adjusted estimation simultaneously adapt the estimation of the constituent models and combine in a manner which is similar to the estimation methods employed in generalized additive modeling [14]. The difference from generalised additive modeling estimation is that the additivity constraint is sacrificed to estimate a more general predictor $f(1 \mid \mathbf{x}) = \alpha + g_1(\mathbf{x}) + \cdots + g_I(\mathbf{x})$ as opposed to $f(1 \mid \mathbf{x}) = \alpha + g_1(\mathbf{x_1}) + \cdots + g_I(\mathbf{x_I})$, where the set $\{\mathbf{x_j} = (x_l)_{l \in J_j}; j : 1, \ldots, I\}$ represents a partition of $\mathbf{x}$ such that $J_1 \cup \ldots \cup J_I = \{1, \ldots, p\}$ and with p the number of predictors. The latter formulation points to the possibility of deriving model combinations which are intermediate between generalized additive modeling and the combinations derived in this paper and by relaxing the partitioning assumption.

3.1 Boosting and Adjusted Estimation

Hastie and Tibshirani discuss the estimation of predictors which are additive on partitions (pages 271-274) and with specific reference to combination of models with regression trees for the modeling of interactions. In addition to the above remarks on additivity however, the analysis described in those pages fits the regression tree last and on the residuals from the previous model fits with no further iteration. The addition of the regression tree thus can have no effect on the fit of the previously added models and most importantly on the definition of the selected basis functions. In contrast, our procedure may be viewed as a method which 'boosts' the performance of each constituent model by implementing a fully alternating estimation. Indeed, as suggested by the simulations, it appears that the method effectively operates by removing influential observations which are inconsistent with a specific constituent model or method from the calibration of that method and then assigns them to the calibration of another classifier. Thus, while traditional Bayesian methods distribute models across data, our method distributes each datum to the most appropriate classifier. Another way to formulate this phenomenon is to say that the algorithm effectively identifies clusters and then assigns these clusters to an appropriate classifier or model. This behaviour of alternating least squares methods has been noted before by Buja [4] who complains about the somewhat anecdotal nature of the evidence with respect to clustering, a problem which our paper unfortunately does not address. Finally, we should note that new work has recently emerged on the analogy between boosting algorithms [9][21] and the generalised additive estimation methods while the research presented in this paper was carried out. [12] describes how the boosting algorithms of Freund and Schapire are of the same form as those used for the optimization of the likelihood function for generalised additive estimation. Perhaps not surprisingly, our algorithm is again of that class, but with the difference that we only keep the final model combination from the sequence of models identified by the alternating algorithm and that we optimize across distinct frameworks of models whereas Hastie, Freund and Schapire apply boosting to the estimation of a single model only. Our remarks may enhance this discussion by pointing to potential links between boosting, influence analysis and clustering, which would provide a more elaborate statistical interpretation of the methodology. Clearly however, further research is required to evaluate such interpretation which the authors may pursue.

3.2   Neural Networks, Modern Classification Methods, and Adjusted Estimation

We have already amply discussed the adaptive nature of the strategies deployed in this paper and their (at least) conceptual similarities to the calibration of models in nodes within neural network prediction structures. From the more classical perspective of generalised prediction equations, and keeping all remarks about adaptive estimation in mind, we should note that the form of the predictors of the combined models discussed in this paper, as well as those from model averaging and more general combination methods, may be viewed as special cases of the general predictor $f(1 \mid \mathbf{x}) = h(g_1(\mathbf{x}), \ldots, g_I(\mathbf{x}))$. This may be constrained to the case of purely linear combinations of predictors $f(1 \mid \mathbf{x}) = \alpha + \sum \beta_i g_i(\mathbf{x})$, which is structurally of the form of the predictors which are constructed in model averaging, generalized discriminant functions [8] and adjusted estimation. We could reduce this further to derive the sequence of subsequent specialisations $f(1 \mid \mathbf{x}) = \alpha + \sum g_i(\alpha_i + \mathbf{x}^T \beta_i)$, as in projection pursuit or neural networks, $f(1 \mid \mathbf{x}) = \alpha + \sum g_i(x_i)$, as in generalised additive modeling and eventually linear prediction $f(1 \mid \mathbf{x}) = \alpha + \mathbf{x}^T \beta$. In terms of the structure of the predictor only,

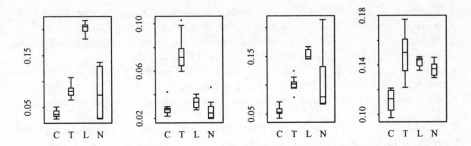

Fig. 3. Boxplots of validated misclassification rates for repetitions of the previously discussed four simulation experiments (first to fourth: from left to right). Misclassification rates are shown for adjusted estimation (C), Tree only (T), LDA only (L) and a neural network (N).

our models may thus be viewed as a generalization of either projection pursuit or neural networks and generalised additive modeling, at least because we allow the interior 'nodes' to be, in principle, any general model. While the methodology may thus be able to provide adequate predictors for a wider class of classification problems, this raises the problem of potential overfitting of the data. Figure 3 shows boxplots of validated misclassification rates for 10 repetitions of the previously discussed four simulation experiments, each time simulating new calibration and validation data. For each simulation, the combination of linear discrimination and tree was fitted and evaluated and similarly for linear discrimination and the classification tree only. It is clear that the combination method compares very favourably. Comparisons with a feed-forward neural network with two hidden logistic nodes as well as a logistic output node and maximum likelihood fitting are also included for the same simulations (courtesy of the nnet procedure [22]). With exception for the second simulation for which neural networks reproduces the linear discrimination results, the method is not competitive for the other problems. Crucially, there is no evidence of overfitting with respect to adjusted estimation. The reasons for this are as yet not clear but may perhaps be found in analogies with penalized least-squares fitting, as is described for the more conventional applications of generalised additive estimation by Hastie and Tibshirani (page 110). Again it is clear that further work is needed to evaluate this.

References

1. Breiman, L. (1992) Stacked regression. Technical report No. 367, August 1992, Department of Statistics, University of California, Berkeley, California 94720.
2. Breiman, L. (1994) Bagging predictors. Technical report No. 421, August 1994, Department of Statistics, University of California, Berkeley, California 94720.

3. Breiman, L. and Friedman, J. H. (1985) Estimating optimal transformations for multiple regression and correlation. *J. Am. Statist. Ass.*, **80**, 580-619.

4. Buja, A. (1990) Remarks on functional canonical variates, alternating least squares methods and ACE. *The Annals of Statistics*, **18**, 1032-1069.

5. Buja, A., Hastie, T. and Tibshirani, R. (1989) Linear smoothers and additive models. *The Annals of Statistics*, **17**, 453-555.

6. Buntine, W. (1992) Learning in classification trees. *Statistics and Computing*, **2**, 63-73.

7. Clark, L. A. and Pregibon, D. (1992) Tree-based models. In: *Statistical Models in S.* (eds. Chambers, J. M. and Hastie, T. J.), Chapter 9. Pacific Grove, CA: Wadsworth and Brooks/Cole.

8. Devijver, P. A. and Kittler, J. V. (1982) *Pattern Recognition. A Statistical Approach.* Englewood Cliffs: Prentice-Hall.

9. Freund, Y. (1995) Boosting a weak learning algorithm by majority. *Information and Computation*, **121**, 256-285.

10. Friedman, J. H. (1989) Regularized discriminant analysis. *J. Am. Statist. Ass.*, **84**, 165-175.

11. Friedman, J. H. (1991) Multivariate adaptive regression splines. *The Annals of Statistics*, **19**, 1-141.

12. Friedman, J. H., Hastie, T. and Tibshirani, R. (1998) Additive Logistic Regression: A statistical view of boosting. Technical report. August 1998, Department of Statistics, Stanford University.

13. Hastie, T. and Pregibon, D. (1990) Shrinking trees. Technical report, AT&T Bell Laboratories, 600 Mountain Avenue, Murray Hill, NJ 07947.

14. Hastie, T. J. and Tibshirani, R. J. (1990) *Generalized Additive Models.* London: Chapman and Hall.

15. Key, J. T., Pericchi, L. R. and Smith, A. F. M. (1998) Bayesian model choice: what and why? Draft paper. Presented at the Sixth Conference on Bayesian Statistics in Valencia, 1998.

16. Madigan, D. and Raftery, A. E. (1994) Model selection and accounting for model uncertainty in graphical models using Occam's window. *J. Am. Statist. Ass.*, **89**, 1535-1545. New York: Wiley.

17. Oliver, J. J. and Hand, D. J. (1996) Averaging over decision trees. *Journal of Classification*

18. Quinlan, J. R. (1992) Learning with continuous classes. In Proceedings of the Fifth Australian Joint Conference on Applied Artificial Intelligence, Eds. A. Adams and L. Sterling. Singapore: World Scientific, pp. 343-348.

19. Ripley, B. D. (1993) Statistical aspects of neural networks. In *Networks and Chaos - Statistical and Probabilistic Aspects* (eds. O.E. Barndorff-Nielsen, J. L. Jensen and W. S. Kendall), pp. 40-123. London: Chapman and Hall.

20. Ripley, B. D. (1994) Neural networks and related methods for classification. *J. R. Statist. Soc.* B, **56**, 409-456.

21. Schapire, R. E. (1990) The strength of weak learnability. *Machine Learning*, **5**, 197-227.

22. Venables, W. N. and Ripley, B. D. (1994) *Modern Applied Statistics with S-PLUS.* New York: Springer-Verlag.

Data-Driven Theory Refinement Using KBDistAl

Jihoon Yang[1], Rajesh Parekh[2], Vasant Honavar[3], and Drena Dobbs[4]

[1] HRL Laboratories, 3011 Malibu Canyon Rd, Malibu, CA 90265, USA
`yang@wins.hrl.com`
[2] Allstate Research & Planning Ctr, 321 Middlefield Rd, Menlo Park, CA 94025, USA
`rpare@allstate.com`
[3] Computer Science Dept., Iowa State University, Ames, IA 50011-1040, USA
`honavar@cs.iastate.edu`
[4] Zoology & Genetics Dept., Iowa State University, Ames, IA 50011-1040, USA
`d_dobbs@molebio.iastate.edu`

Abstract. Knowledge based artificial neural networks offer an attractive approach to extending or modifying incomplete knowledge bases or domain theories through a process of data-driven theory refinement. We present an efficient algorithm for data-driven knowledge discovery and theory refinement using DistAl, a novel (inter-pattern distance based, polynomial time) constructive neural network learning algorithm. The initial domain theory comprising of propositional rules is translated into a knowledge based network. The domain theory is modified using DistAl which adds new neurons to the existing network as needed to reduce classification errors associated with the incomplete domain theory on labeled training examples. The proposed algorithm is capable of handling patterns represented using binary, nominal, as well as numeric (real-valued) attributes. Results of experiments on several datasets for *financial advisor* and the *human genome project* indicate that the performance of the proposed algorithm compares quite favorably with other algorithms for connectionist theory refinement (including those that require substantially more computational resources) both in terms of generalization accuracy and network size.

1 Introduction

Inductive learning systems attempt to learn a concept description from a sequence of labeled examples [13,17,21]. Artificial neural networks, because of their massive parallelism and potential for fault and noise tolerance, offer an attractive approach to inductive learning [10,21,30]. Such systems have been successfully used for data-driven knowledge acquisition in several application domains. However, these systems generalize from the labeled examples alone. The availability of domain specific knowledge (domain theories) about the concept being learned can potentially enhance the performance of the inductive learning system [31]. Hybrid learning systems that effectively combine domain knowledge with the inductive learning can potentially learn faster and generalize better than those based on purely inductive learning (learning from labeled examples alone). In practice the domain theory is often *incomplete* or even *inaccurate*.

D.J. Hand, J.N. Kok, M.R. Berthold (Eds.): IDA'99, LNCS 1642, pp. 331–342, 1999.

Inductive learning systems that use information from training examples to modify an existing domain theory by either augmenting it with new knowledge or by refining the existing knowledge are called *theory refinement* systems.

Theory refinement systems can be broadly classified into the following categories.

- **Approaches based on Rule Induction** which use decision tree or rule learning algorithms for theory revision. Examples of such systems include RTLS [9], EITHER [24], PTR [16], and TGCI [3].
- **Approaches based on Inductive Logic Programming** which represent knowledge using first-order logic (or restricted subsets of it). Examples of such systems include FOCL [27] and FORTE [29].
- **Connectionist Approaches using Artificial Neural Networks** which typically operate by first embedding domain knowledge into an appropriate initial neural network topology and refine it by training the resulting neural network on the set of labeled examples. The KBANN system [34,35] as well as related approaches [6] and [15] offer examples of this approach.

In experiments involving datasets from the Human Genome Project [1], KBANN has been reported to have outperformed symbolic theory refinement systems (such as EITHER) and other learning algorithms such as backpropagation and ID3 [34]. KBANN is limited by the fact that it does not modify the network's topology and theory refinement is conducted solely by updating the connection weights. This prevents the incorporation of new rules and also restricts the algorithm's ability to compensate for inaccuracies in the domain theory. Against this background, constructive neural network learning algorithms, because of their ability to modify the network architecture by dynamically adding neurons in a controlled fashion [14,26,37], offer an attractive connectionist approach to data-driven theory refinement. Available domain knowledge is incorporated into an initial network topology (e.g., using the rules-to-network algorithm of [35] or by other means). Inaccuracies in the domain theory are compensated for by extending the network topology using training examples. Figure 1 depicts this process.

Constructive neural network learning algorithms [14,26,37], that circumvent the need for a-priori specification of network architecture, can be used to construct networks whose size and complexity is commensurate with the complexity of the data, and trade off network complexity and training time against generalization accuracy. A variety of constructive learning algorithms have been studied in the literature [4,8,11,14,26,37]. DistAl [37] is a polynomial time learning algorithm that is guaranteed to induce a network with zero classification error on any non-contradictory training set. It can handle pattern classification tasks in which patterns are represented using binary, nominal, as well as numeric attributes. Experiments on a wide range of datasets indicate that the classification accuracies attained by DistAl are competitive with those of other algorithms [37,38]. Since

---

[1] These datasets are available at ftp://ftp.cs.wisc.edu/machine-learning/shavlik-group/datasets/.

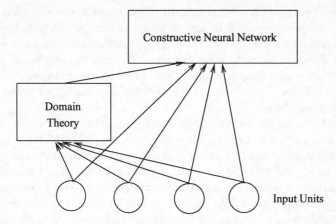

Fig. 1. Theory Refinement using a Constructive Neural Network

DistAl uses inter-pattern distance calculations, it can be easily extended to pattern classification problems wherein patterns are of variable sizes (e.g., strings or other complex symbolic structures) as long as suitable distance measures are defined [18]. Thus, DistAl is an attractive candidate for use in data-driven refinement of domain knowledge. Available domain knowledge is incorporated into an initial network topology. Inaccuracies in the domain theory are corrected by DistAl which adds additional neurons to eliminate classification errors on training examples.

Against this background, we present KBDistAl, a data-driven constructive theory refinement algorithm based on DistAl.

2   Constructive Theory Refinement Using Knowledge-Based Neural Networks

This section briefly describes several constructive theory refinement systems that have been studied in the literature.

Fletcher and Obradović [5] designed a constructive learning method for dynamically adding neurons to the initial knowledge based network. Their approach starts with an initial network representing the domain theory and modifies this theory by constructing a single hidden layer of threshold logic units (TLUs) from the labeled training data using the HDE algorithm [1]. The HDE algorithm divides the feature space with hyperplanes. Fletcher and Obradović's algorithm maps these hyperplanes to a set of TLUs and then trains the output neuron using the pocket algorithm [8]. The KBDistAl algorithm proposed in this paper, like that of Fletcher and Obradović, also constructs a single hidden layer. However it differs in one important aspect: It uses a computationally efficient DistAl algorithm which constructs the entire network in one pass through the training set instead of relying on the iterative approach used by Fletcher and Obradovć which requires a large number of passes through the training set.

The RAPTURE system is designed to refine domain theories that contains probabilistic rules represented in the certainty-factor format [20]. RAPTURE's approach to modifying the network topology differs from that used in KBDistAI as follows: RAPTURE uses an iterative algorithm to train the weights and employs the information gain heuristic [28] to add links to the network. KBDistAI is simpler in that it uses a non-iterative constructive learning algorithm to augment the initial domain theory.

Opitz and Shavlik have extensively studied connectionist theory refinement systems that overcome the fixed topology limitation of the KBANN algorithm [22], [23]. The TopGen algorithm [22] uses a heuristic search through the space of possible expansions of a KBANN network constructed from the initial domain theory. TopGen maintains a queue of candidate networks ordered by their test accuracy on a cross-validation set. At each step, TopGen picks the best network and explores possible ways of expanding it. New networks are generated by strategically adding nodes at different locations within the best network selected. These networks are trained and inserted into the queue and the process is repeated.

The REGENT algorithm uses a genetic search to explore the space of network architectures [23]. It first creates a diverse initial population of networks from the KBANN network constructed from the domain theory. Genetic search uses the classification accuracy on a cross-validation set as a fitness measure. REGENT's mutation operator adds a node to the network using the TopGen algorithm. It also uses a specially designed crossover operator that maintains the network's rule structure. The population of networks is subjected to fitness proportionate selection, mutation, and crossover for many generations and the best network produced during the entire run is reported as the solution. KBDistAI is considerably simpler than both TopGen and REGENT. It constructs a single network in one pass through the training data as opposed to training and evaluating a population of networks using the computationally expensive backpropagation algorithm for several generations. Thus, it is significantly faster than TopGen and REGENT.

Parekh and Honavar [25] propose a constructive approach to theory refinement that uses a novel combination of the Tiling and Pyramid constructive learning algorithms [8,26]. They use a symbolic knowledge encoding procedure to translate a domain theory into a set of propositional rules using a procedure that is based on the *rules-to-networks* algorithm of Towell and Shavlik [35] which is used in KBANN, TopGen, and REGENT. It yields a set of rules each of which has only one antecedent. The rule set is then mapped to an AND-OR graph which in turn is directly translated into a neural network. The Tiling-Pyramid algorithm uses an iterative perceptron style weight update algorithm for setting the weights and the Tiling algorithm to construct the first hidden layer (which maps binary or numeric input patterns into a binary representation at the hidden layer) and the Pyramid algorithm to add additional neurons if needed. While Tiling-Pyramid is significantly faster than TopGen and REGENT, it is still slower than KBDistAI because of its reliance on iterative weight update procedures.

3   KBDistAl: A Data-Driven Theory Refinement Algorithm

This section briefly describes our approach to knowledge based theory refinement using DistAl.

3.1   DistAl: An Inter-Pattern Distance Based Constructive Neural Network Algorithm

DistAl [14,37,38] is a simple and relatively fast constructive neural network learning algorithm for pattern classification. The key idea behind DistAl is to add *hyperspherical* hidden neurons one at a time based on a greedy strategy which ensures that each hidden neuron that is added correctly classifies a maximal subset of training patterns belonging to a single class. Correctly classified examples can then be eliminated from further consideration. The process is repeated until the network correctly classifies the entire training set. When this happens, the training set becomes linearly separable in the transformed space defined by the hidden neurons. In fact, it is possible to set the weights on the hidden to output neuron connections without going through an iterative, time-consuming process. It is straightforward to show that DistAl is guaranteed to converge to 100% classification accuracy on any finite training set in time that is polynomial (more precisely, quadratic) in the number of training patterns [37]. Experiments reported in [37] show that DistAl, despite its simplicity, yields classifiers that compare quite favorably with those generated using more sophisticated (and substantially more computationally demanding) learning algorithms.

3.2   Incorporation of Prior Knowledge into DistAl

The current implementation of KBDistAl makes use of a very simple approach to the incorporation of prior knowledge into DistAl. First, the input patterns are classified using the rules. The resulting outputs (classification of the input pattern) are then augmented to the pattern, which is connected to the constructive neural network. This explains how DistAl is used for the constructive neural network in Figure 1 efficiently without requiring a conversion of rules into a neural network.

4   Experiments

This section reports results of experiments using KBDistAl on data-driven theory refinement for the financial advising problem used by Fletcher and Obradović [5], as well as the ribosome binding site and promoter site prediction used by Shavlik's group [22,23,31,34,35]:

- **Ribosome**
  This data is from the Human Genome Project. It comprises of a domain theory and a set of labeled examples. The input is a short segment of DNA

nucleotides, and the goal is to learn to predict whether the DNA segments contain a ribosome binding site. There are 17 rules in the domain theory, and 1880 examples in the dataset.

– **Promoters**

This data is also from the Human Genome Project, and consists of a domain theory and a set of labeled examples. The input is a short segment of DNA nucleotides, and the goal is to learn to predict whether the DNA segments contain a promoter site. There are 31 rules in the domain theory, and 940 examples in the dataset.

– **financial advisor**

The financial advisor rule base contains 9 rules as shown in Figure 2 [19]. As in [5], a set of 5500 labeled examples that are consistent with the rule base is randomly generated. 500 examples are used for training and the remaining 5000 is used for testing.

1	if (sav_adeq and inc_adeq) then invest_stocks
2	if dep_sav_adeq then sav_adeq
3	if assets_hi then sav_adeq
4	if (dep_inc_adeq and earn_steady) then inc_adeq
5	if debt_lo then inc_adeq
6	if (sav ≥ dep * 5000) then dep_sav_adeq
7	if (assets ≥ income * 10) then assets_hi
8	if (income ≥ 25000 + dep * 4000) then dep_inc_adeq
9	if (debt_pmt < income * 0.3) then debt_lo

Fig. 2. Financial advisor rule base.

4.1   Human Genome Project Datasets

The reported results are based on a 10-fold cross-validation. The average training and test accuracies of the rules in domain theory alone were 87.29 ± 0.22 and 87.29 ± 2.03 for **Ribosome** dataset and 77.45 ± 0.56 and 77.45 ± 5.01 for **Promoters** dataset, respectively. Table 1 and 2 shows the average generalization accuracy and the average network size (along with the standard deviations[2] where available) for **Ribosome** and **Promoters** datasets, respectively.

Table 1 and 2 compare the performance of KBDistAl with that of some of the other approaches that have been reported in the literature. For **Ribosome** dataset, it produced a lower generalization accuracy than the other approaches and generated networks that were larger than those obtained by Tiling-Pyramid. We believe that this might have been due to overfitting. In fact, when the network pruning procedure was applied, the generalization accuracy increased to $91.8 \pm$

---

[2] The standard error can be computed instead, for better interpretation of the results.

Table 1. Results of **Ribosome** dataset.

	Test %	Size
Rules alone	87.3 ± 2.0	–
KBDistAl (no pruning)	86.3 ± 2.4	40.3 ± 1.3
KBDistAl (with pruning)	91.8 ± 1.8	16.2 ± 3.7
Tiling-Pyramid	90.3 ± 1.8	23 ± 0.0
TopGen	90.9	42.1 ± 9.3
REGENT	91.8	70.1 ± 25.1

Table 2. Results of **Promoters** dataset.

	Test %	Size
Rules alone	77.5 ± 5.0	–
KBDistAl (no pruning)	93.0 ± 2.8	12.2 ± 1.0
KBDistAl (with pruning)	95.5 ± 3.3	3.9 ± 2.3
Tiling-Pyramid	96.3 ± 1.8	34 ± 0.0
TopGen	94.8	40.2 ± 3.3
REGENT	95.8	74.9 ± 38.9

1.8 with smaller network size of 16.2±3.7. In the case of the **Promoters** dataset, KBDistAl produced comparable generalization accuracy with smaller network size. As in **Ribosome**, network pruning boosted the generalization accuracy to 95.5 ± 3.3 with significantly smaller network size of 3.9 ± 2.3.

The time taken in our approach is significantly less than that of the other approaches. KBDistAl takes fraction of a minute to a few minutes of CPU time on each dataset used in the experiments. In contrast, TopGen and REGENT were reported to have taken several days to obtain the results reported in [23].

4.2   Financial Advisor Rule Base

As explained earlier, 5500 patterns were generated randomly to satisfy the rules in Figure 2, of which 500 patterns were used for training and the remaining 5000 patterns were used for testing the network. In order to experiment with several different incomplete domain theories, some of the rules were pruned with its antecedents in each experiment. For instance, if sav_adeq was selected as the pruning point, then the rules for sav_adeq, dep_sav_adeq, and $assets\_hi$ are eliminated from the rule base. In other words rules 2, 3, 6, and 7 are pruned. Further, rule 1 is modified to read "*if (inc_adeq) then invest_stocks*". Then the initial network is constructed from this modified rule base and augmented using constructive learning.

Our experiments follow those performed in [5] and [25]. As we can see in Table 3 and 4, KBDistAl either outperformed the other approaches or gave comparable results. It resulted in higher classification accuracy than other approaches in several cases, and it always produced fairly compact networks while using substantially lower amount of computational resources. Again, as in the Human

Genome Project datasets, network pruning boosted the generalization in all cases with smaller network size. For the pruning points in Table 4 (the sequence from *dep_sav_adeq* to *inc_adeq*), the generalization accuracy improved to 89.2, 99.5, 98.4, 92.9, 94.9 and 93.0 with network sizes of 17, 2, 5, 9, 5 and 12, respectively.

Table 3. Results of financial advisor rule base (HDE).

Pruning point	HDE		Rules alone
	Test %	Hidden Units	Test %
dep_sav_adeq	92.7	31	75.1
assets_hi	92.4	23	93.4
dep_inc_adeq	85.8	25	84.5
debt_lo	84.7	30	61.7
sav_adeq	92.2	19	90.9
inc_adeq	81.2	32	64.6

Table 4. Results of financial advisor rule base (KBDistAI and Tiling-Pyramid).

Pruning point	KBDistAI		Tiling-Pyramid		Rules alone
	Test %	Size	Test %	Size	Test %
dep_sav_adeq	88.5	21	91.2 ± 1.7	28.2 ± 3.6	52.4
assets_hi	99.5	2	99.4 ± 0.2	10 ± 0.0	99.5
dep_inc_adeq	98.0	8	94.3 ± 1.5	21.0 ± 3.1	90.4
debt_lo	91.6	16	94.1 ± 2.0	22.1 ± 4.0	81.2
sav_adeq	93.8	10	90.8 ± 1.5	26.4 ± 3.3	87.6
inc_adeq	91.2	18	83.8 ± 2.2	32.7 ± 2.9	67.4

5   Summary and Discussion

Theory refinement techniques offer an attractive approach to exploiting available domain knowledge to enhance the performance of data-driven knowledge acquisition systems. Neural networks have been used extensively in theory refinement systems that have been proposed in the literature. Most of such systems translate the domain theory into an initial neural network architecture and then train the network to refine the theory. The KBANN algorithm is demonstrated to outperform several other learning algorithms on some domains [34,35]. However, a significant disadvantage of KBANN is its fixed network topology. TopGen and REGENT algorithms on the other hand allow modifications to the network architecture. Experimental results have demonstrated that TopGen and REGENT outperform KBANN on several applications. [22,23]. The Tiling-Pyramid algorithm proposed in [25] for constructive theory refinement builds a network of perceptrons. Its performance, in terms of classification accuracies attained, as reported in [25], is comparable to that of REGENT and TopGen, but at significantly lower computational cost.

The implementation of KBDistAl used in the experiments reported in this paper uses the rules directly (by augmenting the input patterns with the outputs obtained from the rules) as opposed to the more common approach of incorporating the rules into an initial network topology. The use of DistAl for network construction makes KBDistAl significantly faster than approaches that rely on iterative weight update procedures (e.g., perceptron learning, backpropagation algorithm) and/or computationally expensive genetic search. Experimental results demonstrate that KBDistAl's performance in terms of generalization accuracy is competitive with that of several of the more computationally expensive algorithms for data-driven theory refinement. Additional experiments using real-world data and domain knowledge are needed to explore the capabilities and limitations of KBDistAl and related algorithms for theory refinement. We conclude with a brief discussion of some promising directions for further research.

It can be argued that KBDistAl is not a *theory refinement* system in a strict sense. It makes use of the domain knowledge in its inductive learning procedure rather than *refining* the knowledge. Perhaps KBDistAl is more accurately described as a *knowledge guided* inductive theory construction system.

There are several extensions and variants of KBDistAl that are worth exploring. Given the fact that DistAl relies on inter-pattern distances to induce classifiers from data, it is straightforward to extend it so as to handle a much broader class of problems including those that involve patterns of variable sizes (e.g., strings) or symbolic structures as long as suitable inter-pattern distance metrics can be defined. Some steps toward rigorous definitions of distance metrics based on information theory are outlined in [18]. Variants of DistAl and KBDistAl that utilize such distance metrics are currently under investigation.

Several authors have investigated approaches to rule extraction from neural networks in general, and connectionist theory refinement systems in particular [2,7,33]. One goal of such work is to represent the learned knowledge in a form that is comprehensible to humans. In this context, rule extraction from classifiers induced by KBDistAl is of some interest.

In several practical applications of interest, all of the data needed for synthesizing reasonably precise classifiers is not available at once. This calls for incremental algorithms that continually refine knowledge as more and more data becomes available. Computational efficiency considerations argue for the use of data-driven theory refinement systems as opposed to storing large volumes of data and rebuilding the entire classifier from scratch as new data becomes available. Some preliminary steps in this direction are described in [12].

A somewhat related problem is that of knowledge discovery from large, physically distributed, dynamic data sources in a networked environment (e.g., data in genome databases). Given the large volumes of data involved, this argues for the use of data-driven theory refinement algorithms embedded in mobile software agents [12,36] that travel from one data source to another, carrying with them only the current knowledge base as opposed to approaches rely on shipping large volumes of data to a centralized repository where knowledge acquisition is performed. Thus, data-driven knowledge refinement algorithms constitute one of the key components of distributed knowledge network [12] environments for knowledge discovery in many practical applications (e.g., bioinformatics).

In several application domains, knowledge acquired on one task can often be utilized to accelerate knowledge acquisition on related tasks. Data-driven theory refinement is particularly attractive in applications that lend themselves to such cumulative multi-task learning [32]. The use of KBDistAI or similar algorithms in such scenarios remains to be explored.

Acknowledgements

This research was partially supported by grants from the National Science Foundation (IRI-9409580) and the John Deere Foundation to Vasant Honavar and a grant from the Carver Foundation to Drena Dobbs and Vasant Honavar.

References

1. Baum, E., and Lang, K. 1991. Constructing hidden units using examples and queries. In Lippmann, R.; Moody, J.; and Touretzky, D., eds., *Advances in Neural Information Processing Systems, vol. 3*, 904–910. San Mateo, CA: Morgan Kaufmann.

2. Craven, M. 1996. *Extracting Comprehensible Models from Trained Neural Networks.* Ph.D. Dissertation, Department of Computer Science, University of Wisconsin, Madison, WI.

3. Donoho, S., and Rendell, L. 1995. Representing and restructuring domain theories: A constructive induction approach. *Journal of Artificial Intelligence Research* 2:411–446.

4. Fahlman, S., and Lebiere, C. 1990. The cascade correlation learning algorithm. In Touretzky, D., ed., *Neural Information Systems 2*. Morgan-Kauffman. 524–532.

5. Fletcher, J., and Obradović, Z. 1993. Combining prior symbolic knowledge and constructive neural network learning. *Connection Science* 5(3,4):365–375.

6. Fu, L. M. 1989. Integration of neural heuristics into knowledge-based inference. *Connection Science* 1:325–340.

7. Fu, L. M. 1993. Knowledge based connectionism for refining domain theories. *IEEE Transactions on Systems, Man, and Cybernetics* 23(1).

8. Gallant, S. 1990. Perceptron based learning algorithms. *IEEE Transactions on Neural Networks* 1(2):179–191.

9. Ginsberg, A. 1990. Theory reduction, theory revision, and retranslation. In *Proceedings of the Eighth National Conference on Artificial Intelligence*, 777–782. Boston, MA: AAAI/MIT Press.

10. Hassoun, M. 1995. *Fundamentals of Artificial Neural Networks.* Boston, MA: MIT Press.

11. Honavar, V., and Uhr, L. 1993. Generative learning structures for generalized connectionist networks. *Information Sciences* 70(1-2):75–108.

12. Honavar, V.; Miller, L.; and Wong, J. 1998. Distributed knowledge networks. In *IEEE Information Technology Conference*.
13. Honavar, V. 1999a. Machine learning: Principles and applications. In Webster, J., ed., *Encyclopedia of Electrical and Electronics Engineering*. New York: Wiley. To appear.
14. Honavar, V. 1999b. Structural learning. In Webster, J., ed., *Encyclopedia of Electrical and Electronics Engineering*. New York: Wiley. To appear.
15. Katz, B. F. 1989. EBL and SBL: A neural network synthesis. In *Proceedings of the Eleventh Annual Conference of the Cognitive Science Society*, 683–689.
16. Kopel, M.; Feldman, R.; and Serge, A. 1994. Bias-driven revision of logical domain theories. *Journal of Artificial Intelligence Research* 1:159–208.
17. Langley, P. 1995. *Elements of Machine Learning*. Palo Alto, CA: Morgan Kaufmann.
18. Lin, D. 1998. An information-theoretic definition of similarity. In *International Conference on Machine Learning*.
19. Luger, G. F., and Stubblefield, W. A. 1989. *Artificial Intelligence and the Design of Expert Systems*. Redwood City, CA: Benjamin/Cummings.
20. Mahoney, J., and Mooney, R. 1994. Comparing methods for refining certainty-factor rule-bases. In *Proceedings of the Eleventh International Conference on Machine Learning*, 173–180.
21. Mitchell, T. 1997. *Machine Learning*. New York: McGraw Hill.
22. Opitz, D. W., and Shavlik, J. W. 1995. Dynamically adding symbolically meaningful nodes to knowledge-based neural networks. *Knowledge-Based Systems* 8(6):301–311.
23. Opitz, D. W., and Shavlik, J. W. 1997. Connectionist theory refinement: Genetically searching the space of network topologies. *Journal of Artificial Intelligence Research* 6:177–209.
24. Ourston, D., and Mooney, R. J. 1994. Theory refinement: Combining analytical and empirical methods. *Artificial Intelligence* 66:273–310.
25. Parekh, R., and Honavar, V. 1998. Constructive theory refinement in knowledge based neural networks. In *Proceedings of the International Joint Conference on Neural Networks*, 2318–2323.
26. Parekh, R.; Yang, J.; and Honavar, V. 1997. Constructive neural network learning algorithms for multi-category real-valued pattern classification. Technical Report ISU-CS-TR97-06, Department of Computer Science, Iowa State University.
27. Pazzani, M., and Kibler, D. 1992. The utility of knowledge in inductive learning. *Machine Learning* 9:57–94.
28. Quinlan, R. 1986. Induction of decision trees. *Machine Learning* 1:81–106.
29. Richards, B., and Mooney, R. 1995. Automated refinement of first-order horn-clause domain theories. *Machine Learning* 19:95–131.
30. Ripley, B. 1996. *Pattern Recognition and Neural Networks*. New York: Cambridge University Press.
31. Shavlik, J. W. 1994. A framework for combining symbolic and neural learning. In *Artificial Intelligence and Neural Networks: Steps Toward Principled Integration*. Boston: Academic Press.
32. Thrun, S. 1995. Lifelong learning: A case study. Technical Report CMU-CS-95-208, Carnegie Mellon University.
33. Towell, G., and Shavlik, J. 1993. Extracting rules from knowledge-based neural networks. *Machine Learning* 13:71–101.
34. Towell, G., and Shavlik, J. 1994. Knowledge-based artificial neural networks. *Artificial Intelligence* 70(1–2):119–165.

35. Towell, G.; Shavlik, J.; and Noordwier, M. 1990. Refinement of approximate domain theories by knowledge-based neural networks. In *Proceedings of the Eighth National Conference on Artificial Intelligence*, 861–866.

36. White, J. 1997. Mobile agents. In Bradshaw, J., ed., *Software Agents*. Cambridge, MA: MIT Press.

37. Yang, J.; Parekh, R.; and Honavar, V. 1998. DistAl: An inter-pattern distance-based constructive learning algorithm. In *Proceedings of the International Joint Conference on Neural Networks*, 2208–2213.

38. Yang, J.; Parekh, R.; and Honavar, V. 1999. DistAl: An inter-pattern distance-based constructive learning algorithm. *Intelligent Data Analysis*. To appear.

Reasoning about Input-Output Modeling of Dynamical Systems

Matthew Easley and Elizabeth Bradley*

University of Colorado
Department of Computer Science
Boulder, CO 80309-0430
{easley,lizb}@cs.colorado.edu

Abstract. The goal of input-output modeling is to apply a test input to a system, analyze the results, and learn something useful from the cause-effect pair. Any automated modeling tool that takes this approach must be able to reason effectively about sensors and actuators and their interactions with the target system. Distilling qualitative information from sensor data is fairly easy, but a variety of difficult control-theoretic issues — controllability, reachability, and utility — arise during the planning and execution of experiments. This paper describes some representations and reasoning tactics, collectively termed *qualitative bifurcation analysis*, that make it possible to automate this task.

1   Input-Output Modeling

System identification (SID) is the process of inferring an internal ordinary differential equation (ODE) model from external observations of a system. The computer program PRET[5] automates the SID process, using a combination of artificial intelligence and system identification techniques to construct ODE models of lumped-parameter continuous-time nonlinear dynamic systems. As diagrammed in Fig. 1, PRET uses domain knowledge to combine model fragments into ODEs, then employs actuators and sensors to learn more about the target

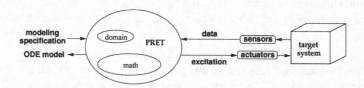

Fig. 1. PRET uses sensors and actuators to interact with target systems in an *input-output* approach to dynamical system modeling.

* Supported by NSF NYI #CCR-9357740, NSF #MIP-9403223, ONR #N00014-96-1-0720, and a Packard Fellowship in Science and Engineering from the David and Lucile Packard Foundation.

D.J. Hand, J.N. Kok, M.R. Berthold (Eds.): IDA'99, LNCS 1642, pp. 343–355, 1999.

system, and finally tests the ODEs against the actuator/sensor data using a body of mathematical knowledge encoded in first-order logic[20].

This *input-output* (I/O) approach to dynamical system modeling, which distinguishes PRET from other AI modeling tools, is very powerful and also extremely difficult. Distilling available sensor information into qualitative form is reasonably straightforward, as described in our IDA-97 paper[3], but reasoning about the information so derived is subtle and challenging. Dealing with actuators is even harder because of the nonlinear control theory that is involved. Among other things, determining what experiments one can perform from the system's present state involves complicated reasoning about *controllability* and *reachability*. In an automated framework, it is also important to reason about what can be learned from a given experiment. During the input-output modeling process, PRET must solve all three of these problems. That is, given a black-box system, a partial measurement of its current state, some knowledge about the available actuators, and some preliminary ideas about a candidate model, PRET must be able to decide what experiments are possible and useful. This is a difficult, open problem for nonlinear systems, even for human experts. The topic of this paper is a set of knowledge representation and reasoning techniques that make it possible to automate this task.

In linear systems these problems are relatively easy. Engineering approaches to linear input-output analysis are well developed; standard techniques for exciting different useful states of the system[13] include changing the type (e.g., ramp, step) or parameters (e.g., amplitude, frequency) of the input. The impulse response of a system — its transient response to a quick kick $x(t_0) = 1$; $x(t) = 0 \, \forall t \neq t_0$ — is particularly useful. The natural resonant and anti-resonant frequencies appear as spikes and the *mode shapes* between those spikes can show whether a vibrating mechanical system is mass- or stiffness-dominated[15].

Nonlinear systems pose a far more imposing challenge to input-output modeling; their mathematics is vastly harder, and many of the analysis tools described in the previous paragraph do not apply. Almost all forms of transient analysis (e.g., step or impulse response) are useless in nonlinear problems, as is frequency response; the concept of a discrete set of spectral components simply does not make sense. Because of this, nonlinear dynamicists typically allow transients to die out and then reason about *attractors* in the *phase* or *state space*, and how the geometry and topology of those attractors change when the system parameters are varied.

Our approach targets the problems that arise in reasoning about multiple set of observations that arise in phase-portrait analysis of complex systems. In particular, we use a combined *state/parameter space* and decompose it into discrete regions, each associated with an equivalence class of dynamical behaviors, derived qualitatively using geometric reasoning. These discrete regions describe the behavior of the system in a uniquely powerful way. As each trajectory is effectively equivalent, in a well-known sense, to all the other trajectories in the same region, one can describe the behavior in that region in a much simpler way, which results in ease of analysis — and great computational savings.

The representation described in this paper — an abstraction/extension of the traditional nonlinear analysis technique termed *bifurcation analysis* — allows PRET's intelligent sensor analysis and actuator control modules to reason effectively about multiple sets of observations over a given system. Coupled with a knowledge representation and reasoning framework that adapts smoothly to how much one knows about the system (e.g., using linear analysis when appropriate), which is described in another paper[9], this representation allows PRET to reason effectively about input-output modeling of nonlinear dynamical systems.

To set the context, the following section gives a brief overview of PRET. We then focus in on the input-output modeling phase, describe our representation and reasoning framework, and show how PRET exploits that framework.

2   PRET

As outlined in the previous section, PRET[5] is an automated tool for nonlinear system identification (SID). Its inputs are a set of observations of the outputs of a black-box system, and its output is an ordinary differential equation (ODE) model of the internal dynamics of that system. PRET's architecture wraps a layer of artificial intelligence (AI) techniques around a set of traditional formal engineering methods like impulse-response analysis, nonlinear regression, etc. The AI layer combines several forms of reasoning,[1] via a special first-order logic inference system[18, 20] to intelligently assess the task at hand; it then reasons from that information to automatically choose, invoke, and interpret the results of appropriate lower-level techniques. This framework lets PRET shift fluidly back and forth between domain-specific reasoning and general mathematics to navigate efficiently through an exponential search space of possible models. This approach has met with success in a variety of simulated and real problems, ranging from textbook systems to real-world engineering applications.

PRET takes a "generate-and-test" approach to model building. It uses domain-specific knowledge to assemble combinations of user-specified and automatically generated ODE fragments into a candidate model;[2] it tests that model by performing a series of factual inferences about the ODE and the observations and then using a theorem prover[19] to search for contradictions in those sets of facts. The technical challenge here is efficiency: the search space is huge, and so PRET must identify contradictions as quickly, simply, and cheaply as possible. The key to doing so is to classify model and system behavior at an appropriate qualitative level and to exploit all available domain-specific knowledge in the most useful way. Symbolic algebra can be used to remove huge branches from the search space. If the target system is known to be chaotic, for instance, all linear ODEs can be immediately discarded, and the computation involved

---

[1] qualitative reasoning, qualitative simulation, numerical simulation, geometric reasoning, constraint propagation, resolution, reasoning with abstraction levels, declarative meta-control, and a simple form of truth maintenance.

[2] In mechanics, for instance, PRET uses Newton's laws to combine force terms; in electronics, it uses Kirchhoff's laws to sum voltages in a loop or currents in a cutset.

— calculating the Jacobian and ascertaining that all of its entries are constant
— requires only simple, inexpensive symbolic reasoning. In other situations,
pruning a single leaf off the tree of possible models can be extremely expensive
(e.g., estimating parameter values for a nonlinear ODE prior to a final corrob-
orative simulation/comparison run, which is a complicated global optimization
problem[4]). Some analysis methods, such as phase-portrait analysis, apply to
all ODEs, whereas others are only meaningful in specific domains (e.g., creep
tests in viscoelastic systems). Orchestrating this complex reasoning process is
a very difficult problem; its solution requires carefully crafted knowledge representation frameworks[9] that allow for an elegant formalization of the essential
building blocks of an engineer's knowledge and reasoning, and powerful automated machinery[20] that uses the formalized knowledge to reason flexibly about
a variety of modeling problems.

The input-output modeling strategies that are the topic of this paper play
important roles in both the generate and the test phase. The "input" half of
PRET's *intelligent sensor/actuator analysis and control* module — which is re-
viewed briefly in the following sections and covered in detail in [3] — uses geometric reasoning and delay-coordinate embedding to distill abstract, useful qualitative information from a highly specific numeric sensor data set. The "output"
part, described in the following sections, reasons about multiple sets of observations about a given system using a new knowledge representation called the
qualitative state/parameter space and an associated reasoning strategy termed
qualitative bifurcation analysis, both of which are AI-adapted versions of well-
known nonlinear dynamics techniques. For more details on the rest of PRET —
issues, solutions, internal representations, encoded knowledge bases, examples
solved, etc. — please consult the papers cited in the previous two paragraphs.

3 Qualitative Bifurcation Analysis

One of the goals of the qualitative reasoning (QR) community[12] is to abstract
specific instances of behavior into more-general descriptions of a system. An
80kg adult bouncing on the end of a bungee cord, for instance, will produce a
different time series from a 50kg child, but both produce similar damped oscil-
latory responses. Reasoning about these two behaviors in their time-series form
can be difficult, as it requires detailed examination of the amplitude decay rate
of and the phase shift between two decaying sinusoids. The state-space representation, which suppresses the time variable and plots position versus velocity,
brings out the similarity between these two behaviors in a very clear way. Both
bungee jumps, for example, manifest on a state-space plot as similar decaying
spirals. Automated phase-portrait analysis techniques[2, 21, 22], which combine
ideas from dynamical systems, discrete mathematics, and artificial intelligence,
generate qualitative descriptions that capture this information.

A discretized version of the state-space representation can abstract away
many low-level details about the dynamics of a system while preserving its important qualitative properties. The cell-to-cell-mapping formalism[14], for instance,

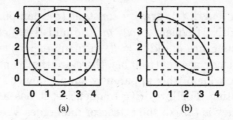

Fig. 2. Identifying a *limit cycle* using the cell-dynamics method.

discretizes a set of n-dimensional state vectors onto an n-dimensional mesh of uniform boxes or *cells*. The circular state-space trajectory in Fig. 2(a), for example, — a sequence of two-vectors of floating-point numbers — can be represented by the *cell sequence* [... (0,0) (1,0) (2,0) (3,0) (4,0) (4,1) (4,2) (4,3) ...]. Because multiple trajectory points are mapped into each cell, this discretized representation of the dynamics is significantly more compact than the original series of floating-point numbers and therefore much easier to work with. Using this representation, the dynamics of a trajectory can be quickly and qualitatively classified using simple geometric heuristics — in this case as a *limit cycle*. PRET's intelligent sensor analysis procedures use this type of discretized geometric reasoning to "distill" out the qualitative features of a given state-space portrait, allowing PRET to reason about these features at a much higher (and cheaper) abstraction level. This scheme is covered in detail in [3].

This is only, however, a very small part of the power of the qualitative phase-portrait representation. Dynamical systems can be extremely complicated; attempting to understand one by analyzing a single behavior instance — e.g., system evolution from *one* initial condition at *one* parameter value, like Fig. 2(a) — is generally inadequate. Rather, one must vary a system's inputs and control parameters and study the change in the response. Even in one-parameter systems, however, this procedure can be difficult; as the parameter is varied, the behavior may vary smoothly in some ranges and then change abruptly ("bifurcate") at critical parameter values. A thorough representation of this behavior, then, requires a "stack" of state-space portraits: at least one for each interesting and distinct range of values. Constructing such a stack requires automatic recognition of the boundaries between these ranges, and the cell dynamics representation makes this very easy. Fig. 2(b), for example, shows another limit cycle trajectory — one with different geometry but identical topology. The key concept here is that a set of geometrically different and yet qualitatively similar trajectories — an "equivalence class" with respect to some important dynamical property — can be classified as a single coherent group of state-space portraits. This is the basis of the power of the techniques described in this paper.

Consider, for example, a driven pendulum model described by the ODE

$$\ddot{\theta}(t) + \frac{\beta}{m}\dot{\theta}(t) + \frac{g}{l}\sin\theta(t) = \frac{\gamma}{ml}\sin\alpha t$$

with mass (m), arm length (l), gravity constant (g), damping factor (β), drive amplitude (γ) and drive frequency (α). m, l, g and β are constants; the state variables of this system are θ and $\omega = \dot{\theta}$. In many experiments, the drive amplitude and/or frequency are controllable: these are the "control parameters" of the system. The behavior of this apparently simple device is really quite complicated and interesting. For low drive frequencies, it has a single stable fixed point; as the frequency is raised, the attractor undergoes a series of bifurcations between chaotic and periodic behavior. These bifurcations do not, however, necessarily cause the attractor to *move*. That is, the qualitative behavior of the system changes and the operating regime (in state space) does not. Traditional analysis of this system would involve constructing state-space portraits, like the ones shown in Fig. 2, at closely spaced control parameter values across some interesting range; this is the *bifurcation analysis* procedure introduced in the previous paragraph. Traditional AI/hybrid representations do not handle this smoothly, as the operating regimes involved are not distinct. If, however, one

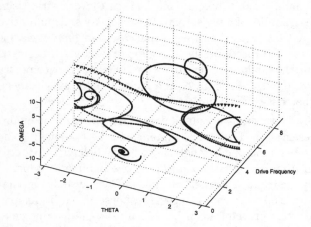

Fig. 3. A state/parameter (S/P) space portrait of the driven pendulum: a parameterized collection of state-space portraits of the device at various Drive Frequencies.

adds a parameter axis to the state space, most of these problems vanish. Fig. 3 describes the behavior of the driven pendulum in this new *state/parameter-space* (S/P-space) representation. Each θ, ω slice of this plot is a state-space portrait, and the control parameter varies along the Drive Frequency axis.

Our final step is to combine this state/parameter-space idea with the qualitative abstraction of cell dynamics, producing the *qualitative state/parameter space* (QS/P-space) representation that is the basis of the KRR framework that is the topic of this paper. A QS/P-space portrait of the driven pendulum is shown in Fig. 4. This representation is similar to the S/P-space portrait shown

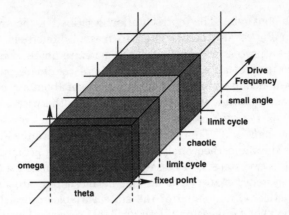

Fig. 4. A *qualitative state/parameter-space* (QS/P-space) portrait of the driven pendulum. This is an abstraction of the state/parameter space portrait shown in Fig. 3; it groups qualitatively similar behaviors into equivalence classes to define the boundaries of qualitatively distinct regions of state/parameter space.

in Fig. 3, but it groups similar behaviors into equivalence classes, and then uses those groupings to define the boundaries of qualitatively distinct regions.

This qualitative state/parameter-space representation is an extremely powerful modeling tool. One can use it to identify the individual operating regimes, then create a separate model in each, and perhaps use a finite-state machine to model transitions between them. More importantly, however, the QS/P-space representation lets the model builder leverage the knowledge that its regions — e.g., the five slabs in Fig. 4 — all describe the behavior of the *same system*, at different parameter values. This is exactly the type of knowledge that one needs in order to plan how to learn more about a system by changing its inputs and observing the results. The remainder of this paper expands upon these ideas, describing how the QS/P-space representation helps PRET perform input-output modeling of dynamical systems.

4   Input-Output Modeling in PRET

The goal of input-output modeling is to apply a test input to a system, analyze the results, and learn something useful from the cause/effect pair. In this section, we describe how PRET reasons about this process using the QS/P representation introduced in the previous section.

As described in Sect. 2, PRET takes a generate-and-test approach, using a small, powerful domain theory to build ODE models and a larger, more-general ODE theory to test those models against the known behavior of the system. I/O modeling using the QS/P representation contributes to this process in a variety of ways. Firstly, it allows PRET to reason effectively about test inputs; a good test input excites the behavior in a useful but not overwhelming way, and choosing such an input is nontrivial. The representation described in the previous section and pictured in Fig. 4 also allows PRET to reason about sensible hypothesis combinations — a process without which the generate phase would be reduced to blind enumeration of an exponential number of candidate models. Finally, qualitative I/O modeling techniques help PRET reason about state variables and observations — information whose sole source would otherwise be the user.

The "input" part of PRET's input-output reasoning takes place in the *intelligent sensor data analyzer*[3]. This module first reconstructs any hidden dynamics from the sensor data and then analyzes the results using geometric reasoning. The first of these two steps is necessary because fully *observable* systems, in which all of a system's state variables can be measured, are rare in normal engineering practice. Often, some of the state variables are either physically inaccessible or cannot be measured with available sensors. This is control theory's *observer* problem: the task of inferring the internal state of a system solely from observations of its outputs. Delay-coordinate embedding[1], PRET's solution to this problem, creates an m-dimensional *reconstruction-space* vector from m time-delayed samples of data from a single sensor. The central idea is that the reconstruction-space dynamics and the true (unobserved) state-space dynamics are topologically identical. This provides a partial solution to the observer problem, as a state-space portrait reconstructed from a single sensor is qualitatively identical to the true multidimensional dynamics of the system.[3] Given a reconstructed state-space portrait of the system's dynamics, the intelligent sensor data analyzer's second phase distills out its qualitative properties using the cell dynamics paradigm discussed in Sect. 3. The results of reconstructing and analyzing the sensor data are a set of qualitative observations similar to those a human engineer would make about the system, such as "the system is oscillating." This information is useful as it not only raises the abstraction level of PRET's reasoning about models but also is critical to the mechanics of the qualitative bifurcation analysis process, as described later in this section.

Reasoning about actuators is much more difficult, so the development of PRET's *intelligent actuator controller* has been slow. The problem lies in the inherent difference between passive and active modeling. It is easy to recognize damped oscillations in sensor data without knowing anything about the system or the sensor, but using an actuator requires a lot of knowledge about both. Different actuators affect different system properties (e.g., the half dozen knobs on the front of a stereo receiver). They also have very different characteristics (range, resolution, response time, etc.); consider the different dynamics of cooking on campfires, gas/electric stoves, or blast furnaces. Identical actuators can affect systems in radically different ways; a gear shift lever in a car, for instance, invokes very different responses, if it is moved into "first" or "reverse." When the sensor and the system are linear, there are some useful standard procedures for choosing test inputs, codifying the results, and reasoning about their implications — e.g., step and impulse response — but these kinds of drive signals

---

[3] This property also allows PRET to estimate an upper bound on the number of state variables in a system.

elicit tremendously complicated responses from nonlinear systems, making output analysis very difficult. In nonlinear systems analysis, one typically applies *constant* inputs, ignores any transients, and reasons about the resulting *attractors* in the state-space representation, as described in Sect. 3. Deciding how to use an actuator is only the first part of the problem. Any planning about experiments must also consider the set of possible states of the system — those that are reachable from the existing state with the available control input. Finally, effective input-output modeling requires reasoning about *useful* experiments: those that increase one's knowledge about the target system in a productive way. The ultimate goal of PRET's intelligent sensor/actuator control module is to find and exploit the overlap between these sets of *useful* and *possible* experiments.

To solve these difficult problems — controllability, reachability, and utility — PRET must reason about multiple sets of observations of a system, each made under a different actuator condition. It must also *plan* those actuator conditions, which involves modeling not only the actuator itself but also the behavior of the actuator-system interface. Our current solution assumes that PRET knows the actuator input range — a reasonable assumption because the actuator normally exists as an external device, unlike the internal workings of an unknown physical system. Using the QS/P paradigm developed earlier, coupled with the cell dynamics technique and a simple binary search strategy, PRET first performs a qualitative bifurcation analysis. It begins at the lower end of the actuator range, setting the drive signal to a constant value, letting the transient die out, and then using cell dynamics to classify the behavior. It then increments the actuator input and repeats the process. When the attractor bifurcates, PRET zeroes in on the bifurcation point by successively bisecting the actuator input interval. The result of this procedure is a QS/P-space portrait of the system, complete with regime boundaries and behavioral descriptions in each regime, such as:

> "in the temperature range from 0 to $50°C$, the system undergoes a damped oscillation to a fixed point at $(x, y) = (1.4, -8)$; when $T > 50°C$, it follows a period-two limit cycle located at..."[4]

PRET then invokes the model-building process in each regime, and finally attempts to unify these models into a single ODE.

In the driven pendulum example, this procedure works as follows. Qualitative bifurcation analysis identifies five separate qualitative state/parameter-space regions, as shown in Fig. 4. PRET then builds an ODE model for each regime using procedures described in Sect. 2. These ODEs are shown in Table 1. Note that four of these five ODEs are different, but all five are, in reality, instances of a single ODE that accounts for the physical behavior across the whole parameter range. PRET's goal is to find that globally valid model, so it must *unify* these ODEs. Unification is reasonably straightforward if it is correctly interleaved with the model-building process. In the driven pendulum, for example, PRET analyzes the system in the small-angle regime,[5] producing the model $\ddot{\theta}(t) = -\frac{g}{l}\theta(t)$. When

---

[4] PRET's syntax is much more cryptic; it has no natural language capabilities.

[5] where $\sin\theta \approx \theta$ and the system acts like a simple harmonic oscillator

Table 1. Valid models of the driven pendulum in different behavioral regimes.

Drive Frequency	ODE	Description
None	$\ddot{\theta}(t) = -\frac{\beta}{m}\dot{\theta}(t) - \frac{g}{l}\sin\theta(t)$	damped oscillator
Low	$\ddot{\theta}(t) = -\frac{g}{l}\sin\theta(t)$	nonlinear solution
Medium	$\ddot{\theta}(t) + \frac{\beta}{m}\dot{\theta}(t) + \frac{g}{l}\sin\theta(t) = \frac{\gamma}{ml}\sin\alpha t$	"true" (full) solution
High	$\ddot{\theta}(t) = -\frac{g}{l}\sin\theta(t)$	nonlinear solution
Very High	$\ddot{\theta}(t) = -\frac{g}{l}\theta(t)$	linear (small angle) solution

the actuator moves the system to the neighboring limit cycle regime, where larger-angle behavior dominates, the small-angle solution no longer holds, forcing a new model search, which yields the model $\ddot{\theta}(t) = -\frac{g}{l}\sin\theta(t)$. PRET then tries to reconcile the two models, applying both of them in both regimes. Since $\ddot{\theta}(t) = -\frac{g}{l}\theta(t)$ is a special case of $\ddot{\theta}(t) = -\frac{g}{l}\sin\theta(t)$, the former holds in only one of the two, whereas the latter holds in both, so PRET discards the $\ddot{\theta}(t) = -\frac{g}{l}\theta(t)$ model and goes on to the next regime, repeating the model building/unification process. Once PRET finds a single model that accounts for all observed behavior in all regimes across the range of interest, its task is complete. Such a model may not, of course, exist; a system may be governed by completely different physics in different regimes, and no single ODE may be able to account for this kind of behavior. In this case, the models in the different regimes would be mutually exclusive, and PRET would be unable to unify them into a single ODE, and so it would simply return the list of regimes, models, and transitions. This is exactly the form of a traditional hybrid model[6] of a multi-regime system.

As is true of automated modeling in general, evaluating the results of this approach can be difficult because the question "How is this model better?" is hard to formalize. From an engineering standpoint, a successful model is one that matches observed behavior to within predefined specifications; PRET is designed to be an engineer's tool, so its judgment of what constitutes success or failure is exactly that. *Parsimony* is another desirable attribute in a model: one wishes to account for the observed behavior using as few — and as simple — ODE terms as possible. Finally, the speed with which PRET produces such a model is another important metric, particularly as we work with more-complex systems and search spaces. Ultimately, the best form of evaluation will consist of whether or not PRET's models are useful for control system design — that is, whether the ODE that PRET constructs of a radio-controlled car can actually be used as the heart of a controller designed to direct that car to perform some prescribed action. We are in the process of evaluating models of real-world systems in several domains — ranging from robotics to hydrology — in this manner.

5   Relationship to Related Work

Most of the work in the AI/QR modeling community builds qualitative models by combining a set of descriptions of state into higher-level abstractions or *qualitative states*[8, 11]. Many tools also reason about equations at varying levels of abstraction, from *qualitative* differential equations (QDEs) in QSIM[16] to ODEs in PRET. PRET's approach differs from many of these tools in that it works with noisy, incomplete sensor data from real-world systems, and attempts not to "discover" the underlying physics, but rather to find the simplest ODE that can account for the given observation. In the QR research that is most closely related to PRET, ODE models are built by evaluating time series using qualitative reasoning techniques and then using a parameter estimator to match the resulting model with a given observed system[7]. This modeling tool selects models from a set of pre-enumerated solutions in a very specific domain (linear visco-elastics). PRET is much more general; it works on linear *and nonlinear* lumped-parameter continuous-time ODEs in a variety of domains and uses *dynamic* model generation to handle arbitrary devices and connection topologies.

PRET shares goals and techniques with several other fields. It solves the same problems as traditional system identification[15], but in an automated fashion, and it relies upon many of the standard methods and ideas found in basic control theory texts such as controllability and reachability[17]. Finally, PRET includes many of the same concepts that appear in the data analysis literature[10], but it adds a layer of AI techniques, such as symbolic data representation and logical inference, on top of these.

6 Conclusion

The goal of the work described in this paper is to automate the type of input-output analysis that expert scientists and engineers apply to modeling problems, and to use that technology to improve the PRET modeling tool, which automatically constructs ODE models of nonlinear dynamical systems. The challenges involved are significant; the nonlinear control-theoretic issues involved in planning and executing experiments routinely stymie human experts. First, PRET must autonomously manipulate a control parameter in order to analyze the system and find behaviorally distinct regimes. Then, it must use knowledge about the behavior and the regime boundaries to reason about what experiments are useful and possible. Finally, PRET must use this information to perform the experiments and analyze the results.

The *qualitative state/parameter-space* representation described in this paper solves some of the problems that arise in phase-portrait analysis of complex systems by combining a state/parameter-space representation with the qualitative abstraction of cell dynamics. This QS/P-space representation, wherein a system's dynamics are classified into discrete regions of qualitatively identical behavior, supports a set of reasoning tactics, collectively termed *qualitative bifurcation analysis*, which allows PRET to reason about multiple sets of observations over a given system.

PRET's sensor-related reasoning is essentially complete, but its reasoning about the relationship between models and excitation sources — as well as final design decisions about how to treat actuator knowledge in an explicit way — are still under development. PRET currently uses very little domain knowledge about its target systems; instead, it relies upon *general* mathematics and physics — principles that are broadly applicable and supported by a well-developed, highly formalized body of mathematical knowledge that applies in *any domain*. The point of this decision was to make PRET easily extensible to other domains; because of this choice, refitting PRET for some new domain is simply a matter of a few lines of Scheme code. However, as we extend PRET into more network-oriented domains, such as electrical circuits, we are discovering that effective use of domain theory may be critical to streamlining PRET's generate phase[9]. A network-oriented modeling approach will also help PRET reason about actuators in a more-intelligent fashion, as the actuator itself, with its various, non-ideal properties, may be represented directly as part of the network. For example, a sinusoidal current source often has an associate impedance that creates a loading effect on the rest of an electrical circuit. With a network approach, these effects naturally become part of the model — just as they do in real systems.

Acknowledgments

Apollo Hogan, Joe Iwanski, Brian LaMacchia, and Reinhard Stolle also contributed code and/or ideas to this project.

References

[1] H. Abarbanel. *Analysis of Observed Chaotic Data*. Springer, 1995.

[2] E. Bradley. Autonomous exploration and control of chaotic systems. *Cybernetics and Systems*, 26:299–319, 1995.

[3] E. Bradley and M. Easley. Reasoning about sensor data for automated system identification. *Intelligent Data Analysis*, 2(2), 1998.

[4] E. Bradley, A. O'Gallagher, and J. Rogers. Global solutions for nonlinear systems using qualitative reasoning. *Annals of Mathematics and Artificial Intelligence*, 23:211–228, 1998.

[5] E. Bradley and R. Stolle. Automatic construction of accurate models of physical systems. *Annals of Mathematics and Artificial Intelligence*, 17:1–28, 1996.

[6] M. S. Branicky, V. S. Borkar, and S. K. Mitter. A unified framework for hybrid control. In *Proceedings of the 33rd IEEE Conference on Decision & Control*, pages 4228–4234, December 1994. Lake Buena Vista, FL.

[7] A. C. Capelo, L. Ironi, and S. Tentoni. Automated mathematical modeling from experimental data: An application to material science. *IEEE Transactions on Systems, Man and Cybernetics - Part C*, 28(3):356–370, 1998.

[8] J. de Kleer and J. S. Brown. A qualitative physics based on confluences. *Artificial Intelligence*, 24:7–83, 1984.

[9] M. Easley and E. Bradley. Generalized physical networks for automated model building. In *Proceedings of IJCAI-99*, 1999. To appear.

[10] A. Famili, W.-M. Shen, R. Weber, and E. Simoudis. Data preprocessing and intelligent data analysis. *Intelligent Data Analysis*, 1(1), 1997.

[11] K. D. Forbus. Interpreting observations of physical systems. *IEEE Transactions on Systems, Man, and Cybernetics*, 17(3):350–359, 1987.

[12] K. D. Forbus. Qualitative reasoning. In J. A. Tucker, editor, *CRC Computer Science and Engineering Handbook*. CRC Press, Boca Raton, FL, 1997.

[13] R. Haber and H. Unbehauen. Structural identification of nonlinear dynamic systems — A survey on input/output approaches. *Automatica*, 26(4):651–677, 1990.

[14] C. S. Hsu. *Cell-to-Cell Mapping*. Springer, New York, 1987.

[15] J.-N. Juang. *Applied System Identification*. Prentice Hall, Englewood Cliffs, 1994.

[16] B. J. Kuipers. Qualitative simulation. *Artificial Intelligence*, 29(3):289–338, 1986.

[17] B. C. Kuo. *Automatic Control Systems*. Prentice Hall, seventh edition, 1995.

[18] R. Stolle. *Integrated Multimodal Reasoning for Modeling of Physical Systems*. PhD thesis, University of Colorado at Boulder, 1998.

[19] R. Stolle and E. Bradley. A customized logic paradigm for reasoning about models. In *Proceedings of the QR-96*, 1996.

[20] R. Stolle and E. Bradley. Multimodal reasoning for automatic model construction. In *Proceedings of AAAI-98*, pages 181–188, July 1998. Madison, WI.

[21] K. Yip. *KAM: A System for Intelligently Guiding Numerical Experimentation by Computer*. Artificial Intelligence Series. MIT Press, 1991.

[22] F. Zhao. Computational dynamics: Modeling and visualizing trajectory flows in phase space. *Annals of Mathematics and Artificial Intelligence*, 8:285–300, 1993.

Undoing Statistical Advice

Russell Almond

Educational Testing Service
Research Statistics Group, 15-T, Princeton, NJ 08541, USA
almond@acm.org

Abstract. Statistical advisors are small pieces of code that are run in response to user actions which provide statistical support for the user, especially users who lack statistical sophistication. These could provide advice in the form of a message, or could automatically perform supplemental actions which change the model according to the advice. However, when the original action is undone, the supplemental actions need to be undone as well. This paper describes an implementation of an intelligent advisory system, NAEPVUE, for analyzing data from the National Assessment of Educational Progress (NAEP). NAEPVUE uses an object-oriented data dictionary for storing statistical advisors. Built in the Amulet user interface development environment, NAEPVUE is able to take advantage of the Myers and Kosbie hierarchical undo model to undo the actions of statistical advisors.

1   Rationale

Many diverse types of expertise are need to analyze a large complex data set. These include: (1) expertise in the scientific domain, (2) an understanding of how the data were collected and what the variables represent, (3) an understanding of the statistical methods used in the analysis and (4) an understanding of how the data are stored and how to extract a meaningful subset for analysis. It is rare to find all of those types of expertise embodied in one person. A statistical advisory system can help by allowing one person to transfer some of their expertise to the analyst. This is particularly true in the case of large government surveys, where the primary analysts can transfer expertise to secondary users through the advisory system.

Consider the National Assessment for Educational Progress (NAEP) – a comprehensive, ongoing study of multiple aspects of educational achievement of United States 4th, 8th and 11th grade students. The data for one grade level of the 1996 survey contains 998 variables, including cognative measurement on the students and background variables on students, teachers, classrooms and schools, taken for 121,000 individuals. To achieve high accuracy estimates of small subpopulations, NAEP employs a complex multi-staged sampling design using both stratification and clustering. To minimize the burden on individual students, items are administered in balanced incomplete blocks which create complex patterns of missing data; to compensate, the public use data tapes provide multiple

D.J. Hand, J.N. Kok, M.R. Berthold (Eds.): IDA'99, LNCS 1642, pp. 357–367, 1999.
© Springer-Verlag Berlin Heidelberg 1999

plausible values for the proficiency variables. To analyze NAEP data, a researcher must be familiar not only with educational policy issues, but also with multilevel models, weighted analysis and multiple imputation techniques, not to mention the meaning of the NAEP background and scale variables. Statistical advisory systems can help secondary analysts by suppling just-in-time advice to suplement the analysts expertise.

NAEPVUE (Sect. 2) is a prototype advisory system for NAEP. Written in Amulet (Myers et al., 1996), it provides a graphical front end to the process of selecting a set of NAEP variable for analysis. Analysts specify models by dragging icons representing variables around on the screen. The placement of the variables on the screen indicates the intended role of the variable in the analysis. NAEPVUE contains a complex data encyclopedia which records information about the variables in a hierarchical taxonomy of variable types. Statistical advisors can be attached to any level of this hierarchy.

Statistical advisors are small pieces of code which run in response to user actions which change the specifications of a model. They can provide advice about possible problems with the model, and recommend or automatically apply changes in the model for statistical reasons. For example, an advisor might suggest a transformation, or automatically select the proper weights based on the response variable. Section 3 describes the NAEPVUE advisory system.

Advisors which change the model present a problem if the user interface supports an undo operation. When a change to the model is undone, the corresponding advise must be undone as well. NAEPVUE can take advantage of the Myers and Kosbie (1996) hierarchical command objects implemented in Amulet to group the action of the advisors with the commands which triggered them. This provides a natural mechanism for undoing the statistical advise. Section 4 describes this in greater details. Section 5 outlines some alternative strategies.

2   NAEPVUE Overview

In order to analyze the NAEP data, researchers must understand a variety of technical issues detailed in the NAEP Technical Reports (O'Reilly et al., 1996). This is a large volume and finding the information can be a daunting task. The NAEPEX program (Rogers, 1995) provides assistance in locating the data on the CD-ROM distribution, but it only provides limited (40 character) description of the variables.

While trying to analyze and interpret the results of NAEP, the analyst's focus is not on the educational policy issues, but on the statistical issues presentd by the NAEP data. Ideally, the focus of the analyst should be on the scientific problem which led to gather and analyze the data; statistical issues should be a secondary concern.

An alternative suggested by Anglin and Oldford (1994) is to focus on the model (and the data) as a vehicle for user interaction. NAEPVUE is one realization of this approach. In NAEPVUE, analysts graphically specify their model by dragging variable icons on a model specification dialog (Fig. 1). This dialog

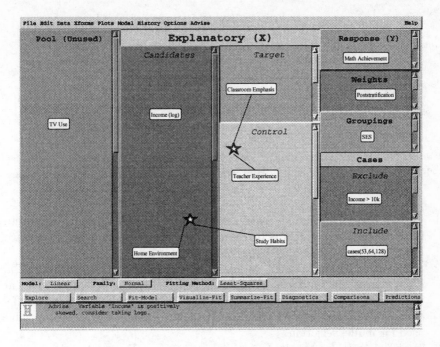

Fig. 1. NAEPVUE Model Specifier Screen

is motivated by the graphical model representation of statistical models (Whittaker, 1990). Section 2.1 describes the main features of the NAEPVUE dialog.

NAEPVUE also employs a data encyclopedia to store metadata about the NAEP variables. This provides rapid (and searchable) access to information about the collection and interpretation of NAEP variables which previously required going back to user manuals or questionnaires. The data encyclopedia is a hierarchical knowledge representation system which allows statistical properties and advice to be attached on any level of the hierarchy. Section 2.2 describes the variable type hierarchy; Section 3 describes the advice system.

2.1 Model Specifier

Figure 1 shows the NAEPVUE model specifier screen from the initial prototype. The central model display is the heart of the NAEPVUE system. It allows the user to specify which variables are to be included in the model and provides a "picture" of the current statistical model under consideration. By focusing on the model instead of the analysis procedure, NAEPVUE promotes this higher level thinking which is closer to the educational policy issues of the analysis.

The model field is divided into four columns. Several of the columns are subdivided into smaller areas. Each of these areas defines a role for the variable. The roles are as follows:

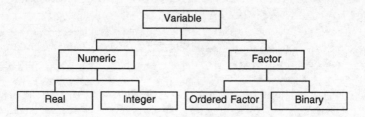

Fig. 2. Top level of Variable Hierarchy. Figures 3 and 4 show lower levels.

1. *Pool* variables have not yet been assigned a role. When a variable is selected from the data encyclopedia or created through transformation, it is placed in the pool until the analyst specifies a role for it.
2. *Explanatory* or independent variables are divided into three subroles: *Target* variables are the focus of scientific interest, while *control* variables are included in the model to reduce variance. These variables are treated differently in graphical displays. *Candidate* variables are possible control variables used for model selection.
3. *Response* variables are the target of measurement. Frequently, these will be the NAEP scores, although other derived scores could be used.
4. *Weight* The weighting variable is filled in with the sampling weight appropriate for the given response variable.
5. *Group* The group variable specifies subpopulations on which to perform parallel analyses; tabulating the results by group.
6. *Cases* Certain cases (or individuals with certain properties) can be *excluded* from the model or *included* in the model by putting appropriate indicator variables in the cases area.

Interactions among the variables can also be manipulated through the model display. An interaction is displayed with a star icon, linked to the constituent variables. As the NAEPVUE data dictionary keeps track of nesting relationships, interactions which should be represented as nestings are automatically treated that way.

Finally, the option buttons below provide the form of the model. In most cases, default values are computed by NAEPVUE. The analyst only needs to worry about these if they wish to override the default values.

2.2   Variable Type Hierarchy

The variable icons in the model display represent more than columns of numbers, they point to rich objects containing both data and metadata. In NAEPVUE, variables are represented as objects within an *ontology* (Gruber, 1991). Important information about a variable, such as the survey question, which level it was collected on, and the primary analyst's notes about the variable are attached as properties of the variable. The variables are part of an object hierarchy relationship, similar to the one described in Almond, Mislevy and Steinberg (1997). This allows the primary analysts to attach "advisor" operators at high level abstract variable types which are inherited by instances of that type. For example, an advisor which suggests square root transformations could be attached to the variable class "count" and would be inherited by all variables representing counts. Hand (1993) suggests other variable type based statistical advice and Roth et al. (1994) suggest selecting visualizations based on the variable types. Mosteller and Tukey (1977, Chap. 5) give some general advice on transformations based on the type of the variable.

Variable type hierarchies aren't new, there are many programs which can now take advantage of the most basic of types such as real or integer vs ordered or unordered factor. For example, both the New S program (Chambers and Hastie, 1992) and the program JMP (SAS Institute) choose the model and fitting procedure based on the type of the predictor variables and on the type of the response. This simple use of functional polymorphism (dispatching the function on the types of the arguments) reduces the program specific knowledge needed by the use to operate the program. The user learns a single syntax for the single fit model command instead of separate commands for each model type (whether accessible via command line or menu, this is a large reduction in user memory requirements).

However, this simple dispatching only scratches the surface of what can be done with a full variable hierarchy. Figure 2 shows the top level of the NAEPVUE heirarchy. Figure 3 shows the NAEPVUE hierarchy for the factor variables. Many NAEP background questions are similar, for example "How often do you ...." NAEPVUE creates abstract variable types for such similar questions which allows all related variables to share the same default attributes. Figure 4 shows the details for numeric meric variables.

3   Statistical Advisors

Statistical advice given by NAEPVUE needs to be sensitive to what has already been specified about the model. This is accomplished by a series of "Agents"— small pieces of code which are run after each user command. The agent can have one of two results:

1. It can deliver a message to be displayed. For example, it could display a message informing the user that a teacher level variable is unsuitable for selection as a response.
2. It can deliver a follow-on command object to be executed. For example, this mechanism can be used to select the appropriate model type and weights in response to the selection of a response variable.

The list of agents appropriate to a situation is computed dynamically. In particular, agents appropriate to a given situation are attached to variables. When

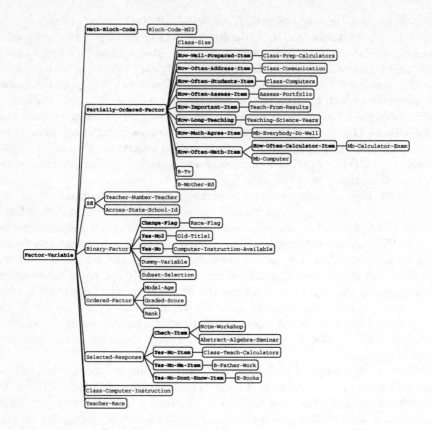

Fig. 3. Variable Hierarchy for Factor Types. Variables lower in the hierarchy inherit default values of attributes and statistical advisors from variables higher in the hierarchy. Another part of the type hierarchy (not shown) contains real and integer valued numeric variables.

agent processing is triggered, NAEPVUE searches the variable type hierarchy looking for all agents attached to this variable or its parents in the hierarchy. Variables can also override agents specified higher in the hierarchy by indicating that they should not be run.

3.1 Need for Advice

Even an analyst with a strong statistical background can use assistance with the NAEP data. Several examples will illustrate the features.

A whole class of issues revolves around tracking the level of analysis of the variables. NAEP cognative variables are collected at the student level and aggregated at the school, state and region levels. NAEP background variables are collected at the student, school and state level, as well as some non-sampling

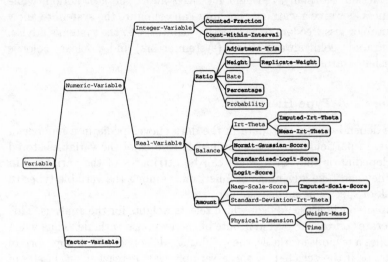

Fig. 4. Variable Hierarchy for Numeric Types

levels such as teacher and classroom. Because teachers are not sampled with equal weights, the teacher level responses are inappropriate for anything but crude exploratory research. As the level of the variable is one of the attributes tracked in the NAEPVUE data encyclopedia, NAEPVUE can do a lot of the bookkeeping about the levels of the variables.

A closely related set of issues revolve around the required sampling weights. In general, the proper set of weights will depend on both the level of response variable (student, school or state) and what the target population of inference will be (i.e., do you apply poststratification). Here, preparing a menu of weights appropriate for each level as well as tracking which jackknife replicates are appropriate for variance calculations is a big help.

3.2   Advisor Feedback

For advice to be truly useful, the analyst must know not only what was done, but why. For this reason, all of the advisors have a common user feedback mechanism. At the bottom of the main screen is a small area for displaying alert messages. A message consists of three parts: (1) A "traffic light" which indicates its severity. (2) The text of the message. (3) An optional help reference which provides a link to on-line information about the nature of the problem or advice offered by the system. The messages are stored in a queue so that the user can scroll backwards through previous messages.

Both immediate commands and advisory agents return messages. The message color indicates how it will be displayed and whether or not to abort the user selected action. Normally, red light messages abort the user action, while yellow light messages give a warning. The user can configure the system to allow themselves more or less freedom to take actions contrary to the system's advise. A special "infrared" color always aborts (system errors) and a "clear" color is used for transient status messages.

3.3   Advisors and Type Hierarchy

The advisors depend on the metadata in the data encyclopedia in a number of different ways. In particular, advisors can use attributes of the variables stored in the encyclopedia, or they themselves can be attributes of the variables. In either case, they can take advantage of inheritance among the variable types to make the task of specifying advice simpler.

For example, consider the advisor which selects weights for the analysis. This primarily operates off of the level attribute of the response variable. Thus when the user specifies a response variable, the weighting advisor selects an appropriate set of weights, or if the selected response variable was at teacher or classroom level, issues a warning that no appropriate responses are available. As the level attribute is copied when a variable is transformed, the weight selection advisor can select an appropriate weight as well.

Any time NAEPVUE performs any action for which there may be advisors, it walks up the variable type hierarchy looking for advisors which are appropriate to the context. Consider the problem of creating a context sensitive menu of candidate transformations for a variable. Possible transformations can be attached at any level of the variable hierarchy. When building the list of candidates, the transformation advisor walks up that hierarchy, gathering candidate transformations.

4   Undo

In the Amulet user interface environment, user manipulations of the interface produce command objects. A command object contains three "Methods" or pieces of code which are run on demand. The "Do Method" performs the action requested by the user. The "Undo Method" reverses the effect of the action and the "Redo Method" repeats the action. When the user performs some gesture which triggers a command – for example, pressing a button or selecting a menu item – the appropriate command object is created, filled in with details about the current context and its "Do Method" is activated. If the command processing does not abort, the command object is then placed in the undo queue so it is available for later undo or redo operations.

However, statistical advisors complicate this simple model. After the action of the command is run, the advisors run. These may in turn make changes to the model, for example, automatically adding the appropriate weights when a response variable is selected. If the action triggering the advisor is undone, the advice commands must be undone as well.

Often commands appear in a nested series which in Amulet is called the *Implementation* hierarchy. (Myers and Kosbie, 1996). For example, consider the operation of moving a variable on the model display. If the variable moves into a new region, this causes the variable to change roles. In NAEPVUE, the "Change Role" command object is the *implementation parent* of the "Move Node" command object. The highest object in the implementation hierarchy is the one queued for undo (or one can use a special top level object to prevent the command from being queued for undo). On a redo, all of the commands in the hierarchy are undone (so in the example both the "Change Role" and the "Move Node" command would be undone).

In NAEPVUE advisory agent invocation is an implementation parent of the active command. Command which should invoke the advisory agents are given a special "Invoke Agents" command as their implementation parent. The "Do Method" for this command has the following steps:

1. Build a list of agents to invoke based on the variables currently specified in the model.
2. Execute those agents one at a time.
   (a) If the agent returns a command object, invoke the do method of the command object and put the command into a queue of actions taken with this command.
   (b) If the agent returns a message object, display that message in the alert area. If the severity of the message is sufficiently strong, abort the command. In this case, that means invoking the undo methods of all of the agent commands and well as the undo mechanism of the command which triggered the "Invoke Agents" command.

The undo mechanism of the "Invoke Agents" command simply triggers the undo method for each command in the queue of agent actions recorded in the original invocation. The redo mechanism runs their redo actions.

Example 1. Suppose that the user selects the 'Data Analysis Scale Score' variable and moves it from the "Pool" to the "Response" areas on the screen. This triggers the parent action which sets the role of the variable to 'response;' the parent action of the change role action triggers the advisors. 'Data Analysis Scale Score' is a continuous student level variable which has multiple plausible values. Thus three advisors will run after the selection: Advisor A selects a linear response model, Advisor B selects the student level weights, and Advisor C configures the model for multiple imputations (averaging over multiple runs of the model.)

Example 2. (undo!) If the user later undoes the selection of 'Data Analysis Scale Score' as a response variable, the following actions take place: (a) Advisor A is undone and the model type is changed back to its previous value (cached with the advisor's command object), (b) Advisor B is undone and the student level weights are removed, (c) Advisor C is undone and the multiple imputation flag is cleared, (d) the selection of 'Data Analysis Scale Score' as a response variable is undone, its rule is restored to 'Pool', and (e) the movement of the variables icon is undone and it is returned to its original location in the 'Pool' area.

Example 3. Suppose the user attempts to move the variable "Teacher's Education" into the response area. Suppose further that the system is set up to query the user on warnings. First, the system would move the "Teacher's Education" icon into the response area. Second, the system would set the role of "Teacher's Education" to "response." Third, the advisory agents would be run. Agent A would set the type of the model to Generalized linear model. Agent B would try and find weights, but would discover that there are no appropriate weights for teacher level variables. It would issue a warning. As the user has selected query on warning, she would be offered the possibility of cancelling the action. If she selects cancel, then Agent A would be undone, as would the "Change Role" and "Move Icon" actions.

5   NAEPVUE Experience

One advantage of working in Amulet (Myers et al., 1996) was the command object and undo mechanism. This forced me to consider the issues raised by undo at an early stage. (Retrofitting an undo mechanism onto existing operational software can be very expensive; personal experience.)

In this approach, the statistical advisors essentially log their undo information with the command object which triggered them. Thus, the advice can be undone when the base command is. An alternative strategy it to always call the advisors based on the current model. Thus after an undo, new advisors would respond to the current state of the model, undoing the effect of previous advisors. Both approaches are feasible. As NAEPVUE is still in a prototype stage, it is difficult to judge the success of this approach.

References

1. Anglin DG and Oldford RW (1994): "Modelling Response models in Software." in Cheeseman P and Oldford RW (eds.) *Selecting Models from Data: Artificial Intelligence and Statistics IV*, Springer-Verlag, 413–424.
2. Almond, R.G., R.J. Mislevy and L. Steinberg (1997) "Using Prototype-Instance Hierarchies to model Global Dependence." *AMS Summer Research Conference on Graphical Markov Models, Influence Diagrams, and Bayesian Belief Networks* Seattle, Washington.
3. Chambers, John M. and Hastie, Trevor J. (1992): *Statistical Models in* S. Wadsworth & Brooks/Cole, Pacific Grove, CA.
4. Gruber TR (1991): "The role of common ontology in achieving sharable, reusable knowledge bases." In Allen JA, Fikes R, and Sandewall E (Eds.), *Principles of Knowledge Representation and Reasoning: Proceedings of the Second International Conference,* Morgan Kaufmann, 601–602.
5. Hand DJ (1993): "Measurement scales as metadata", in Hand DJ (ed.) *Artificial Intelligence Frontiers in Statistics: AI and Statistics III.* Chapman and Hall, 54–64.

6. Mosteller, F. and J.W. Tukey (1977): *Data Analysis and Regression*, Addison-Wesley, Reading, Massachusetts.

7. Myers, Brad A., Guise, Dario A., Dannenberg, Roger B., Zanden, Brad Vander, Kosbie, David S., Pevin Ed, Mickish, Andrew, and Marchal, Phillipe (1990): "Comprehensive Support for Graphical, Highly-Interactive User Interfaces: The Garnet User Interface Development Environment." *IEEE Computer* **23**(11), pp 71-85.

8. Myers BA, Ferrency A, McDaniel R, Miller RC, Doane P, Mickish A, Klimovitski A (1996): "The Amulet Reference Manual." Carnegie Mellon School of Computer Science technical report: CMU-CS-95-166. See also, Amulet Home Page: http://www.cs.cmu.edu/~amulet/

9. Myers BA and Kosbie DS (1996): "Reusable Hierarchical Command Objects," *Proceedings CHI'96: Human Factors in Computing Systems*. Addison-Wesley, pp 260-267.

10. O'Reilly, PF, Zelenak, CA, Rogers, AM and Kline, DL (1996): "National Assessment of Educational Progress 1994 Trial State Assessment Program in Reading Secondary-Use Data Files User Guide". National Center for Education Statistics publication.

11. Rogers, AM (1995): "NAEPEX: NAEP Data Extraction Program User Guide." Princeton, NJ: Educational Testing Service.

12. Roth SF, Kolojejchick J, Mattis J and Goldstien J (1994): "Interactive Graphic Design Using Automatic Presentation Knowledge." In *Human Factors in Computing Systems: CHI '94 Conference proceedings*, ACM Press, 112-117.

13. Whittaker J (1990): *Graphical Models in Applied Multivariate Statistics*, Wiley.

A Method for Temporal Knowledge Conversion

Gabriela Guimarães[1] and Alfred Ultsch[2]

[1] CENTRIA, U. Nova de Lisboa, 2825-214 Caparica and
Department of Mathematics, Universidade de Évora, Portugal
guimas@dmat.uevora.pt
http://kholosso.di.fct.unl.pt/~di/centria/
[2] Department of Mathematics and Computer Science
Philipps University of Marburg, D-35032 Marburg, Germany
ultsch@mathematik.uni-marburg.de
http://www.mathematik.uni-marburg.de/~ultsch/

Abstract. In this paper we present a new method for temporal knowledge conversion, called TCon. The main aim of our approach is to perform a transition, i.e. conversion, of temporal complex patterns in multivariate time series to a linguistic, for human beings understandable description of the patterns. The main idea for the detection of those complex patterns lies in breaking down a highly structured and complex problem into several subtasks. Therefore, several abstraction levels have been introduced where at each level temporal complex patterns are detected successively using exploratory methods, namely unsupervised neural networks together with special visualization techniques. At each level, temporal grammatical rules are extracted. The method TCon was applied to a problem from medicine, sleep apnea. It is a hard problem since quite different patterns may occur, even for the same patient, as well as the duration of each pattern may differ strongly. Altogether, all patterns have been detected and a meaningful description of the patterns was generated. Even some kind of "new" knowledge was found.

1 Introduction

In recent years there has been an increasing development towards more powerfull computers, such that nowadays a great amount of data from, for example, industrial processes or medical applications, is gathered. These measured data are often said to be a starting point for an enhanced diagnosis or control of the underlying process. Particularly interesting for handling noisy or inconsistent data are artificial neural networks (ANN). On the other side, systems with traditional artificial intelligence (AI) technologies have been successful in areas like diagnosis, control and planing. The advantages of both technologies are wideranging. However, the limits of these approaches, namely the incapacity of ANN to explain their behaviour and on the other hand, the acquisition of knowledge for AI systems, are important problems to be adressed.

Recently, there has been an increased interest in hybrid systems that integrate AI technologies and ANN to solve this kind of problems [3]. It its worth

D.J. Hand, J.N. Kok, M.R. Berthold (Eds.): IDA'99, LNCS 1642, pp. 369–380, 1999.
© Springer-Verlag Berlin Heidelberg 1999

to remark here that essentially hybrid systems have been developed that entail several modules, each implemented in a different technology, and that cooperate with another. In contrast, we are mainly interested in hybrid systems that perform a *knowledge conversion*, i.e. a transition between distinct knowledge representation forms [16]. A *symbolic knowledge representation* of a subject should always be in a linguistic, for human beings understandable form. Examples for linguistic representation forms are natural languages, as German or English, but also predicate logic, mathematical calculus, etc. In contrast, a *subsymbolic knowledge representation* always entails numerous elements as, for example, data points from a time series or neurons and weights in ANN that cooperate in a shared and distributed representation of a symbol.

Previous approaches that realize a knowledge conversion [13], [14], [15], [19] do not consider data with temporal dependences. Temporal knowledge conversion always assumes the existence of temporal data, i.e. time series sampled from signals that describe some process. All sampled values are a temporal subsymbolic knowledge representation of the time series. A *temporal knowledge conversion* is an, eventually, successive conversion of multivariate time series or temporal complex patterns in time series to a linguistic, for human beings understandable representation of the time series, i.e. a temporal symbolic knowledge representation [4].

In this paper, we will introduce a new method that enables a temporal knowledge conversion, called TCon [4]. In order to handle this complex problem, several abstraction levels have been introduced. We applied our method TCon to sleep apnea, namely sleep-related breathing disorders (SRBD). SRBD claim to be a very hard problem since quite different patterns for the same temporal pattern may occur, even for the same patient, and the duration of each temporal pattern may differ strongly, as well [11], [12].

2   A Method for Temporal Knowledge Conversion

The method TCon enables a conversion from temporal complex patterns (TCP) in multivariate time series to a linguistic, for human beings understandable temporal symbolic representation in form of temporal grammatical rules (see Fig. 1). The main idea for the detection of TCP in multivariate time series lies in breaking down a highly structured and complex problem into several subproblems. The advantage of such a strategy is the resolution of this highly complex problem into several subtasks, now solvable at a more technical level. Therefore, several abstraction levels have been introduced where at each level TCP are detected successively using exploratory methods, namely unsupervised neural networks [8]. The detection process starts with the identification of primitive patterns, i.e. elementary structures in time series. At the following levels, the time dimension will be introduced smoothly in the detection process until the identification of TCP at the last abstraction level is completed.

At the different abstraction levels temporal grammatical rules are generated for a linguistic description of all TCP. The advantage of a temporal symbolic

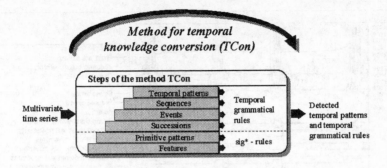

Fig. 1. Abstraction levels and steps of the method Tcon in [4]

knowledge representation in form of temporal grammatical rules is not only the acquisition of a for human beings apropriate representation of the TCP, but also the generation of a knowledge representation form that can be processed by a machine engine, like a prolog interpreter. In order to achieve both, the detection of TCP as well as their description at a symbolic level, we suggest a temporal knowledge conversion. Next, we will introduce the different abstraction levels of TCon and give an overview of the tasks.

Multivariate time series gathered from observed signals of complex processes, as they occur in industrial processes or in medicine, are the input of TCon. We generate a multivariate time series by sampling the observed values at equal time intervals. The result of the method TCon are the detected TCP as well as a grammatical description of the TCP at different abstraction levels.

For example, consider a patient with sleep apnea, namely sleep-related breathing disorders (SRBD), where different types of signals, concerning respiratory flow, i.e. 'airflow', and respiratory effort, are registered during one night [12]. The respiratory effort comprises 'chest wall and abdominal wall movements'. Furthermore, 'snoring' as well as 'oxygen saturation' are considered for the identification of SRBD. Fig. 2 shows such a registration for a short time period. All time series are sampled at 25 Hz. In this paper, we use this example from medicine to illustrate our method.

2.1 Feature Extraction and Preprocessing

First, an extraction of the main features for all time series is advisable, or even a prerequesite for further processing. Therefore, methods, for instance, from statistics or signal processing are applied to time series in order to find a suitable representation. This process usually includes a pre-processing of the time series such that a clustering with unsupervised neural networks becomes possible. However, for most practical applications the choice of an adequate preprocessing will be one of the most significant factors in determining the final performance of the system [2]. An improvement of the whole performance may be achieved by incorporating prior knowledge, which might be used for the extraction of the features.

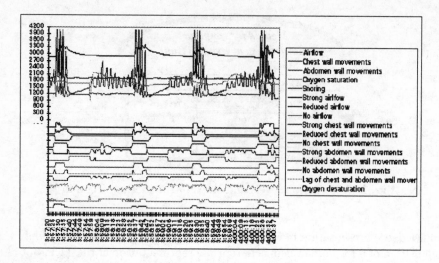

Fig. 2. Small excerpt of multivariate time series and resp. features from a patient with SRBD

For each aplication the feature extraction process may differ strongly. Therefore, we will not focus on this issue in this paper. For a detailed description of the feature extraction see [4]. Nevertheless, it is worth to mention that we considered criteria from the application that usually are applied in sleep laboratories for the identification of SRBD [11].

As multimodal distributions occured in the data for each time series, namely *'airflow'*, *'chest wall movements'* and *'abdominal wall movement'*, fuzzy membership functions for *'no'*, *'reduced'* and *'strong'* averaged amplitude changes have been deduced from histograms. Additionaly, lags between *'chest wall movements'* and *'abdomen wall movements'* may occur that have a high significance for the identification of the SRBD. Therefore, crosscorrelations between *'chest and abdomen wall movements'* have been calculated. Besides, a rescaling of *'snoring'* was performed. As oxygen saturation is not relevant for the pattern detection process, we just will consider the ocurrence of a decay from at least 4% of the oxygen saturation for the past 10 sec. Altogether, twelve features named as *'strong airflow'* $\in [0,1]$, *'reduced airflow'* $\in [0,1]$, *'no airflow'* $\in [0,1]$, *'strong chest wall movements'* $\in [0,1]$, *'reduced chest wall movements'* $\in [0,1]$, *'no chest wall movements'* $\in [0,1]$, *'strong abdomen wall movements'* $\in [0,1]$, *'reduced abdomen wall movements'* $\in [0,1]$, *'no abdomen wall movements'* $\in [0,1]$, *'lag of chest and abdomen wall movements'* $\in [-1,1]$, *'snoring intensity'* $\in [0,1]$ and *'oxygen desaturation'* $\in \{0,0.5,1\}$ have been extracted (see Fig. 2).

2.2 Primitive Patterns

At this level, primitive patterns, i.e. elementary structures in the time series, will be determined from the extracted features. Therefore, we propose to use

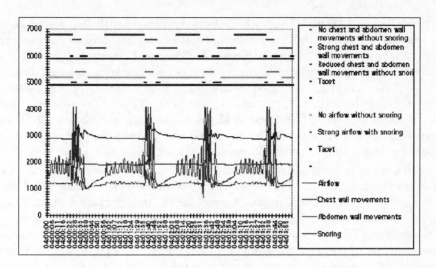

Fig. 3. Multivariate time series and resp. primitive patterns/succession from a patient with SRBD

exploratory methods, in particular, self-organized neural networks (SONN) as proposed by Kohonen [8]. In the last years, SONN enhanced with a special visualization technique, called U-Matrix [18] , have been successfully applied to a wide-ranging number of applications where a clustering of high-dimensional data was afforded [6], [7], [13], [14], [15], [19].

For the detection of primitive patterns several features have to be selected in order to start the learning process. This means, that we have to identify those features that have a lot in common with regard to criteria from the application. But this also means, that several SONN will be learned to detect primitive patterns from different feature selections. We emphasize that one feature may appear in different feature selections. After the learning process and the identification of the clusters using U-Matrices, we are able to determine the primitive patterns. There may appear regions on the U-Matrix that do not correspond to a specific cluster. These regions are regarded as some kind of interruptions, named as tacets. All the other regions are associated to a primitive pattern. Each example is only associated to one class, a primitive pattern class or the tacet class. As a consequence, we now are able to classify the whole time series with primitive patterns and tacets (see Fig. 3). Successions of primitive patterns from one U-Matrix will be called primitive pattern channel.

Without a proper interpretation of the detected structures no meaningful names can be given to the primitive patterns. As a consequence, we cannot generate for human beings understandable temporal grammatical rules at the next higher levels. In order to achieve a meaningful description for primitive patterns, we propose to use machine learning algorithms. For the first time, the rule generation algorithm called sig* [17], was used to generate rules for data in a temporal context. This sig* algorithm selects significant attributes for each class, in this case significant features for each primitive pattern, in order to construct appropriate conditions that characterize each class and generates differentiating rules that distinguish classes from each other, as well. It takes a classified data set in a high-dimensional space as input and produces descriptions of the classes in the form of decision rules. In particular, the generated rules take the significance of the different structural properties of the classes into account. If only a few properties account for most of the cases of a class, the rules are kept very simple. There are two main problems addressed by the sig* algorithm [17].

First, we have to decide which attributes of the data are significant in order to characterize each class. Therefore, each attribute of a class is associated with a "significance value" that can be obtained, for example, by means of statistical measures. In order to define the most significant attributes for the description of a class, the significance values of the attributes are normalized in percentage of the total sum of significance values of a class and sorted in a decreasing order. The attributes with the largest significance value in the ordered sequence are taken until the cumulative percentage equals or exceeds a given threshold value.

Second, we have to formulize apt conditions for each selected significant attribute. For this problem we can use the distribution properties of the attributes of a class. Assuming a normal distribution for a certain attribute, this means that 95% of the attribute values are captured in the limits [mean -2*dev ,mean +2*dev], where dev is the value of the standard deviation of the attribute.

Until now, we just described the part of the sig* algorithm that produces characterizing rules. If the intersection of two classes is nonempty, an additional description of the intersection between the two overlapping classes is necessary. Therefore, we add to the characterizing rule of each class a condition that will be tested by another rule, called differentiating rule. These rules are generated in analogy to the characterizing rules. The significance values, however, are measured between both classes in consideration.

As our main aim is a generation of a meaningful description of the primitive patterns using sig* rules, we just considered characterinzing rules. Of course, both, characterizing and differentiation rules, have been generated. Example 1 shows sig* rules for two primitive patterns from different feature selections. We emphasize that the complexity of each characterizing rule differs a lot, i.e. the number of features characterizing a primitive pattern, since the significance of each feature for each primitive pattern differs. In our case, the conditions for each selected significant feature have a meaning related to the occurence of the feature for the resp. primitive pattern. Values nearby zero mean that this feature will probably not occur, since zero means "no occurence". Values nearby one mean that this feature will occur with a high probability and, therefore, will be used for the generation of a name of a given primitive pattern. This is due to the feature extraction process, where mainly fuzzy functions have been used. For details see [4].

Example 1. Consider the primitive patterns 'A2' and 'B3' that have been detected from different U-Matrices. The following sig* rules have been generated:

```
A primitive pattern is a 'A2'
  if
          'no airflow' in [0.951, 1]
    and
          'reduced airflow' = 0
    and
          'snoring intensity' in [0, 0.241]

A primitive pattern is a 'B3'
  if
          'no chest wall movements' in [0.772, 1]
    and
          'no abdomen wall move-ments' in [0.641, 1]
    and
          'reduced chest wall movements' = 0
    and
          'snoring intensity' = 0
```

Values nearby one mean that this feature occurs with a high probabilty, while values nearby zero mean that this feature probably will not occur.

As the sig* algorithm generates rules with the most significant features for each primitive pattern, the naming of the primitive patterns is straightforward. The primitive pattern 'A2' was named as 'no airflow without snoring' and 'B3' named as 'no chest and abdomen wall movements without snoring'. The names of the primitive patterns have been generated semi-automatically, as they correspond directly to the automatically generated sig* rules. We will see later that they are of crucial importance for the generation of meaningful grammatical rules at the next higher levels. Just now we are able to generate meaningful rules understandable for human beings as domain experts.

2.3   Successions

At this level, we introduce the dimension time where succeeding identical primitive patterns are regarded as a succession (see Fig. 3). Each succession has a correspondend primitive pattern type. The main diference lies in the fact that a succession additionaly has a start and end point and, consequently, a duration. Successions may be identified by trajectories visualized on U-Matrices. We will not focus on this issue in this paper.

A consequence of several feature selections is that several SONN will be learned and, therefore, several U-Matrices will be generated. This means that two or more successions may occur more or less simultaneously. Two overlapping successions are said to occur more or less simultaneously, if and only if the deviation between their start and end points is small enough, i.e. very small.

2.4   Events

At this level, more or less simultaneous successions are joined together to a new unity, called event. In order to focus on the most significant events, we distinguish between events that occur very frequently and those that occur less frequently. Rare events are omitted in the sense that they are regarded as interruptions. These will be named as event tacets. The idea is to select the most frequent events as the most significant events. Then, less frequent events can be associated to them. Similarities among the successions have been considered to join different types of more or less simultaneous successions, i.e. frequent and less frequent events [4]. This means that the number of events will be extremely reduced and that one event consists of different types of more or less simultaneous successions, i.e frequent and less frequent events, as well.

As a consequence, at this abstraction level temporal grammatical rules not only entail a *"more or less simultaneous"* but also an *"or"* for the description of alternations between more or less frequent events. Let us consider the example of the patient with SRBD. In this case, three events have been detected (see Fig. 4). Names of events can be derived straightforward from the generated grammatical rules, as the names for primitive patterns, i.e. successions, are already known (see Example 2). For a detailed description of the whole detection process and generation of the grammatical rules for the events see [4].

Example 2. The following grammatical rules have been generated for *'Event1'* and *'Event3'*:

```
An event is a 'Event1'
  if
            'no airflow without snoring'
       is more or less simultaneous
            ('no chest and abdomen wall movements
               without snoring'
         and
             'tacets')


An event is a 'Event3'
  if
            ('strong airflow with snoring'
         and
             'reduced airflow with snoring'
         and
             'tacets')
       is more or less simultaneous
            'strong chest and abdomen wall movements'
```

The ocurrence of tacets in the rules means that small interruptions in successions may occur or that a succession, for example, from one primitve pattern channel occurs simultaneously with irrelevant information at the other channel. A name of an event contains essentially names of the most frequently ocurring

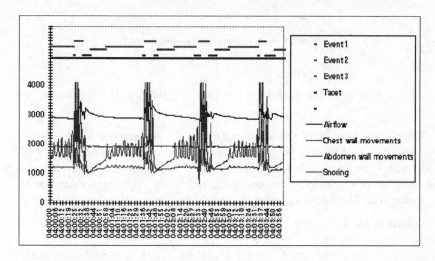

Fig. 4. Multivariate time series and resp. events from a patient with SRBD

successions. Names of rarely occuring successions may be dismissed, since the idea of temporal knowledge conversion also entails an information reduction for the generation of well-understandable rules. If needed, details may then be consulted at lower abstraction levels. The following names have been derived from the rules:

- *'Event1'*: *'no airflow and no chest and abdomen wall movements without snoring'*
- *'Event2'*: *'no airflow and reduced chest wall movements and no abdomen wall movements without snoring'*
- *'Event3'*: *'strong breathing with snoring'*

2.5   Sequences

At a symbolic representation level, an event may be interpreted as a symbol in a temporal context that cannot be further decomposed. Then, at this abstraction level a multivariate time series can be represented as a sequence of symbols, i.e. events. In order to be able to detect TCP in multivariate time series, we just have to identify repeated subsequences of events. The main problem lies in the identification of start and end events, in particular, when dealing with time series that entail several and distinct TCP. Therefore, we builded a probabilistic automat as well as considered delays between the ocurrence of two different events (see [4]).

A sequence of events together with the multivariate time series from the patient with SRBD is illustrated in (see Fig. 4). For this SRBD we identified the following sequence (see Fig. 5) where *'Event2'* follows immediately after *'Event1'* and *'Event3'* follows *'Event2'* after a small interruption.

Fig. 5. A detected sequence from the patient with SRBD

For the generation of the grammatical rules we introduced at this level a "*followed by*" and "*followed after*" interval "*by*". As a sequence always occurs more than once in a multivariate time series, lower und upper boundaries for the duration of the events and sequences may be specified (see Example 3).

Example 3 The following gramatical rule has been generated for '*Sequence1*'

```
A sequence is a 'Sequence1' in [40 sec, 64 sec]
  if
            'Event1': 'no airflow and no chest and abdomen wall
              movements without snoring' in [13 sec, 18 sec]
      followed by
            'Event2': 'no airflow and reduced chest and no abdomen
              wall movements without snoring' in [20 sec, 39 sec]
      followed after [0,5 sec, 5 sec] by
            'Event3': 'strong breathing with snoring'
              in [6 sec, 12 sec]
```

Related approaches that have been used for the generation of grammars from time series usually just consider one time series, as for example ECG´s [9], carotide pulse waves [1] and eye movements [5]. Furthermore, the main structures of the time series are usually known a priori as, for example, PQ segments or QRS complexes of an ECG signal. This means that no exploratory methods are needed for the detection of elementary structures in time series. In contrast, we not only generate grammatical rules from multivariate time series, but also use exploratory methods like unsupervised neural networks for the detection of the main structures in the time series, i.e. primitive patterns.

2.6 Temporal Patterns

Finally, similar sequences will be joined together to a temporal pattern. Therefore, similarities between ocurring events in the sequences as well as the duration of the events have been considered [4]. As the example of the patient with SRBD just contains one sequence, the temporal pattern also just has one sequence. Otherwise, the temporal pattern would be described by an alternation of sequences using an "*or*".

3 Conclusion

Recently, different kinds of hybrid systems that integrate AI technologies and neural networks have been developed [3]. We emphasize that mainly "cooperative" hybrid systems have been developed, i.e. a cooperation between several modules implemented in different technologies exists. The main difference to our approach is that in cooperative hybrid system no transition between different knowledge representation form takes place [16]. The hybrid system WINA [10] is an example for a hybrid system where a knowledge conversion for high dimensional data can be performed. This work was the starting point for the recently developed method for temporal knowledge conversion (TCon) [4].

The main issue of the present paper was to give a brief description of the different abstraction levels introduced by the method TCon. This approach enables a successively and, even, smoothly conversion of temporal complex patterns in multivariate time series to a linguistic, for human beings understandable temporal symbolic knowledge representation in form of temporal grammatical rules. In order to detect elementary structures in the time series, self-organized neural networks, as proposed by Kohonen [8], together with special visualization techniques, called U-Matrices [18], have been used. The realization of the tasks at each level as well as the generation of the temporal grammatical rules was illustrated through an example from medicine, namely sleep-related breathing disorders (SRBD) [12]. SRBD claim to be a very hard problem since quite different patterns for the same temporal patterns may occur, even for one patient. Additionally, the duration of each temporal pattern can differ a lot.

For a lack of space we could just give an overview of the method and present a small example of our experiments with SRBD. We used a much larger data base with the most significant, i.e. most frequently ocurring, SRBD. For details see [4]. Altogether, we detected all temporal patterns with our method TCON and were able to give a, for an expert of SRBD, meaningful description of the temporal patterns with the temporal grammatical rules. Additionally, some kind of "new" knowledge for one temporal pattern, i.e. some not yet well-described SRBD in medicine, have been found.

Acknowledgements

We thank Prof. Dr. J.H. Peter and Dr. T. Penzel, Medizinische Poliklinik, Philipps University of Marburg for making us the data available.

References

1. Bezdek, J.C.: Hybrid modeling in pattern recognition and control. In: Knowledge-Based Systems, Vol. 8, Number 6, Elsevier Science Publisher (1995) 359–371
2. Bishop, C.M.: Neural Networks for Pattern Recognition. Oxford, Clarendon Press, (1995)
3. Goonatilake, S., Khebal, S. (Eds.): Intelligent Hybrid Systems, Wiley & Sons, New York (1995)
4. Guimarães, G.: Eine Methode zur Entdeckung von komplexen Mustern in Zeitreihen mit Neuronalen Netzen and deren Überführung in eine symbolische Wissenrepräsentation. PhD Dissertation, Philipps University of Marburg, Marburg, Germany (1998)

5. Juhola, M: A syntactic Analysis Method for Sinusoidal Tracking Eye Movements. In: Computers and Biomedical Research 24 (1991) 222–233
6. Kaski, S., Kohonen, T.: Exploratory Data Analysis by Self-Organizing Map: Structures of Welfare and Poverty in the World. In: Refenes, A.P.N, Abu-Mostafa, Y., Moody, J., Weigend, A.: Neural Networks in Financial Engineering. Proc. of the Intl. Conf. on Neural Networks in the Capital Markets, London, England, 11-13 October, 1995, Singapore, (1996) 498-507
7. Kohonen, T.: Self-Organizing Maps, Springer Verlag, New York (1995)
8. Kohonen, T.: Self-Organization and Associative Memory. Springer Series in Information Sciences 8, Springer Verlag, New York (1984)
9. Koski, A., Juhola, M., Meriste, M.: Syntactic recognition of ECG signals by attributed finite automata. In: Pattern Recognition, The Journal of the Pattern Recognition Society, Vol. 28, Issue 12, December (1995) 292–297
10. Palm, G., Ultsch, A., Goser, K., Rückert, U.: Knowledge Processing in Neural Architecture. In: VLSI for Neural Networks and Artificial Intelligence, New York (1994) 207-216
11. Penzel, T.: Zur Pathophysiologie der Interaktion von Schlaf, Atmung und Kreislauf - Konzepte der Kardiorespiratorischen Polysomnographie. Habilitationsschrift, Philipps Universität Marburg (1995)
12. Penzel, T., Peter, J.H.: Design of an Ambulatory Sleep Apnea Recorder. In: Nagle, H.T., Tompkins, W.J. (Eds.): Case Studies in Medical Instrument Design, IEEE, New York (1992) 171–179
13. Schweizer, M., Föhn, P., Schweizer, J., Ultsch, A.: A Hybrid Expert System for Avalanche Forecasting. In: Schertler, W., Schmid, B., Tjoa, A.M., Werther, H. Eds.) Informations and Communications Technologies in Tourism, Springer Verlag, Wien (1994) 148–153
14. Ultsch, A., Kleine, T.O, Korus, D., Farsch, S., Guimarães, G.: Pietzuch, w., Simon, J.: Evaluation of Automatic and Manual Knowledge Acquisition for Cerebrospinal Fluid (CSF). In: Keravnu, E. et al. (Eds.): Artificial Intelligence in Medicine, Lecture Notes in Artificial Intelligence 1211, Vol. 934, Springer Verlag (1997) 110–121
15. Ultsch, A., Korus, D., Wehrmann, A.: Neural Networks and their Rules Classification in Marine Geology. In: Raum und Zeit in Umweltinformationssystemen, 9th Intl Symposium on Computer Science for Environmental Protection CSEP'95, Vol. I, GI-Fachausschuß 4.6 "Informatik im Umweltschutz", Band 7, Metropolis-Verlag, Marburg (1995) 676–693
16. Ultsch, A.: The Integration of Neural Networks with Symbolic Knowledge Processing. In: Diday et al. (Eds.): New Approaches in Classification and Data Analysis, Springer (1994) 445–454
17. Ultsch, A.: Knowledge Extraction from Self-organizing Neural Networks, in O. Opitz, B. Lausen and R. Klar, (Eds.) Information and Classification, Berlin: Springer Verlag (1993) 301–306
18. Ultsch, A.: Self-Organizing Neural Networks for Visualization and Classification. In: Proc. Conf. Soc. Information and Classification, Dortmund, April (1992)
19. Ultsch, A.: Konnektionistische Modelle und ihre Integration mit wissensbasierten Systemen. Forschungsbericht Nr. 396, Institut für Informatik, Universität Dortmund, Februar, Dortmund, Habilitationsschrift (1991)

Section V:

Applications

Intrusion Detection through Behavioral Data 383
  D. Gunetti and G. Ruffo

Bayesian Neural Network Learning for Prediction in the Australian
Dairy Industry 395
  P.E. Macrossan, H.A. Abbass, K. Mengersen, M. Towsey, and G. Finn

Exploiting Sample-Data Distributions to Reduce the Cost of
Nearest-Neighbor Searches with Kd-Trees 407
  D. Talbert and D. Fisher

Pump Failure Detection Using Support Vector Data Descriptions 415
  D.M.J. Tax, A. Ypma, and R.P.W. Duin

Data Mining for the Detection of Turning Points in Financial Time
Series 427
  T. Poddig and C. Huber

Computer-Assisted Classification of Legal Abstracts 437
  B. Yang-Stephens, M.C. Swope, J. Locke, and I. Moulinier

Sequential Control Logic Inferring Method from Observed Plant
I/O Data 449
  Y. Ikkai, K. Ikeda, N. Komoda, A. Yamane, and I. Tone

Evaluating an Eye Screening Test 461
  G. Cheng, K. Cho, X. Liu, G. Loizou, and J.X. Wu

Application of Rough Sets Algorithms to Prediction of Aircraft
Component Failure 473
  J.M. Peña, S. Létourneau, and F. Famili

Intrusion Detection through Behavioral Data

Daniele Gunetti and Giancarlo Ruffo

Dept. of Computer Science, University of Torino
corso Svizzera 185, 10149 Torino, Italy
tel: +39 011 7606768, fax: +39 011 751603
{gunetti,ruffo}@di.unito.it

Abstract. We present an approach to the problem of detecting intrusions in computer systems through the use behavioral data produced by users during their normal login sessions. In fact, attacks may be detected by observing abnormal behavior, and the technique we use consists in associating to each system user a classifier made with relational decision trees that will label login sessions as "legals" or as "intrusions".
We perform an experimentation for 10 users, based on their normal work, gathered during a period of three months. We obtain a correct user recognition of 90%, using an independent test set. The test set consists of new, previously unseen sessions for the users considered during training, as well as sessions from users *not available during the training phase*. The obtained performance is comparable with previous studies, but (1) we do not use information that may effect user privacy and (2) we do not bother the users with questions.

1 Introduction

User behavior is probably the rawest form of data available to be processed and exploited. In the case of people using a computer system, monitoring and data collection can be made by specific programs, and we are then left to use the gathered information in a suitable way. "Behavioral Data" can of course be used to classify users and to distinguish them from each other and from unknowns, and the most obvious application of such form of classification is in the field of Computer Security. It is well known that access controls (such as through the use of passwords) are not sufficient by themselves to avoid intrusions, and the connection of computers to local networks and to the Internet is making intrusions not only possible, but more and more likely. In such a situation, we need a way to recognize a user as the legal owner of an account he/she is using, or as an intruder. Ideally, we should be able to do so as soon as possible, with a high level of accuracy, and possibly without affecting the privacy of the user.

In this paper we present an approach to the problem based on the use of data collected through the monitoring of users, and processed via Relational Decision Trees [1]. We obtain a performance comparable with previous studies, but avoiding many of their drawbacks, such as the use of structured typing text,[1] and the

---

[1] That is, predefined text that each user involved in the experiment is required to type in order to "reveal" his/her own keystroke dynamics.

D.J. Hand, J.N. Kok, M.R. Berthold (Eds.): IDA'99, LNCS 1642, pp. 383–394, 1999.
© Springer-Verlag Berlin Heidelberg 1999

use of private information[2]. The classification task is performed after only ten minutes from the beginning of the login session; the approach is very efficient and scales well with the number of users to be monitored. Finally, it is easily kept updated as users change their behavior and acquire new skills.

Intuitively, an *intrusion* is a successful attempt to use system resources without proper authorization. As a consequence, an intrusion detection system can be seen as a classifier: it classifies a particular computer or account state as either safe or unsafe.[3]

To classify intrusions, one may either write a classifier manually, based on expert knowledge, or obtain the classifier from examples of user-system interaction. In the first case, the model must be updated manually when new users are authorized to enter the system, or when new attack paradigms become known. It should be clear that manual approaches are only suitable for very particular situations, especially where a limited number of legal users with very slow-changing habits are involved.

Inductively acquired classifiers, by contrast, could perform well also in large and dynamic environments. In fact, it is easy to obtain a large number of examples of "normal" system and user behavior. From such a large number of examples it is possible to obtain classifiers that perform well on new, previously unseen cases. Specific intrusion detection methods have been proposed, that use neural networks [5], genetic algorithms [6], automata [9] and general statistical approaches [12]. The method presented in this paper is also of this kind, and uses heterogeneous data taken from normal user sessions in a real local network environment. The method is based on a relational decision tree machine learning system.

Within the class of intrusion detection systems using classifiers obtained automatically from examples, we consider user classification. The reason for this choice is the difficulty of obtaining negative examples of what we have called "normal" behavior. The examples of abnormal system behavior or of unauthorized user operations are, and should be, rare. As a consequence, they cannot be used effectively for the purposes of automated induction or statistical analysis.

---

[2] Such as the knowledge of which files were edited and which words were typed.

[3] More precisely, there are essentially two ways to realize that an intrusion is under way or has occurred recently: (1) some users or some known user processes behave in a way that is clearly unusual, e.g. a secretary starts running *awk* and *gcc*; (2) a typical attack pattern is recognized, e.g. some user reads a password file or attempts to delete system logs. In the first case we speak of *anomaly detection*, while the second objective is defined as *misuse detection*. Both approaches have been investigated in the literature. Some recent anomaly detection systems may be found in [9, 7, 8, 12], and misuse detection is discussed in [16, 17]. Some systems combine the two techniques to achieve higher performances (e.g., [13]). However, it should be clear that misuse often implies some form of anomaly, unless a user is accustomed, e.g., to read password files and delete log files, as it could possibly be the case for system administrators. As a consequence, in many cases anomaly detection also includes some form of misuse detection.

We then choose to distinguish one legitimate user from other *known* legitimate users and *unknown* users, instead of recognizing a legitimate user as opposed to an attacker. For the aim of the experiment, the *unknown* are users who behave "normally" w.r.t. their own account. Therefore, they would show potential anomalies when behaving as usual in someone else's account, and hence can well represent intruders. As a consequence, we easily have available a large number of positive and negative examples of user behavior: for each legitimate system user, logs recorded during an interactive session represent the positive examples, while the corresponding information for all the other users represents the negative examples.

Techniques are available for automatically generating accurate classifiers from positive and negative examples, as developed in Machine Learning, Neural Network, and general Pattern Recognition research. Good classifiers will label the available examples as either positive or negative with a low number of errors. However, good classifiers should also make a limited number of errors on *new* examples, i.e. user information obtained in future interactive sessions. And, an even more demanding requirement, good classifiers should perform well even when new users are introduced into the system, users that were not used during the training phase. This is important, as the attacker may not be among the current authorized system users.

2 Inductive Learning of a User Classifier

For obtaining a user classifier from examples of "normal" user sessions, we use a method for the automated induction of decision trees. Together with neural networks and methods derived from genetic algorithms, decision trees are among the most accurate general purpose classifiers that can be obtained inductively [2]. They are also limited in size and very efficient to be learned and used, if compared to other powerful learning techniques (such as, e.g., Horn rules learners [3]). However, they have not been used much in intrusion detection. The only study we know of in this area is [7], where decision trees are used for classifying connection types (e.g. SMTP vs telnet) from network traffic data. For our problem, a decision tree may be seen as a procedure that classifies patterns representing user's behavior and operations, as either related to one specific user (positive), or to another user (negative). Patterns will be described by means of so-called *attributes*, i.e. functions that take a finite number of *values*. For example, an attribute could have as its value the average typing speed of the user, and another attribute could have as its value a symbol indicating the specific command the user typed first during one login session. A node of a decision tree will correspond to some attribute, and the arcs from this node to its children correspond to particular values of the attribute. Leaves will be associated to a classification, positive or negative. A decision tree can then be used for classifying a user login session s as follows: we start from the root of the tree, and evaluate the corresponding attribute for s obtaining a value v; then we follow the arc labeled by v and reach the corresponding node; then, we repeat the procedure until a leaf is reached, and output the associated classification, i.e. the decision tree finally classifies the session as either belonging to the chosen user (a positive classification) or not (a negative classification). We can obtain one decision tree for each user.

For our application we have used ReliC [1], a system that learns *relational decision trees* from both positive and negative examples. Relational decision trees (RDTs) differ from traditional (propositional) decision trees, in the possibility to deal with relations, and not only with attributes. Under this definition, we can say that RDTs are a generalization of decision trees, because the latter are able to work only with unary relations (attribute-value representations). (In [4], the even more general notion of Logical Decision Tree is defined, and it is shown how to map a logical decision tree to a logic program and vice-versa.)

ReliC is based on the older, but excellent work represented by ID3 [14] and C4.5 [15]. C4.5 has become a standard reference in decision tree learning: it has sophisticated pruning mechanisms, and performs well on most applications. Moreover, it is readily available and the implementation is robust. ReliC differs from C4.5 in offering the following advanced options:

- n-ary relations with $n \geq 1$ can be used directly by the system;
- the basic C4.5 post-pruning algorithm can be substituted with a stopping criterion which limitates the expansion of the tree;
- a database interface is provided with the system in order to perform queries for data stored off-line in a DBMS, so as to deal with a very large number of structural examples, as is required in intrusion detection.
- an initial weight can be assigned for each class of examples during learning phase; this is useful in contexts where some examples are considered as more important. In our experiments, positive examples were given higher weights, because they were less numerous.

For the experimental data that we have used, the relational characteristics of the system may have improved the discrimination performances w.r.t. the basic C4.5 system. The experimental setting is discussed in the next two sections.

3   Data Acquisition

The data used in our experiments were collected over a period of three months. Ten volunteers in our department accepted to be monitored as described below. The volunteers were asked to behave as usual, with the only constraint of not allowing other people to sit at the keyboard and use the workstation with the volunteer's account. The monitored people included two system administrators, one PhD student, one professor and six researchers. Each user is monitored with two programs that are launched when the user logs on and runs the X server. After ten minutes, the programs save the relevant data and stop[4].

---

[4] The proposed method, however, would be applicable also to different choices: 1) any windows-like platform that allows for keystrokes to be captured may be used as a

The first program, *time*, connects to the X server and gets the elapsed time between every two keystrokes on the keyboard. To guarantee privacy, typed characters are blurred and are not recorded. Since we want the average elapsed time in continuous typing, *time* does not take into consideration times larger than 600 milliseconds. For such cases we assume the user stopped typing (she is reading her mail or has gone to take a coffee). Elapsed times are summed up together, and after ten minutes this sum is divided by the number of typed keys. Average elapsed time between two strokes and the number of strokes are recorded and then the *time* process dies.

The second program, *command*, records the commands executed by the user in the first ten minutes of his working session, together with the number of times each command was run. This is done through the *lastcomm* command provided by the Unix System. Lastcomm gives information on previously executed commands on the system, but at the same time provides a reasonable level of privacy, since it does not report the arguments of the commands (for example, through lastcomm we may see that a user used 'vi', but cannot know which file was edited). It must be observed that lastcomm, if active, can be used by every user of a system. Hence, *command* does not use more information than that normally available to every non-root user of a Unix system[5].

Together with the above information, the login time is also recorded. Hence, after the first ten minutes of a session, each user produced a set of parameters such as the following:

user: User-1;
login time: 09:15;
number of keystrokes: 157;
average elapsed time between keystrokes: 243 (milliseconds)
command: cat, *how_many:* 3;
command: elm, *how_many:* 1;
command: more, *how_many:* 3;
command: rm, *how_many:* 2;

Every such set is a positive example of User-1, and a negative example for every other user.

Every example must be turned into something that the learning system can handle. The first three parameters can immediately be used as continuous at-

---

platform; 2) instead of stopping after an elapsed time of 10 minutes, the programs could stop after a certain number of commands has been typed, or after a certain number of typed user actions have been performed; 3) mouse clicks labeled with corresponding actions could be used instead of, or in addition to, simple Unix commands. Our experiments prove that users may be characterized and classified on the basis of their interaction with the system, but the kind of interaction that is monitored may be tailored to the installation environment.

[5] For the sake of truth, it must also be said that lastcomm is also one of the most hated Unix command by system administrators, since it tends to produce a very large accounting file in a short time.

tributes[6] by the learning system. To handle the commands we must split them into a set of classes. There are almost five hundred commands in the SunOS release of the Unix systems, and it is not practical to make a class for each command. Hence, the commands are grouped into a set of classes, where each class contains 'homogeneous' commands. For example, a class contains command used to see the contents of files. Commands such as *cat* and *more* belong to this class. In the above instance, User-1 used commands in this class 6 times. Commands used to modify files as a whole (such as *cp* and *mv*) form another class. In the given example, User-1 used one such command, *rm*, twice. We initially identified 24 classes of Unix commands. Later, they were increased to 37.

4   The Experiments

Given a set of positive and negative examples of a user, our goal is to synthesize a decision tree representing a model of that user. When given in input a new example, the decision tree must be able to correctly classify it as a positive or negative example of the user.

It is very important to note that we totally ignored some of the available users during the training phase - these users were only used for testing the system performance, and are equivalent to external, previously unknown intruders. More precisely, six users were selected to learn a model, let us call these the *known* users. The remaining four were left out to be used only in the testing phase, as explained below. We will call them the *unknown* users. The set of positive examples of each known user was randomly split into a training set containing 2/3 of the examples, and a test set containing the remaining examples[7]. A decision tree for a known user was learned from a set of positive and negative examples of that user. The training set of this user's examples were used as positive examples, and the training sets of the other 5 known users were used as negative examples[8]. The learned decision tree was then tested on the set of the testing examples, in order to compute the percentage of positive examples of the user classified as positive, and the percentage of negative examples classified as negative.

The testing set for each known user was made by putting together: *a)* the examples of that user not used in the learning phase (these examples were marked as 'positive'); *b)* the examples of the other five known users not used in the learning phase (marked as 'negative'); *c)* all the examples of the four unknown

---

[6] Actually, the *login time* is first turned into the number of minutes from midnight. In the given example it becomes the number 555.

[7] For each user there was a total number of positive examples varying from 15 to 90: the number of times he logged in at his workstation under X during the three months of monitoring. The total amount of examples from all the users amounts to 343.

[8] Recall that a total of 10 users was available: 6 were called "known" and were used for training, the others were called "unknown and used only for testing", making them equivalent to external intruders

users, marked as 'negative'. The presence, in the testing sets, of negative examples of unknown users is important, because it simulates the real situation when an intruder is coming from the outside, and hence his behavior is completely unknown to the 'guards'. For this reason we selected the four unknown users to be as heterogeneous as possible. The four *unknown* are the professor, the PhD student, one of the researchers and one of the system administrators. As it is common in Machine Learning, the learning/testing process just described was repeated 6 times for each user, each time with a different random split of the set of his examples into a training and a testing set. We then computed the mean error rates out of the six runs available for every known user.

Moreover, the whole procedure was repeated in six different experiments. Experiments differ because of the attributes used to describe the users. The outcomes for these experiments are reported in table 1 and are discussed in the next section. Each entry of the table reports the mean percentage of positive and negative examples that are classified correctly. As an example, table 2 reports the outcomes for the six known users in the last experiment (exp-6) of table 1.

Table 1. Experimental results. Positive (negative) accuracy is the percentage of positive (negative) examples in the test set that are classified correctly. Total Errors is the percentage of positive and negative examples that are not classified correctly. (The total error rate is not the mean of positive and negative error rates, as there are more negative examples.)

Exp.	Pos. Accuracy	Neg. Accuracy	Total Errors
Exp-1	73.3%	89.3%	11.8%
Exp-2	80.5%	90.3%	10.2%
Exp-3	82.8%	89.7%	10.4%
Exp-4	81.6%	90.6%	10.1%
Exp-5	84.1%	90.3%	10.2%
Exp-6	85.4%	89.3%	10.9%

Table 2. Exp-6 results

User	Pos. Accuracy	Neg. Accuracy	Total Errors
researcher 1	79.0%	95.0%	6.2%
researcher 2	88.3%	86.3%	13.3%
researcher 3	94.5%	85.3%	14.1%
researcher 4	81.7%	90.3%	10.2%
researcher 5	75.2%	83.2%	17.6%
sys. admin.	93.8%	95.8%	4.2%
average	85.4%	89.3%	10.9%

The attributes used in the six experiments to describe every example of every user are as follows.

– Exp-1: login time, average elapsed time between keystrokes, number of keystrokes, 24 attributes representing classes of Unix commands (these are binary attributes: the value is 1 if the user used one command of the corresponding class at least once. It is 0 otherwise).
– Exp-2: as in Exp-1, but with 37 classes of Unix commands.
– Exp-3: as in Exp-2, but the average elapsed time between keystrokes is taken into consideration only if the number of keystrokes is larger than 100.
– Exp-4: as in Exp-2, but the Unix commands are counted, so that each attribute indicates the number of Unix commands of the corresponding class run by the user.
– Exp-5: as in Exp-4, but the average elapsed time between keystrokes is taken into consideration only if the number of keystrokes is larger than 100.
– Exp-6: as in Exp-5, but the login time is not taken into consideration.

The classification rules synthesized by the learning procedure are normally meaningful and easy to understand from a "human" point of view. As an example, consider the decision tree learned in the first run of experiment Exp-6 for researcher-4. This tree can be translated into a set of nine clauses. The first two of these clauses correspond to the following rules:

If *monitored user* run a command in class 35 he **is not** *researcher-4*
If *monitored user* run a command in class 30 he **is** *researcher-4*

In fact, class 35 contains commands such as *accton*, *lpc* and *lpstat*, that are typical commands for system administration, and hardly used by normal users. On the other hand, researcher-4 is, in real life, an experienced C-programmer, and class 30 contains command such as *make*, *lint* and *ctrace*.[9]

5   Discussion of the Results

By looking at table 1, we immediately notice an improvement on the ability to classify the positive examples from the first to the second experiment. This is due to a better classification of the Unix Commands into a set of classes. The first experiment is made by using 24 classes of commands, that was raised to 37 in the second experiment (and kept in the other experiments).

To partition the commands into classes, we just looked at the whole set of Unix commands and empirically split them into homogeneous sets. For example, a set contains basic commands used to move around in the file system, such as *cd* and *pwd*. Another set contains the printing commands, such as *lpr* and *lpq*; and another includes commands used to change files and directories, such as *cp*,

---

[9] Actually, because of the second rule listed, we must gather that researcher-4 was the only one using commands in class 30, at least during the monitoring period.

rm, *mkdir* and *rmdir*. After the first experiment, we looked at the 24 classes, and further split some of them up to 37, because some of the initial classes were clearly 'oversized' and meaningless. As an example, there was a class containing the commands used to handle mails, consisting of *elm*, *mail* and *mailtool*. Though reasonable, this class was probably wrong. A user tends to use always the same command to read an answer mails, and avoid the others, especially because these commands have different interfaces, and allow a lot of options that require time to be learned and used. Hence, we made three different classes, one for each of the three mail commands. The adopted partitioning seems reasonable, but is for sure also questionable. For example, we have a class of *basic security commands* containing *passwd*, *su*, and *login*. Whereas the first command can be used by any user to change her own password, the use of the other two may suggest the user knows someone else's password. Hence, it could also be reasonable to put *passwd* and the other two commands in different classes[10].

The third experiment takes into consideration the elapsed time between two keystrokes only if the number of keystrokes is larger than 100. The obvious rationale is that when only few characters are typed the corresponding typing speed is not really meaningful and can be misleading.

In the fourth experiment we tried to take into account the number of times commands of each class were used, and not only whether they were used or not. By itself, this information does not seem to be meaningful, and actually results into a slight decrease of the predictive power on the positive examples. However, combining the information with the threshold on the number of keystrokes (fifth experiment), results into an improvement of the outcomes w.r.t. the previous experiments. The reason lies probably in the fact that, in ten minutes, a user does not normally run a large number of commands. Hence, knowing how many times a particular command was used, does not bring more information than knowing whether that command was used or not at all. But when the number of keystrokes is (relatively) large, then presumably also the number of commands increases, and becomes relevant and useful.

Obviously, a 90% user recognition rate is still inadequate for a fielded intrusion detection system.[11] However, it must be observed that our homogeneous test environment did not help in the classification process. Most of the users are academic people with essentially similar habits and using the same hardware

---

[10] Clearly, this is a point where the knowledge of an expert — a system administrator — would greatly help to define a meaningful set of command classes. Moving from 24 to 37 classes of commands, we also noticed that for every user the results of each run became more stable. That is, the predictive power of the learned tree for a user was roughly always the same regardless of the random set of examples used to learn the tree.

[11] Also, we well understand that a number of ten users involved in the experiments is rather limited. Actually, these users are all those who accepted to be monitored, whereas other refused because were afraid of possible infringements of their privacy. In general, we think this being a very important point that must be faced. Users must understand and accept that every security policy must imply, in some way, a limitation of their privacy.

and software platform. It is likely that classification of external users would yield significantly lower error rates. Consider Table 2. The only system administrator is recognized with a error rate of about 5%. On the other hand, the remaining five researchers are recognized with error rates of 16.3% and 12% for the positive and negative accuracy, on the average. If we assume these people having similar habits, we may reasonably expect larger errors when trying to distinguish every one of them among each other.[12]

Finally, one may observe that a decision tree used to model a user may sooner or later become out of date, as users' habits tend to change (though slowly) over time. New skills are acquired, new programs and commands are used, others are abandoned. This is in itself not a real problem. Suppose a decision tree for a user has been built using - let's say - a set made of the last 30 log in's of that user (plus a set of negative examples automatically provided by the monitoring of other users). When the user logs in and, after ten minutes is recognized as the legal user, the new example replaces the oldest one in the set of positive examples of that user, and a new decision tree is synthesized. This task requires just a few seconds, (whereas using the decision tree is virtually not time consuming), and the older model can be replaced. For the same reason, the method is scalable to larger environments, as one decision tree must be generated for each user, and complexity grows linearly with the number of legal users.

6   Comparisons and Conclusions

The method presented and the above experiments show that we can distinguish effectively one user from other known and unknown users, based on general characteristics such as typing speed and command history. We observed a 10 percent error on an independent test set for about all of our experiments. Higher recognition rates can be obtained if the precise latencies and duration of keystrokes can be measured.[13] Legget et al. [11] report a 5.25 percent error for 36 users, who were required to type the same text, consisting of 537 characters. Brown and Rogers [5] used a neural network approach to obtain one-sided errors between 12 and 21 percent. In this case, users were asked to type names of only 15 characters, in order to create the training data. Frnell et al. [8] share some of the objectives of our study, and obtain an 85% impostor detection rate, using only keystroke analysis data. Monrose and Rubin [12] obtain a 90% rate of correct user recognition, but their experimental setting is different because

---

[12] In the learning phase of the classifier of a researcher, about 84% of the negative examples used belong to other researchers. In the testing phase, only about 60% of the negative examples are from other researchers. This happens because, in the testing phase, *unknown* users' examples are included as negatives, and only one of these *unknown* is a researcher. This also explains why the negative accuracy is better than the positive accuracy.

[13] *Keystroke latency* is the elapsed time between every pair of specific typed keys. *Keystroke duration* is the time a key is held pressed down during typing.

given, "structured" typing text is required, and keystroke duration is used.[14]
However, keystroke duration can only be measured on a local keyboard, as key
release interrupts are not available for a network connection. But even latency is
not easily used for network connections: even small communication delays make
time intervals between individual characters unreliable. Average typing speed
is less affected by network delays, although it may be compromised by severe
bandwidth restrictions.

There are of course many ways to improve the results. First, it is possible to
update and modify a decision tree 'by hand', because decision trees, as opposed
to neural networks and standard genetic classifiers, are easy to understand and
edit. A very precise model of a user can be built in that way, but extending such
procedure to a large set of users would be quite exhausting and time consuming.
Second, improvements are possible along the line adopted in our experiments.
In section 5 we observed that the log in time did not help to classify the users
monitored in our experiments. However, a real intruder would be inclined to
masquerade under some account when the legal owner is not connected, so as to
avoid manual detection. The intruder would then be forced to connect rarely or
to login at times that are unusual for the legal account owner. Login time would
then be a useful attribute in fielded system installations. Also, an intruder would
probably show a high level of activity from the very beginning of the connection,
and this would lead to other useful decision tree attributes. Other parameters
could be useful and, in particular, there is at least one information that would
greatly improve the performances: the argument(s) of commands. Used files are
particularly meaningful in this sense. We have not used file attributes in our
experiments so as to protect user privacy. However, one thing is to know that
a user is just running an editor. Another thing would be to know whether he is
editing one of his files or (let's say) /etc/passwd.

Attacks are often successful just because no monitoring procedure has been
activated, and because different intruding techniques are used. Therefore, it is
important to study different forms of intrusion detection that can also be combined together to achieve a better performance. In this paper we have showed
that heterogeneous data produced by normal user behavior can be used to detect
anomalies and intruders, and can hence be useful to improve the safety of our
systems.

Acknowledgements: This research was partially supported by Esprit Project
20237 ILP^2: Inductive Logic Programming II. We want to thank all the people
in our department who accepted to collaborate to this research.

---

[14] Notice that Frnell's approach infringes in some way users' privacy, since characters
typed by each user must be recorded in order to recognize his/her keystroke dynamics. The other methods bother the users by asking them to type a predefined text.
On the contrary, our approach is essentially transparent to the users.

References

[1] F. Bergadano and G. Ruffo. ReliC: a Relational Learner Using Decision Trees. *Technical Report, Dept. of CS, University of Turin*, 1998.

[2] F. Bergadano, B. Crispo, and G. Ruffo. High Dictionary Compression for Proactive Password Checking. In *ACM Transactions on Information and System Security*, 1(1), 1998.

[3] F. Bergadano and D. Gunetti. *Inductive Logic Programming: from Machine Learning to Software Engineering*. MIT Press, 1996.

[4] H. Blockeel and L. De Raedt. *Lookahead and Discretization in ILP*. In *Proceedings of the 7th International Workshop on Inductive Learning Programming*, Springer Verlag, 1997.

[5] M. Brown and J. Rogers. User identification via keystroke characteristics of typed names using neural networks. *Int. J. of Man Machine Studies*, 39:999–1014, 1993.

[6] M. Crosbie. Applying genetic programming to intrusion detection. In *Proceedings of AAAI Fall Symposium on Genetic Programming*, 1995.

[7] J. Frank. Artificial Intelligence and Intrusion Detections: current and future directions. In *Proceedings of 17th National Computer Security Conference*, 1994.

[8] S. Furnell, P. W. Sanders, and C. T. Stockel. The use of keystroke analysis for continuous user identity verification and supervision. *MediaComm*, 1995.

[9] A. P. Kosoresow and S. A. Hofmeyr. Intrusion Detection via System Call Traces. *IEEE Software*, pages 35–42, 1997.

[10] W. Lee and S. J. Stolfo. Data Mining Approaches to Intrusion Detection. In *Proceedings of 7th Usenix Security Symposium*, 1998.

[11] J. Leggett, G. Williams, and M. Usnick. Dynamic identity verification via keystroke characteristics. *Int. J. of Man Machine Studies*, 35:859–870, 1991.

[12] F. Monrose and A. Rubin. Authentication via Keystroke Dynamics. In *Proceedings od ACM Computer and Communication Security Conference*, pages 48–56, 1997.

[13] P. A. Porras and P. G. Neumann. EMERALD: Event Monitoring Enabling Responses to Anomalous Live Disturbances. In *Proceedings of the 1997 National Information Systems Security Conference*, 1997.

[14] J. R. Quinlan. Induction of Decision Trees. *Machine Learning*, 1:81–106, 1986.

[15] J. R. Quinlan. *C4.5: Programs for Machine Learning*. Morgan Kaufmann, San Mateo, CA, 1993.

[16] S. P. Shieh and V. D. Gligor. On a Pattern-Oriented Model for Intrusion Detection. *IEEE Trans. on KDE*, 9(4):661–667, 1997.

[17] M. Sobirey, B. Richter, and H. Konig. The intrusion detection system AID. architecture, and experiences in automated audit analysis. In *Proceedings of IFIP TC6/TC11 International Conference on Communications and Multimedia Security*, pages 278–290, 1996.

Bayesian Neural Network Learning for Prediction in the Australian Dairy Industry

Paula E. Macrossan[1], Hussein A. Abbass[2], Kerry Mengersen[1],
Michael Towsey[2], and Gerard Finn[2]

[1] Queensland University of Technology, Department of Mathematical Sciences
GPO Box 2434, QLD 4001, Australia
[2] Queensland University of Technology, School of Computing Science
Machine Learning Research Centre, GPO Box 2434, QLD 4001, Australia

Abstract. One of the most common problems encountered in agriculture is that of predicting a response variable from covariates of interest. The aim of this paper is to use a Bayesian neural network approach to predict dairy daughter milk production from dairy dam, sire, herd and environmental factors. The results of the Bayesian neural network are compared with the results obtained when the regression relationship is described using the traditional neural network approach. In addition, the "baseline" results of a multiple linear regression employing both frequentist and Bayesian methods are presented. The potential advantages of the Bayesian neural network approach over the traditional neural network approach are discussed.

1 Introduction

Many different genetic and environmental factors affect the profitability of dairy herds in Australia. Production traits of the individual animals (eg. milk, fat and protein yields), other animal traits such as "workability" traits (eg. temperament) and type traits (eg. size), environmental influences such as climate, season, feed availability, and management practices, all contribute to the profitability of the herd. Complex relationships exist between fertility, milk yield, lactation length and culling which are difficult to model using conventional techniques [22]. Australian dairy farmers face a difficult task in attempting to combine all available information in a mating strategy that will increase profitability in their herds.

Gianola and Fernando [9] describe the objective of a breeding program to be the elicitation, by selection, of favourable trends in a "merit function". The larger issue of selection can be broken down into three sub-problems, each of which must be addressed by the animal breeder for such favourable trends to occur. These sub-problems can be described as:

a) The definition of the breeding goal (or determining worthwhile genetic changes), which in the context of the dairy industry can be expressed in terms of the value of milk, fat and protein yields of dairy cows.

D.J. Hand, J.N. Kok, M.R. Berthold (Eds.): IDA'99, LNCS 1642, pp. 395–406, 1999.

b) The estimation of breeding values (or correctly and efficiently identifying genetically superior animals), currently provided by the calculation of breeding and production values, using performance and pedigree information. These breeding values can then be used in the calculation of a selection index for use in sire ranking or dam appraisal.

c) Mate selection and mate allocation (identifying the most genetically and economically efficient process of matching the selected animals) has always proved the most difficult part of the animal breeding equation to solve, due to the dynamics, and in particular, the non-linearity of the problem. There are two sub-problems to be addressed here. The first is the prediction problem, where the traits of the progeny are predicted from the traits of the sire, dam and the environment. The solution to this problem rests on the solutions to (a) and (b) above. The second component is an optimisation problem, where a simultaneous solution is attempted for mate selection and mate allocation.

This paper is a product of a collaborative project between the Queensland University of Technology Machine Learning Research Centre and School of Mathematical Sciences, and the Queensland Department of Primary Industries. The aim of the project is the solution of (c) above, through the development of a PC based stand-alone program which can predict the optimal mating strategy for mating dairy sires with dams to maximise a "merit function". This paper investigates a role for machine learning, in particular the contribution of neural networks (NNs) and Bayesian statistics, in the solution of the prediction problem. The output of the adopted prediction model will be used as input to the optimisation model in an intelligent decision support environment [2]. There are five objectives in this optimisation model; maximisation of the profit index, the selection index and the profit obtained from culling, and minimisation of inbreeding and semen cost. The prediction model is used to formulate the first two objectives in the optimisation model.

The current approaches to prediction and previous applications of NNs and Bayesian statistics to the dairy prediction problem are discussed in the remainder of Section 1. Section 2 contains an outline of the methods used, Section 3 the results of the study, and Section 4 a discussion of the results, conclusions and future work.

1.1   Current Approaches to Prediction

Since genetic improvement through selection depends on correctly identifying individuals with the highest true breeding value, the accurate prediction of breeding value constitutes an important component of any breeding programme. Genetic parameters, such as heritabilities and genetic correlations, which are necessary for the computation of breeding values, have been established for milk yield, survival, workability and type traits for Australian Holstein-Friesian and Jersey cattle [22]. Estimated Breeding Values (EBVs) or Australian Breeding Values (ABVs) are computed by the Australian Dairy Herd Improvement Scheme (ADHIS) using the Best Linear Unbiased Predictor or BLUP [11]. BLUP has become the most widely accepted method for genetic evaluation of domestic livestock [6]. Using animal model BLUP, the genetic merit of an animal is predicted from its own and its relatives' records compared with records of other animals after adjusting for environmental and managerial factors. When selecting bulls and cows for breeding, an optimum combination of all EBVs is sought. A standard method for combining information on different traits for selection purposes is the selection index (SI) [10].

The problem addressed in this paper is prediction of the performance of daughters from a particular mating. This requires not only information about past performance of the parents and their relatives (integrated using BLUP) but also additional herd and environmental information.

1.2 The Application of Neural Networks to the Dairy Prediction Problem

The problem of prediction of daughter milk production from sire and dam production records appears to have many characteristics which might make an NN solution more attractive than that obtained using other machine learning paradigms. NNs have a tolerance to both noise and ambiguity in data [24]. The dairy database, like most agricultural data sets, is inherently noisy, and is a collection of indicators that represent genetic and environmental influences including climate and farm management [7]. NNs can be applied to problems which require consideration of more input variables than could be feasibly handled by most other approaches [24], a potentially important issue with the present dairy problem. NNs have the ability to approximate non-linear relationships between sets of inputs and their corresponding sets of outputs [13]. The dairy data could be expected to display some degree of non-linearity. The ability of NNs to generalise well [18] and to learn concepts involving real-valued features [5] are potential advantages with this project, since the predicted daughter responses are continuous variables. However an attempt has been made to categorise this data into discrete classes and analyse it using symbolic learning paradigms [1].

On the other hand, many machine learning researchers regard the "black-box" nature of the learning carried out by NNs as a major disadvantage to their use as a learning paradigm. Such researchers argue that the concepts learned by NNs are difficult to understand as they are hidden in the architecture of the network. Nevertheless, there has been some success in identifying the task learned by the network by the extraction of symbolic rules [3]. A second disadvantage of NNs is the high cost of the learning process, which can require large and general sets of training data which might not always be available [24], and which can be very costly in terms of the time needed for the learning to take place [21]. Thirdly, the adaptivity [24] of the most commonly used NN, the multilayer perceptron, does not extend to the architecture of the model chosen.

The potential advantages of a NN solution to the dairy prediction problem are explored in this paper, as well as an investigation of the comparative advantages of a Bayesian framework applied to the NN.

1.3   The Application of Bayesian Statistics to Neural Networks

The essential characteristic of Bayesian methods is their explicit use of probability for quantifying uncertainty in scientific analysis. Gelman et al. [8] break down the process of Bayesian data analysis into three steps:

1. Setting up a full probability model: a joint probability distribution for all observable and unobservable quantities in the problem.
2. Conditioning on observed data: calculating and interpreting the appropriate posterior distribution given the data.
3. Evaluating the model fit: assessing the implications of the posterior distribution.

MacKay [14] and Neal [16] describe a Bayesian neural network (BNN), where a probabilistic interpretation is applied to the NN technique. This interpretation involves assigning a meaning to the functions and parameters already in use. In the Bayesian approach to NN prediction, the objective is to use the training set of inputs and targets to calculate the predictive distribution for the target values in a new "test" case, given the inputs for that case. According to these authors, the hybrid approach of a Bayesian framework applied to the NN overcomes many of the disadvantages of NNs previously discussed. The Bayesian framework allows the objective evaluation of a number of issues involved in complex modelling including the choice between alternative network architectures (eg. the number of hidden units and the activation function), the stopping rules for network training and the effective number of parameters used. MacKay [14] postulates that the overall effect of the Bayesian framework should be realised in the reduction in the high cost of the learning process in terms of the time needed for the learning to take place. The framework allows for the full use of the limited and often expensive data set for training the network.

The Bayesian techniques used in this paper employ Markov Chain Monte Carlo (MCMC) methods to simulate a random walk in θ, the parameter space of interest. The random walk converges to a stationary distribution that is the joint posterior distribution, $p(\theta \mid y)$, where y represents the observed or target data.

2   Methods

2.1   Data Pre-processing

The original data set was obtained from the ADHIS in 1997. The data set consisted of 49 text files containing both raw and summary data of milk production in dairy herds around Australia. The subset of data used in this paper applies to Holstein dairy cattle from the State of Victoria. Records were filtered to remove those containing incomplete milk volume, fat and protein data, those records that lacked sire and dam information, and also to include only those records where the number of test days per lactation was greater than seven. Exploratory data techniques including Stepwise Linear Regression (SLR) and Principal Component Analysis (PCA) were carried out on the resultant data set to determine which variables were to be included in the final feature set. These analyses indicated that some degree of non-linearity existed in the dam season of calving. Dam second milk was used in place of dam first milk because of the large amounts of missing data in the latter, and because of the high correlation between the two (r = 0.81). The final feature set included dam second milk yield, sire ABV for milk, dam herd mean milk yield excluding first lactation and dam season of calving (autumn, summer, winter, spring). Age adjustments were carried out on dam second milk following [19]. In the final data set, dam season of calving was represented as a sparse-coded variable. For the NN, BNN and BLR methods, the continuously-valued variables (representing dam, sire and herd information) were linearly transformed to values between zero and one. Due to the in-built tanh activation function of the BNN software package used, a transformation of these variables to values ranging between -1 and +1 was necessary.

The final data set contained 20682 data records in the training set, and a further 5204 records in the test set. The record for the nth animal consisted of seven input variables, $\tilde{x}_n = (x_{n1}, \ldots, x_{n7})$ with x_{ni} representing the following variables:

1. Dam herd mean milk yield excluding first lactation (x_{n1})
2. Dam second milk yield (x_{n2})
3. Sire ABV for milk yield (x_{n3})
4-7. Dam season of calving (autumn (x_{n4}), summer (x_{n5}), winter (x_{n6}), and spring (x_{n7})).

Each record also contained the daughter milk yield for the first lactation (hereafter referred to as daughter first milk yield), the variable for prediction.

2.2 Analytical Approaches

All four approaches employed the same primary model, which represented daughter first milk yield for the nth animal as $y_n, n = 1, \ldots, 20682$. In each model, $y_n = \mu_n + e_n$ where μ_n represents the expected value of y_n, hereafter referred to as $\hat{y}_n$. Here $e_n \sim N(0, \sigma)$ with σ being the standard deviation of y_n. The full training set of 20682 records was used in all cases, with the full test set of 5204 records used to verify the predictions obtained. For the BNN, an additional run was carried out on a random sub-sample of 1000 records from the training set, with the full test set used for predictions.

Bayesian Neural Network (BNN) The data were modelled using a multilayer perceptron with seven input units, one for each data input, x_{ni} ($i = 1, \ldots, 7$), one hidden layer of J tanh units ($J = 1, 2, 3, 4$ or 8), and a single output unit representing daughter first milk yield. The BNN model [16] was expressed as:

$$\hat{y}_n = b + \sum_{j=1}^{J} v_j h_j(\tilde{x}_n), h_j(\tilde{x}_n) = \tanh\left(a_j + \sum_{i=1}^{7} u_{ij} x_{ni}\right) \tag{1}$$

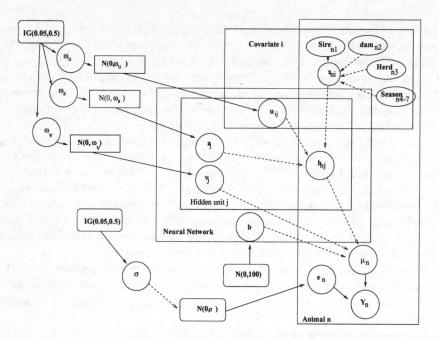

Fig. 1. Graphical representation of the BNN model with seven input units, one hidden layer of one, two, three, four or eight tanh units, and a single output unit

In this model, u_{ij} represented the weight on the connection from input i unit to hidden unit j, v_j represented the weight on the connection from hidden unit j to the single output unit, and a_j and b represented the biases of the hidden units and output unit respectively. The prior distributions [17] used for the network parameters (u_{ij}, a_j, v_j) were taken to be normally distributed $N(0, \omega)$, with standard deviations ω considered to be hyperparameters with inverse Gamma, $IG(\alpha, \beta)$, distributions. Three network hyperparameters with distributions $IG(0.05, 0.5)$ were specified, one for the input-to-hidden weights, u_{ij}, one for the hidden unit biases, a_j, and one for the hidden-to-output weights, v_j. The output unit bias b was given a simple Gaussian prior $N(0, 100)$. The value of the output unit was taken as the mean of a Gaussian distribution for the target, with an associated error term (or network "noise") having a Gaussian prior $N(0, \sigma)$. The standard deviation of this error term was controlled using a hyperparameter with distribution $IG(0.05, 0.5)$. Figure 1 provides a graphical representation of the BNN. Here, circular and oval shapes depict variables (data or parameters), double-edged boxes depict constants, dashed arrows define deterministic relationships and solid arrows show stochastic relationships. For example, the three dashed lines directed toward μ_n reflect the deterministic equation (1) defining μ_n for which $\hat{y}_n$ is an estimate.

The model was implemented using MCMC methods to sample from the posterior distribution. In the initial state of the simulation, each of the hyperparameters (the input-to-hidden weights, the hidden unit biases, the hidden-to-output weights and the "noise" hyperparameters) was given a value of 0.5. The network parameters (u_{ij}, a_j, v_j) were given initial values of zero. Predictions were based on the final 80 of 100 iterations, the first 20 being discarded as "burn-in". The software used to implement the BNN, and the particulars of the implementation used, are described by Neal [17].

Artificial Neural Network (NN) The NN model was as described by equation (1) except that the tanh function was replaced by the logistic function. The data was modelled using a multilayer feed forward NN. Five NN architectures with a single hidden layer of J units, $(J = 1, 2, 3, 4$ or $7)$, with logistic activation functions were trained ten times with different weight initialisations for 20,000 epochs and tested on the test set every 50 epochs using a learning rate of 0.03 and zero momentum. The average of the ten weight initialisations is reported for each network. The software employed for NN is *Tlearn* [15].

Linear Regression (LR) In the LR model, $\hat{y}_n = \alpha + \sum_{i=1}^{7} \beta_i x_{ni}$ with α constant and the $\beta_i (i = 1, \ldots, 7)$ representing the covariates of interest, as outlined in section 2.1. The software used to describe the LR was SPSS for Windows©, Version 8.0.

Bayesian Linear Regression (BLR) The BLR model used is as described for the LR, with priors expressed as $\alpha \sim N(0, 100)$, $\beta_i \sim N(0, 100)$ and σ^2 distributed as $IG(0.001, 0.001)$. MCMC methods were used to carry out the necessary numerical integrations using simulation. A number of preliminary trial runs were carried out on the training set from various starting values and differing numbers of "burn-in" iterations. The final simulation was initiated with values of zero for α and the β_i, and σ^2 equal to one. An initial run of 7000 iterations was generated as "burn-in". Parameters of interest $(\alpha, \beta, \sigma^2)$ were then monitored and 15000 more iterations were performed, giving a total of 22000 iterations performed. A file containing a series of values simulated from the joint posterior of the unknown quantities was used to monitor for convergence. Diagnostics, including output analysis and summary statistics, indicated convergence had occurred after 15000 iterations. The software employed was $BUGS©$, Bayesian Inference Using Gibbs Sampling, version 0.50 [20].

3   Results

The predictions of the different methods on test data were compared using correlations, mean error, root mean square error, and absolute error. The predicted value in all cases is daughter first milk yield but error values cited are for the linearly transformed data as explained in Section 2.1.

3.1   Bayesian Neural Network (BNN)

Table 1 shows the correlations between the target values of daughter first milk yield and the values predicted by the BNN, mean error, RMSE, mean absolute error, and the percentage of target values falling within the 80% prediction quantile for network architectures of one, two, three, four and eight hidden

Table 1. Results for the BNN model. Note that the errors cited here are for a $(-1, +1)$ transformation and as such are twice that which would be expected for a $(0,1)$ transformation used with the NN, BLR and LR models (see Tables 2 and 3 below).

Number of Hidden Units	1	2	3	4	8
Correlation Coeffs.	0.7642	0.7645	0.7649	0.7650	0.7647
Mean Error	-0.0001	0.0000	0.0000	0.0000	0.0002
RMSE	0.1216	0.1216	0.1212	0.1212	0.1212
Mean Abs Error	0.0950	0.0949	0.0949	0.0949	0.0949
% Targets in 10% to 90% prediction quantiles	82.80%	83.00%	82.74%	82.65%	82.80%

units. These results indicate that the architecture using four hidden units gives a slightly higher correlation than that of the other architectures, although the difference is not significant. Note that the errors cited in Table 1 are for a $(-1,+1)$ transformation (used with the BNN model), and as such are twice that which would be expected using a $(0,1)$ transformation (used with the NN, BLR and LR models). Taking this factor into account, the errors referred to in Table 1 are identical to the errors in Tables 2 and 3 (the results for the NN, BLR and LR models below).

In order to briefly investigate the effect of a smaller training set on the performance of the BNN, an additional training run using three hidden units was performed on a random unbiased sample of 1000 records from the training set, the results of which were then analysed on the full test set. The correlation between the target value of daughter first milk yield and the predicted value for this experiment was 0.7591 (cf. 0.7649 for the full training set) whilst the percentage of target values falling within the 80% prediction quantile was 82.51% (cf. 82.74% for the full training set).

3.2 Artificial Neural Networks (NN)

Table 2 shows the correlations between the target value of daughter first milk yield and the value predicted by the NN for network architectures of one, two, three, four and seven hidden units, as well as the error components for the predictions. The correlation coefficient for the three hidden units is slightly better than that for the other architectures, although this difference is not significant.

3.3 Linear Regression (LR)

All seven covariates of interest were employed for LR. However, x_7, representing dam season of calving (spring) was eliminated by SPSS due to the dependency generated in the data from the binary encoding of the seasonal effects. The final regression equation was:

Table 2. Correlations between the target values of daughter first milk yield and the predicted values, the mean of the error, RMSE, the mean absolute error for NN.

Number of Hidden Units	1	2	3	4	7
Correlation	0.7641	0.7645	0.7646	0.7645	0.7645
Mean Error	0.0060	0.0060	0.0040	0.0050	0.0050
RMSE	0.0607	0.0606	0.0605	0.0606	0.0605
Mean Abs Error	0.0480	0.0480	0.0480	0.0480	0.0480

$$\hat{y} = -0.0206 + 0.4390x_{n1} + 0.2170x_{n2} + 0.0972x_{n3} + 0.0125x_{n4}$$
$$+0.0149x_{n5} + 0.0011x_{n6} \tag{2}$$

3.4   Bayesian Linear Regression (BLR)

All seven covariates of interest were employed for BLR. The resultant regression equation was:

$$\hat{y} = -0.0159 + 0.4397x_{n1} + 0.2171x_{n2} + 0.0973x_{n3} + 0.0063x_{n4}$$
$$+0.0089x_{n5} - 0.0050x_{n6} - 0.0059x_{n7} \tag{3}$$

Both types of linear regressions are compared in Table 3. Once again, the two methods gave statistically similar correlation coefficients. Note that both Bayesian and frequentist linear regressions arrived at predictive equations (2) and (3) with similar constants and coefficients for the dam, sire and herd effects. Some degree of variation occurred in the coefficients of the seasonal effects, which can be explained by the omission of the variable x_{n7}, dam season of calving (spring), by the LR. The BLR, having been supplied with all variables, made adjustments in the coefficients of the other seasonal variables to allow for the inclusion of x_{n7}. It is also of interest to note that despite the other indicators being equivalent, there was some increase in the mean error of the BLR compared with LR. In the MCMC simulation it was observed that the main parameters of interest (x_1, x_2, x_3, corresponding to herd, dam and sire effects) were very stable, whilst the seasonal parameters (x_4 to x_7) were inclined to wander, with the constant α also inclined to wander, presumably to counteract the effect of the seasonal digressions. This may have occurred due to the over-specification of the BLR model with the inclusion of x_7.

4   Discussion

Four main conclusions arise from the studies carried out in this paper. Firstly, all four approaches are equivalent in terms of their predictive accuracy on the

Table 3. Correlations between the target values of daughter first milk yield and the predicted values, the mean of the error, RMSE, the mean absolute error for LR and BLR.

	Correlation	Mean Error	RMSE	Mean Abs Error
LR	0.7642	0.0001	0.0608	0.0475
BLR	0.7642	0.0002	0.0608	0.0475

dairy data, as indicated by a test of correlation coefficients between target and predicted value of daughter first milk yield.

Secondly, because of the similarities between the results for all four methods, there is little or no non-linearity in the dairy data. The initial data exploration using SLR and PCA as outlined in Section 2.1 indicated the presence of a possibly non-linear seasonal effect in the data. Some non-linearity in the data may have been removed during the pre-processing stage with the age adjustment for dam second milk yield. The small amount of remaining non-linearity did not impact greatly on the results, which were not significantly different for all four methods.

Thirdly, the predictive power of the BNN trained on the random subset of 1000 records was not significantly different from that of the network trained on the full training set, as indicated by a comparison of correlation coefficients. Moreover, the reduction in training time for the network was dramatic. This finding is significant, not only in terms of clock time necessary to train the network, but also in terms of the amount of data necessary for training. This raises the question of optimal required training set size for both NN and BNN, and further investigation is necessary to determine this.

Fourthly, it is apparent from this study that each different method provided its own particular advantages. On the one hand, both linear regression methods, LR and BLR, provide straightforward descriptions of the relationship being portrayed, as well as some quantification of the importance of each input attribute, by way of the respective predictive equations (2) and (3). On the other hand, both neural network approaches, BNN and NN, have indicated a possible non-linearity in the data by the slight preference for three or four hidden units seen in Tables 1 and 2. Similarly, an advantage of both Bayesian approaches is some quantification of uncertainty in prediction [16] with the BNN predictions expressed in terms of probabilities with credible intervals calculated, plus the added insight gained by the depiction of the Bayesian model using a graphical representation (see Figure 1). Conversely, an advantage of the non-Bayesian approaches, LR and NN, is their relative ease of implementation using readily available software, as opposed to the emerging techniques of both Bayesian approaches, whose implementations were made more difficult by software packages in the early stages of development and refinement.

This study has developed on the work of previous researchers in exploring the potential advantages of BNN over traditional NN learning. It is anticipated a more complete investigation will be undertaken to assess the effect of decreasing the amount of training data [12] on the predictive capability of NN and BNN, and the resulting decrease in the training time necessary. A further investigation of the other potential advantages of BNN including the model fitting aspect [14], the accommodation of missing values [4], and the avoidance of over-fitting when using a large network [12,17], is also foreseen.

Acknowledgement

This work is done as a part of an ARC collaborative grant number C19700273.

References

1. H.A. Abbass, W. Bligh, M. Towsey, M. Tierney, and G.D. Finn. Knowledge discovery in a dairy cattle database: automated knowledge acquisition. 5th Inter. Conf. of the Inter. Society for DSS, Melbourne, Australia, 1999.
2. H.A. Abbass, M. Towsey, and G.D. Finn. An intelligent decision support system for dairy cattle mate-allocation. Proceedings of the third Australian workshop on Intelligent Decision Support and Knowledge Management, pages 45–58, 1998.
3. R. Andrews and J. Diederich. Rules and networks. Proceedings of the Rule Extraction from Trained ANN Workshop, Univ. of Sussex, Brighton, U.K., 1996.
4. J. Besag, P. Green, D. Higdon, and K. Mengersen. Bayesian computation and stochastic systems. Statistical Science, 10:3–66.
5. T.G. Dietterich. Machine learning. Annual Rev. of Comp. Sci., 4:225–306, 1990.
6. J. Dommerholt and J.B.M. Wilmink. Optimal selection response under varying milk prices and margins for milk production. Livestock Production Science, 14:109–121, 1986.
7. G.D. Finn, R. Lister, R. Szabo, D. Simonetta, H. Mulder, and R. Young. Neural networks applied to a large biological database to analyse dairy breeding patterns. Neural Computing and Applications, 4:237–253, 1996.
8. A. Gelman, J.B. Carlin, H.S. Stern, and D.B. Rubin. Bayesian Data Analysis: Texts in Statistical Science. Chapman and Hall, London, 1995.
9. D. Gianola and R.L. Fernando. Bayesian methods in animal breeding theory. Animal Science, 63:217–244, 1986.
10. L.N. Hazel. The genetic basis for constructing selection indices. Genetics, 28:476–490, 1943.
11. C.R. Henderson. Use of all relatives in intraherd prediction of breeding values and producing abilities. Dairy Science, 58:1910–1916, 1975.
12. R. Lacroix, F. Salehi, X.Z. Yang, and K.M. Wade. Effects of data preprocessing on the performance of artificial neural networks for dairy yield prediction and cow culling clasification. Transactions of the ASAE, 40:839–846, 1997.
13. R. Lacroix, K.M. Wade, R. Kok, and J.F. Hayes. Predicting 305-day milk, fat and protein production with an artificial neural network. Proceeding of the third International Dairy Housing Conference: Dairy Systems for the 21st Century, pages 201–208, 1994.
14. D.J.C. MacKay. A practical bayesian framework for backpropagation networks. Neural Computation, 4:448–472, 1992.
15. MIT. Tlearn software. version 1.0.1. Exercises In Rethinking Innateness: A Handbook for Connectionist Simulations. MIT Press, 1997.

16. R.M. Neal. *Bayesian Learning for Neural Networks, Lecture Notes in Statistics No 11*. Springer-Verlag, 1996.

17. R.M. Neal. Software that implements flexible bayesian models based on neural networks, gaussian processes, and mixtures and that demonstrates markov chain monte carlo methods. *http://www.cs.utoronto.ca/~radford/*, 1998.

18. D.E. Rumelhart, B. Widrow, and M.A. Lehr. The basic ideas in neural networks. *Communications of the ACM*, 37:87–92, 1994.

19. G.H. Schmidt and L.D. Van Vleck. *Principles of Dairy Science*. W.H. Freeman and Company, 1974.

20. D.J. Spiegelhalter, A. Thomas, N.G. Best, and W.R. Gilks. *BUGS: Bayesian Inference using Gibbs Sampling, Version 0.50*. MRC Biostatistics Unit, Cambridge., 1995.

21. M. Towsey. *The use of neural networks in the automated analysis of the electroencephalogram*. PhD thesis, 1998.

22. P.M. Visscher and M.E. Goddard. Genetic analyses of profit for australian dairy cattle. *Animal Science*, 61:9–18, 1995.

23. K.M. Wade and R. Lacroix. The role of artificial neural networks in animal breeding. *The Fifth World Congress on Genetics Applied to Livestock Production*, pages 31–34, 1994.

24. B. Widrow, D.E. Rumelhart, and M.A. Lehr. Neural networks: Applications in industry, business and science. *Communications of the ACM*, 37:93–105, 1994.

Exploiting Sample-Data Distributions to Reduce the Cost of Nearest-Neighbor Searches with Kd-Trees

Doug Talbert and Doug Fisher

Department of Computer Science
Vanderbilt University
Nashville, TN 37235
USA
{dat,dfisher}@vuse.vanderbilt.edu

Abstract. We present KD-DT, an algorithm that uses a decision-tree-inspired measure to build a kd-tree for low cost nearest-neighbor searches. The algorithm starts with a "standard" kd-tree and uses searches over a training set to evaluate and improve the structure of the kd-tree. In particular, the algorithm builds a tree that better insures that a query and its nearest neighbors will be in the same subtree(s), thus reducing the cost of subsequent search.

1 Introduction

Kd-trees ([3], [8], [10]) support efficient nearest-neighbor searches for tasks such as instance-based reasoning (e.g., [4], [5], [14]).

KD-DT uses a decision-tree-inspired measure to build a kd-tree with lower cost nearest-neighbor searches than the "standard" approach of [8].

The algorithm starts with a "standard" kd-tree and uses searches over a training set to evaluate and improve the structure of the kd-tree. We test our approach in a nutrition database of 11,697 food instances, each instance described by 56 continuously-valued nutritional components (e.g., protein content and fat content) ([12], [13]).

Section 2 provides background information on kd-trees. Section 3 presents the algorithm with the decision-tree-inspired measure, and Section 4 discusses our experiments with this algorithm. Finally, Sections 5 and 6 describe related and future work, respectively.

2 Kd-Trees

Binary kd-trees organize k-dimensional data for efficient search of nearest neighbors. Internal nodes split dimensions using a threshold, thus partitioning the data, and each leaf lists the instances that satisfy the conditions implied by the path to the leaf.

D.J. Hand, J.N. Kok, M.R. Berthold (Eds.): IDA'99, LNCS 1642, pp. 407–414, 1999.
© Springer-Verlag Berlin Heidelberg 1999

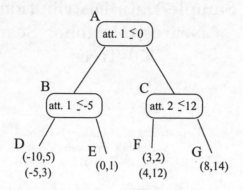

Fig. 1. A Simple Kd-Tree

Figure 1 shows a simple kd-tree on the following data points: (-10, 5) (-5,3) (0,1) (3,2) (4,12) (8,14).

Inputs to a kd-tree search are a "query" instance, a neighborhood size, and a kd-tree. For example, using the tree in Figure 1, we might request the 2 nearest neighbors of (-7, 4).

Two lists help in the search. One list keeps track of nearest neighbors seen thus far along with their distances from the query. The other list keeps track of the geometric boundaries of the current node. These boundaries are defined by the split point values at all of the node's ancestors. For the tree in Figure 1, the bounds on the root, node A, are $(-\infty < att_1 < \infty, -\infty < att_2 < \infty)$ and the bounds for node F are $(0 < att_1 < \infty, -\infty < att_2 \leq 12)$. All data points that lie within the bounds of a node are in the subtree of that node.

The list of nearest neighbors is initialized to contain the necessary number of instance slots with all the associated distances set to ∞.

The query instance is passed to a node. If that node is not a leaf, the query is compared to the node's split point and the appropriate child is identified. The boundaries list is updated, and the recursive call to the child is made. If the node is a leaf, the algorithm computes the distance of each datum at the leaf to the query instance and compares this distance to the farthest distance in the list of neighbors. The list of closest neighbors thus far is updated whenever a closer element is found.

Our example begins with:

Initial boundaries list: $(-\infty < att_1 < \infty, -\infty < att_2 < \infty)$
  Initial neighbor list: (*null*, ∞; *null*, ∞)

The query starts at the root, passes through node B, and reaches a leaf at node D. After searching D's data, the nearest neighbor list is ((-10, 5), 3.16; (-5, 3), 2.24).

After a node has been completely searched, the algorithm uses the boundary information to decide if it is done searching. If all the boundaries are a least as far away from the query as the farthest near neighbor, the algorithm can stop because every point outside that boundary is too far away to be of interest, and every point inside that boundary has already been examined.

In our example, the farther neighbor is 3.16 units away, but according to the current boundary conditions, $(-\infty < att_1 \leq -5, -\infty < att_2 < \infty)$, there is a boundary only 2 units from our query.

Thus, the algorithm backtracks to the previous node and checks to see if the other child needs to be searched. The boundaries of the unexamined child are compared to the distance, d, to the most distant near neighbor. If the space defined by the bounds of that node intersects the region of space within d units of the query, the node needs to be searched because there could be a closer value within that node's subtree.

In our example, the boundary for the unexplored child, node E, are $(-5 < att_1 \leq 0, -\infty < att_2 < \infty)$. We have a neighbor farther away than the boundary, $att_1 = 5$. Therefore, we search the node, but do not find any items close enough to update the neighbor list. E's bounds do not completely enclose the area containing possible near neighbors. So, we continue our search.

Since all of B's children have now been searched, the check to see if we can quit is performed again. The current boundaries are $(-\infty < att_1 \leq 0, -\infty < att_2 < \infty)$. All of those boundaries are more than 3.16 units from our query. Thus, our search stops and returns the current list of neighbors.

The fundamental operation during a kd-tree search is checking the distance from the query instance to a point along a single dimension which happens at varying times, during top-down traversal at each split point, at the leaves, and during backtracking.

A kd-tree learning algorithm [8] recursively partitions the data by the median of the dimension with the greatest range. The "longest" dimension is always split in an attempt to keep each node's geometric region as compact as possible.

The user specifies the number of elements allowed in a leaf node. The algorithm uses this threshold to decide when to stop partitioning a node.

The tree is Figure 1 was constructed in this manner over (-10,5) (-5,3) (0,1) (3,2) (4,12) (8,14).

Attribute 1, with a range of [-10, 8], has a broader spread than attribute 2. Thus, its median value, 0, is chosen as the first split point. The instances are then partitioned, and the process repeats until leaves smaller than the specified threshold (e.g., 2) are formed.

3   KD-DT

For each kd-tree node, the "standard" algorithm [8] examines each attribute in the search space and selects the median of the attribute with the broadest range to be the split point. This produces a balanced tree with informative splits that allow efficient searches. Ideally, the search would be able to proceed directly to the leaf containing all the nearest neighbors and complete its search without any backtracking.

Backtracking occurs when the nearest neighbors of the search item are separated by one of the split points in the kd-tree. KD-DT uses a decision-tree inspired measure to more directly measure the likelihood of backtracking given a particular split point.

Given an initial "standard" kd-tree, KD-DT identifies the nearest neighbors for every item in a training data set. It then builds a new tree, starting at the root, by examining all possible split points for each attribute at the current node. For each side of the split point, KD-DT measures the increase in likelihood that a training item's nearest neighbors lie on that side of the split point given that the item itself lies on that side of the split point over the likelihood that the nearest neighbors lie on that side of the split point without that condition. KD-DT then computes a weighted average of the scores for both sides and weights that score by the probability that the attribute's value is observed in the query.

The potential split point with the greatest score is selected. The training data are partitioned accordingly, and this process repeats at the child nodes until the number of food instances at a node fall below a user-specified threshold.

KD-DT's measure is:

$$Score_{SP_i} = P(a \text{ training instance has a value for } A_i) *$$
$$[P(T_{ji} \leq SP_i)[P(NN_{ji} \leq SP_i | T_{ji} \leq SP_i)^2 - P(NN_i \leq SP_i)^2] +$$
$$P(T_{ji} > SP_i)[P(NN_{ji} > SP_i | T_{ji} > SP_i)^2 - P(NN_i > SP_i)^2]],$$

where

- A_i is the attribute currently under consideration,
- SP_i the split point along A_i currently under consideration,
- T_{ji} is the value for attribute A_i for the jth training (query) instance,
- NN_{ji} is value for attribute A_i for a nearest neighbor of the jth training (query) instance,
- $P(a \text{ training instance has a value for } A_i)$ is the probability that a training (query) instance has a value for its ith attribute,
- $P(T_{ji} \leq SP_i)$ is the probability that the value of the ith attribute for a training instance is less than or equal to the split point currently under consideration,
- $P(NN_i \leq SP_i)$ is the probability that the value of the ith attribute for a nearest neighbor is less than or equal to the value of the considered split point,
- $P(NN_{ji} \leq SP_i | T_{ji} \leq SP_i)$ is the probability that the value of the ith attribute for a nearest neighbor of a training (query) instance is less than or equal to the value of the split point currently under consideration given that the value of the ith attribute for the training instance is less than or equal to the value of the considered split point.

Inspired by the Gini-index used for building decision trees, this measure collectively assesses the extent that a query instance and its nearest neighbors will lie on the same side of a split point. The split point that maximizes the measure is chosen to represent the attribute. The attribute with the maximum score is chosen to split the data.

Finally, KD-DT handles missing values differently than the "standard" algorithm. When a food instance is missing a value needed to compute its distance from a query, KD-DT uses the (global) mean value of that dimension as an estimate, and during tree construction, when a food instance is missing a value needed to decide which subtree the instance belongs in, KD-DT puts the food instances in both subtrees. Since KD-DT estimates missing values during search, this insures that no potential neighbor is missed during the search.

4   Experiments

To test KD-DT we ordered our food instances alphabetically and split them into 10 equal subsets. For each subset, we performed the following 5-fold cross validation test. We randomly split the subset into five equal groups. For each combination of four partition elements, we built a standard kd-tree and measured its average search cost for finding 10 nearest-neighbors for each item in the fifth (test) group. We used a maximum leaf size of 10 food instances. Then we searched the tree for the 10 nearest-neighbors for each food instance in the four (training) groups used to build the tree. For each training instance we processed this way, we recorded its 10 nearest neighbors. Once completed, we have collected a set of ordered pairs: a training instance along with its 10 nearest neighbors, for each instance. We built a new kd-tree using the measure from Section 3 with this (ordered-pair) training data and repeated the search for the 10 nearest-neighbors for each item in the fifth (test) set using the new kd-tree.

Thus each experimental fold measured the cost of finding nearest neighbors using the standard tree over a test set, with the cost of finding nearest neighbors using an alternative tree constructed as described in Section 3. Cost was measured in terms of the number of single dimension distance calculations, which as mentioned in Section 2, is the fundamental operation of kd-tree search.

Table 1 shows the individual results for these experiments, and table 2 shows the average results over all 10 5-fold cross validations.

On average, the nearest neighbors searches in the KD-DT trees was 48% "cheaper" than in the standard kd-trees. Typical cost reduction was around 40–45%. Set 5 showed the least improvement (26%), and set 10 showed the best improvement (64%).

5   Related Work

KD-DT uses more information about the distribution of the search space and its nearest neighbors to build a kd-tree than the standard approach of [8]. It may, however, be the case that user queries exhibit an entirely different distribution than the data (e.g., USDA database) itself. For example, user queries might focus on a small subset of the attributes rather than the entire set. In our nutrition domain, this could occur when a user is focused on a specific nutritional concern.

Table 1. Individual 5-fold cross validation tests

	Default tree	"Trained" tree
Set 1	14479.62	9204.44
	(7599.74)	(6595.23)
Set 2	13727.56	7704.59
	(8659.75)	(5691.19)
Set 3	14542.01	9534.22
	(8067.75)	(6341.54)
Set 4	11432.87	6997.28
	(7586.69)	(6015.32)
Set 5	17335.92	12854.28
	(7751.10)	(6111.17)
Set 6	33788.87	14270.89
	(22038.56)	(9288.01)
Set 7	13661.31	7583.69
	(9785.98)	(6369.20)
Set 8	13580.47	8582.13
	(8657.28)	(6979.09)
Set 9	32000.21	16199.83
	(17745.07)	(8230.35)
Set 10	42690.15	15410.24
	(36097.41)	(12659.85)

Table 2. Summary of experiments

Default tree	Trained tree
20723.90	10834.16
(13398.93)	(7428.10)

For example, a diabetic might only be interested in foods with high protein and low carbohydrates. In [12], we present OPT-KD, an algorithm that exploits information about (simulated-user) query distributions to improve kd-tree search efficiency under such conditions, by excluding those attributes that are not commonly part of user queries. Thus, [12] reexpresses "the data" subsequent to new tree construction, but does not otherwise exploit query distribution information.

There are also other kd-tree algorithms that use different split point selection techniques. [10] uses the mean of the "broadest" attribute as the split point rather than the median, and whereas [8] and [10] partition the data at a node using a plane orthogonal to an attribute, [11] uses matrix computations to select a non-orthogonal partition plane. VP-trees [15] decompose the search space spherically instead of rectangularly as kd-trees do. Another nearest-neighbor approach from computational geometry is Voronoi diagrams ([2], [6], [7]).

Machine learning has been also been applied to diet management in the CAMPER system [9]. This system combines case-based reasoning techniques with a rule-based reasoning technique to use information about an individual's nutritional needs and personal preferences to suggest a daily menu for that person.

6 Future Work

We are very interested in the contrast between the data over which a kd-tree is constructed (e.g., records from the USDA database) and the queries of this data by a particular user or a population of users (e.g., find foods nearest neighbors to a high-protein, low-fat food such as tuna). These queries may themselves serve as data, but with very different distributional properties than the data to which they are being applied. Split measures like the one that we have introduced in this paper can be applied in conjunction with either kind of data set. Future work will investigate ways of exploiting the distribution of both populations, data and user queries, in building customized kd-trees that reduce nearest-neighbor searches for a particular user or group of users.

Since we are using the search space itself as the training set, a natural extension to our current work would be a incremental kd-tree construction algorithm that incorporated queried items into the search space while learning how to organize the tree.

We are examining the effects of training on a subset of the search space rather than on the entire data set as well as the effects of searching for different numbers of neighbors during the training phase.

The relationship of our work to other nearest-neighbor techniques and to applications that rely on nearest-neighbor search (e.g., instance-based reasoning) needs to be examined as well.

Finally, our handling of missing values is simplistic, and other techniques need to be examined. We are exploring other value estimation techniques, and we are considering adopting Aha's IGNORE technique [1]. We also are exploring methods to quantify the utility of these techniques.

References

1. Aha, D. W.: A Study of Instance-Based Algorithms for Supervised Learning Tasks. Technical Report TR-90-42, University of California, Irvine (1990)
2. Aurenhammer F.: Voronoi Diagrams—A Survey of a Fundamental Geometric Data Structure. ACM Computing Surveys **23** (1991) 345-405.
3. Bentley, J. L.: Multidimensional Divide and Conquer. Communications of the ACM **23** (1980) 214-229
4. Dasarathy, B. V. (ed.): Nearest Neighbor (NN) Norms: NN Pattern Classification Techniques, IEEE Computer Society Press, Los Alamitos (1991)
5. Deng, K., Moore, A. W.: Multiresolution instance-based learning. In: IJCAI-95, Morgan Kaufmann, San Mateo (1995)

6. Fortune, S.: Voronoi Diagrams and Delaunay Triangulations. In: Hwang, F., Du, D. Z. (eds.): Computing in Euclidean Geometry (Second Edition), World Scientific, Singapore (1995)

7. Fortune, S.: Voronoi Diagrams and Delaunay Triangulations. In: Goodman, J. E., O'Rourke, J. (eds.): Discrete and Computational Geometry, CRC Press, New York (1997)

8. Friedman, J. H., Bentley, J. L., Finkel, R. A.: An Algorithm for Finding Best Matches in Logarithmic Expected Time. ACM Transactions on Mathematical Software **3** (1977) 209–226

9. Marling, C., Petot, G., Sterling, L.: A CBR/RBR Hybrid for Designing Nutritional Menus. In: Freuder, G. (ed.): Multimodal Reasoning: Papers from the 1998 AAAI Spring Symposium, AAAI Press, Menlo Park (1998)

10. Moore, A. W.: Efficient Memory-Based Learning for Robot Control. Technical Report No. 209 (PhD. Thesis), Computer Laboratory, University of Cambridge (1991)

11. Sproull, R. F.: Refinements to Nearest-Neighbor Searching in K-Dimensional Trees. J. Algorithmica **6** (1991) 579–589

12. Talbert, D., Fisher, D.: OPT-KD: An Algorithm for Optimizing Kd-Trees. In: Bratko, I., Dzeroski, S. (eds.): Machine Learning: Proceedings of the Sixteenth International Conference, Morgan Kaufmann, San Francisco (1999)

13. U.S. Dept. of Agriculture, Agricultural Research Service: USDA Nutrient Database for Standard Reference, Release 12. Nutrient Data Laboratory Home Page, http://www.nal.usda.gov/fnic/foodcomp (1998)

14. Wettschereck, D., Aha, D. W., Mohri, T.: A Review and Empirical Evaluation of Feature Weighting Methods for a Class of Lazy Learning Algorithms. Artificial Intelligence Review **11** (1997) 273–314

15. Yianilos, P. N.: Data Structures and Algorithms for Nearest Neighbor Search in General Metric Spaces. In: Proceedings of the Fourth ACM-SIAM Symposium on Discrete Algorithms (1993)

Pump Failure Detection Using Support Vector Data Descriptions

David M.J. Tax, Alexander Ypma, and Robert P.W. Duin

Pattern Recognition Group
Dept. of Applied Physics, Faculty of Applied Sciences
Delft University of Technology
Lorentzweg 1, 2628 CJ Delft, The Netherlands
{davidt,ypma}@ph.tn.tudelft.nl

Abstract. For good classification preprocessing is a key step. Good preprocessing reduces the noise in the data and retains most information needed for classification. Poor preprocessing on the other hand can make classification almost impossible. In this paper we evaluate several feature extraction methods in a special type of outlier detection problem, machine fault detection. We will consider measurements on water pumps under both normal and abnormal conditions. We use a novel data description method, called the Support Vector Data Description, to get an indication of the complexity of the normal class in this data set and how well it is expected to be distinguishable from the abnormal data.

1 Introduction

For good classification the preprocessing of the data is a important step. Good preprocessing reduces the noise in the data and retains as much of the information as possible [1]. When the number of objects in the training set is too small for the number of features used (the feature space is under sampled), most classification procedures cannot find good classification boundaries. This is called the **curse of dimensionality** (see for an extended explanation [3]). By good preprocessing the number of features per object can be reduced such that the classification problem can be solved.

A particular type of preprocessing is feature selection. In feature selection one tries to find the optimal feature set from a already given set of features [5]. In general this set is very large. To compare different feature sets, a criterion has to be defined. Often very simple criteria are used for judging the quality of the feature set or the difficulty of the data set. See [2] for a list of different measures.

Sometimes we encounter a special type of classification problems, so-called outlier detection or data domain description problems. In data domain description the goal is to accurately describe **one** class of objects, the target class, as opposed to a wide range of other objects which are not of interest or are considered outliers [7]. This last class is therefore called the outlier class. Many standard pattern recognition methods are not well equipped to handle this type of problem; they require complete descriptions for both classes. Especially when

D.J. Hand, J.N. Kok, M.R. Berthold (Eds.): IDA'99, LNCS 1642, pp. 415–425, 1999.
© Springer-Verlag Berlin Heidelberg 1999

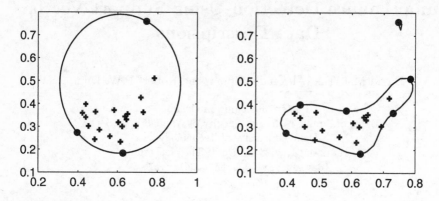

Fig. 1. Data description of a small data set, (left) normal spherical description, (right) description using a Gaussian kernel.

the outlier class is very diverse and ill-sampled, normal (two class) classifiers obtain very bad generalizations for this class.

In this paper we will introduce a new method for data domain description, the Support Vector Data Description (SVDD). This method is inspired on the Support Vector Classifier by V. Vapnik [9] and it defines a spherically shaped boundary with minimal volume around the target data set. Under some restrictions, the spherically shaped data description can be made more flexible by replacing normal inner products by some kernel functions. This will be explained in more detail in section 2.

In this paper we try to find the best representation of a data set such that the target class is optimally clustered and can be distinguished as best as possible from the outlier class. The data set here considered is vibration data recorded from a water pump. The target class contains recordings from the normal behavior of the pump, while erroneous behaviour is placed in the outlier class. Different preprocessing methods will be applied to the recorded signals in order to find the optimal set of features.

We will start with an explanation of the Support Vector Data Description in section 2. In section 3 the origins of the vibration data will be explained and in section 4 we will discuss the different types of features extracted from this data set. In section 5 the results of the experiments are shown and we will conclude with conclusions in section 6.

2   Support Vector Data Description

The Support Vector Data Description (SVDD) is the method which we will use to describe our data. It is inspired on the Support Vector Classifier of V. Vapnik ([9], or for a more simple introduction [6]). The SVDD is explained in more detail in [8], here we will just give a quick impression of the method.

The idea of the method is to find the sphere with minimal volume which contains all data. Assume we have data set containing N data objects, $\{x_i, i = 1, .., N\}$ and the sphere is described by center a and radius R. We now try to minimize an error function containing the volume of the sphere. The constraints that objects are within the sphere are imposed by applying Lagrange multipliers:

$$L(R, a, \alpha_i) = R^2 - \sum_i \alpha_i \{R^2 - (x_i^2 - 2ax_i + a^2)\} \tag{1}$$

with Lagrange multipliers $\alpha_i \geq 0$. This function has to be minimized with respect to R and a and maximized with respect to α_i.

Setting the partial derivatives of L to R and a to zero, gives:

$$\sum_i \alpha_i = 1 \quad \text{and} \quad a = \frac{\sum_i \alpha_i x_i}{\sum_i \alpha_i} = \sum_i \alpha_i x_i \tag{2}$$

This shows that the center of the sphere a is a linear combination of the data objects x_i.

Resubstituting these values in the Lagrangian gives to maximize with respect to α_i:

$$L = \sum_i \alpha_i (x_i \cdot x_i) - \sum_{i,j} \alpha_i \alpha_j (x_i \cdot x_j) \tag{3}$$

with $\alpha_i \geq 0$, $\sum_i \alpha_i = 1$.

This function should be maximized with respect to α_i. In practice this means that a large fraction of the α_i become zero. For a small fraction $\alpha_i > 0$ and these objects are called Support Objects. We see that the center of the sphere depends just on the few support objects, objects with $\alpha_i = 0$ can be disregarded.

Object z is accepted when:

$$(z - a)(z - a)^T = (z - \sum_i \alpha_i x_i)(z - \sum_i \alpha_i x_i)$$

$$= (z \cdot z) - 2 \sum_i \alpha_i (z \cdot x_i) + \sum_{i,j} \alpha_i \alpha_j (x_i \cdot x_j) \leq R^2 \tag{4}$$

In general this does not give a very tight description. Analogous to the method of Vapnik [9], we can replace the inner products $(x \cdot y)$ in equations (3) and in (4) by kernel functions $K(x, y)$ which gives a much more flexible method. When we replace the inner products by Gaussian kernels for instance, we obtain:

$$(x \cdot y) \rightarrow K(x, y) = \exp(-(x - y)^2 / s^2) \tag{5}$$

Equation (3) now changes into:

$$L = 1 - \sum_i \alpha_i^2 - \sum_{i \neq j} \alpha_i \alpha_j K(x_i, x_j) \tag{6}$$

and and the formula to check if a new object z is within the sphere (equation (4)) becomes:

$$1 - 2\sum_i \alpha_i K(z, x_i) + \sum_{i,j} \alpha_i \alpha_j K(x_i, x_j) \leq R^2 \tag{7}$$

We obtain a more flexible description than the rigid sphere description. In figure 1 both methods are shown applied on the same two dimensional data set. The sphere description on the left includes all objects, but is by no means very tight. It includes large areas of the feature space where no target patterns are present. In the right figure the data description using Gaussian kernels is shown, and it clearly gives a superior description. No large empty areas are included, what minimizes the change of accepting outlier patterns. To obtain this tighter description, one training object in the right upper corner is rejected from the description.

This Gaussian kernel contains one extra free parameter, the width parameter s in the kernel (equation (5)). As shown in [8] this parameter can be determined by setting a priori the maximal allowed rejection rate of the target set, i.e. the error on the target set. Applying leave-one-out estimation on the training set shows that non-support objects will be accepted by the SVDD when they are left out of the training set, while support object will be rejected. Therefore the error on the target set can be estimated by the fraction of training objects that become support objects in the data description:

$$E[P(\text{error})] = \frac{\#SV}{N} \tag{8}$$

where $\#SV$ is the number of support vectors.

In [8] it is shown that equation 8 is a good estimate of the error on the target class. The fact that the fraction support objects can immediately be used for the estimate of the error on the target class, makes this data description method a very efficient one with respect to the number of objects needed. Because independent test data is not necessary, all available data can immediately used for estimating the SVDD.

Note we cannot set a priori restrictions on the error on the outlier class. In general we only have a good representation of the target class and the outlier class is per definition everything else.

3   Machine Vibration Analysis

Vibration was measured on a small pump in an experimental setting and on two identical pump sets in pumping station "Buma" at Lemmer. One of the pumps in the pumping station showed severe gear damage (pitting, i.e. surface cracking due to unequal load and wear) whereas the other pump showed no significant damage. Both pumps of the pumping station have similar power consumption, age and amount of running hours.

The Delft test rig comprises a small submersible pump, which can be made to run at several speeds (from 46 to 54 Hz) and several loads (by closing a membrane controlling the water flow). A number of faults were induced to this pump: loose foundation, imbalance, failure in the outer race of the uppermost ball bearing. Both normal and faulty behaviour was measured at several speeds and loads.

In both set-ups accelerometers were used to measure the vibration near different structural elements of the machine (shaft, gears, bearings). Features from several channels were collected as seperate samples in the the same feature space, i.e. inclusion of several channels increases the sample size, not the feature dimensionality. By putting the measurements of the different sensors into one data set, the data set increases in size, but information on the exact position of an individual measurement is lost.

For the Lemmer measurements three feature sets were constructed by joining different sensor measurements into one set:

1. one radial channel near the place of heavy pitting (expected to be a good feature),
2. two radial channels near both heavy and moderate pitting along with an (unbalance sensitive) axial channel, and
3. inclusion of all channels (except for the sensor near the outgoing shaft which might be too sensitive to non-fault related vibration).

As a reference dataset, we constructed a high-resolution logarithmic power spectrum estimation (512 bins), normalized w.r.t. mean and standard deviation and its linear projection (using Principal Components Analysis) on a 10-dimensional subspace. Three channels were included, expected to be roughly comparable to the second configuration previously described.

For the Delft dataset the same procedure was followed: the first set contains data from one channel near a fault location, the second set contains three channels near fault bearings and the third set contains all five channels.

4   Features for Machine Diagnostics

We compared several methods for feature extraction from vibration data. It is well known that faults in rotating machines will be visible in the acceleration spectrum as increased harmonics of running speed or presence of sidebands around characteristic (structure-related) frequencies. Due to overlap in series of harmonic components and noise, high spectral resolution may be required for adequate fault identification. This may lead to difficulties because of the curse of dimensionality: one needs large sample sizes in high-dimensional spaces in order to avoid overfitting of the train set. Hence we focused on relatively low feature dimensionality (64) and compared the following features:

power spectrum: standard power spectrum estimation, using Welch's averaged periodogram method. Data is normalized to the mean prior to spectrum estimation, and feature vectors (consisting of spectral amplitudes) are normalized w.r.t. mean and standard deviation (in order to retain only sensitivity to the spectrum shape).

envelope spectrum: a measurement time series was demodulated using the Hilbert transform, and from this cleaned signal (supposedly containing information on periodic impulsive behavior) a spectrum was determined using the above method. Prior to demodulation a bandpass-filtering in the interval 125 - 250 Hz (using a wavelet decomposition with Daubechies-wavelets of order 4) was performed: gear mesh frequencies will be present in this band and impulses due to pitting are expected to be present as sidebands. For comparison, this pre-filtering step was left out in another data set.

autoregressive modelling: another way to use second-order correlation information as a feature is to model the timeseries with an autoregressive model (AR-model). For comparison with other features, an AR(64)-model was used (which seemed sufficient to extract all information) and model coefficients were used as features.

MUSIC spectrum estimation: if a time series can be modeled as a model of sinusoids plus noise, we can use a MUSIC frequency estimator to focus on the important spectral components [4]. A statistic can be computed that tends to infinity when a signal vector belongs to the so-called signal subspace. When one expects amplitudes at a finite number of discrete frequencies to be a discriminant indicator, MUSIC features may enable good separability while keeping feature size (relatively) small.

some classical indicators: three typical indicators for machine wear are
 − rms-value of the power spectrum
 − kurtosis of the signal distribution
 − crest-factor of the vibration signal

The first feature is just the average amount of energy in the vibration signal (square root of mean of squared amplitudes). Kurtosis is the 4th central moment of a distribution, that measures the 'peakedness' of a distribution. Gaussian distributions will have kurtosis near 0 whereas distributions with heavy tails (e.g. in the presence of impulses in the time signal) will show larger values. The crest-factor of a vibration signal is defined as the peak amplitude value divided by the root-mean-square amplitude value (both from the envelope detected time signal). This feature will be sensitive to sudden defect bursts, while the mean (or: rms-) value of the signal has not changed significantly.

5   Experiments

To compare the different feature sets the SVDD is applied to all target data sets. Because also test objects from the outlier class are available (i.e. the fault class defined by the pump exhibiting pitting, see section 3), the rejection performance on the outlier set can also be measured.

In all experiments we have used the SVDD with a Gaussian kernel. For each of the feature sets we have optimized the width parameter s in the SVDD such that $1\%, 5\%, 10\%, 25\%$ and 50% of the target objects will be rejected, so for each data set and each target error another width parameter s is obtained. For each feature set this gives an acceptance-rejection curve for the target and the outlier class.

We will start with considering the Lemmer data set with the third sensor combination (see section 3) which contains all sensor measurements. In this case we do not use prior knowledge about where the sensors are placed and which sensor might contain most useful information.

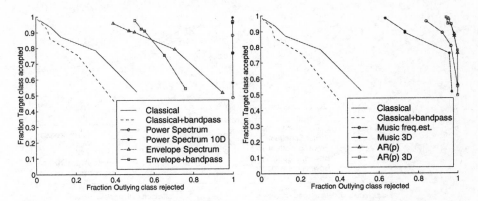

Fig. 2. Acceptance/rejection performance of the SVDD on the features on the Lemmer data set, with all sensor measurements collected.

In figure 2 the characteristic of the SVDD on this data is shown. If we look at the results for the power spectrum using 512 bins (see left figure 2) we see that for all target acception levels we can reject 100% of the outlier class. This is the ideal behavior we are looking for in a data description method and it shows that in principle the target class can be distinguished from the outlier class very well. Drawback in this representation though is that each object contains 512 power spectrum bins, it is both expensive to calculate this large a Fourier spectrum and expensive in storage costs. That is why we try other, smaller representations.

Reducing this 512 bin spectrum to just 10 features by applying a Principal Component Analysis (PCA) and retaining the ten directions with the largest variations, we see that still we can perfectly reject the outlier class.

Looking at the results of the classical method and the classical method using bandpass filtering, we see that the target class and the outlier class overlap significantly. When we try to accept 95% of the target class only 10% or less is rejected by the SVDD. Also considerable overlap between the target and the outlier class is present when envelope spectra are used. When 5-10% of the target class is rejected, still about 50% of the outlier class is accepted. Here also bandpass filtering does not improve the performance very much, only for large target acceptance rates, the bandpass filtering is useful.

Finally in the right figure 2 the results for the MUSIC estimator and the AR-model features are shown. The results on the AR-model feature set and the MUSIC frequency estimation feature are superior to all other methods, with the AR model somewhat better than the MUSIC estimator. The AR model approximates almost the 512 bin power spectrum, only for very large acceptance rates of the target class, we see some patterns from the outlier class being accepted. Applying the SVDD on the first three principal components deteriorates the performance of the MUSIC estimator. The AR model still performs almost optimal.

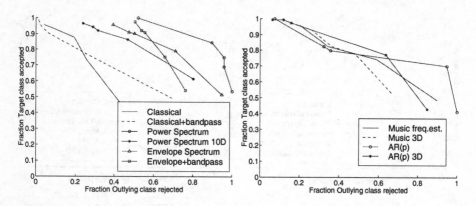

Fig. 3. Acceptance/rejection performance of the SVDD on the features on the Delft data set, with all sensor measurements collected.

In figure 3 similar figures are shown for the Delft measurements. Looking at the performance of the 512 bin power spectrum, we see that here already considerable overlap between the target and the outlier class exist. This indicates that this problem is more difficult than the Lemmer data set. The performances by the different features do not vary much, the MUSIC estimator, AR-model and the envelope spectrum perform about equal. In all cases there is considerable overlap between target and outlier class. This might indicate that for one (or more) of the outlier classes the characteristics are almost equal to the target class characteristics (and thus it is hard to speak of an outlier class).

The analysis was done on a data set in which all sensor information was used. Next we look at the performance of the first and the second combination of sensors in the Lemmer data set. In figure 4 the performance of the SVDD is shown on all feature sets applied on sensor combination (1) (on the left) and combination (2) (on the right). Here also the classical features perform poorly. The envelope spectrum works reasonably well, but both the MUSIC frequency estimator and the AR-model features perform perfectly. The data from sensor combination (1) is clearly better clustered than sensor combination (3). Only the AR model features and the Envelope detection with bandpass filtering on the single sensor data set shows reasonable performance.

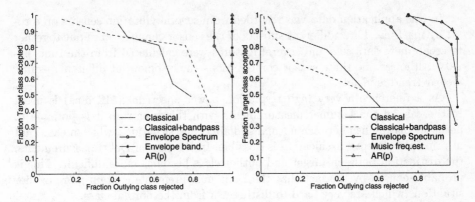

Fig. 4. Acceptance/rejection performance of the SVDD on the different features for sensor combination (1) and (2) in the Lemmer data set.

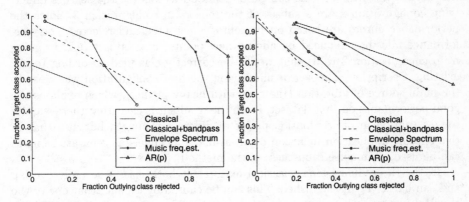

Fig. 5. Acceptance/rejection performance of the SVDD on the different features for sensor combination (1) and (2) in the Delft data set.

We can observe the same trend in figure 5, where the performances are plotted for sensor combination (1) and (2) in the Delft data set. Here also the MUSIC estimator and the AR model outperform the other types of features, but there are large errors, which can be expected considering the complexity of this problem.

6   Conclusion

In this paper we tried to find the best representation of a data set such that the target class can best be distinguished from the outlier class. This is done by applying the Support Vector Data Description, a method which finds the smallest sphere containing all target data. We applied the SVDD in a machine diagnostics problem, where the normal working situation of a pump in a pumping station (Lemmer data) and a pump in an experimental setting (Delft data) should be distinguished from abnormal behavior.

In this application data was recorded from several vibration sensors on a rotating machine. Three different subsets of the sensor channels were put together to create new data sets and several features were calculated from the time signals. Although the three sensor combinations show somewhat different results, a clear trend is visible.

As a reference a very high resolution power spectrum (512 bins) is used. In the case of the Lemmer measurements with this spectrum it is possible to perfectly distinguish between normal and abnormal situations, which means that in principle perfect classification is possible. In the case of Delft measurements, the distinction between target and outlier class becomes more difficult. This is probably caused by the fact that the Delft measurements contain more outlier situations which are very hard to distinguish from the normal class.

Performance of both MUSIC- and AR-features was usually very good in all three configuration data sets, but worst in the second configuration and best in the third configuration. This can be understood as follows: the sensors underlying configuration 2 are a subset of the sensors in configuration 3. Since the performance curves are based on percentages accepted and rejected, this performance may be enhanced by adding new points to a dataset (e.g. in going from configuration 2 to 3) that would be correctly classified according to the existing description. The sensor underlying the first configuration was close to the main source of vibration (the gear with heavy pitting), which explains the good performance on that dataset. From the results it is clear that there is quite some variation in discrimination power of different channels, but also that in this specific application inclusion of all available channels as separate samples can be used to enhance robustness of the method.

In the three dimensional classical feature set both classes severely overlap and can hardly be distinguished. This can be caused by the fact that one of the classical features is kurtosis, whose estimate shows large variance. Increasing the time signal over which the kurtosis is estimated might improve performance, but this would require long measurement runs.

When all sensor combinations and both Lemmer and Delft data sets are considered, the AR-model allows for the tightest description of the normal class when compared with all other features. We can conclude that if we want to use shorter representations of vibration data to overcome the curse of dimensionality, the AR-model is best choice.

7   Acknowledgments

This work was partly supported by the Foundation for Applied Sciences (STW) and the Dutch Organisation for Scientific Research (NWO). We would like to thank TechnoFysica B.V. and pumping station "Buma" at Lemmer, The Netherlands (Waterschap Noord-Oost Polder) for providing support with the measurements.

References

[1] C.M. Bishop. *Neural Networks for Pattern Recognition.* Oxford University Press, Walton Street, Oxford OX2 6DP, 1995.

[2] P.A. Devijver and J. Kittler. *Pattern Recognition, A statistical approach.* Prentice-Hall International, London, 1982.

[3] R.O. Duda and P.E. Hart. *Pattern Classification and Scene Analysis.* John Wiley & Sons, New York, 1973.

[4] J.G. Proakis and D.G. Manolakis. *Digital signal processing - principles, algorithms and applications, 2nd ed.* MacMillan Publ., New York, 1992.

[5] P. Pudil, J. Novovicova, and J. Kittler. Floating search methods in feature selection. *Pattern Recognition Letters*, 15(11):1119–1125, 1994.

[6] D.M.J. Tax, D. de Ridder, and R.P.W. Duin. Support vector classifiers: a first look. In *Proceedings ASCI'97.* ASCI, 1997.

[7] D.M.J. Tax and R.P.W Duin. Outlier detection using classifier instability. In Amin, A., Dori, D., Pudil, P., and Freeman, H., editors, *Advances in Pattern Recognition, Lecture notes in Computer Science*, volume 1451, pages 593–601, Berlin, August 1998. Proc. Joint IAPR Int. Workshops SSPR'98 and SPR'98 Sydney, Australia, Springer.

[8] D.M.J. Tax and R.P.W Duin. Data domain description using support vectors. In Verleysen M., editor, *Proceedings of the European Symposium on Artificial Neural Networks 1999*, pages 251–256. D.Facto, Brussel, April 1999.

[9] V. Vapnik. *The Nature of Statistical Learning Theory.* Springer-Verlag New York, Inc., 1995.

Data Mining for the Detection of Turning Points in Financial Time Series

Thorsten Poddig and Claus Huber

University of Bremen, Chair of Finance
FB 7, Hochschulring 40
D-28359 Bremen, Germany
poddig@uni-bremen.de
huberc@uni-bremen.de

Abstract. One of the most challenging problems in econometrics is the prediction of turning points in financial time series. We compare ARMA- and Vector-Autoregressive (VAR-) models by examining their abilities to predict turning points in monthly time series. An approach proposed by Wecker[1] and enhanced by Kling[2] forms the basis to explicitly incorporate uncertainty in the forecasts by producing probabilistic statements for turning points. To allow for possible structural change within the time period under investigation, we conduct Data Mining by using rolling regressions over a fix-sized window. For each datapoint a multitude of models is estimated. The models are evaluated by an economic performance criterion, the Sharpe-Ratio, and a testing procedure for its statistical significance developed by Jobson/Korkie[3]. We find that ARMA-models seem to be valuable forecasting tools for predicting turning points, whereas the performance of the VAR-models is disappointing.

1 Introduction

Facing the task of forecasting with a quantitative model, an economist usually estimates a single model to produce point forecasts. Thereby the uncertainty inherent in any kind of forecast is neglected: "The generation of a forecast is of no great practical value if some measure of the uncertainty of that forecast cannot also be provided."[4]. In this paper, our intention is to explicitly incorporate this uncertainty into probabilistic statements for turning points in monthly financial time series. We implement a Monte-Carlo-based regression introduced by Wecker[1] and enhanced by Kling[2], which is described in section 2. To decide which models (ARMA or VAR) perform better we take the view of a participant in the financial markets. Here one is not interested to optimize statistical criteria, like Mean Squared Error etc., but in an acceptable profit for the taken risk. The Sharpe-Ratio is a performance criterion which allows to relate the profits to the risk of an investment. In section 3 we briefly review its basics and a test for statistical significance of the Sharpe Ratio of two investments. Section 4 describes our Data Mining approach to out-of-sample model selection

D.J. Hand, J.N. Kok, M.R. Berthold (Eds.): IDA'99, LNCS 1642, pp. 427–436, 1999.

with the rolling regressions and the research design to compare the ARMA- and VAR-models. Section 5 presents empirical results and concludes.

2   Probabilistic Statements for Turning Points in Time Series

As a first step to obtain a probabilistic statement about a near-by turning point one has to define a rule when a turning point in the time series is detected. The turning point indicator

$$z_t^P = \begin{cases} 1, & \text{if a peak occurs at time } t \\ 0, & \text{otherwise} \end{cases} \tag{1}$$

is defined as a local extreme value of a certain amount of preceding and succeeding datapoints:

$$z_t^P = \begin{cases} 1, & \text{if } x_t > x_{t+i}, i = -\tau, -\tau+1, \ldots, -1, 1, \ldots, \tau-1, \tau \\ 0, & \text{otherwise} \end{cases} \tag{2}$$

The trough indicator z_t^T is defined in an analogous way.[1] As we investigate monthly time series, we define $\tau = 2$. Choosing $\tau = 1$ would result in a model too sensitive to smaller movements of the time series, whereas with $\tau > 2$ the model would react with inacceptable delay. At time t the economist knows only the current and past datapoints $x_t, x_{t-1}, \ldots, x_{t-\tau+1}, x_{t-\tau}$. The future values $x_{t+1}, \ldots, x_{t+\tau-1}, x_{t+\tau}$ have to be estimated. Since the turning point indicators $z_t^P, z_{t+1}^P, \ldots$, respectively $z_t^T, z_{t+1}^T, \ldots$, are functions of the future datapoints $X_{t+1}, X_{t+2}, \ldots$, they are random variables. Using econometric models and the known $x_t, x_{t-1}, \ldots, x_{t-\tau+1}, x_{t-\tau}$, one can estimate $\hat{x}_{t+1}, \ldots, \hat{x}_{t+\tau-1}, \hat{x}_{t+\tau}$. Here it becomes clear that the ability for the detection of turning points critically depends on the forecasting model. The time series (X_t) could be generated by a univariate autoregressive process. In this case the following model is adequate to describe the true data generating process (DGP):[2]

$$x_{t+1} = \beta_0 + \beta_1 x_t + \beta_2 x_{t-1} + \ldots + \beta_R x_{t-R+1} + \epsilon_{t+1} \tag{3}$$

where β_i are the regression coefficients, R is the order of the AR process, and ϵ_{t+1} is a white noise disturbance term. Using optimisation techniques, such as Ordinary Least Squares, a model can be estimated from the data so that $E[\hat{\beta}_i] = \beta_i$. The model reflects the supposed DGP. The standard deviations $\sigma_{\hat{\beta}_i}$ of the estimated regression coefficients $\hat{\beta}_i$ and the standard deviation $\sigma_{\hat{\epsilon}_{t+1}}$ of the disturbance term are measures of the uncertainty of the forecast by the model and can be used to judge the ability of the model to mimic the true DGP. High $\sigma_{\hat{\beta}_i}$

---

[1] Furtheron we do not explicitly distinguish between peaks and troughs.

[2] The simple AR-process only serves for illustration purposes. More complex processes (e.g. VAR-, non-linear processes) could be relevant as well. The time series (X_t) here is meant to decribe a scalar. Generalisations to vector notation are straightforward.

resp. $\sigma_{\hat{\epsilon}_{t+1}}$ correspond to high uncertainty, whereas low values of $\sigma_{\hat{\beta}_i}$ resp. $\sigma_{\hat{\epsilon}_{t+1}}$ mean low uncertainty. After estimating $\hat{x}_{t+1}, \ldots, \hat{x}_{t+\tau}$ the indicators z_t^P and z_t^T can be computed. We are interested in a statement for the next turning point, so we define

$$w_t^P = w(z_{t-\tau+1}^P, z_{t-\tau+2}^P, \ldots) = k \tag{4}$$

where k is such that $z_{t+k}^P = 1$ and $z_{t+j}^P = 0, j < k$. Verbally interpreted w_t^P expresses the number of periods until the next turning point. The following 6-step Monte-Carlo procedure can be used to derive probabilistic statements for near-by turning points:

1. Draw random numbers $\tilde{\beta}_1(1), \tilde{\beta}_2(1), \ldots, \tilde{\beta}_R(1)$ from a multivariate normal distribution with mean vector[3] $(\hat{\beta}_1, \hat{\beta}_2, \ldots, \hat{\beta}_R)^T$ and empirical variance-covariance matrix of the regression coefficients.
2. Draw a random number $\tilde{\epsilon}_{t+1}(1)$ from a univariate normal distribution with mean 0 and variance $\sigma_{\hat{\epsilon}_{t+1}}^2$.[4]
3. Compute $\tilde{x}_{t+1}(1) = \tilde{\beta}_0(1)x_t + \tilde{\beta}_1(1)x_{t-1} + \ldots + \tilde{\beta}_R(1)x_{t-R+1} + \tilde{\epsilon}_{t+1}(1)$. If $\tau > 1$, draw $\tilde{\epsilon}_{t+2}(1), \ldots, \tilde{\epsilon}_{t+\tau}(1)$ and iterate step 3 to obtain $\tilde{x}_{t+2}(1), \ldots, \tilde{x}_{t+\tau}(1)$.
4. Compute $z_{t-\tau+1}^P(1), \ldots, z_{t+h-\tau}^P(1)$ and $z_{t-\tau+1}^T(1), \ldots, z_{t+h-\tau}^T(1)$.
5. Compute $w_t^P(1)$ and $w_t^T(1)$.
6. Repeat steps 1 to 5 N times.

The predictive distributions P_t^P and P_t^T for a near-by turning point can be approximated by the empirical distributions $w_t^P(1), \ldots, w_t^P(N)$ and $w_t^T(1), \ldots, w_t^T(N)$. As an example take the following table derived from a Monte-Carlo-Simulation with $N = 10$ drawings: There are three entries for a turning point in

Table 1. Example for determination of the turning point probabilities

n	1	2	3	4	5	6	7	8	9	10
$w_t^P(n)$	3	0	2	1	2	2	1	2	2	1

$t + 1 : w_t^P(4) = 1, w_t^P(7) = 1, w_t^P(10) = 1$. It follows that $P_t^P(W_t^P = 1) = \frac{3}{10} = 0.3$. The probabilities for one period are characterised by $P_t^P + P_t^T \leq 1$. A turning point ist detected, if P_t^P reaches or exceeds a certain threshold θ, e.g. $\theta = 0.5$. Summarizing section 2, we explicitly incorporate uncertainty of the forecasts by producing probabilistic statements for near-by turning points. Furthermore, by not only considering one single model, but a family of N models, our forecasts are more reliable than those of single models. To compare the ARMA and VAR models, we need a measure of performance we base our decision on. It is discussed in the next section.

---

[3] The exponent T symbolizes transposition of the vector.

[4] Kling[2], p. 212, estimates the turning points with a VAR model. He draws the residual vector from a multivariate normal distribution with mean 0 and empirical variance-covariance matrix of the residuals.

3   Evaluation of Performance

The econometric model classes (ARMA and VAR) applied in this paper have to be evaluated concerning their task to forecast turning points. Hence it does not make sense in this context to rely on error measures of function approximation, such as MSE, MAE, etc. A participant in the financial markets usually is not interested in function approximation but in economic performance. Unfortunately error measures of function approximation show little coherence with trading profits[5]. Criteria especially developed to evaluate a model's ability to forecast turning points were developed, amongst others, by Brier[6] and Diebold/Rudebusch[7]. But those performance measures are similar to the error measures and a statistical test of significance is not available. One of our main goals in this study is evaluation based on economic criteria such as profits from a trading strategy. Since our models do not produce return forecasts but probabilities for turning points, we have to measure performance indirectly by generating trading signals from those probabilities: A short position is taken when a peak is detected ($P_t^P \geq \theta$, implying that the market will fall, trading signal s=-1), a long position in the case of a trough ($P_t^T \geq \theta$, market will rise, s=+1), and the position of the previous period is maintained if there is no turning point. One possibility to evaluate the quality of the trading signal forecasts is to count the number of correct forecasts and relate it to the number of incorrect ones. Unfortunately, this type of performance measurement does not discriminate between trading signals attributed to large and small movements of the time series. A participant in the financial markets usually is interested to get the large movements rather than the small ones. Correctly predicting the large movements corresponds to the idea of maximising a profit-oriented criterion. The Sharpe-Ratio, which is briefly described in the following, is such a criterion. With the actual period-to-period return $r_{actual,t}$ we can calculate the return $r_{m,t}$ from a turning point forecast of our model:

$$r_{m,t} = s \cdot r_{actual,t} \tag{5}$$

Subtracting the risk-free rate of interest $r_{f,T}$ from the average return of the model $\bar{r}_m = \frac{1}{T}\sum_{t=1}^{T} r_{m,t}$ over T periods yields the average excess return $\bar{e}_m = \bar{r}_m - r_{f,T}$. The Sharpe-Ratio SR[8] relates $\bar{e}_m$ to the return's standard deviation σ_m:

$$SR = \frac{\bar{e}_m}{\sigma_m} \tag{6}$$

The Sharpe-Ratio measures the excess return a model produces for a unit of risk the model takes. Jobson/Korkie[3] developed a test for the null hypothesis

$$H_0 : SR_m - SR_{BM} = 0 \tag{7}$$

of no significant difference between the Sharpe-Ratios of a forecasting model and a benchmark.[5] By re-arranging (7) and relating it to the variance δ of the two Sharpe-Ratios[6], Jobson/Korkie find that the test statistic

$$z_{m,BM} = \frac{\bar{e}_m \cdot \sigma_{BM} - \bar{e}_{BM} \cdot \sigma_m}{\sqrt{\delta}} \tag{8}$$

asymptotically follows a standard normal distribution and is powerful in moderately large samples. A positive and statistically significant $z_{m,BM}$ means that the model outperforms the benchmark in terms of the Sharpe-Ratio. The next section shows how the Jobson/Korkie-test was used within our Data Mining approach.

4   Data Mining in Financial Time Series

To test the ability of the ARMA and VAR models to predict turning points, we investigated the logarithms of nine financial time series, namely DMDOLLAR, YENDOLLAR, BD10Y (performance index for the 10 year German government benchmark bond), US10Y, JP10Y, MSWGR (performance index for the German stock market), MSUSA, MSJPA, and the CRB-Index. The data was available in monthly periodicity from 83.12 to 97.12, equalling 169 datapoints. One was lost because of differencing. 100 datapoints were used to estimate the models, so that we can base our decision which model class performs better on 68 out-of-sample forecasts. To allow for the possibility of structural change in the data, we implemented rolling regressions: After estimating the models with the first 100 datapoints and forecasting the succeeding datapoints, the data-"window" of the fixed size of 100 datapoints was put forth for one period and the estimation procedure was repeated. We estimated a multitude of models for each model class: 15 ARMA-models from (1,0), (0,1), (1,1),..., to (3,3) and 3 VAR models VAR(1), (2), and (3). We do not specify a model and estimate all rolling regressions with this model. Rather we specify a class of models (ARMA and VAR). Within a class the best model is selected for forecasting. As an extreme case, a different model specification could be chosen for every datapoint (within the ARMA class e.g. the ARMA(1,0) model for the first rolling regression, ARMA(2,2) for the second etc.). This model selection procedure is purely data-driven, so it can be regarded as Data Mining. Since it is well known that in-sample evaluation is a poor approximation for out-of-sample performance [10], reliable model selection has to be based on true out-of-sample validation. Therefore we divided the data in three subsequent, disjunct parts: a training subset (70 datapoints), a validation subset (30 datapoints), and a forecast subset ($\tau = 2$ datapoints, see Fig. 1).[7]

---

[5] Jobson/Korkie[3] developed a test statistic which allows to compare the Sharpe-Ratios of more than two portfolios simultaneously, too.

[6] $\delta = \frac{1}{T} 2\sigma_m^2 \sigma_{BM}^2 - 2\sigma_m \sigma_{BM} \sigma_{m,BM} + \frac{1}{2} \bar{e}_m^2 \sigma_{BM}^2 + \frac{1}{2} \bar{e}_{BM}^2 \sigma_m^2 - \frac{\bar{e}_m \bar{e}_{BM}}{2\sigma_m \sigma_{BM}} (\sigma_{m,BM}^2 + \sigma_m^2 \sigma_{BM}^2)]$.

[7] τ symbolizes the number of periods that have to be forecast in order to make a turning point decision at time t, cf. section 2.

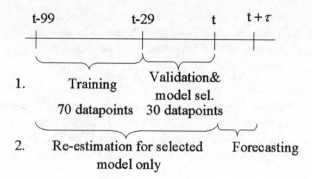

Fig. 1. Division of the database

The first 70 datapoints from t-99 to t-30 were used to estimate the models, which were validated with respect to their abilities to predict turning points on the following 30 datapoints from t-29 to t. This is true out-of-sample validation of the models, because at time t-30 the datapoints from t-29 to t are unknown. For each model and each datapoint in each rolling regression N=200 Monte-Carlo-simulations in order to calculate the turning point probabilities were performed. If the model at the beginning of the validation period in t-29 decided "no turning point" (results in maintenance of the previous period's trading signal), there is no trading signal originally stemming from the model. In this case we used the last trading signal which could be produced with certainty. With $\tau = 2$ the last certain signal for a turning point can be generated for t-31. Then the best model on the validation subset was selected. For each of the two model sequences (ARMA and VAR) only one model was selected at each time. The specification of this model, e.g. ARMA(2,2), then was re-estimated with the 100 datapoints from t-99 to t to forecast the at time t unknown τ values of the time series, which are necessary to decide whether there is a turning point at time t. The decision which model is the "best" was made with respect to the Jobson/Korkie-test on the difference between the Sharpe-Ratio of the models and a benchmark. Thus each of the multitude of models of each sequence had to be tested against a benchmark. Since our goal is the comparison of the two competing classes ARMA vs. VAR models, each sequence has to consist of representatives of this model class. The simplest model of each class served as a benchmark in the statistical tests: for the ARMA-sequence the benchmark was the (1,0)-model, in the other case the VAR(1)-model. Using the Jobson/Korkie-test as a criterion for selection, each of the multitude of ARMA models was tested against the (1,0) model. If e.g. the ARMA(2,2) model could reject the null hypothesis $z_{m,BM} = 0$ with a significantly positive $z_{m,BM}$ on the validation subset (t-29 to t), this model specification was selected and re-estimated with t-99 to t to forecast the τ unknown values of the time series for $t + 1, ..., t + \tau$. If more than one model qualified, the one with the highest SR was selected. If the null could not be rejected, the forecasts were conducted with the (1,0)-model.

Table 2. ARMA- and VAR-sequence as an example for the rolling regressions

				ARMA		VAR	
R.R	training	validation	forecast	Spec.	$z_{m,BM}$	Spec.	$z_{m,BM}$
1	84.1-89.10	89.11-92.4	92.5-92.6	(1,0)	*	(3)	3.3563 (.0008)
2	84.2-89.11	89.12-92.5	92.6-92.7	(2,2)	1.9823 (.0475)	(1)	*
⋮	⋮	⋮	⋮	⋮	⋮	⋮	⋮
68	89.8-95.4	95.5-97.10	97.11-97.12	(3,0)	2.1486 (.0317)	(3)	1.9987 (.0456)

This procedure was implemented for the VAR-sequence in an analogous way. As we solely rely on economic performance to select the best model, we do not consider statistical criteria, like t-values etc. The variances resp. standard deviations of the regression coefficients are needed for the drawings of the random numbers to incorporate the uncertainty in the forecasts. Badly fitted models with high variability in the coefficients and according high variances will not be able to detect the relevant turning points in the validation subset and so be disqualified in the selection procedure. Two sequences with a threshold $\theta = 0.5$ and a significance level of 0.1 could look like Table 2. The first four columns refer to the number of the rolling regressions and the training, validation, and forecast period, respectively. The 5th (7th) column gives the specification of the selected ARMA (VAR) model, the 6th (8th) column gives $z_{m,BM}$ (the entry (*) in the column "$z_{m,BM}$" means that in this period no model qualifies against the benchmark; p-values in parenthesis below the $z_{m,BM}$-value):

The first turning point forecast was done for 92.4 (with the unknown values of 92.5 and 92.6), the last for 97.10. The primary objective of this paper is to make a statement about the relative performance of ARMA- vs. VAR-models to detect turning points in time series. We created two model sequences with a sample size of 68 forecasts each. In order to produce a statistically significant result, we compare the ARMA sequence with the VAR sequence. Therefore we compute the Sharpe-Ratios of the ARMA excess returns (SR_{ARMA}) and the VAR excess returns (SR_{VAR}) over the 68 out-of-sample rolling regression forecasts. Comparing those two Sharpe-Ratios with the Jobson/Korkie test statistic $z_{ARMA,VAR}$ (thereby using SR_{VAR} as the benchmark) allows to make a statement which model class performs better on the 68 datapoints. A result might be that $z_{ARMA,VAR} > 0$ and statistically significant (e.g. $z_{ARMA,VAR} = 1.96$ is significant at the 5%-level). In that case the conclusion is that ARMA models outperform VAR models.[8] This does not mean that ARMA models are valuable forecasting tools. In order to be sure that ARMA models in this example are valuable forecasting tools, one would like to test if this model class is able to

---

[8] In the case $z_{ARMA,VAR} < 0$ VAR-models outperform ARMA-models.

outperform a simple benchmark as well. When forecasting economic time series, a simple benchmark is the naive forecast. The naive forecast uses the status of the current period to forecast the next period. In the context of return forecasts, the return of the current period is extrapolated as a forecast of the next period. As we deal with turning point predictions and do not produce explicit return but trading signal forecasts derived from turning point predictions, the extrapolation of returns is not adequate. One could think of using the actual return from t-1 to t as an indicator for the trading signal of the future period: a past positive return means a trading signal +1 for the future period, a negative return means a trading signal -1. One goal of turning point predictions is to detect the longer term trend reversals. Using the past return as a benchmark is more adequate for short-term, period-to-period forecasts. Hence we need a naive benchmark which works in a similar way as our model and thereby reflects the idea of turning point forecasts.[9] Using the last certain turning point statement can be regarded as a benchmark in this sense. As $\tau = 2$, the last certain turning point statement can be made for $t - 2$, using the datapoints from $t - 4$ to t. A valuable forecasting model should be able to outperform this Naive Turning Point Forecast (NTPF), so it is straightforward to test the ARMA- and VAR-sequences against the NTPF. E.g. a significantly positive $z_{ARMA,NTPF}$ ($z_{VAR,NTPF}$) calculated with the Sharpe-Ratios for the ARMA- (VAR-) and NTPF-sequences over the 68 out-of-sample forecasts implies that e.g. the ARMA- (VAR-) models are valuable tools for forecasting turning points in financial time series. If $z_{ARMA,NTPF}$ is negative, the NTPF produces a higher Sharpe-Ratio over the 68 datapoints. The next section presents empirical results from the turning point forecasts with our Data Mining approach.

5   Empirical Results

The following Table 3 exhibits the results for the turning point forecasts with a significance level of SL=.1 for the Jobson/Korkie-test and a threshold of $\theta = .75$. Results with different threshold values $\theta = .5$ and $\theta = .95$ showed that overall $\theta = .75$ produces the best results of the model classes vs. NTPF. The lower the level of significance for the Jobson/Korkie-test, the higher is the required difference between the two Sharpe-Ratios to be considered as statistically significant. With SL=.01, the sequences almost solely comprised the simplest (=benchmark) model (ARMA(1,0) resp. VAR(1)) in each model sequence. To a lesser degree this was valid for the turning point forecasts with a significance level SL=.1, whose results are presented in Table 3. Another point in this direction comes from the sample size of only 30 datapoints in the validation subset, which results in low discriminative power of the test. Hence the bias for the selection of the simplest model in each sequence is relatively high. The nine financial time series are considered as a closed market system, where every variable influences each other. Therefore the VAR models consisted of nine equations with lags of all

---

[9] For a detailed discussion of the problem to select an adequate benchmark for turning point models see Poddig/Huber[11], p. 30ff.

Table 3. Empirical results

				ARMAvsVAR		ARMAvsNTPF		VARvsNTPF	
$\theta = .75$	SR_{ARMA}	SR_{VAR}	SR_{NTPF}	z	$p(z)$	z	$p(z)$	z	$p(z)$
MSWG	.0124	-.1419	-.0038	1.44	.1488	.13	.8897	-.94	.3450
MSUSA	.1149	-.0287	.0341	1.10	.2703	.71	.4774	-.49	.6265
MSJPA	-.0398	.1300	-.0700	-1.14	.2544	.13	.8955	1.07	.2862
BD10Y	-.2206	-.3545	-.2602	1.39	.1653	.47	.6402	-.78	.4352
US10Y	-.1253	-.0851	-.1597	-.36	.7187	.27	.7855	.50	.6178
JP10Y	.0883	.0480	-.0824	.58	.5613	1.35	.1764	1.16	.2450
DMDO	-.2569	-.3169	-.3098	.45	.6520	.39	.6977	-.05	.9636
YEND	-.1966	-.1931	.1015	-.03	.9755	-.52	.5992	-.56	.5778
CRB	-.3458	-.4307	-.4759	.44	.6597	1.05	.2920	.24	.8132

variables in the system and a constant. Table 3 exhibits in the first column the name of the time series under consideration. The three following columns show the values of the Sharpe-Ratios of the ARMA- and VAR-models, and the NTPF, respectively. For each change from a long- into a short-position transaction costs of 0.75% were subtracted. The 5th column and 6th column give the z-values for the Jobson/Korkie-test statistic and its corresponding p-value for the test of the ARMA- vs. the VAR-sequences. The two following columns present z- and p-values for the comparison of the ARMA- vs. NTPF-sequences. The 9th and 10th column exhibit those values for the VAR- vs. NTPF-sequences.

Looking at the results for e.g. MSWGR in detail, only the ARMA-models were able to produce a positive Sharpe-Ratio ($SR_{ARMA} = .0124$) in the out-of-sample forecasts for the 68 months under consideration. This means that the ARMA-models on average reward each unit of risk, measured in standard deviations of the return, with an excess return of 1.24% per month. From the positive $z_{ARMA,VAR} = 1.44$ ($p = .1488$) for the nullhypothesis $H_0 : SR_{ARMA} - SR_{VAR} = 0$ it can be seen that they outperformed VAR models, although not significantly at the usual levels (1% to 10%). ARMA-models outperformed the NTPF as well ($z_{ARMA,NTPF} = .13, p = .8897$). VAR-models underperformed even the NTPF, so they do not seem to be a valuable tool for forecasting turning points in the German stock market. ARMA-models managed to produce positive Sharpe-Ratios for three out of the nine markets (MSWGR, MSUSA, JP10Y), VAR (MSJPA, JP10Y) and NTPF only twice (MSUSA, YENDOLLAR). In six markets ARMA-models outperformed VAR-models (positive $z_{ARMA,VAR}$-values), and in all markets but YENDOLLAR they outperformed the NTPF (positive $z_{ARMA,NTPF}$-values), but not significantly. VAR-models manage to beat the NTPF only four times (positive $z_{VAR,NTPF}$-values for MSJPA, US10Y, JP10Y, CRB). MSJPA is the only market in which VAR-models remarkably outperform ARMA-models ($z_{ARMA,VAR} = -1.14, p = .2544$). In two more cases VAR at least produce higher Sharpe-Ratios ($z_{ARMA,VAR}$ negative for US10Y and YEN-DOLLAR). Only the Japanese stock market MSJPA could be predicted remarkably more successfully by VAR- than by ARMA-models and NTPF (MSJPA: $z_{VAR,NTPF} = 1.07; z_{ARMA,VAR} = -1.14$. For JP10Y the VAR outperformed the NTPF, but so did the ARMA-models. The CRB-index seems to be unpredictable: none of the three sequences produced a positive Sharpe-Ratio, but the ARMA-(SR=-.3458) and VAR-models (SR=-.4307) still performed better than the NTPF (SR=-.4759). Summarizing the results in brief, it seems that ARMA-models are better tools for forecasting turning points in financial time series. In all but one case they managed to outperform the NTPF, although not in one single case statistically significant. The bad performance of the VAR-models might be due to their possible overparameterisation with nine variables and one to three lags. The simplest VAR(1)-model comprises nine variables plus a constant in each equation, which results in (9+1)·9=90 regression coefficients. Future research in the area of turning point forecasts will concentrate on smaller VAR-models and the derivation of portfolio weights from the turning point probabilities. This can be accomplished by "rewarding" forecasts with a high degree of certainty in the forecasts (e.g. $P_t^P \approx 1 \Rightarrow$ certainty of a peak, or $P_t^P \approx 0 \Rightarrow$ certainty of no peak) and "penalizing" the ones with a low degree of certainty ($P_t^P \approx \theta$).

References

1. Wecker, W. (1979): Predicting the turning points of a time series; in: Journal of Business, Vol. 52, No. 1, 35-50
2. Kling, J.L. (1987): Predicting the turning points of business and economic time series; in: Journal of Business, Vol. 60, No. 2, 201-238
3. Jobson, J.D.; Korkie, B.M. (1981): Performance Hypothesis Testing with the Sharpe and Treynor Measures, in: Journal of Finance, Vol. XXXVI, No. 4, 889-908
4. McLeod, G. (1983): Box-Jenkins in Practice, p. 11-130, Lancaster
5. Leitch, G.; Tanner, E. (1991): Economic Forecast Evaluation: Profits versus the conventional error measures, p. 584; in: American Economic Review, Vol. 81, No.3, 580-590
6. Brier, G.W. (1950): Verification of forecasts expressed in terms of probability; in: Monthly Weather Review, Vol. 75 (January), 1-3
7. Diebold, F.X.; Rudebusch, G.D. (1989): Scoring the Leading Indicators; in: Journal of Business, Vol. 62, No. 3, 369-391
8. Sharpe, W.F. (1966): Mutual Fund Performance; in: Journal of Business, 119-138
9. Swanson, N.R.; White, H. (1997): Forecasting economic time series using flexible versus fixed specification and linear versus nonlinear econometric models; in: International Journal of Forecasting, Vol. 13, 439-461
10. Poddig, Th. (1996): Analyse und Prognose von Finanzmärkten, Bad Soden/Ts., p. 380ff.
11. Poddig, Th.; Huber, C. (1998): Data Mining mit ARIMA-Modellen zur Prognose von Wendepunkten in Finanzmarktzeitreihen; Discussion Papers in Finance, No. 1, University of Bremen, available at http://www1.uni-bremen.de/~fiwi/

Computer-Assisted Classification of Legal Abstracts

Bokyung Yang-Stephens, M. Charles Swope, Jeffrey Locke, and
Isabelle Moulinier

West Group, 610 Opperman Drive, Eagan, MN 55123, USA

Abstract. This paper describes a Memory-Based Reasoning application that generates candidate classifications to aid editors in allocating
abstracts of judicial opinions among the 82,000 classes of a legal classification scheme. Using a training collection of more than 20 million
previously classified abstracts, the application provides ranked lists of
candidate classifications for new abstracts. These lists proved to contain
highly relevant classes and integrating this application into the editorial environment should materially improve the efficiency of the work of
classifying the new abstracts.

1 Introduction

There is much research in the fast growing field of automated text classification in both the Information Retrieval (e.g. [9]) and the Machine Learning (e.g.
[3]) communities. Text classification is all the more important for information
providers and publishers generally. Classification systems have been applied to
collections of news articles [10,9], medical records [15,8], or the Web [4]. Despite the research in this area, reports of applications of automatic classification
techniques in production environments are rare [5,7].

This paper focuses on an application in the area of legal abstracts. West
Group's legal classification system (known as the Key Number system) is used
to classify more than 350,000 abstracts per year among approximately 82,000
separate classes. This work is performed manually by a staff of highly specialized
attorney/editors. This application is designed to provide computer-aided support
for this time-consuming task.

The hypotheses upon which this application is based are:

- a Memory-Based Reasoning approach utilizing the more than 20,000,000
  already existing classified abstracts can produce relevant candidate classifications for new abstracts and will improve the efficiency of classification
  editors,
- in a Memory-Based Reasoning system [13] (a k-nearest neighbor method),
  the accuracy of the candidate classifications is proportional to the amount
  of training data, and
- a small number of neighbors (k) is inappropriate given the nature of our
  data.

D.J. Hand, J.N. Kok, M.R. Berthold (Eds.): IDA'99, LNCS 1642, pp. 437–448, 1999.
© Springer-Verlag Berlin Heidelberg 1999

Section 2 describes the problem. In Sect. 3, we briefly present our classification approach. Information on our text collections is provided in Sect. 4 while Sect. 5 presents our evaluation strategy. Results are reported in Sect. 6 and discussed in Sect. 7.

2   The Headnote Classification Task

2.1   Key Number System - Background

The American legal system is based in substantial part upon judicial precedent. That is, the pronouncements of judges in their written and published decisions declare the law and, theoretically at least, establish the law that will be followed in similar cases. Therefore, it is necessary that American lawyers and judges have access to the entire body of judicial opinions in order to determine what the law is in any given situation.

West Publishing, a predecessor of West Group, first began publishing judicial opinions in 1872, and its National Reporter System (NRS) now contains approximately 5 million published opinions from virtually every federal and state jurisdiction. Using its proprietary Key Number classification system, West categorizes the points of law stated in judicial opinions. This system has been the principal tool for the location of judicial precedent since the turn of the century.

At the top level, the Key Number system has over 400 topics. Topics are generally further subdivided with large subjects having a number of hierarchical layers (up to 8 levels deep). At the bottom of the hierarchical tree structure are the individual Key Numbers. There are approximately 82,000 of these Key Number categories, each one of which delineates a particular legal concept.

2.2   Key Number Assignment

Attorney/editors at West read each opinion to be published in the NRS and make individual abstracts for each point of law enunciated or discussed in the opinion. These abstracts, or headnotes as they are called, are then given a Key Number classification by experienced editors (see Fig. 1 for an example). The classification editors often examine classification of headnotes in cases cited in the opinion, and also use Westlaw®[1] Boolean search techniques in attempting to achieve accuracy and consistency.

About 350,000 headnotes are classified each year. These classified headnotes appear with case law documents on Westlaw® and in print digest publications. To function properly as a reliable tool for finding precedent, these classifications must be consistent. With a legacy collection of 20 million classified headnotes, maintenance is also a priority. Changes in the law require modification of existing topics and creation of new topics. Redefinition of existing concepts by the courts requires new classification of older material. Between the classification of new headnotes and the reclassification of legacy headnotes, a substantial and expensive manual effort is required.

---

[1] Westlaw® is West Group's computer-aided legal research system.

134	DIVORCE
134V	Alimony, Allowances, and Disposition of Property
134k230	Permanent Alimony
134k235 k.	Discretion of court

Abuse of discretion in award of maintenance occurs only where no reasonable person would take view adopted by trial court

Fig. 1. Example of a headnote and its associated Key Number hierarchy

2.3 The Computer-Assisted Task

We are interested in a system that eases the burden of manually classifying the headnotes and increases the consistency of classification. Headnotes are considered easy or difficult to classify. An easy classification is one for which no research is needed by the editor. Approximately 40 percent of headnotes are difficult to classify, but an editor spends over 60 percent of his/her time classifying these headnotes. Thus, from a production standpoint, the system's value lies in assisting classification of difficult headnotes.

The system described below attempts to accomplish this task by locating legacy headnotes similar to new, unclassified headnotes and suggesting candidate Key Numbers. It displays to editors lists of likely Key Numbers or hierarchically defined ranges of Key Numbers. The system also makes available for review the similar headnotes. This type of information is currently available only by running complicated Boolean searches on Westlaw® and gleaning the Key Number information from the search results. In effect, the system emulates the kind of manual research that is done by editors to discover correct Key Numbers for newly created headnotes.

Ideally, the system will rank the most likely Key Numbers highest. Furthermore, it should be capable of displaying the list of Key Numbers in the context of the Key Number classification hierarchy. Doing so will direct editors to the neighborhood of relevant Key Numbers even if none of the Key Numbers displayed is exactly applicable. If several key numbers are found under the same parent, relevant key numbers are likely to appear in the neighborhood even if the individual Key Numbers themselves are weak evidence. The system lists the most promising key numbers in a ranked order. The editors view the list of suggested Key Numbers and select the relevant Key Numbers.

3   The Classification Algorithm

We chose Memory-Based Reasoning, a variant of a k-nearest neighbor method, as our core classification algorithm. That choice was motivated by the following: first, we wanted to leverage the existing huge collection of manually classified headnotes (over 20 million); secondly, we needed an inductive method that could handle classification over 82,000 classes (Key Numbers); finally, we wished to get preliminary results with a minimum effort in development.

Given a test instance, the k-nearest neighbor classifier retrieves stored instances that are closest to the test instance with respect to some distance function; it then outputs the most probable class, given the classes of the retrieved instances. Our k-nearest neighbor approach relies on a full text retrieval engine. First, training documents are indexed. Then, a test instance is transformed into a structured query, and a search is run against the indexed collection. The result of that search is a ranked list of document-score pairs. A score corresponds to the similarity between the retrieved document and the test instance. We use this similarity score as the metric for finding the nearest neighbors. Finally, we extract the Key Numbers (classes) associated with the k top documents (i.e. the k nearest neighbors to the test instance), and rank those Key Numbers according to a scoring function. We rank Key Numbers as the system is intended to propose candidate classification for human review.

We used research implementations of the indexing program at West Group and of the natural language version of Westlaw®(both referred to as NL-Westlaw in the remainder of this paper). NL-Westlaw is based on the work by H. Turtle [14], and is related to INQUERY, another implementation of the same theoretical model [2].

3.1   Collection Indexing

Indexing involves the following steps:

- tokenization: tokenization reads in documents, removes stop-words (in our case, there are 290 stop-words) and single digits[2]), stems[3] terms using Porter stemming algorithm [11].
- transaction generation: a transaction is a tuple grouping a term t, a document identifier n, the frequency of t in n, and the positions of t in n.
- inverted file creation: an inverted file (see [12] for instance) allows efficient access to term information at search time. Records in the inverted file store the term, the number of documents in the collection the term appears in, and the transactions created at the previous stage.

3.2   Similarity Score as a Distance between Documents

Two components are involved in retrieving documents strongly related to the query: concept resolution and search. Concept resolution turns a natural language query (here a headnote) into a structured query and identifies concepts. Concepts may be individual terms, or query operators and their operands. One example is the phrase operator, where operands are terms. Concept resolution

---

[2] We removed single digits as they tended to appear as item markers in enumerations.
[3] A word "stem" corresponds to the root of a word after removal of predefined affixes.

additionally gathers global information for each concept, such as the number of documents in the collection containing the concept. This information is then used during the search phase.

The search process is responsible for computing the similarity between documents in the collection and the query, given the identified concepts. Individual terms are scored using a *tf-idf* formula:

$$w(t, d) = 0.4 + 0.6 \times tf(t, d) \times idf(t).$$

The inverse document frequency factor (*idf*) favors terms that are rare in the collection, while the term frequency factor (*tf*) gives a higher importance to terms that are frequent in the document to be scored. In our current setting, we use:

$$idf(t) = \frac{\log(N) - \log(df(t))}{\log(N)} \text{ and } tf(t, d) = 0.5 + \frac{0.5 \times \log(f(t, d))}{\log(\max tf)}$$

where N is the total number of documents in the collection, $df(t)$ is the number of documents where term t appears, $f(t, d)$ is the number of occurences of term t in document d and $\max tf$ is the maximum frequency of a term in document d.

More generally, concept scores are derived from the score of their operands and the scoring rule associated with the operator (see [2]). The similarity score between a document and the query is then obtained by averaging the scores of the concepts. In the end, the search returns a ranked list of documents and their associated scores.

3.3   Ranking Key Numbers

In order to display a list of candidate Key Numbers, we extract the Key Numbers assigned to the top documents in the search results. We then group the Key Numbers using a scoring function. We choose to experiment with the following scoring functions:

- the raw frequency of a Key Number, i.e. the number of retrieved documents with that Key Number. We expect this function to yield ties frequently.
- the sum of the similarity scores of retrieved documents assigned a given Key Number, in an effort to eliminate ties.
- the sum of rank weights. These functions give a higher weight to a Key Number assigned to a document at the top of the retrieved set, and a lower weight when the document is at a lower position. We consider two functions, $w(r) = r^{-1}$ and $w(r) = (1 - r\epsilon)$, where $\epsilon = 1/(k + 1)$, k being the number of nearest neighbors.

For each test instance, the system sorts the Key Numbers by their scores and displays the ranked list of Key Numbers.

4   The Corpus

4.1   Document Collections

We constructed two collections of headnotes from the databases available at West. The first one, hnotes-all, contains all headnotes ever written and classified. The second one, hnotes-25, is a subset of hnotes-all and contains headnotes written and classified in the past 25 years. As Table 1 indicates, hnotes-25 represents 42.81% of the headnotes in hnotes-all.

Table 1. Summary of the headnotes collections

Collection	Number of headnotes	Number of unique terms indexed	Total number of terms indexed
hnotes-all	20,481,882	308,112	759,928,514
hnotes-25	8,767,630	188,516	345,348,582

Although several Key Numbers can be assigned to a single headnote, 90% of the headnotes have a unique Key Number. When a headnote is assigned several Key Numbers, it becomes several training documents, each with a unique Key Number. Consequently, a simple 1-nearest neighbor approach is bound to fail.

Also, topics and Key Numbers are not uniformly assigned to headnotes as is reflected by the noticeable discrepancy between the mean and median number of headnotes per topic and Key Numbers as shown in Table 2.

Table 2. Summary of the distribution of headnotes per Key Number and topic

Topics		
Collection	Median	Mean
hnotes-all	8,903	45,834.5
hnotes-25	2,956	21,661.1

Key Numbers		
Collection	Median	Mean
hnotes-all	90	224.2
hnotes-25	23	121.9

4.2   Test Collection

The test collection is a set of 200 queries (recent headnotes) selected by an experienced editor. The selection was constrained to yield a representative sample of headnotes whose classification was judged as easy or difficult. Easy and difficult to classify headnotes represent 60 and 40 percent of the editor's work load, respectively. Thus, the queries were selected to reflect the ratio.

Each query went through an automatic process that identified legal phrases, removed stopwords and stemmed terms, in a way similar to the indexing program. There was a wide variation in the length of the resulting queries. The shortest was 4 terms (including phrases) long, the longest was 86 terms long. The average length of a query was 24 terms and phrases.

5   Evaluation Strategy

Our task is not a usual classification task as we are not required to output a unique class. As an application of classification techniques, we report the accuracy of our classifier when only the top candidate is returned.

To properly evaluate our classifier given our requirements, we report the percentage of times we found the correct Key Numbers within the top n positions of the ranked list; we used the values 2, 3, 4, 5 and 10 for n.

An editor would consider a support system that suggests relevant Key Numbers for a large proportion of headnotes more valuable than a system that is somewhat more accurate but that succeeds on fewer headnotes. Therefore, we also report the percentage of queries where we failed to retrieve the relevant Key Numbers.

Even if our classifier cannot find the correct Key Number, it would be considered useful (see Section 2.3) if the editor was pointed in the right direction. To reflect the interest, we report all above measures at the topic level, i.e. the first level in the Key Number hierarchy.

6   Results

In our approach, only the number of neighbors and the scoring function have to be chosen empirically. We evaluated performance on both collections when $k = 5$, $k = 10$, $k = 25$, $k = 50$, $k = 75$, and $k = 100$. The scoring functions are those from Section 3.3 for Key Numbers and topics.

Table 3 reports the percentage of queries for which the classifier failed to retrieve the correct Key Number or topic at any rank. This percentage depends on k, but is independent of the scoring function. The lower the number of retrieved documents, the lower the probability that the editor will find the relevant assignment. We observe but a negligible difference between the two collections. In addition, the good performance at the topic and Key Number level suggests that the system will be a useful support tool.

Table 4 reports, for both collections, the percentage of correct assignments within the first n candidates at the topic and Key Number level using the sum of similarity scores. We fixed k at 100, the best performing setting above. On average, the rank weight $w(r) = 1 - r\epsilon$ performed slightly better (by 1 or 2%)

Table 3. Percentage of queries for which the system failed to produce a correct answer when the number of neighbors k varies.

Topics						
Collection	$k = 5$	$k = 10$	$k = 25$	$k = 50$	$k = 75$	$k = 100$
hnotes-all	7.5%	6%	2.5%	2%	1.5 %	1.5%
hnotes-25	7%	5%	2.5%	2.5%	1.5%	1.0%

Key Numbers						
Collection	$k = 5$	$k = 10$	$k = 25$	$k = 50$	$k = 75$	$k = 100$
hnotes-all	31.5%	24.5%	18.0%	11.0%	9.5%	8.0%
hnotes-25	33.0%	23.5%	15.5%	12.0%	9 %	8.5%

than the sum of similarity scores for Top 1, Top 2 and Top 3. However, there was no difference for Top 4, Top 5 and Top 10. The raw frequency was found as effective as the sum of similarity scores, except in cases of ties (4 at the Key Number level at Top 1) where a random choice picked out the incorrect answer. The rank weight $w(r) = r^{-1}$ performed the worst: this function gives too much importance to the first retrieved headnote. Once again, the difference between the two collections was insignificant.

Table 4. Percentage of correct assignments after the first n Key Numbers or topics. The number of neighbors k is set to 100. The scoring function is the sum of similarity scores.

Topics						
Collection	Top 1	Top 2	Top 3	Top 4	Top 5	Top 10
hnotes-all	80.5%	91.5%	94.5%	95.5%	96.0%	97.5%
hnotes-25	80.5%	91.5%	95.5%	96.5%	97.5%	98.5%

Key Numbers						
Collection	Top 1	Top 2	Top 3	Top 4	Top 5	Top 10
hnotes-all	50.0%	63.5%	69.5%	77.0%	78.0%	83.5%
hnotes-25	48.5%	61.0%	67.5%	73.5%	76.0%	83.5%

The accuracy of the classifier is 50% at the Key Number level on hnotes-all and 48.5% on hnotes-25 (i.e. the percentage of correct answers at Top 1). We consider this result encouraging as the classifer has to pick among 82,000 Key Numbers.

Finally, we studied how our classifier performed relative to the difficulty of headnote classification. Remember that our support system will be more valuable if it can provide meaningful help with the difficult headnotes. Table 5 breaks down the percentage of correct assignments at Top n between the easy and difficult to classify queries. We present results on the hnotes-25 collection only as results were similar for hnotes-all. While our classifier performed better on the easy queries than the difficult ones, the number of correct assignments for the difficult queries appears more than sufficient to be valuable to editors.

Table 5. Percentage of correct assignments on the hnotes-25 collection, broken down by ease of classification. The number of neigbors k is set to 100. The score function is the sum of similarity scores.

Topics						
Difficulty	Top 1	Top 2	Top 3	Top 4	Top 5	Top 10
easy	82.5%	94.2%	95.8%	97.5%	98.3%	99.2 %
difficult	77.5%	87.5%	95.0%	95.0%	96.2%	97.5%

Key Numbers						
Difficulty	Top 1	Top 2	Top 3	Top 4	Top 5	Top 10
easy	57.5%	70.0%	74.2%	80.8%	82.5%	88.3%
difficult	35.0%	47.5%	57.5%	62.5%	66.2%	76.2%

Although a test collection of 200 queries is not small in information retrieval, it may be considered small by classification and machine learning standards. Consequently, the results presented here are meant to be more suggestive than conclusive.

7   Discussion

With the help of expert classifiers, we conducted a failure analysis of the 17 queries for which the system failed to retrieve the correct Key Number. For 10 out of these 17 queries, the system retrieved a Key Number related to the correct Key Number within the 5 top ranked candidates. In two of the test cases, headnotes had been assigned 2 Key Numbers manually. The k-nearest neighbor approach retrieved the other Key Number in the top 5 candidates. Three queries were found to be incorrectly formatted. To sum up, the analysis showed that there were only 4 queries that could be considered true failures.

It has been conjectured that the more documents there are, the better the results will be [5]. However, using all 20 million headnotes did not improve performance over using 8.7 million headnotes. For each query, we compared the headnotes retrieved in both collections: 78% of the headnotes retrieved in hnotes-25 also appeared in the retrieved set from hnotes-all. Overall, 81.5% of the retrieved headnotes from hnotes-all were written in the past 25 years (the additional 3.5% results from a difference in term weights in the collections).

Typical values for k in previous research range from 1 to 15. [15] reported that a larger value of k (30 in her experiments) may be more suitable when documents can appear multiple times in the training collection. We were able to use a larger number for k because of some characteristics of our training collection: its size and the average number of headnotes per Key Number.

We believe that our system succeeded in proposing relevant Key Numbers since NL-Westlaw can choose from a very large number of headnotes. Furthermore, we suspect that NL-Westlaw is successful because the queries and the documents are of the same length and style, which is unusual in information retrieval applications.

The performance of the classifier leads us to believe that we are justified in going forward to deploy the support system in a production environment. The percentage of the queries with the correct Key Numbers in Top 10 is especially encouraging. The system found relevant topics and Key Numbers for the difficult to classify headnotes almost at the same level as for the easy to classify headnotes.

7.1 Related Work

Nearest neighbor classification (see [6] for an overview), also referred to as instance-based learning [1] or Memory-Based Reasoning [13], has been widely studied. Three papers reported applying a nearest neighbor approach to textual data. They used a full text retrieval engine to assess similarity between documents to be classified and previously classified documents. Masand et al. [10] first used Memory-Based Reasoning to classify news stories. Yang's ExpNet [15] is a nearest neighbor method applied to documents extracted from the MEDLINE database. Larkey and Croft [8] used a nearest neighbor classifier in combination with other classifiers to assign codes to inpatient discharge summary. Cohen's WHIRL system can also be viewed as a k-nearest neighbor technique, when used for classification [4]. WHIRL extends the join operator for relational databases to handle textual fields of varying length, and has been applied to data collected from the Web.

Although we adopted a similar approach, we differ in terms of the size of the training collection (20 and 8.7 million documents) and the number of classes (82,000 Key Numbers), several orders of magnitude larger than the largest collection reported: [10] used a collection of around 50,000 news stories and 350 classes, while [8] used 3,261 codes and about 11,600 documents.

It is hazardous to compare two systems on two distinct problems. However, we find the performance of our classifier encouraging, when compared to that of [8]. At the full code level (similar to our Key Number level), their k-nearest neighbor classifier found the correct code for 38.5% of the test collection at Top 1 and 72.2% at Top 10; at their higher level the performance was 55.1% at Top 1 and 84.1% at Top 10.

8 Conclusion

We showed that with a minimum effort, using a full text retrieval engine, our Memory-Based Reasoning approach is successful at suggesting candidate Key

Numbers or hierarchically defined ranges of Key Numbers (here the top most informative node in the hierarchy, the topic). While we are confident that the performance of the classifier will increase the efficiency of the classification process, work remains to be done to integrate this system into the overall editorial environment.

We used two test collections in this experiment. The first consisted of 20 million headnotes (hnotes-all), the entire collection of abstracts. The second consisted of only those abstracts produced in the last 25 years (hnotes-25). We were somewhat surprised to discover that the accuracy of the candidate Key Numbers produced by the system was as great with the smaller collection as with the larger.

Our experiments showed that the Memory-Based Reasoning system worked best when the number of neighbors (k) was more than 50. This confirms our hypothesis that the nature of our data requires a larger value for k than is usually reported in the literature.

In the future, we first plan to further reduce the size of the training collection to include only headnotes specific to the jurisdiction of the query. We believe that this would result in retrieval of even more similar headnotes. Another advantage would be to reduce the processing time. Then we will investigate query modification, especially reducing the length of the queries based on some statistical evidence. This will also allow us to reduce computation, as long queries require more processing. Finally we need to assess whether the system (with its graphical interface) will help increase classification consistency and accuracy of new or legacy headnotes. Additionally, a similar approach could be adopted in suggesting Key Numbers to be used for query enhancement for on-line customer queries.

References

1. D. W. Aha, D. Kibler, and M. K. Albert. Instance-based learning algorithms. *Machine Learning*, (6):37–66, 1991.
2. J. P. Callan, W. B. Croft, and S. M. Harding. The inquery retrieval system. In *Proceedings of the Third International Conference on Database and Expert Systems Applications*, pages 78–83, Valencia, Spain, 1992. Springer-Verlag.
3. W. Cohen and Y. Singer. Context-sensitive learning methods for text categorization. In *Proceedings of the Nineteenth Annual International ACM SIGIR Conference on Research and Development in Information Retrieval*, Zürich, Switzerland, 1996.
4. W. Cohen and H. Hirsh. Joins that generalize: Text classification using whirl. In *Proceedings of the Fourth International Conference on Knowledge Discovery and Data Mining (KDD-98)*, pages 169–173, New York City, New York, 1998. AAAI Press.
5. R. H. Creecy, B. M. Masand, S. J. Smith, and D. L. Waltz. Trading MIPS and memory for knowledge engineering: Classifying census returns on the connection machine. *Communication of the ACM*, (35):45–63, July 1992.
6. B. V. Dasrathy, editor. *Nearest Neighbor (NN) Norms: NN Pattern Classification Techniques*. IEEE Computer Society Press, 1990.

7. P. Hayes and S. Weinstein. CONSTRUE/TIS: a system for content-based indexing of a database of news stories. In *Second Annual Conference on Innovative Applications of Artificial Intelligence*, 1990.
8. L. S. Larkey and W. B. Croft. Combining classifiers in text categorization. In *Proceedings of the Nineteenth Annual International ACM SIGIR Conference on Research and Development in Information Retrieval*, Zürich, 1996.
9. D. D. Lewis. Feature selection and feature extraction for text categorization. In *Proceedings of Speech and Natural Language Workshop*, Arden House, 1992.
10. B. Masand, G. Linoff, and D. Waltz. Classifying News Stories using Memory Based Reasoning. Copenhagen, 1992.
11. M. F. Porter. An algorithm for suffix stripping. *Program*, 14(3):130–137, July 1980.
12. G. Salton. *Automatic Text Processing: the Transformation, Analysis and Retrieval of Information by Computer.* Addison Wesley, 1989.
13. C. Standfill and D. Waltz. Toward memory-based reasoning. *Communications of the ACM*, 29(12):1213–1228, December 1986.
14. H. Turtle. *Inference Networks for Document Retrieval.* PhD thesis, Computer and Information Science Department, University of Massachussetts, October 1990.
15. Y. Yang. Expert network: Effective and efficient learning from human decisions in text categorization and retrieval. In *Proceedings of the Seventeenth Annual International ACM SIGIR Conference on Research and Development in Information Retrieval*, 1994.

Sequential Control Logic Inferring Method from Observed Plant I/O Data

Yoshitomo Ikkai, Kazuhisa Ikeda, Norihisa Komoda, Akira Yamane, and
Isao Tone

Department of Information Systems Engineering
Faculty of Engineering, Osaka University
2–1, Yamadaoka, Suita, Osaka 565–0871, JAPAN
phone: +81-6-6879-7823 ; fax: +81-6-6879-7827
{ikkai,kazuhisa,komoda}@ise.eng.osaka-u.ac.jp

Abstract. Today, there are many needs to replace or maintain many
plants built in the 1960s. However, it is difficult to replace or maintain
them, because the documents of installed sequential control logic are
seldom remain.

Therefore, we propose an automatic regeneration method(SPAIR) in order to solve this problem. SPAIR regenerates sequential control logic
that is expressed on a ladder diagram from the input and output data
of a target control unit and its supplementary specifications, which indicate the information about timers, etc. SPAIR consists of two parts,
namely basic logic inferring engine and interior coil logic inferring engine. In basic logic inferring engine, time series data is compressed and
translated into training data using the specifications. The training data
are processed by inductive learning and transformed into control logic.
In the interior coil logic inferring, the target logic of the interior coil is
acquired by the selective attachment of logic parts.

1 Introduction

To replace sequential control systems that are made up of vacuum tubes or
relay circuits, the control logic that is installed in the control systems should
be transform to the form of a ladder diagram for modern programmable logic
controllers (PLCs). However, documents of control logic often no longer exist or
most of the remaining documents are mostly incorrect, because of modifications
of the control logic. For this reason, it is necessary to automatically extract the
currently installed control logic from the information of the target logic that we
can observe, for example, input-output data and other action specifications.

Even though methods for the automatic programming of sequential control
programs have been developed[1][2], they require complete and exact models and
plant specifications. Therefore, these methods are not suitable for regenerating
sequential control programs for operating plants.

Therefore, We have proposed automatic regeneration of sequence programs
for operating plants: Sequential control Program Automatic Inductive Regener-

D.J. Hand, J.N. Kok, M.R. Berthold (Eds.): IDA'99, LNCS 1642, pp. 449–460, 1999.

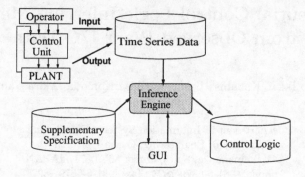

Fig. 1. SPAIR Outline.

ation(SPAIR) method[3]. SPAIR regenerates sequence programs by using inductive learning from input-output data of a controller(time series data) and action specifications.

SPAIR consists of two engines, namely basic logic inferring engine and interior coil logic inferring engine. In the basic logic inferring engine, in order to apply inductive learning, training data, is needed. Therefore, target control logic is divided into "set" or "reset" conditions for each output signal. We have defined a training data format for learning each condition.

In the regeneration of logic, interior coils, which do not appear in time series data, cause some problems. Generally, some logic variables which do not appear in output data, called "interior coils", are used in some cases, for example, in recognizing action mode. If the target logic contains interior coils, it is impossible that SPAIR regenerates the target logic. Therefore, we proposed an efficient inference method for interior coil logic, called Logic Part Attaching Algorithm. In this method, the target logic of interior coil is acquired by repeated selective attachment of logic parts, which are points of contact in ladder diagram. This method contains two phases, which are the attaching phase and the selecting phase. In the attaching phase, some logic parts are attached to a current tentative logic in order to generate several candidate logic. In the selecting phase, the most promising logic is selected as the next tentative logic.

2   Outline of SPAIR

SPAIR regenerates a target plants' logic. An outline of SPAIR is shown in Fig. 1. The inputs of SPAIR are time series data patterns(input-output data) from the target plants, and action supplementary specification of the target plants, such as information about timers. In SPAIR, a basic logic inference engine is firstly applied. Then, if the target logic has interior logic, a interior coil logic inferring engine is performed.

3   Basic Logic Inferring Method

The composition of the basic logic inferring engine of SPAIR is shown in Fig. 2. The basic logic inferring algorithm consists of four phases: preprocessing, training data generating, inductive learning, and the ladder transforming phases. The descriptions of the details of each phase are followed.

In the preprocessing phase, when the same data patterns continue in time series data that is accumulated from the controller, time series data is compressed and continuous time is added. The reduced data is called arranged time series data. The purpose of this function is to limit the quantity of the data and to reduce the time of inductive learning. When the time series data is accumulated from the objective plant, the arranged time series data is generated.

In the training data generating phase, the training data sets of each target output logic are generated from the arranged time series data. A training data set consists of some attributes and a class. The training data set is applied to ID3, which is a typical type of inductive learning[4]. When the value of the target output is changed, peculiar inputs and outputs are usually changed within the current time of the time series data. Therefore, the attributes of the training data set are made up of the current time data, and the class of training data is made up of the target output at the current time and at the previous time.

The class of the training data set is divided into four classes; "set", "reset", "1-continue" and "0-continue". If the target output on current time is 1 and the previous output is 0, the class of the training data set is "set". Similarly, if the present output is 0 and the current output is 1, the class is "reset". If both previous the output and current time output are 1 or 0, the class is "1-continue" or "0-continue," respectively.

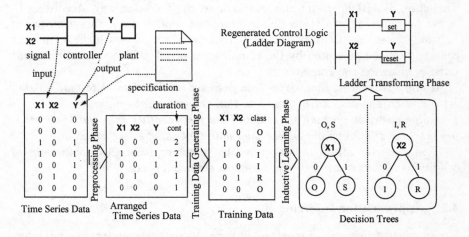

Fig. 2. The Composition of the Basic Logic Inferring Engine.

In the inductive learning phase, decision trees are made from the training data set by using ID3. The decision tree can specify which class the training data whose class is unknown belongs in. The set and reset conditions are acquired resoectuvely, because they are independent of each other. The training data sets whose class is "set" and "0-continue" are used in order to find the set conditions. The reset condition is learned from the training data sets whose class is "reset" and "1-continue".

In the ladder transforming phase, the decision trees are converted into control logic in the form of a ladder diagram, which we can easily understand. Finally, when all of the generated logic of each output is merged, a completed control logic in a ladder diagram is regenerated.

4   Interior Coil Logic Inferring Method

4.1   Problem of Interior Coil

When control logic contains interior coils, a state of interior coil can or may change a signal of output, as shown in Fig.3. In the figure, the signal of M does not appear in the time series data, because M is the interior coil, and the training data made from the time series data includes "conflict data," which have the same attributes but have different classes. A control logic that contains interior coils can not be acquired by using inductive learning, because of conflict data. Therefore, it is necessary to infer interior coil logic when conflict data is contained in the training data, and add attributes about interior coil to training data.

There are two problems in the inference of interior coils: when the interior coil is set or reset is unknown. Also, it is impossible to acquire set or reset conditions of the interior coil independently or separately, because of their mutual relation. Therefore, SPAIR infers interior coil logic in the following way. According to target output, conflict data is divided into "set conflict data" target output is "1" and "reset conflict data" target output is "0", as shown in fig.3. Interior coil logic can be presented by the combination of set and reset condition that satisfies following two consistents:

Going upstream on time series data from set conflict data, data that satisfies set condition appears earlier than data that satisfies reset condition

Going upstream on time series data from reset conflict data, data that satisfies reset condition appears earlier than data that satisfies set condition

Then, interior coil logic is acquired by searching from all combinations of conditions. But this method requires much time and space.

4.2   Approach for Inferring

For an efficient inferring of interior coil logic, we proposed an interior coil inference method called Logic Parts Attaching Algorithm[5]. In this method, interior coil logic is made by repeatedly and selectively attaching logic parts, as shown in

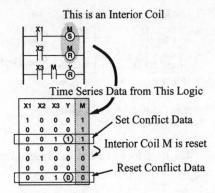

Fig. 3. Problem of Interior Coils.

Fig. 4. This method acquires interior coil logic by repeatedly using two phases, the attaching phase and the selecting phase.

In the attaching phase, some candidates for interior coil logic, called "candidate logic", are made. If all of candidate logic are made, the number of candidates is enormous and the inference is inefficient.

In the selecting phase, when the logic that can classify all of conflict data exists in candidate logic, the logic is just interior coil logic. Otherwise, the most promising candidate logic that is close to interior coil logic is selected and attached logic parts again in the next attaching process. The selected logic is called "tentative logic". We defined that the distance to interior coil logic is accuracy when a candidate logic classifies the conflict data.

Then, the problems are the following two points. One is how to define the distance to interior coil logic in the selecting phase, the other is how to judge a logic that becomes the interior coil logic. We propose definition of the distance to

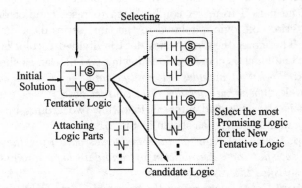

Fig. 4. Logic Parts Attaching Algorithm.

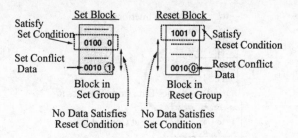

Fig. 5. Classify Blocks to Set or Reset Group.

interior coil logic and the method of selecting tentative logic in 4.3, and judgment of candidate logic which have the possibility to become interior coil logic and the method of attachment in 4.4.

4.3 Selecting Tentative Logic

In this method, the candidate logic that is the closest to the interior coil logic needs to be selected for the next tentative logic. We defined that the distance to interior coil logic is determined by degree how correctly a candidate logic can classify the conflict data. In the judgment of the distance, the signal of the interior coil is not acquainted from output of the control unit. Therefore, it is necessary to assume the signal. Additionally, searching the logic from all over the time series data, causes a large amount of complexity. Therefore, the time series data is divided into blocks before starting the inference.

First, it is assumed that the signal of the interior coil is "1" at set conflict data, and the signal is "0" at reset conflict data. It does not matter that the assumption is wrong, because the logic by exchanging between set condition and reset condition is logically the same as the actual target interior coil logic.

Interior coil is set in the period from reset conflict data to set conflict data, and reset in the period from set conflict data to reset conflict data. In other words, the interior coil logic is related to the time series data downside of the conflict data. Therefore, the time series data is divided to blocks between the conflict data. The block is classified to following two blocks, as shown in Fig. 5.

Set block: *Block that includes set conflict data.*

Reset block: *Block that includes reset conflict data.*

The block is also classified into the following two groups by applying the conditions of candidate logic, as shown in Fig. 5.

Set group: *Going upstream on the time series data from the conflict data, the data that satisfies the set condition of candidate logic appears earlier than the data that satisfies the reset condition.*

Reset group: *Going upstream on the time series data from the conflict data, the data that satisfies the reset condition of candidate logic appears earlier than the data that satisfies the set condition.*

In set block, interior coil is set at the set conflict data, so that data that satisfies the reset condition does not appear after data that satisfies the set condition. That is, that all of the set blocks should be classified to the set group by the interior coil logic. Similarly, all of the reset blocks should be classified to reset group.

Second, the distance to interior coil logic is defined by the following method. The distance to interior coil logic is determined by the degree of how the blocks of the time series data are correctly classified. Correct classification means that a set block is classified to set group and a reset block is classified to reset blocks. When the candidate logic that can exactly classify all blocks to the correct groups, the candidate logic is just the interior coil logic.

While any candidate logic can not classify all blocks correctly, the candidate logic that can classify the blocks most efficiently is selected as the new tentative logic. Then, the concept of entropy is introduced for the quantitative expression of classification correctness. We defined that the most promising candidate logic is the candidate logic whose entropy gain is the largest of all.

As shown in Fig. 6, entropy gain[4] is calculated for each result of classifying blocks by all candidate logic. Then, the candidate logic whose entropy gain is the largest of all is selected as the next tentative logic. In the figure, candidate logic 2 has the largest entropy gain of all, therefore, candidate logic 2 is selected as the next tentative logic.

4.4   Attaching Logic Parts

In order to enable the tentative logic become interior coil logic by attaching a new logic part, it is necessary that the candidate logic can correctly classify conflict data that the tentative logic cannot. In an attaching process, candidate logic that can improve the current tentative logic should be made for an effective inference.

In Fig. 7, block E is a block that is classified to incorrect group, called an "error block", because block E is a set block but is classified to reset group. The reason why block E is classified to reset group is that the data which satisfies reset condition appears earlier than the data that satisfies set condition, going upstream on time series data from set conflict data in block E. The data should to satisfy the set condition earlier than the data that satisfies the reset condition, in order to classify block E to set group.

Therefore, we propose the following method. Attaching logic parts to reset condition in series(AND connection) enable data that has satisfied reset condition to become not to satisfy the reset conditoin. It reduces the probability of classifying blocks to the reset group. Similarly, attaching logic parts to set condition in rows(OR connection) enable data which has not satisfied the set condition satisfies the set condition. It raises the probability of classifying blocks to the set group, because set conditions may be satisfied again after the reset condition is satisfied. Further, these operations raise the number of blocks that are classified to the reset group, and blocks that are classified into the set group is not affected by that. Similarly, if reset blocks are classified to the set block,

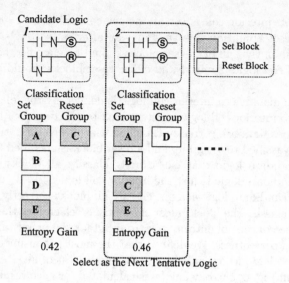

Fig. 6. Selecting the Most Promising Logic.

it is necessary to attach logic parts to the set condition in series or to the reset condition in rows.

5   Application Result

In order to confirm the effectiveness of SPAIR, we applied it to an automatic well model, as shown in Figure 8. The installed control logic is shown in Figure 9. This logic has one interior coil. "Mode 1 Switch" (S_1), "Mode 2 Switch" (S_2) and "Tank B Valve" (V_B) turn on and off at random. "Drug Tank Valve" (V_D) and "Mixer" (M_i) are turned off automatically after a given amount of time has passed.

10,000 steps time series data were accumulated from this model. They were edited into 1,500 arranged time series data during preprocessing. Basic logic inferring method and interior coil logic inferring method of SPAIR are applied to these data. As a result, generated the control logic is shown in Figure 10.

Comparing the control logic that is inferred by this system to the installed control logic, $y_1 \sim y_6$ are equal except for the fact logic that does not occur while the time series data is being accumulated.

We also applied the proposed method to another 2 model (one of them is a real conveyer plant), and confirmed the effectiveness of the method.

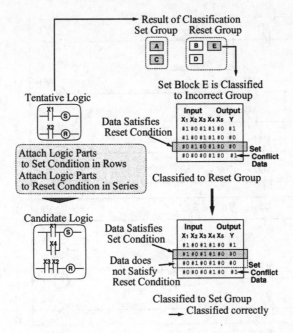

Fig. 7. Modification by Attaching Logic Parts.

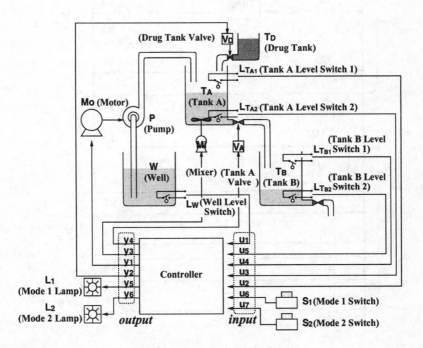

Fig. 8. Automatic well model.

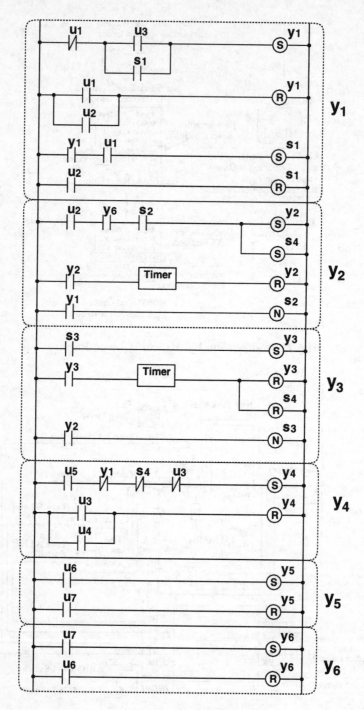

Fig. 9. Installed control logic.

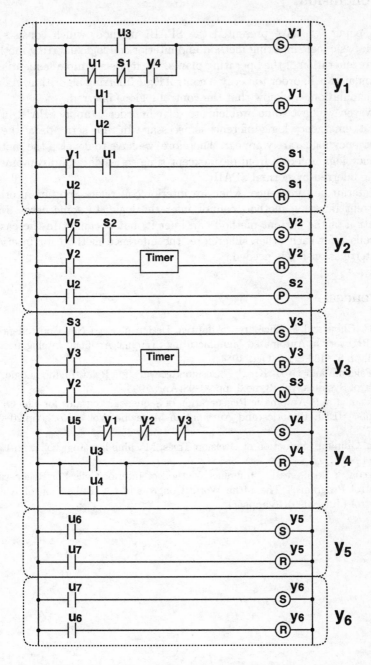

Fig. 10. Control logic inferred by the SPAIR method.

6   Conclusion

In this paper, we have presented the SPAIR method, which consists of two method: basic logic inferring method and interior coil logic inferring method, for a logic regeneration of the operating plants. We made a sample sequential model and simulated it in order to verify a control logic inferring algorithm. As a result of this simulation, we know that the control logic is inferred.

However, we have some problems to solve in order to apply SPAIR in practical. First, emergency logic inference is necessary. In time series data, the signals by emergency logic rarely appear. Therefore, we have to develop the method for emergency logic inferece from data except time series data and combine it and the logic inferred by normal SPAIR.

In interior coil inference, when an interior coil refers another interior coil, the current inferring method cannot infer the logic. In some cases, repeated apprication of the current method can infer it, but it cannot in the cases that those coils refer each other. Therefore, the inference method for interior coils with interrelationship is needed.

References

1. E. C. Chou and F. Dicesare: "Adaptive Design of Petri Net Controllers for Error Recovery in Automated Manufacturing System," Artificial Intelligence, vol.24, no.3, pp.85–168(Sept./Oct. 1984).
2. A. Falcione and B. H. Krogh: "Design Recovery for Relay Ladder Logic," IEEE Control Systems, vol.13, no.2, pp.90–98(Apr. 1993).
3. Y.Ikkai, et al.: "Automatic Regeneration of Sequence Programs for The Operating Plants," IEEE Robotics and Automation Magazine, Vol.4, No.2, pp.20–26(June 1997).
4. J. R. Quinlan : Induction of Decision Trees, Machine learning, vol.1, no.1, pp.81–106(1986).
5. K.Ikeda, Y.Ikkai, eta l.: "Inference Method of Interior Coils For Regeneration of Control Programs," The 14the World Congress of Int. Federation of Automatic Control (July 1999)(to appear).

Evaluating an Eye Screening Test

Gongxian Cheng[1], Kwawen Cho[1], Xiaohui Liu[1], George Loizou[1], and
John X. Wu[2]

[1] Department of Computer Science, Birkbeck College, University of London,
Malet Street, London WC1E 7HX, United Kingdom
[2] Moorfields Eye Hospital, Glaxo Department of Ophthalmic Epidemiology,
Institute of Ophthalmology, Bath Street, London EC1V 9EL, United Kingdom

Abstract. Field evaluation of AI systems or software systems in general
is a challenging research topic. During the last few years we have developed a software-based eye screening system. In this paper we describe our
work on evaluating several important aspects of the system. We have systematically studied the key issues involved in evaluating software quality
and carried out the evaluations using different strategies. After a brief
introduction of the system, this work is described from a data-analysis
problem-solving perspective, involving problem analysis, data collection,
and data analysis.

1 Introduction

A sensible evaluation of AI systems or software systems in general has always
been a challenging research issue [1,5,9]. A careful assessment of such systems
in laboratory environments is important but is no substitute for testing them in
real-world environments where they are developed for. This is especially important in medical informatics applications where their use in clinical situations is
vital [15].

In the last few years, we have developed a software-based visual field screening system that integrates a visual stimuli generating programme with a number
of machine learning components [11]. This system was developed in response to
the practical need to screen subjects in various public environments where the
specialised instruments for examining the visual field cannot be made available.
In particular, the system was designed to detect glaucoma and optic neuritis
effectively. It was based on the Computer Controlled Video Perimetry (CCVP)
[12], the first visual stimuli generating programme implemented on portable
PCs. CCVP had demonstrated some early success in detecting visual field damage, especially under certain controlled test environments [13,14]. In particular,
CCVP introduces to the test subject various stimuli at predetermined locations
in the visual field and obtains *repeated measurements* over these locations. The
subject's response to each stimulus is recorded as having recognised, or having failed to recognise the stimulus. The results are subsequently analysed to
determine the possibility of eye disease.

D.J. Hand, J.N. Kok, M.R. Berthold (Eds.): IDA'99, LNCS 1642, pp. 461–471, 1999.
© Springer-Verlag Berlin Heidelberg 1999

One of the extensions to the CCVP programme is the development of a user-friendly interface. One key consideration in the development of this interface was how to handle the problem of human behavioural instability during the test so that the subjects would make fewer mistakes (false positive or false negative responses). As learning, inattention and fatigue are among the major behavioural factors, various measures have been taken to address these issues in the interface development. These include a feedback system to indicate the subject's performance using sound and text, the design of interesting test stimuli, and customised test strategies for individuals. Moreover, attempts were made to develop an adaptive interface using machine learning techniques where the number of repeated measurements from each individual may vary [11].

To deal with the possibility of collecting unreliable data, an on-line neural network "stability analyser" component was adopted to clean the data, to judge whether the current test is *stable* and whether an immediate *follow-up test* should be conducted on the subject [2]. This turns out to be an important addition to the system capability since major field studies are typically expensive, and therefore not conducted often. It is important to collect reliable data from the subjects in the investigation under consideration.

To evaluate this screening system, various characteristics affecting software quality were systematically studied and clinical data collected from laboratory-based and field-based investigations in different communities were carefully analysed. This paper examines this evaluation effort, describes it from a data-analysis problem-solving perspective, and discusses what has been learned.

2   Problem Analysis: Evaluation Issues

Understanding and formulating of an analysis task is the first step to addressing the problem. In this context, various factors affecting the application development are analysed, including the key requirements from the application, human and organisational constraints, what data should be collected, and possible legal implications. The nature of the problem solving task is defined. It was found that problem formulation is one of the most challenging parts of the data analysis process, which has yet to receive sufficient attention [6].

Much research has been carried out on how to evaluate software systems [1,9]. In particular, there is an ISO International Standard (ISO/IEC 9126) which defines and details various software evaluation characteristics, including functionality, reliability, usability, efficiency, maintainability, and portability [8]. The space limit here prevents us from giving a detailed analysis of all the characteristics for our application, so we shall focus on functionality, reliability, and efficiency. These are among the most important characteristics for screening applications.

Functionality: This is used to refer to a set of functions that satisfy stated needs for an application [8]. For the screening application we want to see the system to be able to detect as many as possible of those subjects in the community who suffer from an eye disease at an early stage, and at the same time, to minimise the number of "false positives" - those who failed the test, but have no eye disease. Note that "in the community" implies that it is of crucial importance that the system be tested in different public environments.

Reliability: This is defined as the capability of software to maintain its level of performance under stated conditions for a stated period of time [8]. One of the most important criteria for screening applications is how reliably the data collected by the system reflect a subject's visual functions or damages. We have proposed two criteria for measuring such reliability: 1) the consistency between the repeated test results from the same subject; 2) the agreement between disease patterns discovered from our test and those from other established screening instruments.

Efficiency: Efficiency is concerned with the relationship between the level of performance of the software and the amount of resources used [8]. In the screening context, this is about how to minimise the amount of time a subject has to spend on a single test visit, while maintaining the quality of the test results. Since immediate follow-up tests may be recommended to obtain *reliable* test results during a single visit (see section 1), the following two questions are worth asking: 1) What is the minimum number of repeated measurements during a test to maintain the quality of test results? 2) If there is a need for on-line follow-up tests, what is the minimum number of follow-ups for subjects?

Apart from a detailed examination of what should be evaluated, one should also consider other issues regarding what needs to be done in order to allow for an effective evaluation. For example, how should we select the target population? The answer to this question depends very much on what kind of disease one aims to screen for. If one tries to screen for glaucoma, the second largest cause of blindness in the developed world that affects one-in-thirty people over the age of 40, then it probably makes sense to set up such a test in GP clinics and to screen mainly those over 40. On the other hand, if one aims to screen for optic neuritis, the most common optic-nerve disease affecting young people, it is desirable to set up such a screening test in African or Central/South American countries where this disease is particularly common.

Naturally what kind of data are to be collected and the size of target populations should be important concerns. These are closely related to the particular operating constraints imposed by the corresponding investigation, and in screening applications, it often means taking as large a sample as time or cost would allow. Amongst the data collected from subjects are the following two items: subject's responses to the repeated measurements, and subject's *response time* (time taken from a stimulus displayed on the screen to the moment the subject responds).

Another important concern would be the possible legal implications should a patient sue a doctor who had access to the screening system. This is a complex issue and several guidelines are listed in [15] to avoid negligence claims, including that the system has been carefully evaluated in laboratory conditions, the system provided its user with explanations or the opportunity to participate in the decision-making process, and no misleading claims are made regarding the capability of the system.

3   Data Collection

The screening system has been used in both hospital-based and field-based investigations. In this section we briefly describe the settings of two major field studies. The first is the World Health Organisation programme for preventing optic neuritis in the Kaduna State, Nigeria [2]. Kaduna was chosen since this is an area particularly known for being endemic for optic neuritis. The exact cause for this disease is still unknown, but the symptoms are blurred central vision, reduced colour vision, and reduced sensation of light brightness. The other is a pilot study to detect people with glaucoma, a common disease with the elderly in the UK, sponsored by the Medical Research Council [11]. Glaucoma is a condition, sometimes associated with high pressure in the eye, that over many years can damage the retinal nerve fibres at the back of the eye. If left untreated, glaucoma can lead to complete blindness.

In the optic-neuritis study, the subjects were from a farming community in Kaduna, who were largely computer-illiterate. The visual field tests were carried out in village huts on consenting subjects aged 15 years and over in several rural communities that were endemic for optic neuritis in the guinea savannah of Kaduna State, Northern Nigeria. These tests were conducted on a random sample of all those subjects that had failed some standard visual function tests. In addition, a population which was not endemic for optic neuritis with similar ethnic, cultural, educational and geographic backgrounds to the endemic population was examined as a control population. In all, 3182 test records from 2388 different eyes were collected using six notebook computers operated by ophthalmic nurses.

In the glaucoma study, the test was offered during routine attendance at a large urban general practice in North London and was conducted in a corner of the main waiting room separated by a cotton screen. Although the test is conducted by patients themselves, a nurse was on side to communicate with patients before or after the test, e.g. inviting the patient, conducting a questionnaire, and obtaining a hard copy of the test results. For a three-month period during the pilot study, all patients aged 40 or over who routinely attended the practice were offered the test. Upon entering the clinic, each patient was given an information sheet explaining the purpose of the pilot study, the nature of glaucoma and the visual field test, what to expect during and after the test, and information about whom to contact if they wished to know more about the test in general or were concerned about their own results. A consent form for taking the test was then signed by each interested patient. Patients with known glaucoma were excluded from the study, so were those too ill or incapable of completing the test. More than 900 people were screened and over 2000 test records were collected during the screening period.

In each of these two studies, there were a number of subjects who were subsequently invited back to undertake a thorough re-examination by ophthalmologists where various other tests were conducted to determine the nature of disease. The test data corresponding to these subjects were then used to evaluate the screening system.

4   Data Analysis

This section describes the methods and results of evaluating the screening system from the following software characteristics: **functionality, reliability, efficiency**. Since the main **functionality** for the screening system is its "discriminating power", we aim to establish the system's capability in maximising the chance of detecting those in the community who suffer from an eye disease at an early stage, while minimising the number of "false positives" - those who failed the test, but have no eye disease. We have used the *Receiver Operator Characteristic* (ROC) analysis [7] and associated methods for this purpose.

In assessing **reliability**, we are interested in seeing how reliably the data collected by the system reflect a subject's visual functions. To this end, we devised two evaluation strategies. The first is based on the notion of *reproducibility* of test results: the results should be reproducible for the same subjects if the tests are carried out in close time proximity in the same testing environments. The second strategy is based on checking the *agreement* of disease patterns between this and other conventional visual field tests. Since many conventional visual-field testing instruments have been clinically demonstrated to be reliable, it would be useful to check if results produced by our system are consistent or not with those from established testing instruments.

Regarding the **efficiency** assessment, we researched into two different ways of finding out the minimum number of repeated measurements for an individual test while maintaining the quality of the test results. Further, since one of the major features of the system is the capability of judging whether the current test applied to a subject is stable, and whether an immediate follow-up test should be conducted, how efficient is this aspect of the screening system?

4.1   Functionality

To .examine the *discriminating power* or the main *functionality* of the test, ROC analysis was considered as the most direct method. ROC curves are drawn to assess a test's diagnostic performance by displaying pairs of sensitivity and specificity values throughout the whole range of a test's measurements (see Figure 1). While curves shifted towards the upper left of the diagram, performance of the test is improved in terms of both sensitivity and specificity. The decision threshold used for discriminating between normal and abnormal subjects is the average percentage of positive responses within a test [2].

We applied ROC analysis to both the original CCVP data and the data collected by the integrated screening system. Amongst the 3182 test records collected in Nigeria, we have 181 different eyes which have been assessed to have optic neuritis and 352 who have no such disease. These findings were made by ophthalmologists who examined other signs, symptoms or test results, which are considered to be independent of the CCVP test. Figure 1 gives the sensitivity and specificity results from those 533 different eyes obtained under both the original CCVP and the integrated screening system. The results of the original CCVP with regard to the disease are represented in solid curve, while those of

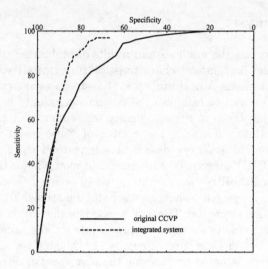

Fig. 1. Sensitivity and specificity from the two systems

the integrated system are given in dashed line. Although there are areas where the CCVP test has shown better sensitivity (bounded between 20% and 55% sensitivity, and between 90% and 100% specificity), the integrated screening test has higher sensitivity and specificity than the CCVP test for all other areas, particularly in the top left corner. This area is the most important since we are trying to find out which test can maximise both sensitivity and specificity for detecting the disease.

The ROC analysis was also applied to the glaucoma data collected from the opportunistic glaucoma study in London and overall results obtained are similar to those from the optic neuritis data. Among all the 925 people screened during the three-month period, 33 failed the test. All these 33 people, together with 45 chosen from those who passed the test (controls), were later assessed clinically in the practice by an ophthalmologist. The group who failed the test had many more eye problems than the group who passed the test. For example, 70% of those who passed the test (controls) had a normal visual field, and there was not a single confirmed glaucoma case found in this group. On the other hand, 82% of the people who failed the test had various visual defects including 34% confirmed glaucoma cases, 9% glaucoma suspects, 24% cataract cases and 15% other visual defects. It is encouraging to note that, among those whose visual defects were first detected by our screening system, most did not consider themselves to have any eye problem when they visited the clinic.

4.2 Reliability

Reproducibility of Test Results. As glaucoma is a long term progressing disease, the visual function should remain more or less the same during a short period of time. Therefore results from two such repeated tests within this time

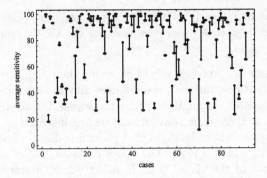

Fig. 2. Results of the original CCVP system

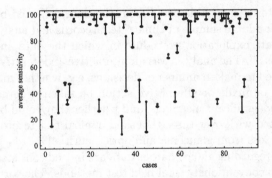

Fig. 3. Results of the integrated screening system

period should be very close. However, this is not always true under real clinical situations as measurement noise is involved in each test, perhaps for different reasons. Thus it is not surprising to note that there are a large number of repeated tests, which were conducted within an average time span of one month, and whose results showed disagreements of varying degrees (see the CCVP results in Figure 2). In the figure the dot is used to indicate the result of the first test, the oval is used for the result of the second test, and the difference between the two results for each case is illustrated by the line in between them. There are a number of repeated measurements for each test, and the "average sensitivity" is the average of the percentages of positive responses within all those repeated measurements.

Since one of the main reasons for the disagreement is the measurement noise, it is natural to expect that the sensitivity results of two consecutive tests should agree (to varying degrees) after the noise is discarded. As the integrated system has the data cleaning capability, we can then see whether the results of repeated tests are consistent or not. And this is indeed the case: the lines between two consecutive tests are in general shortened in Figure 3, shown by the results of experimenting with nearly 100 pairs of test records which had significant disagreements between two consecutive tests for the CCVP test (Figure 2) [10].

Pattern Agreement. Another way of assessing the reliability of the screening system is to analyse how different eye diseases may manifest themselves on the test data. A reasonable assumption is that the visual damage patterns detected should be similar to those from conventional testing instruments, or from clinical topographic analysis. It is understood that glaucoma damages tend to first occur in one "hemifield", which is either the upper or lower half of the retina, or the corresponding area of the visual field. In other words, abnormal locations are more likely to be found within a single hemifield, according to findings from conventional testing instruments. However, this pattern is not found for optic neuritis studies.

So what patterns can be detected from the data collected by our screening system? We took a large sample of clinical test records and analysed them using an interactive data exploration procedure in which the data analyst steers the discovery process [3]. The analysis was an interactive and iterative process where the analyst needed to make a number of decisions, e.g. whether more specific data selection should be made or alternative action be taken, whether any patterns detected had any significant meanings, and whether they could be validated. We have experimented with over three thousand clinical test records from patients with visual field loss from glaucoma and optic neuritis [3].

Our findings regarding glaucomatous data are indeed consistent with those of early research on conventional visual field test methods. The correlations among locations within either hemifield were found to be strong, whereas correlations between any two locations across hemifields were much weaker. For optic neuritis data we have also found strong correlation between certain pairs of retinal locations, but in this case across the two hemifields [3]. Topographic analysis of clinical chorioretinal changes related to the sensitivity at these test locations was conducted for optic-neuritis subjects, which has confirmed this finding.

4.3   Efficiency

To evaluate the efficiency of our system in terms of testing time versus reliability, we tried to find out the minimum number of repeated measurements for an individual test. Two strategies have been suggested. The first was based on the idea of *prediction/classification* and was tested on a set of visual field data involving six test locations, four test stimuli and ten repeated measurements. Various techniques such as neural networks, multiple regression and decision tree induction were used to do the prediction. The other strategy was based on the idea of *clustering* and was applied to a set of clinical glaucomatous test records. The results from these experiments have found the two strategies in general capable of keeping the number of repeated measurements low for individual subjects, while maintaining the quality of the test results [4]. However, further research is required to have a thorough and careful comparative study of these two strategies as they have different underlying assumptions as well as different theoretical foundations.

To evaluate the efficiency of on-line follow-up tests for a single test visit, a strategy was proposed and applied to the data from the optic-neuritis study in Nigeria [2]. In particular, follow-up tests were carried out irregularly on 532 different eyes. We have found that 371 (70%) subjects were stable and the remaining 161 subjects were unstable in their first tests. Among those *unstable* subjects, 95 became stable in their second test. In the rest of 66 subjects, 51, though indicated unstable, have similar patterns to those from the first test. Only 2.8% of subjects are still left undecided. These observations indicate that one test is sufficient to obtain stable test results for 70% of subjects, while *one* immediate follow-up test is normally adequate for the rest of the population.

5   Concluding Remarks

We have applied a software quality evaluation process to the assessment of an eye screening system and we have learned a lot, particularly the following:

1. Problem analysis: we have found it very important to carefully analyse various factors affecting the system evaluation, including evaluation objectives, target populations, related operating constraints, and what and how data should be collected. The feedbacks from early system trials have contributed in no small part to the continuing refinement of the screening system.
2. Data collection: Data collection from large-scale field studies is expensive and it is crucial to have the necessary resources and close collaboration from field staff. For example, we were fortunate to be supported by the British Council for the Prevention of Blindness and the World Health Organisation for the field study in Nigeria to make the data collection possible. In all, two Land Rovers and six portable PCs were used by dedicated staff in screening several thousand villagers who collaborated in the trial.
3. Evaluation: we have adopted a systematic way of evaluating different aspects of the screening system. Although we only have space to present results from the evaluation of the three main characteristics: functionality, reliability and efficiency, results from other characteristics are encouraging too. For example, the system has been found to have a higher than expected *acceptability*. During the three-month glaucoma study the test was offered to 1215 subjects of whom 925 (76%) accepted (the acceptance of opportunistic tests in city practices ranged from 50% to 70% in general). This was achieved despite there being little work to increase the number of patients taking part in the study (no advertising, and little stimulation from staff in the clinic). This is an encouraging finding regarding the "usability" of the system.
4. Future research: this will include further usability testing of the screening system. Moreover, the consistency checking between the results obtained by subjects' responses and subjects' response time may offer yet another interesting way of assessing the system's reliability. A more thorough evaluation using various methods [5] will also be attempted.

Finally, this is a truly interdisciplinary project in which community health experts, computer scientists, epidemiologists, eye specialists, general practitioners, and ophthalmic nurses have worked together in identifying the system requirements, designing and implementing the system, testing the system in different operating environments, analysing the data collected, and continuously refining the software. The collaboration from the trial communities is also vital as this is directly related to the quality of data collected. Currently the test is being used in more public environments and the data collected will allow us to improve the system further.

Acknowledgements

The work reported in this paper is in part supported by the British Council for Prevention of Blindness, International Glaucoma Association, UK's Medical Research Council and the World Health Organisation. We are grateful to B Jones, R Wormald, S Corcoran, R Hitchings, F Fitzke, J Collins and A Abiose for their collaborations. Finally, we thank the referees for their helpful comments.

References

1. Basili, V, Selby, R and Hutchens, D, Experimentation in Software Engineering. IEEE Transactions on Software Engineering, **SE-12** (1988) 733-743.
2. Cheng, G, Liu, X, Wu, J X and Jones, B, Establishing a Reliable Visual Function Test and Applying it to Screening Optic Nerve Disease in Onchocercal Communities. International Journal of Bio-Medical Computing, **41** (1996) 47-53.
3. Cheng, G, Liu, X, Wu, J X, Jones, B and Hitchings, R, Discovering Knowledge from Visual Field Data: Results in Optic Nerve Diseases. Medical Informatics Europe '96, (1996), 629-633.
4. Cho, K W, Liu, X, Loizou, G, and Wu, J X, An AI Approach to Dynamic Visual Field Testing. Computers and Biomedical Research, **31** (1998) 143-163.
5. Cohen, P R, Empirical Methods for Artificial Intelligence. MIT Press, (1995).
6. Hand, D J, Deconstructing Statistical Questions (with discussion). Journal of the Royal Statistical Society, Series A, **157** (1994) 317-56.
7. Hanely, J X and McNeil, B J, The Meaning and Use of the Area under a Receiver Operator Characteristic (ROC) Curve. Radiology, **143** (1982) 29-36.
8. ISO International Standard, Information Technology – Software Product Evaluation – Quality Characteristics and Guidelines for Their Use. ISO/IEC 9126, (1991).
9. Kitchenham, B, Towards a Constructive Quality Model: Software Quality Modelling, Measurement and Prediction. Software Engineering Journal, **2** (1987) 105-113.
10. Liu, X., Cheng, G. and Wu, J.X.: Noise and Uncertainty Management in Intelligent Data Modelling. Proc. of 12th National Conference on Artificial Intelligence (AAAI-94), 263-268
11. Liu, X, Cheng, G and Wu, J X, AI for Public Health: Self-Screening for Eye Diseases. IEEE Intelligent Systems, **13:5** (1998) 28-35.
12. Wu, J X, Visual Screening for Blinding Diseases in the Community Using Computer Controlled Video Perimetry, PhD thesis, University of London, (1993).

13. Wu, J X, Fitzke, F, Poinoosawmy, D, Hitchings, R, and Johnson, G, Variability in Glaucomatous Visual Damage Measured with Motion Detection. Investigative Ophthalmology and Visual Science, **34** (1993) 1475.
14. Wu, J X, Jones, B, Cassels-Brown, A, Murdoch, I, Adeniyi, F, Alexander, N, Minassian, D, and Abiose, A, Preliminary Report on the Use of Laptop Computer Perimetry with a Motion Sensitivity Screening Test to Detect Optic Nerve Disease in Onchocercal Communities of Rural Nigeria. Perimetry Update 1992/93, (1992) 323-329.
15. Wyatt, J and Spiegelhalter, D, Field Trials of Medical Decision-Aids: Potential Problems and Solutions. Proc. of the 15th Symposium on Computer Application in Medical Care, Washington, 3-7, (1991).

Application of Rough Sets Algorithms to Prediction of Aircraft Component Failure

José M. Peña[2], Sylvain Létourneau[1], and Fazel Famili[1]

[1] Institute for Information Technology, National Research Council, Ottawa, Canada
{sylvain.letournau, fazel.famili}@iit.nrc.ca
[2] Department of Computer Science, Universidad Politécnica de Madrid, Spain

Abstract. This paper presents application of *Rough Sets* algorithms to prediction of component failures in aerospace domain. To achieve this we first introduce a data preprocessing approach that consists of case selection, data labeling and attribute reduction. We also introduce a weight function to represent the importance of predictions as a function of time before the actual failure. We then build several models using rough set algorithms and reduce these models through a postprocessing phase. End results for failure prediction of a specific aircraft component are presented.

1 Introduction

Rough Sets theory was first defined by Pawlak [10,11]. During the last few years it has been applied in Data Mining and Machine Learning environments to different application areas [9,7]. As demonstrated by these previous applications and its formalized mathematical support, *Rough Sets* are efficient and useful tools in the field of knowledge discovery to generate discriminant and characteristic rules. However, in some cases the use of this technique and its algorithms requires some preprocessing of the data. In this paper, we explain the application of the *Rough Sets* algorithms and the preprocessing involved in order to use these techniques for prediction of component failures in the aerospace domain.

In today's aerospace industry the operation and maintenance of complex systems, such as commercial aircraft is a major challenge. There is a strong desire to monitor the entire system of the aircraft and predict when there is a potential for certain components to fail. This is specially true when in modern aircraft there is access to complex sensors and on-board computers that collect huge amounts of data at different stages of operation of the aircraft and transmit this data to ground control center where it is available in real-time. This information usually consists of both text and parametric (numeric/symbolic) data and it exceeds 2-3 megabytes of data per month for each modern aircraft. In most cases this data may not be used or even properly warehoused for future access. Several reasons exist: (i) engineers and operators do not have sufficient time to analyze huge amounts of data, unless there is an urgent requirement, (ii) complexity of the data analysis process is in most cases beyond the ordinary

D.J. Hand, J.N. Kok, M.R. Berthold (Eds.): IDA'99, LNCS 1642, pp. 473–484, 1999.
© Springer-Verlag Berlin Heidelberg 1999

tools that they have, and (iii) there is no well defined automated mechanism to extract, preprocess and analyze the data and summarize the results so that the engineers and technicians can use it.

Several benefits could be obtained from proper prediction of component failures. These are: (i) reducing the number of delays, (ii) reducing the overall maintenance costs, (iii) potential increase in safety, and (iv) preventing additional damage to other components.

The data used in this research comes from automatically acquired sensor measurements of the auxiliary power units (APU) of 34 Airbus A320 aircraft. This data has been acquired between 1994-97 and it consists of two major parts: (i) all repair actions taken on these aircraft, and (ii) all parametric data acquired during the operation of these power units. Examples of problems with this data were: missing attributes, out-of-range attributes and improper data types. After cleaning the original data, a data set consisting of about 42000 cases was prepared.

Our goal was to use this data to generate models (in the form of rules) that explain failure of certain components. These rules would then be used in a different system in order to monitor the data and generate alerts and inform the user when there is a potential for certain components to fail. This paper explains the process and the results of our research for the use of *Rough Sets* in prediction of component failures. In Section 2 we provide an overview of the approach. Section 3 includes the data preprocessing procedure and in Section 4 we explain the process of building a model. Section 5 contains the results and Section 6 is conclusion and future work.

2   Overview of the Approach

The aim of the rule extraction process described in this paper is to generate a valid set of prediction rules for aircraft component failures. These rules will have to accurately recognize particular patterns in the data that indicate an upcoming failure of a component.

The rule inference process starts by the selection of the data related to the component of interest. This is done in two steps. First, we retrieve, from the historical maintenance reports, the information about all occurrences of failure of the given component. The information retained is the failure dates along with the identifiers of the aircraft (or engine) on which the failures happened. Then we use this information to retrieve all the sensor measurements observed during the preceding days (or weeks) of each failure event. We also keep some data obtained during the days following the replacement of the component. Two new attributes are added to the initial raw measurements: the time between the observation is collected and the actual failure event, and a tag identifying each observation to a specific failure case. The data from all failures are finally combined to create the dataset used to build the predictive model.

In order to use a supervised learning approach such as *Rough Sets* algorithms as well as many others [13,12], we must add another attribute to the dataset just created. That is the CLASS (or LABEL) attribute. The algorithm used to generate this new attribute is also called *labeling algorithm*.

In our case, the labeling algorithm creates a new attribute with two different values (0 and 1). This new attribute is set to 1 for all cases obtained between the time of the failure and the preceding n days (these n days define the window that we target for the failure predictions), and set to 0 for all other cases observed outside that period of time. Following the labeling of the data, some data preprocessing is performed which is explained in Section 3.

The next step is to build the models. This includes: selection of the relevant attributes, execution of *Rough Sets* algorithms, and post-processing of the results. Finally, the end results are evaluated. The overall process is summarized in Figure 1.

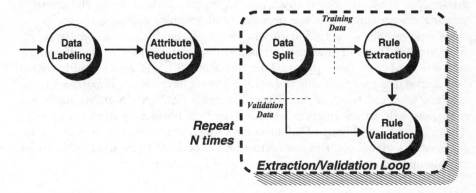

Fig. 1. General rule extraction procedure.

3   Data Preprocessing

This section explains preprocessing steps required before the application of the *Rough Sets* algorithms.

3.1   Discretization Algorithm

One of the requirements of all standard *Rough Sets* algorithms is that the attributes in the input data table need to be discrete (also known as nominal attributes). However, in the aerospace domain, the sensored data usually consists of continuous attributes and therefore a discretization process is required.

Discretization algorithms can be classified by two different criterion. The first division of these techniques is between *local* or *global* algorithms. *Local* algorithms are considered as some form of an induction algorithm (like C4.5 [13]). These algorithms perform partitions that are applied in some iterations of the induction process such as in a number of nodes during tree construction. *Global* algorithms are used to transform continuous attributes into nominal attributes in a preliminary preparation task and with no direct interaction with the subsequent analysis processes. The second classification of discretization techniques defines *supervised* and *unsupervised* methods. *Supervised* algorithms use label (or class) information to guide discretization process and *unsupervised* methods apply different kinds of discretization criteria (such as equal interval width or equal frequency intervals).

In our experiments, we have discarded *local* methods because: (1) *global* algorithms are less prone to variance in estimation from small data size (some experiments [3] with C4.5 have been improved using preliminary global discretizations before C4.5 induction with no local discretization) and (2) our rule extraction process is performed by *Rough Sets* algorithms that require the previous discretization. We have chosen *supervised* techniques because using classification information we can reduce the probability of grouping different classes in the same interval [8]. Some typical *global supervised* algorithms are: *ChiMerge* [8], *StatDisc* [14] (both of them use statistical operators as part of the discretization function), *D-2* (entropy-based discretization [2]), and *MCC* (find partition boundaries using contrast functions [16]). But we have chosen *InfoMerge* [1], an information-theoretic algorithm, that substitutes *ChiMerge/StatDisc* statistical measures with an information loss function in a bottom-up iterative process. This approach is similar to C4.5 local discretization process but in order to apply it into a global algorithm a correction factor need to be used. This factor adjusts information function using interval weight (number of elements).

3.2   Weight Function

The second transformation operation is not so closely related to algorithm requirements and its application is motivated by a better rule quality at the end of the process. As described in Section 2, the labeling mechanism selects all the records in the last 30 days before the failure as positive data (the rules generated by the model will discriminate this time window from the data before and after this period). But the importance of the detection of this situation is not the same during all this period. For example, a component failure alert 20 days before the possible failure is less important than 5 days before and alerts too close to the failure do not allow any corrective actions. This domain characteristic can be described as a weight function as shown in the Figure 2. This weight function example defines three different values connected by a step function and it is an example of the distribution of the importance of alerts for this component. All algorithms of the procedure have been revised in order to use this weight function.

4   Building a Model

In this section, the three main steps of the model building phase are described in detail. These steps are: i) attribute reduction, ii) rules extraction, and iii)

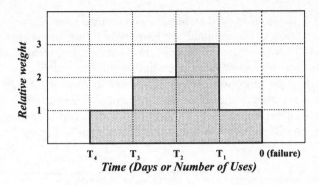

Fig. 2. Weight function example.

rules post-processing. In this research, *Rough Sets* algorithms have been used to implement each of these phases.

4.1   Attribute Reduction

In this phase of the process, we select from an original set of attributes, provided by the user, a subset of characteristics to use in the rest of the process. The selection criteria are based on the reduct concept description, as defined by [11]. The term REDUCT is defined as *"the essential part of knowledge, which suffices to define all basic concepts occurring in the considered knowledge"*. In this problem's context we can define reduct as the reduced set of features that are able to predict the component failure.

Many different algorithms have been developed in order to obtain this reduced set of attributes [15,6]. Not all of them are suitable for our domain. For instance, the *Discernibility Matrix* algorithm [15] defines a triangular matrix with a size equal to the number of records in both dimensions. This algorithm would not be appropriate due to the size of the matrix it requires (e.g. for a problem of 20000 records it is necessary to handle a matrix of about 200 million cells). Another traditional method to calculate this set is to generate all combinations of attributes and then evaluate the classification power of each combination. The usual way to perform this evaluation is to calculate the *Lower* approximation [11]. *Lower* is a set of original records that belong to the concept and they are selected by an equivalence relation described by some attributes. These attributes are used to define this *Lower* region. If an element belongs to this approximation then it *surely* belongs to the class (the set of records we want to classify).

$$U : \; Universe \; (all \; the \; records). \tag{1}$$

$$X : \; Elements \; that \; belong \; to \; the \; CLASS \; (concept). \; X \subseteq U \tag{2}$$

$$R : \; Equivalence \; relation \; (defined \; by \; the \; attributes). \tag{3}$$

$$Lower = \{x \in U : [x]_R \subseteq X\} \tag{4}$$

In our experiments, we have used a simple reduct calculation algorithm. The main goal was not to obtain the minimal attribute reduct, but to provide a good result at a reasonable cost in terms of computation time and memory used. The algorithm implemented also uses the *Lower* approximation calculation [11] to evaluate the classification power of a set of attributes in each of the iterations. This approximation represents the set of data records successfully classified by a set of attributes. Therefore, the set of attributes is designed to preserve this original *Lower* region. The algorithm pseudo code is shown in Figure 3.

```
 1:AttributeSet Calculate_Reduct(Data data,AttrSet attr)     1:Float Lower_Approximation(Data data,AttributeSet attr)
 2:{                                                          2:Pre: "'data' must be sorted by 'attr'"
 3:  AttributeSet red={};                                     3:{
 4:  Float acc,maxAcc=0.0,attrAcc[attr.size()];               4:  Float pos=0.0,neg=0.0; cls=0.0; tot=0.0;
 5:  Attribute at1,at2,a,b;                                   5:  Tuple reference,current;
 6:                                                           6:
 7:  while(maxAcc<REQUIRED_ACCURACY) {                        7:  reference=data.first();
 8:    maxAcc=0.0;                                            8:  for(current in data) {
 9:    for(a in attr) {                                       9:    if(IsEqual(current,reference,attr)) {
10:      attrAcc[a]=Lower_Approximation(data,red+{a});       10:      if(IsPositive(current)
11:      for(b in attr) {                                    11:        pos+=current.weight;
12:        acc=Lower_Approximation(data,red+{a,b});          12:      else
13:        if(acc>=maxAcc) {                                 13:        neg+=current.weight;
14:          maxAcc=acc;                                     14:    else {
15:          at1=a;                                          15:      tot+=pos;
16:          at2=b;                                          16:      if(pos/(pos+neg)>VPRSM_THRESHOLD) {
17:        }                                                 17:        cls+=pos;
18:      }                                                   18:        Write_Rule(reference,pos,pos+neg);
19:      attr=attr-{a};                                      19:      }
20:    }                                                     20:      reference=current;
21:    if(attrAcc[at1]>attrAcc[at2])                         21:      if(IsPositive(current)
22:      red=red+{at1};                                      22:        pos=current.weight; neg=0.0;
23:    else                                                  23:      else
24:      red=red+{at2};                                      24:        neg=current.weight; pos=0.0;
25:  }                                                       25:    }
26:  return(red);                                            26:  }
27:}                                                         27:  return(cls/tot);
                                                             28:}
```

Fig. 3. Non-optimal reduct calculation / Lower approximation calculation algorithms.

In each iteration, this algorithm first selects the best subset of two attributes based on the classification power (calculated with `Lower_Approximation`). It then selects the best attribute from these two. This algorithm is very efficient since it limits the search for the best subset of two attributes only. However, that limitation may also have an impact on the results obtained. It might be appropriate to run a modified version of this algorithm that can also search for the best subset of 3 attributes, or even more.

In Figure 4 there is a comparison between the combinatorial calculation of the reduct and the calculation using our approximative algorithm. The figure pictures the number of times Lower Approximation function has to be executed. For example, to calculate a 5-attribute reduct from 80 original attributes, with the combinational approach over 30 millions Lower regions must be calculated, but with the other algorithm there are only 13450 regions to calculate.

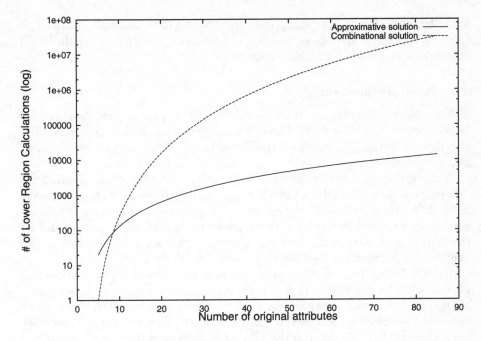

Fig. 4. Calculation of a 5-attribute reduct

4.2 Rule Extraction

At the core of the building model process we find the rule extraction step. The algorithm to perform that step scans the training data and extracts discriminant rules for the the target concept using the selected subset of attributes (obtained from the attribute reduction algorithm, see section 4.1). In our experiments, we have selected a fixed number of attributes for the reduct computation (the most discriminant ones, according to the reduct criteria). In other words, we forced the rule extraction algorithms to work with only a small subset of features. This constraint was necessary to limit the size of the rules generated and helped in keeping a good level of comprehensibility for domain experts that will have to review the results.

In our experiments, we also used *Lower* approximation calculation to generate the rules that describe the concept (i.e. the situations for which we should predict a specific component failure). Using this approach, each rule obtained consists of a conjunction of attribute value conditions (one condition per input attribute). As we will see in Section 4.3, this set of rules had to be processed before being used to predict component failure.

The implementation developed in our research supports Variable Precision Rough Set Model (VPRSM as defined by [17]) and the algorithm used is based on the design proposed by [5]. VPRSM extends traditional rough sets theory providing an inclusion threshold that allows more flexibility. With VPRSM an element x belongs to *Lower* region if more than $\alpha\%$ of elements in the same equivalence class ($[x]_R$) belong to the concept. The only variation of this algorithm is related to the use of the weight function and its effect on threshold comparison process in VPRSM (see figure 3).

4.3   Rule Postprocessing

The number of rules obtained from the rule extraction process described above is typically very high. This section first explains why so many rules are generated and then, it explains an approach developed to transform the rule set obtained into a smaller one.

First, one of the characteristics of rules extracted by the *Lower* approximation calculation is that all the rules are expressed in terms of all the attributes provided to the algorithm. Each rule extracted using this technique is a conjunction of predicates. The format of these predicates is *attribute* = *value*, and all the attributes appear in all the rules. Clearly, with such a representation, the number of rules required to cover all possibilities is very large.

The quality of the discretization process may also have an impact on the total number of rules generated. Because the discretization process is independent of the rule extraction algorithm used, an attribute may be splitted into more intervals than required to generate the rules. In these cases, two or more rules are generated that only differ in the value of a discretized attribute and this two or more values represent consecutive intervals. Such a non optimal splitting of the attributes will contribute to enlarge the number of rules obtained.

In order to reduce the number of rules, a two-phase algorithm has been developed. In the first phase all the initial rules are combined to generate new rules, these new rules are more general (include all the elements described by both of the combined rules) than previous ones. This process is repeated until no new rule can be generated. In each of the iterations any initial or previously generated rules can be combined. In a second phase, all the rules that are described by a more general rule (all of the elements represented by the rule are also represented by another rule) are removed. The result of this second phase is a final set of rules equivalent to the original one but smaller (or in the worst case equal). This process cannot be achieved by a single combination/pruning phase since some rules may be used to generate more than one new rule. An example of execution of this algorithm is shown in Figure 5.

The final output of this algorithm is a smaller set of postprocessed more general rules. These rules are finally sorted by their support. The support being defined as the ratio between the number of cases in which this rule can be applied and the total number of cases.

5   Performance and Results

In this section, we report the results obtained by our approach to learn models to predict failure of the Auxiliary Power Unit (APU) starter motor. We also study the relationship between two important parameters of the approach. The process for our experiment is as follow:

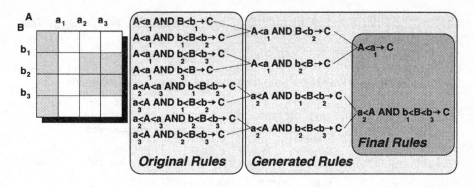

Fig. 5. Rule postprocessing example.

1. The data is splitted into batches. One batch being created for each failure case. For the APU starter problem, we had data from 30 failure cases (30 batches were then created).

2. We execute our approach to learn the rules using data form 29 cases and then use the data from the remaining case for validation. We repeat this step until data from each case has been used for validation (which means 30 iterations for the current component).

3. We use the validation results from the different runs to compute: (i)the number of cases for which we have at least one good alert generated during the prediction window(see Section 2), and (ii)the number of cases for which we have one ore more alerts generated outside the prediction window. In Table 1, these two numbers are referred to as Good Alert and False Alert, respectively.

We repeated the above process several times with different settings for two important parameters in our approach: the VPRSM threshold and the maximal number of intervals generated by the discretization algorithms. We experimented with VPRSM thresholds of .99, .97, .95, .90, and .80. Similarly, we experimented with values of 2, 3, 5, 7, and 10 for the maximal number of discretization intervals. Table 1 presents the results from our experiments. The impact of these two parameters on the final results is very significant. In the top left side of the table, with high restrictive thresholds and a small number of intervals, the percentages of correct failure predictions and false alerts are both very low. On the other hand, low VPRSM thresholds and large number of intervals for discretization (bottom left corner of the table) lead to a high percentage of correct failures predictions along with an important ratio of false alerts. It is very interesting to note the impact of the maximal number of intervals for discretization. For instance, with a VPRSM threshold of .97, increasing the maximal number of intervals from 5 to 7 lead to an increase of 20% in the number of failures predicted and to a 26% decrease of the false alert ratio.

Finally, the most interesting result was obtained with a threshold of .97 and a maximal of 7 intervals. This result shows a good ability of the model in predicting failures of the APU starter motor (70%) with a reasonable percentage of false alerts (6.7%).

Table 1. VPRSM threshold vs maximun number of intervals

Threshold	# Intervals	2	3	5	7	10
0.99	Good Alert:	3.3%	6.7%	20.0%	33.3%	26.7%
	False Alert:	10.0%	6.7%	10.0%	6.7%	10.0%
0.97	Good Alert:	3.3%	20.0%	50.0%	**70.0%**	23.3%
	False Alert:	10.0%	33.3%	33.3%	**6.7%**	10.0%
0.95	Good Alert:	6.7%	26.7%	40.0%	56.7%	40.0%
	False Alert:	16.7%	23.3%	10.0%	93.3%	33.3%
0.90	Good Alert:	10.0%	23.3%	63.3%	83.3%	86.7%
	False Alert:	16.7%	20.0%	43.3%	66.7%	96.7%
0.80	Good Alert:	10.0%	36.7%	70.0%	83.3%	93.3%
	False Alert:	16.7%	30.0%	66.7%	96.7%	96.7%

The rules extracted by our model never have more than five attributes (predicates). This rule size is close to the limit above which human comprehensibility becomes difficult. This characteristic is quite important because the predictive rules are processed by an automated monitoring tool that generates alerts with these rules and for each of the alerts the associated rule needs to be shown to an expert user who decides on corrective actions to be taken. An example of a rule obtained is:

```
IF 50.000<=SMIN15<52.000 AND 713.000<=EMIN20 AND 522.000<=EMAX
THEN "APU starter motor will fail within 15 days"
```

Similar rules can be generated by other algorithms. We are experimenting with other systems such as C4.5 and other algorithms accessible trough MLC++ [4]. Results obtained so far tend to show that the approach developed in this paper is competitive with well known decision tree systems in both the execution time and the accuracy of the results. For instance, the best model obtained so far with C4.5 has been able to correctly predict 77% of the failures with a false alert rate of about 9%. In terms of execution time, our *Rough Sets* implementation and C4.5 are also quite similar; each experiment for the selected component takes about 25 minutes with both systems.

6   Conclusions and Future Work

In this paper we present a new approach to the use of *Rough Sets* algorithm for prediction of component failures. Our data came from a real world aerospace application for which accurate predictions of component failures will be extremely useful. The approach consists of an extensive data reduction process, use of a global supervised algorithm for discretization and a weight function to evaluate the performance of our experiments. The experiments carried out in our research revealed that the large number of rules generated by the algorithms had to be reduced to a smaller set for human comprehensibility. This was done using a novel approach that significantly reduces the number of rules without affecting the accuracy of the results.

An extensive experiment has been run to verify the impact of two parameters: the VPRSM threshold and the maximal number of intervals generated during discretization. The experiment has shown that the quality of the results is heavily affected by the maximal number of discretization intervals chosen. The experiment has also demonstrated that the overall approach is useful for obtaining rules that can predict up to 70% of the APU starter motor failures (prediction of the component targeted in this research) with a very reasonable rate of false alerts (less than 7%). This kind of models could lead to important savings for an airline.

The research framework described in this paper can be used as a basis for our future research in this area. Different discretization algorithms, weight functions and attribute reduction techniques along with other forms of rule postprocessing strategies can be experimented.

Acknowledgments

J.M. Peña thanks Dr. C. Fernández and Dr. E. Menasalvas for helpful comments and suggestions and also thanks all IIT group at NRC for support and help.

References

1. Alves Freitas, A. and Lavington, S. H.: Speeding up Knowledge Discovery in Large Relational Databases by Means of a New Discretization Algorithm. BNCOD 1996: 124–133.
2. Catlett, J.: On Changing Continuous Attributes into Ordered Discrete Attributes. EWSL 1991: 164–178.
3. Dougherty, J., Kohavi, R. and Sahami, M.: Supervised and Unsupervised Discretizations of Continuous Features. ML 1995: 194–202.
4. Kohavi, R., Sommerfield, D., and Dougherty, J.: Data Mining Using MLC++: A Machine Learning Library in C++. Tools with Artificial Intelligence. IEEE Computer Society Press 1996: 234–245.
5. Fernández-Baizán, C., Menasalvas, E. and Peña, J.M.: Rough Sets as a Foundation to Add Data Mining Capabilities to a RDBMS. CESA 1996: 764–769.
6. Fernández-Baizán, C., Menasalvas, E. and Peña, J.M.: A New Approach for the Calculation of Reducts in Large Databases. JICS 1997: 340–344.
7. Hadjimichael, M.: Discovering Fuzzy Relationships from Databases: CESA 1996: 830–835.
8. Kerber, R.: ChiMerge: Discretization of Numeric Attributes. AAAI 1992: 123–128.
9. Lin, T.Y.: Rough Set Theory in Very Large Databases. CESA 1996: 936–941.
10. Pawlak, Z.: Rough sets. IJICS 1982: 344–356.

11. Pawlak, Z.: Rough Sets - Theoretical Aspects of Reasoning about Data. Kluwer Ed., 1991.
12. Quinlan, J.R.: Induction of Decision Trees. ML 1986: 81–106.
13. Quinlan, J.R.: C4.5: Programs for Machine Learning. Morgan Kaufmann Ed., 1993.
14. Richeldi, M. and Rossotto, M.: Class-Driven Statistical Discretization of Continuous Attributes (Extended Abstract). ECML 1995: 335–338
15. Skowron, A. and Rauszer, C.: The Discernibility Matrices and Functions in Information Systems. ICS PAS Report 1/91 (Technical University of Warsaw): 1–44.
16. Van de Merckt, T.: Decision Trees in Numerical Attribute Spaces. IJCAI 1993: 1016–1021.
17. Ziarko, W.: Variable Precision Rough Set Model. Journal of Computers and System Sciences (49), 1993: 39–59.

Section VI:

Media Mining

Exploiting Structural Information for Text Classification on the WWW.... 487
  J. Fürnkranz

Multi-agent Web Information Retrieval: Neural Network Based
Approach 499
  Y.S. Choi and S.I. Yoo

Adaptive Information Filtering Algorithms 513
  D.R. Tauritz and I.G. Sprinkhuizen-Kuyper

A Conceptual Graph Approach for Video Data Representation and
Retrieval 525
  N. Fatemi and P. Mulhem

Exploiting Structural Information for Text Classification on the WWW

Johannes Fürnkranz

Austrian Research Institute for Artificial Intelligence
Schottengasse 3, A-1010 Wien, Austria
juffi@ai.univie.ac.at

Abstract. In this paper, we report on a set of experiments that explore the utility of making use of the structural information of WWW documents. Our working hypothesis is that it is often easier to classify a hypertext page using information provided on pages that point to it instead of using information that is provided on the page itself. We present experimental evidence that confirms this hypothesis on a set of Web-pages that relate to Computer Science Departments.

1 Introduction

The advent of the World-Wide Web has rejuvinated the interest in text categorization problems. Vast amounts of documents are available on-line, and categorizing them into meaningful semantic categories is a rewarding and challenging research problem.

However, current approaches to text categorization on the Web mostly concentrate on simple representation schemes that are based on word occurrence and word frequency. The structural information that is inherent to documents on the Web is often neglected. There are at least two different kinds of structural information on the Web that could be used to enhance the performance of current text classification algorithms:

- the structure of an HTML representation which allows to easily identify important parts of a document, such as its headings and its title, and
- the structure of the Web itself, where pages are linked to each other in various ways.

In this paper, we report on a set of experiments that explores the utility of such structural information. Our working hypothesis is that (at least in some domains) it is easier to classify hypertext pages using information provided on pages that point to a page instead of using information that is provided on the page itself. There are several reasons for this:

Redundancy: Quite often there is more than one page pointing to a single page on the Web. The ability to combine multiple, independent sources of information can improve classification accuracy.

D.J. Hand, J.N. Kok, M.R. Berthold (Eds.): IDA'99, LNCS 1642, pp. 487–497, 1999.
© Springer-Verlag Berlin Heidelberg 1999

Independent Labeling: Being able to rely on the information provided by multiple authors (the authors of the pages that point to the page to be classified) is less sensitive than having to rely on the vocabulary used by one particular author [11].

Page Sparseness: Web pages are often very sparse or contain mostly images. Using the links to a page increases the chances of encountering informative text about the page to classify.

To investigate our hypothesis, we represent a Web page with features derived from information of pages that point to the page. To that end, we encode each hyperlink pointing to a document with its anchor text, the headings structurally preceding it, and the text of the paragraph in which it occurs. Then we learn a set of classification rules with the inductive rule learning algorithm RIPPER [1]. The predictions of links pointing to the same page are then combined to yield a prediction for this page.

Our results show that documents can often be classified more reliably with information originating from pages that point to the document than with features that are derived from the document text itself.

2   Motivation

Our approach for the use of structural information for classifying Web-pages was motivated by the following observation that we made while working with conventional text classification techniques on the WebKB data set.[1]

Observation 1: *The text on the pages themselves is often insufficient or irrelevant for a reliable classification.*

For example, home pages of computer science departments often only consist of images with pointers to information about offered courses, student and faculty home pages, research projects, etc. Even if this information is contained on a single page, the words on the page itself do not provide many clues for the fact that we are dealing with the home page of a computer science department as opposed to any other page in a computer science department.

Observation 2: *Information on the pages that contain a pointer to a given page is much more helpful. Very often, at least one of the following three pieces of information contains an obvious clue for the intended classification of the page.*

1. *the anchor text*
2. *the context in which the anchor text appears*
3. *the headings that structurally precede the section of the document in which the link occurs*

For example, department pages typically have a large number of links pointing to them that are marked with anchor texts that include phrases like "computer science department", "CS department", "dept. of computer science", or

---

[1] A brief description of this domain can be found in section 5

similar. Each of them should be sufficient to identify the link as pointing to the page of a computer science department. Student home pages very often contain a pointer to their advisor's home page. Thus, faculty home pages can often be identified by the occurrence of the word "advisor" in the neighborhood of a link that points to the page. Furthermore, many computer science departments have a page that lists all students, faculty, staff, projects, courses, or other information. Typically such a page (or segment of a page) starts with a heading that identifies the type of information that is listed below it. Clearly, this information can also be very useful for classifying the pages that the list items below this heading point to.

3   Document Representation

In order to capture its structural information, we represented a document in the following way. First, the entire text of the document itself was discarded. Instead, we identified a set of pages that contain a pointer to the current page.[2] Each of these pages was turned into a separate training example using the following pieces of information:

Anchor: All words that occurred in the anchor text of the link (between the opening `<A ...>` and the closing `</A>` of the HTML link).

Heading: All words that occurred in headings that *structurally* precede the hyperlink in the HTML document. This means a heading of type `<Hi>` is included iff it appears before the hyperlink and no heading of type `<Hj>` with $j \leq i$ appears in the segment between the heading and the hyperlink. Page titles and titles for definition lists (`<DT>`) were also included as headings (with $i = 0$ and $i = 7$ respectively).

Paragraph: All words of the paragraph in which the hyperlink occurs. Our method for determining the paragraph is somewhat heuristic and certainly not perfect. Pieces of text separated by `<P>` or an empty line are paragraphs, as are structural entities such as items in a list `<LI>`.

The three features described above were each encoded as a separate set-valued feature [2] for the separate-and-conquer rule learner RIPPER [1], which achieves noise-tolerance through an extension of incremental reduced error pruning [7]. A set-valued feature may be viewed as an efficient encoding of a group of binary features that correspond to the occurrences of words in the document. We will also refer to set-valued features as *feature sets* and use the terms *feature* and *word* interchangeably. Each training example was labelled with the appropriate class information, which is the class of the page the link points to.

---

[2] We did this by scanning a collection of pages of Computer Science departments for all occurrences of an HREF that contains the address of the current page. In principle, this could also be performed on-line using a search engine like ALTAVISTA that allows to query for pages that point to a given address.

4   Voting Schemes

As discussed above, the training sets for RIPPER consist of one example for each hyperlink. From such a set, RIPPER induces a set of unordered rules[3] that discriminate the examples of each class from the examples of all other classes. At prediction time, RIPPER selects among all rules that fire for a given example the one that has the highest confidence associated with it and uses it to classify the example.

Quite frequently, however, several links point to the same page. As our goal is to the predict the class of a page (and not of each individual link) we can try to exploit the redundancy that is provided by such multiple links. In order to do so, we have to device strategies for combining the predictions of all hyperlinks pointing to a page into a single prediction for the class of the page. We implemented the following five straight-forward techniques:

Voting *(Vote (all))*: The simplest technique is to give each link that points to a page one vote, and predict the class that receives the most votes. Ties are broken in favor of larger classes. Links that are classified using the default rule learned by RIPPER (i.e., the rule specifying that if no other rule applies, predict the majority class among all unexplained examples in the training set) are eligible to vote.

Restricted Voting *(Vote)*: It is reasonable to assume that there will always be a few links that are classified by the default rules. Thus we implemented another version of the voting scheme, where votes of such links are ignored and only links that were classified by non-default rules are eligible to vote. If a page only receives votes from default rules, it is classified with the majority class.

Weighted Sum *(Weight)*: We also associate a confidence score with each of RIPPER's predictions, which simply consists of the Laplace-estimate $\frac{p+1}{p+n+2}$ of the probability that an example covered by the rule is positive (estimated on the training set). If the prediction originates from a default rule, it is assigned a score of 0. Such a score is computed for each possible class of each link. The *Weight* voting scheme simply returns the sum of all weights as the confidence score of the prediction.

Weighted Normalized Sum *(Norm)*: This voting scheme is identical to the previous one, except that the confidence scores are first normalized in a way that distributes a total weight of 1 among the different candidate classes for each link. This is necessary because the confidence score that is associated with each class only depends on the number of positive and negative examples covered by the best rule that predicts this class and covers the example. Therefore the confidence scores associated with each class cannot be interpreted as class probability estimates unless they are normalized.

---

[3] We have also experimented with ordered rule sets, but the results were usually a little worse. Besides, in "ordered" mode, RIPPER treats one class as the default class and does not learn rules for that class.

Maximum Confidence *(Max)*: The last combination method simply chooses the class prediction that receives the highest score over all links that point to the page to classify and predicts that class. This is an attempt to use only the most accurate of all applicable rules to classify a page.

From a Machine Learning perspective, the problem can be viewed as combining the predictions for different training examples, for which it is known that they have the same class label. To the extent to which the predictions of the classifier for different training examples are independent of each other (which roughly corresponds to the extent to which the feature vector representation of the examples differ), it can be expected that combining the predictions may yield a performance gain [5].

5   Experimental Setup

We performed a series of experiments on 1050 pages of the WebKB domain. These pages are classified into one of the categories *Student*, *Department*, *Faculty*, *Research Project*, *Research Associate*, *Post Doc*, and *Course*. Within these pages, 5803 hyperlinks point to another page within this set. Each of these is turned into a separate training example using the set-valued features described above.

The pages/links were collected from four universities. All reported results are from a 4-fold leave-one-university-out cross-validation, i.e., for each experiment we combined the examples of three universities to learn a classifier which was then tested on the data of the fourth university. Because of the different test set sizes for each of the four results, we used micro-averaging for evaluating the accuracy of the predictors, i.e., we lumped the predictions from all four runs together and computed an accuracy measure on the entire set of predictions.

More details on the experimental setup can be found in [8], while the dataset is described in [4].

6   Results

6.1   Page Accuracy

Table 1 shows the accuracies measured for predicting the page labels. The rows list the different representation schemes, starting from the default prediction accuracy (using no features), to the classifier that uses all features. The columns of the table give the accuracy for each of the 5 implemented prediction combination techniques, starting with the voting scheme including default prediction, voting without default prediction, normalized weighted average, weighted average, and finally the maximum method (see section 4).

In terms of representation, it becomes apparent that using additional feature sets will generally result in higher accuracies. The exception to the rule is the *Paragraph* feature set. Whenever its features are added to a representation that

Table 1. Accuracies for classifying the 1050 pages using various methods for combining link predictors to page predictors.

Classifier	Combination Method				
	Vote (all)	Vote	Normal	Weight	Max
Default	51.81	51.81	51.81	51.81	51.81
Anchor	67.52	74.67	74.38	74.19	**74.76**
Headings	60.48	72.29	72.38	**72.95**	72.95
Paragraph	63.05	66.86	66.86	**66.95**	66.29
Anchor+Headings	74.48	85.33	84.95	85.14	**86.57**
Anchor+Paragraph	68.00	74.29	74.00	73.90	**74.67**
Headings+Paragraph	70.48	79.90	80.19	81.14	**81.33**
All	74.19	82.29	81.71	82.67	**83.24**

already includes the *Anchor* features, the result is a loss of predictive accuracy. A reason for this might be that these two feature sets are much less independent of each other than other pairs of feature sets.[4] The best results were achieved when relying only on the anchor text and the information from the headings.

Among the five different techniques for combining the link predictions to a page prediction, taking the prediction with the maximum confidence is a clear winner. In 7 out of 8 runs, using this method gave the best results (shown in **bold** face). However, in general, the differences among the combination methods are not nearly as large as the differences among the different document representations. The only exception is the voting scheme that also allowed the default rule to vote (first column of table 1). Apparently, the learned rules have a fairly low coverage, so that many of the links have to be classified using the default rule. It happens quite frequently that a few good rules are outnumbered by a number of default predictions. We have also found that the performance deteriorates similarly when default predictions are included into the weighted prediction combiner (results not shown). The maximum technique remains mostly unaffected by this because it is unlikely that a default prediction receives the maximum confidence score among a number of competing link predictions (results also not shown).

6.2   Link Accuracy

One question that remains unanswered by table 1 is how much has actually been gained by combining the prediction of different links pointing to a single page. To investigate this question, we computed a weighted accuracy estimate by weighting each page with the number of links that point to that page. In

---

[4] Note, however, that even though the set of words occurring on the anchor text is a subset of the set of words occurring in its surrounding paragraph, the resulting *Anchor* feature set is *not* a subset of the resulting *Paragraph* feature set because the feature $x\_occurs\_in\_anchor\_text$ is semantically different from the feature $x\_occurs\_in\_paragraph$, the former being more specific than the latter.

Table 2. Accuracies for classifying the 5803 links with various predictor combination methods.

Encoding	No	Combination Method				
		Vote(all)	Vote	Normal	Weight	Max
Default	36.67	36.67	36.67	36.67	36.67	36.67
Anchor	57.92	58.80	75.93	75.56	75.37	**76.05**
Headings	43.34	40.01	66.62	69.89	**70.77**	64.33
Paragraph	53.40	55.09	65.91	65.81	**66.33**	58.59
Anchor+Headings	62.49	61.66	86.18	85.46	**86.25**	83.22
Anchor+Paragraph	58.40	59.23	**73.70**	73.67	73.46	71.81
Headings+Paragraph	58.50	56.69	78.67	78.98	**80.30**	76.63
All	57.99	61.43	79.15	77.74	**79.44**	79.20

other words, all links that point to the same page perform an internal vote to decide upon a common classification for the page they point to. Each link of such a group is then classified with this common label. The resulting accuracy estimate counts the number of correctly predicted links over all links, and can thus be directly compared to the accuracies of the base classifiers that predict the class labels of each link independently.

These results are shown in table 2. The first thing to note is a substantial difference between the independent classifier (first column) and the classifiers that rely on combining the predictions for different links for all methods except voting with inclusion of default predictions. Obviously, many mistakes could be corrected by combining the predictions of different links and thus being able to rely on good features that appeared in a different link pointing to the same page.

Secondly, the differences between the voting scheme that includes default predictions (second column) and the voting schemes that ignore them is more remarkable than in table 1. We explain this with the fact that for pages with many incoming links, there are good chances that many of the links are classified by default rules, and that the combination of these predictions overrides the few "educated" guesses. With the voting schemes that ignore default predictions, the situation is the opposite: A few correct rule-base classifications can override many wrong default classifications and thus gain substantially in accuracy.

It is also interesting to observe that in table 2, the *Max* prediction method (last column) is not as dominant as in table 1 and, in some cases, it performs substantially worse than its competitors. The reason for this is that the maximum prediction is much less susceptible to variations in the number of link predictions that are combined to a single page prediction. If an erroneous link prediction has the maximum confidence score, it is used for predicting the class of the page. The voting and weighting methods, on the other hand, can make use of a number of unanimous predictions with lower confidence scores to override a prediction with a higher confidence score. Thus, it can be expected that pages with a higher number of incoming links are classified more reliably by voting or weighting,

Table 3. Recall and Precision for the page predictors. *Recall* is the percentage of pages that are not classified with the default rule and *Precision* is how many of these classifications were correct.

Classifier	Recall	Precision			
		Vote	Normal	Weight	Max
Anchor	40.76	83.64	82.30	82.48	83.88
Headings	74.10	88.05	88.19	88.95	88.95
Paragraph	46.67	75.71	75.91	75.92	74.49
Anchor+Headings	85.90	92.35	91.91	92.13	93.79
Anchor+Paragraph	60.19	83.23	82.81	82.59	83.86
Headings+Paragraph	82.38	88.44	88.79	89.94	90.17
All	78.00	86.94	86.20	87.42	88.16

while pages with a lower number incoming links are better classified by taking the prediction with the maximum score. As the latter category is more frequent, the page accuracies tend to be higher for the maximum prediction method, while the link accuracies tend to be higher for the voting and weighting schemes.

6.3   Recall and Precision

We have discussed above that many of the test examples are classified using the default rule and that it seems to be advisable to ignore these default link predictions for computing the page predictions. But what happens in cases where *all* links that point to a page are classified by default rules, i.e., no link contains any information that could be used for a justified prediction? In the experiments reported in the previous section, we have simply predicted the majority class *Student* for each of these pages. What if we ignore these predictions? It can be expected that the classification accuracy goes up at the expense of classifying fewer pages. This trade-off is commonly measured in terms of precision and recall.

Table 3 lists recall and precision estimates that shed some light upon this question. *Recall* is the percentage of pages which were classified using at least one rule different from the default rule. Note that this estimate is the same for all combination methods because the underlying link classifiers are the same and hence the links that are classified with default rules are the same. *Precision* is the percentage of classified pages that were correctly classified. In general, the precision scores are much higher than the accuracy results of table 1. This is not surprising because accuracy can be viewed as a weighted sum between the precision on the recalled examples and the precision on the examples classified by default rules (which should be about the default accuracy, although the variance can be very high). The recall scores are more differentiated. *Headings* features not only have the highest, but also achieve this precision at significantly higher recall scores.

Table 4. Accuracy and number of features for using feature subset selection on the full-text classifier.

Classifier	# Features	Accuracy
Link-Based	8,075	85.05%
Full-Text	20,322	70.67%

Table 5. Accuracy results for feature subset selection on the full-text classifier.

# Features	Accuracy
100%	70.67
50%	73.90
10%	74.19
5%	74.76
1%	71.33
0.1%	54.67

6.4 Comparison to Full-Text Classifier

We also compared the predictive accuracies of the link-based page classifiers to those of a classifier that uses the words occurring on the page as a feature. Table 4 shows a comparison between the link-based classifier using all four feature sets and a full-text classifier in terms of predictive accuracy and the number of features used by both representations.[5] The link-based classifiers discussed in this paper are considerably more accurate while using less than half of the number of features.

An obvious question at this point is, of course, whether the differences in accuracy are at least partly due to the different number of features. Could we produce a similar effect by employing feature subset selection on the full-text classifier? We have already seen, that in general, adding additional feature sets improves accuracy. On the other hand, it is also known that too many features can lead to overfitting. Table 5 shows the results for using only the top n% of the features of the full-text classifier (selected by entropy). Feature subset selection results in some improvement, but the best result is still more than 10% behind the link-based classifiers. We have not checked whether feature subset selection would improve the link-classifiers as well.

7   Conclusion

Our results show that it is possible to classify documents more reliably with information originating from pages that point to the document than with features that are derived from the document text itself. Furthermore, it proved to be beneficial to be able to exploit redundant information on the WWW by combining multiple predictions (one for each hyperlink pointing to a page). However, we have shown this for one domain only, so our results can only be considered as preliminary. More experimental work in other domains must be conducted in order to establish a conclusive result.

---

[5] The reported number of features is the total number of features in the entire dataset. Each of the four training sets of the cross-validation contained on average a little more than 80% of the features for both types of classifiers.

Although the encoding scheme we used is quite straight-forward, it illustrates that the use of information about the HTML structure of pages and about the structure of the WWW itself can be useful for improving text categorization on the WWW. The use of more elaborate representation schemes (e.g., distinguishing different types of headings or even using an entire HTML-tree [6] as background knowledge) suggests itself as a rewarding topic for further research as does the use of relational learning techniques (see, e.g., [3,10]). We have already performed preliminary experiments using linguistic phrases of the kind used in [9] as an additional feature set, but found that they did not make much difference [8]. Such approaches also need to be investigated in more detail.

Acknowledgements

This work was performed during the author's stay at Carnegie Mellon University, which was enabled by a *Schrödinger-Stipendium* (J1443-INF) of the Austrian *Fonds zur Förderung der wissenschaftlichen Forschung (FWF)*. The author has benefited greatly from discussions with Mark Craven, Tom Mitchell, and Ellen Riloff. Thanks to the CMU text learning group for making the WebKB dataset available, in particular to Dayne Freitag and Tom Mitchell for providing a preprocessed version.

References

1. William W. Cohen. Fast effective rule induction. In A. Prieditis and S. Russell, editors, *Proceedings of the 12th International Conference on Machine Learning (ML-95)*, pages 115–123, Lake Tahoe, CA, 1995. Morgan Kaufmann.
2. William W. Cohen. Learning trees and rules with set-valued features. In *Proceedings of the 13th National Conference on Artificial Intelligene (AAAI-96)*, pages 709–716. AAAI Press, 1996.
3. Mark Craven. Using statistical and relational methods to characterize hyperlink paths. In D. Jensen and H. Goldberg, editors, *Artificial Intelligence and Link Analysis: Papers from the 1998 AAAI Fall Symposium*, pages 14–20, Orlando, Florida, 1998. AAAI Press. Technical Report FS-98-01.
4. Mark Craven, Dan DiPasquo, Dayne Freitag, Andrew McCallum, Tom Mitchell, Kamal Nigam, and Seán Slattery. Learning to extract symbolic knowledge from the World Wide Web. In *Proceedings of the 15th National Conference on Artificial Intelligence (AAAI-98)*. AAAI Press, 1998.
5. Thomas G. Dietterich. Machine learning research: Four current directions. *AI Magazine*, 18(4):97–136, 1997.
6. Dan DiPasquo. Using HTML structure to aid in automatic information retrieval from the world wide web. Senior Honors Thesis, School of Computer Science, Carnegie Mellon University, May 1998.
7. Johannes Fürnkranz. Pruning algorithms for rule learning. *Machine Learning*, 27(2):139–171, 1997.
8. Johannes Fürnkranz. Using links for classifying web-pages. Technical Report OEFAI-TR-98-29, Austrian Research Institute for Artificial Intelligence, 1998.

9. Johannes Fürnkranz, Tom Mitchell, and Ellen Riloff. A case study in using linguistic phrases for text categorization on the WWW. In M. Sahami, editor, *Learning for Text Categorization: Proceedings of the 1998 AAAI/ICML Workshop*, pages 5–12, Madison, WI, 1998. AAAI Press. Technical Report WS-98-05.
10. Seán Slattery and Mark Craven. Combining statistical and relational methods for learning in hypertext domains. In D. Page, editor, *Proceedings of the 8th International Conference on Inductive Logic Programming (ILP-98)*, pages 38–52, Madison, WI, 1998. Springer-Verlag.
11. Ellen Spertus. ParaSite: Mining structural information on the Web. *Computer Networks and ISDN Systems*, 29(8-13):1205–1215, September 1997.

Multi-agent Web Information Retrieval: Neural Network Based Approach

Yong S. Choi and Suk I. Yoo

Department of Computer Science, Seoul National University,
Shilim-dong, Kwanak-ku, Seoul,151-742, Korea,
{cys,siyoo}@hera.snu.ac.kr
http://hera.snu.ac.kr/index.html

Abstract. The Web is full of information sources. Currently, retrieving useful information on the Web is a time-consuming process. In this paper, we propose a multi-agent learning approach to information retrieval on the Web, where each agent collaboratively learns its environment from user's relevance feedback using a neural network mechanism. Our approach makes it possible to discover information sources associated with useful information and then retrieve that information effectively. First, we present a framework of IR agent and its operation for our multi-agent learning approach. Secondly, we define the multi-agent IR system based on our approach and then describe its training procedure for collavorative information retrieval. Finally, we present the experimental results of our approach, comparing them to those obtained by the approach of traditional meta-search service.

1 Introduction

As the number and diversity of distributed information sources on the Web increases rapidly, there has been an increased demand for Web Information Retrieval (IR) systems which help people search for useful information. Thus a number of automated Web IR systems for retrieving information on the Web have been developed. Conventional Web IR systems usually build database indices for each information in a single platform and use a well-known retrieval model such as the vector space model based on TFIDF algorithm [1]. These approaches however often cause massive bottlenecks and unacceptable access delays under highly competitive access situations as in search tools such as Lycos [2] and WebCrawler [3]. This shortcoming becomes more severe as the amount of information stored as the form of database indices increases. This problem has led to meta-search services such as IBM InfoMarket[1] and MetaCrawler[2] that distribute IR task into several search tools. The traditional meta-search service broadcasts a user query to several search tools simultaneously and then merges the results submitted by these search tools and presents them to the user as

---

[1] The URL of *IBM Infomarket* is www.infomarket.ibm.com.
[2] The URL of *MetaCrawler* is www.metacrawler.com/index_text.html.

D.J. Hand, J.N. Kok, M.R. Berthold (Eds.): IDA'99, LNCS 1642, pp. 499–511, 1999.
© Springer-Verlag Berlin Heidelberg 1999

an HTML page with clickable URLs [4]. Therefore, the traiditioanl meta-search service provides its user a layer of abstraction over multiple search tools and serves as a Web search interface.

The traditional meta-search service broadcasts a user query to all accessible search tools even when the index of useful information may be located at only one or some of search tools, which results in ineffective and wasteful competition for network resources with considerable communication cost. Therefore, the indiscriminant broadcast of traditional meta-search service is inefficient in the Web environment where the indices of information related to each other are often clustered according to the categories of search tools so that the useful information will be given by only one or a few search tools. These considerations for the Web IR raise an interesting problem, which we call the multiple access problem of IR: If there exist many information sources like search tools that have or might have the seeking information, how many queries should be issued and to which sources should the queries be given?

To solve this problem, we propose a multi-agent cooperative learning approach for the Web IR. In the proposed approach, a number of information agents interact effectively utilizing the distributed search tools and learn their environment from the user's feedback so that they can retrieve useful information to the user efficiently from the widely spread information sources on the Web. We adopted the BackPropagation neural Network (BPN) [5] as the learning and generalization mechanism that each information agent uses to build up and employ knowledge about information resources relevant to user's interests or preferences. The knowledge is acquired by means of user's relevance feedback judgement. The multi-agent IR system constructed on our approach, for any query, locates the search tools which could give the information useful to user, and then retrieves that information as long as it is sufficiently trained based on the BPN learning mechanism.

The remainder of this paper is organized as follows. In Section 2, we define an IR agent for our multi-agent learning approach and then describe its operation procedures. In Section 3, we define the multi-agent IR system constructed from a number of IR agents and search tools, and then describe its training procedure for effective information retrieval. In Section 4, we evaluate our approach with the performance measurement of an experiment system and compare the performance measurement to that obtained by the approach of traditional meta-search service.

2   IR Agent

The term agent system (or agent) has been increasingly used within information technology to describe various computational entities. Especially, the exceedingly voluminous and readily available information on the Web has given rise to developing agents as the computational entities for accessing, discovering and retrieving information. This agent for IR (IR agent) can be described as a self-contained problem solving entity usually (but not necessarily) equipped with

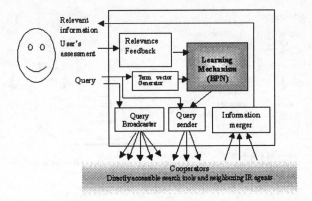

Fig. 1. Framework of an IR Agent

internal knowledge, sensor, effector and data pertinent to IR problem; it also has its own built-in control mechanism [6]. The following two subsections defines an IR agent and then describes its operation for information retrieval and training.

2.1   Definition

To solve the multiple access problem of IR, our approach has, as a problem domain, the environment where there exist a number of Web search tools. The Web search tool is an information source that receives a query and returns some information relevant to that query based on its own IR database indices. In this environment, each IR agent locates search tools associated with useful information and then retrieves that information from those search tools by communicating with its neighboring IR agents if necessary. Each IR agent sends a given query to and then receives the information relevant to that query from its directly accessible search tool or neighboring IR agent, which we call a cooperator of that IR agent. Therefore, each IR agent can retrieve useful information for a given query from its cooperators by sending that query to them. Fig. 1 shows the main components of an IR agent and the control flows among them. Thus, an IR agent α is defined by the 6-tuple $a=< QB, IM, RF, TG, LM, QS >$, where each component is described in the following subsections.

Query Broadcaster (QB) The Query Broadcast broadcasts a given query to all cooperators of its IR agent in order to receive all information relevant to that query from them.

Information Merger (IM) The Information Merger merges the information submitted by the cooperators of its IR agent and then presents it to the issuer of query.

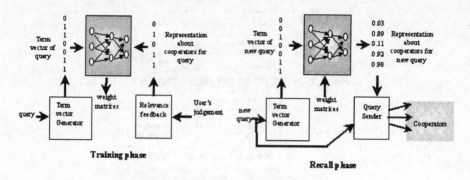

Fig. 2. Training and recall phase of BPN

Relevance Feedback (RF) The Relevance Feedback receives the user's judgement for the information presented by the IM for a given query q and then generates a binary vector representation $c_q = (c_{q1}, c_{q2}, \ldots, c_{qM})$ where if S is an ordered set of all cooperators, $S = < a_1, a_2, \ldots, a_M >$, of the IR agent that the RF belongs to, then, for $i = 1, 2, \ldots, M$,

$$c_{qi} = \begin{cases} 1 & \text{if the information submitted by } A_i \text{ for a given query } q \text{ is judged to} \\ & \text{be relevant by the user,} \\ 0 & \text{otherwise.} \end{cases}$$

Term Vector Generator (TG) The Term Vector Generator transforms a query q, which is expressed as a set of index terms by eliminating non-content words and stemming the plural noun to its single form and inflexed verb to its original form [7], into a binary vector representation (called term vector) $s_q = (s_{q1}, s_{q2}, \ldots, s_{qN})$ where if T is an ordered set of all index terms, $T = < t_1, t_2, \ldots, t_N >$ and $q \subseteq T$, then, for $i = 1, 2, \ldots, N$,

$$s_{qi} = \begin{cases} 1 & \text{if } t_i \in q \\ 0 & \text{otherwise.} \end{cases}$$

Learning Mechanism (LM) To learn from user relevance feedback and recall when retrieving information, each agent has its Learning Mechanism as the form of the neural network associative memory that is shown by the shaded rectangle in fig. 1. Backpropagation neural network (BPN) is used for this neural network associative memory to take advantage of its learning and generalization properties. Fig. 2 shows that the BPN of each IR agent acts in two phases: a training phase and a recall phase.

During the training phase, the input and the output layer of the BPN are set to represent a training pair (s_q, c_q) where s_q is produced by the TG and c_q is produced by the RF for a given query. The well-known BPN learning procedure

Procedure *Learning(BPN, T)* *// This procedure trains BPN with T*
BPN : a backpropagation neural network
T : a training query set
begin
 repeat
  for each training pair $(s_q, c_q) \in T$
  begin
   Apply s_q to the input layer of *BPN*;
   Calculate the output of *BPN*;
   Calculate the error ε between the output of *BPN* and the desired output c_q;
   Adjust the link-weight matrices of *BPN* in a way that minimizes ε;
  end
  until the error is acceptably small for all $(s_q, c_q) \in T$;
 Store the link-weight matrices of *BPN*;
end

Fig. 3. BPN learning procedure

is performed for all training pairs made of the outputs produced by the TG and the RF for given training queries. Fig. 3 shows the overall BPN learning procedure for a set of training pairs T. The BPN learning procedure adjusts the link-weight matrices of BPN using the backpropagation learning rule [8], and its result is stored as the IR knowledge about user's interests or preferences.

During the recall phase, the input layer of the BPN is activated by applying the term vector produced by the TG for a newly given query. This activation of the BPN spreads from the input layer to the output layer using the link-weight matrices stored during the training phase. This spreading activation[3] produces, as the output of BPN, a vector representation whose components are all between 0 and 1.

The learning mechanism using BPN is the core of IR agent and thus the parameter configuration of BPN may have a crucial effect on the performance of our IR approach. We illustrate the configuration of BPN for the experiment IR system in Section 5.

Query Sender (QS) The Query Sender sends a given query selectively to the cooperators of its IR agent according to the output of the BPN recall phase as follows: Let S be the ordered set of all cooperators, $S = < a_1, a_2, \ldots, a_M >$, of the IR agent that the QS belongs to, and let $o_q = (o_{q1}, o_{q2}, \ldots, o_{qM})$ be an output vector of the BPN recall phase for a given query q and let τ be a tolerance constant[4] such that $0 < \tau < 1$. Then, for $i = 1, 2, ..., M$, the QS sends q to a_i if and only if $o_{qi} \geq \tau$.

---

[3] This spreading activation procedure is more detailed in [8].
[4] In the experiment system, we have used 0.75 as the tolerance constant.

2.2   Operation

In this section, we explain how an IR agent is trained to retrieve useful information for a given query. First, we describe the procedure of how an IR agent retrieves information for a given query and then we describe a training procedure of an IR agent using user's relevance feedback. In the followings, we describe the procedures using the key components of an IR agent explained in the previous section.

Information Retrieval An IR agent $a =< QB, IM, RF, TG, LM, QS >$ receives a query expressed as a character string from the human user or some other IR agent, and then returns the information for that query as the following steps.

Step 1: TG transforms a given query q into its term vector s_q.
Step 2: LM (BPN) activated by s_q produces an output vector o_q by its recall phase.
Step 3: QS selects cooperators based on o_q and sends q to the selected cooperators.
Step 4: IM merges all information submitted by the cooperators selected on o_q in step 3, and presents it to the issuer of q.

In step 2 and 3, an IR agent locates its cooperators that is expected to give useful information for a given query using the IR knowledge stored as the link-weight matrices of BPN and send that query to those cooperators to retrieve information.

Training The training procedure of an IR agent acquires the IR knowledge about the user's interests or preferences using the user's relevance feedback. If a query is given from the user, the IR agent broadcasts that query to all its cooperators by QB, and then waits for the information from them. If all information is returned, the IM merges and displays that information to the user. The RF asks the user to mark the pieces of information judged as relevant to his/her query and then extracts the information about from where each marked piece of information was returned. This extraction produces the binary vector representation, which indicates which of the cooperators of an IR agent gave the information relevant to the user's interests or preferences for a given query, as described in Section 2.1. The term vector and the binary vector representation, which are produced for a given query by the TG and the RF respectively, compose a training pair. The BPN of an IR agent is trained with the set of training pairs obtained from all the queries given by the user. Fig. 4 shows the entire training procedure of an IR agent a for the training queries given by the user. With no training, the BPN as the learning mechanism of an IR agent has a random initialization of its link-weight matrices so that for any query, its recall phase does not produce any heuristic knowledge about the location of useful information. But, as the BPN is trained with the more training pairs, it produces

Procedure *ATrains*(α) :
α : an IR agent
Let α = < *QB, IM, RF, TG, LM, QS* >   *// LM is BPN*
begin
trainingpairset ← ∅
for each training query *q* given by user
  begin
  TG generates the term vector s_q ;
  QB broadcasts *q* to all cooperators of α ;
  Wait for all information returned from all cooperators of α ;
  IM displays all information from all cooperators of α to the user ;
  RF produces the binary vector representation c_q from the user's relevance
    feedback ;
  trainingpairset ← *trainingpairset* ∪ { (s_q , c_q) } ;
  end
Train *LM* by calling *Learning*(*LM, trainingpairset*) ;
end

Fig. 4. Training procedure of an IR agent

the more heuristic knowledge. Eventually, after trained with sufficient training pairs, it can produce the heuristic knowledge about the location of useful information for any query because by the White theorem [9], the probability of the BPN error exceeding any tolerance level goes to zero as the size of the training set increases. This potential is experimentally discussed in detail in Section 4.

3   Multi-agent IR System

In the previous section, we defined an IR agent and then described its operation procedures. In this section, we define a multi-agent IR system based on IR agents and their accessible search tools, and then describe the training procedure of multi-agent IR system for collaborative information retrieval.

3.1   Definition

From some search tools as information sources and IR agents retrieving information from those search tools, a multi-agent IR system is constructed, which may be defined as follows:

Definition: A multi-agent IR system is a 3-tuple $M = < A, S, R >$ where A is a set of IR agents, S is a set of search tools and R is a binary relation on $A \times (A \cap S)$ such that $< x, y > \in R$ if and only if y is a cooperator of x.

As it can be noticed, a multi-agent IR system $M = < A, S, R >$ can be represented as a directed graph diagram where the elements of A are IR agent

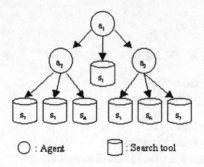

Fig. 5. Graph diagram of a multi-agent system

nodes, the elements of S are search tool nodes and $< x, y >\in R$ is an arrow (directed link) from x to y. For example, let $M =< A, S, R >$, where $A = a_1, a_2, a_3$, $S = s_1, s_2, s_3, s_4, s_5, s_6, s_7$ and $R=< a_1, s_1 >, < a_1, a_2 >, < a_1, a_3 >, < a_2, s_2 >, < a_2, s_3 >, < a_2, s_4 >, < a_3, s_5 >, < a_3, s_6 >, < a_3, s_7 >$. Then, M is represented as a graph diagram of fig. 5, where any arrow from a node representing an IR agent outgoes to a node representing a cooperator of that IR agent.

3.2   Operation

In this section, we explain how a multi-agent IR system is trained to collaboratively retrieve useful information. First, we describe a training procedure based on the definition of multi-agent IR system and then we explain about the collaborative information retrieval of multi-agent IR system.

Training Using the training procedure of each IR agent and the definition of multi-agent IR system, we describe the training procedure of a multi-agent IR system. For an IR agent to be trained, any of its cooperators that is not a search tool should have been already trained. If not so, the information submitted by some cooperators of that IR agent can be inaccurate and thus that IR agent can be trained with the inaccurate information. Based on this restriction, fig. 6 shows the training procedure of a multi-agent IR system M. For example, for the multi-agent IR system represented as the graph diagram of fig. 5, the IR agents are trained in the order of a_2, a_3, a_1 or a_3, a_2, a_1 by the procedure of fig. 6. In this procedure, we assume that the directed graph diagram representing a multi-agent IR system is acyclic. The training method in the multi-agent IR system represented by a cyclic directed graph diagram is also being developed, but we will not deal with this work in this paper but put it to the future work.

Collaborative Information Retrieval Each IR agent in a multi-agent IR system sends a given query to some of its cooperators according to its trained BPN and then presents the information submitted by them to the issuer of

```
Procedure MTrains(M) :
M : a multi- agent IR system
Let M = < A, S, R >
begin
agentset←A ;
while agentset ≠ ∅ do
  begin
  untrained←agentset ;
  for each a∈untrained ;
    if c∉agentset or c∈S for all c∈A∪S such that <a, c>∈R then
      begin
      Train a by calling ATrains(a ) ;
      agentset←agentset - {a} ;
      end
  end
end
```

Fig. 6. Training procedure of multi-agent IR system

that query by the information retrieval steps of IR agent described in Section 2.2. For example, let us assume that the multi-agent IR system represented as the graph diagram of fig. 5 was trained with sufficient training queries by the training procedure of 6. If a human user gives a query q whose relevant information is indexed in the search tool s_6 to an IR agent a_1, a_1 sends q to a_3, which is determined by a_1's BPN and then a_3 also sends q given by a_1 to s_6, which is determined by a_3's BPN. Then, if s_6 submits the information relevant to q to a_3, a_3 presents them to a_1 and then a_1 presents them submitted by a_3 to the human user. As a result, the IR agents in a multi-agent IR system can collaboratively retrieve useful information without exhaustively traversing all search tools in that multi-agent IR system by their learning mechanisms. This may result in the significant improvement in terms of communication cost and also make it possible to filter out the information irrelevant to the user's interests or preferences, which will be experimentally discussed in the following section.

4   Experiment

We evaluated the performance of our multi-agent learning approach to IR on the popular search directories of $Yahoo!$ $Korea$[5]. $Yahoo!$ $Korea$ provides hierarchically organized directories in Korean language according to various categories, which are both browsable and searchable. We chose seven directories from them, each of which serves as a search tool that retrieves the descriptions of documents relevant to a given query for its category. On these seven directories of

---

[5] The URL of $Yahoo!$ $Korea$ is http://www.yahoo.co.kr.

Yahoo! Korea, we constructed a multi-agent IR system composed of three IR agents each of which has its three cooperators as shown in fig. 5. In this figure, s_1, s_2, s_3, s_4, s_5, s_6 and s_7 represent the chosen seven directories of *Yahoo! Korea* for respectively *Medicine, ComputerScience, ElectricalEngineering, Mechanics, Physics, Chemistry* and *Biology* categories. For this multi-agent IR system, we used the following configuration for BPN of each IR agent.

• The number of input and output units is respectively 200 and 3: The number of input units is obtained from experiences as a number that is large enough to represent all training queries as different binary vectors. The number of output units represents the number of cooperators of each IR agent.

• Only one hidden layer has been used because by the *Kolmogorow theorem* [10], three layers are theoretically sufficient to operate as an approximate associative memory.

• The number of hidden units was set to 125: The number of hidden units is also obtained from experiences as a small number as possible to succeed in training each IR agent.

We extracted 200 representative keywords from short descriptions of documents provided by the chosen seven directories of *Yahoo! Korea* and used these keywords as training queries. We gave all the 200 training queries to each IR agent of our multi-agent IR system and then trained our multi-agent IR system by the procedure of fig. 6. For comparison, we implemented an another IR system based on the indiscriminant broadcast of traditional meta-search service on the same directories of *Yahoo! Korea* as those in our approach. For performance test, 50 test queries were used. The test queries were generated as follows. First, we randomly selected 50 documents from the document descriptions provided by the chosen seven directories of *Yahoo! Korea*. Next, we manually extracted terms and phrases from those 50 documents. Finally, we randomly chose 50 ones from those terms and phrases, and used them as the test queries. These test queries were given to both the root IR agent (a_1 in fig. 5) of our trained multi-agent IR system and the traditional meta-search service system to retrieve information. We evaluated the documents retrieved for each test query and considered the ones interesting to us as relevant. We used the precision, the recall and the communication cost as the measurements of performance, which are defined as follows.

$$\text{precision} = \frac{\text{the number of relevant documents retrieved}}{\text{the total number of documents retrieved}}$$

$$\text{recall} = \frac{\text{the number of relevant documents retrieved}}{\text{the total no. of relevant documents existing in the seven directories}}$$

communication cost = the total number of query passes to retrieve information

Results obtained by evaluating the entire set of 50 test queries for various dimensions of the training query set are reported in fig. 7. In this figure, the average values of the results from the 50 test queries are used.

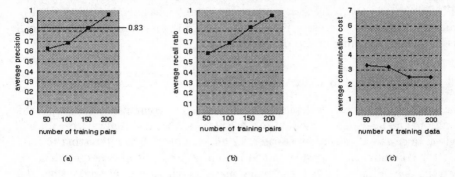

Fig. 7. Experimental results

4.1   Precision

Fig. 7-(a) shows the precision curve for our multi-agent IR approach. The horizontal line across this curve indicates the average precision in the traditional meta-search service approach. As it can be noticed, the precision of our approach gets better as each IR agent possesses larger amounts of knowledge from the user. Especially, when the size of training query set is over 150, our approach is always better than the traditional meta-search service approach in terms of precision. We may suppose that as the size of training query set goes over 200, the precision approaches 100%. However, the precision did not increase any more but converges on 96% in this experiment. The most probable explanation for this result is in the tolerable error permitted by the BPN learning procedure.

4.2   Recall

Fig. 7-(b) shows the recall curve for our multi-agent IR approach. In this graph, we used a recall ratio to the traditional meta-search service approach, which is defined as follows.

$$\text{recall ratio} = \frac{\text{recall in our approach}}{\text{recall in the traditional search service approach}}$$

Because the traditional meta-search service always retrieves information from all search tools, the recall of our approach cannot surpass that of the traditional meta-search service approach. Therefore, the recall ratio is a good measurement for comparison. From this graph, we can notice that the recall ratio is also proportional to the amount of knowledge of each IR agent. When each IR agent was trained with more than 200 training pairs, the recall ratio was kept close to 95%. As a result, when each IR agent was sufficiently trained, the precision showed a gain of nearly 16% and the recall showed a loss of 5% in comparison with the traditional meta-search service approach. In many cases, IR tasks suffer from too-much problem: for a given query, the IR system in question often returns too many pieces of information to deal with in a reasonable manner [11]. This means that precision is more important measurement than recall in many IR situations. Therefore, more improvement in precision than loss in recall has significant meaning in the IR performance.

4.3   Communication Cost

The communication cost is depicted in Fig. 7-(c). The communication cost of the traditional meta-search service approach is always 7 because it always broadcasts a given query to all seven directories of *Yahoo! Korea*. It is interesting to note that the communication cost obtained by our approach is always quite smaller than the one obtained by the traditional meta-search service. For more than 150 training query pairs, the communication costs do not show the big difference. This means that the communication cost converges earlier than precision and recall. The result of communication cost implies that our approach heavily reduces the workload for network resources and thus considerably mitigates the bottleneck problem under highly competitive IR situations.

4.4   Training Cost

The BPN learning procedure used for training each IR agent requires a number of training cycles for every training pair in order to converge to a stable state minimizing errors. In our experimental multi-agent IR system, the number of training cycles during the training phase of BPN of each IR agent did not exceed 56 for all dimensions of the training query set. This means that the number of feedback propagations that occurred during the training phase of BPN was not more than 11,200 (56×200) in each IR agent. Actually, each training phase was finished within 39 seconds in the experiment on the *UNIX SPARC* station. Therefore, this additional training cost is acceptable when the significant improvement of IR performance is considered.

5   Conclusion and Future Work

In this paper, we proposed a multi-agent learning approach to the Web IR using a neural network. Our multi-agent learning approach provides a method for locating the information sources that will give useful information and then retrieving that information. Our approach also can capture the knowledge about user's interests or preferences for efficient and effective IR. From the results of experiment, we identified the notable improvements of performance at the expense of some training cost in our approach, as compared with the traditional meta-search service. We also observed that the learning and generalization capability of a BPN could be effectively utilized as an internal learning mechanism of an IR agent. Since none of the current generation of IR methods incorporates a learning mechanism of artificial neural network into cooperative multi-agent IR techniques, the experiment system for our multi-agent IR approach may be an interesting application of artificial neural network. The work presented in this paper is an early stage of our research plan. Currently, we are investigating how the performance changes as various parameters change in the experimental system. We are also looking into an automated method to find an optimal parameter setting. We plan to continue our research for developing more general training procedure feasible even for the multi-agent IR system represented as a cyclic directed graph diagram. We will also extend our work into an adaptive IR agent system that will retrieve information from highly dynamic information sources whose theme, content and structure are subject to asynchronous changes.

References

1. Salton, G. Developments in automatic text retrieval. Science 253 (1991), 974-979.
2. Mauldin, M., and Leavitt, J. Web agent related research at the Center for Machine Translation, in Proceedings of the ACM SIGNIDR '94, 1994.
3. Pinkerton, B. Finding what people want: Experiences the webcrawler, in Proceedings of 2nd International WWW Conference, 1994.
4. Gudivada, V.N. and et. al. Information Retrieval on the World Wide Web. IEEE Internet Computing (September 1997), 58-68.
5. Werbos, P. Beyond Regression: New Tools for Prediction and Analysis in the Behavioral Sciences. PhD thesis, Harvard, Cambridge, MA, 1974.
6. O'leary, D.E. The Internet, Intranets and the AI Renaissance. Computer 30, 1 (January 1997), 71-78.
7. Salton, G. and McGill, M. Introduction to Mordern Information Retrieval. McGraw-Hill, New York NY, 1983.
8. Freeman, J.A. and Skapura D.M. Neural Networks Algorithms, Applications, and Programming Techniques. Addison-Wesley, MA, 1992.
9. White, H. Connectionist Nonparametric Regression: Multi-layer Feedforward Networks Can Learn Arbitrary Mappings. Neural Networks 3, 5 (1990), 535-549.
10. Hertz, J. and et. al. Introduction to the theory of Neural Computation. Addison-Wesley, New York NY, 1991.
11. LaMacchia, B.A. Internet Fish. PhD thesis, MIT, MA, 1996.

Adaptive Information Filtering Algorithms

Daniel R. Tauritz and Ida G. Sprinkhuizen-Kuyper

LIACS, Leiden University
{dtauritz,kuyper}@cs.leidenuniv.nl

Abstract. Adaptive Information Filtering is concerned with filtering information streams in changing environments. The changes may occur both on the transmission side (the nature of the streams can change) and on the reception side (the interests of a user can change). The research described in this paper details the progress made in a prototype Adaptive Information Filtering system based on weighted trigram analysis and evolutionary computation. The main improvements of the algorithms employed by the system concern the computation of the distance between weighted trigram vectors and a further analysis of the two-pool evolutionary algorithm. We tested our new prototype system on the Reuters-21578 text categorization test collection.

1 Introduction

We live in what is often termed the "information age". It might more appropriately be called the "data age", for only relevant data is information, and finding relevant data among the ever greater accumulations of available data is becoming increasingly more difficult. One of the fields dealing with this problem is Information Filtering (IF). IF is the process of filtering data streams in such a way that only particular data are preserved, depending on certain information needs. The IF environment is the combination of data stream and information needs. When the data stream and the information needs are not changing over time the IF environment is said to be static. When, however, the IF environment is dynamic, as opposed to static, an adaptive information filtering (AIF) system is called for. An AIF system is an IF system capable of adapting to changes in both the data stream and the information needs.

One of the essential ingredients in any information retrieval (IR) or IF system is its ability to match a query (in the case of an IR system) or a profile (in the case of an IF system) with the documents available for perusal. While optimally a semantical match should be performed, that is not currently feasible and we have to be satisfied with a syntactical match. A good general reference to the field of IR/IF is [4].

The most widely employed syntactical representation of textual documents is based on term indexing (see for example [6]). In manual indexing keywords are manually assigned to a document, while in automatic indexing the frequencies of all the terms occuring in a document are indexed. Term indexing has several drawbacks, such as its sensitivity to spelling variations and errors, its static

D.J. Hand, J.N. Kok, M.R. Berthold (Eds.): IDA'99, LNCS 1642, pp. 513–524, 1999.
© Springer-Verlag Berlin Heidelberg 1999

nature (the terms need to be known beforehand which is fine for IR but not for IF) and its reliance on linguistic preprocessing, such as stop word removal and word stemming, to make it effective.

Another approach which in the last decade has received quite a bit of attention is based on the so-called n-gram analysis [3]. The n stands for a positive integer. The application of n-gram analysis produces an n-gram frequency vector which holds the frequencies of all the distinct character combinations of length n. In 1-gram analysis the occurrence of single letters is determined, in 2-gram analysis that of pairs of letters, in 3-gram analysis that of triplets, etc. When talking about a specific value of n, especially for lower values of n, often its Latin name is used instead of the numeric value, so 2-grams are often called bi-grams or bigrams, 3-grams trigrams, 4-grams quadgrams, but 7-grams usually just 7-grams. For example, the word "coconut" consists of the bigrams "co", "oc", "on", "nu" and "ut", all with a frequency of one except for "co" which has a frequency of two. The trigrams are "coc", "oco", "con", "onu" and "nut", all with a frequency of one. The use of n-gram analysis has many advantages over term-based systems, such as being more robust when dealing with spelling variations or errors and not requiring linguistic preprocessing which facilitates the deployment of n-gram-based systems in multi-topic/multi-language environments [2]. However, also an n-gram-based system can potentially benefit from preprocessing, since for example when the stop word 'the' is removed, the trigram 'the' becomes of significance.

In [9] it was shown that term indexing — traditionally used in IR/IF systems — is in general not suited for AIF, but that weighted trigram analysis is. See [8] for an example of a term-based AIF system for use in a restricted domain. A prototype AIF system based on weighted trigram analysis was introduced in [9] and [10]. For $n < 3$ n-gram analysis does not provide sufficient syntactical information [7] and for $n > 3$ advanced sparse vector representations are required which will be employed in future versions of our AIF system.

The matching technique used in the original prototype AIF system was based on the Euclidean metric, which is a special case of the Minkowski ℓ_p-metric, namely for p equal to two (p equal to one is called the Manhattan metric). This paper details the advances made in the matching technique. An important improvement is normalizing the weighted trigram vectors instead of the trigram vectors themselves. It also introduces the Manhattan metric as a possible alternative to the Euclidean metric in the prototype AIF system. For a general introduction to measurements in information science see [1].

A crucial step in working with weighted trigram analysis is to find the right weight vector. Our first prototype AIF system introduced a novel two-pool evolutionary algorithm (EA) for optimizing weight vectors. EAs are a class of optimization algorithms which come in handy when no a-priori solutions to a specific optimization problem are available. They work by evolving a population of trial solutions using techniques inspired by evolutionary biology. For an easy introduction to evolutionary computation (EC) see chapter 4 of [9]; for a more comprehensive introduction to EC see [5]. This paper provides a full derivation of the two-pool EA, showing that it is a special case of a whole family of classification EAs.

A new prototype AIF system based on the improved matching technique has been constructed. This paper describes the new system and presents the results of testing it on the Reuters-21578 text categorization test collection. Using a standard test collection will facilitate comparing these results with other case studies. The Reuters collection has embedded tags indicating common usage in text categorization tests. They were not suitable for our purposes which prevents our results from being compared to previous studies which did employ those tags. However, as the collection is readily available and later in this paper we describe how we obtained the training and test sets for our research, we facilitate conducting studies which can be compared to our results.

The paper is structured as follows. In section 2 we give a global description of the complete system. In section 3 we describe the distance measures. The details of the two-pool EA are presented in section 4. In section 5 our new prototype AIF system is explained, while section 6 describes the Reuters-21578 test collection and the results of our experiments with that collection. Finally, section 7 gives our conclusions.

2   Overview of the AIF System

This section is meant to illustrate the working of the system as a whole without drowning the reader in all the details which are given later in this paper. The core of the system is the clustering cycle (see figure 1). The clustering algorithm uses a weight vector to compare the trigram frequency vector of a document with the prototype vectors of the clusters and decides in what cluster the document will be classified. Depending on the parameters of the cluster algorithm, the prototype vector of the chosen cluster will shift a bit in the direction of the newly presented document vector. The prototype vectors are initialized by averaging the trigram vectors of a number of documents belonging to each cluster (class).

The weight vector and the parameters of the cluster algorithm (the cluster radius and the shift factor) are determined by the EA. So the EA works on a population of individuals each containing a chromosome with genes existing of the components of the weight vector and the parameters of the cluster algorithm. The fitness of an individual is determined by dividing the number of documents it has correctly classified by the total number of documents it has classified.

3   Measuring Distance in Weighted Trigram Frequency Vector Space

The performance of a matching technique is called its discriminating power. The higher the discriminating power, the better a technique is able to separate documents which are semantically dissimilar and to group together documents which are semantically similar. In [9] it was shown that the combination of weighted

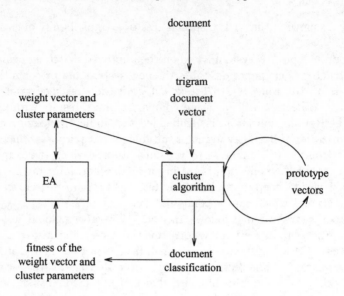

Fig. 1. Schematic overview of the adaptive IF system.

trigram analysis (each trigram is assigned a weight indicating its relative importance) and the Euclidean distance metric has sufficient discriminating power for document classification.

The size of the alphabet used will be indicated with $|a|$. Consider two document vectors d_1 and d_2. Let $f = (f_1, f_2, \cdots, f_n)$ and $g = (g_1, g_2, \cdots, g_n)$ with $n = |a|^3$ be the corresponding trigram frequency vectors for these documents. Let $w = (w_1, w_2, \cdots, w_n)$ with $w_i \geq 0$, $i = 1, \cdots, n$ be the weight vector giving the relative importance of the different trigram frequencies. The weighted trigram vectors $x = (x_1, \cdots, x_n)$ and $y = (y_1, \cdots, y_n)$ corresponding to f and g respectively are defined as follows: $x_i = f_i w_i$ and $y_i = g_i w_i$ for $i = 1, \cdots, n$.

In [9] it was argued that the trigram frequency vectors had to be normalized to prevent the length of a document influencing the distance metric. However, if we want to measure the distance between two weighted trigram frequency vectors then those are the vectors that need to be normalized, not the trigram frequency vectors. This can be accomplished by introducing $\overline{x} = (\overline{x}_1, \cdots, \overline{x}_n)$ with $\overline{x}_i = x_i / \sum_{j=1}^{n} x_j$ and $\overline{y}_i = y_i / \sum_{j=1}^{n} y_j$.

The match between d_1 and d_2 can then be estimated by applying the Euclidean distance metric to $\overline{x}$ and $\overline{y}$:

$$\rho(\overline{x}, \overline{y}) = \sqrt{\sum_{i=1}^{n} (\overline{x}_i - \overline{y}_i)^2} \tag{1}$$

An alternative to the Euclidean metric is the Manhattan metric. Using it the match between d_1 and d_2 can be estimated as follows:

$$\rho'(\overline{x}, \overline{y}) = \sum_{i=1}^{n} |\overline{x}_i - \overline{y}_i| \qquad (2)$$

4 Applying Evolutionary Computation to Classification

In our AIF system the classification of a document vector is dependent on the weight vector being used. We determine this vector by using an evolutionary algorithm (EA). In this section we will consider the development of classification EAs (CEAs) more generally, but for our concrete system the members of a population are weight vectors, the score of a member is the number of correctly classified documents and its age is the total number of documents it has classified.

The set of objects to classify will be denoted with S and the number of objects in S with $|S|$. For short σ will stand for an object and $c(\sigma)$ for the class σ maps to. The set $P = \{P_1, P_2, \cdots, P_{pop\_size}\}$ is the population of trial solutions with pop_size a positive integer. For the purpose of indexing the population members we define i as an integer between 1 and pop_size. Two essential components of any CEA are the evaluation of all the population members and, based on that, the evolvement of the population. The evolvement component will be denoted with $EVOLVE(P)$. The evaluation component will be denoted with $EVAL(S, P)$ and is defined as follows:

$$EVAL(S, P) : \quad \forall P_i \in P \text{ determine } FITNESS(S, P_i) \qquad (3)$$

The fitness of a trial solution given an object set is the average score of that trial solution on classifying all the objects in the object set. The range of the fitness is from zero to one with zero being the worst (all classifications incorrect) and one the best (all classifications correct). The fitness function is defined as follows:

$$FITNESS(S, P_i) = \frac{\sum_{\forall \sigma \in S} RESULT(\sigma, P_i)}{|S|} \qquad (4)$$

The result of classifying an object given a trial solution is either zero (incorrect) or one (correct). The result function is defined as follows:

$$RESULT(\sigma, P_i) = \begin{cases} 0 & \text{if } classify(\sigma, P_i) \neq c(\sigma) \\ 1 & \text{if } classify(\sigma, P_i) = c(\sigma) \end{cases} \qquad (5)$$

The result function works by comparing the actual mapping of an object to the mapping of that object computed using a trial solution. The function which performs that computation is defined as:

$$CLASSIFY(\sigma, P_i) = \text{the class } \sigma \text{ maps to using } P_i \qquad (6)$$

The CEA can then be defined as given in Algorithm 1.

Algorithm 1 Static object set

---
initialize S, P
$EVAL(S,P)$
while (not termination condition) do
    $EVOLVE(P)$
    $EVAL(S,P)$
end

4.1 Expanding Object Set

If S expands in time we can simply execute Algorithm 1 after each expansion to find a mapping from object space to class space at any given time. If the set of objects is smaller than the object space and represents it better as it expands, then the mapping found by the CEA will better approximate the mapping from object space to class space as time progresses. In this case it is likely that the mapping found at any particular time is a good approximation of the mapping to be found the following time and therefore would make a good starting point for the next search. Time will be denoted with τ and the object added to S at $\tau = \hat{\tau}$ with $\sigma_{\hat{\tau}}$. The new algorithm is given as Algorithm 2.

Algorithm 2 Expanding object set

$\tau \leftarrow 1$
initialize S, P
repeat forever
    $EVAL(S,P)$
    while (not termination condition) do
        $EVOLVE(P)$
        $EVAL(S,P)$
    end
    $\tau \leftarrow \tau + 1$
    add σ_τ to S
end

4.2 Shifting Window

There are a number of reasons why we may not want to use an ever expanding set of objects to find a mapping from object space to class space. For one, this requires an ever increasing amount of computational resources, both in terms of memory and in CPU cycles. And secondly, the mapping may change over time so that obtaining $c(\sigma)$'s might prove to be an expensive operation or it is even possible that old $c(\sigma)$'s are not obtainable at all. In this case we can impose a shifting window on S limiting the number of objects to be used in the evolutionary process at any given time. The size of the shifting window will be indicated with w. The new algorithm is given in Algorithm 3.

Algorithm 3 Shifting window

$\tau \leftarrow 1$
initialize S, P
repeat forever
    $EVAL(S, P)$
    while (not termination condition) do
        $EVOLVE(P)$
        $EVAL(S, P)$
    end
    $\tau \leftarrow \tau + 1$
    add σ_τ to S
    if $(\tau > w)$ then remove $\sigma_{\tau-w}$ from S
end

4.3　Age

One thing we lose by employing a shifting window is the information on how well trial solutions performed on objects no longer contained in S. And the smaller w is, the greater this loss. To preserve this information in our shifting window CEA we introduce the concepts of member age and member score. The age of a member is defined as the number of population generations since the creation of that member and is denoted with P_i^{age}. The score of a member is defined as the number of correct classifications it has made since its creation and is denoted with P_i^{score}. The fitness function is now defined as:

$$FITNESS(P_i) = \frac{P_i^{score}}{P_i^{age}} \ . \tag{7}$$

And the evaluation component becomes:

$$EVAL(S, P) : \forall P_i \in P : \forall \sigma \in S :$$
$$P_i^{age} \leftarrow P_i^{age} + 1, P_i^{score} \leftarrow P_i^{score} + RESULT(\sigma, P_i)$$
$$\text{and compute } FITNESS(P_i)$$

4.4　Two Pool

One of the consequences of the new way of determining fitness is that as the age of a member increases so does its statistical reliability in approximating the *true* fitness of a member, that is, its fitness if computed using S equal to the entire object space. If, when producing offspring, the new member's score and age are set to zero, as opposed to basing them on those of its parent(s), its statistical reliability plunges and time is needed to recover some measure of reliability. In that case it is necessary to prevent the new member from participating in the evolution process until it *matures*. This can be accomplished by splitting the population into two pools, namely a child pool P^c and an adult pool P^a with $P = P^c \cup P^a$, $|P^c|$ the number of members in P^c , $|P^a|$ the number of members in P^a and *age_threshold* the age at which members are moved from P^c to P^a. The resulting algorithm is given in Algorithm 4.

Algorithm 4 Two pool

$\tau \leftarrow \tau + 1$
initialize S, P^c
repeat forever
    $EVAL(S, P)$
    while (not termination condition) do
        if $(|P^a| > 0)$ $EVOLVE(P^a)$
        $EVAL(S, P)$
        $\forall P_i \in P^c$: if $(P_i^{age} = age\_threshold)$ move P_i from P^c to P^a
    end
    $\tau \leftarrow \tau + 1$
    add σ_τ to S
    if $(\tau > w)$ then remove $\sigma_{\tau-w}$ from S
end

---

5 A New Adaptive Information Filtering System Prototype

The prototype AIF system introduced in [9] was completely rewritten incorporating the new distance measures presented in section 3 and using the two-pool CEA derived in section 4. Another change is that the weights are expressed in floating point numbers instead of integers, allowing much more gradual change during mutation. A significant improvement has been made in how the system measures its performance; in addition to tracking the lowest, average and highest fitness values, the new system also measures the actual system performance. System performance is expressed in correct classifications per document, ranging from zero for all documents classified incorrectly, to one for a perfect classification record. While the fitness values offer insight into how the CEA is doing and can, to a certain degree, be indicative of how the system is performing, system performance is by far the best basis for comparisons.

In order to accurately measure the performance of the system thousands of documents need to be classified. The $c(\sigma)$'s should to be provided via user feedback. Until the system is ready for trial deployment, however, it will be necessary to simulate this user feedback. One way this can be accomplished is by employing a test set of documents for which the $c(\sigma)$'s are known. The CEA is a special case of Algorithm 4, namely with shifting window size set to one and with a termination condition such that the inner loop is executed only once for each outer loop. The population members each consist of their score, their age, the radius parameter used by one of the $CLASSIFY$ functions and a full set of weights. The system can then be described as given in Algorithm 5.

The prototype vectors representing the category cluster centers are initialized by calculating for each the average of a certain number of trigram vectors. The initialization of the population is done by setting the scores and ages to zero, the radius to a random value within a user specified range and assigning positive random values to the weights.

Algorithm 5 AIF two pool

$\tau \leftarrow 1$, initialize prototype vectors
initialize P^c
repeat forever
    $EVAL(\sigma_\tau, P)$
    if $(|P^a| > 0)$ $EVOLVE(P^a)$
    $\forall P_i \in P^c$: if $(P_i^{age} = age\_threshold)$ move P_i from P^c to P^a
    $\tau \leftarrow \tau + 1$
end

There are two $CLASSIFY(\sigma, P_i)$ functions. The one determines if the distance between σ and the closest class to σ is within the maximum class radius as set in the parameter file. If so, it returns the index of that class, if not, it returns a value indicating no class was close enough. The other simply determines the class closest to σ. The distance functions used are the Manhattan distance function $\rho'(\overline{x}, \overline{y})$ and the Euclidean distance function $\rho(\overline{x}, \overline{y})$ as derived in section 3.

There are two evolvement algorithms, one with crossover (resulting in two children produced by two selected parents) and one without crossover (resulting in one child which is a copy of the selected child). In both algorithms the generated child(ren) are mutated (see below) and the weakest adult(s) is (are) removed for the generated child(ren). The form of crossover employed is uniform crossover, in which each gene of a child has an equal chance to come from either parent. Mutation is performed by adding with a certain probability Gaussian noise to the genes of a member. Parent selection is done by selecting fitter members with an exponentially higher probability; this causes selective pressure. If no adult gets selected by this process, the fittest adult is selected by default.

The user definable parameters for the new AIF system are as follows. For the CEA the user can specify the size of the population (positive integer), the age threshold (positive integer), the number of adults to replace after each evaluation (positive integer), the selective pressure rate (real value between 0 and 1), crossover (enabled/disabled), the chance that a gene gets mutated (real value between 0 and 1) and the amount of Gaussian noise used during mutation (real value between 0 and 1). Note that after two times the age threshold generations, the size of the child pool is the age threshold times the number of adults to replace after each evaluation, assuming the total population size is larger or equal. So, for example, if the size of the population is 100, the age threshold 10 and the number of adults to replace after each evaluation is 4, then after 20 generations the child pool will stabilize at size 40 and the adult pool at size 60. For the clustering algorithm the user can specify the distance function to be used (Manhattan or Euclidean), the number of vectors used for averaging during the initialization of the prototype vectors (positive integer) and the range of the radius values (positive real values). For each experiment the user can further specify the number of clusters and the size and number of passes for the training and the test set.

6   The Reuters-21578 Text Categorization Test Collection

The experiments conducted with the first prototype of the AIF system used Internet newsgroup articles from a number of carefully selected moderated news-
groups. This is not satisfactory for two reasons. First, while the moderation
process tends to eliminate most of the personal messages, it allows a lot of meta-
messages, such as announcements, the topics are often interpreted very broadly
and the article contents can be relevant to multiple topics. And secondly, unless
one carefully archives, indexes and makes available, the articles used in an experiment, it is not possible for other researchers to reproduce reported experimental
results. A collection of documents without the above mentioned drawbacks was
desired to facilitate experimentation with the new AIF system. The construction of a large high-grade text categorization test collection is extremely time
consuming, therefore we decided to use a standardized collection instead of creating one of our own. The collection we selected was the Reuters-21578 text
categorization collection.

The documents in the Reuters-21578 collection appeared on the Reuters
newswire in 1987. The collection is downloadable from David D. Lewis' profes-
sional home page[1]. The documents in the Reuters-21578 collection are in SGML
format and tagged for the purpose of splitting into training and test sets as used
in published studies concerning text classification. This was done to allow the
results of different studies to be compared. For our purposes, however, a subset
of the collection was needed. First of all it was required that a document be
indexed with only one topic, which limited the subset to 9494 documents. And,
secondly, it was required that the document be a regular text document which
further limited the subset to 8654 documents. From that subset only those documents belonging to the ten most frequent topics in the subset, as listed in Table
1, were employed. For the purpose of trigram analysis, a document is treated as
a string of characters. Letters are handled case-insensitive and all other characters are interpreted as the space character. Any sequence of spaces is replaced
by a single space. Thus the trigram alphabet consists of 27 characters, namely
'a' through 'z' and the space delimeter. The number of distinct trigrams is then
$27^3 = 19683$.

We did experiments using a growing number of the selected topics in Table
1 from the Reuters-21578 collection. Our results are given in Table 2. The experiments used the Manhattan metric as distance measure. It was decided to
classify in closest cluster regardless of distance to that cluster. We averaged 30
document vectors in order to properly initialise the prototype vectors. For each
experiment the training set was comprised of thirty document vectors for each
topic and the test set of fifty document vectors for each topic (except for Money-
Supply the sample was slightly smaller). The population size was 200, the age
threshhold 25, the number of adults which got replaced each generation was 2,
the selective pressure was 0.1, crossover was enabled, the mutation chance was
0.5, the mutation rate was 0.00001 and the training set was presented 20 times.

---

[1] currently at http://www.research.att.com/home/lewis

Table 1. Subset of Reuters-21578 used in experiments

tag	topic	size
acq	Mergers/Acquisitions	2125
coffee	Coffee	114
crude	Crude Oil	355
earn	Earnings and Earnings Forecasts	3735
interest	Interest Rates	211
money-fx	Money/Foreign Exchange	259
money-supply	Money Supply	97
ship	Shipping	156
sugar	Sugar	135
trade	Trade	333

Table 2. Test set results (percentage correctly classified)

Topics	Unweighted	Average	Best	System
Coffee, trade	99.0	99.5	100	100
+ crude	93.3	98.6	100	98.7
+ money-fx	89.5	96.6	98.1	96.5
+ sugar	89.2	97.0	100	95.6
+ money-supply	83.1	93.9	100	89.7
+ ship	78.5	89.2	96.3	85.9
+ interest	77.2	88.2	93.7	84.9

The first column of Table 2 lists the test set results for classifying without the use of weights. The second column lists the average adult population member score, the third column the best adult population member score and the fourth column the system score. The results show that the new matching technique presented in this paper allows even unweighted trigram analysis to perform reasonably well for a small number of topics. When the number of topics increases the superiority of weighted trigram analysis is clearly demonstrated by the system scores. Preliminary results indicate that when progressively more training time is allocated as the number of topics increases, the test set results for weighted trigram analysis are greatly improved.

7   Conclusions

In this paper we described a complete revision of the prototype AIF system introduced in [9] and [10]. From the results presented in section 6 we can draw a number of conclusions. First of all, the discriminating power has been significantly increased as a result of the new matching technique presented in section 3. Secondly, the combination of the new matching technique and the AIF two-pool CEA delivers greatly improved system performance. As a result of the improved system performance it is now feasible to experiment with eight and more clusters instead of only four clusters (more than four clusters caused strong degradation of performance in the old system). But while the case for generalization and scalability has been further strengthened, there is still a lot of work to be done to prove it conclusively.

Obviously a lot more experimental data is needed. A major hurdle has been the amount of computational time required to perform an experiment, as well as huge long term storage and RAM requirements. The recent move in long term storage from huge sparse trigram frequency vectors to compact trigram frequency vectors resulted in a reduction in the amount of storage space required of between 90 and 95 percent. We are now looking into doing the same for the internal representation of the trigram frequency vectors and possibly the weight vectors too, which should reduce RAM requirements comparably. It should also reduce the amount of computational time significantly allowing much larger experiments. Another area we have to concentrate on is the fine tuning of the two-pool EA. Other potential improvements to our AIF system we will investigate are support for n-grams with user definable values of n and larger alphabets. Further in the future we will be looking at more advanced clustering algorithms which will be able to add new clusters and in which each cluster would have an independent radius.

References

1. Boyce, Bert R., Meadow, Charles T., Kraft, Donald H. (1994). Measurement in Information Science, Academic Press.
2. Cavnar, William B. (1994) "Using An N-Gram-Based Document Representation With A Vector Processing Retrieval Model" in "Overview of the Third Text REtrieval Conference (TREC-3)", D.K. Harman (ed.), National Institute of Standards and Technology (NIST) Special Publications 500-225, April 1995.
3. De Heer, T. (1982). "The Application of the Concept of Homeosemy to Natural Language Information Retrieval", Information Processing and Management **18**, No.5, pp.229–236.
4. Jones, Karen Sparck, Willett, Peter (eds.) (1997). Readings in Information Retrieval, Morgan Kaufman, July 1997.
5. Michalewicz, Zbigniew (1996). Genetic Algorithms + Data Structures = Evolution Programs, 3rd revised and extended edition, Springer-Verlag.
6. Rijsbergen, C.J., van (1979). Information Retrieval, 2nd edition, Butterworths, London.
7. Schmidt, S., and Teufel, B. (1988). "Full text retrieval based on syntactic similarities", Information Systems, Vol. 13, No. 1, pp. 65–70.
8. Sheth, Beered Dilip (1994). "A Learning Approach to Personalized Information Filtering", M.Sc. thesis, Massachusetts Institute of Technology, U.S.A.
9. Tauritz, Daniel R. (1996). Adaptive Information Filtering as a means to overcome Information Overload, M.Sc. thesis, Internal Report 96–35, Department of Computer Science, Leiden University, The Netherlands.
   Available via:
   http://www.wi.leidenuniv.nl/MScThesis/IR96-35.html
10. Tauritz, Daniel R., Kok, Joost N., Sprinkhuizen-Kuyper, Ida G. (1997). "Adaptive Information Filtering using Evolutionary Computation", Joint Conference of Information Sciences 1997, Vol.1, pp.77–80.

A Conceptual Graph Approach for Video Data Representation and Retrieval

Nastaran Fatemi[1,2] and Philippe Mulhem[1,3]

[1] Clips, BP 53, 38041 Grenoble Cedex, France
{Nastaran.Fatemi,Philippe.Mulhem}@imag.fr
[2] EPFL-DI-LITH, Ecublens, 1015 Lausanne, Switzerland
fatemi@di.epfl.ch
[3] IPAL, School of Computing, National University of Singapore
Lower Kent Ridge Road, Singapore 119260
mulhem@krdl.org.sg

Abstract. We present in this paper a video representation and retrieval model using the conceptual graphs and based on the characteristics of the perception of video content in time. We propose a new semantic structure for video content representation based on the notion of *event*. This new vision of content representation takes into account the different levels of abstraction of video content. On the other hand the model covers the temporal dimension of video and so presents a temporal model based on two time dimensions defined as *video* and story time.

1 Introduction

Video is a media which contains an enormous variety of information. The temporal dimension of video documents due to their particular image presentation frequency creates the illusion of animation and so makes the perceivable content of video documents reach to a very high degree comparing to still image and text. Thus the modeling of the video content information needs a comprehensive attention in order to take into account the maximum of this information and also to present a suitable schema permitting the efficient utilization of this information. The present study aims to provide a video model to be used in a video information retrieval system. In such systems despite the information concerning the general characteristics of a document (as title, author, etc.), we insist on the content information of the documents. In order to define such information, we have based our work on the study of the characteristics of the perception of video content in time. This study revealed us some characteristics of the video content which we afterwards applied as the principles of our model. The introduction of the notion of *event* as the unit of video content description and also the consideration of two dimensions of time:*video time* and *story time*, are amongst these principles. As we will explain later, we believe the conceptual graphs as an adequate formalism to describe the proposed video data model and also to support the logical basics of the retrieval procedure.

D.J. Hand, J.N. Kok, M.R. Berthold (Eds.): IDA'99, LNCS 1642, pp. 525–536, 1999.

One of our important viewpoints in the conception of the present model has been to provide a *general model*: a model to be simply adaptable to different types of video and application contexts. To fulfill this objective we propose the model in two distinct parts concerning the *generic* and *specific* aspects of videos. The flexible construction of the *event* unit has particularly facilitated the achievement of the recalled generality.

In the following, we first give in section 2 a concise review of the existing approaches of video modeling. In section 3 we describe the features of the video content perception. These features lead to the principles of our model described in section 4. Section 5 provides an introduction to the conceptual graphs formalism and their relation to information retrieval. We present the description of the video model using the conceptual graphs in section 6. An exemple showing the interest of our approach is given in section 7. Finally we conclude in section 8.

2   Related Works

In order to give a concise overview of the principal approaches adopted in existing video models and to note their inadequacy in serving as a general representation and retrieval model, we classify them into three main categories. The first category and the most well known consists of the models based on the hierarchical cinematographical structure of video documents [1], [2], [3], which insist on the cutting of video into scenes, shots and images. The utilization of this structure is adequate for video documents with a semantic structure which follows the so-called cinematographical structure, for example the television news. For other types of video documents where such a structure does not exist, these models are restrictive. Another category are the models based on the representation of the objects [4] and spatio-temporal relationships between the objects [5]. These models are restricted to object description and do not permit more elaborate semantic description of video content. Between the existing approaches of video modeling, stratification [6] and [7] seems more oriented to semantic description of video. However, as stratification has been initially proposed for editing and annotating video systems, it does note provide a precise definition of what the content of each strata may be, how this content description is organized and how it is possible to retrieve a video document by describing its content through a set of strata. We will see in this paper how the semantic structure we define for video documents overcomes the above restrictions. To understand the foundations of our proposed model, the following section describes the characteristics of the video content perception which we have taken into consideration.

3   Video Content Perception

A video document is a sequence of images played at an accurate frequency to create the illusion of animation. All information we receive from this media, either temporal or non-temporal, is the result of this succession of images in time. To show the different aspects of the time-based perception of video, in the following, we first explain the different levels of perception of video content and then the different time dimensions related to these levels.

3.1 Different Levels of Perception of Video Content

In a first time, we define two principal levels of perception of video content: *visual perception* and *semantic perception*. Visual perception corresponds to the elementary information received when watching a video, independent of any abstraction attached to them. These information are: the presence of pictorial elements[1] and the change of spatio-temporal characteristics of these elements. An example of visual perception is the perception of the presence of a circle and its going up and then coming down in a sequence of images. This level of perception is independent of the different video and application contexts.

Once pictorial elements are observed, abstractions are made through these elements towards different concepts[2]. Such abstractions depend mainly on the context of the presentation of video. For example, the circle of last example can be perceived in a particular context as the sun and its going up and coming down as the sunrise and the sunset. This abstraction process may continue in a hierarchical way: new concepts can be created as abstraction of one or several other concepts. Then, in the last example, the sunset followed by the sunrise may be considered as a "day" and so on.

The abstraction of the content information explained above does not end with the construction of concepts (and relations). The understanding of the video content leads finally to the perception of a *story*. In fact, the story is first created by the maker of the video document by the intermediate of the techniques and the art of cinematography (the cutting of video into shots and scenes is part of this artwork). Then, the comprehension of the cinematographical language by the spectator reshapes the story. The notion of story has a primordial importance in the semantic content information perceived in a video as it represents the conceptual description of the video content for the spectator.

Each story contains a set of *events*, which are the dominant facts happenings during the story. An event is formed by a set of concepts and relations abstracted in the semantic level. According to the context of video, an event may represent the presence of certain objects or persons, an action realized by/on some objects or persons, etc. The events have temporal continuity in the story and so a description of the whole story may be formed by describing the events in time. Here we note that whereas the concepts and relations forming the interior structure of events are context dependent, the construction of the whole semantic structure of video by events related in time is independent of video and application contexts and consists a general semantic structure for video documents.

---

[1] A pictorial element is defined as a set of pixels that verify common criteria in a sequence of images. Such criterion may be the form or texture created by the set of pixels, their color, etc.

[2] For the sake of simplicity, we use the term of concept for the result of an abstraction process. We will see later that in fact there exist concepts and also relations between concepts.

In the next section, we precise the modalities of temporal description of video by presenting two dimensions of time we define for a video document.

3.2   Two Dimensions of Time for Video

The notion of story creates a new time dimension perceived by the user, namely the *story time*. The story time is the time dimension during which the story of video "takes place". This time dimension is different from the real time dimension of the video called the *video time* during which the story is "shown". Events are then present in the story and also in the video. But the temporal characteristics of the events in the story and video are different. These differences are essentially present in time intervals of the events and also their temporal relationships as they happen in story and as they are shown in video. For example, an event shown in video during a few minutes may create the illusion of its happening during one day in the story. Another example is two concurrent events of story which happen in different places. To show this, the events are cut into a few smaller parts and shown alternatively. The flashback is another example where an event happening in story before another, is shown after in video. We have presented a detailed description of the temporal aspect of the video and its modeling in [8].

4   The Principles of Video Data Model

Following the results of our study of time-based perception explained earlier, we now describe the principles of the proposed video model. Before passing to such detailed description, in order to present an intuitive vision of the kinds of queries that we would expect the model to reply, we present here a few such examples[3].

Q1 : The video portions in which we see Garry Cooper dancing with a woman.
Q2 : The video portions in which we see Alfred Hitchcock for at least 1 minute.
Q3 : The video portions in which we see a car falling down to a valley after a car pursuit.
Q4 : The video portions in which an explosion happens at the same time that two persons are talking together.
Q5 : The video portions in which we see soldiers the day after the war.

Considering the characteristics of the time-based perception of videos from one side and the type of queries that are excepted to be resolved on the other side, here we present the principles, which will be provided by our model:

1. *The representation of the event as the base unit of content description.* The example of an event in the above queries is "Garry Cooper dancing with a woman" in Q1 or "Two persons talking together" in Q4.

---

[3] For the sake of simplicity the examples given here are taken from the film videos, however, as the principles described just after will reveal, any other type of video (medical, object tracking, etc.) may be represented using this approach.

2. *The representation of the interior construction of events from concepts and relations.* For example the event in Q1 is constructed from the concept instances "Garry Cooper" and "woman" and the relation "dancing" between these two concepts.

3. *The representation of the temporal relations between the events.* For example the relation "after" between the two events "a car falling down to a valley" and "a car pursuit" in Q3. We remind from the definition of the event given in 3.1 that events are considered as temporal units of description and so we may have temporal relations only between the events and not inside each one. Another important point is: as we aim to represent both the video and the story time, we need to represent both types of video and story temporal relations between the events.

4. *The attribution of story and video time intervals to the events.* The video time interval has the extra utility of determining the boundaries of the video portion containing each represented event. We precise here that as described in the section 3.2 an event can be related to several video intervals. In this case, we consider the use of *minimum surrounding interval* of a set of intervals of *S*, namely *MSI(S)*, as the interval that begins with the first begin of the intervals of *S*, and that ends with the last ending of the intervals of *S*. The video temporal relations are then based on the *MSI* of the intervals related to the events.

Despite the so-called principles, there are some other key points, which give to the presented model a high power of expression. One of these aspects is the possession of the hierarchies of concepts and relations which describe the specialization relation existing between the concepts (and relations). We have described these hierarchies using the concept and relation lattices of the conceptual graph formalism (ref. 5.1). These hierarchies are specially used during the matching phase of the video retrieval.

In order to describe the details of our video model with precision and to avoid giving separate pieces of description, we prefer describe the model directly using the conceptual graphs, which we find quite adequate as a relational knowledge representation formalism and specially to support the logical basis of the retrieval model. Amongst the most important advantages of using this formalism, we name the three following:

1. There exists a strong relation between the conceptual graph formalism and the first order logic and consequently with the logical model of information retrieval [9].

2. There exist algebraic operators that are in accordance with the logical interpretation of conceptual graphs. This leads to a strong theoretical validation of the formalism synonym to the strong validation theory [10].

3. The algebraic interpretation gives a basis to achieve query processing with polynomial complexity when adequate preprocessing is performed [10].

5   Conceptual Graphs

To facilitate the understanding of the model proposed in section 6, we present in the following, first an introduction to the conceptual graphs formalism and then its application to the information retrieval.

5.1   An Introduction to the Conceptual Graphs Formalism

Conceptual graphs are knowledge representation formalism based on the linguistics, psychology and philosophy defined by Sowa [11]. A conceptual graph represents information as a finite, connected, oriented, bipartite graph having two types of nodes: *concepts* and *relations*. Concepts have a *type* (which corresponds to a semantic class) and possibly a referent (which corresponds to an instantiation to an individual of the class). There exist two categories of referents: individual referents, each of which designates a particular individual and the generic referent noted by * which designates any individual referent conform to the type of the concept. Conceptual relations specify the relation which exists between the concepts of the graph. The relations are identified by a type and they give a direction to the conceptual graph containing them.

An example of a conceptual graph is given below. This graph represents the fact "A young man is talking to Mary".

$$[\text{Man: *}] \rightarrow (\text{Talking}) \rightarrow [\text{Woman: Mary}]$$
$$\rightarrow (\text{Has\_Character}) \rightarrow [\text{Character: Young}]$$

The formalism defines a knowledge base that contains a *concept lattice* and a *relation lattice*. The concept lattice, T_C, is a set of concept types. T_C is provided with a partial ordering relation $\leq_C$. The relation lattice, T_R, is a set of relation types. T_R is provided with a partial ordering relation $\leq_\delta$ (The partial ordering relations $\leq_C$ and $\leq_\delta$ represent the notion of Generalization/Specialization). The set of concepts and relations in T_C and T_R are relatively restricted between Top_C, $Bottom_C$ and Top_R , $Bottom_R$.

In the conceptual graphs formalism, *canonical graphs* represent the possible situations of the real world. These graphs express the valid combinations of the concepts and relations. There exists a set, namely the *base*, of canonical graphs that are defined *a priori* and which express the elementary semantic constraints of the represented domain. Other canonical graphs are *derived* from the canonical base by the *canonical operations* of copy, join, restriction, and simplification proposed in the conceptual graph formalism.

If a graph g2 is derived from a graph g1, g2 is a specialization of g1: g2 ≤ g1.

5.2   Conceptual Graphs and Information Retrieval

The important advantage of the conceptual graphs, besides their flexibility and expressive power is specially their connection with the logical model of information retrieval [9]. This connection is due to the explicit relation of the formalism with the first order logic. Sowa [11] defined an operator Φ, which permits to associate to each graph u a formula $\Phi(u)$ expressed in first order logic. This operator has the property of conserving an order on the graphs: if $u \leq v$ (u is a specialization of v) then the associated logical formulas verify the following implication: $\Phi(u) \supset \Phi(v)$.

The conceptual graph formalism permits a translational semantic towards the first order logic: using the operator Φ the conceptual graph expressions are translated to the first order logic expressions. The relationship between this formalism and a retrieval process is: a document indexed by a conceptual graph D is relevant to a query represented by the graph Q if D is a specialization of Q, i.e., $\Phi(D) \supset \Phi(Q)$. The realization of such implication is achieved on conceptual graphs using the projection operation: if $u \leq v$ then there exists a projection of v on u. So using the projection operation of conceptual graphs we can affirm that $D \leq Q$ and hence $\Phi(D) \supset \Phi(Q)$.

6   Video Data Model Presented by Conceptual Graphs

An information retrieval model is usually presented in three distinct parts: document model, query model and the matching function. Using the conceptual graph formalism, the queries and documents are represented each one as a graph and the matching function consists of the projection of the document graph into the query graph. To describe the video model, we give in the following the details of the document model, which are exactly the same ones for the query model.

To describe the document model, we present the canonical base C, the concept lattice T_C and the relation lattice T_R.

Each video document is composed of a set of *events*. The content of each event is described by a graph. The initial graphs of C are thus the following:

$$[\text{Video}] \rightarrow (\text{ Is\_Composed\_Of }) \rightarrow [\text{Event}]$$
$$[\text{Event}] \rightarrow (\text{ Has\_Content }) \rightarrow [\text{Content}]$$

The referents of the concept *Video* are unique identifiers for the instances of the video concept type. *Content* is itself a graph whose construction, as explained before, depends on the characteristics of each particular domain. To distinguish clearly between the generic and specific aspects of the model, we present the description of the Content graph by providing separate specific canonical base: C_{SP}, specific concept lattice: T_{CSP}, and specific relation lattice: T_{RSP}.

As example, we describe the construction of the content graph for film video documents. In that case, between the most important elements of events we may consider *Persons*, *Objects*, *Actions* and *Locations*. *Persons* and *Objects* are regrouped to a more general concept, *Entity*. *Actions* are performed by *Entities* on other *Entities*. They may be simple or complex.

For example holding is considered as a simple action: someone holds something, whereas taking is an action which may be complex: someone takes something from some other one. The following graphs of the canonical base, C_{SP},

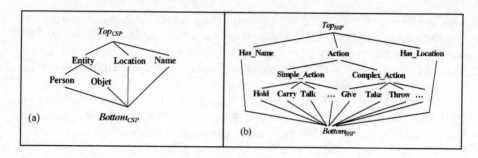

Fig. 1. An example of (a) specific concept lattice and (b) specific relation lattice.

represent the above descriptions.

$$[\text{Entity}] \rightarrow (\text{Simple\_Action}) \rightarrow [\text{Entity}]$$
$$[\text{Entity}] \rightarrow (\text{Complex\_Action}) \rightarrow [\text{Entity}]$$
$$\rightarrow [\text{Entity}]$$

The referents of the concept types Entity, Person and Object are unique identifiers for the relative instances. Besides the unique identifier, each entity may have a name, normally of string type. The following graph of C_{SP} represents the attribution of a *Name* to each *Entity*.

$$[\text{Entity}] \rightarrow (\text{Has\_Name}) \rightarrow [\text{Name}]$$

On the other side entities are related to certain *Locations*, represented by the two following graphs of C_{SP}.

$$[\text{Entity}] \rightarrow (\text{Has\_Location}) \rightarrow [\text{Location}]$$
$$[\text{Location}] \rightarrow (\text{Has\_Name}) \rightarrow [\text{Name}]$$

The related T_{CSP} and T_{RSP} are represented in the figure 1. In the above lattices more specialisation of the concepts and relations may be added to include more details on the information related to the domain.

Besides the content graph related to each event, there exist important temporal information representing the time interval of the event and its temporal relationships with other events. These information are part of the generic characteristics of the model as they do not depend to the particular domains: whatever are the elements inside the event, the temporal characteristics of the event unit is the same in different domains. In the section 4 we explained that to each event we accord a video and a story time interval and that the events are related by video and story temporal relations. To represent the temporal relations we use the Moulin relations [13] which are a refinement of the well known Allen Relations [12]. In fact, Moulin proposes the representation of all Allen Relations by only two relations *Before* and *During* and the parameter *Lap* bound to *Before* and *DB* and *DE* bound to *During*. The attribution of the negative, zero,

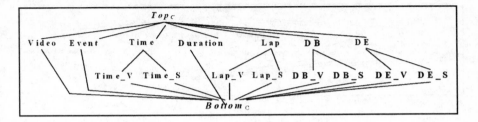

Fig. 2. Generic concept lattice.

or positive values to these parameters permit at the same time, the distinction of Allen relations and also the quantification of these relations [4]. The detailed description of the temporal modeling of video using these relations is given in [8].

These temporal information are represented by the following graphs in the generic canonical base, C. We distinguish between the concepts and relation used relatively to represent the video and story time using the postfixes " _V" and " _S".

[Event] → (Before_V) → [Event] → [Lap_V] [Event] → (During_V) → [Event] → [DB_V] → [DE_V]	[Event] → (Has_Beg_V) → [Time_V] [Event] → (Has_End_V) → [Time_V] [Event] → (Has_Duration_V) → [Duration]
[Event] → (Before_S) → [Event] → [Lap_S] [Event] → (During_S) → [Event] → [DB_S] → [DE_S]	[Event] → (Has_Beg_S) → [Time_S] [Event] → (Has_End_S) → [Time_S] [Event] → (Has_Duration_S) → [Duration]

The generic concept and relation lattices are presented in figures 2 and 3. In the generic relation lattice we note that the existence of the concepts *During* and *Before* which are the more generic concepts of *During_V*, *During_S* and *Before_V*, *Before_S*, allows to have queries which are careless of the distinction between the the two times and which insist on finding the events which are just concurrent or not.

---

[4] Defining an interval by its beginning and end points as Intvl = (Beg , End) Moulin relations are as following:

$$\text{Before(Intvl 1, Intvl 2, Lap) } where \text{ Lap = End2- Beg1}$$
$$\text{During(Intvl 1, Intvl2, DB, DE) } where \text{ DB = Beg1 - Beg2}$$
$$and \text{ DE = End2 - End1}$$

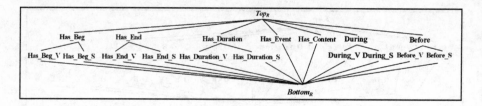

Fig. 3. Generic relation lattice.

We remind also that the instances of the concepts *Time_V*, *Time_S*, *Lap_V*, *Lap_S*, *DB_V*, *DB_S*, *DE_V* and *DE_S* should indeed represent a coding for the exact video and story time-points. To be precise, we propose a BNF-like notation for the representation these two kinds of times. We represent the story time-points by the notation [-][YYYY]:[MM]:[DD]:[HH]:[MM]:[SS]. For example, to represent the time 10:00 PM, we use the string ":::22:00:". The video time-points are represented using the SMPTE timecodes in a string format of [HH]:[MM]:[SS]:[FF].

7 Example

Finally, in order to give a whole viewpoint of typical graphs (document or query), we consider here the example of news: an interview of 6 minutes, during which a person called *A* is interviewed by a person called *B*. During this interveiw we first see a one minute report on *A* in Japan in September 1998 and then another one minute report on *A* in Africa in May 1999. As we see in the following, the proposed model permits the description of 3 events. By using two different dimensions of times, it is possible to represent the exact video temporal features of these events (specially the concurrency of the events 2 and 3 with the event 1) and also the story temporal features (here the dates of the trips).

$$[\text{Video}:\#v1] \rightarrow (\text{Has\_Event}) \rightarrow [\text{Event}:\#e1]$$
$$[\text{Video}:\#v1] \rightarrow (\text{Has\_Event}) \rightarrow [\text{Event}:\#e2]$$
$$[\text{Video}:\#v1] \rightarrow (\text{Has\_Event}) \rightarrow [\text{Event}:\#e3]$$

[Event:#e1] → (Has_Content) → [[Person:#b] → (Talk) → [Person:#a]]

[Person: #b] → (Has_Name) → [Name:"B"]

[Person: #a] → (Has_Name) → [Name:"A"]

[Event: #e1] → [Has_Duration_V] → [Duration:"00:00:06:00"]

[Event:#e2] → (Has_Content) → [[Person:#a] → (Has_Location)
→ [Location:#l1]]

[Location:#l1] → (Has_Name) → [Africa]

[Event:#e2] → (Has_Beg_S) → [Time_S:"1998:09::"]
[Event:#e2] → [Has_Duration_V] → [Duration:"00:00:01:00"]

[Event:#e3] → (Has_Content) → [[Person:#a] → (Has_Location)
→ [Location:#l2]]
[Location:#l2] → (Has_Name) → [Japan]
[Event:#e3] → (Has_Beg_S) → [Time_S:"1999:05::"]
[Event:#e3] → [Has_Duration_V] → [Duration:"00:00:01:00"]

[Event:#e2] → (During_V) → [Event:#e1]
→ [DB_V:"00:00:00:30]
→ [DE_V:"00:00:04:30]
[Event:#e3] → (During_V) → [Event:#e1]
→ [DB_V:"00:00:02:00]
→ [DE_V:"00:00:03:00]

This description allows to find :

1. interviews including reports on the same person (using co-referents),
2. interviews including the events that happaend in a given date or time,
3. interviews including reports on a person in a given place,
4. any combination of above queries, etc.

8   Conclusion

This paper described a new approach to the modeling of the content information of video documents besides a retrieval schema corresponding to the proposed model. We have used conceptual graphs as the support to represent the proposed model. Using this formalism facilitated the description of the semantic structure we propose for the video documents through the representation of the legal bindings of concepts and relations and also the hierarchies describing the relations of specialization/generalization existing between them. Using separate canonical bases and concept and relation lattices, we arrived at presenting the model separating the generic and specific aspects of video and so offering a more generic model. The representation of the temporal aspect of the videos using the same formalism is one of the other important points of the proposed model.

The presented video model may be extended in different axes. At query level, studies should be done to determine the different modalities of temporal description in natural language and their correspondence to the temporal description using the well-known Allen relations. This study will permit the definition of a simple and natural query interface and also the principles of processing of such queries. To extend the matching function, we consider the study of the possibilities of involving temporal characteristics during the matching process. This may provide us useful measures permitting the determination of different levels of relevance replacing the exact matching.

Finally we consider the continuation of the current study from an indexing point of view. The challenge in this direction will be the determination of a set of physical characteristics permitting to automate as much as possible the process of derivation of events and their temporal characteristics from the video content.

References

1. H. J. Zhang, Y.Gong, S.W.Smoliar, and S.Y.Tan, "Automatic parsing and indexing of news video", Proceedings of IEEE conference on multimedia computing systems, Boston, Massachusetts, (1994) 45-54.
2. D. Swanberg, C. F. Shu, and R. Jain, "Architecture of a multimedia information system for content-based retrieval", Proceedings of 2nd international workshop on network and operating system support for digital video, Heidelberg, (1993) 387-392.
3. B. L. Yeo and M. M. Yeung, "The front pages of video database: Retrieving and visualizing video content", IBM research division, RC 20901, (1997).
4. A. Nagasak and Y. Tanaka, "Automatic video indexing and full-video search for object appearances", Proceedings IFIP TC2/WG 2nd Workshop conference on database systems, Budapest, (1991) 120-133.
5. M. Aritsugi, T. Tagashira, T. Amagasa, and Y. Kanamori, "An approach to spatio-temporal queries: Interval-based contents representation of images", Proceedings of 8th international conference on database and expert systems applications (DEXA'97), Toulouse, France, (1997) 202-213.
6. G. Davenport, T. A. Smith, and N. Pincever, "Cinematic primitives for Multimedia", in *IEEE computer graphics and applications on multimedia*, (1991) 67-74.
7. R. Weiss, A. Duda, and D. K. Gifford, "Composition and search with a video algebra", in *IEEE multimedia*, (1995) 12-24.
8. N. Fatemi, "La modlisation temporelle d'un systme de recherche d'information vido", Report MRIM-RAP98-02, CLIPS-IMAG, Grenoble, June (1998).
9. C. J. v. Rijsbergen, "A new theoretical framework for information retrieval", Proceedings of ACM conference on research and development in information retrieval, Pisa, (1986): 194-200.
10. I. Ounis, "Un modle d'indexation relationnel pour les graphes conceptuels fond sur une interprtation logique", PhD thesis, Grenoble: University of Joseph Fourier, (1998).
11. J. F. Sowa, "Conceptual Structures: Information Processing in Mind and Machine", Addison-Weseley Publishing Company, (1984).
12. J. F. Allen, "Maintaining knowledge about temporal intervals", *Communications of ACM*, vol. 26, num. 11, (1983) 832-843.
13. B. Moulin, "Conceptual graph approach for the representation of temporal information in discourse", *Knowledge based systems*, vol. 5, num. 3, (1992) 183-192.

Author Index

Abbass, H.A.	395	Hand, D.J.	235, 317
Adams, N.M.	235	Hashimoto, K.	123
Aladjem, M.	223	Hemert, J.I. van	281
Almond, R.	357	Herrera, F.	15
Andrienko, G.	149	Hofmann, Th.	161
Andrienko, N.	149	Honavar, V.	331
		Huang, X.	111
Bauer, H.	137	Huber, C.	427
Béjar, J.	211	Hüllermeier, E.	257
Berthold, M.R.	87		
Bioch, J.C.	187	Ikeda, K.	449
Biswas, G.	245	Ikkai, Y.	449
Bradley, E.	343		
		Jappy, P.	27
Cheng, G.	461		
Cho, K.	461	Keller, A.	291
Choi, Y.S.	499	Kelly, M.G.	235
Cohen, P.	99, 199	Klawonn, F.	291
Cordón, O.	15	Komoda, N.	449
		Kosters, W.A.	39
Davis, J.	199		
Dobbs, D.	331	Létourneau, S.	473
Duin, R.P.W.	415	Li, C.	245
		Liu, X.	51, 461
Easley, M.	343	Locke, J.	437
Eggermont, J.	281	Loizou, G.	461
Eiben, A.E.	281		
Elomaa, T.	63	Macrossan, P.E.	395
		Marchiori, E.	39
Famili, F.	473	Matsumoto, K.	123
Fatemi, N.	525	Mengersen, K.	395
Finn, G.	395	Mertens, B.J.A.	317
Firoiu, L.	99	Mirkin, B.	269
Fisher, D.	407	Moulinier, I.	437
Flexer, A.	137	Moura-Pires, F.	269
Fürnkranz, J.	487	Mulhem, P.	525
Guimarães, G.	369	Nascimento, S.	269
Gunetti, D.	383	Nock, R.	27

Oerlemans, A.A.J.	39	Tax, D.M.J.	415
		Tone, I.	449
Parekh, R.	331	Towsey, M.	395
Peña, J.M.	473	Tucker, A.	51
Poddig, T.	427		
Potharst, R.	187	Ultsch, A.	369
Ramoni, M.	199	Valtchev, P.	303
Richard, G.	3		
Ruffo, G.	383	Warwick, J.	199
		Wu, J.X.	461
Sebastiani, P.	199		
Sebban, M.	3	Yamane, A.	449
Silipo, R.	87	Yang, J.	331
Sprinkhuizen-Kuyper, I.G.	513	Yang, L.	173
Swift, S.	51	Yang-Stephens, B.	437
Swope, M.C.	437	Yoo, S.I.	499
		Ypma, A.	415
Talavera, L.	75, 211		
Talbert, D.	407	Zhao, F.	111
Tauritz, D.R.	513		

Lecture Notes in Computer Science

For information about Vols. 1–1569
please contact your bookseller or Springer-Verlag

Vol. 1570: F. Puppe (Ed.), XPS-99: Knowledge-Based Systems. VIII, 227 pages. 1999. (Subseries LNAI).

Vol. 1571: P. Noriega, C. Sierra (Eds.), Agent Mediated Electronic Commerce. Proceedings, 1998. IX, 207 pages. 1999. (Subseries LNAI).

Vol. 1573: J.M.L.M. Palma, J. Dongarra, V. Hernández (Eds.), Vector and Parallel Processing - VECPAR'98. Proceedings, 1998. XVI, 706 pages. 1999.

Vol. 1572: P. Fischer, H.U. Simon (Eds.), Computational Learning Theory. Proceedings, 1999. X, 301 pages. 1999. (Subseries LNAI).

Vol. 1574: N. Zhong, L. Zhou (Eds.), Methodologies for Knowledge Discovery and Data Mining. Proceedings, 1999. XV, 533 pages. 1999. (Subseries LNAI).

Vol. 1575: S. Jähnichen (Ed.), Compiler Construction. Proceedings, 1999. X, 301 pages. 1999.

Vol. 1576: S.D. Swierstra (Ed.), Programming Languages and Systems. Proceedings, 1999. X, 307 pages. 1999.

Vol. 1577: J.-P. Finance (Ed.), Fundamental Approaches to Software Engineering. Proceedings, 1999. X, 245 pages. 1999.

Vol. 1578: W. Thomas (Ed.), Foundations of Software Science and Computation Structures. Proceedings, 1999. X, 323 pages. 1999.

Vol. 1579: W.R. Cleaveland (Ed.), Tools and Algorithms for the Construction and Analysis of Systems. Proceedings, 1999. XI, 445 pages. 1999.

Vol. 1580: A. Včkovski, K.E. Brassel, H.-J. Schek (Eds.), Interoperating Geographic Information Systems. Proceedings, 1999. XI, 329 pages. 1999.

Vol. 1581: J.-Y. Girard (Ed.), Typed Lambda Calculi and Applications. Proceedings, 1999. VIII, 397 pages. 1999.

Vol. 1582: A. Lecomte, F. Lamarche, G. Perrier (Eds.), Logical Aspects of Computational Linguistics. Proceedings, 1997. XI, 251 pages. 1999. (Subseries LNAI).

Vol. 1583: D. Scharstein, View Synthesis Using Stereo Vision. XV, 163 pages. 1999.

Vol. 1584: G. Gottlob, E. Grandjean, K. Seyr (Eds.), Computer Science Logic. Proceedings, 1998. X, 431 pages. 1999.

Vol. 1585: B. McKay, X. Yao, C.S. Newton, J.-H. Kim, T. Furuhashi (Eds.), Simulated Evolution and Learning. Proceedings, 1998. XIII, 472 pages. 1999. (Subseries LNAI).

Vol. 1586: J. Rolim et al. (Eds.), Parallel and Distributed Processing. Proceedings, 1999. XVII, 1443 pages. 1999.

Vol. 1587: J. Pieprzyk, R. Safavi-Naini, J. Seberry (Eds.), Information Security and Privacy. Proceedings, 1999. XI, 327 pages. 1999.

Vol. 1589: J.L. Fiadeiro (Ed.), Recent Trends in Algebraic Development Techniques. Proceedings, 1998. X, 341 pages. 1999.

Vol. 1590: P. Atzeni, A. Mendelzon, G. Mecca (Eds.), The World Wide Web and Databases. Proceedings, 1998. VIII, 213 pages. 1999.

Vol. 1592: J. Stern (Ed.), Advances in Cryptology – EUROCRYPT '99. Proceedings, 1999. XII, 475 pages. 1999.

Vol. 1593: P. Sloot, M. Bubak, A. Hoekstra, B. Hertzberger (Eds.), High-Performance Computing and Networking. Proceedings, 1999. XXIII, 1318 pages. 1999.

Vol. 1594: P. Ciancarini, A.L. Wolf (Eds.), Coordination Languages and Models. Proceedings, 1999. IX, 420 pages. 1999.

Vol. 1595: K. Hammond, T. Davie, C. Clack (Eds.), Implementation of Functional Languages. Proceedings, 1998. X, 247 pages. 1999.

Vol. 1596: R. Poli, H.-M. Voigt, S. Cagnoni, D. Corne, G.D. Smith, T.C. Fogarty (Eds.), Evolutionary Image Analysis, Signal Processing and Telecommunications. Proceedings, 1999. X, 225 pages. 1999.

Vol. 1597: H. Zuidweg, M. Campolargo, J. Delgado, A. Mullery (Eds.), Intelligence in Services and Networks. Proceedings, 1999. XII, 552 pages. 1999.

Vol. 1598: R. Poli, P. Nordin, W.B. Langdon, T.C. Fogarty (Eds.), Genetic Programming. Proceedings, 1999. X, 283 pages. 1999.

Vol. 1599: T. Ishida (Ed.), Multiagent Platforms. Proceedings, 1998. VIII, 187 pages. 1999. (Subseries LNAI).

Vol. 1601: J.-P. Katoen (Ed.), Formal Methods for Real-Time and Probabilistic Systems. Proceedings, 1999. X, 355 pages. 1999.

Vol. 1602: A. Sivasubramaniam, M. Lauria (Eds.), Network-Based Parallel Computing. Proceedings, 1999. VIII, 225 pages. 1999.

Vol. 1603: J. Vitek, C.D. Jensen (Eds.), Secure Internet Programming. X, 501 pages. 1999.

Vol. 1604: M. Asada, H. Kitano (Eds.), RoboCup-98: Robot Soccer World Cup II. XI, 509 pages. 1999. (Subseries LNAI).

Vol. 1605: J. Billington, M. Diaz, G. Rozenberg (Eds.), Application of Petri Nets to Communication Networks. IX, 303 pages. 1999.

Vol. 1606: J. Mira, J.V. Sánchez-Andrés (Eds.), Foundations and Tools for Neural Modeling. Proceedings, Vol. I, 1999. XXIII, 865 pages. 1999.

Vol. 1607: J. Mira, J.V. Sánchez-Andrés (Eds.), Engineering Applications of Bio-Inspired Artificial Neural Networks. Proceedings, Vol. II, 1999. XXIII, 907 pages. 1999.

Vol. 1608: S. Doaitse Swierstra, P.R. Henriques, J.N. Oliveira (Eds.), Advanced Functional Programming. Proceedings, 1998. XII, 289 pages. 1999.

Vol. 1609: Z. W. Raś, A. Skowron (Eds.), Foundations of Intelligent Systems. Proceedings, 1999. XII, 676 pages. 1999. (Subseries LNAI).

Vol. 1610: G. Cornuéjols, R.E. Burkard, G.J. Woeginger (Eds.), Integer Programming and Combinatorial Optimization. Proceedings, 1999. IX, 453 pages. 1999.

Vol. 1611: I. Imam, Y. Kodratoff, A. El-Dessouki, M. Ali (Eds.), Multiple Approaches to Intelligent Systems. Proceedings, 1999. XIX, 899 pages. 1999. (Subseries LNAI).

Vol. 1612: R. Bergmann, S. Breen, M. Göker, M. Manago, S. Wess, Developing Industrial Case-Based Reasoning Applications. XX, 188 pages. 1999. (Subseries LNAI).

Vol. 1613: A. Kuba, M. Šámal, A. Todd-Pokropek (Eds.), Information Processing in Medical Imaging. Proceedings, 1999. XVII, 508 pages. 1999.

Vol. 1614: D.P. Huijsmans, A.W.M. Smeulders (Eds.), Visual Information and Information Systems. Proceedings, 1999. XVII, 827 pages. 1999.

Vol. 1615: C. Polychronopoulos, K. Joe, A. Fukuda, S. Tomita (Eds.), High Performance Computing. Proceedings, 1999. XIV, 408 pages. 1999.

Vol. 1616: P. Cointe (Ed.), Meta-Level Architectures and Reflection. Proceedings, 1999. XI, 273 pages. 1999.

Vol. 1617: N.V. Murray (Ed.), Automated Reasoning with Analytic Tableaux and Related Methods. Proceedings, 1999. X, 325 pages. 1999. (Subseries LNAI).

Vol. 1618: J. Bézivin, P.-A. Muller (Eds.), The Unified Modeling Language. Proceedings, 1998. IX, 443 pages. 1999.

Vol. 1619: M.T. Goodrich, C.C. McGeoch (Eds.), Algorithm Engineering and Experimentation. Proceedings, 1999. VIII, 349 pages. 1999.

Vol. 1620: W. Horn, Y. Shahar, G. Lindberg, S. Andreassen, J. Wyatt (Eds.), Artificial Intelligence in Medicine. Proceedings, 1999. XIII, 454 pages. 1999. (Subseries LNAI).

Vol. 1621: D. Fensel, R. Studer (Eds.), Knowledge Acquisition Modeling and Management. Proceedings, 1999. XI, 404 pages. 1999. (Subseries LNAI).

Vol. 1622: M. González Harbour, J.A. de la Puente (Eds.), Reliable Software Technologies – Ada-Europe'99. Proceedings, 1999. XIII, 451 pages. 1999.

Vol. 1625: B. Reusch (Ed.), Computational Intelligence. Proceedings, 1999. XIV, 710 pages. 1999.

Vol. 1626: M. Jarke, A. Oberweis (Eds.), Advanced Information Systems Engineering. Proceedings, 1999. XIV, 478 pages. 1999.

Vol. 1627: T. Asano, H. Imai, D.T. Lee, S.-i. Nakano, T. Tokuyama (Eds.), Computing and Combinatorics. Proceedings, 1999. XIV, 494 pages. 1999.

Col. 1628: R. Guerraoui (Ed.), ECOOP'99 - Object-Oriented Programming. Proceedings, 1999. XIII, 529 pages. 1999.

Vol. 1629: H. Leopold, N. García (Eds.), Multimedia Applications, Services and Techniques - ECMAST'99. Proceedings, 1999. XV, 574 pages. 1999.

Vol. 1631: P. Narendran, M. Rusinowitch (Eds.), Rewriting Techniques and Applications. Proceedings, 1999. XI, 397 pages. 1999.

Vol. 1632: H. Ganzinger (Ed.), Automated Deduction – Cade-16. Proceedings, 1999. XIV, 429 pages. 1999. (Subseries LNAI).

Vol. 1633: N. Halbwachs, D. Peled (Eds.), Computer Aided Verification. Proceedings, 1999. XII, 506 pages. 1999.

Vol. 1634: S. Džeroski, P. Flach (Eds.), Inductive Logic Programming. Proceedings, 1999. VIII, 303 pages. 1999. (Subseries LNAI).

Vol. 1636: L. Knudsen (Ed.), Fast Software Encryption. Proceedings, 1999. VIII, 317 pages. 1999.

Vol. 1638: A. Hunter, S. Parsons (Eds.), Symbolic and Quantitative Approaches to Reasoning and Uncertainty. Proceedings, 1999. IX, 397 pages. 1999. (Subseries LNAI).

Vol. 1639: S. Donatelli, J. Kleijn (Eds.), Application and Theory of Petri Nets 1999. Proceedings, 1999. VIII, 425 pages. 1999.

Vol. 1640: W. Tepfenhart, W. Cyre (Eds.), Conceptual Structures: Standards and Practices. Proceedings, 1999. XII, 515 pages. 1999. (Subseries LNAI).

Vol. 1642: D.J. Hand, J.N. Kok, M.R. Berthold (Eds.), Advances in Intelligent Data Analysis. Proceedings, 1999. XII, 538 pages. 1999.

Vol. 1643: J. Nešetřil (Ed.), Algorithms – ESA '99. Proceedings, 1999. XII, 552 pages. 1999.

Vol. 1644: J. Wiedermann, P. van Emde Boas, M. Nielsen (Eds.), Automata, Languages, and Programming. Proceedings, 1999. XIV, 720 pages. 1999.

Vol. 1645: M. Crochemore, M. Paterson (Eds.), Combinatorial Pattern Matching. Proceedings, 1999. VIII, 295 pages. 1999.

Vol. 1647: F.J. Garijo, M. Boman (Eds.), Multi-Agent System Engineering. Proceedings, 1999. X, 233 pages. 1999. (Subseries LNAI).

Vol. 1649: R.Y. Pinter, S. Tsur (Eds.), Next Generation Information Technologies and Systems. Proceedings, 1999. IX, 327 pages. 1999.

Vol. 1650: K.-D. Althoff, R. Bergmann, L.K. Branting (Eds.), Case-Based Reasoning Research and Development. Proceedings, 1999. XII, 598 pages. 1999. (Subseries LNAI).

Vol. 1651: R.H. Güting, D. Papadias, F. Lochovsky (Eds.), Advances in Spatial Databases. Proceedings, 1999. XI, 371 pages. 1999.

Vol. 1652: M. Klusch, O.M. Shehory, G. Weiss (Eds.), Cooperative Information Agents III. Proceedings, 1999. XI, 404 pages. 1999. (Subseries LNAI).

Vol. 1653: S. Covaci (Ed.), Active Networks. Proceedings, 1999. XIII, 346 pages. 1999.

Vol. 1654: E.R. Hancock, M. Pelillo (Eds.), Energy Minimization Methods in Computer Vision and Pattern Recognition. Proceedings, 1999. IX, 331 pages. 1999.

Vol. 1663: F. Dehne, A. Gupta. J.-R. Sack, R. Tamassia (Eds.), Algorithms and Data Structures. Proceedings, 1999. X, 367 pages. 1999.